PELICAN BOOKS

A411

THE AGE OF ELEGANCE

ARTHUR BRYANT

Arthur Bryant

THE AGE OF ELEGANCE

ELEGANCE

1812-1822

PENGUIN BOOKS

Penguin Books Ltd, Harmondsworth, Middlesex

U.S.A.: Penguin Books Inc., 3300 Clipper Mill Road, Baltimore 11, Md

AUSTRALIA: Penguin Books Pty Ltd, 762 Whitehorse Road,
Mitcham, Victoria

—

First published by Collins 1950
Published in Pelican Books 1958

Made and printed in Great Britain
by R. & R. Clark Ltd
Edinburgh

To
FIELD-MARSHAL MONTGOMERY
VICTOR OF ALAMEIN

CONTENTS

LIST OF MAPS

PREFACE

In *The Years of Endurance* and *Years of Victory*, I tried to trace the course of our ancestors' long struggle against the French Revolution and Napoleon. The second of these, published in 1944, left the tale unfinished with the capture of Ciudad Rodrigo in January, 1812, and the opening of the offensive which was to carry Wellington's army, first to Madrid and then to the Pyrenees. I have completed my ten years' task by taking the story to its conclusion at Toulouse, the Vienna Conference table, and Waterloo. The war and its termination, so often recorded by Continental writers, has never been presented in its entirety from the British angle by a modern historian, though its different phases have been definitively treated in the great classics of Oman, Fortescue, Holland Rose, Fisher, Corbett, Mahan, and Webster.

Living in a post-war and revolutionary age, I have also tried to describe, in the second and longer part of the book, the impact of the bewildering economic, social, and ideological phenomena of the time on victorious Britain. The seven years that followed the Napoleonic Wars were among the most confused in our history; they appear so to the student because they were so to those who lived through them. Britain, without realizing what was happening, was undergoing a major revolution, one which had been hastened but concealed by her long struggle and splendid victory. The Industrial Revolution and its aftermath have been presented by a succession of great economic and social historians – Cunningham, Toynbee, Smart, the Webbs and Hammonds, Halévy, and, more recently, Clapham, Cole, Fay, and Ashton. The political and literary society it both supported and undermined has been brilliantly reconstructed in the work of such distinguished living scholars and critics as Professor Aspinall, Sir Herbert Grierson, Edmund Blunden, Lord David Cecil, Roger Fulford, John Gore, Harold Nicolson, Peter Quennell, and Professor Willey. What I have attempted, however inadequately, is to show the synthesis between the two: to depict on a single canvas the nation's wealth and splendour, its tough, racy, independent, rustic and sporting life, its underlying poverty and degradation, and the clash between its ancient faith and polity and its newer needs and aspirations. In this I have been immeasurably assisted by Professor Woodward's *Age of Reform*, and the earlier and monumental work of Élie Halévy.

It remains to thank those who have helped me so generously: my constant guide and critic, Milton Waldman, and my patient amanuenses, my wife and secretaries; Colonel Alfred Burne who, as before, has helped me with the maps and military history; Commander John Owen, H. J. Massingham, Ludovic Kennedy, Bernard Knowles, General Sir Bernard Paget, and Colonel Sir James Neville, who have all read the book in part or in whole and have made invaluable suggestions for its improvement. I am particularly indebted to Henry Newnham and Herbert van Thal who again have read my proofs, to Professor L. B. Namier who, in the midst of his own work has placed at my disposal his immense historical knowledge and wisdom, and to Professor A. Aspinall who has given me the benefit of his unrivalled knowledge of the period and helped to eliminate many errors. I must also record my gratitude to Lord Hamilton of Dalzell, for allowing me the use of his ancestor's manuscript, referred to in these pages as the *Hamilton of Dalzell MS.*, to Lady Gurney of Walsingham Abbey for so kindly sending for my inspection Robert Blake's MS. diary, to Brigadier C. E. Hudson, V.C., and General Sir Henry Jackson for the use of unpublished Waterloo letters, and to the Duke of Wellington for generous permission to use extracts from Mrs Arbuthnot's *Journal* which he and my kind friend, Francis Bamford, have edited.

Smedmore, ARTHUR BRYANT
July, 1950

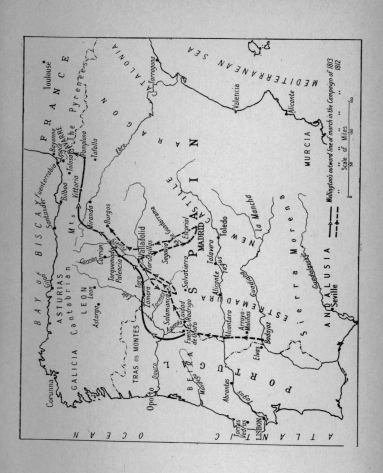

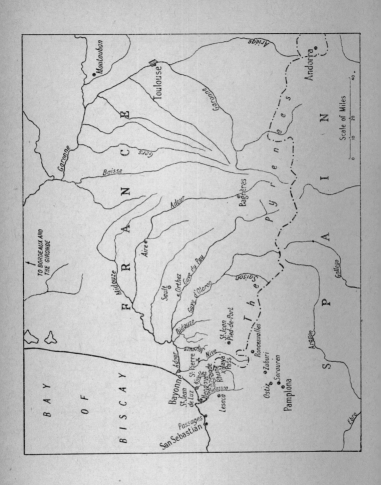

CHAPTER I

ENGLAND TAKES THE OFFENSIVE

And what are noble deeds but noble truths realised?
COLERIDGE

IN the spring of 1812 every road across Germany was thronged with horses, guns, and wagons bound for Poland. The ditches were strewn with dead horses, farms were stripped of livestock, villages requisitioned and looted. A British prisoner in a fortress on the frontiers of France watched for weeks the interminable train of men, horses and supplies, until the refrain of his jubilant jailers grew intolerable: 'The Emperor will soon subdue England.'[1] More than half a million troops were marching east. Their aim was to drive back Russia into her Asian steppes and open a way to world empire.

The *Grande Armée* was the most concentrated instrument of power yet seen on earth. It surpassed the armies of Alexander and Caesar, of Darius, Attila, and Tamerlane. The restless energy of the Revolution, superimposed on the martial tradition of France, had been forged by the organizing genius of Napoleon into an irresistible weapon. The names of Lodi, Marengo, Austerlitz, Jena, Friedland, and Wagram were inscribed on its banners; in fourteen years it had entered every Continental capital except St Petersburg, Stockholm, and Constantinople.

Yet there remained one force it had been unable to subdue. The sea, and the floating batteries of England that barred the sea's channels, had set bounds to its conquests. And neither threats nor guile could induce the island rulers to make peace. True to the beaconlight of their dead leader, Pitt, they had refused to accept the universal hegemony which was Napoleon's prescription for human government. The will and genius of the crowned Jacobin was matched by the stubborn refusal of British aristocrats, squires, traders, and lawyers to accept his dictatorship. And for all the strains and injustices of British social life, that refusal – so far as they had any say in the matter – was endorsed by the common people of Britain. The rude Wapping boatmen who sailed

1. Stewart, 57.

13

with Nelson and Collingwood, the hungry North Country weavers who enlisted for liquor to drown the memory of their ill-usage and cares, the Irish peasants who fought so valiantly by their side, had stood, for a generation, between Napoleon's armies and the domination of the world. As the spring of 1812 crept northwards over a cowed Europe, they stood there still.

It was England's mysterious art of commanding the waves that now impelled those armies eastwards. Westwards they could not go: four great sea-battles fought during the past fifteen years off Europe's shores had made that plain, even to Napoleon. On their own element the English were invincible. Nor was their power confined to the Atlantic. Southwards, too, in Europe's inland sea, their invisible ring extended. Twice Napoleon had tried to break it: once when, taking advantage of their Fleet's absence from the Mediterranean, he had seized Malta and landed in Egypt; again when he had treacherously invaded the territories of his ally, Spain, with the intention of closing the Straits of Gibraltar. In each case the logic of sea-power and its stranglehold on military communications had thwarted him. Striking back from the sea at the point where his own lunge was over-extended, a handful of stiff, red-coated British soldiers had landed from their ships and called on the conquered to rise. Ten years before, Napoleon had wheedled them out of Egypt by a truce. Yet when, in an attempt to renew his drive on Asia and Africa, he had broken that peace, their fleets had closed round him again. And since their landing in Portugal, all his Marshals' attempts to expel them from that seabound extremity of Europe had been in vain. After four years they were still there and, because of their presence, his brother's Spanish subjects were in a state of permanent eruption.

Everything the Emperor had done to destroy the English had failed. Since Trafalgar he had turned Antwerp into a naval arsenal, and filled it, as well as the dockyards of Venice, Toulon, Brest, Rochefort, and Cherbourg, with the hulls of new battleships. But as the British kept watch outside and their cruisers prevented all coastal trade, his ships could neither get out nor obtain stores. Ceaselessly contained by more than a hundred British battleships, Napoleon's Navy, which by 1812 numbered seventy capital ships with fifty more building, was a fleet in embryo but never one in being. His intricate plans for transporting

200,000 men into an England denuded of troops by the Spanish War remained a fairy tale: one so insubstantial that English mothers could no longer frighten their children with it.

Because England drew her strength from trade, Napoleon sought to destroy her by ruining trade. Since his conquest of Germany in 1806, he had shut Europe's ports to everything she made or carried, which meant everything from the outer world. Yet, though he made bankrupt thousands of her traders and manufacturers by extending his power – and Decrees – south to Seville and north to Stockholm, he had failed to break her stranglehold. While he closed old markets to her with one hand, he opened new ones with the other. The more he conquered in Europe, the more England conquered beyond the seas. As her remaining colonial and trading rivals became satrapies of France, she seized the bulk of the trade of Asia, America, and Africa. And, as the exigencies of war forced her Government, in the teeth of its own economic convictions, to create abundant loan-credit to buy and maintain the flow of arms and equipment from her new machines and factories, she was able to supply on an ever-growing scale, not only her own fleets and armies, but all the discontented forces which, first in one part of Europe and then in another, sought to challenge Napoleon's new *imperium*.

For, by denying to the peoples he had conquered the colonial and manufactured wares, the coffee, spices, tea, sugar, and cloths, to which they were accustomed, and so depriving their traders of their livelihood, Napoleon's Decrees against England robbed the Continent of the very unity he was trying to impose. The bonfires on the quaysides burning British colonial imports became beacons that heralded a Continental crusade, not against England but against himself. Bereft of commercial intercourse, his Empire remained in a state of constant ferment. More than a hundred thousand *douaniers* were permanently engaged in trying to stop its middle and upper classes from obtaining the things they wanted. The will of one man, however dynamic and lucid, proved incapable of controlling the diverse purposes and activities of man. It was the virtue of England – the historic nursery of freedom – that, while she resisted the regimented march of mankind to the theoretical liberty of the aggregate, she continued to be the champion of the real liberties of the individual.

Napoleon, and the brave and intelligent French people who followed him so blindly, failed to see this. To them England, in opposing the Revolutionary will and the military power that enforced it, was prolonging the old, corrupt institutions and discriminatory laws that everywhere repressed human energies and preserved inequalities. She alone stood out against the reforming Emperor and the great natural force he embodied. Yet, in doing so, while her terrifying adversary came increasingly to regard all opposition as treason to be crushed without mercy, England, old-fashioned, aristocratic, and conservative, became the rallying-point for all who resented injustice and oppression. And as in her sea-power England enjoyed a weapon which, though useless for enforcing uniformity on others, was perfectly adapted for preventing anyone else from doing so, she turned the Continent Napoleon had conquered into a cage.

To break out of it and complete his unification of mankind, Napoleon, therefore, prepared to strike at Russia. There was no other way. Five years before, when his victories had convinced the Russians of his overwhelming might and of England's impotence, the Czar had signed with him a treaty of peace and mutual friendship. Together, the two rulers had agreed, they would advance across southern Asia and divide the empire of the world. But neither trusted the other. Alexander, like every Russian ruler, coveted Constantinople and all Poland, an outlet to the Mediterranean, and the hegemony of Asia. Napoleon wanted the whole earth. There was, thus, from the start a rift in their friendship.

It was one which the Continental Decrees widened. At first the young Czar, seeing the British as usurers who relied on their sea-barriers to avoid martial sacrifices for their allies, joined in the great blockade. But, though Russia was a land of peasants, her ruling class depended on sea-borne trade for their luxuries and standard of living. As commerce languished, the Czar changed his policy. At the end of 1810, chafing at Napoleon's annexations in northern Germany, he readmitted colonial produce under neutral flag into his dominions. Sooner than see his blockade broken, the French Emperor thereupon threatened war.

The Czar did not want another war with Napoleon. But there was in his nature, as in that of his race, a fund of fatalism; driven beyond a certain point, he was prepared to fight without counting the cost. He continued to protest his desire for friendly relations with France, but persisted in his policy. Like everyone else in Europe, he was impressed by the success of Wellington's Fabian retreat in Portugal; he had been heartened, too, by the resistance of the Spanish guerrillas. He therefore increased his army, called out the Cossacks, and began to build entrenchments on the road to St Petersburg.

At the time, however, it needed a Slav set in impenetrable space, or an Englishman with the cloak of ocean about him, to suppose Napoleon resistible. The rulers of central and southern Europe had felt his lash too often. When at the beginning of 1812 he ordered them to arm against Russia, they obeyed. The Prussian King, though it meant ruin to his people, promised free passage and forage to the *Grande Armée* and sent the remnants of his own to join it. The Austrian Emperor, who as Napoleon's father-in-law enjoyed a special position of servile favour in his entourage of puppets, offered to guard his southern flank. The lesser Sovereigns of Germany raised 150,000 troops, Italy 40,000, the Duchy of Warsaw nearly 100,000. Frenchmen, Poles, Germans, Dutchmen, Spaniards, Italians, Danes, Croats, Swiss, Illyrians, all marched under the new Caesar's banner. The only Continental State which stood out was Sweden, which, given the choice between the ruin of her commerce and the invasion of her trans-Baltic province, tacitly chose the latter.

In order to free a quarter of a million French veterans for a campaign which was to start a thousand miles from Paris, Napoleon called up 120,000 more conscripts. No Frenchman was exempt; a bevy of young exquisites whom he encountered at a hunting party were sent to the colours next day. On May 9th, ignoring the Czar's final plea for a settlement, he set out to join his army. At Dresden, the home of the puppet King of Saxony, an emperor and seven kings waited in his ante-chamber and thirty reigning princes paid him homage. Europe, he announced, was an old prostitute who must do his pleasure; an unwieldy, medieval realm of barbarous serfs and wandering Asian tribes could not hope to resist him. Britain would inevitably fall when he had destroyed her influence at St Petersburg. The Continent would become a single state and Paris its capital.

Napoleon was the embodiment of the dreams of a hundred years. He was the child of nature, the personification of reason and energy, the irresistible Figaro, who, always triumphing, proved the force of natural genius. This stern, plump, iron-faced little Italian, with his aquiline nose and eagle eye, his sword, sash, and laurel-wreath, had shattered the pretensions of mankind's 'legitimate' rulers. Strong as tempest, swift as lighting, he had only to will and strike.

Yet, just because Napoleon shared this view of himself, he was doomed. Having risen by observing natural law, he had come to suppose himself above it. He acknowledged no morality but his own appetite and will. He cheated, lied, bullied, and exploited until in the end no one who had had dealings with him trusted him. Viewing treachery as inherent in human nature, he betrayed and was betrayed. He even denied arithmetic. Believing from repeated success that he could do anything, that the word *impossible* existed only in the dictionary of fools and that he alone was exempt from folly, he essayed that summer what he himself had declared the greatest of military follies: a campaign against a desert. No one was better able to assess the arithmetical impossibility of supporting half a million men and their horse-borne transport in the Russian wastes. But with all the intensity of his passionate nature he was resolved to make the diversionist crawl, and when the Czar Alexander, sooner than do so, called on his Gods and the valour of his people, Napoleon turned his back on the Europe he had conquered and strode to destruction.

*

As he did so, the little British army, whose fighting power he despised, struck in his rear. Before the end of February it had left its winter quarters in the lonely Beira mountains and begun the long southward march to Badajoz – a place which Napoleon had repeatedly declared it would never dare attack. 'You must think the English mad,' he had written to Marmont, 'if you suppose them capable of marching there while you are at Salamanca and able to reach Lisbon before them.' But the Emperor, as so often in his correspondence with his distant Marshals in Spain, overlooked the facts. For, in obedience to his own earlier orders, half Marmont's army was on the far side of Spain helping Suchet to capture Valencia, while the British, exploiting the fact, had possessed themselves of the Spanish frontier fortress that barred Marmont's road to Lisbon. With Ciudad Rodrigo in his hands, Wellington could for the moment ignore the French Army of Portugal and concentrate against Badajoz.

Since its loss a year before by Spanish neglect and treachery, the great fortress, with its towers dominating the Guadiana and the southern road into Spain, had been the thorn in Wellington's flesh. So long as the French held it, the British could neither advance into Estremadura, nor concentrate against Marmont in the north without exposing southern Portugal to Soult's Army of Andalusia. Only with both his frontier-fortresses could Wellington take the offensive. Napoleon's arrogance in supposing him incapable of a winter campaign had already given him Ciudad Rodrigo. If he could now take Badajoz before the summer, the Peninsular War might take a new turn.

When their destination became known, the British, fresh from their triumph at Ciudad Rodrigo, broke into cheers. Twice in the previous summer they had laid siege to Badajoz and, for lack of proper battering and sapping equipment, had thrown themselves at its half-breached defences; twice they had had to draw off as Soult's and Marmont's armies marched to its relief. Now Marmont, with his hands tied by his master's orders and his troops scattered in the interior, was left to watch the bolted door into northern Portugal, while Soult, unaware of the sudden threat to his Estremaduran bastion, was far away in Andalusia, holding down his wide province and laying interminable siege to sea-guarded Cadiz. 'Proud' Badajoz, with its fever-laden mists, its rich, collaborating *alfrancesados*, its record of disaster to the Allied cause, was at Wellington's mercy.[1]

While the long, winding columns of men and mules followed the two-hundred-mile mountain-track along the frontier, the guns of the siege-train moved eastwards from Lisbon, sliding up the Tagus to Abrantes and jolting over rough unmetalled roads behind bullock teams, while hundreds of peasants followed, bearing shot and shell. In every wooded valley climbing into Spain, droves of mules, laden with food and ammunition, converged on Badajoz, their bells mingling with the shouts of muleteers and the screeching ox-wagons. For Britain's power to strike in that barren land of sierras and far horizons depended on her ability to feed and supply; to purchase stores from neutral Morocco, America, and Turkey, to carry them across the seas

1. Grattan, 175; Gomm, 249–50; Bessborough, 221; Tomkinson, 145.

to Lisbon and Oporto and distribute them over mountain, gorge, and forest to the fighting columns on the frontier. The commissaries in their travel-soiled cocked-hats, the hardy, active muleteers with their bright trappings and guitars, the ragged, muddy escorts marching beside them with musket and pack, the bucking mules and patient bullocks, the wicker-sided, wooden-wheeled country carts, piled with provender, were England's life-line and the conduit along which her power ran. So were the transports and merchantmen courting the winds as they followed their ocean courses to Tagus, Mondego, and Douro. And guarding them, far away, the battleships that had fought under Nelson and St Vincent still kept their vigil outside the ports of Napoleon's closed empire. On Pellew, Collingwood's successor in the Mediterranean, watching Toulon and Venice; on Lord Keith, Commander-in-Chief of the Channel Fleet guarding Rochefort, Brest, and Cherbourg; on William Young – 'stiffo Rumpo' to the Navy which had bred him since his tenth birthday – blockading Antwerp and the Texel; on Saumarez in the Baltic; and on the rough, hard-used men who served under them, the fortunes of England and the world continued to revolve. Without them Wellington's eight fighting divisions would have counted for as little on the battlefields of Europe as they did in Napoleon's computation. It was maritime power that magnified their strength.

That, and the patient genius of their commander. When at the darkest hour of their country's struggle Nelson, Pitt, and Fox had followed one another to the shades, it had seemed as if Britain had been left leaderless. Sir John Moore's death at Corunna had completed the desolation of the landscape. Then a young Lieutenant-General, appointed before his fortieth birthday to command her expeditionary force in Portugal, had not only enabled England to retain her foothold in the Peninsula, but in three years of unspectacular success had steadily expanded it.

Though contemptuously called a Sepoy general by Napoleon, who had never crossed swords with him, Lord Wellington had already outmatched his finest lieutenants. Notwithstanding their superior numbers, Masséna, Soult, Victor, Jourdan, Marmont, Junot, and Kellermann had all in turn tasted the iron he administered. Repeatedly on the point of being driven into the sea, he stood at the end of four campaigns undefeated on the Spanish frontier with a liberated Portugal behind him and an expectant Spain ahead. And by opening a fifth campaign in the depth of winter, he had raised the temper of his troops to the highest expectancy. They felt sure now he would always 'out-manoeuvre Johnny'; of the impossibility of his suffering defeat.[1]

Yet Wellington was not a commander who readily inspired emotion. He never embraced his veterans like Napoleon, spoke of them as comrades, or wasted fine words on them. He had, as one of them put it, a short manner of speaking and a stern look. Save for an occasional brisk, 'Now, my lads,' when he required some more than ordinary effort, he confined his communications to general orders of the most sparing kind. These, however, never admitted of misunderstanding. Everyone knew where they stood with him, and though this may not have generated enthusiasm – a quality he suspected – it engendered a steady growth of confidence. His men did not love him, but they relied on him; they knew that, while he commanded them, their sacrifices would not be wasted. 'Whare's ar *Arthur*?' asked one fusilier of another as, under Beresford's blundering command, they tramped up the blood-stained hill of Albuera. 'I don't know, I don't see him,' replied his comrade. 'Aw wish he wore here.'[2]

For, little sentiment though he spared them, no commander ever took greater pains to deserve his men's confidence. He was as frugal with their lives as with his words. He looked after what they most valued – their stomachs. Regard to what he called regular subsistence was his first article of war. 'The attention of commanding officers,' ran one of his bleak, laconic orders, 'has been frequently called to the expediency of supplying the soldiers with breakfast.' Of all generals he was the most commissariat-minded. Having done most of his fighting in deserts, he had learnt to be.

He once defined the key to victory as the pursuit of all means, however small, which might promote success. He, therefore, left undone no duty which might enable his men to do theirs. He rose at six, applied himself in the absence of a trained staff to every detail of administration, and only rested when he had done the work of the day, falling asleep

1. Granville, II, 147. See also Bessborough, 221; Kincaid, 196; Simmons, 183; Oman, *Wellington's Army*, 38; Smith, I, 93–4.

2. S. Cooper, *Rough Notes of Seven Campaigns*, 63.

with the same ease, regularity, and promptitude as he did everything else. It was characteristic of the man that he called himself, shaved himself, and brushed his own clothes.[1]

As with all great soldiers, action worked on him like a tonic, sharpening the edge of his cool, incisive mind. In the field his temper grew calmer as storms arose. Then his strong common sense acquired the quality of genius. It was this which enabled him to forecast with such accuracy his enemies' movements; to guess what was 'on the other side of the hill'; to do what he defined as the main business of life – finding out what he didn't know by what he did.

Having once or twice faced disaster and having, like most British commanders, suffered disappointment at the miscarriage of his plans through his country's failure to supply what he had a right to expect, he shunned projects built on grandiose anticipations. He relied only on what he was sure he could count on, and adapted his ends strictly to his means. The French Marshals, he once said, planned their campaigns like a splendid set of harness which answered very well until it got broken: after that it was useless. 'Now I,' he added, 'made my campaigns of ropes. If anything went wrong, I tied a knot and went on.'

He was a man without enthusiasms or illusions. He saw life and men very much as they were, and this enabled him to steer a steady course amid the passions, stratagems, and treacheries of a war-racked, revolutionary land. He put little trust in others and tended to do everything that was vital himself. 'I am obliged,' he once said, 'to be everywhere.' Of his generals he only really confided in Hill and Graham. This was sometimes costly, for, when he was not there himself, his subordinates were afraid to act. Yet, when they blundered, he took full responsibility and indulged in no public reproaches. No part of his character was more admirable and more rare, wrote a member of the Government that supported him, than his temper and fortitude under great disappointments arising from the weakness and neglect of others.

Though a stern disciplinarian who would order a man five hundred

1. On a visit to Cadiz in 1812 he astonished his hostess by his simple habits. When her servants called him at seven they found him fully dressed and packing his shaving apparatus. Leslie, 24. Gronow, I, 213. See also Stanhope, 37, 47; Larpent, I, 85; Lady Shelley, I, 46.

lashes or string him up on the gallows without mercy if he thought it necessary, his troops bore him no ill-will for it. 'Atty,' they called him among themselves; 'the ould chap that leathers the French!' When they saw, silhouetted against the tawny landscape, the familiar equestrian figure with the trim grey cloak, oilskin cocked-hat, telescope and neatly buckled boots, or found themselves under the unrelenting scrutiny of those high-arched inquiring eyes, they cheered till the rocks rang. 'Here he comes with his long nose, boys,' they cried, 'now you may fix your flints!' Once in an exposed spot an emotional Irish sentry, finding his Commander-in-Chief had forgotten the countersign, brought his musket to the salute with a 'God bless your crooked nose; I would sooner see it than ten thousand men!'[1]

For between leader and led – though he gruffly called them 'they' and, in his worse moments, the scum of the earth – there had grown a confidence that could not be shaken. Horse and rider were one, and in that lay a priceless asset for their country. And if the rider was acknowledged now by all Europe, the steed he rode was worthy of him. It was a very different force from that which, gallant but raw, had landed in Portugal in 1808. Though its staff was a trifle amateur and its engineers, as befitted the men of an island race, lacking in knowledge of Continental fortification, and its cavalry over-apt to dash after the enemy like a field of fox-hunters, 'as if,' in Wellington's words, 'incapable of manoeuvre except on Wimbledon Common,' its infantry were the finest in the world. Again and again its patiently husbanded volleys had halted the French columns at the moment of triumph; again and again Napoleon's advancing, cheering veterans had wavered, huddled together and broken before its terrible musketry. Being accustomed to operating with little support from other arms, it had evolved a combination of fire-power and movement perfectly fitted to the stony hills of the Peninsula. 'We cracked them out with our muskets,' wrote their Commander-in-Chief.

Three and a half years of campaigning had produced a wonderful synthesis between the men of four nations. Shepherds from the Dorset hills, rollicking blades from Cashel and Clonmel who had enlisted for drink and a fight, sober Nottinghamshire weavers, breechless giants

1. Bell, I, 34, 79. See also Cooke, 47r8; Bessborough, 221; Greville (Suppl.), I, 457; Kincaid, 190; Guedalla, 209; Simmons, 183.

with flaming hair from the Highlands, wastrels from London gaols and sponging-houses, prudent Lowland Scots who had learnt their Latin at Aberdeen Grammar School or Glasgow Academy, were blended, under the command of country squires, fox-hunters, grizzled captains too poor to buy promotion, and eager boys fresh from school, into an entity that represented as nothing else at that moment the national spirit. Since they had sailed from England, cooped up in minute, leaky, rat-infested hulks, they had shared ceaseless short commons, discomfort, and danger. They had slept on arctic sierras and drenched fields, marched under blazing suns, weighed down by knapsack, firelock, and ball-cartridge, with stiff leather girdles round their throats and as many belts as would harness a donkey, cantoned for years among poor, stinking mountain villages where the houses were so full of vermin that if a man lay down he was certain to rise bitten from head to foot.[1] When they fell sick or wounded, they had to endure a hell unimaginable by gentlemen in England, jolting in open bullock-carts with solid wheels or lying under clouds of flies with their wounds crawling with maggots while the surgeons went their round with cauterizing iron and dripping knife. 'No ventilation, twenty sick men in the room, of whom about eighteen died,' ran the diary of a wounded sergeant. 'Shirt unchanged and sticking to my sore back, ears running with stinking matter, a man lying close on my right side with both his legs mortified nearly to the knees and dying.' Those who survived had small hope of pension or gratuity. Even their pay, thanks to the Treasury, was usually months in arrears.

Yet these hard-used men were filled with a burning love of their country and a resolve which no odds or injustice could daunt. They went into battle with shouts of 'Hurrah for old England!' and drums playing 'The British Grenadiers' or 'Garryowen,' wild for a dash at the French. Their pride in their corps was a religion; when, at Albuera,

---

1. Larpent, I, 21. See also *idem*, 12, 17; Grattan, 223; *Johnny Newcome*, 40, 54; Kincaid, 89. Young Sir Thomas Styles of the 1st Foot Guards, who as a small boy at Eton had thrashed the poet Shelley, was bitten so badly on his way through Portugal to join his unit that he committed suicide. The girls in the Portuguese villages on the road made high jest of his sufferings, shaking the fleas out of their petticoats over pails of water and shouting with laughter. Gronow, II, 205-6. See Bell, I, 5-7; Anderson, 4-5; Grattan, 2; Gomm, 132; Blakeney, 15; Boothby, II, 134-5; Dyott, I, 268; *Johnny Newcome*, 11.

two-thirds of the Gloucesters had fallen and all their officers, one of the latter, finding he could still stagger, hobbled back into the fight. 'Twas the system,' he explained, 'of the Old Slashers.' A soldier of the 43rd, that glorious regiment, dying on a straw palliasse, refused to lie still when a badly wounded superior was borne in; his nature would not let him die in peace when an officer was laid beside him on the stones. This was not servility but the spirit of proud subordination which makes an army. So was the sacrifice of the private of the Royal Artificers who exclaimed, when Masséna was sweeping towards Lisbon and a temporary bridge over the Murcella failed to blow up, 'It shall not fail, they shall not pass,' and standing on the structure, held the match to the mine. It was conscience, not fear of the lash, that kept men like these to the sticking-point. 'I heard an old soldier,' wrote a new-comer after his first engagement, 'answer to a youth like myself who inquired what he should do during the battle, "Do your duty!"'[1]

Under their rough exteriors these men were philosophers and humorists. Before a fight jokes and quips ran through the ranks; 'Ah! if me poor mother saw me now!' the men of the 28th would shout when things went awry, rocking with rude laughter at the time-honoured sally. In the same spirit, when the famous rub-a-dub of the French *pas de charge* was heard, the riflemen called out to one another from behind the boulders, 'Holloa there! Look sharp! for damme, here comes Old Trousers!'

Among the Irish, who crowded the ranks of almost every regiment, this joking spirit was often carried to the point of riot. 'A parcel of lads that took the world aisy,' they tended to turn their surroundings into a Donnybrook Fair. They nearly drove Wellington's Provost Marshals mad with their plundering; a few minutes after they bivou-acked, the sheep and hens would start bleating and cackling for miles round. Nor, though their escapades sometimes brought them to the gallows, were they ever at a loss for an answer. 'And I know you, sir, and the "boys of Connaught" know you too,' replied a Connaught Ranger whom General Picton had observed from the far side of an un-fordable river making off with a goat, 'and I'd be sorry to do anything

1. *Journal of a Soldier*, 22, 24. See also Donaldson, 211; Bell, 1, 26–7, 83; Charles Napier, 1, 163–4, 172; Blakeney, 204; Grattan, 112; Gomm, 226; Simmons, 80, 134, 249; Bessborough, 221.

that would be displaising to your honour; and, sure, iv you'd only let me, I'd send your sarvent a leg iv him to dhress for your dinner, for, by my sowl, your honour looks cowld and angry – hungry I mane.' After which, this experienced campaigner, knowing himself safe, held up the old goat by the beard and shook it genially at the General's aide-de-camp.[1]

No discipline could wholly tame such inveterate plunderers. 'I have no fear of your conduct in face of the enemy,' Wellington told an Irish regiment. 'I know you. You are where you wish to be, leading the army. But if I hear of any straggling or irregularities in pursuit, I'll punish you as severely as the worst corps in the army, and *you know me.*' Upon which there arose from the rear rank an agonized cry of 'Glory be to God! there'll be no plundering, after all!' The 'Pat-landers'' wives, who did the army's washing, were as incorrigible. 'Bad luck to his ugly face – the spy of our camp!' cried Mrs Skiddy of the 34th after one of her brushes with the Provost Marshal, 'may he niver see home till the vultures pick his eyes out, the born varmint!' Bestriding the rocky hill-tracks on her celebrated donkey, 'the Queen of Spain,' the little, squat, turtle-backed woman, with her uncontroll-able tongue and invincible courage, was the type of all her ragged race. She and her sisters were always ready to risk their lives to be in at the the bivouac before their husbands and 'have the fire and a dhrip of tay ready for the poor craythers after their load and labour.'

For fighting's sake these 'Teagues' would endure without com-plaining an almost Roundhead discipline. In the whole army no corps was so severely drilled as the Connaught Rangers, the celebrated 88th – a regiment, as one of its veterans wrote, whose spirit it was impossible to break. If a man coughed in the ranks, if the sling of his firelock left his shoulder when it should not, if he moved his knapsack when stand-ing at ease, he was punished. 'Yet, if it came to a hard tug and we had neither rations nor shoes,' wrote Captain Grattan, 'then indeed the Rangers would be in their element and outmarch any battalion in the Service! Without shoes they fancied themselves at home, without food they were nearly at home.' An officer of another regiment has left us a picture of them as they passed him in a moment of crisis, merry

1. Grattan, 21. See also *idem* 87, 123–5, 128, 136–8; Blakeney, 18–19, 165; Schaumann, 23, 202; Leslie, 97.

as larks, singing and cracking their jokes, with bronzed faces and frames hard as nails, and as eager for the fight as for a ration of rum. Danger seemed to inspire them; George Napier recorded how one worthless, drunken dog ran up to a thirteen-inch shell which had dropped into a crowded trench and, knocking off its spluttering fuse, presented it to him with a 'By Jasus, your honour, she'll do you no harm, since I knocked the life out of the cratur!'

With its 'hard cases', inveterate drunkards, and jailbirds – one colonel reckoned the criminal element at from fifty to a hundred men in every battalion – the British Army was no school for saints. The recruiting sergeant took what he could get. Yet nearly all were game-cocks in a fight; as one of their officers said, there never was such an army. And many of these rough men displayed at times a touching affection and kindness. George Napier, when wounded, was visited by an Irish private of his company who, after having his arm amputated, walked seven miles to assure himself of his captain's safety. His brother, William Napier, related how John Henessy of the 50th, a drunken, thieving brute, several times flogged for his evil ways, who was captured with him at Corunna, tramped two hundred miles on his return home in order to deliver to Napier's sister a silver spur entrusted to his charge.

The British soldier's incurable vice was drink. An old woman of Pontalegre, after four years' acquaintanceship with Wellington's army, always assumed, when an Englishman asked a question, that he was after wine. To obtain it, he would commit every species of depredation; rob a house, plunder a church, steal from his comrade, and strip his own dead officer after death. Sergeant Donaldson of the 94th, who wrote an account of life in the ranks, thought that the craving for liquor was often pathological – the result of harsh usage and brutal punishment. Soldiers had to endure so much and had so few normal pleasures that they turned automatically to drink when they relaxed. Men who could take three or four hundred lashings without a groan, chewing a musket ball or a bit of leather to keep themselves from crying out while the blood ran down their backs, were scarcely likely to restrain themselves when they got into a wine vault.

Yet Wellington's remark that the bulk of his men enlisted for drink concealed the representative character of his army. Though poverty was its recruiting ground, many of its soldiers were thoughtful and serious men of refinement and education. One Scottish private related how he found a comrade on guard reading Cromek's *Remains of Nithsdale and Galloway Song*; another how the eyes of himself and his comrades filled with tears as they sang the songs of their native land before a battle.[1] And running through the tough fibre of the rank and file was a strain of chivalry. Foul-mouthed, obscene, irreligious, they would yet give their last bit of biscuit to a starving Portuguese peasant or shoulder the burden of a woman or child. When he was sober and his blood not roused, the British soldier, so fierce and implacable in battle, could show an almost childlike tenderness towards an enemy: would tear the shirt off his own back to bind his wounds, carry him to safety, or share the contents of his flask. Having never known invasion at home, he seldom evinced the revengeful spirit of his German and Iberian allies. A Scottish sergeant who was shot at by a wounded Frenchman for whom he had gone to fetch a drink, after a moment's reflection with raised firelock, quietly went on with his mission of mercy. A private of the same race, finding a Portuguese muleteer robbing a peasant girl, faced his knife with his bare fists and knocked him down.

Among the officers this chivalrous sense of honour was more than an instinct; it was a code. They were almost too ready to take on a bully or punish a cheat; Charles Napier flattered himself that his leg was as straight a one as ever bore up the body of a gentleman or kicked a blackguard. He regarded the treatment of women as the measure of civilization; tenderness towards the helpless and adherence to one's word constituted for him the tests of a gentleman. A man who broke his parole was beneath contempt; George Napier held it up to his children as the unforgivable offence – that and cowardice. One rode straight, spoke the truth, and never showed fear. There was little outward religion in Wellington's officers; skylarking and often uproariously noisy, they were like a pack of schoolboys. Yet under the surface was a deep fund of Christian feeling; their *beau idéal* was a man like John Colborne of the 52nd – upright, fearless, and gentle – or John Vandeleur, whom his friends never heard speak harshly of any man. 'The British Army is what it is,' Wellington said long afterwards,

1. Donaldson, 180; *Journal of a Soldier*, 115–16.

'because it is officered by gentlemen; men who would scorn to do a dishonourable thing and who have something more at stake than a reputation for military smartness.'[1]

It was this that kept them so staunch at the testing time. They fought, not for public applause, but for an inward satisfaction that each man bore in his soul. 'I should never have shown my face again,' wrote one of them of a bout of fever, 'had I applied for sick leave.' They took their knocks as they came, believing that nothing mattered so long as they were true to code and comrade. 'How did you sleep?' asked a young officer of a newcomer after a night in the clouds on the march to Arroyo-Molinos. 'Slept like a fish,' came the reply, 'I believe they sleep very well in water.' 'Bravo,' said he, 'you'll do!' 'Begin to like my trade,' wrote the same apt novice a few weeks later, 'seeing all my comrades as jolly and fearless as if they were fox-hunters.'[2]

The Prussian rigidity which the Horse Guards with pipeclay and lash had imposed on the eighteenth-century Army had long been shed. Wellington's force was as knowing, adaptable, and individualistic as a field of fox-hunters. After four years' campaigning in the toughest country in western Europe, it could, he claimed, go anywhere and do anything. Its courage was the cool, resourceful kind of men with complete confidence in their own skill. 'Now, my lads,' said Colonel Colborne, 'we'll just charge up to the edge of the ditch, and, if we can't get it, we'll stand and fire in their faces.'[3] Alert and wiry veterans as the French were, they had met their match. 'Their soldiers got them into scrapes,' Wellington replied when asked to explain his success, 'mine always got me out.' They were up to every trick of the game and, like their hardy adversaries, able to make themselves comfortable anywhere. Captain Leslie of the 29th and Kincaid of the Rifles have each

1. Fraser, 207; Charles Napier, 1, 316; Gomm, 375; George Napier, 55, 76, 174–5, 218, 221; Grattan, 57, 229, 303; Kincaid, *Random Shots*, 288; Tomkinson, 222; Blakeney, 178, 281–2; Leslie, 193–4, 198; Bessborough, 231; Oman, v, 453; Anderson, 14; *Journal of a Soldier*, 106; Boothby, 159; Costello, 74; Donaldson, 200; Bell, 1, 42, 83–4; Smith, 1, 46–7.

2. Bell, 1, 13–14, 22. See also Simmons, 193; Tomlinson, 22. 'I knew no happier times, and they were their own reward.' Kincaid, *Random Shots*, 252.

3. *Random Shots*, 273. 'I am confident if Colborne was suddenly woken out of his sleep and told he was surrounded by treble his numbers, it would only have had the effect of making him, if possible, still more calm and collected.' George Napier, 220–1.

described the scene at their nightly bivouac: the rough sedge-mats spread under a tree, the accoutrements hanging on the branches, the parallel trenches dug on festive occasions to form a table with candles stuck in the sockets of upturned bayonets, the soup made from stewed ration-beef and vegetables; the partridges and hares roasting on a turning thread suspended from a tripod of ramrods; the rough wine of the country cooled under moist cloths in canteens hung from the trees. Then with a bundle of fine branches to lie on and a green sod or saddle for pillow, the young victors would sleep in their cloaks till reveille. 'The bugles sounded,' wrote Ensign Bell, 'I rolled my blanket, strapped it on my back and waited for the assembly call.'

It was not the French now who hunted the British, but the British the French – 'to pot them, kill them and cook them in their own fashion.' 'Damn my eyes,' the men shouted to one another when on short rations, 'we must either fall in with the French or the Commissary to-day; I don't care which!' 'It was like deer-stalking,' wrote another, 'a glorious thing to whack in amongst a lively part with their flesh-pots on the fire of well-seasoned wood, a chest of drawers, perhaps, or the mahogany of some hidalgo in the middle of the street blazing away and the crappos calling out, "*Bonne soupe, bonne soupe!*"' Officers and men were always thinking out new ways of surprising and harrying the enemy; Captain Irvine of the 28th taught himself to sling stones with such accuracy that, if he encountered two or three Frenchmen, he would bowl one over with a well-placed rock, flatten another with his firelock, and petrify a third with a shout, tripping him up or, if he bolted, pelting him with pebbles – a spectacle which never failed to delight his men.[1]

It was this offensive spirit – itself the outcome of perfect training, fitness, and teamwork – that made Wellington's army so formidable. It was always on its toes; healthy, collected, well-provisioned, wary, impudent, and out to make trouble. Apart from the old Scots champion, Sir Thomas Graham, and Picton, who was fifty-three, the average age of its divisional commanders in the spring of 1812 was slightly under forty. Stapleton Cotton, who commanded the cavalry, was thirty-

1. Bell, I, 163. See *idem*, I, 24, 64, 81-2; Grattan, 176; *Johnny Newcome*, 170; Tomkinson, 137; Kincaid, 33, 42-8, 60, 211; *Random Shots*, 87-90; Leslie, 83-5; Donaldson, 206-7; Tomkinson, 37; Simmons, 15-16, 57.

eight; Alexander Dickson of the Artillery thirty-four; George Murray, the Quartermaster-General and Chief-of-Staff, forty.

Of those they led, the crown and exemplar was still the Light Division – capable, as Harry Smith claimed, of turning the tide of victory any day. 'There perhaps never was, nor ever again will be,' wrote Kincaid, 'such a war brigade as that which was composed of the 43rd, 52nd, and the Rifles.' Its officers, who took a pride in being gay of heart, were always ready to enter into whatever amusement was going – a practical joke, a hare- or fox-hunt, an impromptu donkey-race, a day after the partridges, a dance with guitar, cakes and lemonade in some draughty, candle-lit barn where the raven-haired, garlic-scented village señoritas, screeching with excitement, pinned up their dresses for *bolero* and *fandango*. At the head of this famous Division went the green-jacketed Rifles – 'the most celebrated old fighting corps in the Army' – who in the whole war never lost a piquet. And the scarlet-coated 43rd and 52nd – that beloved corps of George Napier's, 'where every officer was a high-minded gentleman and every private a gallant and well-conducted soldier' – were their equals. 'We had only to look behind,' wrote Kincaid, 'to see a line in which we might place a degree of confidence equal to our hopes in Heaven; nor were we ever disappointed.' Grattan of the 88th – though a member of the rival 3rd Division – acknowledged the 43rd to be the best regiment in the Army.[1]

There were many competitors: the peerless Fusilier regiments which snatched victory out of defeat at Albuera; the Guards with their grace and nonchalance and unbreakable discipline; the fiery Highlanders; the great, undemonstrative regiments of the Line – the 5th, the 28th, the 29th, the 45th, the 48th, the 57th. On their capacity to rise, when called upon, to the highest capacity of human endurance and valour, their commander, though he seldom misused it, knew he could rely. 'Ah,' he said during a near-run fight to an officer who informed him that he had placed the Royal Welch in a dangerous gap, 'that is the very thing!'

Pride in the continuing regiment – the personal individual loyalty

1. Grattan, 120; Bell, I, 12, 37, 54–5, 156; George Napier, 207–8; Kincaid, 96, 153–4, 179; *Random Shots*, 16; Simmons, XXI, 279; Smith, I, 185, 190; Schaumann, 339; Larpent, I, 89, 102; Costello, 148; Cooke, 71–2.

which each private felt towards his corps – gave to the British soldier a moral strength which the student and administrator ought never to underestimate. It enabled him to stand firm and fight forward when men without it, however brave, would have failed. To let down the regiment, to be unworthy of the men of old who had marched under the same colours, to be untrue to the comrades who had shared the same loyalties, hardships, and perils were things that the least-tutored, humblest soldier would not do. Through the dusty, tattered ranks the spirit of companionship ran like a golden thread. 'Years of hard fighting, fatigues and privations that we now wonder at,' wrote Grattan, 'had a charm that in one way or another bound us all together; and, all things considered, I am of opinion that our days in the Peninsula were amongst the happiest of our lives.' 'You may laugh at me,' wrote George Napier after leading a storming party, 'but it made me cry with pleasure and joy to find myself among the men and to see their rough, weather-beaten countenances look at me with every expression of kindly feeling.'

There was little outward pageantry now about Wellington's army – little except the bronzed faces, the level eyes, the indefinable air of resolution and alertness. The dandified uniforms of peace-time England, the powder, pipeclay, brilliant colours, shining brass-work, had become things of the past. Wellington cared little for these; provided his men brought their weapons into the field in good order and sixty sound rounds of ammunition, he never asked whether their trousers were blue, black, or grey.[1] Their jackets were faded and ragged, their breeches patched with old blankets, their shakos bleached by sun and twisted into fantastic shapes. When an officer, returning wounded from Portugal, saw the Portsmouth garrison in their smart white small clothes and black gaiters, they seemed to him like the troops of another nation. And the Life Guards, arriving in Spain from England, mistook the Rifles from their dark clothing and sunburnt visages for Portuguese. The slouching gait, the motley wear, the alert, roving gaze of the Peninsular men were as far removed from the Prussian gait of the

1. Grattan, 50. 'There is no subject of which I understand so little. ... I think it indifferent how a soldier is clothed provided it is in a uniform manner, and that he is forced to keep himself clean and smart as a soldier ought to be.' Wellington, *Supplementary Dispatches*, VII, 245. See Oman, *Wellington's Army*, 296; Kincaid, 203–4.

barrack square as was the fustian of Cromwell's Ironsides. Only their firelocks were always bright and clean.

*

Yet as they assembled in the March of 1812 before Badajoz, there was no mistaking their power. On the 17th – the day after the city was invested – they paraded before Wellington, their bullet-ridden colours, bare and faded, floating in the wind and the band of each regiment breaking into the march, 'St Patrick's Day'. That night the work of entrenching began under heavy fire from the fortress and in icy rain. The men had to dig up to their knees in slime under continuous bombardment; for the next week, while the rest of the army covered the siege, they spent sixteen out of every twenty-four hours in the trenches. At one moment floods swept away the pontoon bridge that linked them with headquarters at Elvas. Every morning of that anxious week as Wellington waited for news of Soult's army beyond the Sierra Morena, the Portuguese Governor of Elvas and his Staff in full uniform solemnly waited on him to ask, with a wealth of old-world compliment, how he had passed the night.[1]

On the afternoon of March 24th the weather cleared. Next night five hundred volunteers of the Light and 3rd Divisions stormed Fort Picurina, an outlying bastion on the south-east of the town. As the last stroke of the cathedral bell tolled eight, the storming detachments rose from the trenches and raced towards the glacis. Two hundred fell, but, before the enemy could recover, they were swarming up the ladders, the men of the 3rd Division crying out to their old rivals: 'Stand out of the way!' to which the latter, shoving fiercely by, shouted back, 'Damn your eyes, do you think we Light Division fetch ladders for such chaps as you to climb up!'[2]

The capture of Picurina enabled the breaching batteries to begin the bombardment of the south-eastern corner of the city wall which the engineers had selected as its weakest point. It was now a race between the British guns and Soult's troops. Fortunately, Marmont, who in the previous summer had successfully marched to the relief of Badajoz,

1. Stanhope, 327.
2. Smith, I, 62. See also Grattan, 188; Bell, I, 28; Tomlinson, 143; Blakeney, 261; Fortescue, VIII, 286; Oman, V, 239–40.

had been expressly commanded by Napoleon to invade Portugal in Wellington's absence – a futile demonstration as he knew, since not only did Ciudad Rodrigo bar the road to Lisbon, but he had no means of supporting his army in the Portuguese hinterland.

By April 4th, the day Soult emerged from the Sierra Morena, two breaches had been made. Next day, every gun was directed to making a third in the curtain wall between. By the rules of siegecraft, no assault should have been made until the batteries had blown in the counter-scarp. But as this was beyond Wellington's power, an unmilitary Parliament and parsimonious Treasury having failed to provide him with trained sappers, he had to use his infantry to do the work of mine and shell.

Badajoz was held by nearly 5000 veteran troops under General Phillipon, a past-master of fortification. Faced by Napoleon's threat to shoot the Governor of any fortress who surrendered before it had been stormed – a defiance of the eighteenth-century convention that allowed the Governor of a besieged town to yield as soon as a practicable breach had been effected so as to avoid casualties and the horrors of a sack – he had sealed off the breaches with tiers of trenches and strewn the un-bridged ditch before them with thousands of mines, iron harrows, crows' feet, and *chevaux de frise*. Believing the rest of the city's defences to be impregnable, he had then concentrated half the garrison at the point and armed every man with eight loaded muskets.

It was Wellington's plan that of the four divisions besieging the town, the 7500 men of the 4th and Light should storm the breaches. At Picton's eleventh-hour entreaty, the 3rd Division on their right had been given the supplementary task of trying to take the main castle by *escalade* – a feat apparently impossible, for part of its walls rose a hundred feet sheer above the ditch and the Guadiana. Meanwhile, on the other side of the town, which was known to be heavily mined, General Leith's 5th Division and some Portuguese were to pin down as many of the garrison as possible by a demonstration. At the last moment a few ladders had been allotted to them to attempt the ramparts of the San Vincente bastion at the extreme north-west corner of the town.

By the afternoon of April 6th the third breach had been made. The order for the assault was immediately given. Though it was certain that there would be terrible losses, the troops received it with grim satisfaction. Even officers' servants insisted on taking their places in the ranks. The gaiety of the southward march had now been succeeded by something in the men's bearing that told that, though during the siege they had made no complaint of their fatigues and had seen their comrades fall without repining, they smarted under the one and felt the other. Their expression of anxiety to seize their prey was almost tiger-like.[1]

As evening approached, a hush fell on the camp. The men sauntered about, many for the last time, while bands played airs which recalled distant homes and bygone days. The time for the assault had been fixed for seven-thirty, but owing to various mishaps it was postponed till ten, giving the enemy several further hours of darkness in which to sow the ditch and breaches with explosives. Ghostlike sheets of mist rose from the Guadiana, hiding the lanterns of the working-parties; only the rippling waters, the croaking of frogs along the bank, and the sentinel's cry on the ramparts broke the silence. Grattan has left a picture of the waiting columns: the men without knapsacks, their shirts unbuttoned, trousers tucked to the knees, tattered jackets so worn as to make the insignia of regiment and rank indistinguishable, the stubby, keen-set faces, the self-assurance, devoid of boast or bravado, that proclaimed them for what they were – an invincible host.

Soon after nine the order was given to move to the storming positions, and without a word and in pitch blackness the men went forward. Those approaching the castle were discovered shortly before zero hour by the light of a flaming carcass thrown from the ramparts. Immediately every gun opened up. In front of the breaches the storming parties, creeping up to the glacis, had already begun to descend into the ditch. As the first fireball rose, the scene was lit up like a picture; the ramparts crowded with dark figures and glittering arms, and, below, the long red columns coming on 'like streams of burning lava'. Then there was a tremendous crash, and the leading files were blown to pieces as hundreds of shells and powder barrels exploded.

For an instant, wrote an officer, the men stood on the brink of the ditch amazed at the sight; then, with a shout, flew down the ladders or, disdaining their aid, leaped, reckless of the depth, into the gulf below.

1. Grattan, 193–7; Kincaid, 130; Bell, i, 27.

Hundreds fell, but their comrades, trampling over them, pressed forward through a storm of grape-shot and cannister. The ditch became a writhing mass of dead and wounded, across whose bodies fresh assailants struggled through flame and darkness towards the breaches. Many were shot or burnt; some, losing their bearings in the darkness, stumbled into the flooded part of the ditch and, weighed down by their packs, sank beneath the waters. Others were blown to pieces by the exploding grenades, mines, and powder-barrels. Yet still little groups of men forced their way through that surf of fire and 'went at the breach like a whirlwind. ... Hundreds fell, dropping at every discharge which maddened the living; the cheer was for ever on, on, with screams of vengeance and a fury determined to win the town; the rear pushed the foremost into the sword-blades to make a bridge of their bodies rather than be frustrated. Slaughter, tumult and disorder continued; no command could be heard, the wounded struggling to free themselves from under the bleeding bodies of their dead comrades; the enemy's guns within a few yards at every fire opening a bloody lane amongst our people, who closed up and, with shouts of terror as the lava burned them up, pressed on to destruction – officers, starting forward with an heroic impulse, carried on their men to the yawning breach and glittering steel, which still belched out flames of scorching death.'[1] All the while the bugles continued to sound the advance.

But, though the breaches were three times cleared by the bayonet, none penetrated them. There were soldiers who in the frenzy of attack thrust their heads through the hedge of swords at the summit and allowed the foe to smash them with the butts of their muskets, or, enveloped in streams of fire, died trying to tear with lacerated hands the blades out of the *chevaux de frise*. All was in vain. No troops could have passed through that curtain of death.

Yet, 'though valour's self might stand appalled,' the British refused to withdraw. They stood sullenly facing that terrible fire until some officer, rallying fifty or a hundred tired men, led them forward once more, only to meet the same inevitable fate. For two hours the slaughter continued until a third of the Light Division had fallen. The 95th alone lost twenty-two officers.

About midnight Wellington, who was waiting in a neighbouring

1. Bell, 1, 30–1.

quarry, called off the attack. His face, lit by the flame of a candle, was grey and drawn, and his jaw fell as he gave the order. In that bitter hour he ordered one of his aides to hasten to Picton and tell him that he must try at all costs to succeed in the castle. He was unaware that the castle had already fallen. While the buglers on the glacis before the breaches still sounded the retreat and the stubborn survivors of the 4th and Light Divisions began to fall back to the quarries, an officer galloped up with the news that Picton's men were inside the walls. For, by their refusal to admit defeat, the men of the breaches had given their comrades the chance to achieve the impossible. Those struggling to breast the castle's towering cliffs had, too, suffered terrible casualties, and, baffled by a murderous cross-fire from the bastions and shells, stones and logs thrown from the ramparts, had fallen back in defeat. But Picton, who never did things by halves, wounded though he was in the groin, returned to the ditch and formed up his entire division, 4000 strong, at the base of the wall. Though ladder after ladder was flung down by the defenders and the rungs were slippery with blood, those below took the places of those who fell so swiftly that in the end a lodgement was made, the ramparts cleared, and, after nearly a fifth of its numbers had fallen, the 3rd Division swarmed into the fortress. Among the casualties was Colonel Ridge of the 5th Fusiliers – the third to reach the summit. 'No man,' wrote Napier, 'died that night with more glory – yet many died, and there was much glory.'

By capturing the castle, and with it the enemy's reserves of food and ammunition, Picton had made the fall of Badajoz certain. He could not alter the immediate situation in front of the breaches because the castle gates leading to the ramparts had been bricked up, and only a single postern, hastily closed by the enemy, gave access to the town. But while his men were dragging up a gun from the embrasure to blow it in, Wellington, still waiting in the quarries near the breaches, thought he heard the sound of an English bugle in the tower of San Vincente at the far side of the town. Here, though the walls were more than thirty feet high and the ladders too low, a detachment of General Walker's brigade of Leith's 5th Division, consisting of men of the 4th and 44th Regiments, managed in the darkness to secure a foothold on the undermanned ramparts. They had at once gone to the assistance of their comrades below, and by midnight had lifted the whole brigade into the town. Though there was fierce fighting on the walls and Walker himself was wounded, Leith brought up the rest of his division with such speed that the enemy was given no chance to recover. It was the appearance in the rear of the breaches of a detachment of this force, marching in haste through the deserted streets, that caused the French to collapse. Unable to imagine how their foes had entered, they threw down their arms or fled. The exhausted survivors of the Light and 4th Divisions, returning to the attack, found the breaches deserted. Badajoz had fallen.

What followed tarnished the night's glory. The men, separated in the darkness from their officers, parched with thirst and half-mad from the fury of the attack, broke into the cellars and wine-shops. By dawn they had become a mob of fiends. They had been promised, in accordance with the rules of war, that, if the garrison resisted after the breaches had been made, the city would be given up to sack; they did not now mean to lose a prey so hardly won. The worst horrors were the work of the scoundrel minority of an army recruited in part from the jails, and of the Spanish and Portuguese camp-followers. For two days and nights packs of drunkards rushed from house to house, blowing in doors, firing through windows, and looting everything. Women were dragged screaming from hiding holes and raped, wine casks were broached in the streets, and satyrs with blackened faces drank till the liquor ran from their mouths and ears. No officer could control them. It was not till the third day that Wellington, marching in fresh troops and erecting a gallows in the square, restored order.[1]

Yet even during these scenes soldiers risked their lives to stay the tumult. Groups of officers fought their way through the streets escorting women to the church of St John's where a guard was mounted; others kept watch over Spanish families and drove back the mobs who assailed them. Down at the camp below the town, where the British wounded lay in thousands, two young officers, standing at their tent door on the day after the attack, saw two Spanish ladies approaching, the elder of whom, her ears torn and bleeding from the grasp of drunken savages, confided to their protection her sister, a girl of fifteen. Such

1. Blakeney, 270–8; Grattan, 158, 208, 210–16; Gomm, 202; Costello, 120–1; Bell, I, 33–4; Tomkinson, 146; Simmons, 233; Kincaid, 139; *Random Shots*, 285; Stanhope, 49; Napier, IV, 430–1.

was her faith in the British character, she declared, that she knew the appeal would not be in vain. 'Nor was it,' wrote one of the officers, 'nor could it be abused, for she stood by the side of an angel – a being more transcendently lovely than any I had ever before beheld. To look at her was to love her – and I did love her, but I never told my love, and in the meantime another and a more impudent fellow stepped in and won her!' Two days later Juanita Maria de los Dolores de Leon was married to Captain Harry Smith of the Rifles. The Commander-in-Chief gave her away, and she became the darling of the Army, henceforward sharing all its adventures and hardships. Many years later, when her husband, the victor of Aliwal, had become the hero of Victorian England and Governor of the Cape, she gave her name to a South African town destined to become the scene of another famous siege.

CHAPTER 2

SALAMANCA SUMMER

I made a mistake about England, in trying to conquer it.
The English are a brave nation.

NAPOLEON

THE price of Badajoz had been 5000 British and Portuguese casualties, 3500 of whom, the flower of the army, fell in the assault. When the sun rose on the morning after the attack the ditch before the breaches was a lake of smoking blood. Yet the price had been worth the sacrifice.[1] The key fortress of western Spain with nearly 5000 prisoners was in Wellington's hands. So, for the first time in the war, was the initiative. Possessing Badajoz as well as Ciudad Rodrigo, he could now concentrate against either of the two French armies barring the road to Spain. With the use of interior lines, he could attack Marmont in the north or Soult in the south before either could come to the other's aid. Nor could either, with the Spanish frontier fortresses in their way, effectively invade Portugal in his absence. On Napoleon's orders, Marmont had attempted to do so during the siege of Badajoz, but though his marauding troops, helped by a panic among the Portuguese militia, had penetrated fifty miles, they were quickly forced back starving to their base at Salamanca. Three weeks later, after returning to the north, Wellington sent Hill's corps of observation in Estremadura to seize Almaraz – Soult's last bridge across the Tagus below Toledo. Thus all direct communication between Soult and Marmont was lost, and the two Marshals could henceforth only communicate through Madrid. Simultaneously, Wellington's engineers improvised a suspension-bridge of ropes and cables – the first of its kind in Europe – across the Tagus gorge

1. 'The capture of Badajoz affords as strong an instance of the gallantry of our troops as has ever been displayed, but I anxiously hope that I shall never again be the instrument of putting them to such a test as that to which they were put last night. ...When I ordered the assault I was certain I should lose our best officers and men. It is a cruel situation for any person to be placed in, and I earnestly recommend to your lordship to have a corps of sappers and miners formed without loss of time.' Wellington to Liverpool, April 7th, 1812. Oman, *Wellington's Army*, 284–5.

at Alcantara, so giving him direct north-to-south communication along the frontier. It was for this he had been campaigning for the past year.

Yet Napoleon could still make Spain secure. He had a quarter of a million troops in the Peninsula to Wellington's 45,000 British and 25,000 Portuguese regulars. He had only to call off his attack on Russia to reinforce these to a point beyond which they could not be challenged by so few. But the flaw in his character which Wellington had always seen gave England her chance. Instead of regarding the loss of Badajoz as a warning, the Emperor greeted the news with one of his famous fits of rage, and then, forbidding all reference to it, behaved as though it had never happened. Turning his back on Wellington, he marched on June 24th into Russia with half a million men.

By that time Wellington was himself across the frontier. As in 1809, the outbreak of war in eastern Europe enabled him to take the offensive. Throughout May he had been preparing magazines for an advance towards the Douro. True to his unchanging strategy of doing nothing to distract Soult from his selfish preoccupation with his Andalusian viceroyalty, and leaving a token force under Hill to watch the Tagus and the road over the Sierra Morena, he concentrated against the northern highway from Ciudad Rodrigo to Salamanca and Valladolid. It was the road Moore had followed when he struck at Napoleon's communications. It offered a greater strategic prize than an advance through Badajoz towards Madrid or Seville, since if he could reach Burgos – two hundred miles to the north-east – Wellington would cut off both these places from south-western France and dominate the whole of Spain except the eastern coast. Between him and his goal lay Marmont's army, which, when assembled, equalled his own. Beyond it, holding down the country, were three other armies almost as large.

Yet Wellington, though numerically inferior, had certain advantages; it was his genius as a commander that, seeing the war whole and steadily, he never lost sight of any of them. One was that, so long as he could keep it supplied, his entire force was free for field operations, while the French were preoccupied in garrisoning a vast, turbulent country. Neither General Caffarelli's Army of the North, nor Marshal Suchet's Army of the East, nor King Joseph's and Marshal Jourdan's Army of the Centre, still less Soult's Army of Andalusia, could reinforce the Army of Portugal without abandoning a large part of Spain to the guerrillas and the Spanish hill armies. Here Wellington's second asset operated: that, thanks to Napoleon's system of ruling by division, no one of his Marshals trusted any other or would willingly send troops from his own domain to help the common cause. His third asset was that the Peninsula was almost surrounded by sea over which his country enjoyed complete mastery. Her ships could succour the Spanish guerrillas at any point and keep the French in continual alarm and uncertainty. Because of this, Caffarelli in Biscaya, Suchet in Catalonia, and Soult in Andalusia instinctively faced, not westwards towards Wellington, but north, east, and south towards the sea. Even Marmont, on Napoleon's orders, had had to send part of his army to the Asturias, where the Cantabrian guerrillas and the Spanish Army of Galicia were armed and supplied by the Royal Navy.

In planning his summer campaign Wellington made use of these factors. His object was to destroy Marmont while keeping the latter's colleagues busy elsewhere. The Spanish general, Ballasteros, with his raggle-taggle army in the mountains round Seville, supported by Hill's corps of observation in distant Estremadura, was to tie down Soult by threatening as many Andalusian towns as possible. In the east a British expeditionary force of 10,000 men, temporarily released from garrison duty in Sicily by the departure of Murat's Neapolitan army for Russia,[1] together with 7000 Spanish troops from Alicante and Majorca, were to be landed by the Mediterranean Fleet on the Valencian coast to harry Suchet's communications. And in the north, along the Atlantic cliffs, that erratic champion of amphibious war, Commodore Sir Home Popham, with two battleships, half a dozen frigates, a battalion of marines, and a company of marine artillery was to keep the coastline from Gijon to the French frontier in an uproar. So sustained, the guerrillas of the Basque country and Navarre – the most serious of all the thorns in King Joseph's flesh – were to make it impossible for the harassed Caffarelli to reinforce Marmont. At the same time the Spanish army of Galicia was to take the offensive against the latter's northern wing, lay siege to Astorga, and prevent even the Army of Portugal from concentrating.

On June 13th Wellington crossed the Agueda with 51,000 men,

1. By April, 1812, such was the concentration of troops for the impending march to Moscow, only one French division remained in Italy. Oman, v, 342.

including 18,000 Portuguese and 3000 Spaniards. Marmont, with one division in the Asturias and the rest of his army dispersed, could offer little immediate resistance. Ordering a concentration, he fell back across the Tormes. As the British entered Salamanca on the 17th, a surge of ecstatic humanity broke over the red-coated columns in the sun-bathed Palaza Mayor. It was the first Spanish city to be liberated in three years. Even Wellington, as he sat writing orders on his sabretache, was almost unhorsed by a charge of ladies.[1]

He remained, however, cautious. During the next ten days he blockaded three small forts which Marmont had built outside Salamanca. He made no attempt to bring the French to battle. Instead he covered the siege and awaited their attack in one of those innocent-looking but carefully chosen positions which had so often proved fatal to them. But Marmont, taught by experience, was cautious too. After several half-hearted attempts at relief, he allowed the forts and their garrisons to fall.

Thereafter he fell back for thirty miles across the rolling Leon plain to the Douro. Here, with his army concentrated and almost equal in size to Wellington's, and with ample reserves behind, he had only to hold the crossings from Toro to Tordesillas to bring the British offensive to an end. If he could stay there until the harvest was gathered, the French position in northern Spain would be secure for another year. For a fortnight at the beginning of July, while far away Napoleon's interminable columns drove through Lithuania into Russia, the two armies faced one another across the shallow, sunlit Douro. Then on the 16th, seeing nothing to stop him, Marmont recrossed the river at Tordesillas and feinted at Wellington's right flank. Next day, as the latter parried the stroke, he deftly shifted his forces eastwards and, crossing again at Toro, struck at his left. Like a true son of the Revolution and a Marshal of France, he was in search of glory: to survive he had to outshine his rivals.

To the disgust of his army Wellington promptly retreated. Unlike his adversary, who could live by plundering the country, he was dependent on his commissariat wagons. Rather than risk his communications with Portugal, he fell back towards the hillier and more barren

1. Tomkinson, 162. See also Gomm, 272; Kincaid, 150; Oman, v, 360; Simmons, 236.

terrain whence he had come and where he would have Marmont once more at a disadvantage. For the next six days the two armies within easy striking distance of one another marched and manoeuvred under a burning sun, steadily moving south-westwards as Marmont tried to cut off Wellington from his base and Wellington gave ground to prevent him. Both, like skilful fencers, kept their forces closely concentrated, neither for a moment lowering his guard. On July 18th, when there was some skirmishing, and again on the 20th, the two armies marched within gunshot all day in parallel columns, their accoutrements glittering in the sunlight, while swarms of vultures cruised overhead.[1]

The French, who were slightly the better marchers, reached the Tormes first, crossing the river at the ford of Huerta, ten miles east of Salamanca, at midday on the 21st. Wellington recrossed the river the same evening about two miles above Salamanca. Marmont was driving straight for his communications, and, though the gloom of the liberated city now surpassed its ecstasy of a month earlier, the British commander resolved that night to abandon it and retire on Ciudad Rodrigo. Without a major blunder by his opponent he could not hope for a decisive victory or for one without losses which he could not replace. The two armies were by now almost equal, the French having 48,500 men with a marked superiority in guns to the Anglo-Portuguese 50,000. And thanks to the guerrillas' interception of French dispatches Wellington, unlike Marmont, knew that 15,000 men under King Joseph and Jourdan were hastening to Marmont's aid from Madrid. He had also learnt that the British Commander-in-Chief in Sicily had failed to make a diversion on the Valencian coast and was contemplating instead an expedition to Italy. Faced with the possibility of Suchet also reinforcing Marmont, there seemed nothing for it but to abandon the offensive for another year. He could not afford to be cut off from Portugal or to fight a battle which he was not reasonably sure of winning.

To those whose lives he was so prudently husbanding Wellington's decision to retreat came as a bitter disappointment. Their confidence in their own prowess, the warmth of their welcome from the Spanish people, the hopes of diving deeper into the romantic land before them, had ended in the old way. To add to their humiliation, that night as

1. 'I was frequently impressed with the horror of being wounded without the power to keep them off.' Tomkinson, 190.

they lay tentless and hungry in the open fields they were assailed by a fearful thunderstorm. Flashes lit the blackness of the plain, horses broke from their piquets and galloped into the enemy lines, and the earth threw up multitudes of drowning worms. The summer dawn of the 22nd found the British soaked, aching, and sullen.

In Marmont's mind Wellington's iron self-restraint had by now established the idea that he was incapable of any but a defensive role. It had even eradicated the painful impression of British invincibility forced on the French consciousness by the battles of the past four years. It caused the Marshal to throw all caution to the winds. On the morning of July 22nd he saw his chance – the greatest of his career. Before the elusive British could slip away again to the Portuguese mountains, he would treat them as his master had treated the Austrians and Prussians. By reverting to the *élan* of revolutionary tradition, he would do to the stiff-necked redcoats what Junot, Victor, Soult, Ney, Masséna, even Napoleon had failed to do.

With this intention the Marshal resumed his westward march on the morning of the 22nd, edging as he had done before round the right flank of the mainly invisible British, while his guns maintained a brisk cannonade against such of their positions as he could see. Presently, mistaking adjustments in Wellington's disposition for signs of an immediate retreat, he resolved to hasten the pace of his march towards the Salamanca-Rodrigo highway. He therefore ordered his advance-guard – the left flank of the line he presented to the British – to hurry ahead to envelop their right and cut their communications. By so doing he extended his force in the presence of an enemy still concentrated.

The British Commander-in-Chief, guardian of the only army England possessed, had told his Government that he would never risk a general encounter at a disadvantage. But he had never said that he would not seize victory if it was offered him. Between two and three in the afternoon the leading French division, which was marching across his front along a low ridge about a mile away, began to race ahead. Seeing the gap between it and more slowly moving centre widen, Wellington dropped the chicken leg he was eating and seized a telescope. Then, with a quick, 'That will do,' he sent off his aides with orders to his divisional commanders, and, mounting his horse, galloped three miles across the stony fields to the village of Aldea

Tejada where, about two miles north of the point on which the French advance-guard was moving, he had posted the 3rd Division in reserve. Here he bade his brother-in-law, Edward Pakenham, move forward, take the heights in his front, and drive everything before him. Then, before the colours could be encased and the men receive their orders to prime and load, he was on his way back to his position in the British centre. He had three hours of daylight and a chance that might never recur.

Before him the French army was spread out on a series of low rolling hills, moving in column of march in a great semicircle westwards and on a scattered front of more than five miles. It was a sight not dissimilar to that which confronted Nelson at Trafalgar. The marching columns had their right flanks towards him. Because of the rolling and wooded nature of the country and the skill with which he had placed his own formations out of sight, they seemed unaware of the compact force which they were so hopefully passing and attempting to encircle. Indeed, misled by the westering movement of Wellington's baggage-train on the Salamanca-Rodrigo highway, Marmont was under the impression that the British army had already begun its retreat. Between his leading division, that of Thomières, and those of Maucune, Clausel, and Brennier in his centre there was a gap of more than a mile, while another of equal size separated the centre from the four scattered divisions following.

Wellington, as always in an enemy's presence, had his force closely in hand. While his left, consisting of the 1st and Light Divisions and Bock's German cavalry – just over 10,000 men – faced eastwards, the bulk of his army, which in view of the French encircling movement he had earlier in the day wheeled towards the south, was grouped around the little village of Arapiles. Here 14,000 British infantry of the 4th, 5th, 6th, and 7th Divisions, most of Cotton's cavalry, nearly 14,000 Portuguese and España's 3000 Spaniards – a force of some 34,000 – were drawn up in line of battle within a mile of the 18,000 marching men of Marmont's centre. Farther to the west another 6000 British and Portuguese, under Pakenham, were moving up from Aldea Tejada to strike at the head of Thomières's strung-out advance-guard of 4500 infantry and attendant cavalry. The rest of the French army, more than 24,000 strong, was still coming up from the east.

Marmont, as Wellington remarked to his Spanish aide-de-camp, was lost. Supported by D'Urban's Portuguese cavalry, the 3rd Division cut across Thomières's line of march, in Napier's phrase, like a meteor. As it reached the summit of the plateau, it deployed and opened fire. The French were caught strung out on the march, surprised and at a hopeless disadvantage. Thomières was killed, half his division mown down and all its guns captured. The survivors were driven back into the ranks of those behind.

Here the British 4th and 5th Divisions, with their flanks covered by Bradford's Portuguese and Cotton's cavalry, had been moving in line

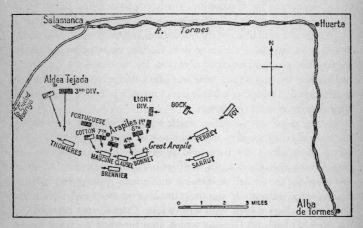

across a shallow depression towards the French centre. As soon as Marmont had seen the British coming up over the opposing ridge, he had realized his mistake: Wellington was not a purely defensive general after all. But it was too late to retrieve it; a few minutes later, while galloping forward, he was struck down by a shell. Though his artillery, with 78 guns to the British 54, raked the oncoming scarlet lines, nothing could break that confident advance; it came on like the bore of a tidal river. Behind, in support, followed the 6th and 7th Divisions. For some reason Maucune's men awaited the attack in square, a little in rear of the crest along which they had been moving. They could not have chosen a more disastrous formation. The 5th Division, marching with review precision, breasted the ridge and, at an order from General Leith, fired a tremendous volley. Then, through the smoke and darkness, it charged the shattered French squares with the bayonet.

As the latter broke, a terrible fate overtook them. At that moment the first of Cotton's cavalry brigades, consisting of the 5th Dragoon Guards and the 4th and 5th Dragoons under Major-General Le Marchant, appeared on the sky-line. Le Marchant was a brilliant officer who had recently joined the army after serving as the first Commandant of the Royal Military College at High Wycombe. He at once led his men to the charge. Though he himself fell, they caught Maucune's flying infantry in the flank with their heavy swords and drove right into Brennier's division behind; many of the former were so disfigured by sabre cuts that all traces of the human face and form were obliterated. Wellington, watching the scene with Cotton, declared he had never seen anything so well executed in his life. By the time Leith's infantry had finished the massacre, as little was left of Brennier's and Maucune's divisions as of Thomières's. More than a third of Marmont's army had been destroyed in forty minutes.

Further to the east the Allied attack was less successful. Here Pack's Portuguese failed to carry the rocky side of the Great Arapile knoll which, dominating the battlefield at the point where the original British line turned northwards, had been occupied by Bonnet's division as a pivot for the French enveloping movement. Charged by the defenders when gallantly trying to scramble up its steep side, the Portuguese were thrown back with serious loss. Their repulse exposed the left flank of Cole's 4th Division which, after breasting the ridge, found itself assailed on two sides by Clausel's and Bonnet's men. It, too, was forced back in confusion.

For a moment it seemed to Clausel, who had succeeded to the command, that the battle might be retrieved. While the remnants of the French left were flying into the wood, the right centre, consisting of his own and Bonnet's divisions, with Ferey's support, struck boldly at the ridge from which Wellington's attack had been launched. But as they pursued Cole's and Pack's retreating men, they encountered Clinton's 6th Division coming up in an unbroken line, with the 1st and 7th Divisions on either flank. As so often before, the unexpected appearance of Wellington's carefully husbanded reserves was decisive.

In twenty minutes Bonnet's and Clausel's men were as badly beaten as their comrades.

It was left to Ferrey's and Sarrut's divisions, forming line across the edge of the forest to the south-east, to cover the escape of the French army. For half an hour in the failing light they fought with splendid steadiness, inflicting the heaviest British casualties of the day on Clinton's men who were trying to dislodge them.[1] As at Talavera, the dry grass was kindled by the fire of the guns, so that the British, fighting up the slope towards the forest, seemed to be attacking a burning mountain. As darkness fell, the heroes of the French rearguard, almost naked and besmeared with blood and dust, withdrew, still firing, into the woods.

Without the failure of a Spanish officer whom Wellington had placed in the castle of Alba to guard the crossing of the Tormes, scarcely a man would have got away. Believing the bridge there to be securely held, Wellington assumed that the only escape for the French was to the north-east by Huerta and sent the unused Light Division and Ponsonby's cavalry to seize the ford there. But with the incorrigible individualism of his race, the commander at Alba had not only abandoned his post, but refrained from informing his British chief that he had done so. And it was to the bridge which he had left open, eight miles south-east of the battlefield, that the demoralized survivors of the French army fled. As a result Wellington was robbed of a victory as complete as Ulm or Jena.

Yet though more than 30,000 of Marmont's men escaped, they did so without cohesion and with no immediate hope of being able to re-form as a fighting force. As Foy, the commander of the only undamaged division, confided to his diary, the catastrophe of the Spanish war had come. With the Army of Portugal's rout the balance of Napoleon's dispositions in the Peninsula had been destroyed. So had the legend of French invincibility. Suffering 15,000 casualties to Wellington's 5000, the French left in his hands two eagles, six colours, twenty guns, and 7000 prisoners. Their Commander-in-Chief and four divisional commanders were among the casualties. The battle, Foy thought, raised Wellington almost to the level of Marlborough. 'Hitherto,' he wrote,

1. Two British regiments, the 11th and 61st, lost 340 out of 516 and 366 out of 546 men. Oman, v, 462.

'we had been aware of his prudence, his eye for choosing a position, and his skill in utilizing it. At Salamanca he has shown himself a great and able master of manoeuvre. He kept his dispositions concealed for almost the whole day; he waited till we were committed to our movement before he developed his own. ... He fought in the oblique order – it was a battle in the style of Frederick the Great.'[1] Not since the victor of Blenheim supped with two captive Marshals of France in his coach had a British army won such glory.

*

Wellington's pursuit was not the spectacular affair that followed Napoleon's victories. He had only 3000 cavalry; his tired men had fought three major engagements in six months, and many of his regiments were gravely depleted. Sweeping gestures and risks were beyond his means. Apart from his German, Portuguese, and Spanish auxiliaries, he had still less than 40,000 troops in the Peninsula. Unlike Napoleon he could not look to conscriptions to fill his ranks; he was the servant of a parsimonious Parliament. And there were still four other French armies in Spain.

Except for two regiments of Foy's rearguard, who were annihilated in square by a brilliant charge of German cavalry on the day after the battle, the retreating French received little injury from their pursuers. They moved too fast for them. The British commander was more concerned to feed his advancing columns and to prevent King Joseph's army from Madrid from joining and rallying Clausel's fugitives.

Only when he learnt that Joseph was withdrawing again across the Guadarramas, did Wellington push on to Valladolid where he took another 17 guns and 800 sick on the 29th. Here he waited a week till he was satisfied that the shattered Army of Portugal, falling back on Burgos, was not being reinforced by Caffarelli's Army of the North. Then, finding that the latter was fully occupied by Popham's coastal operations, he turned his face to the south. On August 5th, a fortnight

1. The sources used for the account of the battle are Oman, v, 418–74; Fortescue, VIII, 480–98; Wellington's *Dispatches*; Napier, Book XVIII, Ch. iii; Colonel A. H. Burne's *The Art of War on Land*; Foy; Gomm, 272–80; *Dickson Papers*, II, 685–97; Granville, II, 437, 450; Simmons, 241–2; Grattan, 238–60; Granville, I, 75; Vere, 31–7; Tomkinson, 168–89; Lynedoch, 236–7; Leith Hay, II, 46–58.

after Salamanca, leaving Clinton with the 6th Division to watch Clausel, he marched with 36,000 troops to Segovia and Madrid. His resolution was reached after learning that the British expedition from Sicily had arrived after all on the Mediterranean coast. Reckoning that this would keep Suchet from reinforcing his colleagues, he decided to seize the Spanish capital before Soult's 45,000 troops from Andalusia could come to the rescue of Joseph's outnumbered Army of the Centre. For its liberation would not only hearten the Spaniards, stiffen the Russians in their resistance, and suggest to a restless Europe that French power was on the wane, but would give the British the advantage of interior lines in any future operations against Soult. With the whole Tagus valley and both ends of the Madrid-Badajoz highway in his hands, Wellington then could bring up Hill's 21,000 men from Estremadura more quickly than Soult could attack him. He would also gain the main French arsenal in Spain.

In glorious weather the army crossed the Guadarramas and began to move on Madrid. Never had Spain shown such a welcoming face. In every village were bands of music, girls with streamers and laurel crowns to shower kisses on the victors, shouts of 'Viva el gran Capitan,' and 'Vivan los Heroes Ingleses los Salvadores.' The rough, battle-worn men responded in character to this romantic Iberian flattery, and for once, though there were many opportunities for drink, drunkenness was almost unknown. At the royal summer-palace of San Ildefonso there was a fête in the gardens under the blue mountains; bands played in the walks, and the waterworks threw up glittering cascades. At twilight, as Wellington, surrounded by generals and grandees, entered the gardens, every band broke into 'See the Conquering Hero Comes,' and thousands swelled the chorus, while hundreds of ladies saluted and embraced him as their saviour.[1]

Meanwhile in Madrid Joseph's satellites prepared for flight. All night carriages and carts rolled out of the city on the southern road, laden with household goods and terrified collaborators flying from their countrymen's ferocious patriotism. As there was no news of Soult, who

[1]. Those present remembered it as one of the most intoxicating nights of pleasure they had ever known. 'When the shrill note of the bugle aroused us from our sleep all that had passed seemed but as a dream.' Grattan, 261-4; Granville, II, 454-5; Simmons, 247; Kincaid, 176; Bell, I, 55.

was still ignoring all orders to quit his beloved Andalusia, the King, after probing the strength of Wellington's army, abandoned the capital. To have fought the victor of Salamanca with only 15,000 men would have been madness. Once more summoning the disobedient Duke of Dalmatia to join him, he set out across the high barren hinterland for Valencia.

Next day, August 12th, Wellington entered Madrid, with every bell pealing, palms waving, fountains flowing wine, and women casting shawls before his horse. Everyone was shouting 'God save King Ferdinand!' 'Glory to the English Nation!' 'Long live Wellington!' Ballet-dancers pirouetted before the columns; the ranks were broken by householders with gifts and wine; soldiers were dragged into doorways and feasted. All night the triumph continued, and even next day when the 3rd Division, still followed by an immense and excited multitude, advanced against Retiro; as the troops moved up to the attack, every roof-top within sight of the fortress resounded with *vivas*. Fortunately the French commander, recognizing that his defences were untenable, surrendered after a few shots, leaving the victors possession of nearly 200 cannon, 20,000 stands of arms, and 2500 more prisoners. After that the city gave itself up to a round of fêtes, balls, and bull-fights, while blissful parties of ill-looking patriots roamed the streets, breaking into houses and dragging off to dungeons and midnight executions anyone who was believed to have held a post under King Joseph. No one gave a thought to making any preparations for further military operations. That was left to the British and the mountain guerrillas.

Wellington did not remain in Madrid. He moved three divisions south to the Tagus to counter any move by Soult and quartered the remainder of his troops at the Escorial, twenty miles to the north. Then, learning that Soult was still lingering in Andalusia and that no attack from the south was likely for four or five weeks, he marched north again with half his army to rejoin Clinton at Valladolid, ordering Hill in Estremadura to reinforce Madrid if Soult moved against it. His object was to take the fortress of Burgos, eighty miles beyond Valladolid on the road to France, and so pin the Armies of Portugal and the North beyond the upper Ebro. For if he could barricade them out of central Spain and return to Madrid in October, he might, with Hill's aid and his interior lines, be able to fend off Soult and Joseph, especially if the Spanish Army of Murcia and the British expedition from Sicily, which had now landed at Alicante, continued to keep Suchet occupied.

Yet he was under no illusions. With less than 80,000 troops of mixed nationality, half of them operating north of the Guadarramas and the other half a hundred and fifty miles away on the Tagus, he had to face an attack before the winter by two French armies from the north, and two – possibly three – from the south. For his very success had exposed him to the danger he had hitherto contrived to avoid – a concentric movement of all the French forces in the Peninsula. Beyond that lay a still worse threat: the return of Napoleon and a victorious *Grande Armée* from Russia. The news from the east was ominous: the Emperor, over-coming all resistance, was driving towards Moscow at tremendous speed to compel the Czar's surrender before the winter. 'Though I still hope to be able to maintain our position in Castile and even to improve our strength,' Wellington wrote to his brother on August 23rd, 'I shudder when I reflect upon the enormity of the task which I have undertaken, with inadequate powers myself to do anything and without assistance of any kind from the Spaniards. ... If by any chance I should be overwhelmed or should be obliged to retire, what will the world say? What will the people of England say?'

On September 16th, having marched another hundred and sixty miles, he appeared before Burgos with four of his eight divisions. Two days earlier Napoleon had entered Moscow after defeating the Russians in a great battle at Borodino. About the same time Soult, who had at last abandoned Seville and his lines before Cadiz, sulkily set out from Granada with 45,000 troops to join King Joseph and Suchet in Valencia. Meanwhile the guerrilleros, intoxicated by their success, began to congregate in the liberated cities to plunder and murder colla-borators. Their pressure on the French, therefore, relaxed.

The attack on Burgos castle did not go as Wellington had intended. Despite the lessons of Ciudad Rodrigo and Badajoz, he had under-estimated the strength of the place, and failed, until it was too late, to order up enough heavy artillery. Nor had the sappers for whom he had asked yet reached him from England. As before, he had to use storming parties to do the work of guns and mines. Yet, shaken by the casualties of Badajoz, he did not dare to use them decisively. After losing 2000 men in five minor assaults, he was forced on October 21st to abandon the siege. By that date not only were the French Armies of Portugal and the North, half again as strong as his own, marching to the fortress's relief, but Soult and Joseph with 60,000 men were threatening Madrid from Valencia. The British were in danger of being crushed between the upper and nether mill-stones.

In victory Wellington had displayed some of the weaknesses of his country. He had been a little too easy-going and sanguine, and had shown signs, most unusual in him, of preferring to hope for, rather than to ensure, success. But when the storm broke he acted with wonderful resolution and presence of mind. Years later, when asked what was the test of a great general, he replied, 'To know when to retreat and to dare to do it.' Marching his men in silence through the streets of Burgos on the night of October 21st, he gained a day on the relieving army before the French were aware that he had gone. Yet, with 6000 cavalry to his own 1300 dragoons, they were able to press him very hard. The weather, too, turned against him, making muddy rivers of the primitive Castilian roads.[1] His men were weakened by sickness and sulky at having to withdraw; in the little wine town of Torquemada 12,000 of them broke into the wine vaults with the usual disgraceful results. None the less, he brought them back with few casualties to the Douro in five days. Here he intended to stand, facing northwards across the river, while Hill, a hundred miles to the south on the other side of the Guadarramas, faced southwards across the Tagus to keep Joseph and Soult from Madrid. With 55,000 Anglo-Portuguese and 25,000 Spaniards operating on interior lines, there seemed at least a hope of being able to hold the summer's gains and prevent the 50,000 men of the French Armies of Portugal and the North from uniting with the 60,000 of the Armies of the South and Centre.

But that autumn Wellington's star was not in the ascendant. He failed to hold the Douro because, during the evening of October 29th, a party of French volunteers with splendid daring swam across what was thought to be an impassable reach near the shattered bridge at Tordesillas and surprised and routed a regiment of German infantry, thus enabling Foy's sappers to get a pontoon bridge across the flooded

1. In England the equinoctial gales that stormy October strewed the Channel with wrecks, and the Thames at Westminster rose so high that it flowed into Westminster Hall. See Colchester, II, 466–7; Daniell, I, 106.

stream. And Hill was unable to hold the Tagus because the autumnal rains which had set in with such violence north of the Guadarramas had still to fall in New Castile. Not only did the rivers south of Madrid fail as a result to bar Soult's and Joseph's advance, but General Ballasteros, the erratic commander of Spain's southern army, omitted, in a fit of sulks, to make his promised move against the French flank in La Mancha. Both halves of the British army were thus forced into the open, and both, being outnumbered – particularly in cavalry – were left with no alternative but retreat.

Ordering Hill to blow up the Retiro and cross the Guadarramas to join him, Wellington prepared to fall back on Salamanca. On the last day of October the British marched out of Madrid, watched by reproachful multitudes. Then, knowing there was an end to peace and pleasure so long as a Frenchman remained in Spain, the men, bronzed and strapped under their packs, swung out in the familiar columns towards the snow-capped mountains. 'A splendid sight it was,' wrote Bell, 'to see so grand an army winding its way zig-zag up that long pass so far as the eye could see. The old trade was going on, killing and slaying and capturing our daily bread.' On either side of the track lay dead beasts and murdered peasants, slain no one knew how or by whom. Spain was like that.

As soon as Hill was through the Guadarrama, Wellington resumed his retreat, their roads converging. By November 9th 30,000 British and Germans, 20,000 Portuguese, and 25,000 Spaniards were concentrated on the Tormes in front of Salamanca, while 50,000 Frenchmen moved cautiously against them from the north-east and 60,000 from the south-east. With perfect judgement Wellington had brought the two halves of his army back two hundred miles in the face of a superior enemy without losing a gun and hardly a prisoner. It would have been possible for him at that moment to throw his united force against either of his still divided adversaries. There was not a man in the British ranks who did not hope and believe that he would. But without counting the Spaniards who, through lack of discipline, were still almost impossible to manoeuvre, Wellington had not sufficient men to win a decisive victory over either French army – to one of which, without the Spaniards, he was inferior, and to the other about equal. And in the event of victory over one adversary, he would still, with depleted ranks, have had to encounter the other; while, had he failed, he must have been crushed between their approaching pincers. True, therefore, to his unchanging principle, he avoided needless risks and, allowing the French to join armies – that grand concentration which he had so long and successfully avoided – awaited their attack in one of his usual well-chosen positions. As they were a third again as strong as his own force, he had every reason to expect one.

But the French, remembering Salamanca, were taking no risks either. Pursuing the same strategy as Marmont, Soult crossed the Tormes on the 14th and began to work his way southwards and west-wards round Wellington's southern flank, while the Army of Portugal faced him from the east. But, unlike Marmont, who had tried to en-velop Wellington by cutting straight across his front, Soult took so broad and cautious a sweep that his adversary was never in any danger of being encircled at all. And as it was clear that the French were not going to attack him on his own ground but were merely hoping, with-out an encounter, to cut his communications with Portugal, the British commander resolved to fall back to his base at Ciudad Rodrigo. It meant abandoning Salamanca, but there was nothing now to be gained by remaining there for the winter.

On the afternoon of November 15th, therefore, he gave the order to retreat, so bringing the campaign of 1812 to an end. Though he had been forced to relinquish his gains in Castile and Leon, it had proved more profitable than any he had yet undertaken. Twenty thousand French prisoners had been sent to England and 3000 guns had been taken or destroyed, the fortresses of Ciudad Rodrigo, Badajoz, Al-maraz, and Alcantara were in his hands, and Santander and the Asturian coast ports had been won by Popham and the guerrillas as a sea base for future operations. A British force from Sicily was established at Alicante in the east, and Estremadura and the whole of the south had been liberated. Indeed, the very concentration of French armies that had driven Wellington from Madrid and Valladolid had given to the Spanish guerrillas and patriot armies the control of vast new areas. With the Cortes installed at Seville instead of being penned in Cadiz, Joseph's pretence of being King of Spain was almost at an end. His very capital, though he did not know it, had been reoccupied as soon as his troops left by the guerrilla chief, El Empecinado.

Still, it was humiliating for the British to have to retrace their steps and withdraw from the scene of their triumphs to the bleak hills of the Portuguese frontier. On the day their retreat began, the equinoctial gales set in with an intensity of cold and rain unprecedented at that season. Within a few hours every stream and watercourse was a torrent and the roads rivers of icy mud which, rising to men's ankles and some-times to their knees, sucked the boots off their feet. For four days, until the Agueda could be reached, there was no prospect of any bivouac but the drenched ground. That night it became known that there was small hope of food either.

For through an administrative blunder the rations had gone astray. Like every British commander in the field, Wellington suffered much from the War Office or, as it was then called in its administrative part, the Horse Guards. In pursuit of some time-honoured formula of trans-fer and promotion that institution, with an Olympian disregard of his wishes, had posted his Quartermaster-General, George Murray, to Ireland and replaced him by an inexperienced nominee of its own. This functionary, on receiving orders to retire to Ciudad Rodrigo, sent off the supply-train by a route far to the north of the army's line of re-treat on the assumption that the road farthest from the enemy was the safest. By forgetting that his first business was not to preserve his stores but to feed the troops, he inflicted greater suffering and loss on them than the concentration of four French armies. Had it not been for the excessive caution of Soult's pursuit – a legacy of Corunna and Albuera – they might have had to fight without the strength to do so.

For four dreadful days, as they fell angrily back, the men were with-out rations. Not knowing why, they assumed some disaster had oc-curred and that the French in some unaccountable way had out-manoeuvred them and won a bloodless victory. For the veterans the retreat revived memories of the race to Corunna. No coat could keep out the wet and icy wind from hungry bodies; soaked, foot-sore, their old wounds aching and their teeth chattering with ague, weighed down with heavy packs and arms, the frostbitten men trudged across that bitter upland without comfort or hope. At night they bivouacked in drenching woods and fed on acorns or raw carrion cut from dead bul-locks and on such unmilled wheat as the harassed commissariat officers could find. 'Queer music it was,' wrote one, 'to see and hear an army

sitting on the sod, each man with two big stones grinding his dinner.'
Kincaid confessed he was so sharply set he could have eaten his boots.[1]

On the second night an encounter with a herd of swine in a forest
provided an unexpected dinner for several thousands. But the greater
part of the army remained without rations for four days. As a result
more than three thousand men fell by the way out of sheer exhaustion
and were gathered up by the French.

Yet, though in some regiments, especially those fresh from England,
discipline momentarily failed, there was little grumbling. Famished,
with bleeding feet, racked with ague and dysentery, the men still had
the heart to make light of their lot. Courage, pride, and comradeship
kept the army together. In the rearguard, formed by the Light Division,
the rough veterans of the 95th offered their precious biscuits to the
eighteen-year-old son of Lord Spencer as he sat pale and shivering over
the acorns he had gathered: in such times, wrote Rifleman Costello,
lords found they were men and men that they were comrades.[2]

There was one incident of the retreat that deserves to be recorded,
for it belongs to the heritage of the British race. It was taken down by
a subaltern of the 34th – to-day the Border Regiment – from the lips of
his laundress, the wife of one of his Irish soldiers.[3] 'Yer honour minds,'
she said, 'how we were all kilt and destroyed on the long march last
winter, and the French at our heels, an' all our men droppin' an' dyin'
on the roadside, waitin' to be killed over agin by them vagabones
comin' after us. Well, I don't know if you seed him, sir, but down
drops poor Dan, to be murdered like all the rest, and says he, "Biddy
dear, I can't go no furder one yard to save me life." "O, Dan jewel,"
sis I, "I'll help you on a bit; tak' a hould av me, an' throw away your
knapsack." "I'll niver part wid my knapsack," says he, "nor my firelock, while I'm a soger." "Dogs then," sis I, "you 'ont live long, for the
Frinch are comin' up quick upon us." Thinkin', ye see, sir, to give him
sperret to move, but the poor *crather* hadn't power to stir a lim'; an' now
I heerd the firin' behind, and saw them killin' Dan, as it it was! So I
draws him up on the bank and coaxed him to get on me back, for, sis I,

1. Bell, 1, 66-7, 73-4; Kincaid, 186-7, 192. See also Gomm, 290; Grattan;
291-4, 304-6; Larpent, 1, 20, 29, 42; Bessborough, 231; Kincaid, 187-8, 194;
Simmons, 255-6, 265; Costello, 142; Oman, VI, 143-8, 159.

2. Costello, 142; Grattan, 293.   3. Bell, 1, 182.

"the French will have ye in half an hour, an' me too, the pagans"; in thruth I was just thinkin' they had hould av us both, when I draws him up on me back, knapsack an' all. "Throw away your gun," sis I. "I won't," says he, "Biddy, I'll shoot the first vagabone lays hould av your tail," says he. He was always a *conthrary crather* when anyone *invaded* his firelock. Well, sir, I went away wid him on me back, knapsack, firelock, and all, as strong as Samson for the fear I was in; an' fegs, I carried him half a league after the regiment into the bivwack; an' me back was bruck entirely from that time to this, an' it'll never get strait till I go to the Holy Well in Ireland, and have Father McShane's blessin', an' his hands laid over me!' She had saved, as her auditor told her, a good man for herself and the army.

*

To Wellington – and to England when the news of the retreat and its sufferings arrived – it seemed like a defeat. Those four days of famine and cold had temporarily reduced a victorious army to an assemblage of famished tramps. Though food in plenty was waiting on the Agueda, it was long before the hospitals would restore to the ranks the thousands laid low by typhus, enteric, and ague. Until the end of January the death-rate averaged five hundred a week, and a third of Wellington's force was on the sick-list. So shaken was he by the transformation of his army that he drafted an impatient Order denouncing the failure of regimental officers to maintain discipline. When this document, addressed to senior officers, became known, it caused deep resentment; it was even whispered that the strain of the past few weeks had been too much for the Commander-in-Chief's mind. 'The officers asked each other,' one of them wrote, 'how or in what manner they were to blame for the privations the army had endured. Their business was to keep their men together and, if possible, to keep up with their men on the march. Many were mere lads, badly clothed and without a boot to their feet, some attacked with dysentery, others with ague, others with a burning fever raging through their system; they had scarcely strength to hobble on in company with their more hardy comrades, the soldiers. Nothing but a high sense of honour could have sustained them.'[1]

1. Grattan, 307. See *idem* 311–12; Simmons, 265; Bell, I, 73–4, 77; Costello, 144; Fortescue, IX, 100; Larpent, I, 6, 19, 54, 74, 127; Oman, VI, 181.

Wellington was not alone that November in having to retreat across a desert. After waiting five weeks in a burnt-out Moscow for a Russian surrender that never came, Napoleon had set out on October 18th for Kaluga and the warmer lands of the Ukraine with 115,000 fighting troops, 20,000 sick in wagons, and 40,000 camp-followers. But the Russian army under Kutusov, heartened by the news of Wellington's liberation of Madrid,[1] had barred his way at Malo-Yaroslavitz, and, after a bitter fight, had forced him back on the more northerly route by which he had come. Here the countryside had been completely stripped by his advance – one of the most destructive even in the annals of Revolutionary war – and partisans from the forests were already harrying the long lines of communication. Apart from what it carried, there was nothing for the *Grande Armée* to eat until it reached its advance magazines at Smolensk, two hundred miles to the west.

As the starving host retraced its steps through charred villages, the immensity and savage gloom of the Russian landscape struck a chill in every heart. The germs of typhus were already in men's veins; near the battlefields of Borodino, where thousands of corpses lay unburied, gangrenous cripples from the hospitals, fearful of Russian vengeance, fought for places on the plunder-laden wagons. Vast numbers, unable to obtain food, fell by the wayside; hundreds of baggage-carts and ammunition wagons were left abandoned with the horses dead at the shafts.

On November 5th, when they were still a few days short of Smolensk, the first cold set in. Prisoners had warned the French that when it came their nails would drop from their fingers and the muskets from their hands. A deadening and penetrating fog rose from the ground; then out of the darkness the snow began to fall. As it did so a terrible wind swept out of the north, howling through the forests and piling the snow in the path of the blinded invaders. Famished and exhausted, the vast predatory army lost hope and cohesion, began to disintegrate and dissolve.

From November 9th to 14th, while Wellington was awaiting the French attack at Salamanca, Napoleon was at Smolensk. He had already lost 40,000 men since leaving Moscow. But he was forced to resume the retreat, for the supplies in the town were insufficient to feed the

1. Chambray, 303–7.

survivors. On the 14th, with 40,000 fighting men and 30,000 followers, he set out westwards. In the next four days, while the British were re-treating to the Agueda, the Grand Army suffered an unparalleled disaster. As the long procession of famished ghosts struggled through the snow, the Russians, almost as severely decimated by the rigours of that terrible climate, took the offensive at Krasnoi. In three days' fight-ing, 10,000 of the invaders were killed, 26,000 taken prisoner, and more than two hundred guns captured. Only the Emperor's resolution and the discipline of the Imperial Guard prevented the destruction of the entire army. By the 19th scarcely 12,000 men remained with the colours.

The dying agony of the great host lasted another three weeks. The dwindling column struggling to reach Europe was joined by division after division summoned from the lines of communications and rear areas. All suffered the same fate. On the Beresina in the last days of November two Russian armies, closing in from north and south, barred the retreat. The Emperor broke through, but left another 12,000 drowned in the river and 18,000 more in Russian hands. On December 5th he abandoned the survivors and set out by sleigh for Warsaw. 'All that has happened is nothing,' he explained on his arrival, 'it is the effect of the climate, and that is all. From the sublime to the ridicu-lous is but a step. ... I am going to raise 300,000 men. In six months I shall be again on the Niemen.' A week later he reached France for the second time in his career, without the army with which he had set out to conquer the east. About the same time ten thousand typhus-ridden cripples – all that remained of half a million men – staggered across the bridge at Königsberg into Prussia.

CHAPTER 3

NEPTUNE'S GENERAL

He rode a knowing-looking thorough-bred horse, and wore a grey
overcoat, Hessian boots and a large cocked hat.
GRONOW

THE news from Russia did not begin to reach England until the second
week of December. There had always been a few far-sighted Britons,
as well as some very romantic ones like the Prince Regent and Walter
Scott, who had seen in their adversary's eastern adventure a chance that
he might get himself into a scrape. Among the former was the commissariat-minded Wellington, who had written that, if the Czar was
prudent and his Russians would fight, Bonaparte could not succeed.[1]
But most Englishmen had seen too many countries succumb to believe
it. The Government, while rejecting a peace offer that would have
enabled Napoleon to concentrate his entire force in the east, had so little
faith in Russia that it refused her a loan and warned the Czar that, if he
chose to resist, it must be at his own risk. 'I cannot have one particle of
hope for Russia,' wrote the Secretary for War as late as August 31st.
The long Russian retreat, the news of the French victories at Smolensk
and Borodino, the capture of Moscow, had had the usual effect. The
average British reaction was typified by David Wilkie's remark: 'Ah!
but he has got there!'

*

For it had become almost impossible for Britons not to despair of the
Continent. The difficulties from which they suffered as a result of its
enforced unification under Napoleon were too great. The last two
years had been the worst of the war: as the tyrant's grip on the European
ports tightened, British warehouses and quays became bogged with
unexportable goods. The social economy of the industrial districts had
momentarily been disrupted. Those whom the demand for British

1. Gurwood, July 25th, 1812. 'I trust in God,' wrote Walter Scott in August,
'that all will go well and Europe will yet see peace before the present generation
are in their graves.' Scott, III, 153. See also Dudley, 159; Ashton, I, 143–4; *Two
Duchesses*, 349–50.

goods and the paper money created to finance their manufacture had drawn into the factory towns found themselves without livelihood or alternative employment.

Early in 1811 the United States struck Britain a further blow. By an act forbidding commercial intercourse with her to prevent incidents arising from the Continental Blockade, she deprived the Lancashire mills of raw cotton, reduced British exports to North America from £11,000,000 to under £2,000,000 and forced the British Government – since it could no longer pay with goods – to expend its dwindling reserves of bullion on American corn for Wellington's army. This harsh measure of the young Republic did not even have the preventative effect intended. In the summer of 1812 popular clamour against the blockade and the seizure of British naval deserters from American vessels and, above all, the American backwoodsman's desire for the fertile, empty country beyond the Canadian frontier, tempted Congress, hopeful of a quick victory, into declaring war against England. It did so at the very moment that the Foreign Secretary was announcing in Parliament the repeal of the Orders in Council to appease American opinion.

The effect on industry was calamitous. In Glasgow the average weekly wage of hand-loom weavers fell from 17s. 6d. to 7s. 6d. All but six of Manchester's thirty-eight mills had to close, and a fifth of the population of urban Lancashire was driven on to the rates.[1] The rise of the latter further aggravated the deflationary situation. By the beginning of 1812, in part of Nottinghamshire alone 15,000 frame-workers were in receipt of poor relief. The most alarming feature was that, while wages fell and unemployment increased, the price of food – which could not be multiplied by machinery – tended to rise. In 1811 after a wet summer the harvest failed and a famine was only averted by a purchase of French, Italian, and Polish corn which Napoleon allowed to be exported in order to drain England of bullion, on the assumption that a hungry nation needed gold more than corn. Even with this aid from the enemy, food-prices in 1812 were 87 per cent above pre-war level. The cost of potatoes and oatmeal, the staple food of many workers, was almost trebled.[2]

1. *Leeds Mercury*, Feb. 22nd, 1812.
2. Mathieson, 135–6; Porter, II, 188; Felkin, 231; Lilian Knowles, 336; Darvall, 20–46, 53–6; Colchester, II, 408.

The ruling classes, immersed in the life-and-death struggle with France, had no remedy. Their sole cure for economic stresses and strains was to leave them to the laws of supply and demand; the Home Secretary's advice to a delegation of unemployed Stockport weavers was to be patient. To starving workers unaware of the teaching of economic philosophers, such a policy seemed heartless inertia. Illiterate and helpless, they turned in their anger on their employers – the only representatives of power with whom they were acquainted – and against the machines which had brought wealth and opportunity to these ambitious men and ruin to themselves. Napoleon's decrees and American policy were outside their cognisance. But the machines, which did the work of ten men for the wages of one, were within their reach.

Towards the end of 1811 riots broke out in Nottinghamshire, where unemployment had been aggravated by the collapse of a speculative market in revolutionary South America. Mobs of starving framework-knitters, calling themselves Luddites, openly assembled in every village to break the machines which robbed them of their livelihood. When the Government to restrain them sent down a brigade of dragoons – urgently needed in the Peninsula – they continued their operations by night. The trouble spread to the neighbouring counties of Derbyshire, Leicestershire, Staffordshire, Lancashire, and Yorkshire. By the spring of 1812 to conservative minds the whole of the manufacturing districts of the North and Midlands seemed engaged in a gigantic conspiracy. Men with blackened faces handed anonymous threats to machine-owners, factories were gutted, arms seized from householders and militia depots. While Wellington's men were storming Badajoz, their countrymen in the West Riding and Lancashire were engaged, with axes, hammers, and muskets, in battering down the doors of moorside mills under the fire of their equally pugnacious and stubborn owners.

To all this society's only answer was repression. A military camp was formed in Sherwood Forest, the yeomanry were called out, watch committees were set up, and special constables enrolled. More troops were used that spring to hold down the manufacturing districts than had been sent in the original expeditionary force to Portugal. Cavalry patrolled the disaffected districts night and day, spies were employed to track down the ringleaders, and Parliament made frame-breaking a capital offence.[1] More than forty rioters were sentenced to death at special Assizes and as many transported.

Yet any weakness might have been fatal. But for the Government's firmness England could easily have failed its army in the hot, restless summer of Salamanca. While the country was at war with a militant revolution that had overthrown every State in Europe, a rough and illiterate populace, rendered desperate by suffering, had taken the law into its own hands. The reports of the Home Office spies were full of allusions to mysterious agitators, midnight drillings, and sanguinary Jacobin resolutions. There was no police force, and even the loyalty of the Militia was uncertain. On May 11th, 1812, the Prime Minister, Spencer Perceval, was assassinated in the House of Commons. Though it subsequently turned out that his murder had nothing to do with industrial unrest, the savage joy with which it was greeted by the hungry workers of the North terrified the rest of the nation.[2] In the new manufacturing towns – a neglected, nightmare world cut off from the ancient civic and rural polity of England – the ruling classes had become intensely unpopular.

The little group of Pitt's disciples, who under Perceval and his successor, Lord Liverpool, were carrying on the administration, made up in courage and common sense for what they lacked in brilliance. They were practical men who loved their country and, though they had made mistakes, learnt from them. They both dealt firmly with violence and refused to be stampeded into defeatist economic measures which, though agreeable to the theories of pedants and most of their own class, might have destroyed England's ability to wage war. When a Parliamentary Committee on currency reform, presided over by the Whig Horner, attributed the country's economic plight, not to the closing of Europe's and America's ports, but to the inconvertibility

1. *Hansard*, XXI, 603, *et seq.* Byron made his maiden speech in the Lords against the measure. 'Can you commit a whole country to their own prisons?' he asked. 'Will you erect a gibbet in every field and hang up men like scarecrows?' Moore, *Byron*, 157.

2. *Wilberforce*, IV, 29. See also *Two Duchesses*, 364; Colchester, II, 394–403; Dyott, I, 299; Scott, III, 112; H. M. C. Bathurst, 188; Dudley, 151–2; Lord Coleridge, 201; Bury, I, 92; II, 285; Shelley, I, 8–9. At the execution of his murderer, the hangman was pelted. Alderson, 20.

of her enlarged paper money, and proposed as remedy a deflationary resumption of cash payments, Castlereagh, as Leader of the Commons, and Vansittart, the Chancellor of the Exchequer, refused to accept it. Had they done so, the run on the country's dwindling gold might have brought trade to a standstill and even forced the recall of Wellington's army from Spain. It was not the first time that Ministers in their resolve for victory had defied economic theory to keep the wheels of industry turning. When the first wave of bankruptcy was sweeping the industrial areas, they had boldly resisted the growing restriction of currency by advancing six million pounds free of interest to embarrassed traders.

*

The opening of the ports of Russia and of her ally, Sweden, brought about a resumption of exports in the nick of time. So long as the French were advancing on Moscow and St Petersburg this revival of trade was precarious, but when in October it became known that the Russians were fighting on and the French were in retreat, it was as though a great weight had been lifted. 'Glorious news from the north,' wrote Walter Scott on December 10th, '*pereat iste!*' Men could not at first believe it. When Napoleon's flight to Paris and the destruction of his army became known at Cambridge, the Fellows of Trinity leapt on the tables, danced, sang, and hugged one another; 'you never saw such a scene,' Adam Sedgwick told Montague Butler many years afterwards, 'and you never will!' A grateful Parliament and country joined in voting funds and subscribing to the Russian National Relief Fund; even Wellington's veterans in their cantonments along the Portuguese border contributed their pennies and celebrated by impromptu dancing to the strains of 'The Downfall of Paris'.[1]

With the Baltic open and a prospect of Europe liberating itself, England once more put forth her full strength. By the spring of 1812 the export entries at the Leith Customs were higher than ever in their history. That year, with a population of less than 13 millions in

1. 'Bravo Russians,' wrote Simmons of the Rifles. 'They are worthy of the country they inhabit !' Simmons, 270, 278. See Bury, 1, 202; Costello, 158; Dudley, 179, 183; Gomm, 291; Tomkinson, 291; Letter to *The Times* by J. P. Bidder, Jan. 20th, 1943; Colchester 11, 413–14; Leigh Hunt, *Autobiography*, 222; *Paget Brothers*, 252; *Peel*, 1, 41.

Great Britain and 5 millions in Ireland, Britain subsidized the armies of every State in Europe willing to rise against Napoleon. Her expenditure rose to £118,000,000 – nearly five times its pre-war figure – £68,000,000 of it raised out of current taxation.

And after twenty years of war her Government knew how to use her strength. Composed of men whom clever folk regarded as mediocre, it represented the nation's continuing resolve to win. All but two of them still in their forties, they were Pitt's pupils. To his inflexible will they had added, through bitter experience, a tough horse-sense and a knowledge of the fundamental rules of war. They had learnt to concentrate. 'Bonaparte has conquered the greatest part of Europe by doing but one thing at a time,' wrote the Master-General of the Ordnance to the Secretary for War, 'and doing that with all his heart, with all his soul, and with all his strength. If you succeed in the Peninsula, nothing of yours will go on ill elsewhere; if you fail, nothing will go on at all anywhere else.'[1] As the news of Napoleon's Russian disaster spread across the world, Ministers staked everything on success in Spain. Disregarding the possibility of invasion, they kept back only 25,000 regulars to guard the British Isles.

*

The Peninsular campaign of 1813 was planned against the background of a new war beyond the Pyrenees and Alps. In the last days of the old year, while the remnants of the *Grande Armée* were trying to rally on the Vistula, General Yorck, in command of its Prussian contingent, concluded an armistice with the Russians. Though at first repudiated by King Frederick William, who was still mesmerized by Napoleon, it was received with wild enthusiasm by every patriot. Six weeks later the Prussian king, surrendering to popular clamour, signed an alliance with the Czar at Kalisch. On March 4th, Cossacks entered Berlin as the French fell back to the Elbe. Twelve days later Prussia declared war on France. On the 25th, in a joint proclamation, the Russian and Prussian sovereigns summoned all Germany to rise.

Meanwhile Napoleon had called up half a million more conscripts. Many were lads of sixteen: France was reduced to its last man and horse. But, though the possessing classes had lost all faith in him, the

1. Mulgrave to Bathurst, Oct. 7th, 1812. H.M.C. Bathurst, 216.

Emperor's resolution rallied the nation for one last great throw. He rejected his Austrian father-in-law's offers of mediation, refused to withdraw his troops from a single fortress in eastern Europe and made it clear that he would accept nothing less than his full former authority.

*

To provide cadres for his new army Napoleon again ignored Wellington. In the teeth of the evidence, he chose to assume that the latter had only 30,000 British troops. By recalling the remaining units of the Imperial Guard and drafts of veteran non-commissioned officers and men from every regiment in Spain, he reduced his forces there to little more than 200,000 effectives. The only reinforcements he sent to Spain to replace the heavy casualties of 1812 were boys. Many of them, unable to stand the hardships of the march, died on the road.

Already, though the British had scarcely fired a shot since the autumn, King Joseph was in trouble. So strong was the guerrilla stranglehold on his communications that the news of the retreat from Moscow took a month to travel from the Pyrenees to Madrid; Napoleon's return to Paris on December 18th only became known to Joseph on February 14th. After Wellington's triumphs of the previous summer the Spanish partisans were past holding. They behaved no longer as outlaws but as men certain of victory, and the whole country was either behind them or terrorized into acquiescence. In Navarre the great guerrillero, Mina, levied taxes and maintained a personal army of eight thousand; in February, with the help of guns landed from British ships, he force the French garrisons of Tafalla to surrender. One of his detachments stormed the castle of Fuentarrabia on the frontier, threw its armament into the sea, and made a funeral pyre that was visible far into France. Every village along the trunk roads had to be garrisoned, every church and farm made a fortress. To reach its destination a French dispatch needed a regiment, sometimes a brigade in escort.

In the opening months of 1813, while Germany was arming, the long Spanish war of Independence reached its climax of ferocity. A French officer told a British prisoner that there was scarcely a family in France that was not in mourning for it. It was a struggle in which yellow fever and typhus played their part: a shadow war pictured in

Goya's cartoons of disaster – the women raped in the broken mill, the squat, brutal troopers with their vulture faces, the haggard peasants mutilating their captives with axe and knife or facing, with despairing eyes, the levelled guns of the firing squads; the burning town, the rifled tomb, the atrocious vengeance; the naked corpses transfixed to charred lintel or broken tree; the famine-stricken fugitives with skull-like heads and match-stick limbs; the vampire forms of men and women transformed by hatred and terror into the likeness of beasts. The struggle had set its impress on the campaign long before the British guns began to rumble over the stony roads towards the French frontier. On March 17th, 1813, Uncle Joe – 'the King of the Bottle' – left Madrid for ever. On Napoleon's orders he took up his headquarters at Valladolid and dispatched half his field-forces to hunt down guerrillas in the valleys of Biscaya and Navarre. Clausel with the Army of the North and almost the entire infantry of the Army of Portugal was sent to chase Mina out of Navarre, Foy with another corps to pacify the Biscayan coast. In their attempts to restore their communications, Joseph and his master reduced the forces facing Wellington to little more than 50,000 men.

The British army had no guerrillas to hunt: the people of Spain were its friends. And with the centre and south now liberated, it was all concentrated in the north within fifty miles of the Leon plain. Thanks to the fine work in emptying the hospitals of James McGrigor, the chief of the Medical Staff, there were more men with the colours than there had ever been before. All that winter and spring the roads to Portsmouth and Plymouth had been full of troops bound for the Peninsula: jangling Household Cavalry with splendid accoutrements and fresh, beefy faces, the spoilt 'householders' of army jest; the reserve battalions marching to join their consorts; detachments of rosy-cheeked militia-men under raw young ensigns 'in fine new toggery', the drums and fifes playing before them and the village boys running beside, while housewives at their cottage doors mourned over the poor lambs going to the slaughter, and the confident young soldiers, not knowing what was coming to them, jested back. Thence, drawn by the invisible strings of Wellington's design, they crossed the Bay and saw for the first time the barren, tawny shoes of the Peninsula, felt the stones and smelt the stink of Lisbon town, and marched out of Belem barracks on the long mountain track to the frontier. When, bug-bitten, footsore, and dusty, they found themselves among the tattered, cheery veterans who were to be their comrades, their education began. 'Do you see those men on the plain?' barked old Major O'Hara of the Rifles to the latest batch of 'Johnny Newcomes' as they looked down from their rocky fastness. 'Es, zur.' 'Well, then, those are the French and our enemies. You must kill those fellows and not allow them to kill you. You must learn to do as these old birds do and get cover where you can. Recollect, recruits, you come here to kill and not be killed. Bear this in mind; if you don't kill the French, they'll kill you!'[1] Every fresh arrival was ruthlessly probed by the old hands for weak points; if he was game and survived their rough chaff, he was accepted; if not, he was dealt with unmercifully.

By the end of April 1813, Wellington was in command, not of the 30,000 British troops Napoleon supposed, but of 52,000, together with 29,000 well-disciplined Portuguese – a striking-force of over 80,000 men. To these, following his appointment – grudgingly made after the liberation of Madrid – as Generalissimo of the Spanish Armies, were now added 21,000 Spaniards under his direct command. He was still, however, unable to get regular rations and pay for them out of the jealous, quarrelling Regency and Cortez.

During the winter he had made many improvements in his army. The defects of the previous campaign had been carefully corrected. The former Chief-of-Staff, George Murray, was back at his post; tents were issued for the first time; portable tin kettles substituted for heavy iron vessels; every soldier equipped with three pairs of shoes and a spare set of soles and heels in his knapsack. Discipline, too, had been tightened: a new Judge-Advocate had spent the winter speeding up courts martial, hanging deserters, and flogging plunderers. Even a small corps of trained sappers had arrived from England, and a properly organized siege train.

With a force embodying the accumulated experience of five years' campaigning and with his adversary facing a war on two fronts, Wellington was more hopeful than he had even been before. 'I propose,' he wrote, 'to take the field as early as I can and to place myself in for-

1. Costello, 70. See also *Johnny Newcome*, 16, 18, 30, 151; Bell, 1, 3–5, 79; Simmons, 124, 232; Grattan, 311–12; Kincaid, *Random Shots*, 238.

tune's way.' Of his plans for doing so, however, he said little, even in his dispatches to the Secretary of State. They depended on surprise and on the use of sea-power. Instead of a frontal attack against the broad and easily defensible Douro as in 1812, he proposed to outflank the river by secretly transferring the bulk of his troops while still in Portugal to its northern bank and sending them, first north and thence east, to cross its mountain tributary, the Esla, and appear in the rear of the enemy's defences. To do so, with their guns and supplies, they had first to negotiate a wild and almost roadless region on the borders of northern Portugal and Spain. But for months Wellington's engineers and commissariat officers had been probing the Tras-os-Montes, and he was satisfied that it could be done.

Once across the mountains and the Esla, the British Commander planned a further surprise – one which Commodore Popham's capture of Santander had made possible. While threatening the French communications by driving round their right or northern flank towards the Bayonne trunk road, he would put it out of their power to threaten his own supply-lines by switching these from Portugal to the Bay of Biscay. For Lisbon and Oporto he would substitute Santander and later, perhaps, Bilbao and Pasages. By doing so he would shorten his communications with England by four hundred land-miles and as many sea-miles. Instead of advancing away from his supplies, he would move towards them. And with every mile he drove into the north-east, edging nearer the sea from which his strength came, his communications would become, not more exposed, but safer. Scarcely ever had the offensive use of sea-power on land been more clearly envisaged by a soldier. Being England's, he was Neptune's general.

In the utmost secrecy and under pretence of equipping the Spanish Army of Galicia, Wellington assembled supply-ships, guns, and ammunition in Corunna for transference to Santander Bay, two hundred and fifty miles to the east. The operation was attended by difficulties. For the war with the young American Republic, begun in the previous summer, had taken an unexpected course. While the long-impending American attack on the defenceless Canadian frontier had been thwarted by a few hundred regulars under the British Commander-in-Chief, Isaac Brock, American frigates, more heavily manned and gunned than their British counterparts, had triumphed in three spectacular duels which, though of little strategic importance, caused an immense sensation in both countries. Thus encouraged, American privateers had begun to appear on the Portuguese coast in search of Wellington's supply ships. The menace was never serious, for the strength of the Royal Navy was immense and the United States had not even a single capital ship. But during the early months of 1813, as the campaign which was to decide the fate of Spain took shape in his mind, Wellington waxed very bitter over naval slackness and inefficiency.[1]

He possessed, however, another asset. Thanks to the guerrillas, he knew the enemy's dispositions while having his own concealed. When the campaign started, 55,000 men under King Joseph and Marshal Jourdan were strung out across a front of nearly two hundred miles from the Douro to the Tagus. Far behind them, as many more were hunting partisans in the tangled mountains near the French frontier or garrisoning fortresses and blockhouses. And four hundred miles away, on the east coast, cut off from the rest of Spain by mountain and desert, Marshal Suchet with 68,000 troops was holding down Valencia and Catalonia. To make sure that no reinforcements from this quarter should reach Joseph through the Ebro valley, Wellington made a further use of his country's command of the sea. In April he ordered Lieutenant-General Sir John Murray, who had just successfully repulsed Suchet at Castalla, to embark his force of 18,000 Britons, Germans, Italians, and Spaniards for an attack on Tarragona two hundred miles up the coastal road to the north. Confronted by such a threat to his communications, as well as by the unpredictable movements of the Spanish Army at Murcia and the guerrillas of Catalonia and Aragon, Suchet, a selfish man at the best of times, was unlikely to spare any help for his colleagues.

1. Fortescue, IX, 104; VIII, 545. See also, for an interesting illustration of naval slackness as seen through a soldier's eyes, Blakeney, 286–90. Larpent, the Judge-Advocate, took a more dispassionate view. 'People here', he wrote from Wellington's headquarters on January 2nd, 'are all very sore about the Americans and our taken frigates. I think we deserve it a little. Our contempt of our descendants and half-brothers has always rather disgusted me. ... The reverse may set things right. The Americans have faults enough; we should allow them their merits. Our sailors all thought Americans would not dare look them in the face. I think the Army rather rejoice and laugh aside at all this falling on the Navy, as they bullied so much before.' Larpent, I, 76.

Yet everything depended on the British striking quickly. Clausel and Foy were bound before long to disperse the northern guerrillas and rejoin King Joseph. And events in Europe might soon release far larger French forces. On April 15th Napoleon had left Paris to join his army on the Rhine; on the 24th he reached Erfurt, intending to fall on the Prussians and Russians before the Austrians could intervene. It was, therefore, irritating for Wellington to be delayed by a late spring and consequent lack of green forage; it had been a bitter winter all over Europe, and in London the Thames had been frozen for eight weeks. Accidents, due to fraudulent contractors, had also held up the pontoon bridge on its way from Tagus to Douro. And with a succession of rivers to cross, Wellington's plan depended on pontoons.

During the second week of May the main British army began its northward march through the Tras-os-Montes. To distract the enemy's attention, Wellington and Hill with the remaining 30,000 moved on the 22nd on Salamanca. As he crossed the frontier the British Commander-in-Chief turned in his stirrups and bade farewell to Portugal. He and his men were leaving for ever the rocky upland villages, the stunted trees and stony fields, the boggy woods and heaths; the smoky, flea-ridden billets, the dances with ivory-teethed peasant girls in bat-haunted, windy barns, the hunts and horse-races among the vineyards and olive trees, the days after partridge, snipe, and hare; the gallina and garlic sausages, the black bread and sour country wine, the rain and mountain wind in the desolate square of lonely Frenada.[1]

The French were taken completely by surprise. On May 25th, Hill's troops drove in their outposts before Salamanca. The single French division in the neighbourhood of the town, after losing two hundred prisoners, withdrew towards the Douro. Everything pointed to a British advance in that direction, and orders were given at Joseph's headquarters to meet it, between Toro and Tordesillas, as Marmont had done in the previous summer.

On reaching the Tormes, however, Wellington and Hill halted. Screened by their cavalry, they remained there for a week, while to the north the main body under Graham completed its two-hundred mile

---

1. Simmons, 277–8, 281; Costello, 148; Kincaid, 89, 203–4; Schaumann, 317–18; Tomkinson, 22; Grattan, 223; Gronow, II, 205–6; Larpent, I, 12, 17, 44, 63, 75; Boothby, 162–3; *Johnny Newcome*, 40.

outflanking march through the Tras-os-Montes. Guns had to be lowered over precipices by ropes, and the infantry to climb at times on hands and knees. But by May 28th the entire force was across the frontier and marching in three columns on the Esla. They reached the river on the 29th and 30th, and, finding it in flood, crossed it on the last day of the month, partly by pontoons and partly by fords waded chin-deep. Except from a few scattered cavalry patrols, there was no resistance. Next day the advance-guard entered Zamora. Before Joseph and his Chief-of-Staff could realize what had happened their entire line had been taken in flank.

By that time Wellington himself had joined the northern wing of his army. Leaving Hill to direct the southern part, he had left Salamanca at dawn on the 29th, ridden all day, and crossed the swollen Douro at Miranda in a basket slung from ropes. Everything was happening as he had intended. The French now knew that his army was across the Esla, but it was too late for them to do anything about it. On June 2nd, realizing that their Douro defences were useless, they evacuated Toro. Here on the following day, covered by Graham, Hill's 30,000 also crossed the river. By June 4th the whole British army, 81,000 strong, was concentrated north of the Douro.

It at once set out north-eastwards towards the Carrion and Pisuerga. For the next ten days it marched without a halt in parallel columns across the great corn plain of Old Castile – the waving Tierra de Campos – its cavalry screen interposing between it and the retreating French. 'The sun shone brilliantly,' wrote an officer, 'the sky was heavenly blue, the clouds of dust marked the line of march of the glittering columns. The joyous peasantry hailed our approach and came dancing to meet us, singing and beating time on their tambourines; and when we passed through the principal street of Palencia the nuns, from the upper windows of a convent, showered down rose-leaves upon our dusty heads.'[1] Thanks to Murray's staff work, supplies were plentiful. All was cheerfulness and anticipation.

Against this unexpected march the French were powerless. They

---

1. Maxwell, *Peninsular Sketches* (1845), II, 37. See also Tomkinson, 239; Schaumann, 371; Oman, VI, 352–3; Smith, I, 93–4; Gomm, 301; Simmons, 285–6; Fortescue, IX, 147. For a rhymed description of this wonderful march see *Johnny Newcome*, 213–15.

had either to retreat or be cut off. Valladolid was evacuated on June 2nd, Palencia on the 7th, Burgos itself on the 12th. Fear of hunger sped their steps, for, unlike the rich corn-lands of the Douro, the country along the royal *chaussée* to the north-east was a desert. Though their fighting troops still mustered less than 60,000, they were impeded by a vast host of useless courtiers, officials, and refugees as well as by thousands of wagons laden with ladies of pleasure and loot. 'We were a travelling *bordel*,' a French officer complained.

On June 13th, the British were awakened by a tremendous explosion reverberating through the mountains. It was the end of Burgos castle, which the retreating French had blown up in despair. Yet even had it been defended, it could no longer have stopped Wellington. For, having outflanked the Douro and its tributaries, he had already turned north again to encircle the French defences in yet another river valley, the Ebro. His staff, seeing they had covered more than two hundred miles from the Portuguese frontier, were in favour of a halt; the French were falling back on reinforcements, and the news from Germany was bad. On May 2nd Napoleon had defeated the Russo-Prussian army at Lützen on the Saxon plain; on the 8th he had entered Dresden, and, two days before Wellington set out from Portugal, had won a second, though not decisive, victory at Bautzen. The possibility of another Continental peace was in every mind; in fact, though the news had still to reach the Peninsula, a five weeks' armistice had already been signed at Plaswitz. Yet Wellington knew that, whatever happened on the Elbe, time must elapse before its effect would be felt on the Ebro. His safest plan now was to go forward. For once on the Pyrenees, whatever the French might do, he would have an easier front to defend than a Spanish river.

Without a halt, therefore, the advance continued. Once more the army struck out across desert and mountain. Only the cavalry screen remained in the neighbourhood of the Burgos-Bayonne highway to deceive and shadow King Joseph. Wellington's plan was to cross the headwaters of the Ebro between Rocamonde and Puenta Arenas, and thence, turning eastwards, to strike the road at Vittoria twenty miles in rear of the French defences. By this sweep to the north he would link up with Giron's Galicians and Longa's guerrillas and open his new communications with Santander and the Bay of Biscay.

For the next three days the footsore, dusty army toiled northwards through iron-bound hills and defiles which no artillery had ever passed. Again the guns had to be brought down precipices by hand with locked wheels; the sweating infantry, spoiling for a fight, muttered that they would make the French pay for it. By the 14th, the marching columns found themselves looking down from the stony plateau to the green and wooded valley of the infant Ebro. By nightfall tents were rising among the cherry trees and the men were garlanded with blossom by dancing peasant girls. Next day, having crossed the river, they turned once more into the east, marching in torrential rain through richly cultivated valleys and along the base of forest-clad mountains. They had covered three hundred miles through enemy territory and had scarcely fired a shot. 'It was a most wonderful march,' wrote Harry Smith, 'the army in great fighting order, and every man in better wind than a trained pugilist.'[1]

On June 17th, two days after crossing the Ebro, the army regained touch with the French. The men, in high spirits, began to fix their flints, for they could smell, they said, the frog-eaters' baccy and onions. Next day the Light Division was in action at San Millan. As the French outposts fell back, Jourdan, still waiting for Clausel twenty miles to the south-west, ordered a general retreat. The line of the Ebro had gone the same way as those of the Douro, Carrion, and Pisuerga.

On the 20th the French army, 58,000 strong, with 20,000 useless followers, came pouring into the valley of Vittoria. Here the river Zadora, winding between mountains, made a miniature plain twelve miles by seven, tapering towards its eastern end into a bottleneck where the little twin-spired town of Vittoria nestled under the spurs of the Pyrenees and the great high-road to France ran into the hills. Here a number of lesser roads met, one going eastwards to Salvatierra and Pamplona – the only way of escape left to the French should the Bayonne *chaussée* be cut.

The British did not stay for the attack. They meant to destroy Joseph before he could get his baggage-train through the guerrilla-haunted mountains and before Clausel, still labouring in the Navarrese defiles, could join him. They waited a day in the Bayas valley to collect their

1. Smith, I, 97; Tomkinson, 256. See also Bell, I, 82–3; Kincaid, 209–10; Simmons, 305; Gomm, 306; *Pakenham Letters*, 211–14.

forces; then at dawn on June 21st advanced for battle. They came out of the west in three columns, 75,000 strong. The southernmost under Rowland Hill crossed the Zadora and Madrid highway eight miles below Vittoria and in the clear morning sunlight climbed the rocky Puebla ridge that enfiladed Joseph's lines to the south. Ever since his first fight against them at Rolica, Wellington had realized the sensitiveness of Napoleon's intelligent and imaginative infantry to any threat to their flanks. And, as he intended, Hill's eastward feint along the ridge drew off their reserves in that direction.

It was not till the early afternoon that the main British attack developed on the other side of the valley. It was directed partly against the French centre over the bridges of the winding Zadora, and partly four miles further east where Graham, with the 1st and 4th Divisions and Longa's Spaniards, was driving along the Bilbao–Vittoria road towards the vital highway to France. Unfortunately both Graham and the four divisions attacking in the centre were delayed by the rough ground they had to cover between the Bayas and their battle stations. The difficulty of Wellington's convergent attack – forced on him by the character of the *terrain* – was its timing; inter-communication between his widely separated columns was almost impossible, and they had to be guided mainly by the sound of one another's fire.

But for the resource of the Light Division, one of whose brigades crossed the Zadora unseen and took up a position in the very heart of Joseph's lines, and the fiery spirit of General Picton, the attack in the centre might have come too late. Lord Dalhousie, who had recently arrived from England to command the 7th Division and who was to have led the attack, failed to bring up his men in time, and, though aide-de-camp after aide-de-camp arrived with orders, the assault on the bridges hung fire. Picton, who alone had reached his station punctually, waited till he could stand it no more. Conspicuous in a blue frock-coat and a broad-brimmed top-hat,[1] he rode up to one of Wellington's messengers to ascertain his orders. On hearing that they were for the 7th Division to attack the Mendoza bridge, he shouted back, 'Then you may tell Lord Wellington that the 3rd Division under my

---

1. To protect an inflamed eye. He swore, wrote his admirer Kincaid, as roundly as if he had been wearing two cocked ones. Kincaid, 222. See Robinson, *Picton*, ii, 195–6.

command shall in less than ten minutes attack that bridge and carry it!' Upon which he set his men in motion towards the valley, calling out with customary oaths as he rode beside them, 'Come on, ye rascals! Come on, you fighting villains!'

Supported by the 4th and the remainder of the Light Division, the Fighting Third crossed the river and broke the enemy's centre. Though the ground was suitable for defence – vineyards, woods, and standing corn, interspersed with ditches and villages – the French infantry did

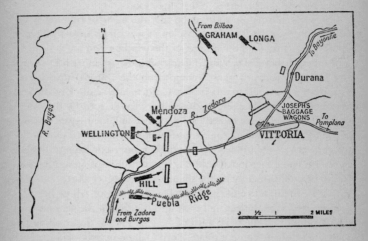

not fight well that day. They were depressed by their long retreat, had lost confidence in their leaders, and knew that the British outnumbered them. And as the threat to their flanks grew, they began, commanders and privates alike, to look over their shoulders.

Thereafter the end was certain. About five o'clock Longa's guerrillas on Graham's left flank cut the Vittoria–Bayonne *chaussée* at Durana, two miles beyond the town. The direct line of retreat to France was gone. Only the valour of General Reille's men in delaying Graham's advance prevented a complete encirclement. Holding the last high ground before Vittoria, their muskets flashing like lightning and the guns shaking the earth as the gunners bounded to and fro through the smoke, the remnants of the old Army of Portugal kept back the left prong of Wellington's pincers until the rest of the French could escape to the east.

But they did not go as an army or stand upon the order of their going. Hitherto they had retired with their guns and train; now they went without. A mile beyond Vittoria, on the narrow road to Pamplona, the treasure-wagons and carriages of King Joseph's Court were blocked in indescribable confusion. As the British shot crashed overhead and pursuing cavalry appeared on the skyline, panic broke out. Soldiers and civilians cut the draft-horses' traces and rode off, leaving their vehicles to the victors: ladies were thrown off their mounts or flung from their carriages; sacks of dollars and jewels were torn open by the retreating infantry and spilt about the road. Among those carried away in the tumult were King Joseph and Marshal Jourdan; the latter's baton was picked up by a British hussar, and sent to the Prince Regent.

The battle of Vittoria was over. As the victorious columns moved forward across the plain and the artillery galloped to the front, the sun began to sink behind the western hills, gilding the helmets of thousands of horsemen. Before them the French empire in Spain was dissolving. Had the pursuing cavalry been led by Cotton, Uxbridge, or Le Marchant, few of the enemy would have reached the safety of Pamplona and the mountains. But Le Marchant had fallen at Salamanca; Uxbridge was in disgrace expiating a scandalous elopement with Wellington's sister-in-law; and Cotton, who had been on sick leave in England, was detained by contrary winds in the Bay. There was no one at that moment with the initiative to weld the British cavalry into a cohesive and destroying whole. The rest of the army was tired out after five weeks' continuous marching and the long day's battle.[1]

As a result the French were able to escape along the single road to the east. They reached Pamplona two days later. 'They robbed and plundered everywhere,' wrote one of their pursuers, 'women and young girls were found on their own hearthstones outraged and dead; houses

---

1. The account of the battle is based on Oman, VI, 384–450; Fortescue, IX, 152–87; Napier, Book XXX, Ch. viii; Gurwood, *Supplementary Dispatches*; Bell, I, 83–91; Tomkinson, 243–54; Schaumann, 374–81; Kincaid, 217–26; *Johnny Newcome*, 223–32; Simmons, 289; Gomm, 304–6; Costello, 157–65; Smith, I, 95–102; Blakiston, *Twelve Years of Military Adventure*, II, 206–10; Jourdan, *Mémoires*; Maxwell, II, 40–3; Leith Hay, II, 10–208; Robinson, *Picton*, II, 195–200.

fired and furniture used for hasty cooking. Such is war!'[1] They left to the victors all but one of their 152 guns, every vehicle they had, and more booty than had fallen to the lot of a modern European army in any single battle.

There was another reason why the pursuit flagged. To Wellington's rage the King's baggage train proved too much for his men's discipline. Around it the soldiers of three nations, with powder-blackened faces, fought one another for boxes of dollars, rummaged state papers, pictures, and furniture, dressed up in fine clothes, and feasted on the wines and foods of a luxurious court. 'Come, boys,' shouted an Irish grenadier, 'help yourselves wid anything yez like best, free gratis and for nothing at all! The King left all behind him for our day's trouble. Who'll have a dhrink o' wine?' For miles the Pamplona road was strewn with the plunder of six years' predatory war: here the personal baggage of a king, there the decorations of a theatre, war stores and china, arms, drums, trumpets, silks, jewellery, and plate; 'wounded soldiers, deserted women and children of all ages imploring aid and assistance – here a lady upset in her carriage – in the next an actress or a *femme de chambre*; sheep, goats, and droves of oxen roaming and bellowing about, with loose horses, cows and donkeys.' That night the abandoned carriages were turned into the stands of an impromptu torchlit fair. According to Wellington's dispatch to the Secretary for War, nearly half a million pounds passed into the hands of his soldiers. When next day the pursuit was resumed, they were so gorged and laden they could scarcely move.

Yet, though as a result only 2000 prisoners were taken, and more than 50,000 French escaped by Pamplona and the Pyrenean passes to France, Vittoria was one of the decisive battles of the war. It liberated Spain, exposed France to invasion, and heartened Europe to make the final effort to break its chains. When on the night of June 30th the news reached the Allied camp on the Silesian border, Count Stadion broke into Prince Metternich's bedroom with a short of '*Le roi Joseph est – en Espagne!*' At that moment Austria's attitude and the prolongation of the armistice were in the balance. Next day Napoleon, who had been on the point of taking the field again against the still inadequately

1. Bell, 1, 96–8. See also Simmons, 291; Smith, 1, 102–3. 'The seat of war', wrote the latter, 'is hell upon earth.'

equipped Russians and Prussians, agreed to a conference and a six weeks' extension of the truce. It was the period the Austrians needed to complete the mobilization of their army. For a moment Britain became the idol of resurgent German youth; in Vienna Beethoven wrote an overture on the theme of 'Rule Britannia', and even the Russians sang, for the only time in their history, a *Te Deum* in gratitude for a foreign victory.

CHAPTER 4

ACROSS THE PYRENEES

> *Beating from the wasted vines*
> *Back to France her banded swarms,*
> *Back to France with countless blows,*
> *Till o'er the hills her eagles flew*
> *Beyond the Pyrenean pines,*
> *Follow'd up in valley and glen*
> *With blare of bugle, clamour of men,*
> *Roll of cannon and clash of arms,*
> *And England pouring on her foes.*
> *Such a war had such a close.*
>
> TENNYSON

BEFORE Napoleon had signed the extension of his truce with the eastern Powers Wellington's men were on the Pyrenees. Graham with the left wing reached the sea and Bidassoa on June 25th. The centre and right, stretching south-eastwards along the frontier, rested on the mountain passes of Maya and Roncesvalles. 'We fired our last shots into the *parlez-vous*,' wrote Bell, 'as we slashed them over the hills into their own country, while they carried along with them the curses of a whole kingdom.' It was five years since Canning had predicted that one day Europe would see a British army looking down on France from the Pyrenees.

Napoleon was not the man to brook invasion of his territories. He reacted to the news of Vittoria with passionate rage. Forbidding all reference to it in his closed Press, he put Joseph and Jourdan under house arrest and replaced them by the man whose disobedience had been the cause of half their troubles. On July 1st Soult left Dresden for Bayonne with orders 'to re-establish the imperial business in Spain.' He reached the headquarters of the demoralized army on the 12th and at once set to work to restore its morale. A superb organizer and, when driven to it, like all the great Revolutionary leaders, a dynamo of energy, the big, bullying Marshal completed his task in less than a fortnight. After five years of sulkily serving under others, he had at last achieved his ambition. In a flamboyant proclamation he told his troops that they had been expelled from Spain through the incompetence of their leaders and that under his command they would annihilate the enemy's 'motley levies'.

At that moment Wellington was occupied with the reduction – by storm or starvation – of the two remaining Spanish fortresses in French hands behind his lines. Profoundly distrustful of the armistice in Germany and of his country's new allies, he had no intention of advancing into France without securing his rear. His front, extending for fifty miles into the mountains, necessitated the division of his force into a number of isolated posts along the frontier passes. His left under Graham, who was in charge of the operations against San Sebastian, was on the coastal plain; his centre under Hill in the mountain *massif* called the Bastan; his right under Picton and Lowry Cole on the high Roncesvalles road from Pamplona to St-Jean-Pied-de-Port in France. His strategy, for the present a defensive one, was to hold the passes with small delaying forces against any French thrust until his main strength could be concentrated to give battle behind them. It meant reposing more trust in his scattered subordinates than he cared for, but Pyrenean geography left him no alternative. His own headquarters was at the hill village of Lesaca, half-way between San Sebastian and the Bastan. It was far nearer his ocean left than his mountain right, but it was at the former, where the main road from France crossed the Bidassoa, that he expected trouble. He had ordered San Sebastian to be stormed at once and he believed that Soult would try to relieve it. Reports of French movements towards the passes in the south he regarded as feints to distract his attention from the coastal sector.

In this he was wrong. Soult's plan, a most daring one, was to throw 35,000 bayonets – two-thirds of his force – against the Allied right at Roncesvalles, while D'Erlon with the remainder stormed the Maya pass to the north and, dominating all roads through the Bastan, interposed himself between Wellington and his threatened right in front of Pamplona where 5000 veteran troops and the main French artillery park were besieged by the Spaniards. Once the fortress was relieved, the whole army was to drive towards Tolosa or Vittoria in Wellington's rear, so turning on him the tables of his own campaign and forcing him to retreat. It was a gamble, for, being without transport since its defeat, the French army was bound to starve unless it could reach

Pamplona and capture its besiegers' stores within four days. But it was helped by the existence of a lateral road system on the French side of the Pyrenees that was lacking on the other, and by the fact that Wellington, being about to storm San Sebastian, was expecting Soult to strike in the north to relieve it.

At dawn on July 25th Graham's storming parties moved against San Sebastian. By midday Wellington, listening in Lesaca churchyard to the guns ten miles away, knew that the attack had failed. But hardly had he left Lesaca for the coast to discuss the next move with Graham, when heavy gunfire was heard from the opposite direction. Here D'Erlon had launched his attack on the Bastan against Hill's outposts in the Maya pass. A further twenty miles to the south-east 6000 British, Portuguese, and Spaniards under Major-General Byng had been defending the defiles of Altobiscar and Linduz since dawn against 35,000 assailants.

Despite the odds against them Byng's men had held their positions before Roncesvalles without difficulty, for Soult's columns, strung out along narrow mountain roads, had no room to deploy. But at five that evening a dense fog fell, and Sir Lowry Cole, the commander of the 4th Division, fearful for his flanks, decided against orders to fall back along the Pamplona road on Picton and the 3rd Division behind him. Nearer Wellington, in the Bastan, Sir William Stewart's two brigades repulsed D'Erlon's three divisions, thanks to a desperate stand by the 92nd Highlanders. 'They stood there', wrote an eyewitness, 'like a stone wall, until half their blue bonnets lay beside those brave Highland soldiers. ... I can see now the line of their dead and wounded stretched upon the heather.'[1] At nightfall all the ground lost was regained by a sudden attack on the French flank by two battalions from Lord Dalhousie's 7th Division under a young brigadier named Barnes. Yet here, also, what the pluck of the rank and file had held, the fears of their commanders yielded. For, with the Maya pass sealed once more against the French, Sir Rowland Hill arrived with news that Cole was overwhelmed at Roncesvalles and that a retreat was necessary to straighten the line. So it came about that on the morning of the 26th, both Soult and D'Erlon found to their surprise the British gone and the passes open. Instead of having to admit failure, the Duke

1. Bell, i, 104.

of Dalmatia was able to send a flamboyant dispatch to Dresden, which caused Napoleon, going one better, to announce that Pamplona and San Sebastian had been relieved and the British decisively defeated.[1]

Owing to his visit to San Sebastian and the failure of his subordinates to send prompt warning of what was happening, Wellington only learnt of the French attack late that night. At four o'clock next morning he set out post-haste for the Bastan where he found Hill and Stewart with 9000 men at Irutita, ten miles south of the abandoned Maya pass. As they were now strongly posted and as there was no sign of D'Erlon, he continued his journey southwards along the wooded mountain tracks, ordering a general concentration of reserves on Pamplona. After travelling all day he learnt at eight in the evening that Cole had abandoned Roncesvalles on the previous night and had fallen back to join Picton at Zuburi, twenty miles north-east of Pamplona. He at once sent Picton orders to hold his ground at all costs, promising to join him next day.

Yet Picton had already abandoned Zuburi without a fight. This fine soldier, who normally could never bridle his ardour in the presence of the French, had joined Cole at Linzoain that morning. At the sight of his tall hat and umbrella the men had supposed their retreat at an end; 'Here comes old Tommy,' they cried, 'now, boys, make up your minds for a fight!' But, after consulting Cole, Picton, paralysed by the responsibility, decided that it was not safe to stand in a defile where his flanks might be turned. He ordered instead an immediate retreat to the foothills north of Pamplona. By doing so he needlessly abandoned a further ten miles of difficult country and placed the relief of the fortress almost within Soult's reach. It was this that caused Wellington to write to the Prime Minister that all his victories had not yet given his generals confidence in themselves, and that, though

1. 'You had better,' wrote the Emperor to his Foreign Secretary, 'circulate the news that in consequence of Marshal Soult's victory on July 25th, the siege of San Sebastian has been raised and 30 siege guns and 200 waggons taken. The blockade of Pamplona was raised on the 27th; General Hill, who was in command at that siege, could not carry away his wounded and was obliged to burn part of his baggage. Twelve siege-guns were captured there. Send this to Prague, Leipzig and Frankfort.' *Lettres de l'Empereur Napoléon, non inserées dans la Correspondance*. 1909, p. 3.

heroes when he was present, they were like children in his absence. It was the price he paid for trusting them so little.

In the race to reach Pamplona before the British, Soult had gained the initial advantage. By the morning of the 27th – two days after he started – there were only six hilly miles and 19,000 British and Spanish troops between him and his goal. But at dawn Wellington had resumed his southward ride at Almandoz, half-way down the Maya-Pamplona road. Ten miles farther on, at Ostiz, he learnt of Picton's retreat and of what was happening ahead. Out-distancing all but a single aide, he galloped the remaining four miles to Sorauren village, reaching it just before Soult's outposts. Here he could see Cole's men spread across the heights with the French skirmishers moving towards them. He had just time before the enemy cut the road to scribble orders to his chief-of-staff for a general concentration on the spot. Then he galloped on to join Cole and Picton. It was, as he said, 'a close run thing.'[1]

At the sight of the erect, lithe figure on the thoroughbred, the Portuguese light infantry broke into a shout of 'Douro! Douro!' Soon the whole ridge was cheering; everyone knew that there would be no more retreat. It is possible, as Napier suggests, that the familiar sound, reverberating up the mountain valleys, caused Soult to postpone his attack until the morrow. Since Albuera – indeed, since Corunna – Soult, or General Salt as the British called him, had always hesitated in the immediate presence of the redcoats. There was an Achilles-heel in this fine strategist's armour which became apparent on the day of battle, when his magnificent self-assurance always temporarily deserted him.[2] With Pamplona only two hours' march away and his adversary for the moment outnumbered by two to one, he shrank from an immediate attack. Instead, he took his siesta and waited till next day.

By then it was too late. Wellington had made his dispositions, and

1. Larpent, II, 70. See also Oman, VI, 658–62; Fortescue, IX, 269–72; Bell, I, 106–7; Blakeney, 297–8; Smyth, *History of the XXth*, 396; H. M. C. Bathurst, 234.

2. Maximillien Lamarque, II, 182. 'He loved vigorous enterprises,' wrote one of his aides, possibly a little unfairly, 'provided they did not involve too much personal danger.' *Mémoires de St Chamans*. See also Lemonnier-Delafasse, 219, *cit*. Oman, VI, 590–1, 663; Cooper, *Rough Notes*, 24.

four British divisions – one, at least, certain to arrive during the day – were marching on the battlefield. He had won the race after all. Within twenty-four hours he would outnumber the enemy; till then he had only to hold his position and trust to his men's proved steadiness. Soult's ensuing attack was like Busaco, with the Allied line drawn up behind the skyline of a ridge. Twice the densely packed French columns reached the summit only to be expelled by the volleys and charges of the defenders. By four o'clock the battle of Sorauren was over.[1]

The French, who had lost nearly 4000 to the Allies' 2600, had shot their bolt. They had failed either to relieve Pamplona or capture supplies. They had now either to retreat or starve. In an effort to save something from the wreck, Soult ordered a march across Wellington's flank towards the Pamplona-Tolosa road, hoping to raise the siege of San Sebastian. By doing so he gave his adversary, whom he had already presented with a Busaco, the opportunity for a Salamanca. During the 30th Wellington struck at his rearguard and all but annihilated it. Famished and demoralized, Soult's troops abandoned all pretence of order and ran for safety. Scarcely half of them regained France with the colours.

Had Wellington chosen to pursue he could probably have reached the Garonne. But the truce in Germany was still continuing and, for all he knew, might already have culminated in a peace, freeing Napoleon's full strength for operations against him. At that moment his was the only Allied army actively engaged. It amounted, after its Vittoria and Pyrenean casualties, to little more than 80,000 men, of whom 25,000 were ill-fed and ill-disciplined Spaniards. To have invaded France with the latter – unpaid by their politicians and burning with a savage desire to revenge themselves on their country's oppressors – might have provoked a partisan resistance which the British commander was resolved to avoid. He therefore forwent his chance of glory and halted his army once more on the summit of the Pyrenees.

Throughout August, while the Spaniards resumed the blockade of Pamplona, he completed his preparations for a second assault on San

1. 'Nothing could stand against the ragged redcoats of old England.' Bell, I, 107–8. See Oman, VI, 667–80; Fortescue, IX, 275–80; Larpent, II, 20–1; Garwood; Maxwell, *Peninsular Sketches*.

Sebastian. On the last day of the month, while Soult from beyond the Bidassoa vainly strove to relieve it, his men stormed the fortress in daylight. The casualties were appalling; one British brigade lost more than half its number, another a third and another a quarter. But by the early afternoon, after Graham's artillery had opened fire on the curtain only a few feet above the heads of the stormers, the little fortress town, blazing to the stormy summer sky, was in British hands. 'Such was the ardour and confidence of our army,' wrote one of its officers, 'that if Lord Wellington had told us to attempt to carry the moon we should have done it.' Next day Soult, having lost nearly 4000 men in his attempt to raise the siege, fell back across the Bidassoa.

Again the Fabian Wellington refrained from following up his success. He was still awaiting news from the North. It came two days later, on September 3rd, when a fast vessel, which had been waiting at Portsmouth, entered Pasages with the tidings – brought to London on the 27th and semaphored at once to the south coast – that Austria had joined with Russia and Prussia in war against France. Napoleon had refused to accept the Rhine frontier; on August 12th the ten weeks' armistice had ended. Of the course of the new campaign Wellington knew nothing save for a rumour from the French lines of a Napoleonic victory at Dresden on the 27th. He was unaware that the Emperor's success had been offset by two disasters: the defeat of Marshal Macdonald by Blücher at Kätzbach on the 26th, and Vandamme's surrender at Kulm on the 30th.

Without further delay, however, he decided to invade France. Though nothing would induce him to risk his army needlessly, he knew that a concentric attack on Napoleon could only succeed if pressure was simultaneously exerted at every point on the circumference. He therefore prepared for an assault on Soult's mountain defences. He had to face the price of his earlier prudence: the time given to the Duke of Dalmatia to reorganize his troops and defence. For weeks that officer had been constructing an immense line of redoubts running southwards from the sea – a substitute for the offensive spirit his men had lost and a strange reversion for a Revolutionary general to eighteenth-century practice. But they were too extended; all but 8000 of his 47,000 infantry had to be strung along them, leaving too small a reserve to repel a concentrated attack. In this Soult was the victim of his country's political system; he dared not shorten his lines by a withdrawal because he knew that Napoleon would visit his wrath on any subordinate who retreated or gave up anything. He was also afraid that his troops, accustomed to living on the countryside, would provoke a rebellion in France by their excesses.

Wellington's plan was to attack the seaward end of the enemy line and, by pinching out a westward bulge on Spanish soil, capture the frontier town of Hendaye on the lower Bidassoa and advance his line to the Nivelle. By doing so he hoped to secure the little port of St-Jean-de-Luz for his supply-ships. His objectives, as always, were carefully attuned to his resources – a fact which assisted his project, since Soult, who attributed to him the more daring designs he himself would have favoured, had concentrated his reserves at the other end of his line to guard against an enveloping drive from Roncesvalles to the sea. As a result, only 10,000 men were holding the mouth of the Bidassoa.

During the early days of October, Wellington unobtrusively moved unit after unit to his seaward flank until more than 25,000 were concentrated near the river. At dawn on the 7th the light companies of the 5th Division opened the battle of the Bidassoa by wading armpit deep across the estuary. They reached the northern bank before the French were even aware of what was happening. When Soult arrived from the other end of his long line, the British were firmly established inside the frontier. Farther inland the Light Division and Freire's Spaniards simultaneously assaulted the mountain bastion of the Grande Rhune. By the evening of the next day all Wellington's objectives had been gained, and the French right was in retreat to the Nivelle. The operation, giving him possession of a whole chain of carefully prepared entrenchments,[1] had cost less than 1500 casualties.

Though the French had shown little of their old spirit and had abandoned the strongest positions as soon as their flanks were turned, Wellington again made no pursuit. He was still waiting for more certain news from Germany and for the fall of Pamplona to release more troops. He contented himself, therefore, with consolidating the rocky ledge of France he had won and preparing for the next move.

1. 'We found the soldiers' huts very comfortable; they were built of trees and furze and formed squares and streets, which had names placarded up such as Rue de Paris, Rue de Versailles, etc.' Gronow, 1, 4.

Looking down from the Pyrenean heights in those days of waiting, the way ahead – the final straight of the long race begun twenty years before – was already visible to the British. To the right ran a great wall of peaks stretching into the remote distance towards the Mediterranean: to the left the Bay of Biscay, with the warships of the Royal Navy perpetually on the move. In front lay France. 'From these stupendous mountains,' wrote Simmons of the Rifles, 'we had a most commanding view of a vast extent of highly cultivated French territory, innumerable villages, and the port and town of St-Jean-de-Luz. We could also see our cruisers sailing about near the French coast which gave an additional interest to the view before us. ... One morning one of our ships was observed to be chasing a brig of war and got between her and the shore. As the boats from the English went to board her, the Frenchman got into theirs and made for the shore. A short time after she was one mass of fire and blew up. It was a beautiful morning and some thousands of veteran Englishmen, having a bird's-eye view of the whole affair, took a lively interest in the manner our brave tars performed their duty.'

Had the vision of the watching soldiers been able to penetrate the October horizon, they would have seen beyond the Biscay bay the sails of British battleships in the swell off Brest and Lorient; the transports bearing men and supplies to feed the battlefields; the ocean merchantmen coming and going with the tribute of trade which sustained their country's alliances; the smoking chimneys of the North Country towns and Midland forges; the tax-collectors gathering their harvest and the money-lenders at their ledgers; the politicians debating in the forum at Westminster; the semaphore watchers on the Admiralty roof gazing across the river to the wooded Surrey heights. And far away in the north-east beyond the Alps they might have seen, amid the wooded folds of great rivers serpentining across the Saxon plains, the steely glint of marching armies set in motion by British faith and fortitude and paid by British gold, as they converged from north and east and south on the city of Leipzig, where Napoleon, clinging to his conquests, stood at bay with an army of veteran marshals and young, sickly conscripts.

For on October 16th, 1813, three hundred thousand Russians, Austrians, Prussians, and Swedes, with more than 1300 guns, closed in on a hundred and ninety thousand Frenchmen, Italians, and Saxons under the greatest captain of all time. Three days later the battle of Leipzig ended with the desertion of Napoleon's last German allies and the utter rout of his army, scarcely a third of it escaping. Britain's part in the victory was confined to the doings of a single battery of Congreve rockets, commanded by a young officer who a generation later was to fall fighting against his country's Russian allies. Yet, though its scale made the battles of the Peninsular War seem insignificant, it was the redcoated watchers on the Pyrenean heights and their sea-going comrades in the Bay who had laid its foundations.

Three weeks later, as the first authentic news of Leipzig chilled the hearts of France's southern army, the British stormed the heights of the Nivelle and broke into the Gascony plain. Pamplona, reduced to its last rat, had surrendered at the end of October; early in November a spell of cold and storm was succeeded by brilliant sunshine. The French, brought by conscript drafts up to 62,000 men, were holding the hilly south bank of the Nivelle, their redoubts and entrenchments bristling with guns. Confident in this wall of rock and iron, which was reputed as strong as the Lines of Torres Vedras, Soult boasted that it would cost the attackers a third of their force to dislodge him. But Wellington, unbending over the port, told his generals that he meant to prod the fat Marshal till he came to terms.[1] 'Those fellows think themselves invulnerable,' he remarked, 'but I will beat them out with ease.'

Once again the French were holding lines longer than they could man, and the British commander could bring a force against any point greater than they could concentrate to meet it. And he had an instrument with which to do so which, as he said, could go anywhere and do anything: 'the finest army,' in the words of one of its officers, 'in better order, better discipline, in better health and more effective than any British one in the Continent ever was before.' On November 10th, a month after the battle of the Bidassoa, he put it to the test as 'the two game-cocks of England and France' grappled all day on the hills to the south of the Nivelle. The British columns, which had moved up to their stations overnight, waded the river in the half-light of dawn and,

1. *Blackwood's*, Dec. 1946. 'A Gallant Pack,' by Peter Carew. No. 1574, Vol. 260.

scaling the heights, broke through the redoubts of Soult's centre like a screen of reeds. 'Nor did we ever meet a check,' wrote Harry Smith, 'but carried the enemy's work by one fell swoop of irresistible victory.' There is a lyrical quality in all the eye-witness accounts of that day; in no engagement of the war was the supremacy of Wellington's army shown more clearly than in that of the Nivelle. 'The fierce and continued charge of the British was irresistible,' recalled one who, wounded in the heather, watched his comrades storm the incredible crags of the Petite Rhune; 'onwards they bore nor stopped to breathe, rushing forward through glen, dale and forest. ... The star of three united nations shone victorious on the summits of the lofty Pyrenees, gilding the tall pines which capped their heads and foreboding downfall to Imperial France.'[1] By sundown the British spearheads were many miles behind the French lines, pressing after the fugitives with a running fire till nature could do no more, when the tired men stretched their limbs on the sod, pulled out their captured rations of cheese and onions, and went to roost.

Once the chain of Soult's line was broken, no link could hold. Units in almost impregnable fortresses, finding themselves surrounded, surrendered without a shot; others, fearful for their flanks, fell back leaving their comrades isolated. The morale of France's southern army could no longer withstand the attack of the British infantry.[2] Only the shortness of the November day saved Soult's right between the hills and the sea. It fled from encirclement towards Bayonne, leaving the port of St-Jean-de-Luz, over fifty guns, and 1200 prisoners in the attackers' hands. The latter's casualties, which Soult had expected to number 25,000, were less than half the defenders'.

The tidings of these victories set the hearts of the British people rocketing. From the Prince Regent, who hugged the Speaker when he announced the news of Sorauren, to the smock-frocks around the ale-house fire, they were kept that winter in a state of continuous excitement. The harvest had been good, the opening of the European ports had revived trade, and the hopes of twenty years of endurance were

1. Blakeney, 320–3; see also Bell, I, 119–25; Granville, II, 471–8; Smith, I, 145–6; Simmons, 321–5; Larpent, II, 155–7; Smith, I, 125–6; 142–54; *MS. Diary of Robert Blake*, 5–6; Schaumann, 390–4; William Napier, I, 132; Kincaid, 272.
2. 'They always met us like lions, but in the end it was like hares.' Bell, I, 151.

being suddenly fulfilled. The guns sounded for triumphs in France, Germany, and Italy; day after day the clanging bells of the mails, as they dashed by in a bower of laurel branches, set country folk along the highways cheering. Oxen were roasted in provincial market-squares, transparencies lit on Georgian balconies, and crackers and bonfires in London streets amid the roar of mobs: 'the tumult and train-oil and transparent flippancies,' wrote the scornful Byron, 'and all the noise and nonsense of victory!' On October 18th a chaise-and-four with a flag waving from the window dashed on to the Horse Guards Parade with the news of Wellington's crossing of the Bidassoa; a fortnight later the Tower salvoes proclaimed the victory of Leipzig.[1] Boney, men told one another, was back on the Rhine; his routed army, dripping with typhus, was crawling like a dying beast from the Europe it had ravaged. On November 4th the Allied Sovereigns entered Frankfurt; a few days later German troops reached the Rhine, kneeling with joy at the sight. Even the Dutch, who had placidly borne the conqueror's yoke for twenty years, caught the infection and drove the feeble French garrisons from their cities with shouts of 'Orange Boven!' A Prussian army stormed Arnhem, liberating Cossacks clattered over the cobbles of Amsterdam, and the Guards, repeating their initiating act of twenty-one years earlier, marched through cheering streets to embark for Holland. Five days later the old Prince of Orange, at the invitation of his people, sailed in a British seventy-four from the shores which had sheltered him for a generation. It was like the final scene in a play: the hero was almost weighed down with fortune's favours.

Yet the war was not over. Though the road behind stank with half-buried corpses and only a tenth of the army that had set out in the spring recrossed the Rhine, Napoleon was still set on conquest. He would not recall a garrison from Germany or Italy for the defence of France. When on the day before the battle of the Nivelle the Allied Sovereigns from Frankfurt offered him the 'natural frontiers' of Rhine, Alps, and Pyrenees, he refused to consider such humiliating terms. 'The word peace is ever in my ears,' he told his Council of State, 'when

1. Moore, *Byron*, 187–8, 202–5; Ashton, I, 174–5, 185–7; Festing, 192; Croker, I, 53; Colchester, II, 454–60; Granville, II, 482–3, 492; Scott, III, 366, 389; Gomm, 336–8; Ham, 188; Auckland, IV, 394–5; Austen, 243–4; Dudley, 223; Haydon, I, 239.

all around should echo with the cry, War! Peace! No peace till Munich is in flames!' The Corps Législatif, who petitioned him to declare that he was only fighting for the independence of France, were denounced as traitors in the pay of England. Regardless of the cost, the Emperor meant to win back all he had lost. He might lose his throne, he assured Metternich, but he would bury the world in its ruins.

Everything, therefore, depended on the hunters holding together. In their failure to do so, as Napoleon knew, lay his one hope. Three times a European Coalition had dissolved before him; once again divisions in the victors' councils might save him. Already they were quarrelling; the homesick Russian generals wished to turn back; the Prussians, avid for loot, to go on; the Austrians, conscious of dynastic ties and afraid both of Russia and Prussia, to temporize. Even after Napoleon had rejected their terms the statesmen of Austria still continued, over his head, to offer the French people the Rhine frontier – 'an extent of territory,' they pointed out, 'such as France has never had under her ancient kings.'

It was England who cemented Europe's wavering purpose. She was already underwriting the Grand Alliance by maintaining nearly a quarter of a million Russian, Austrian, and Prussian troops. She now reminded those who were taking her subsidies of the purpose for which they had been granted. On November 15th, before the news of Wellington's invasion of France had reached him, the Foreign Secretary, Lord Castlereagh, informed the British representative at Vienna that England would consent to no peace that did not give solid securities for a permanent settlement. Though for the sake of one prepared to surrender the greater part of her colonial conquests, she demanded the independence of Holland, Spain, and Portugal, the demilitarization of Antwerp and the mouth of the Scheldt, and the freedom of the seas. To ensure these the Foreign Secretary set out for Allied headquarters in southern Germany. He left London in the last week of the year in a dense fog, with men walking before the horses' heads carrying flambeaux. 'We have now the bull close-pinioned between us,' he wrote, 'and if either of us let go our hold till we render him harmless, we shall deserve to suffer for it.'[1]

Long before Castlereagh, travelling across a Continent gripped by

1. Castlereagh, IX, 41.

frost, reached his destination, Wellington had resumed his advance. The Pyrenean roads were sodden with rain, but on December 9th, having learnt of Napoleon's losses at Leipzig, he struck once more. To break out of the restricted triangle between the mountains and the Lower Adour and Nive, he threw four of his eight divisions under Hill across the latter. It was a daring move, for until the flooded river could be bridged, it enabled Soult, whose force was concentrated round Bayonne, to hit back with superior numbers at either half of the British army. Yet Wellington, who never took risks without weighing them, felt complete confidence in his men's ability to beat off any assault the French might make.

The event proved him right. For though Soult with nearly 50,000 troops attacked, first Hope's 30,000 between the sea and the Nive on December 10th and 11th, and then Hill's 14,000 on the right bank of the Nive at St-Pierre on the 13th, he was held in both cases until the arrival of Wellington's reserves. In the second battle the British were nearly overwhelmed; one nervous colonel, fresh from England, withdrew his indignant men from the slaughter: another – a braggart – was found behind the lines attending to the wounded. But the rank and file and rosy-faced 'Farmer' Hill, their commander, rose gloriously to the occasion; it was almost the only occasion the latter had ever been heard to swear. For three hours the 'thin red line of old bricks' stood between the cheering French columns and a victory that seemed at last within their grasp; 'dead or alive,' cried Colonel Brown of the Gloucesters, 'we must hold our ground.' And they did. The field was so thickly strewn with corpses that Wellington said afterwards that he had never seen its like. General William Stewart of Albuera fame – 'auld grog Willie,' as the men called him – had every member of his staff struck down: 'a shell, sir, very animating!' he remarked as one exploded at his feet, and went on with his conversation. The battle ended with a counter-attack by the 92nd Highlanders, who went into the fight with tossing plumes and a piper with a broken leg playing 'Hey! Johnny Cope.' 'This,' wrote Bell, recalling the blue bonnets' advance, 'was to understand war.' As the French began to stream back to Bayonne, the victors threw up their caps and gave 'a long, thrilling cheer.'[1]

1. Bell, I, 126–41; Gomm, 331; Larpent, II, 223; Gronow, I, 19–21; Fortescue, IX, 469–72; Oman, VII, 223–81.

Having established himself on the east bank of the Nive, a new prospect opened before Wellington. By remaining in his entrenched camp at Bayonne, the enemy could still bar his road to Bordeaux and the North, but only at the expense of leaving unguarded a broad and fertile expanse of France stretching eastwards for more than two hundred miles. On this Soult depended not only for his supplies – for the country north of Bayonne was mainly sand and wood – but for his communications with Suchet, who was still trying to hold the Catalonian fortresses.

Before he could advance Wellington had to win a victory of another kind over his own army. For, if it was to retain numerical superiority in the field, he could spare no troops to hold down territory in his rear. While the midwinter rains temporarily bogged down the armies, he devoted himself to winning the goodwill of the civilian population. In this he was helped by his opponents who, after twenty years of pillage, rape, and arson abroad, could not deny themselves these pleasures in their homeland. This had the effect of making the invaders appear as liberators instead of conquerors. There was a little difficulty at first in imposing this conception on them; one private, tried and hanged for a rape, explained that, as he was now in France, he thought it must be in order. Most of the Spaniards had to be sent home; as Wellington told their commander, he had not sacrificed thousands of men merely to enable the survivors to rob the French. Their British comrades, who included a liberal proportion of gaolbirds,[1] he treated in his usual realist way by sending a strong force of military police up and down the columns with orders to string up on the spot every man found pilfering. After a few examples there was no more plundering.

Such a manner of making war much astonished the French. They could scarcely believe their eyes; an innkeeper veteran of Napoleon's Italian campaigns was speechless when Brigadier Barnard of the Light Division asked him how much he owed for his dinner. Having long repudiated the idea of gentility, the people of south-western France found themselves quartering an army of gentlemen. It was worth a

1. When Wellington, having occasion to coin money for the occupied territories, called for a return of professional forgers, he was supplied with enough to man a mint. Oman, VII, 289. See *idem*, VII, 215–19; Durwood, XI, 288–9, 296, 306; Larpent, II, 5, 106–7, 161, 164–5, 167, 226; III, 36, 68; Gronow, I, 12–13; Bell, I, 131–3, 153; Smith, I, 150; Simmons, 329; Bessborough, 237–8; George Napier, 251–2; Fortescue, IX, 443; Schaumann, 394–5.

dozen victories to the Allies. The British Commander-in-Chief even invited the *maires* of the towns where he stayed to his table: a thing undreamt of in a French Revolutionary general. Those who had fled came flocking back to their homes: the British, it was said, only waged war against men with arms in their hands. What was more, they paid for all they needed. Before long the inhabitants were coining money; fowls were selling at 14s. apiece and turkeys at 30s. The Commissariat was inundated with cattle, grain, and fodder. Even bankers offered the British cash and credit. If this, wrote an English officer, was what making war in an enemy country was like, he never wished to campaign in a friendly one again.

This wise humanity increased the size of Wellington's striking force by at least two divisions. Lines-of-communication troops were rendered needless. Men and supplies could travel about the country unescorted, while the wounded could be billeted and nursed in French households. In vain Soult circulated proclamations exhorting the people to raise partisan bands; they declined to do anything so unprofitable. The only guerrilleros were disgruntled conscripts who took to the hills and fought, not the British, but the Emperor's recruiting officers. Instead, the people of Aquitaine looked on their nice, orderly conquerors as harbingers of peace and prosperity who had come to put an end to conscriptions and war taxes. Some even expressed a wish to be governed by them permanently.[1]

*

By the second week in January, Wellington knew that his fears of a premature peace were groundless and that the Austrians, Russians, and Prussians had crossed the Rhine and invaded France. He did not approve of their dispersed line of advance in Napoleon's presence – a system, he said, on which he would not have marched a corporal's guard: his own advice would have been to 'run in upon him' by a concentrated drive on Paris. None the less, he was resolved to give them what support he could, and on February 12th, after a week's sunshine had dried the roads, resumed his offensive. Napoleon had drawn off

1. Larpent, III, 42; see *idem*, II, 181, 211, 221–2, 231; III, 30, 35, 44, 76–7, 90–1; George Napier, 241–2; Simmons, 342; Lynedoch, 610–11; Oman, VII, 286, 291–2, 390; Fortescue, X, 1819; Smith, I, 166; Bell, I, 150–1; Gronow, I, 12; Simmons, 335; Schaumann, 402; Bessborough, 237–8.

14,000 of Soult's men for his own campaign in the north, so offsetting the Spanish divisions that had had to be left behind on the frontier. As usual, the Marshal, facing south across the Adour and digging himself in, had taken up too wide a front. This gave Wellington the initiative. Dividing his army, he left 30,000 men under Sir John Hope in front of Bayonne and struck eastwards into the interior with the remaining 45,500. By doing so he caused the defensive-minded Soult to suppose that the line of the Adour was about to be attacked at its eastern end and to draw away his reserves from Bayonne.

Instead, however, of turning north against the line of the Adour, Wellington continued his eastward march. The country east of the Nive was an open plateau, crossed by five swift Pyrenean rivers – the Joyeuse, Bidouze, Saison, Gave d'Oloron, and Gave de Pau – running from south to north and joining the Adour in its long westward reach above Bayonne. By using his slight superiority in numbers to maintain a strong flanking column under Hill to the south, Wellington turned the defence lines of each river without a fight and compelled the French to fall back ever farther eastwards. As was his wont, he guarded against a counter-blow by keeping a strong reserve under his own command behind his marching columns. Then, having by February 19th driven Soult's field army as far east as the Gave d'Oloron, forty miles from Bayonne, he halted and, while his opponent tried to anticipate his next move, proceeded to do the one thing he was not expecting. On the 23rd, instead of attempting to cross the Adour above Bayonne, he threw Hope's 18,000 men across it at its broadest point between the fortress and the sea.

Wellington had returned to St-Jean-de-Luz on the 19th to supervise this delicate operation. But the gunboats which were to have bridged the estuary being delayed by a Biscay gale, he had been forced to return to his main army on the Gave d'Oloron, leaving the task to Sir John Hope. Undeterred by the continuance of the gale and the non-appearance of the flotilla, this gallant Scotsman succeeded on the morning of the 23rd in shipping five companies of the Guards and two of the 60th in rowing boats to the north bank of the Adour. Here they maintained their position under the noses of 14,000 Frenchmen. In this feat they received unexpected help from a battery of the new Congreve rockets which, at the instance of the Prince Regent, had arrived from England,

and about which, on account of their erratic aim, both Wellington and the Army had been very scornful.[1] The frightful noise they made and their capacity for setting things on fire kept the French from investigating the crossing too closely. By the evening of the 24th, when the British naval vessels at last forced the bar and came up the river, Hope had contrived to get the bulk of the Guards Division across. By the 26th the bridge of boats was complete and 15,000 British troops were beyond the Adour encircling Bayonne and its garrison.

On the day the fortress was invested – February 27th – Wellington, sixty miles away, struck at Soult on the Gave de Pau, the last river line that barred his advance into the central plain of southern France. Having been driven from the Gave d'Oloron by yet another march of Hill's flanking column, the Marshal had concentrated 36,000 men to dispute the crossing at Orthez. Though the attacking force only numbered 7000 more, Wellington again divided it, sending two of his seven divisions to cross the river above the town and threaten the French line of retreat. Since his victories on the Nive he no longer feared Soult's counter-attacks. He knew that the latter lacked resolution and his men fighting spirit: he knew, too, of what his own army was capable.

The battle took place, not in front of the town, where the river was impassable, but to the west of it, where the British left wing under Beresford had crossed on the previous day while the French cavalry, expecting a repetition of Hill's out-flanking movement, had been watching the fords on the other side of Orthez. Soult's position was one of great natural strength, not dissimilar to those from which Wellington had repulsed so many attacks in the past. But, instead of, like Wellington, keeping a strong reserve in hand, and using it for counterblows, he hoarded it to cover a withdrawal. Retreat from the start was his dominating idea. Throughout the six hours' fight the initiative remained with the British, who, even after their first assault had failed, were able to renew it elsewhere without interference. The day's crowning achievement was an attack by the 1st Battalion of the 52nd Light Infantry, which at a critical moment deployed and, supported by a cloud of sharpshooters, drove with review precision up a bullet-swept

1. 'I don't want to set fire to any town and I don't know any other use of rockets.' Wellington, *Dispatches*. See also Larpent, II, 256–8; Fortescue, IX, 485.

height; Harry Smith thought it the most majestic advance he had ever seen. The battle ended, as Wellington had reckoned when he sent Hill's two divisions on a flanking march against Soult's communications,[1] with the French scurrying to the bridge of Sault, ten miles to the north-east. Had the country been favourable for cavalry or had the British commander followed up more vigorously – he had been slightly wounded by a spent bullet – the French might have suffered major disaster. As it was, their losses were over 4000, including 1350 prisoners: casualties almost double those of the attackers. During their retreat they lost as many more from desertion.

*

Two days before the battle of Orthez, five hundred miles away in the little town of Bar-sur-Aube, the British Foreign Secretary conferred with the representatives of his country's allies – the Czar of Russia, Prince Hardenberg of Prussia, Prince Metternich, and the Austrian Commander-in-Chief, Prince Schwarzenberg. At that moment, Napoleon, flushed with victory, was a few hours' march away at Troyes, which his troops had just recaptured. Yet, a fortnight before, the Allies, after advancing two hundred and fifty miles in a month, had overrun more than a third of France and were sweeping towards Paris in two great armies, one of 60,000 under Blücher driving westwards down the Marne, and the other of more than 100,000 under Schwarzenberg down the Seine, thirty miles to the south, while the advance-guard of a third army in the north under Bernadotte – the renegade French Marshal who had become Crown Prince of Sweden – was moving down from Flanders and had occupied Laon, Rheims, and Soissons. The morale of Napoleon's troops, outnumbered by three to one and disastrously defeated at La Rothière at the beginning of the month, was visibly disintegrating, and hordes of deserters were pouring towards a silent and appalled Paris, while Cossack patrols, spreading far across the country, had penetrated as far as Orleans and had reached the imperial palace of Fontainebleau. Everywhere the Emperor's cause seemed in ruin; from

1. 'The cry "We are cut off, the enemy is across the road," began to be heard in our ranks!' Lapéne, 264. See Fortescue, IX, 498–514; Oman, VII, 282, 343–75; Baeston, *Orthez Campaign*; Gurwood; Smith, I, 163–5; Bell, I, 147–8; Foy, 238–242; *Narrative of a Soldier*; Brown, 259–60; Seaton, 201–2; Cooper, 110–11; Col. A. Burne, *The Enigma of Toulouse* (*Army Quarterly*, January, 1927).

Italy news had come that his brother-in-law, Murat, in return for an Austrian guarantee of his Neapolitan throne, had joined the Allied cause, while in the north Flanders and Denmark had been overrun by his fellow traitor, Bernadotte. All Europe was hunting down Napoleon. Antwerp was closely besieged, Brussels taken, and a British force under Sir Thomas Graham was investing Bergen-op-Zoom, while in Germany the last surviving French garrisons faced starvation. In England, which had been blanketed by the worst frost of living memory – the Thames was frozen over at Blackfriars and there had been twenty-foot drifts in the Midlands – glorious rumours percolated. On February 21st a post-chaise, decked with laurels, dashed up the Dover road with news of a great victory won at the gates of Paris and of Napoleon's death at the hands of Cossacks. On 'Change, Government stocks rose six points, only to fall a few hours later after the owners of the chaise had made a fortune.

For at that moment the campaign in France had taken a very different turn. Field-Marshal Blücher, in his zeal to be the first in Paris, had allowed his army of Prussians and Russians to become dangerously strung out. Taking advantage of the leisurely pace of the main Austrian army down the Seine valley, Napoleon drove his famished and exhausted men northwards during the day and night of February 9th through the deep clay forest of Traconne and unexpectedly appeared at Champaubert on the morning of the 10th. Here, after annihilating a Russian division, he cut across Blücher's line of march; then turning westwards towards the head of his column, defeated another of his corps commanders at Montmirail on the 11th, another at Château-Thierry on the 12th, and Blücher himself at Vauchamps on the 14th. In four swift battles that seemed to reach back across the years to Rivoli, in every one of which he brought superior numbers against the enemy's isolated columns, he inflicted 20,000 casualties and took fifty guns. Then, having flung back Blücher towards Chalons, he hurried back to the Seine where Schwarzenberg's army had driven Victor's and Oudinot's weak screen to within fifty miles of Paris. At Nangis on the 17th and Montereau on the 18th he inflicted a further 5000 casualties on the leading German and Russian corps. Appalled by the successive tidings of disaster, the Austrian Commander-in-Chief ordered a general retreat. By the 21st the Allies were back at Troyes; three days later, after a council of war, they began to retire – like Brunswick's army twenty-two years before – towards the Vosges. Against all probability Napoleon had saved his capital. His decision, speed, and the legend of his name had snatched victory from defeat. The miracle of Marengo had been repeated. Or so it seemed to those whom he had so often defeated in the past.

Thanks to the Royal Navy the British Foreign Secretary had never suffered that experience. While the Austrians were counselling retreat and even the brave Czar was sunk in a wave of despair, Castlereagh remained serene. He reminded his allies of their overwhelming superiority in numbers: even now, after their losses of the past fortnight, they commanded within or near the borders of France more than half a million men. He was supported by Blücher who, despite his recent drubbing, was all for trying again and marching on Paris. Only a few days' march away on the Aisne and the Flemish frontier were two Russian and one Prussian corps; joined to Blücher's depleted troops they would bring his army up to 100,000 men, a force greater than any Napoleon could interpose between it and Paris. When the sovereigns and statesmen round the council table at Bar-sur-Aube pointed out that these three corps formed part of Bernadotte's Army of the North and could not be taken from it without trenching on the jealously guarded rights of that crafty and exceedingly dilatory commander, Castlereagh replied that if Bernadotte refused the transfer, his monthly subsidies from London would be cut off. At this the decision to let Blücher advance was taken.

The Austrians, however, continued their retreat and only stopped when Napoleon, turning back to chase Blücher away from his capital, ceased to pursue. Since Wagram it had been a canon of Austrian policy that it was better to try to civilize the revolutionary dictator of the West than to fight him. Only Napoleon's refusal to be content with less than the domination of all Europe had induced the Emperor Francis to throw in his lot with the Allies after the failure of his attempts at mediation. Napoleon's son and heir, the infant King of Rome, was his grandson, and, to a cautious and far-sighted Austrian, an imperial France reduced to reasonable limits and governed in due course by a half-Habsburg seemed safer company than an enlarged Russia and Prussia unchecked by any Western counterpoise. The revolutionary barbarism of France might be redeemed by the civilizing influence of the Habsburgs. That of Russia and her jackal, Prussia, were fundamental. To an Austrian, with his knowledge of the Orient, Russians and Prussians were barbarians in the bone.

To this view the British had never subscribed. Since their unsuccessful attempt to live on terms with Napoleon twelve years before, they had refused to countenance any compromise with him. Their view was that, so long as he reigned, permanent peace was unobtainable. Anyone who would fight him relentlessly like themselves was their friend, Latin, Slav, or Teuton. His insane resolve to yield nothing at all, and his persistence, even after Leipzig, in rejecting the Rhine frontier, gave them the chance to impress on their allies the need for restraining him once and for all. Castlereagh's instructions were to insist that France should relinquish all claims in Germany, Italy, and Spain, that Holland should become an independent kingdom with sufficient territory to secure her from future French invasion, and that Antwerp should be placed in friendly hands.

When, therefore, negotiations for a peace had been opened at Châtillon-sur-Seine in February, the terms offered France were no longer the 'natural frontiers' of Rhine, Alps, and Pyrenees, but merely those she had enjoyed under her ancient kings. At one moment, after his defeat at La Rothière, Napoleon had reluctantly given his Foreign Minister, Caulaincourt, authority to accept them if no other way of saving Paris seemed possible. But after his victories he had cancelled the recall of his troops from Italy and announced that he would carry the war to Munich. Despite lambent flashes of his old genius, his sense of reality seemed to have completely deserted him. He persisted in behaving as though he was at the head of a vast army, spoke of skeleton formations of disorganized survivors as though they were army corps in full strength, and stormed at his Marshals when, with hopelessly attenuated forces, they failed to carry positions that only the vanished legions of his imagination could have taken. He cared nothing for peace; he was only concerned with recovering his former empire. The question whether it was arithmetically possible to do so interested him no more than whether it was morally desirable.

His only hope of success lay not in his military prowess – for the sword was already broken in his hand – but in the likelihood of his enemies falling out. Throughout the Châtillon negotiations he continued to address secret proposals for a separate peace to his father-in-law; if Austria could be detached, he felt he could deal with Russia and Prussia. It was Castlereagh's service that he defeated these efforts. Not only did he hearten the Czar, but he overcame the suspicions of Metternich. On March 1st, the day that the Austrians, finding that Napoleon had turned back in pursuit of Blücher, cautiously resumed their advance, he secured the adhesion of his allies to a treaty which spelt the end of the usurper's power.

By the Treaty of Chaumont the four contracting Powers, in the now certain event of Napoleon continuing to refuse their terms – for nothing would now induce him to give up the Rhine frontier and Antwerp – undertook to prosecute the war till he was overthrown. Each was to maintain 150,000 troops in the field and adjure a separate peace, while Britain, in addition, was to contribute an annual subsidy of five millions sterling to her allies. Secret clauses provided for a federal union of the liberated German states, an Austrian hegemony in Italy, the return of the Bourbons to Spain, the independence of Switzerland and, at Britain's instance, the enlargement of Holland to include Antwerp and the former Austrian Netherlands. The alliance was to last for twenty years. Its creation was almost wholly Castlereagh's.

*

Meanwhile, Wellington, unaware of what was happening in the North, was exploiting his victory. The French rearguard made a show of standing at Aire on March 2nd but disintegrated when attacked. 'It was all in vain,' wrote Bell of the 34th, 'the blood of the old bricks was up and we drove them into and right through the town.' A few nights later he slept in a bedroom, with damask drapery, mirrors, and polished furniture; it was the first time he had been in a bed since the occupation of Madrid two summers before. The campaign had suddenly become a picnic, with fowls to roast at the camp fires, wine at fifteen *sous* a bottle, and riflemen slicing slabs of bacon on their bread like English haymakers.[1]

By his retreat eastwards Soult left the road to the north open. More than a hundred miles up the Atlantic coast from besieged Bayonne lay

1. Bell, I, 151–8; Smith, I, 175; Larpent, III, 32–3, 46, 75, 87–9; Gronow, I, 24–5; Pellot, *Guerre des Pyrénées, cit.* Alison, XIII, 33.

the great city of Bordeaux, the third in France and the capital of Gas-
ony. While his field-army halted its eastward march to consolidate
its communications, the British Commander-in-Chief extemporized
a flying force under Beresford to seize the city and secure the Gironde
estuary for his transports. Reports had reached him that its merchants,
ruined by the blockade, were talking of a Bourbon restoration, and,
though scrupulously anxious not to encourage any Frenchman to a step
which might prove fatal in the event of an Allied peace with Napoleon,
he could not afford to ignore a civil movement so favourable to his
operations. On March 12th Beresford reached Bordeaux with two
regiments of hussars. The mayor met him at the gates and, tearing off
his tricolour scarf, trampled it in the mud with cries of '*A bas les
aigles!*' '*Vivent les Bourbons!*' Subsequently, ignoring the delicate
negotiations at Chaumont, he proclaimed, to Wellington's embarrassment and indignation, that he had been authorized by the Allies to
conduct the administration of the city in King Louis' name.

For under its own momentum the war was gathering speed at a rate
transcending sober political calculations. Faced by the recoil upon itself of the revolutionary maxim of making war support war, and bled
white by successive conscriptions and taxations, Napoleonic France
was disintegrating. Her people could not take the medicine they had
so often inflicted on others. Everywhere, save in her Emperor's immediate presence, her soldiers were on the run, watched by apathetic
civilians who made no response to his proclamations enjoining them
to emulate the Spanish guerrilleros and fall on the invaders' rear. The
only result of his injunctions in the south was the formation of local
guards to protect the villages from the depredations of these hypo-
thetical partisans. On March 20th, two days after Wellington resumed
his eastward advance against Toulouse, Lyons, the second city of
France, fell to an Austrian column advancing from the Jura as Augereau's men, unsupported by the countryside, withdrew hastily before
it.

As the British swept forward, in sunshine at last, across a flat, water-
logged meadow-country of orchards, vineyards, and trout-streams,
after Soult's scarecrow army, the people flocked out of their houses to
greet them. At Bagnères Spa, even before the first redcoat appeared,
the National Guard turned out to present arms to a party of English

civilians. When Wellington reached the outskirts of Toulouse on March 26th, he had less than a battalion guarding the two hundred miles that separated him from his ships in the Bay of Biscay. The reinforcements which should have reached him from England had been deflected by the politicians, who, in their excitement at the news from the Continent, had forgotten their hard-earned lessons and sent every available man to Holland to enable Graham to capture Bergen-op-Zoom and Antwerp – places which were bound to fall in any case if the French armies were defeated in the field. But, since Wellington's discipline enabled him to dispense with lines-of-communication troops, it mattered little, except to Graham's unfortunate soldiers who were repelled from Bergen with heavy loss on March 8th.

Meanwhile in the confused fighting on the misty, shivering heights above the Aisne – though no news of it had yet penetrated to the south across a disorganized France – Napoleon had made his last throw and lost. As Wellington had always said, he lacked the patience for defensive operations. Having forced back the Russians in a bloody battle at Craonne but failed to prevent their junction with Blücher's Prussians, he was repulsed at Laon on March 9th and 10th. Three days later, in a night attack on Rheims, he took his last town. His army was by now a horde of famished desperadoes in ragged greatcoats and bare feet, its guns and wagons worn out, its units inextricably confused. More than 70,000 veterans who might have brought its depleted ranks up to strength were locked up in fortresses beyond the Rhine which Napoleon, in his insane desire to retain the unretainable, had refused to relinquish. Even Blücher's army was now twice the size of his own. And along the Seine valley, Schwarzenberg's host, stirred into activity by the expostulations of Castlereagh and the Czar, was moving once more on Paris. On March 20th Napoleon, marching in haste to intercept it, fell on its flank at Arcis-sur-Aube and was again repulsed. Henceforward, while it pursued its way towards the capital, he was left to roam, furious but impotent, across its lines of communication with an army of ghosts; still sending hourly messages to Paris and his Marshals to resist, still summoning to his aid armies that had ceased to exist, still breathing threats of vengeance against Rhineland, Danube, and Vistula.

On March 28th, ignoring these demonstrations and driving Marmont's and Mortier's weak forces before them, the two Allied armies joined hands at Meaux, less than thirty miles from Paris. Two days later, while Napoleon desperately marched by way of Fontainebleau, with his men dropping in hundreds by the roadside, to rescue his capital, 180,000 invaders stormed its northern heights. Thirteen thousand fell as the Russian and Prussian columns fought their way up the slopes of Montmartre and the Butte de Chaumont and boys from the *École Militaire* served the defenders' guns. That afternoon, with the Allied artillery commanding its streets, Paris surrendered. Its citizens had no stomach for a fight, and the bourgeois National Guard, called out to reinforce the hopelessly outnumbered regulars, was more concerned with guarding the shops from the mob than in dying for a lost cause.

*

On the afternoon of April 5th, a British officer, who had set out from Paris with dispatches on the evening of March 30th, reached London via Antwerp. As men heard the news in street or counting-house, or stood breathless with the newspaper in their hands, they seemed to be in a dream. 'It is the Lord's doing,' wrote Sir William Pepys to Hannah More, 'and it is marvellous in our eyes.' All over England houses were decked with laurel, transparencies and coloured candles lit in windows, and the populace, dancing and singing, poured into the streets. The church bells rang and the mob joyously chalked rude notices on the doors of those who were supposed to have sympathized with Boney, and Wilberforce wished his old friend Pitt were alive to witness the end of the drama.

During the Easter week-end – with warm sunshine thawing men's hearts after the long frost – it became known that Napoleon's Marshals had abandoned him, that his servile Senate had decreed his deposition and the recall of the Bourbons, and that the Allied Sovereigns had resolved on his abdication. 'This dreadful scourge is at last removed from us,' wrote Lord Auckland, who had been Ambassador at The Hague when the Revolutionary armies invaded Holland, 'and after twenty years of distress and difficulty we breathe and live again.' Only a handful of cantankerous radicals protested: to Lord Byron, who wrote an ode to the fallen tyrant, it seemed that the blockheads had won and Prometheus was chained. But most Englishmen at that moment could see nothing to admire in Napoleon; after keeping the world in oceans of blood, it seemed shameful that he should wish to survive the ruin he had created instead of perishing, sword in hand, at the head of his men. 'This,' wrote Walter Scott, 'is a poor Devil!'[1]

One thing gave almost universal pleasure. The Czar, in the hour of victory, seemed to have no other thought than how to restore peace to Europe. However much the French might deserve to be punished for the injuries they had inflicted, there was to be no revenge; the war had been waged against one man, and now that he had fallen, enmity was at an end. The Allied Sovereigns had come to France, Alexander declared, neither to conquer nor to rule, but to establish peace for all. 'It is like a dream,' wrote Dorothy Wordsworth, 'peace, peace all in a moment – prisoners let loose, Englishmen and Frenchmen brothers at once! – no treaties, no stipulations!' For one magnanimous moment humanity seemed to stand in the dawn before the Bastille fell.

But the war was not quite over. Six hundred miles away to the south, on the Languedoc plain, the British army was still fighting. Its commander did not yet know that Napoleon had abdicated, though he had learnt of the occupation of Paris. Soult, whose love of digging-in had become an obsession, had got his troops behind the walls of a fortified city with a flooded river between them and the British, and, in a dissolving world, it seemed as safe a place as any he could hope to find. Wellington would have preferred to have advanced northwards from Bordeaux through the traditionally royalist Bocage to the Loire, so carrying the war which he had begun on the circumference of Napoleon's empire to its heart. By doing so and making Nantes his base, he would have drawn, as in his march to the Bay of Biscay in the previous summer, towards his sea-borne supplies.[2] But with the reinforcements he should have received sent by the Cabinet to besiege fortresses in Holland, he had not the men both to advance towards the Loire and contain Soult in the east. The latter might at any time be joined by Suchet who, at last, was withdrawing from Catalonia; and, though

1. Scott, III, 451. See idem, 428–9, 441; De Selincourt, 592–4; Moore, Byron, 227, 324; Two Duchesses, 386–7; Colchester, II, 482; Broughton, I, 87, 103–5; Haydon, I, 239; Lord Coleridge, 212; Gaussen, 317; Scott, III, 427–9; Ashton, I, 251–3; Wilberforce, 395; Auckland, IV, 413; Robinson, 429.

2. See his conversation in Stanhope, 21.

the two Marshals hated each other, they could together constitute a formidable force.

As Wellington also feared that Napoleon might try to prolong the war by marching south to join his last two armies, and, as the capture of Toulouse might precipitate a Royalist rising throughout Languedoc, he resolved to drive Soult out of the town. It involved a grave risk, for he was in an enemy country far from his base, only slightly superior in numbers, and without any siege-train. Before he could even reach the city and attack its eastern and only superable side, he had to move the bulk of his troops across the Garonne – swollen by floods to a width of over 500 feet. 'How the devil,' asked the cheery Patlanders, 'are we to get over that big strame of a river to leather them vagabones out o' that!'

It proved an operation of great difficulty. The troops had to trudge barefooted through knee-deep clay; at one point on the road six oxen and four horses, in addition to its own six mules, had to be fastened to Wellington's travelling carriage to drag it through the quagmires. The first attempt to cross the river below Toulouse failed owing to the inadequacy of the pontoon bridge; a second, made by Hill's corps a mile lower down, was abandoned owing to the state of the roads. But Wellington, with the resilience that always came to his aid when thwarted, chose a new crossing-place above the town, withdrew Hill's troops, and on the stormy night of April 4th renewed his attempt. While the operation was only half completed the bridge was broken by floods, and for three days 18,000 British troops under Beresford were isolated and exposed to the attack of more than double their numbers. Yet Soult refused to attack. 'You do not know what stuff two British divisions are made of,' he is reported to have said; 'they would not be conquered so long as there was a man left to stand.' Instead, he continued to dig himself in.

On three sides, where the walls were surrounded by water defences, Toulouse was impregnable. Its weakness lay in a 600-foot ridge named Mont Rave to the east from which a besieger's artillery could dominate the city. It was this that Soult had been so busy fortifying. Here, behind his field-works, he had concentrated nearly half his 42,000 troops on a two-and-a-half-mile front, with a strong reserve behind. As Toulouse was the chief magazine of southern France, he had been able to re-

equip them with plentiful arms and ammunition. In artillery he out-
gunned the British – a fortnight's march from their nearest base – by
two to one. Thus, with 49,000 troops – only 700 more than the defenders – Wellington had to attack a fortified city from the side farthest
from his communications and with a flooded river dividing his army.
His own headquarters at Grenade were guarded by less than twenty
men with a French garrison at Montauban only an hour's ride away.

Yet he never hesitated. His moral ascendancy over the enemy was
now complete. As one of his officers put it, six years of almost uninter-
rupted success had engrafted a seasoned confidence into his soldiers
that made them invincible. Leaving sufficient forces to contain the defenders round the city's circumference and to act as a reserve, Wellington at dawn on April 10th – Easter Day – moved up two British
and two Spanish divisions against the eastern heights. To reach their
assault stations at the south end of the ridge the British had to march,
or rather flounder, through three miles of swamp under heavy fire
from Mont Rave, closely crossing the enemy's front with an unford-
able river behind them. There was only one thing to prevent Soult
descending from the hill to destroy them: his fear, founded on repeated
experience, of what would happen if he did.

Before Beresford's British divisions could deploy, the Spaniards,
who had begged to be allowed to share in the glory of the day, rashly
attempted to storm the northern end of the ridge without waiting for
orders. During the ensuing rout, as Wellington hastily plugged the
gap in his line with the Light Division, he remarked that he had never
before seen ten thousand men running a race. Their absence till they
could be re-formed for another attack gave Soult two hours to complete his preparations for dealing with the British, who were still
plodding across his front through the marshes. Bringing up his reserve
to the south end of the ridge, he concealed it in almost Wellingtonian
fashion behind the skyline, ready to fall on Cole's 4th Division – the
men of Albuera – as they came toiling in a thin, extended line up the
slope. But instead of driving them in rout down the hill, Soult's charging columns were stopped dead in their course. Closing their ranks and
forming square on either flank, the English regiments, though taken
by surprise, riddled their assailants with volley after volley. The French
divisional commander fell pierced by three bullets; his men, as the red-

coats resumed their advance, fled up the hill. Their panic spread to the garrison of the Sypière redoubt on the summit. Within a few minutes the British were in possession of the southern crest of the ridge.

During the remainder of the day Beresford's two divisions, exploiting their success, fought their way northwards along the ridge, enfilad-

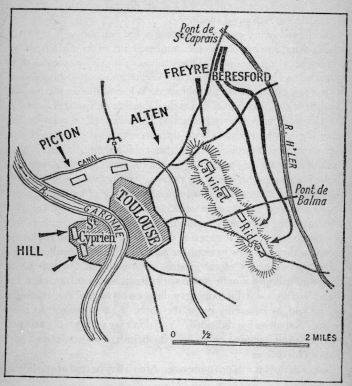

ing successive redoubts. Though the French fought fiercely back, repeatedly counter-attacking, the issue was never in doubt. The battle ended with a magnificent charge by General Pack's 42nd and 79th Highlanders with the 91st in support. By five o'clock, twelve hours after the first shot, the whole ridge was in British hands. Though the guns had still to be brought up, Toulouse was at Wellington's mercy. Of the attackers 4568 had fallen, to the French 3236, the Black Watch alone losing more than half and the Camerons nearly half their strength. Four hundred of the casualties were needlessly contributed by Picton, who, haunted by the memories of his achievement at Badajoz, disobeyed his orders and converted a sham diversion against the city's water defences into a real attack.[1]

On the following evening Soult began the evacuation of the city, withdrawing southwards, to the immense relief of its inhabitants, to join Suchet along the only road remaining open. He left behind 1600 wounded and half his guns. Next day Wellington entered amid scenes of, to him, rather distasteful jubilation. When at dinner the leading royalists of the place hailed him as the Liberator of Spain, France, and Europe, he bowed shortly and called for coffee. His troops, on the other hand, were charmed with their reception as they marched in their tattered coats through the city, their colours flying, drums beating, and the ladies waving to them from the balconies and throwing garlands. They supposed, after their victory, that they were now to enjoy this garden of Eden with its flowers and pretty girls. A smirking aide-de-camp in a cocked hat soon undeceived them, and by nightfall they were marching along the Carcassonne road after the old familiar stink of tobacco and onions. It appeared that, having boxed them round the compass, they had now to chase the *parlez-vous* back to Spain.

But that evening Colonel Frederick Ponsonby of the 12th Light Dragoons galloped into the town with dispatches from Bordeaux. He found Wellington in his lodgings pulling on his boots. 'Ay, I thought so,' he said, as Ponsonby broke the news, 'I knew we should have peace.' 'Napoleon has abdicated.' 'You don't say so, upon my honour. Hurrah!' And, spinning on his heel, the British Commander-in-Chief snapped his fingers.[2]

Yet even now it was not quite over. After a day or two of argument,

1. The account of the battle is based on Oman, VII, 465–95; Fortescue, x, 79–80; and a brilliant article by Colonel Alfred Burne, *The Enigma of Toulouse*, in *The Army Quarterly* for January, 1927. See also Lapéne, 370–85; Bell, I, 164–9; Seaton, 205; George Napier, 257–9; Gurwood; Vidal de la Blache, *L'Évacuation de l'Espagne et l'invasion dans le midi*.

2. Broughton, I, 189–90. See Oman, VII, 498; Bell, I, 170; Larpent, III, 137; Fortescue, x, 91.

Soult laid down his arms. His rival, Suchet, had already done so. But at Bayonne the Governor decided to fight on. On the night of April 13th, three days after the battle of Toulouse, General James Hay, going the round of the besieging trenches, told his men that the war was finished and that they would soon be home with their wives and sweethearts. Two hours later he was dead, slain with several hundred British and French soldiers after a sortie as wanton as it was useless. Among those taken prisoner was the British commander, Sir John Hope, whose love of fighting drew him into the trenches as soon as firing began. Not till April 26th did the French Governor condescend to do like the rest of the world and make peace.

Thereafter the British army took its ease. The cavalry, by arrangement with the new Bourbon Government, rode home across France to Boulogne and Calais, feasting off champagne at a shilling a bottle and delighting in a countryside unravaged by war. The infantry marched to Bordeaux to await transportation to England or America, where war with the United States was still continuing. As the troops tramped the sunny roads of southern France or glided in barges down the silver stream, a new world of peace seemed to be opening before them and mankind: a world in which there should be no more parades and piquets, no more midnight alerts, no more broken bones, no more slaying and being slain. After hard commons for so long they found it difficult to accustom themselves to down beds and no danger; an officer of the Rifles, who had never lost a piquet in six years' campaigning, woke in a cold sweat in his château bed with dreams of sentries unposted and lines surprised.[1]

Here at the camp of Blanquefort, among fruit, flowers, wines, and friendly people, the veterans who had begun the liberation of Europe bade farewell to one another and, as an army, dissolved. Their skill and comradeship and hard-won experience were no longer needed. They left behind the bones of their companions and the memory of their victories, of their invincible endurance in adversity and their magnanimity and good conduct in triumph. When the time came for them to sail, the host of one subaltern – a worthy Bordeaux merchant – took his bronzed, youthful lodger aside and, with tears in his eyes, offered to led him any money he might need, adding that he had every confi-

1. Smith, I, 189–90; Costello, 183, 186; Bell, I, 173–4.

dence in the word of an Englishman, and expressing a desire that their two countries might henceforward live together in peace. Then he accompanied him to the ship, kissed him on both cheeks and parted from him for ever.[1]

1. Bell, I, 185–7.

CHAPTER 5

TRIUMPHANT ISLAND

For States, as for individuals, true prosperity consists, not in acquiring or invading the domains of others, but in making the best of one's own.

TALLEYRAND

PART ONE: THE COURT OF PRINCE FLORIZEL

The papers have told you, no doubt, of the fusses,
The fêtes and the gapings to get at those Russes,
Of his Majesty's suite up from coachman to Hetman
And what dignity decks the fat face of the great man.

BYRON

ON June 6th, 1814, six weeks after the last shot was fired, the Czar Alexander and his ally, the King of Prussia, arrived at Boulogne. They were accompanied by the ruling princes, statesmen, and generals of the greater part of Europe. Among them were the Chancellor of the Austrian Empire, Prince Metternich, the hero of the hour, Field-Marshal von Blücher, the snowy-haired Chancellor of Prussia, Prince Hardenberg, and his colleague, the famous scholar, von Humboldt, the still more famous Hetman Platoff of the Don Cossacks, the young royal princes of Prussia – boys in years but veterans in battle[1] – and the rulers or heirs of half a dozen German kingdoms and principalities. They were bound for England – the heart of the coalition which had overthrown the revolutionary dictatorship of Europe. It was a spontaneous act of homage to the nation which, in De Quincey's words, had for twenty years 'put a soul into the resistance to Napoleon, wherever and in whatever corner manifested,' to 'the moral grandeur which had yielded nothing to fear, nothing to despondency,' and the resources which had enabled her to support the united exertions of Christendom.[2]

Before the travellers lay the sea and the harbour where ten years earlier Napoleon had tried to embark his army for the expedition which

1. One of whom, more than half a century later, was to be proclaimed German Emperor at Versailles.
2. De Quincey, III, 62-3.

was to have completed his conquest of the world. Now the barges he had built were mouldering at their moorings, the harbour-works silted up with sand, and he himself, caged in the little Mediterranean island of Elba, a poor pensioner of those he had once controlled. Close to the harbour lay one of the floating castles with which England's sailors, from their remote haunts of waves and clouds, had halted his armies. Even in that far, dark hour her admirals had predicted that one day the power they wielded would free the world from slavery.

At midday the sovereigns were received on board H.M.S. *Impregnable* by the King of England's sailor son, the Duke of Clarence. Around him were the symbols of his country's strength: the masts and yards with their forest of ropes, the scrubbed decks and spotless brasswork, the triple lines of guns, the smart, self-assured officers and gaunt, taut-buttocked tars in blue jackets, checked shirts, and bell-bottomed trousers, moving so resiliently that they seemed, like the escorting frigates, part of the sea itself. The piping of whistles, the trampling of feet, the clanking and creaking of pulleys, the hammering of the waves and the smell of tar and brine were new to the lords of the Continent. So was the ship's uneasy motion.

At six o'clock on the same evening, after waiting for two hours for the tide under the white cliffs, the kings and captains went ashore among the bathing-boxes, piers, and marine terraces of Dover. Crowds thronged the beaches, and the Scots Greys and three of the most famous regiments in the British Army – the 43rd, 52nd, and 95th – were waiting on the quayside. The little tough light-infantrymen, who had fought the French out of every stony acre from the Tagus to the Garonne, saw walking swiftly down their ranks a tall, moon-faced potentate in a short-skirted, bottle-green uniform, a high gold collar, and a tunic so padded and laced that his arms hung down like a doll's beneath his gilded epaulettes. Behind, at a respectful distance, came the King of Prussia – a gaunt, melancholy, wall-eyed man, with high cheekbones and closely-cropped hair, wearing top-boots and white pantaloons. He, too, had a surprisingly short waist and showed, in an uncompromising, soldier-like way, a good deal of bottom. After them came the Prussian princes – fine erect lads with blonde hair and rosy faces – and a clinking cavalcade of generals with whiskers, epaulettes, spurs, and feathered hats.

Next morning they set out for the capital. As their carriages bowled along the fine metalled highways, they were able to see something of England's wealth with their own eyes: the emerald downs with their immense flocks of sheep, the fat meadows and cattle, the yeoman farms and orchards; the weather-boarded cottages smothered in flowers; the painted hay-wains with straked wheels and tilted bows; the country houses with classical façades and cool, creeper-framed windows set among lawns and trees. In this thriving countryside, with its corn-mills and hop-yards, ancient barns and churches, neat hedgerows and chestnut coppices merging into blue horizons, everything seemed cared for down to the minutest blade of grass. To the Czar, fresh from scenes of destruction, it all looked like a garden.[1]

Five hours after leaving Dover the travellers reached the outskirts of London. They saw from the top of Shooter's Hill a canopy of vapour on the eastern horizon, and then, as the low-slung landaus, with their varnished, panelled sides, sped across Blackheath, the stately hospital of Greenwich rising among woods, the windmills and straggling hedgerows of the Isle of Dogs, and, winding in and out of trees, a river of masts. And beyond, under the green hills of Highgate and Hampstead,

> *a mighty mass of brick and smoke ...*
> *A wilderness of steeples peeping*
> *On tiptoe through their sea-green canopy;*
> *A huge, dun cupola, like a foolscap crown*
> *On a fool's head – and there is London Town!*

*

The people of the capital were wildly excited. They had been waiting for this for twenty years. There was nothing narrow or ungenerous in their rejoicing. For having fought so long to save their own liberties, they had been thrilled when the princes and peoples of the Continent had taken up arms by their side. They had forgotten all that had gone before: the defeats, the betrayals, the abuse, the collaboration with the

1. Colchester, II, 502. For some contemporary accounts of the dazzling appearance of rural prosperity which England presented to foreign visitors, see Bury, I, 242; Lord Coleridge, 223-4; Simond, I, 3, 10, 14, 16, 146-7, 201-2, 206; II, 86, 100, 224, 228, 235, 246, 254, 283; Leigh Hunt, *Autobiography*, II, 154; Bamford, I, 94; Lady Shelley, I, 1-3; Washington Irving, *Sketch Book*; *Don Juan*, Canto X; Wansey, 115.

foe. 'The Emperor of Russia,' wrote an English lady, 'is my hero, and everybody's hero!' Since the retreat from Moscow she and her compatriots had lost all sense of proportion about the northern heroes who had chased their enemies across Europe. The first Cossack to appear in London had been followed by cheering thousands and given three-times-three by the Lord Mayor on the steps of the Royal Exchange. The almost hysterical enthusiasm with which everything that had happened was now attributed to Russia caused the Czar's sister, who was not given to understating Russian achievements, to reply impetuously: 'Oh, no! the emancipation of Europe is owing to the steady and persevering conduct of this great and happy country! To this country Europe owes its deliverance!'[1]

*

And now the greatest Russian of all, the noble magnanimous Czar, was coming to London. Since dawn the streets had been filled with a great multitude, pouring into the south-eastern suburbs. The Prince Regent's gold and scarlet postilions, sent to meet the sovereigns, were submerged in the tumult. No one wanted them, anyway, for the word had gone round that the carriages were to be unhorsed and dragged in triumph over London Bridge. The route to St James's Palace was lined with coaches and carts, wooden stands had been erected at the street corners, and the windows were black with heads. Every vehicle approaching from Kent was set upon by a joyous, perspiring mob. The noise, the sweat, the honest stink were earnest of a free-born people's welcome.

Having been warned of the unpoliced state of the British capital and of the populace's excitement, the sovereigns scattered. The Czar, sitting back in his ambassador's carriage, left the highway for the Surrey lanes to the south, travelling through a landscape of buttercup meadows, dingly heaths, and wooded hills from whose slopes, dotted with gentlemen's villas, the dome and steeples of the city could be occasionally glimpsed. Shortly after one o'clock, after passing the villages of Camberwell and Clapham, he crossed the pastoral Thames by Battersea's wooden toll-bridge. He saw the trees of Chelsea Hospital, the high-sailed barges skimming the rushes, the winding, well-wooded shores.

1. Farington, VII, 253. See also Ashton, I, 155-9; *Lieven Letters*, 2; Havelock, 230, 233, 267; Lockhart, III, 428.

The market-gardeners were at work in the fields as he drove through rustic Sloane Street and the little elm-shaded, white-brick suburb of Hans Town. Skirting the grounds of Hans Place, he reached the western highway into London at the Cannon Brewery, Knightsbridge. So, having outflanked the British capital, the Emperor entered it by the turnpike at Hyde Park Corner and, unannounced and unexpected, arrived in front of the stone pillars and bow windows of the Pulteney Hotel which the Grand Duchess, his sister, had rented for her stay. A young man named De Quincey, who happened to be walking down Piccadilly at the time, saw a plain carriage dash up to the hotel steps, and a file of waiters rush out to form a line across the pavement, before a smiling foreigner ran into the hotel, kissing his hand to a lady at a first-floor window.

A moment later the Czar was in his sister's arms. Between this fair-haired, vivacious widow of twenty-six and her impulsive, lonely, and secretly unstable brother there was a deep bond. Having lost her husband, Prince George of Oldenburg, during the Moscow campaign, the Grand Duchess had come to England to cement the Anglo-Russian alliance by a second marriage. But though impressed by Britain's material achievements – particularly the steam-engine – she had not taken to its reigning house. The Dukes of Clarence and Sussex had struck her as uncultivated boors, while for their brother, reputed to be the first gentleman in Europe, she had conceived an almost passionate dislike. 'Handsome as he is,' she had told the Czar, 'he is a man visibly used up by dissipation. His much-boasted affability is the most licentious, I may even say obscene, strain I ever listened to.'[1] Finding her impervious to his charms, he had not even troubled to flatter her.

The Grand Duchess found that many shared her dislike of the Regent. The English Whigs had never forgiven him for keeping his father's Ministers in office. Discredited during the war by their defeatism, they were now seeking an opportunity for revenge. Nineteen years before, in order to get his debts paid, the object of their hatred, then their ally, had espoused the daughter of the Duke of Brunswick who had failed at Valmy and fallen at Jena. It had been the most

[1]. 'With him and his brothers, I have often had not only to get stiffly on my stiffs, but not to know what to do with my eyes and ears. A brazen way of looking where eyes should not go!' Havelock, 22.

unhappy act in his life and deservedly so, for he had long been secretly and morganatically married to a woman who loved him and to whom he afterwards returned. His Princess had retaliated by allowing herself freedoms which, though less heinous than his, had brought her under suspicion of high treason. Her habit of sitting up all night in the company of embarrassed sea-captains, her flippant, rattling, and indelicate conversation,[1] and her ostentatious parade of an adopted docker's child whom she called Willikin, had caused a public scandal. Among those suspected, though probably wrongly, of being her lovers were the defender of Acre, Sir Sidney Smith, the painter Lawrence, one of her own footmen, and the Tory statesman, Canning. In the year after Trafalgar the Whig Government of Fox and Grenville had been compelled by an alarmed royal family to institute an investigation into her conduct. Its findings, opposed by the Tories more out of party feeling than conviction, had exonerated her from the graver charges but stressed her persistent indecorum. Thereafter she had been banished from royal society.

The political wheel had now come full circle. King George III was mad and under restraint, the Princess's husband was Regent, and his erstwhile friends, the Whigs, had been jilted in favour of the Tories. It had now fallen to the latter as his Ministers to disapprove the Princess of Wales' doings and to support, as best they could, her husband's. It had become the function of the Whigs to champion the Princess. The Allied Sovereigns' visit gave them their opportunity. For when this stout, grievously-wronged, and outrageous lady announced in her comical English her intention of attending the next Drawing-Room to meet the Prussian King in whose service her father had died, she was informed by the prim, tyrannical old Queen, her mother-in-law, that she could not be received. Thereupon jubilant Whig gentlemen rose in the House to ask Ministers by whose advice the Princess of Wales was denied her constitutional right of attending the royal Drawing-Room. For the first time for years they had the public on their side. Though the Princess's indiscretions were notorious, everyone knew they had been caused by her husband's: that he had sent his mistress to

1. 'And when I did look round at them I said to myself, "*A quoi bon* this dull assemblage of tiresome persons." ... *Mein Gott!* dat is de dullest person Gott Almighty ever did born!' Bury, II, 298; I, 158.

receive her on her first landing, that he had spent his wedding night drunk in the fender, that he had left her as soon as her child was born. Her guilt had never been proved, his own was flagrant, and it seemed outrageous that he should insult her. For weeks he had been unable to pass through the streets without being hooted and pelted.

*

All this the Czar learnt from his sister as he looked out across Piccadilly on the Green Park's browsing deer and cattle, the white-stuccoed Ranger's Lodge among the trees, and the red-brick façade of Buckingham House framed by the Abbey towers and Surrey hills. Sooner than share his host's unpopularity he resolved, on the impulse of the moment, not to proceed to the State apartments prepared for him in St James's Palace but to stay at his sister's hotel. The fact that the Lord Chamberlain, two bands, and half the great Officers of State had been waiting since dawn to receive him did not cause him a moment's concern; he was an eastern autocrat, and in Russia things were done that way. Nor did it worry him or his sister that the Regent would be placed in a position of acute embarrassment; it was what the Grand Duchess wanted. The Pulteney being outside the private reserve of his parks and palaces, he would now have to face the howls of the populace in the streets. Already a vast cheering crowd had gathered outside the hotel and was growing larger every minute. At the end of three hours the ruler of England was forced to admit his inability to wait on his guest.

Thus it came about that at the moment to which the Prince Regent had been so eagerly looking forward, he was confronted with the hideous contrast between his own unpopularity and the people's adulation of another. Instead of receiving Alexander as a fellow-conqueror, he appeared as one afraid to show himself in his own streets. This was the more galling because, never having been allowed to lead his country's armies, he was particularly sensitive on the subject of military glory. He greeted the Czar, not with his wonted ease and affability, but in his stiffest, haughtiest vein. The latter could scarcely conceal his contempt. 'A poor prince,' he remarked to his ambassador as he left the palace.[1]

1. On which Count Lieven, who had been contending for some weeks with a similar attitude in the Grand Duchess, murmured 'who has helped your Imperial Majesty to wage a glorious war and a peace to match.' Havelock, 277.

Having recovered from their morning's disappointment, which they attributed to the Regent's dislike of being hissed, the crowds were by now mobbing the other potentates as they straggled into the capital. The greatest reception of all was for Blücher. As the old man, standing erect to salute the colours, passed through the Horse Guards, the populace seized the shafts from his carriage, knocked over the sentries at the garden gates of Carlton House, and practically carried him, carriage and all, into the Palace. Lest worse should follow, the doors were flung open and the Field-Marshal was swept into the Regent's presence on a Rowlandsonian wave of cheering Britons. Meanwhile the Czar, looking like a big, benign angel, was bowing to the crowds from the balcony of the Pulteney. Everyone except the Regent seemed to be thoroughly happy, and the huzzaing and trampling continued far into the night. Every building was illuminated with candles, fairy lamps, and transparencies.

When the Czar and Grand Duchess sallied forth next day the crowd was waiting for them in the roadway. Before they reached their carriage they had to suffer the grasp of hundreds of hands. When, after driving a mile along the leafy, western highway, they alighted for a walk in the private gardens of Kensington Palace, they underwent a similar ordeal. Back at the hotel steps, after a sightseer's visit to the Abbey and British Museum, they had to fight their way once more through a tumult of well-dressed women who clung to their wrists and stared adoringly into Alexander's eyes. Some of them, by bribing the porter, managed to get into the hotel.

That afternoon, Joseph Farington, the artist, found Piccadilly thick with people, horses, and carriages, waiting to see the Emperor and Grand Duchess leave for a banquet at Carlton House. The Regent's state chariot, with its magnificent footmen and hammer-cloth of scarlet and gold, was drawn up outside the Pulteney behind a troop of Household Cavalry. Before setting out, the Czar came to the balcony to receive the popular acclamations. Then, with his sister by his side, her hair clustered with enormous pearl-drops, he drove off in the great coach towards St James Street, bowing from side to side through the windows.[1]

*

1. *Ann. Reg.* 1814. Chron. 45; Ashton, I, 261–3, 266–7, 274–5; Broughton, I, 113, 139–40; Brownlow, 108; Farington, VII, 255–7; De Quincey, III, 67;

Unlike the Czar, the Prince Regent had not risen early. His country's Constitution had not allowed him to form a soldier's habits, and his own inclined him to a luxurious indolence. So did his practice of sitting up late drinking cherry brandy. Though not yet fifty-two, he was enormously fat; his great backside, tightly swaddled in bright white inexpressibles, was one of the sights of Society. The public saw it less often, for, owing to his dislike of being stared at, he divided his time between Carlton House and the exquisite seaside Pavilion he had built for himself at Brighton. His tastes, despite a talent for designing military uniforms – he had recently devised a Field-Marshal's attire for himself and the Duke of Wellington[1] – were aesthetic and epicurean rather than soldierly. He knew more about architecture, painting, books, and music than any prince in Europe; he was shrewd, intelligent, and witty and, when younger, had been the idol of society, 'with fascination,' Byron wrote, 'in his very bow:

> ... *the grace too rare in every clime*
> *Of being, without alloy of fop or beau,*
> *A finish'd gentleman from top to toe.*'

But age and self-indulgence had not improved him; his affability had grown vinous and, though he could on occasion show an affecting dignity and courtesy, he was Prince Charming no longer. He still possessed an immense Hanoverian zest for life: could be at times a flamboyant, impulsive, overgrown baby, halloing over the supper-table, sobbing because his newest inamorata was cruel, or presiding over his private band, beating time on his thighs and accompanying himself the while at the top of his voice. But the gusto was degenerating into an irritable itch to domineer, and the surges of exuberant energy were succeeded now by long periods of torpor, bile, and self-pity. A younger and less tolerant generation, which had never known the court of Prince Florizel or the enchanted days before the Bastille was

---

Nicolson, 112; Lady Shelley, I, 58–60; Pyne, *Royal Residences*, III, 12–14; Stanley, 84.

1. 'How sure Ben was to make up a Field-Marshal's uniform according to his own fancy. Not only the cuffs, collars and front of the coat were richly (2 inches wide) embroidered but the very seams – all the seams!' *Paget Brothers*, 198–9. See *idem*, 222; *Creevey Papers*, I, 47, 63, 147–9; Farington, VII, 89, 161; Lady Shelley, I, 35; Wynne, III, 188–9.

stormed, took an increasingly dark view of this epicurean veteran. To
the young writers of the middle-class – the men who were to have the
ear of the future – he appeared not as the grotesque, flouncing spoilt
playboy, Big Ben, whom his contemporaries had once known as a
fairy-court prince, but as something more sinister. To them he was
Swellfoot, the tyrant, who had betrayed the nascent cause of reform,
imprisoned the martyrs of liberty, persecuted his wife, and impounded
her child. The radical poet, Leigh Hunt, described him in his weekly,
the *Examiner*, as 'a libertine over head and ears in debt and disgrace, a
despiser of domestic ties, the companion of gamblers and demireps, a
man who has just closed half a century without one single claim on the
gratitude of his country or the respect of posterity.'[1] And Charles
Lamb, the punning East India clerk, made him the subject of a lampoon
called ' The Triumph of the Whale ':

> *By his bulk and by his size,*
> *By his oily qualities,*
> *This (or else my eyesight fails)*
> *This should be the Prince of Whales.*[2]

'What a fellow Prinny is!' wrote one of his old Whig cronies. He
was at once a national scandal, a national disaster, a national achievement, and national entertainment. He was the representative – the not
very decorous but full-blooded one – of England in the last age in which
men of all classes felt at liberty to let themselves go. And he happened
by the accident of birth to be heir to and, for all practical purposes,
occupant of the throne. In the new, more restrained, more decorous
age into which England was moving, this made things very difficult
for his Ministers. But for those who could afford to see the jest – and
peril – of the situation, the fun while it lasted was uproarious.

Yet, though Society, which once had idolized him, passed him by,
and the holy place of the highest fashion was no longer Carlton House
but Almack's assembly rooms, the Regent had been the ornament of a
far more cultivated and polished circle than any known to the Lady

---

1. A freedom which cost him two years' imprisonment for seditious libel.
2. 'Who is there,' wrote 'Monk' Lewis, 'that may not be caricatured when
the most avowedly graceful man of his time, or perhaps of any time, can thus
be personally ridiculed!' Bury, I, 77.

Patronesses of that haughty, dull, and exclusive establishment. When he chose, he could talk with judgement and taste on almost any subject. He knew how to be gracious and caressing, to set his auditors at ease by his exquisite manners, and send them away convinced of his personal interest.[1] With such gifts he might have made himself as popular as Charles II or Henry VIII. But, while he loved to impress, he suffered from a fatal dread of ridicule. Any threat to his vanity aroused in him a ruthless, almost hysterical self-protectiveness. It was his wife's unforgivable offence that, in her rattling, missish way, she had quizzed him on his growing belly. He could not even endure the casual glance of housemaids: any servant who stared at him was threatened with instant dismissal. Nor could he tolerate boredom. He would break the most important engagement because it irked him, and kept his dependants in constant uncertainty by his eleventh-hour changes of plan. Nothing in his disorderly life was ever decided until the last moment.[2]

Being, for all his impulsive generosity and tender-heartedness, utterly inconsiderate where his own feelings were concerned, he was a lonely man. Most of his intimates were women. Of these, having enjoyed the society of the liveliest and most cultivated of the age, he was a fastidious judge. For years he had oscillated mainly between Mrs Fitzherbert and the Countess of Jersey – both women of over fifty when he parted with them. His latest *confidante* was the Marchioness of Hertford, an imperceptibly fading grandmother of the most exquisite fashion. When first he fell for her, regardless of their years he behaved like a lovesick boy, weeping continuously, not speaking, and even at times refusing nourishment. Since then, despite a spasmodic attempt to transfer his affections to Lady Bessborough[3] – another fascinating

1. That sharp observer, Captain Harry Smith of the Rifles, bearing dispatches from America, recorded that his interview with him was 'the most gentleman-like and affable' he could possibly imagine. Smith, I, 215. See also D'Arblay, III, 243, 300; Colchester, II, 272; Bury, I, 283; Lockhart, IV, 371; Havelock, 278.
2. Farington, VIII, 142–4 for a curious example of this, describing how his architect, Nash, had been compelled at the last minute to ask a hundred and twenty neighbours to eat the dinner he had prepared for him, and how a few days later the local yeomanry were vainly called away from the harvest in the expectation – again disappointed – of welcoming him.
3. 'He threw himself on his knees and, clasping me round, kissed my neck before I was aware of what he was doing; I screamed with vexation and fright; he continued, sometimes struggling with me, sometimes sobbing and crying ...

grandmother – he had been ruled with a rod of iron. According to the Marchioness's account, their relationship was entirely platonic: they even, she averred, read the Bible to one another. But she enjoyed the traditional fruits of her office: her husband became Lord Chamberlain and her rather disreputable son, Lord Yarmouth, Vice-Chamberlain.

Of one activity the Regent never tired. He would have made, it was said, a splendid upholsterer. He filled Army Orders with instructions about epaulettes, gold lace, and feathers, sent the 23rd Dragoons to Spain so arrayed that they could not be distinguished from the French, and rigged out his own Regiment of Hussars like padded monkeys in crimson breeches and yellow boots. 'His whole soul,' a friend wrote, 'is wrapped up in Hussar saddles, caps, cuirasses, and sword belts!' The Whig bard, Tom Moore, suggested – with prophetic insight – that the next victims of his sartorial enthusiasm would be his political advisers:

> 'Let's see,' said the Regent, like Titus, perplex'd
> With the duties of empire, 'whom shall I dress next?'
> So what's to be done? There's the Ministers, bless 'em!
> As he made the puppets, why should not he dress them?

Yet wonderful as were the costumes he designed, they were surpassed by the settings he chose for them. His guests complained that the splendour of his rooms made their clothes insignificant. There was no limit – except the faith of moneylenders in the patience of British taxpayers – to his adventures in interior decoration. His palaces were continually being rebuilt. The oriental fantasy he made of the Pavilion at Brighton, with its Kremlin domes and pagodas, 'looking,' as Sydney Smith remarked, 'as if St Paul's had gone to the sea and pupped,' was one of the wonders of the age, its walls decorated with mandarins and fluted yellow draperies to resemble the tents of the Chinese, its peach-blossom ceilings and canopies of tassels and bells, its imperial, five-

vows of eternal love, entreaties and promises of what he would do – he would break with Mrs Fitzherbert and Lady Hertford, I should make my own terms, I should be his sole *confidante*, sole adviser ... I should guide his politics, Mr Canning should be Prime Minister ...; then over and over again the same round of complaint, despair, entreaties and promises ... that immense, grotesque figure flouncing about, half on the couch, half on the ground.' Lady Bessborough to Lord Granville Leveson-Gower, Dec., 1809. Granville, II, 349.

clawed dragons darting from every chandelier and overmantel. *Outré* and grotesque, it was yet informed by its creator's exquisite taste. On its statuary, carpets, pictures – he was an early collector of Dutch masters – china, and ormulu he lavished an inexhaustible care. Scarcely a day passed without some new artist or craftsman being ushered into his presence. In three years he spent £160,000 on furniture alone.

The crown of this royal impresario's achievement was Carlton House. Here, under the successive supervision of Henry Holland, James Wyatt, and John Nash, he had transformed a modest two-storied mansion into a palace worthy of the ruler of an eastern empire. Its armoury contained the sceptre of the King of Candy, the dagger of Ghengis Khan, and the palanquin of Tippoo Sahib. Taxpayers regarded it with jaundiced eyes; it struck them, like its occupant, as extravagant and un-English. But though its portico in Pall Mall was too large for its façade,[1] and its Ionic screen out of keeping with the homely red brick houses between which it was wedged, once inside the marble entrance hall the effect was overwhelming. When, after Napoleon's retreat from Moscow, foreign ambassadors began to return to London, they were astounded and pronounced it not only the finest house in England, but the rival of Versailles and St Cloud.

When the foreign potentates dined with the Prince Regent on the evening of June 8th Carlton House was at the height of its glory. Its pillars were hung with thousands of lanterns and its screen was silhouetted by topaz and scarlet flares set between palm trees. One after another its great rooms, lit by magnificent chandeliers, revealed their owner's taste and splendour: the Entrance Hall with porphyry columns and cornices adorned by Etruscan griffins; the Throne-Room with its canopy of helmets and ostrich-plumes and its fender supporting the eagle of Jupiter subduing prostrate dragons; the Circular Dining-Room whose walls were lined with silver and whose pier-glasses reflected forests of Ionic columns with silver capitals; the Crimson Drawing-Room with the blue velvet carpet adorned with the insignia of the Garter and the lovely chandelier, whose three circles of lights surrounded a cascade of glass which played for ever in mirrored vistas;

1. To-day the portico of the National Gallery. Ackermann, *Microcosm*, I, 113. See also Ackermann, *Repository*, I, 398; VII, 29; XIV, 189; Pyne, *Royal Residences*, III (*Carlton House*); L. C. C. *Survey of London*, XX, 73–6; Hughson, II, 231; Gronow, II, 255; Plumer Ward, 399–400; *Paget Brothers*, 195, 197.

the Vestibule, Ante-Room, Rose-Satin Drawing-Room, Blue Velvet Room, and Closet. From the ground floor the Regent led his guests in procession down the circular double staircase, past the giant bronzes of Chronos with his clock and Atlas bearing the map of Europe, to a still more wonderful set of apartments below. From a vestibule whose windows looked on to a quiet garden where nightingales sang, they swept left to Library, Golden Drawing-Room, and Gothic Dining-Room, and right to Ante-Room, Dining-Room, and Conservatory. The open double doors between made a continuous chamber three hundred and fifty feet long. Its ceilings were spandrelled and traceried in the Gothic taste, its walls panelled with golden mouldings and shields emblazoned with the quarterings of England, its windows curtained with crimson, its fairy-like chandeliers suspended from carved monastic heads. The climax of this fantastic splendour – the Regent's reply to Erfurt and the Tuileries – was the Conservatory, which was not so much an adjunct to a palace as a miniature Gothic cathedral conceived by a *fin-de-siècle* voluptuary, with a nave and aisles formed by clusters of carved pillars, stained glass windows, and a ceiling whose glazed traceries flooded the marble pavement with light. And at the west end a low, wide Gothic door opened on to lawns, weeping trees, the multi-coloured fans of peacocks' tails, and the setting sun.

Yet in spite of all that the Regent had to show his guests, his florid affability, the magnificent food and wine, the gold plate and candles, the evening was not a success. The heat – as always in his palaces – was intense. The old Queen, who during half a century in England had preserved the rigid etiquette of the petty German Court of her youth, petrified the conversation. Throughout the stately and interminable meal the Regent made repeated attempts to break the ice, but the Grand Duchess – the only member of the party who could converse in all three languages – was determined to help no one. Afterwards, when the palace filled with guests, the stiff little Queen took her place under the canopy in the Throne-Room and hundreds of women in low-necked, high-waisted satin dresses, attended by sworded, white-stockinged gentlemen in court-dress and uniform, defiled before her, their heads adorned with plumes. The Czar was left with nothing to do but stand and watch. He amused himself by quizzing the younger and prettier women.

The failure of the evening was complete when the Regent, with portly grace, brought forward his exquisitely groomed but ageing favourite, the Marchioness of Hertford. Like all English ladies, she was dying to talk to the saviour of Europe. But when his host presented her, the Czar, who had been told all about her by the Grand Duchess, merely bowed. The Regent, knowing him to be a little deaf and supposing he had not heard, repeated loudly, 'This is my Lady Hertford.' Alexander still said nothing. The lady made a deep curtsey, gave him the haughtiest of glances and withdrew. The fate of the visit, Countess Lieven thought, was written in that glance.[1]

*

Next morning the Czar rode almost round London before breakfast. Emerging from the royal parks, he saw it first from Westminster Bridge as it lay asleep in the morning sun – upstream the terraced trees and grey, ghostly houses in front of Westminster Hall, the new Millbank Penitentiary and the low, willowed banks; downstream the tottering old taverns and warehouses of Scotland Yard, the gardens of Northumberland House, the conical water-tower of York Buildings, Somerset House rising like a Venetian palace from the water, and Paul's dome floating above the houses and spires. And binding Westminster to the city, the city to the world, and man to the ages, the great stream flowed seawards, green and grey, with white and brown sails and wherries and tossing barges on its bosom. Then, having gazed on that famous spectacle, the Czar rode on over the high, balustraded bridge, with its bays and hooped lamp-posts, towards the Surrey shore.

A few years before, St George's Fields had been an open plain crossed by highways, crowded all day with horsemen and carriages and forming at night a constellation of twinkling lamps across the marshy meadows. But now its view of London and Westminster was blotted out by a mass of mean, ill-constructed buildings. All that the Czar saw were rows of small dwellings and bleak factories rising on the last remaining meadows – a poor, unsavoury, squatters' town. Passing the Obelisk at the junction of the Borough and Greenwich roads, he followed the dull, wide highway into Southwark.

Suddenly emerging from the Borough High Street he came once

---

1. Havelock, 271, 278.

more on the river. Beyond it lay a city with a straight, uniform sky-line, its parapets crowned with a halo of stone belfries, almost as many, it seemed, as there were masts in the river. Above them the cliffs of an immense cathedral carried the eye upwards to a remote golden cross and ball. The dome on which these symbols rode belonged to a differ-ent world from the houses below which, shrouded by the smoke of the chimneys,[1] were so close round the temple's base that they seemed to be crowding into its portals. For, if above the level of the houses the city belonged to God, below it Mammon reigned, grudging every foot of ground. Yet the worshippers of God and Mammon alike had observed in their building the rules of proportion and good sense. In all London north of the river there scarcely seemed a house not in keeping with its neighbours.

Between the eye and this classical city lay the source from which it drew its wealth – the river, no longer, as in the reaches below West-minster, given over to purposes of pleasure but lined with wharves, warehouses, timber-yards, and manufactories. Spanning it was a bridge dating from the remote past. Its dark camel-back was no longer crowned with houses and shops, but beneath it the stream, narrowed into cataracts, poured down through arches where wheels sucked water into iron cylinders with a noise like artillery. On either side of the steep slope, crowded with carts and pedestrians, were bowers in whose recesses old women sat selling apples and sweetmeats.[2] Below the bridge the sky was dark with masts, and the river almost hidden by the throng of barges and wherries.

Then up the cobbled, odoriferous incline of Fish Street the Czar passed into 'the great emporium of men, riches, arts, and intellectual power' – Georgian London. It was a city built without a plan and yet with a common and clearly conceived purpose, not imposed by some grandiloquent King but to serve the needs of a community of mer-chants who, nursed in a classical tradition, had learnt that, to be free, man must express himself within a framework of order. Controlled

1. The cross, 340 feet high, was approximately eight and a half times higher than the 40-foot skyline of the principal streets below. Ackermann, *Microcosm*, III, 151; Summerson, *Georgian London*, 45.

2. Among them the good woman whom George Borrow found there read-ing 'blessed Moll Flanders.' *Lavengro*.

since the Great Fire by Building Acts which laid down the ceiling-heights, types of materials, and number of storeys to be used in every class of street, London in 1814 was at the acme of its ordered and man-nered beauty, mellowed by time and still untouched by the hand of the Gothic improver. There were no palaces and few large buildings, but street after street of unpretentious, uniform, exquisitely propor-tioned three- and four-storeyed houses of brown and grey brick, their skylines of parapet, tile, and chimney-stack broken only by trees and the white stone of Wren's belfries. The roadways were mostly straight and, in relation to their height, wide, with flagstoned pavements guarded from the traffic by posts and with wrought-iron railings be-fore the houses. Every house had the same sober, unadorned face of freestone-bordered sash, the same neat white pillars on either side of the pedimented door, the same stone steps over the area crowned by a lamp-post. Only in the beautifully moulded doors and brightly polished knockers, with their lion masks, wreaths, and urns, did the English instinct for individuality break through that all-pervading, almost monotonous framework. There, and in the narrow, winding lanes and courts behind the Georgian façade, glimpsed through arch-ways from which came whiffs of laystall and stable and where ragged children swarmed in darkness and cobblers sat at hutches with low open doors.

Unlike the fashionable West End, the City was awake. Postmen in scarlet coats with bells and bags were going from door to door, porter-house boys were scurrying home with pewter mugs from last night's suppers, bakers in white aprons were shouting 'Hot loaves!'. Small chimney-sweeps carrying brushes, hawkers with bandboxes on poles, milk-maids, with the manure of suburban cowsheds on their feet and pails suspended from yokes across their shoulders, were crying their wares, competing with the bells of dust-carts and the horns of news-vendors. On the pavements apprentices, freshly risen from their masters' counters, were taking down the shutters of bow-fronted, multi-paned windows, and ragged urchins were leap-frogging over the posts. When they saw the tall horseman and his Cossack attendants with their sheepskin cloaks and long lances, they came shouting after. Brewers' drays, drawn slowly by draught-horses as big as elephants, vast hooded wagons with wheels like rollers, carts with hay for the

London markets, stopped in the middle of the road; bullocks on their way to Smithfield were driven by drovers into corners and yards, women with baskets left their pitches in the gutter, and the aged Jehus of the rickety hackney-coaches, waiting at their stands, stood up on their boxes to huzza. So did slaveys in mob caps leaning out of upper windows, and pale-faced merchants' clerks hurrying along the pavements to their counting-houses. Even the old blind Tobits, who leant against the railings of the Mansion House, came running after the clattering hoofs, clutching their wallets, staves, and crutches, their dogs barking beside them.

As the stately Muscovite, with a smile on his little curving mouth, threaded his way through the long defile of Coleman Street and across the cobbled immensities of Finsbury Square, the wealth and splendour of the City became ever more apparent. The shop windows with their silks, muslins and calicoes, china and glass-ware, jewels and silver, glittered with everything the heart of man could desire. The streets, unlike those of Continental cities, were wide and clean, with sweepers plying their trade with doffed cap at every crossing. The pavements were thronged with citizens in high hats and neat broadcloth, men with big noses, lantern jaws, and resolute mouths, loose-limbed young giants whose frank looks bespoke the assurance of perfect freedom, brightly-coloured, elegant gowned girls carrying shopping baskets, children bowling hoops, females with exuberant faces and billowing breasts, paunchy old men with grog-blossom complexions and heaving buttocks, workmen in aprons and padded leather jackets, raree-show men carrying the mysteries of their trade on their backs, women selling canaries from wicker cages on church walls. There were no police to control them, yet there was no confusion. And behind the façade of the unassuming houses the commerce of the universe was being carried on, as clerks entered into ledgers transactions which had drawn into the Thames the products of America, Africa, and the Indies and sent them out again, enriched and transformed by the skill of England's artificers and the foresight and courage of her capitalists.

Along either side of the long straight City Road the houses grew thinner. The Czar crossed Old Street, catching a glimpse of the gloomy façade of St Luke's hospital for the insane, with its Hogarthian figures of Melancholy and Raving Madness; then followed the highway westwards across decaying fields where market gardens and scraggy hedgerows gave way to the sprawl of monotonous, unfinished rows and crescents of thin-bricked, two-storeyed, jerry-built houses. The scents of June meadows mingled with the acrid smell of brick-kilns, labourers in dust-stained fustian leant against the posts, and vegetable carts, donkeys with paniers, and top-heavy, elongated stage-coaches competed for the crest of the road. Beyond the premises of the New River Water Company and the half-rustic theatre of Sadler's Wells, where nightly a young clown called Grimaldi held the Cockney apprentices entranced, the highway passed through Pentonville. Here wooden palings took the place of pavements, and cottages with cobbled roofs succeeded streets and terraces, and, where the City stretched its long, polypus arm into the Middlesex meadows, a new town of small houses nestled among the elms to the north, inhabited by clerks and retired tradesmen, some of whom could be seen at their door, tending minute gardens. A mile farther on, past the Islington turnpikes another brand-new settlement of terraced brick boxes, each with fan-light and tenuous, pathetic aspiration to gentility and elegance, housed yet another community of clerks – the acolytes of England's new commercial religion.[1]

As the Czar continued westwards along the old track from Islington to Paddington – now the northern border of the capital – the landscape took on a more countrified aspect. The highway was lined with gardens and pleasure-bowers with wooden arbours and mulberry trees – the resort of city tradesmen's families on summer Sabbaths. To the north the fields, dotted with dairy-farms and merchants' week-end boxes, gently climbed the wooded crests of Highgate and Hampstead. To the south the new streets and squares of Bloomsbury and Marylebone were only a meadow's length away, ending – a little incongruously for so much magnificence – in a rough builder's paling covered with advertising bills. It seemed incredible to the Czar that so many private citizens should have the wealth to build and inhabit such houses. At one point on the highway workmen were busy on the foundations of a new town which the Regent, taking advantage of the reversion of

1. It was here, at Somers Town, that a few years later Charles Dickens, who was to voice their aspirations and chronicle their lives of seedy struggle, came to live with his father.

Marylebone Park to the Crown, was planning to rival Napoleon's unfinished western *faubourg* of Paris. Here an enormous circus of aristocratic mansions, grouped round elysian groves and lawns, was to look southwards to Carlton House down an imperial avenue.

After passing the Yorkshire Stingo pleasure gardens at Lisson Grove and Mr Lord's cricket ground – now scheduled for building – the Czar reached the Edgware Road at the half-mile stone and, turning south, saw before him the wooden Tyburn turnpike and the northern wall of Hyde Park. Even here, where a few years before all had been country, a continuous line of houses bordered the roadway to the east. Only westwards, where their windows looked across the Paddington meadows to the heights beyond Westbourne, and herds of pigs were fattening for the London hotels, did the country seem secure from the encroachments of the town.[1]

*

During the next three weeks the Czar and his companions saw – from the outside – something of London's life. They visited its public buildings, though these, in a land where almost everything was left to individual initiative, were few: the Abbey among the little, shabby, ancient streets of Westminster, with its sooty walls and crumbling monuments; the Tower where the unaccountable English exhibited their King's jewels and a menagerie of wild animals collected during their commercial voyages; the British Museum beside the Bloomsbury fields where, thanks to the combination of British sea-power, a persistent artist and the discrimination of a great nobleman, the Parthenon marbles had recently been brought from the brigand-infested wastes

1. Leigh Hunt, *Autobiography*, II, 18. See also Chancellor, Plate 79; Simond, I, 29–30. For this description of London as seen by Alexander on his early morning ride through the City, see *inter alia*, Ackermann, *Microcosm*, *passim*; Ackermann, *Repository*, I, 102, 187, 330; II, 50; Ashton, II, 200–1, 213, 228, 232–6, 277–9; John Britton, *passim*; Borrow, *Lavengro*; Broughton, II, 153, Campbell, II, 257; Chancellor, *passim*; De Quincey, *Works*, *passim*; *Life in London*, *passim*; *Real Life in London*; Farington, VII, 257, 267–8, 283; Feltham, *passim*; Festing, 193, 195; Havelock, 280–1; Haydon, I, 199, 251; Hazlitt, *Essays*; Hughson, *passim*; Keats, IV, 61, 92; Lamb, *Essays of Elia*; L.C.C. *Survey of London*; Leigh, *passim*; Malton, *passim*; Partington, *passim*; Pennant, *London*, *passim*; Pyne, *Costume of the British People*; Robinson, I, 358; Simond, I, 3, 18–22, 26, 50–2, 195; II, 29–30, 116–17, 142, 199–200, 260; Southey, *Espriella*, *passim*; Stanley, 89; Summerson, *passim*; *English Spy*; Wood, *passim*.

of Athens. They visited, too, what to a shop-keeping people seemed of more importance than any of these, the corporate institutions formed by their merchants. They saw the Royal Exchange with its piazza where traders in the garb of every nation haggled with top-hatted John Bulls; the Bank of England where a private company of financiers successfully monopolized the most precious of all royal prerogatives, the issue of money, and were now engaged in raising the handsomest building in the country behind high walls; the great docks built during the war by the East and West India merchants to protect their growing imports from the quick-fingered Cockneys. They even visited a brewery – a prodigious place where the Englishman's favourite drink was stored in vessels as large as ships and in quantities which, translated into money, would have maintained a Continental army for months, and where they partook of the brewer's traditional hospitality of a steak done on a shovel and washed down with a pint of the firm's 'best entire'. And this, they were told, was only one of a dozen other London breweries as large or larger. It added to their amazement to learn that their host, that plebeian master of vats and dray-horses, was a leading member of the House of Commons and the proprietor of the Theatre Royal.

The visitors saw something, too, of the great charities – the offspring of private benevolence – with which the islanders had endowed their capital. They visited the Charterhouse, the Foundling Hospital in the northern fields, the palaces built for naval and military pensioners at Greenwich and Chelsea, and dined in the halls of the Goldsmiths and Merchant Taylors – representatives of corporations which spent between them as much on relieving and educating the poor as a Continental sovereign on maintaining his Court. The British capital had twenty voluntarily supported hospitals, a hundred and twenty alms-houses, fifty free dispensaries, forty-five endowed free schools, and two hundred and fifty parochial schools, educating, clothing, and feeding nearly twenty thousand children. Though the palace of St James's was the smallest and least imposing in Europe, London could claim that her real palaces were hospitals. Wren's Greenwich and Chelsea; Gibbs' St Bartholomew's with its Hogarth staircase; St Thomas's with its four great quadrangles, treating and discharging 11,000 patients a year; the new 'Bethlem' and St Luke's for the insane, with their enormous classical façades, were buildings that a king might have been proud to inhabit. In no other country was there so much voluntary corporate goodness towards the hungry, diseased, and weak. When on Holy Thursday six thousand London charity children marched in procession to St Paul's, the Prussian General Yorck declared that nothing had ever moved him so deeply. Blake, the poet, has left a picture of that famous service:

> Grey-headed beadles walked before with wands
>   as white as snow
> Till into the high dome of Paul's they like
>   Thames waters flow ...
> The hum of multitudes was there, but multitudes
>   of lambs,
> Thousands of little boys and girls raising
>   their innocent hands.

*

As a patron of liberal institutions, the Czar also took the opportunity to investigate English methods of government. He visited the man who, though an untitled and private member of Parliament, had succeeded, in the teeth of vested interest, in abolishing the Slave Trade, and sat under the famous mulberry tree in Wilberforce's country garden at Kensington Gore expounding to the frail little philanthropist his views on the welfare of Humanity. On another occasion he drove with his sister to Westminster to hear a debate in the House of Commons – the Horse Guards with their swords riding up and down the roadway to keep back the crowds, while gentlemen, with muslined, high-waisted ladies, raised curved top-hats, and screeching urchins clung to lamp-posts to catch a glimpse of their coach. Alighting in a green precinctual square between a Norman hall and a hackney-coach stand, they found themselves, after threading a maze of ancient passages, in the gallery of a modest chamber, about ninety feet long, panelled in the plainest style of Queen Anne and fitted with tiers of green leather benches. With its arched casement windows, it might have been the chapel of one of the severer Protestant sects. This impression was quickly dispelled by the irreverent behaviour of its occupants, who were lolling about the benches, with arms akimbo and hats over their eyes, some lying on their backs, some propped against the pillars snoozing, others talking and cracking jokes. At the end, on a candle-lit throne surmounted by the Royal Arms, sat the Speaker in a black gown and long wig; in front of him three clerks wrote at a green baize table on which lay a golden mace. It was very stuffy and, but for the light cast by a brass chandelier, extremely dark. Here the astonished Czar and his sister listened to the speeches of those who governed England, including one from their late host, Mr Whitbread – that stout, vehement Whig who in private life, to the infinite amusement of his fellow legislators, sold beer and liked, despite his Eton education and aristocratic wife, to be thought of as Sam, the People's man. The subject of his oratory[1] was the family affairs of the Prince Regent – scarcely a proper theme, his royal auditors reflected, for a brewer. Throughout the speeches members continued to cough, shuffle their boots, utter goose-like honks of 'Hear, hear' and 'Order, order,' snort into their napkins, whinny, bark, crow, groan, and even howl like hounds. The only respect they showed was for their Speaker and his baubles. Half the time of his clerks was spent in laying the Mace alternately on top of the table or under it in accordance with his movements. Members on entering or leaving the Chamber bobbed at his chair; seen from the strangers' gallery they looked like boys practising before a dancing master. Indeed, in its exaggerated respect for illogical rites and in its bantering, halting, schoolboy oratory the House was not unreminiscent of the noisier kind of school. It even had a kind of egalitarian tuck-shop – a place called Bellamy's – with an open fire, a roasting jack, and little tables along the walls lit by candles where the Czar and his sister, sitting among the members, supped on broiled rump-steaks, Stilton cheese, and salad.[2] It enabled them to realize more fully the extraordinary way in which England, for all its wealth and success, was governed.

1. The Duchess of Gordon spoke of his eloquence as 'teaching his drayhorse to caper.' Holland, I, 234. See Creevey, I, 164; Simond, II, 163; Wilberforce, IV, 339; Moore, Byron, 184.

2. For the description of the House of Commons and the Czar's visit to it see Ackermann, Microcosm, I, 185; Bamford, II, 27–8; Byron, Vision of Judgement; Colchester, II, 503–4; Feltham, 107–11; Havelock, 281; Hansard, XXVIII, 104–116; Hughson, II, 201–5; Lady Shelley, I; Malton, Street Views in London and Westminster; Simond, I, 52–60; II, 163–4.

Set against the foliage and blossom of the West End parks and squares, the glittering balls and dinners of that June revolved round the bestarred and epauletted presences of the Allied sovereigns. They danced – for the Czar was a great waltzer – at the houses of the higher aristocracy, breakfasted at the Star and Garter at Richmond, and went to the Opera. On their first Sunday they appeared at the afternoon parade in Hyde Park when everybody who was anybody drove and rode round the Ring to see and be seen. It was a wonderful spectacle of silks, laces, and glossy horses made more beautiful by the plumes and cuirasses of the Emperor's bodyguard dancing among the trees. The throng was so great that when the Sovereigns passed through the private gates of Kensington Gardens, eight thousand cavaliers followed them in. When they galloped down the avenue from Kensington Palace to the Serpentine there was almost a disaster. Boots were dragged off in the crush, ladies screamed, and the Master of the Horse, Garter ribbon and all, was thrown on to the grass. Poor Blücher, always the centre of attraction, was so set upon that he had to stand with his back to a tree to keep his admirers at bay.[1]

The aristocratic gaiety of that gala midsummer mingled with the pageantry of state – the horses of the guard of honour in the glory of scarlet and gold striking sparks from the cobbles, the Coldstream band with its giant Negroes striking their cymbals with high, rhythmic blows, the Knights of the Garter marching in procession for an investiture. In an age when men of rank were expected to spend their wealth on display, pageantry was as much a public prerogative as the utilitarian social services of to-day. Bright uniforms and liveries, music, banners, and gilding, the spectacle of fine horses, equipages, and jewelled women were part of the Londoner's birthright. Ceremony and pageantry provided, too, in that unpoliced England, a sounding-board for public opinion. As they drove through the crowds, the great and powerful learnt from their reception how they stood in popular esteem. For months the Regent, surrounded by all the pomp of state and in the floodtide of a great national triumph, had been unable to raise an huzza. In contrast, the Czar could not appear without an

1. Ashton, II, 279–80; Brownlow, 108–9; Colchester, II, 502; De Quincey, III, 68; Festing, 193–5; Lady Shelley, I, 59–60; Stanley, 86–8. See also Chancellor, Plate 79; Feltham, 99, 375; Gronow, I, 52.

hysterical ovation. There were never less than ten thousand people waiting outside the Pulteney to see him. During those first days in London he moved in an unbroken halo of glory. The whole population, silks, rags, and broadcloth, seemed to be in the streets, rushing after him and asking which way he had gone. The very horses of his escort had their tails plucked for souvenirs.

*

All this was made more humiliating for the Regent by the acclamations for his wife. Her presence in the capital at such a time was a constant aggravation. He was forced to inform his guests through the Foreign Secretary that any notice taken of her would be regarded as an insult. There was a terrible occasion when he and they attended the opera in the Haymarket. The theatre was crammed to its flame-coloured dome, the boxes filled, row after row, with women in white satin gowns and diamonds and men in orders and gold lace. But though the whole house rose and sang the National Anthem and the cheering continued for several minutes, the Regent – an unhealthy contrast to the rosy-cheeked Monarchs beside him – was seen to be gazing apprehensively at an empty box. And just as the second act was about to begin, there was a stir, every head turned, and there, noisily entering, was the injured Princess, shapeless and spangled, her brightly rouged face set off by a leonine mane of yellow curls. In the awful silence that ensued she curtsied to the Emperor, who rose to his feet and bowed, thus compelling the Regent to do the same. At this everyone cheered frantically. The situation was only saved by the Regent, who, always at his best in a crisis, took the applause as meant for himself and bowed until it ceased.[1] But the Princess had spoilt his evening and delighted the Opposition *frondeurs* who had incited her to go. Afterwards, as she left the theatre, the mob surrounded her carriage, huzzaing, snatching her hands, and offering to burn down Carlton House.

There was another embarrassment. Eighteen years earlier the Princess

1. 'His toadies ... to save him the imputation of this ridiculous vanity chose to say that he did the most beautiful and elegant thing in the world and bowed to his wife.' Lady Charlotte Bury. Bury I, 210–11. See Anderson, 76; Ashton, I, 279; Broughton, I, 141–2; Colchester, II, 501; Feltham, 260; Havelock, 284; Nicolson, 114; Simond, I, 89–91.

of Wales had borne her husband a daughter. As after him she was next in the succession the Regent had done his best to keep the little Princess Charlotte in obscurity. But 'the young 'un,' as the Whigs called her, was not easy to ignore. With a full and shapely bosom, protuberant Hanoverian eyes, and a fine pair of legs, which, like her father, she delighted to show, she was, despite many excellent qualities, a rather flamboyant little puss. According to the old Queen, she was forward and dogmatical, buckish about horses, and full of expressions very like swearing. While still in the schoolroom she had become involved, with her mother's connivance, in a foolish correspondence with a young cavalry officer, and this had given her father the opportunity of stopping her weekly visits to the Princess of Wales. The girl had rebelled, and her plight had become a public question. The Opposition asked questions in Parliament, Lord Byron, the darling of Whig society, outraged conventional loyalty by publishing a poem beginning, 'Weep, daughter of a royal line,' and the Princess refused to appear at the Queen's Drawing-Room because her mother was not allowed to be present. The mob adopted her cause; insulting processions marched past Carlton House, and mother and daughter, meeting accidentally in the Park, delighted the disaffected by embracing from their carriage windows.[1]

The Regent, therefore, was grateful when an opportunity arose to marry her and ship her out of England. Having gone to war to prevent a military domination of the Low Countries and having, after twenty years, achieved its object, the British Government was anxious to establish a strong, friendly, and united Netherlands under the Stadtholder of Holland. Nothing could, therefore, seem more appropriate after the liberation of Holland and Belgium than a match between his heir, William of Orange, who had been serving on Wellington's staff, and the daughter of England. The Princess felt little enthusiasm for the young man, but, as anything seemed better than her present confinement, she had allowed her father's impetuous announcement of her

1. See Aspinall, *Princess Charlotte, passim*; Ashton, I, 192, 195–6, 216; *Bessborough*, 232; Bury, I, 10–11, 38–9, 85, 125–6, 129, 151, 154–5, 162–3, 202; II, 290–2, 435; Colchester, II, 376, 416; *Creevey Papers*, I, 146, 176; Creston, *passim*; Farington, VII, 153, 200, 244, 266; Greville (Suppl.), I, 103–4; *Marlay Letters*, 157, 244–6; Lady Shelley, I, 47–8, 55–6; Simond, II, 32; Stanhope, 92; Woodward, 64.

engagement to pass. But the train of events that seemed about to unite the dynasties of Britain and the Netherlands had also brought the Grand Duchess Catherine to England. As a Russian, she did not wish to see such a combination – a threat to her country's Continental paramountcy – formed inside the grander alliance of European thrones of which her brother was the genius. Nor as a woman did she wish to see the Regent happy or his daughter obedient. Making a dead set at Charlotte, she implanted in her mind a strong dislike for her uninspiring fiancé and a fancy for one of the Prussian princes – fine creatures, brave as lions, it was said, and conveniently within the Russian orbit. In this she was aided by the wiles of the young Opposition lawyer, Henry Brougham – 'wicked shifts,' as his colleagues called him – who insinuated into the girl's head the notion that if she went to Holland, the Regent would procure a divorce, marry again, and deprive her of the succession. 'The effect upon the young 'un,' wrote a Whig, 'was almost magical.' A few days later, provided by her father with a list of wedding guests which omitted her mother's name, she returned it with her own erased.[1]

Thus the arrival of the foreign Sovereigns had not only brought to a head the Regent's unhappy relationship with his wife, but had deflected his daughter from the marriage his Ministers had planned for her. Instead of ministering to his pride as the head of the first nation on earth, his principal guest, egged on by his intolerable sister, had consistently humiliated him. It was in vain that, with florid condescension and in ever more wonderful clothes, he took his allies to Ascot or went with them down the river to Woolwich attended by sixty barges manned by liveried musicians and watermen. The Czar, like his ancestor, Peter the Great, was greatly impressed by the wonders of England's shipyards and the resources of her national arsenal; they resembled, he declared, the preparations for the commencement of a war rather than the stores remaining at its end.[2] But he managed to convey that, while he was responsible for Russia's achievements, England's were in no way due to the Regent. Throughout his conversation he insinuated an unmistakable tone of contempt.

1. Brownlow, 45, 78, 107; Bury, I, 202, 207; II, 292-3, 315; Festing, 193; Grenville, I, 230; *Paget Brothers*, 263-5.
2. Croly, *Life of George IV*, II, 67.

There was policy in this. For the Czar welcomed the opportunities for intrigue offered by British politics. He could rule, it seemed, by dividing. The Regent was only a figurehead – the butt of the luxurious society over which he presided in his father's absence. The position of his Ministers, creatures of the hour, was constantly undermined by the factious opposition of other nobles and members of Parliament. For all her wealth England was only another Poland; with France out of the way, nothing could stay the predestined advance of Russia, with her clear, inspired leadership, vast numbers, and heroic soldiers. It was not only an amateur Spartan's contempt for an epicurean that made the Czar scorn the Regent's society.

Indulging in the occupation, so dear to his country's policy, of fishing in troubled waters, he and his sister ostentatiously appeared at Opposition gatherings to which the Regent was not invited. In his rôle of liberal-minded philosopher, Alexander sought to convey the impression that he was not so much a prince as a gentleman among gentlemen. When a Whig Earl presented him with an ice on a salver, he insisted on putting the empty glass down himself. It was the great year of Almack's – the assembly rooms where the Whig hostess, Lady Jersey, set the tone for the highest fashion. With this excitable, imperious, and rather obtuse beauty from Ireland, the Czar pretended to be in love. On the day of her midsummer ball the Regent had arranged for his guests to be in Oxford. After the academic junketings – the Latin orations, the banquet in the Radcliffe at which the military had to be called in to quiet the enthusiastic students, the Encaenia with the Regent arrayed in silken cap and gown – the Czar took sudden leave in the middle of a dinner in Christ Church hall and, driving through the night, reached London at three in the morning, where Byron saw him in

> *a starless blue coat and kersey –*
> *mere breeches whisk'd round with the Jersey,*
> *Who, lovely as ever, seem'd just as delighted*
> *With majesty's presence as those she'd invited.*[1]

The climax of this contest of pinpricks between the two vainest men in Europe occurred on June 18th when the monarchs dined with the

1. Moore, *Byron*, 255. See *Ann. Reg.* 1814; Chron. 47–8; Ashton, I, 281–4; Farington, VII, 258; Havelock, 288; Howitt, 11; Nicolson, 114; Lady Shelley, I, 63.

Lord Mayor. Knowing that if he went to the Guildhall unaccompanied, he would be insulted by the mob, the Regent had arranged to drive with the Czar. But at the last moment the Grand Duchess decided to come too. In vain it was pointed out that the arrangements had all been made and that women were excluded from civic feasts. Argument merely strengthened her resolution. All day frantic letters passed between the Pulteney and Carlton House. The Czar was adamant; unless the Grand Duchess drove with him by his side, he would not go to the Guildhall at all. As it was impossible for all three to occupy the same seat, and none could sit with dignity on the opposite one, there was nothing for the Regent to do but resign his state coach to the Czar and proceed in a separate one. His reception in the City streets was such as to make him vow he would never visit it again. Despite the two Prussian princes hastily requisitioned to sit opposite him, the Lord Mayor riding ahead with the Sword of State, the Yeomen of the Guard and the massed escort of cavalry, the Regent was greeted with hisses, groans, and shouts of 'Where's your wife? Love your wife!'

Nor did his humiliation end at the Guildhall. In the presence of his Ministers, the King of Prussia, and the foreign princes, the head of the British State was forced to await the arrival of the Russians for a whole hour, the end of which was rendered the more agonizing by the frantic cheering which greeted them in the streets outside. And as the royal procession at last entered the banqueting hall to the strains of 'The Roast Beef of Old England', the Czar deliberately stopped to talk to Lord Grey and Lord Holland, two of the Regent's bitterest enemies. The enraged Prince had to wait behind him under the gaze of thousands. For the rest of the evening he preserved a haughty and chilling silence. Under the gold-fringed canopy of velvet over the thrones of England, Russia, and Prussia the air was electric: a little island of ice in the midst of the crowded, chattering, perspiring hall. While the Lord Mayor stood majestic behind, while the traditional baron of beef, surmounted by the royal standard and attended by sergeant carvers, was borne with musical honours to the table, and toast followed toast, the Regent said not one word to the imperial barbarian at his side.

But the Russians had not finished with him. When after the toasts and 'Hip! Hip! Hurrahs,' at which the Grand Duchess laughed deliciously, the fiddlers and opera-singers in the gallery struck up the

time-honoured songs appropriate to each sentiment – 'Rule Britannia!'
'Hail! Star of Brunswick,' 'To Arms, to Arms!' – she began to make
signals of distress. If the caterwauling went on, she declared, she would
be sick. She became so hysterical that out of common courtesy the
Regent was forced to ask the music to stop. But this caused so much indignation in the body of the hall that, to placate his hosts, he had to
appeal to the Calmuck beauty to allow the National Anthem to be
sung. She was merciless; 'as if,' she replied with a toss of the head,
'that was not music!' At this, however, a murmuring began and a note
was passed to the Russian Ambassador: 'If your Duchess does not allow
the music, we won't answer for the royal table.' Faced by a national
obstinacy as great as her own, the lady gave way: 'Well, let them
bawl, then!' And in the silence that ensued the Prime Minister was
heard to mutter, 'When folks don't know how to behave, they ought
to stay at home!'

On the way back to Carlton House the Regent's coach, tightly surrounded by guards, was followed by a groaning crowd. When he got
home he learned that at the opera that night the whole house had
applauded his wife. 'God bless you,' the crowd had called to her afterwards, 'we'll make the Prince love you before we have done with
him!' 'Prinny,' wrote one of his old cronies, 'is exactly in the state one
would wish; he lives only by protection of his visitors. He is worn out
with fuss, fatigue, and rage.'[1]

*

During the closing days of the visit popular enthusiasm began to wane
and the English to grow insular again. Those who came in contact
with the Russians, like Dr Johnson's old friend, Mrs Piozzi, who let
them her house at Streatham, found that, though they might have
saved civilization, they were not very civilized themselves. Nor did
their ruler, for all his condescension and fine manners, escape criticism.
His flirting and waltzing scarcely accorded with his character of Christian paladin; he was gallant enough to the young ladies, it was noted
but had nothing to say to their elders. A nearer approach showed him

---

1. *Creevey Papers*, I, 196. See *Ann. Reg.* 1814, Chron. 48–50; Ashton, I, 114–15,
287–8; Bury, I, 123, 205, 234; Colchester, II, 502–3; Dyott, I, 311; Farington,
VII, 268; Festing, 193, 195; Jerningham, II, 54; Nicolson, 114–15.

to be a foolish, good-natured, dancing dandy: Byron's

> coxcomb Czar,
> The autocrat of waltzes and of war.

Even the Opposition leaders ceased to be responsive; Whig aristocrats, as Napoleon also had found, welcomed reforming dictators in theory, but in practice were allergic to all rulers. They particularly resented Alexander's insistence, while putting off the monarch, on the royal privilege of monopolizing the conversation.[1]

'I hope,' wrote Jane Austen from Chawton on June 23rd, 'Fanny has seen the Emperor, and then I may fairly wish them all away!' That day the foreign Sovereigns left London.[2] At Portsmouth they inspected the dockyards and witnessed a naval review from the deck of the royal yacht. Then, after a night at Petworth, they bade farewell to the Regent, and set out for Dover. To the last the Czar and his sister continued to play to the gallery. At Hastings they stopped their carriage on the outskirts of the town, shook hands with the astonished peasantry, and distributed cakes among the children. George Cruikshank commemorated the incident in a cartoon called *Russian Condescension or the Blessings of Universal Peace.*

A few of the visitors lingered in England a little longer. The Hetman Platoff, whose ugliness much endeared him to the English, was seen at an Essex country-house party in July joyously stamping his feet like a horse and nodding his head in a Cossack dance. Blücher, who was also there, danced mazurkas with the bright-eyed English ladies like a subaltern. He retained his wonderful popularity to the end, his mere appearance in a London street automatically emptying every shop in a matter of seconds. The courtyard of St James's Palace where he lodged was filled all day with sightseers; with the greatest good humour the old warrior never failed, sometimes at five-minute intervals, to appear

1. Lord Grey described him as a vain, silly fellow who thought himself clever but was a damned fool. *Creevey Papers*, I, 195–6. See Ashton, I, 275–6; Broughton, I, 153; Brownlow, 76; Lady Burghersh; Colchester, II, 503–41; Dudley, 230; Farington, VII, 261–2; Havelock, 272, 280–1; Jerningham, II, 54; *Lieven Letters*, 10; *Paget Brothers*, 262–3; Lady Shelley, I, 58, 60–3; Wynne, III, 373.

2. 'The Grand Duchess and the Czar left £200 among the thirty servants at the Pulteney and nothing at all for the State coachmen and cooks. A country baronet, it was felt, would have done better.' Broughton, I, 153.

at the window. He seemed to like the English as much as they liked him; he once paid them the compliment of remarking what a fine capital theirs would be to sack. When he sailed from Dover, he stood watching the white cliffs, murmuring as he turned away, 'That's a fine country!'[1]

*

The rest of the victory summer passed like a dream. 'I rejoiced,' wrote De Quincey, 'with the universal nation then rejoicing.' The return to England of Wellington – a Duke now – was the signal for a new out-burst of celebrations. At Dover he was seized by the crowd and borne shoulder-high to the Ship Inn; all the way to London, through the Kentish hayfields, where old men in white smocks stood bareheaded to see him pass, the cheering and fêting continued. 'It was quite refresh-ing,' wrote Mary Mitford, who saw him driving in an open carriage without the slightest affectation of bowing, 'after all those parading foreign emperors.' He took the lionizing calmly, as he had taken worse things, rode about London in a plain blue coat with a single groom, and made it clear that, while promiscuous pawing might do for an Emperor, it was too much for an English gentleman. In the Commons, after the Government had proposed to vote him £300,000 to buy an estate, the leader of the Opposition tabled an amendment increasing the grant to £400,000. 'When the will of Heaven and the common destinies of our nature,' the Speaker told him as he sat, in Field-Marshal's uniform, within the bar of the House, 'shall have swept away the present generation, you will have left your great name and example as an imperishable monument, exciting others to like deeds of glory and serving at once to adorn, defend and perpetuate the existence of this country among the ruling nations of the earth.'

While England commemorated its victories, it dismissed the forces that had won them. All June and July the troops from Bordeaux – except those dispatched across the Atlantic to fight the Americans – were returning in dark, crowded transports, the decks packed with hungry men asleep in blankets and the holds with wounded. When Ensign Bell reached his father's house in Ireland, his brethren waited

1. Haydon, I, 282. See Ashton, I, 270, 272–3, 274–5, 279–80; Broughton, I, 113–14; De Quincey, III, 66–7; Festing, 193–5; Moore, *Byron*, 305; Lady Shelley, I, 58–60.

for him at the end of the avenue, bonfires blazed on the hills, and, penniless younger son though he was, he danced for a week with every pretty girl in the county. The rank and file were less fortunate. They were recruited from the gutter, and to the gutter they returned. They had done what the nation needed and were wanted no more. They were given their arrears of pay – without interest – and disbanded so that taxes could be reduced. The seamen released from French prison camps were dismissed by the port authorities without a penny and left to beg their way home. At Chelsea thousands of idle soldiers, awaiting demobilization, lined the streets and lounged before the doors of public-houses. 'There,' wrote Rifleman Harris, discharged after seven years' campaigning with a wound-pension of 6d. a day, 'hobbled the maimed light-infantryman, the heavy dragoon, the hussar, the artilleryman, the fusilier ... the Irishman shouting and brandishing his crutch, the Englishman reeling with drink, and the Scot with grave, melancholy visage sitting on the step of the public-house amongst the crowd.' Others never came home at all; at Gibraltar, where several regiments were awaiting transport, yellow fever broke out, and, the army doctors being free to take fees from the rich Jews and Moors of the Rock, the men were left to die in the care of drunken orderlies.[1]

The summer's rejoicings – marred by a July day when the Princess Charlotte flounced out of Carlton House, hailed a hackney coach and took refuge at her mother's house – culminated in a jubilee celebration on August 1st, the centenary of the Hanoverian accession. The Regent, having dispatched his daughter under close guard to the country, superintended the preparations himself, throwing open the royal parks to the populace. St James's Park was hung with coloured lanterns, its lawns set for dancing and its canal spanned by a Chinese bridge, crowned with a seven-storeyed, gas-lit pagoda. In front of Buckingham House a platform was built for the ascent of a balloon, and a royal pavilion for the Regent and his guests. The Green Park had a sham castle a hundred and thirty feet high, before which the storm of Badajoz was to be staged, and Hyde Park had refreshment and gambling booths and a representation of the Battle of the Nile on the Serpentine, enacted by model three-deckers made out of ship's barges and fitted with miniature cannon.

1. Leslie, 256–7. See Harris, 189; Haydon, 1, 286–7; Stewart, 92–3.

Usually Parliament and the country opposed and, when they could not prevent, deplored the Regent's grander flights of extravagance; on this occasion he expected to have them with him. With his own hands, forgetting for a moment the vexation of being a husband and a father, he helped to design the dual-purpose Castle of Discord and Temple of Peace, with its symbolic illuminations of the devastations of War and the evils of Despotism and Tyranny, its mechanical fountains, imitation porphyry columns, rainbows, vestal virgins, and transparencies depicting the Golden Age Restored. He also selected the fireworks – girandoles, jerbs, Roman candles, and *pots de brin* – and insisted on the inclusion of a battery of Colonel Congreve's rockets of which, unlike his country's naval and military commanders, he had always been an ardent patron.

Despite rain in the morning, the Jubilee was an immense success. Piccadilly, the Strand, and Oxford Street were completely blocked for hours, and by the afternoon half a million people had assembled. For all the alarmist predictions in the Press, the crowds were orderly and good-humoured. Spreading across the grass of the royal parks, they settled down to enjoy their unwonted treat. Some picnicked under the trees, some climbed the branches, some vanished into the gaming booths, while others gaped at the mimic three-deckers and frigates on the Serpentine ocean. Sunshine had now succeeded rain, and it was a beautiful evening, the air fresh and delightful. Providence seemed to be smiling on the Regent and his people. The balloon soared away 'in a most solemn and majestic manner,' dropping coloured parachutes and landing, after hair-raising adventures, forty minutes later in the Mucking Marshes. The rockets rose in golden clusters, galloping about the heavens, wrote Charles Lamb, like young stars in the making and descending in sheets of fire on the deserted streets of Westminster. There were maroons and mines, redcoats with blackened faces creeping through the dark with glinting bayonets, and diabolical Frenchmen gesticulating on the battlements of the Castle of Discord. The illumination was increased by the burning of four of the model ships and the noise by the screeching of the Serpentine swans.

The Regent's *coup d'œil* was timed for midnight. There was a deafening explosion and the canvas walls of the Green Park fortress – emblem of destructive war – suddenly lifted to reveal the revolving Temple of

Peace, glittering with coloured lamps, while water flowed from the jaws of lions into golden basins, and a detachment of Foot Guards on the roof held aloft the Royal Standard and self-consciously gave three cheers. At almost the same moment the pagoda in the other park burst into flames and, after blazing for a quarter of an hour, fell into the lake, killing two spectators. The crowd, which supposed this to be part of the performance, continued to gape until the last flames and fireworks were expended. Then, having satisfied its love of wonders, the respectable part set off homewards through the darkness. The pressure in the Strand was so great that a Hanoverian commissary, on his way home from the Peninsula, was borne far past his lodgings. The rest of the crowd stayed behind in the drinking booths. It was still there, despite the Home Secretary's efforts to expel it, a week later.[1]

It was not only in London that England celebrated the peace. In little country towns from one end of the island to the other there were thanksgiving sermons and anthems, bands of music in the streets, processions with ribbons and banners, emblems in cars drawn by gaily-decked teams of horses, illuminations, crackers, and bonfires. There was a general public holiday, and the rich subscribed to feast their poorer neighbours. At Lichfield more than three thousand people sat down to roast beef, plum-pudding, and ale; at Blandford home-made transparencies were erected over every door with hovering doves, flags, trumpets, and the figure of Plenty shedding corn and fruit from her cornucopia. The more rustic the scene, the more artless the commingling of neighbours. At East Coker in Somerset the tents and tables were set at the bottom of a field, backed by a stream and row of elms, at the neighbouring village of Yetminster under the eaves of a farmhouse. 'It was pleasant,' wrote an onlooker, 'to see the hilarity and good humour that prevailed between Master and Men, to say nothing of the hearty gourmandizing of men, women, and children.

1. 'All that was countrified in the Parks,' Charles Lamb wrote to Words-worth, 'is all but obliterated. The very colour of green is vanished, the whole surface dry crumbling sand ... the stench of liquors, bad tobacco, dirty people and provisions conquer the air, and we are stifled and suffocated.... The whole beauty of the place is gone – that lake-like look of the Serpentine – it has foolish ships upon it. But something whispers to have confidence in nature and its revival.' Lamb, VI, 436. See *Ann. Reg.* 1814; Ashton, I, 331–50; Chancellor, Plate 55; Brownlow, 113–14; Bury, I, 270; Colchester, II, 514; Schaumann, 413–15.

After all sorts of loyal toasts drunk in beer and cider, the company rose from the table for a dance on the green. Mr Barrett took an old woman for his partner and, after giving her the last whirl, kissed her to the great delight of all present, one man exclaiming, "God Almighty will bless you, Master, for that. If he don't I'll be damned!"[1] At Gainsborough in Lincolnshire little Thomas Cooper – the future Chartist leader – and his schoolfellows, dressed up as the Allied Sovereigns, serenaded the neighbouring squires and farmers, singing 'Awake, my soul, and with the sun,' and 'Glory to Thee, my God, this night.' 'The beloved and venerated Sir Charles himself,' he wrote, 'stood and smiled to hear us, and called us very good boys as he gave us a real silver half-crown.'

*

The old King, in whose honour these simple pieties were observed, was a prisoner in his castle, blind, mad, helpless, and living in a world that had ceased to exist. The bells still rang to celebrate his birthday; the sentries still stood outside his palaces; the enactments of Government were issued in his name. Men, mostly old, prayed for him, spoke of him with affection and thought of him wistfully in their rejoicings at the triumph of his arms. But he himself was impervious to all: a ghost left over from the days of Pitt and Chatham, who had conversed with Johnson and Wolfe, been painted by Ramsay, and who now, dressed in velvet cap and dressing-gown, wandered from room to room or flitted across the terrace at Windsor with sightless eyes and unkempt snowy beard, his long, tapering, kingly fingers, feeling for an imaginary sceptre. And, as in the days of his sanity, he still, though alone, talked continuously: those who loved him comforted themselves with the thought that it was with angels.[2]

1. 'Mr B. forced himself to look grave and pointed to one of the flags which bore the motto, "Fear God and honour the King."' Ham, 191. See also *Ann. Reg.* 1814, Chron., 215; Dyot, I, 310; Cooper, 23–4; Lucas, I, 35.
2. D'Arblay, III, 267. See Ashton, II, 130–2; Bessborough, 223; Colchester, II, 353–4; Dyott, I, 306, 373, 581; Gaussen, II, 322; Gronow, II, 305–6; *Paget Brothers,* 149; Simond, II, 115.

PART TWO: HER FRESH GREEN LAP

There lives not form nor feeling in my soul
Unborrowed from my country.
COLERIDGE

A FOREIGNER with a more extended view of Britain than that enjoyed by the Allied Sovereigns would have seen two islands – a dominant one with a population of ten million English, two million Scots, and half a million Welsh, and a subordinate one inhabited by five million Catholic Irish peasants and a million Protestants of Anglo-Scottish descent who alone held the right to sit in Parliament, and enjoy high office. The condition of the two islands was thus dissimilar: the one a closely-knit commonwealth pursuing its own interest, the other a dependency garrisoned by a ruling caste, foreign in religion and partly so in race. The gulf between them had been widened by the Act of Union which had merged the Irish Parliament into an imperial legislature at Westminster in which its members could always be outvoted.

Neither this, nor the periodic racial and religious risings and the permanent agrarian unrest of Ireland had kept its sons out of Britain's fleets and armies, to which they were drawn by their love of fighting, craving for drink, and extreme poverty. This last, because of bad farming and a vicious system of land tenure, was chronic. It was intensified by an alarming rise in population which drove thousands of Irish emigrants every year into the cotton factories of Lancashire and Clydeside and into the London slums. They constituted the chief residuum of unskilled labour for Britain's new machinery – a development whose influence on the national life of England had yet to be realized.

For except in Protestant Ulster the Irish were a very different race from the sober, law-abiding English and the thrifty, tenacious Scots. The difference was partly one of climate, partly of religion, economics, and history, partly of diet. The English lived on meat, beer, and wheaten bread, the Irish on potatoes and whisky. They were at once a tragic, reckless, kind-hearted, superstitious, and, by English standards, lawless and unreliable race, always doing wild things and in so gay and absurd a manner that their irresponsibility was a jest rather than a reproach. Their only point in common with the English, apart from their courage, was their passion for horses. Ireland's vivid green Atlantic landscape, with its mournful bogs and misty mountains, its stinking hovels and elegant, filthy, drunken capital, seemed to belong to a foreign country. Here women, half-naked, with matted hair hanging over their bosoms, sat at cabin doors smoking pipes and staring at melancholy horizons, and men in blue cloaks and slouching hats carrying shillelaghs stood jesting at street corners in sinister groups. In this other island the most savage crimes were constantly being committed for religious, patriotic, or agrarian reasons by a peasantry whom Harry Smith found the lightest-hearted, kindest, most generous creatures he had ever known.[1]

Ireland was not the only part of the British Isles which presented a contrast to the wealth and splendour of London and the garden of Kent and Sussex. There were the marshes and fens with their half-animal fishermen and fowlers, poor primitive villages along the rocky, western coasts with mud walls and blackened, ragged thatch, the northern moors and the Welsh valleys where a sturdy people – almost as broad as they were high – talked in a strange tongue, wore traditional dress and lived a life apart.[2] Scotland, too, though its wealth had increased immeasurably in the past half century, was a poor land compared with England. The country women still went about barefooted, except on Sundays when they attended kirk in fine shawls, black velvet bonnets, and looks of ineffable piety. They lived in bare, unfloored cottages, mostly of one room, with dung piled against sodden turf walls. Even in its noble capital – 'Auld Reekie' – with its labyrinth of crooked closes and tall medieval houses, the cry of 'gardy loo' still warned the passer-by that the ordure of the past twelve hours was

1. Smith, I, 337. See Mrs Arbuthnot, *Journal*, 5th Jan., 1822; Ashton, II, 201–2, Bell, I, 181, 187, 192; Bury, II, 109, 112, 115–16; Colchester, II, 591–2; Farington, VIII, 64, 121; Granville, II, 456–7, 458; Grattan, 327–8; Gronow, II, 87; *Hamilton of Dalzell*, MS. p. 277; Keats, *Letters*, 6th July, 1818; *Lavengro*, 57–9; Lockhart, V, 179; Nevill, 56–60; Newton, 193; Peel, I, 206–7, 231, 236–7; Simond, I, 65; II, 135, 259, 324–6, 332, 339; Woodward, 314–24.

2. When Richard Ayton landed in the Pwllheli peninsula in 1814, Cymric amazons emerged from filthy wigwams and proceeded to twist and pull about his umbrella with cries and grunts of amazement. Daniell, I, 167. See *idem*, 69 *et seq.*; Festing, 159–60; *Marlay Letters*, 256; Simond, I, 210–37.

about to descend into the roadway. For all the fine new farms of the Lothians and the Lanarkshire cotton mills, Scotland's chief wealth was still the frugality and honesty [1] of its deeply religious people.

Beyond the Lowlands were the feudal Highlands – the primitive land of mountain and flood made fashionable by Walter Scott's poems and novels. Here, in poor shepherds' huts full of animals and peat-smoke, lived a race whose splendid physique and proud bearing recalled the soldiers of ancient Rome or the noble savages of North America.[2] There were only 300,000 in all, but, their former loyalty to the House of Stuart having been gloriously expiated on England's battlefields, their kilts, pipes, and sporrans had lately become a national institution.

*

Of England's own ten millions, a tenth lived in the capital. Apart from its suburbs of new villas engulfing ancient villages it was really five towns, the mercantile City, the royal West End, the riverside port, the Borough of Southwark, and the slums. These last crowded out of sight – though not always out of smell – of the rich, behind the grander houses, and spread ever further eastwards into the Essex and Kentish meadows, leaving a string of low, dingy towns on either side of the Thames. They were still what they had been in the Middle Ages, fever-ridden haunts of vice and wretchedness: a maze of alleys and lanes fading into the unwholesome vapour that always overhung them, of dirty, tumbledown houses with windows patched with rags and blackened paper, and airless courts crowded with squabbling women and half-naked children wallowing in pools and kennels. The improvements effected by eighteenth-century humanitarians were constantly being counteracted by the influx of newcomers from every part of the kingdom.

1. Simond noted in 1810 that the woman attendant at the Edinburgh Penitentiary to whom he gave half a crown, at once put it into the box for poor prisoners. Simond, I, 273–4. In the Highlands the inns were without locks and travellers' luggage could be safely left all night in unguarded carriages in the highway. *Idem*, 302. See Lockhart, IV, 218. Keats, III, 166; *idem*, 170–1; Clapham, , 28–9, 37; Simond, I, 28–9, 263–4; II, 39–40, 56; Lady Shelley, II, 57–8.

2. 'The same proud indolence, the same carelessness, the same superiority to want, the same courage, the same hospitality and unfortunately, I hear, the same liking for spirituous liquors.' Simond, I, 301. See *idem*, I, 302–24; Bewick 74–7; Keats, III, 164, 191–213; Letts, 247.

Apart from London and the Scottish and Irish capitals there were only two towns in Great Britain, Manchester and Liverpool, with 100,000 inhabitants, and five others – Bristol, Glasgow, Birmingham, Leeds, and Sheffield – with over 50,000. At Liverpool, which had taken Bristol's place as the country's first outport, rows of warehouses, eight or nine stories high, extended for half a mile along the waterfront, where thousands of men perpetually unloaded ships from the far ends of the earth. Here was the former base of the slave trade – the sinister, golden traffic on which the port's wealth had been raised – and the chief home, supplanting Bristol, of the West Indian interest. Richard Ayton, in his *Voyage round Great Britain*, thought Liverpool, with its fine residential houses, elegant Grecian buildings, clean broad streets and spreading smoke pall, silhouetted against the Cheshire hills, the most beautiful town in England after London; it brought to his mind 'the country in the pride of its industry and enterprise and under the most striking signs of its wealth, consequence, and power.'

The manufacturing towns, or rather overgrown squatters' villages – for they had none of the traditional dignity associated with English cities – now spreading fast around the new steam factories, iron works, and mines of the Midlands, South Lancashire, Clyde, and Tyne, were astonishing phenomena. As travellers approached them through the encircling mists, they heard the rumbling of wheels and the clang of hammers, and saw long rows of furnace fires. Pückler-Muskau's picture of Birmingham serves for all: flame and smoke belching from diabolical chimneys, factories larger than palaces with every window blazing through the night as men made goods and weapons for the destruction of Bonaparte, and, gleaming above the lurid town, the spires of ancient churches silhouetted in the moonlight. Classically-minded young ladies, passing through such places, were reminded in their journals of 'the realms of Plutus'.[1]

*

1. Wynne, III, 343. The author of *A Guide to all the Watering and Sea-Bathing Places* (1815 ed.), 349–51, thought Birmingham a wonderful town, 'the houses well built, the streets ... broad and well paved and the spirit of industry so universally predominant that scarcely a child is unemployed.' See Bamford, II, 333, 335; Hammond, *Rise of Modern Industry*, 221–32; Letts, 127, 129–30; Newton, 25–6; Simond, I, 278; II, 76, 79, 83; Smart, 249–51; Lady Shelley, II, 41.

Yet, though increasing fast, the industrial population was only a small fraction of the country, hidden out of sight on remote heaths and in lonely Pennine valleys. More than three-quarters of the English people still lived in ancient villages or small market towns. Even a generation later, after a further feverish expansion, only one in eighty was working in the cotton trade – the country's largest urban industry. There were far fewer miners than there were tailors and bootmakers, and more domestic servants than cotton-workers. Set against 'Britain's calm felicity and power', London's Alsatias and the helot settlements beside the Irk and Swayle seemed accidental and unimportant. Only a prophet could have foreseen that, in these, and not in the pastoral and still feudal south, lay the England of the future. Here, Washington Irving wrote, everything was the growth of ages, of regular and peaceful existence, conveying an impression of 'a calm and settled security, an hereditary transmission of home-bred virtues and attachments that spoke deeply and touchingly for the moral character of the nation.'

One saw this traditional life on Sundays in the villages: the well-dressed family groups converging through the fields and lanes as the church bells pealed – a continuous chain of sound at that hour across England – the spacious pews of the gentry lined with black leather, the old peasants in the aisle, the choir with their strings, clarinets, and serpents in the gallery, the old men and girls in white gowns on either side of the chancel, the dignified high-church rector and parish clerk intoning 'England's sublime liturgy', the happy neighbours meeting afterwards in the churchyard that Harry Smith and his fellow warriors recalled with such nostalgia on a Sabbath morning in the little Pyrenean town of Villa Alba.[1] One saw it in the market towns with their beautiful houses – Georgian, Queen Anne, Tudor, and Gothic – the romantic eaves and latticed windows of the old, and the classical cornices and pediments of the new, the broad high streets with driven cattle and umbrellaed market tables, the fine trees casting their shade over garden walls, the pillared market-halls, the criers with scarlet coats and bells proclaiming the news. Such towns crowned nearly a thousand years of unbroken civilization. From their upper windows one looked across gardens to fields, woods, and clear rivers whose waters carried trout

1. Smith, I, 108. See Cooper, 16; Farington, VII, 125; Howitt, 570–3; *Lavengro*, 2; *Old Oak*, 57–8; *Romany Rye*, 65.

and crayfish. 'One of those pretty, clean, unstenched and unconfined places,' Cobbett called Huntingdon, 'that tend to lengthen life and make it happy.' At Winchester, when Keats stayed there in 1819, nothing ever seemed to be happening in the still, cobbled streets; nothing but the sound of birds in the gardens, the echoing, unhurrying footsteps of passers-by, the roll of market carts flooding in or out of the city with the tides of the encircling shire. Everywhere, as one travelled this rich, ancient land, one saw the continuity and natural growth of a community that had never known invasion and where the new, not confined as on the Continent by fortifications, had been free to develop without destroying the old. At Norwich, capital like York and Exeter not of a shire but of a province, the city was grouped round an episcopal tower, a Norman castle, and a vast market square from whose stalls poured that abundance of foodstuffs which so astonished the German, Meidinger. 'The most curious specimen at present extant of the genuine old English town,' Borrow called it, 'with its venerable houses, its numerous gardens, its thrice twelve churches, its mighty mound.' Farington was impressed by the universally neat appearance of the houses; he could not recollect any other town with such an air of being inhabited by people in good circumstances.

*

The first thing that struck every visitor to England was her beauty. It derived from her exquisite turf and foliage and soft, aqueous atmosphere: what Leigh Hunt, pining among the Apennines for the buttercup meadows and elms of the vale of Hampstead, called the grassy balm of his native fields. Everywhere was the sense of peace, wealth, and security: the avenues of huge elms, the leafy Middlesex landscape, the great trees on Hampstead's airy height, the blue horizons, the farmhouses of beautifully fashioned brick and stone, the pastoral Thames still set, as Horace Walpole had pictured it, amid enamelled meadows and filigree hedges, with brightly-painted barges, solemn as Exchequer barons, moving slowly up to Richmond or down to Syon, the sculptured, classical bridges, the wayside alehouses with placid drinkers under their spreading oaks and chestnuts, the old grey churches and barns, the ghostly trees in the evening twilight, the drinking cattle and homing rooks, the mystery and the mist.

Though England's forests had long been shorn to feed her fleets and furnaces, the sense of fine trees remained all-pervading. She was still, as Constable painted her, carpeted with her native hard-woods, which gave moisture to her soil, shade to her cattle and depth and mystery to every horizon. From the terrace at Richmond, or from Harrow hill, one looked across a vast plain from which trees rose in endless waves of blue. Every commentator dwelt on the same phenomenon: the great oaks, the hedgerows of elm and ash, the forest trees scattered about the meadows. Cobbett, stumbling for the first time on the Hampshire hangars, sat motionless on his horse, gazing down on that mighty flood spilling into every valley. In Sherwood Forest avenues stretched for miles in every direction, the solitude broken only by the whirring of partridges and pheasants. Cranborne Chase in Dorset had still nearly ten thousand deer; Windsor Forest, Burnham Beeches, and Epping, close to the capital, almost as many. In the Berkshire woodlands south of Reading, Mary Mitford described the forest-like closeness – a labyrinth of woody lanes, crossroads, and cartways leading up and down hill to farm-houses buried in leaves and wreathed to their clustered chimneys with vines, and little enclosures so closely set with growing timber as to resemble forest glades. One could scarcely peep, she wrote, through the leaves.[1]

Probably at no period was England so beautiful. Man had everywhere civilized nature without over-exploiting and spoiling it. The great landscape-painters and water colourists of the closing decades of the eighteenth century and the first of the nineteenth are the testimony to its inspiration. Gainsborough, Morland, de Wint, Farington, Cozens, Rowlandson, Crome, Cotman, Girtin, Turner, Bonington, and Constable, the Suffolk miller's son who revolutionized European painting, all sprang from that countryside. So did the poets – Wordsworth, Coleridge, Blake, Shelley, Keats – who were not isolated phenomena but men inheriting, though in expression they transcended,

1. Mitford, *Our Village*, 74–5, 115; *Cranbourn Chase, passim*; Grote, *passim*; West, II, 51; Cobbett, I, 10, 25, 53, 57–9, 91–2, 121; Bamford, II, 98, 338; Cundall, *Bygone Richmond*; Edlin's *Woodland Crafts in Britain*; Howitt, 366–92; Simond, I, 16, 150–3, 201, 335; II, 98, 103, 150–3, 230, 255, 282; *Old Oak*, 2–3; De Selincourt, II, 886; Raumer, III, 136–7; Varley. Raumer thought that, though England might not be the richest land in forests, she seemed the most abounding in trees. Clapham, I, 9–12.

the common feelings of their countrymen. Even in the unlovely manufacturing towns the English carried the memory of their landscape
with them; Cooper, the Chartist leader, thanked God in old age that
he was still familiar with the name of every English flower.[1] Cobbett,
who prided himself on being a plain man with no nonsense about him,
travelling from Redbourne to Chesham described how in every field
the haymakers had left a closely-mown strip between the hedgerow
and the corn; 'this,' he wrote, 'is most beautiful. The hedges are full
of shepherd's rose, honeysuckles, and all sorts of wild flowers, so that
you are upon a grass walk with this most beautiful of all flower-gardens
and shrubberies on your one hand and with the corn on the other.
And thus you go on from field to field, the sort of corn, the sort of
underwood and timber, the shape and size of the fields, the height of
the hedgerows, the height of the trees, all continually varying. Talk
of pleasure-grounds, indeed! What that man ever invented under the
name of pleasure-grounds can equal these fields in Hertfordshire?'

*

This landscape was constantly being enriched. It was ditched, hoed,
and hedged to an extent elsewhere unknown. Stacks over forty feet
high, meticulously finished and roofed with straw, barns built to outlast the centuries, outhouses, windmills and watermills which were
miracles of fine workmanship, sturdy gates and fences made by men
who were masters of their craft, were the commonplaces of the English scene. The thrifty and loving use of nature's resources and the
spirit of active and methodical enterprise seemed almost universal.
'The white farms ... the well-stocked rickyards behind,' wrote Mary
Mitford, 'tell of comfort and order.'

Yet every shire, every parish, differed in its farming methods, being
cultivated in the way which soil, climate, and immemorial experience
had proved best. Every district had its particular abundance, the bleak
lands as well as the fine. From sandy Norfolk came the enormous
turkeys – 'the grand Norfolkian holocaust' that at Christmas smoked
round Elia's nostrils from a thousand firesides. The stony fields round

1. 'I was invariably on the hills or in the lanes or woods or by the Trent by
sunrise. I often stood to gaze down the vista of a wood or upon some feature
of beauty in a landscape with a thrill of joyous feeling that I could not have
defined.' Cooper, 61. See also Bamford, 1, 85.

Bridport were blue with hemp and flax. Salisbury Plain and the Dorset uplands were cropped and fertilized by immense flocks of sheep: 'it is the extensive downs in its vicinage,' explained the Weymouth guide-book, 'which produces the sweetest herbage and gives a peculiarly fine flavour to the mutton.' And all over England the folded sheep, fed from the turnip-root, made it possible to grow good crops on marginal lands otherwise too light to bear them: on the Wiltshire downs Cobbett counted four thousand hurdled on a single acre.

The golden creed of 'Hoof and Horn', use and return, was the firm and, as it seemed, unalterable base of the country's wealth. The meadows that fed the suckling ewes and lambs in spring yielded hay by midsummer; and, when the corn was cut, the stubble kept the pigs. A Yorkshire squarson – for the very priests were farmers – recorded as the crown of a holiday tour the spectacle of a hundred and twenty shorthorns tethered and fed where they stood in open sheds on successive crops of vetch, mown grass, clover, and tares from fields manured by the straw they had soiled. The yields of such rotational agriculture, judged by the standards of other lands, were amazing. The Isle of Wight, with its fine wheat crops, pastures stocked with Alderneys, and downs bearing vast flocks of sheep, grew seven times more than its inhabitants consumed. At Milton in the Vale of Pewsey, where three thousand five hundred acres produced annually three thousand quarters of wheat and six thousand of barley and the wool of seven thousand sheep, as well as eggs, milk, and poultry, Cobbett reckoned that every labourer raised enough food to support from fifty to a hundred persons.

Necessity acted as a spur. A fast-rising population, which, through medical advances, had doubled in a century, and which for a generation had been cut off by war from foreign supplies, needed ever more grain, meat, and ale and was prepared to pay for it. Landlords and farmers, sowing root crops and clovers, liming, marling, and draining, carrying the plough and hurdled sheep to the hills, reclaiming moor and marsh, breeding ever fatter livestock, and pursuing husbandry as a high science, had obtained from the soil the utmost output of which it was capable. The productivity of Norfolk doubled in two decades, largely through the genius of one of its squires, Coke of Holkham, who, working in a smock-frock like a labourer, first taught himself to farm and then taught his tenants. The heaths to the west of London, the haunt from time immemorial of highwaymen, were turned into the finest market gardens. New methods were constantly being tried; horses superseded oxen in the plough, thrashing machines the flail, and drills broadcast sowing, turnips and swedes eliminated the bare fallow of the past and fed the livestock in winter. 'Everyone,' wrote a foreigner, 'has planted or is planting his thousands or millions of timber trees, has his flocks, talks of turnips, cloves, and lucerne, drains and enclosures.' Scott took greater pride in his compositions for manure than in his literary ones and boasted that his oaks would outlast his laurels.[1]

This wonderful performance was achieved by organic farming without injury to the capital of the soil. Its object was not to seize the maximum profit from sales against costs in the minimum time, but to secure over the years the highest possible increase from soil, plant, and beast. The goal was the productive fertility of the land rather than the immediate saleability of particular crops in relation to wage-costs: output per acre instead of output per wage-earner. The farming was multi-, never mono-, cultural, and much of the all-pervading plenty arose from by-products like the snow-white ducks of the Vale of Aylesbury. 'Whenever cows are kept, so must pigs,' wrote a country gentleman, 'or the profit of buttermilk and whey will be lost.' The beautiful thatched roofs of the cottages and barns were made from the combed straw left over by the threshers. When timber was cut, a temporary shed was erected round it so that every piece could be worked for the exact purpose for which it was suited, without leaving a splinter on the ground.[2]

*

1. Bewick, 8, 155; Clapham, I, 15–19; Lord Coleridge, 223–4; Cobbett, *Rural Rides*, I, 19–21, 24; Grote, I, 19–21, 24; Eland, 50, 64; Ernle, 190–223, 225; *Hamilton of Dalzell*, MS, 151–6; Howitt, 125; Lockhart, IV, 263–4; V, 133; Mitford, *Our Village*, 104–5; Newton, 185–8; *Paget Brothers*, 271–2; Simond, I, 181–182, 330–1, II; 75–6, 223, 291; Smart, 138–50; Wansey, 22.

2. See Bamford, II, 21, 260; Cobbett, *Rural Rides*, I, 49, 87–9, 108; II, 363–6; *Cranbourn Chase*, 47, 65–7; Daniel, VII, 36; Edlin; Eland, 97–101; Fowler, 241; Grote, 21; Howitt, 109–11; *Boy's Country Book*, 89–90; Lamb, VI, 480; Mitford, *Our Village*, 32; Newton, 184–5, 195; *Paget Brothers*, 180–1; Lady Shelley, I, 38; Simond, I, 13, 170–1, 195, 206, 209, 216, 239, 330–2; II, 54, 72, 75–6, 242, 245, 291; *Sea-Bathing Places*, 504.

All this abundance, though directed by landlords and farmers applying the knowledge gleaned from the great agricultural experiments of the past three generations, was founded on the plentiful labour of an hereditary race of husbandmen bred in the cumulative lore of centuries. In a single field in East Lothian a traveller counted forty-eight reapers; near Bury St Edmunds he saw ten ploughs turning at the same hedge. In haymaking time squads of labourers moved from tract to tract, leaving the fields cleared behind them, the mowers going before with their scythes, the haymakers following. There were gangs of boys to pull the charlock and keep the land clean, and women to pick stones, weed, reap, and glean. Few complained of their hours of labour or the aches they suffered for the enrichment of others and the support of their country: their heart was in the land they served, and their pride in their strength and skill.

These skilful, simple, and generous-hearted men, with the gaunt bony frames, slow gait, and stolid, patient eyes, followed husbandry in all its branches, including wood-cutting, hurdling, thatching, and sheep-shearing. They were more efficient than any machine, for their exactitude was based on a sensitive knowledge of nature learnt from childhood. Their industry was prodigious. They worked from first light till dusk. In a day a good dibbler would sow a bushel and a peck and a mower cover two acres. They wasted little or nothing; a reaper with his sickle would cut the ears of corn with so short a straw that scarcely a weed found its way into the sheaf. In their spare time – often only achieved after a walk of several miles home – they kept pigs and bees and cultivated their gardens, those long irregular slips with gooseberry bushes, neatly tended vegetables and flowers, which Cobbett thought distinguished England from the rest of the world; 'we have only to look at these gardens to know what sort of people English labourers are.'[1]

While their husbands and fathers toiled in the fields, the wives and children at home added their own contribution to England's wealth. They worked at the loom, made lace – particularly in Buckinghamshire and Nottinghamshire – buttons, string, netting, pack-thread,

1. Cobbert, *Rural Rides*, I, 81; *idem*, I, 61; Clapham, I, 199–201; Eland, 21, 70–1, 127–8; Grote, 22–3; Howitt, 107–18; *Boy's Country Book*, 83; Mitford, *Our Village*, 7–8, 14, 43, 65; Newton, 188; Simond, I, 181, 184; II, 86, 293.

and gloves, and plaited straw into a thousand useful and beautiful shapes.[1] In season they tramped into the woods or orchards to gather fuel, nuts, and fruit, or worked in gangs in the hay and harvest fields. In the pasture lands the unmarried women watched and milked cows, going out in traditional fashion with cans balanced on their heads and wooden milking-stools in their hands.[2] Their younger brothers, in patched round smocks, took service on the farms at eight or nine years of age, learning their fathers' lore of life and working as long as their elders. For all their hard usage they seemed healthy and happy – 'wild, nimble, gleesome beings,' as Bamford, looking back, remembered: the 'open, spirited, good-humoured race' of Mary Mitford's village, with brown and ruddy cheeks and merry eyes, always ready for a bird's nesting or a game of cricket, 'batting, bowling, and fielding as if for life' at the end of twelve or fourteen hours' field labour.[3] They grew up to be farmers' boys or 'chawbacons' – bucolic, round-faced, hardy – the 'clods' of whom the county regiments were made and who held the ridge at Waterloo. With their grey slouch hats, bright neck cloths and ribbons and proverbial pitchforks, they could be seen in the aggregate at the hiring fairs in the county towns or at the traditional farm feasts of harvest and sheep-shearing.

The farm labourer's work was supplemented by a host of rustic craftsmen. The drover with his lacquer-back curry-comb, the swearing carter, the shepherd with his dog and crook and eye watchful for tick, foot-rot or blow-fly, the wood-cutters, sawyers, hurdlers, spoke-choppers, faggoters, rake and ladder-makers of the forest lands, the village blacksmiths, saddlers, tailors, wheelwrights, masons, carpenters, glaziers, clockmakers, millwrights, carriers, reddlemen, shoemakers, and pedlars who kept the rustic economy self-sufficient, were

1. Bamford stumping the country in the summer of 1808 encountered in the fields north of Loughborough a company of young women with forks and rakes on their shoulders; the kind, merry creatures made a ring around him and danced, afterwards regaling him with brown bread and cheese and a draught of home-brewed ale.

2. In the north at Keswick the girl who served the town with milk rode a pony with two large barrels slung on either side. Newton, 184.

3. Witnesses as temperamentally diverse as Mary Mitford, William Howitt, Samuel Bamford, the handloom weaver, and Mrs Grote of East Burnham, the Radical's wife, paint the same picture from close personal observation in four different counties.

part of an army many times larger than Wellington's and without which his could neither have been recruited nor maintained. Many were craftsmen of exquisite quality, like Miss Mitford's humble neighbour, 'famed ten miles round and worthy all his fame,' whom few cabinet-makers, even in London, surpassed. They were the hard core of England, and her wealth rested on the fact that they were able and willing in their lifetime of unresting work to do so much in return for the food, clothing, shelter, and modest comfort which in all ages, whatever the nominal money-level of wages and prices, remains the reward of manual labour. The nation which employed them received for their keep a *per capita* return in skill and industry probably greater than that enjoyed by any other in history.

*

Outside their homely circle, yet auxiliary to it, were the independent *tirailleurs* of the industry – the vermin-catchers with their skin caps, gaiters, and leather bags, the samphire and herb-gatherers of the cliffs and moors, the twine-makers of the Derbyshire caves, the hurdle-makers of Cranborne Chase and the bodgers of the Chilterns, the dog-breakers and gamekeepers, understrappers and wild rovers who were all to be found labouring in their place and season. These, too, were masters of their crafts, like the rat-catcher in the *Romany Rye* who described his trade as the best in the world and the most diverting and one that was likely to last for ever.[1] So were the raggle-taggle gypsies – makers of saucepans and basket-weavers – encamped with their ponies and beautifully painted caravans in the dingles and grassy rides: *Can you*, ran their song,

> speak the Romany tongue?
> Can you make the fiddle ring?
> Can you poison a jolly hog
> And split the stick for the linen string?

[1] 'When you see the rats pouring out of their holes and running up my hands and arms, it's not after me they comes, but after the oils I carries about me they comes.' *Romany Rye*, 226–7. See also Cooper, 18–19; Daniel, I, 23; Harris, 1–2; Eland, 42, 65, 74–5, 127–8; Bamford, I, 33, 37, 71; Bewick, 10–11; Clapham, I, 66, 73, 169–70; *Cranbourn Chase*, 59–60, 65–7; Grote, 21–2; Howitt, 112; *Lavengro*, 13, 29, 240, 319–20; *Old Oak*, 3; Simond, I, 109; II, 103; Mitford, *Literary Life*, 177; *Our Village*, 10, 13, 89, 155; *Sea-Bathing Places*, 272.

A grade higher in the national economy were the yeomen – the men who worked and owned, whether by freehold or copyhold, their own land. They ranged from the great Norfolk yeoman, ninety years old and worth £90,000, whom Borrow remembered riding into Norwich in a white corduroy suit and snuff-coloured greatcoat, to the 'smock-frock farmer' who entertained the Romany Rye on a holding of two acres cultivated with four kinds of grain – wheat, barley, peas, and beans – and whose garden, pollinated by bees, was as full of scents as an orange grove. Such men knew how to keep themselves and their families self-sufficient, quartering their lands in husbandly rotation and manuring them from cow, mare, foal, sow, and poultry that filled their little yards, fortressed round by hayrick, beanstack, wheatrick, and orchard. They followed the plough and carted muck like labourers, while their wives handled the churn, pressed curd in cheese-pan, boiled whey, salted and turned cheese, fed calves, geese, turkeys, and fowls, and, seated on a stuffed sack, jogged weekly to market, bringing up their children in the process and starching flounces and shirt-frills for their richer neighbours. On such holdings the whole family worked without cessation but enjoyed liberty and a share of the good things they created.[1] They were most numerous in the unenclosed north, where the 'statesmen' of Westmorland and Wensleydale lived in grey mossy stone houses on the hillsides; 'to this day,' wrote Bewick, recalling them in old age, 'I can see their broad shoulders and their hardy sunburnt looks.' Historically speaking, the yeomen were fast declining, but in 1815 between a quarter and a fifth of England's farmlands was

1. '... The father, mother and children returning from the wheatfield, the little ones laden with bristling, close-tied bunches of wheat-ears, their own gleanings, or a bottle and a basket which had contained their frugal dinner, whilst the mother would carry her babe hushing and lulling it, and the father and her elder child trudged after with the cradle, all seeming weary and all happy.' *Our Village*, 73. Mary Mitford, though an educated woman, knew rustic life at first hand, for after her father's ruin she spent her life in a tiny cottage in a country parish. See also *idem*, 32, 70–1, 73, 86, 125–6; Ackerman, *Microcosm*, III, 73; Bamford, I, 22, 71, 206; II, 21; Bewick, 30–1, 40–1; Cobbett, I, 12, 50–1; Clapham, I, 33–4, 111, 113–14, 183–4; Fowler, I, 260; Grote, 9, 21–3; Howitt, 108–9, 124; Jekyll and Jones, 114; Larpent, III, 68; *Lavengro*, 120; Mitford, *Literary Life*, 199–201; Newton, 184; *Picturesque Representation*, Plate II; St John Priest, *General View of Agriculture of Buckingham* (1810); Simond, I, 338; Smith, I, 331; Woodward, 8.

still owned and cultivated by them. Their greatest contribution was the immense quantity of poultry, ducks, and geese they kept on the commons and marginal lands; Cobbett saw ten thousand on a single common between Chobham and Farnham. What they did not eat themselves they sold to feed the nearest town, setting up their standings of butter, eggs, poultry, and vegetables in the market place. Like their neighbours, the cottage labourers, they also kept pigs fed on household waste and surplus milk products. Theirs, measured by England's needs, was the truest economy.

With the agricultural changes which were uprooting them, the yeomen were yielding to the large tenant-farmers who paid the rents that supported the aristocratic splendour and display of the English capital and country-houses. Some of these farmed a thousand or more acres, employed sixty or seventy labourers, and kept hunters and banking accounts – a thing almost unknown on the Continent. They laid out lawns and shrubbed gardens before their substantial farmhouses and had their daughters taught the piano. They would sometimes pay more for a prize-bull or blood-stallion than their fathers had handled in a year. Such a one was Thomas Bates of Halton, later of Kirklevington, who laid the foundation of his herd of shorthorns in 1810 with a cow bought for 185 guineas. To their landlords, though not always to their labourers, they seemed fine fellows 'who talked of beef and ate pudding and drank like true-born Britons.' Ruddy and broad of beam, in their blue tailcoats, Kersey small-clothes, top boots, and waistcoats of crimson or yellow swansdown, they represented the very substance of the England of their time; John Bull himself in his hour of thriving. 'Everything prospers with him,' wrote Mary Mitford, 'money drifts about him like snow. ... There is a sturdy squareness of face and figure and a good-humoured obstinacy, a civil importance. He never boasts of his wealth or gives himself undue airs; but nobody can meet him at market or vestry without finding him the richest man there.' The same observer drew the greatest farmer of them all, as she remembered him in the closing years of the war at his massive red house at Botley by Bursledon River. 'I never saw,' she wrote, 'hospitality more genuine. ... There was not the slightest attempt at finery or display of gentility, and everything was in accordance with the largest idea of an English yeoman of the old time. They called it a farmhouse and ... everything was excellent, everything abundant – all served with the greatest nicety by trim waiting damsels.'[1] The garden was full of wonderful wall-fruit, Indian corn, Caroline beans, and water-melons, and glowing in the autumn sun with pyramids of hollyhocks and masses of China-asters, cloves, mignonettes, and geranium. Over all towered Cobbett himself, tall, stout, sunburnt, with his good-humoured face and never-tiring activity, rising at dawn to mow the lawn with a giant's sweep and rewarding the first of his children downstairs and at work in farm or garden with the coveted title of Lark of the Day and the privilege of making his mother's nosegay.

*

In one of his outbursts against the social changes that were destroying the England of his youth Cobbett declared that, though no theologian, he loved any religion that gave men plenty to eat and drink. In this he spoke for his country. The English ate as though eating were an act of grace; the very sick were prescribed beefsteaks and port. They ate more than any people in the world, because they grew more. A Hampshire farmer at his wedding dinner fed his guests from his own land on beef, fowls, a gammon of bacon and a sucking pig, a green goose, river-fish, plum pudding, apple-pie, cheese-cakes, custards, home-brewed beer, home-made wine, and syllabub. From the wholemeal bread baked at home according to some immemorial family recipe[2] to the oysters which the seamen of the Ratcliffe Highway ate with such relish on their holidays, the English enjoyed the best of everything. Their seas afforded harvests as rich as their fields; the submarine plants round their shores sustained the world's finest eating fish, and cross-Channel passengers, wind-bound off the Kentish coast, would borrow lines from the captain and fill their baskets with whiting, mackerel, and gurnet.

England's fat cattle were among the wonders of the age. On feast days the roast beef of Old England was eaten with musical honours,

1. Mitford, *Literary Life*, 199–201. See also Howitt, 87–106.
2. Walter Scott always insisted on a brown loaf made and cut according to his neighbour Mrs Shortrede's recipe for making yeast, baking and cutting bread; a specially designed bread-barrel and knife were kept at Abbotsford for the purpose. Lockhart, IV, 194, 242.

and legislators rounded off debates with beefsteaks broiled over a clear, strong fire and served hot, juicy, and tender. Borrow thought that nothing in nature surpassed a leg of Welsh mutton, 'rich but delicate, replete with juices derived from the aromatic herbs of the noble Berwyn and cooked to a turn.' Yet in other cuts the mutton of many parts of England excelled it. The verdure that raised such meat produced also the butter and cheeses, the delicious draughts from the can which the Manchester handloom weavers bought on Sunday rambles from their loves, the milkmaids of Hoolswood and Gerrard-hey, the curds and clotted cream which Mother Hundrell, the Devonshire milk-woman, gave little Thomas Cooper and of which he used to dream in hungrier years. 'Then we went to the dairy,' wrote a young Englishwoman, 'so fresh and cool and clean – glittering with cleanliness, overflowing with creamy riches! And there I had the greatest enjoyment of my whole day, the printing with my own hands a pat of butter.'[1]

Every part of the island had its peculiar delicacies: Lincolnshire acelet and collared eel, Norfolk dumpling, Oxford John, Dee salmon, Pegwell Bay shrimps, Solomon Gundy, Banbury cake, Mansfield gooseberry pie, Isle of Wight crabs, and the cheeses – Stilton, and Cheddar, Cheshire, Double Gloucester, Blue Vinney, Lancashire Leigh, York, Colwick, Wensleydale – which were among England's regional glories. There seemed so much to eat that many found it hard to stop eating. A Yorkshire squire at a single sitting absorbed a plateful of haddock, another of veal, two of tongue, three of mutton, two of roast pig, a wing of duck, and half the tail of a lobster. It was not surprising that bulging veins, mottled noses and what was politely termed a full habit were common among the English upper and middle classes. Statesmen, judges, merchants, poets, all engaged in the national vice of stuffing; when Coleridge dined with a rich friend in the victory summer of 1814, it was on turbot, lobster sauce, boiled fowls, turtle, ham, a quarter of lamb and cauliflowers, ducks, green peas, a gooseberry and currant pie, a soft pudding, grapes, pineapples, strawberries,

1. Mary Mitford, *Literary Life*, 116–19. See *Our Village*, 154; Bamford, I, 109, 143, 154, 168, 188, 217; Borrow, *Wild Wales*, 47; Cobbett, *Cottage Economy*, 98; Cooper, 5; Eland, 12, 23; Fowler, I, 251; Howitt, 91–6; Lucas, I, 35; Simond, II, 164; Osbaldeston, 30; Raumer, III, 142–3.

cherries, champagne, burgundy, and madeira. Charles Lamb, celebrating the glories of roast pig, was writing for a ready public. Even divines shared the ruling passion; Dr Paley, author of the *Evidences*, always ate everything on the table and finished with a raid on the side dishes which he called skirmishing.[1]

What there was on the table is shown by contemporary menus. Spiced mulligatawny and turtle soup, salmon and turbot set in smelts, saddle of mutton and roast beef, boiled fowls, tongue and ham followed one another at dinner parties with splendid, indigestible monotony. When the Reverend Benjamin Newton stayed with his wife and daughter at a Cockermouth inn, they sat down with twenty-two other guests to dine on a trout, a salmon, a pair of soles, a fillet of veal, a ham, two boiled fowls, a round of beef, a loin of mutton, pies, puddings, gooseberries, currants, and cherries. For supper they had roast rabbits, a round of cold beef, shrimps – a local speciality – potatoes and 'etceteras', and for breakfast meat and eggs. The inclusive charge was four shillings a head a day. 'My wife and Anne ate ravenously,' the parson noted, adding that, while so long as they were moving such liberties did no harm, now that they were stationary the salmon, gooseberries, and currant-and-apple pies were beginning to tell.[2]

After the salads and cheeses the servants set on the table, with oranges and nuts, the brandy-primed sherries, ports, marsalas, and madeiras in which Englishmen delighted. Except in Scotland and the exotic little world of the higher aristocracy, which remained gallicized even during the war, clarets were little drunk by men; such thin, washy stuff was thought unworthy of gentlemen of bottom, at least until the port was finished. By that time there were better things to crown a festive evening: broiled bones and a bowl of punch or 'Bishop', that noble concoction of steaming port and roasted lemons so loved of the higher Anglican clergy. Or, if it was Scotland, there would be a salver of silver quaighs brimful of Glenlivet. Those who

1. He was described by a friend as 'a great sensualist in eating.' Farington, VIII, 180. See *idem*, II, 194; VII, 185; Bamford, II, 330; Brownlow, 125; Coleridge, *Unpublished Letters*, II, 122; *English Spy*, II, 98; Gronow, I, 217–18; Jekyll and Jones, 109; Leigh Hunt, II, 65; Mytton, 18–19; Newton, 122–3; Simond, I, 8, 22, 284; II, 35, 242.

2. Newton, 188–91; Fowler, 222–4. 'Good apple pies are a considerable part of our domestic happiness,' wrote Jane Austen. Austen, II, 424–5.

survived would top up, before retiring, with a night-cap of hot brown brandy or a glass of Hollands gin with a lump of sugar in it.[1]

*

The poor, of course, did not fare like this. In days when international trade was confined mainly to goods of small bulk, the price of grain fluctuated widely with the season. Though England was normally better off in this respect than any other country, the prolonged closure of Europe's ports hit her hard. There were times during the blockade when, under her dazzling appearances of wealth, she had faced famine and the shadow of social collapse. Five times during the war, with the Baltic shut to her ships, the harvest had failed. Though the rich and middle classes suffered little, those who lived largely on bread had been reduced almost to starvation. 'For two seasons,' wrote a poor dyer, 'the corn was spoiled in the fields with wet, and when the winter came we would scoop out the middle of the soft distasteful loaf; and to eat it brought on sickness.'[2] Such seasons had fallen with particular severity on the manufacturing districts where the workers, divorced from the land, were dependent on shop prices and where, at the height of the Continental blockade, there had appeared a new phenomenon, mass-unemployment, which, sweeping the young manufacturing districts of the North and Midlands like a pestilence, temporarily deprived whole populations – producing for export instead of subsistence – of the wherewithal to buy. Scarcity prices for grain, while benefiting the landlord and farmer, hit, with what seemed a monstrous injustice, the landless labourer in the newly enclosed villages of the east Midlands. For having forfeited his ancient copyhold or manorial rights, he had lost with them the grain, grazing, and firewood which had enabled him, regardless of price and wage levels, to provide his own milk, eggs, poultry, and cooking fuel. In time of shortage he was now reduced to living on baker's bread, occasional cheese, and weak tea.

Such times, however, had been the exception, not the rule, and had lasted only a season. If the population had doubled, the agricultural improvements of the past sixty years enabled the soil to support twice

1. Ashton, I, 331–3; *Creevey Papers*, II, 92–3; *English Spy*, I, 134; II, 233; Farington, VIII, 104; Fowler, 221; Gronow, II, 208–10; Letts, 206; Lockhart, I, 89; IV, 167; Nevill, 41; *Romany Rye*, 10; Simond, I, 46–7; II, 164.
2. Cooper, 26.

as many mouths as before. The war which quickened the threat of famine had also brought new markets and means of livelihood; after the Baltic had been reopened by Nelson's victory at Copenhagen, and again in 1812, a period of widespread prosperity and full employment ensued. At the time of their victory over Napoleon the British did not look like a people used to going hungry. The very bitterness of their resentment when they did so implied that, unlike the poor of other lands, they regarded it as something out of the course of nature. The peasants in the south, it is true, tended to be rather small and pallid, suggesting to one foreign traveller that, for all their neat appearance, they were better dressed than fed. But in the north they were more often giants, with stiff bony frames and rugged majestic features, like 'the fearless, sword-heaving English dragoon, engrafted on the simple, incredulous, ineradicable rusticity of the old Lancashire moorlander' whom Bamford remembered keeping the gate of the Manchester infirmary. And many of the London labourers – draymen, coal-heavers, bargees – were huge fellows with massive shoulders and ruddy faces, the kind of Englishmen who figured in the patriotic cartoons belabouring whole packs of starveling Frenchmen. There was about the race an unmistakable air of health and good living; an Italian lady was amazed by the beauty of the adventuresses in the theatres. The country lasses whom Simond saw as he travelled through Lancashire had rosy cheeks, cherry-lips, fine shapes, and arms red as apples. The carpenter's daughter in *Our Village* was 'of square, sturdy, upright form with the finest limbs in the world, a complexion purely English, a round, laughing face, sunburnt and rosy, large, merry, blue eyes, curling brown hair, and a wonderful play of countenance.'[1]

Even in the worst times of the war the dietary of the English had never fallen to the dreadful level of many parts of Europe where periodically starvation and typhus took toll of thousands. Frederic Eden, in his survey of the condition of the poor made during the famine of 1795 and 1796, analysed the budget of a Leicester wool-comber with two children, who, out of an income of £47 a year, made

1. Mitford, *Our Village*, 76, 82, 126. 'Oh! how I admire the Devonshire girls of about fifteen!' wrote Keats. There was one at the inn-door, holding a quartern of brandy; the very thought of her kept me warm a whole stage.' See also Bewick, 104; Campbell, II, 270–1; Letts, 211–12; Simond, I, 3; II, 143; Green, *Stendhal*, 128.

up of his own and his wife's and elder son's earnings and an £11 grant from the Poor Law guardians, was able to buy weekly ten pounds of butcher's meat, two pounds of butter, three and a half of cheese, and about nineteen pints of milk, as well as potatoes, vegetables, tea, sugar, and beer. He was not even a particularly industrious man, for he was said to spend several days every month in the alehouse lamenting the hardness of the times.[1] Another case instanced by Eden was that of a Manchester dyer who only earned, with his wife's help, £42 p.a., yet bought five pounds of meat weekly. Even in the workhouses meat usually figured on the dietary three or four days a week. When six Lancashire weavers were consigned by the Home Office to the Cold Bath Fields prison on a charge of treason, they were allowed between them for breakfast six pound-loaves of bread, two pounds of butter, two of sugar, and one of tea, for dinner a quarter of pork with vegetables, potatoes, and a pot of porter a-piece, and for supper cold meat and tea. On another day they were given a leg of mutton weighing thirteen and a half pounds.

By and large, as the population increased, the feeding standards of the poor were declining. It was probably no longer true, as Defoe had claimed a century before, that the English labourer ate and drank three times more than any foreigner. In counties like Kent, where before the war farm-workers had enjoyed meat almost daily, there had been a big falling-off, but they were still better off than Continental peasants who lived part of the year on roots.[2] Even after enclosure many cottagers still contrived, so long as the war lasted, to keep a pig; ham and eggs and 'a bit of frizzle' figure with cheering frequency in Bamford's account of his early days of poverty. William Howitt in his youth once saw bacon ten inches thick on a farm-servant's breakfast flanked by a peck of boiled beans and a brown loaf the size of a beehive.[3] Even in the enclosed villages, where wholemeal bread, cheese, and ale had come to form the landless labourer's main dietary, there was in normal times

1. Eden, 228–9.
2. Gronow of the Guards, comparing French soldiers with British, noted that the broth on which the latter campaigned would never do for the former, who required meat twice a day. Gronow, II, 299.
3. Howitt, 115–16. See Bamford, I, 157; Clapham, I, 118, 316–17; De Selincourt, II, 878; Lord Coleridge, 233–4; Eden, passim; Simond, I, 256; II, 224; Woodward, 9.

as much of all three as he could eat or carry with him into the fields. Many country folk still baked and brewed at home; the germ remained in the wheat, and the oven, like the porch and tank, was part of the peasant's birthright. So were the ale brewed in the copper, the mead, sweet and mellow but strong as brandy, made from home-raised honey, the cowslip and other rustic wines distilled from traditional recipes and drunk on special occasions. The old skills and habits were dying out with enclosure, but large numbers of country workers still quenched their thirst on untaxed ale of their own making. And what they bought in the alehouse, if not always wholesome, was at least strong and cheap: an old Buckinghamshire labourer declared he didn't think nothing of no beer if it didn't give him three falls for a shilling. A poor man could drink his skinful; Jack Birt, the Berkshire shepherd in *Our Village*, had a pot of double X placed before his sheepdog, Watch, every evening.[1]

In the north the poor man's food was usually much more varied. Its staples were oatmeal crowdie, riddle and girdle-cakes, thick porridge with buttermilk, pease-kail, dumpling, oaten jannocks and barley-bread, butter, treacle, and plentiful milk. Thomas Bewick, who grew up among the Northumbrian peasantry, reckoned that, though they lived almost entirely on oatmeal, barley cakes, broth, potatoes, and milk, they enjoyed better health than any men he knew. The Duke of Argyll recalled how as a boy he watched the farmhands eating their breakfast with spoons and mugs of horn out of a bowl of steaming porridge as big as a footbath. 'I went to rest betimes,' wrote Bamford, describing his early dietary, 'and rose clear-headed and with a strength and buoyancy of limb that mocked toil and weariness.' The same witness has left the picture of a Lancashire weaving family's meals at the beginning of the century: the brown earthenware dish on a low table, the breakfast of boiling water-porridge poured into it from the pan, the children standing round, each with his spoon, oaten-cake, and dish

1. Mitford, *Our Village*. Cobbett a decade later, when conditions had worsened, mentioned that the haymakers at Redbourne got two quarts a day of what they called strong beer and as much small beer as they could drink. *Rural Rides*, I, 81–2. See *idem*, 62; Austen, 27; Bamford, I, 60, 120–1, 129–30, 152, 208, 217; II, 212, 279; Bewick, 73; Clapham, I, 170–1; Cobbett, *Rural Rides*, I, 62–3, 82; Eden, 107; Fowler, I, 25, 251; *Old Oak*, 36; *Romany Rye*, 123; Howitt, 115–16; Lockhart, IV, 194, 242; Grote, 21.

of milk, the fatherly blessing before the eager, silent feast; the dinners of crisp-crusted potato pie, dumpling, meat-broth or butcher's meat taken in the same patriarchal fashion, the meat apportioned to each child on a piece of oatcake, the potatoes poured into the central dish from which all helped themselves until it was empty, after which the children stole out to their play munching the remnants of meat and cake. And all the while not a word was spoken.[1]

Some idea of the London workers' dietary can be seen from the capital's feeding statistics. In 1807, London, with a population of just over a million, consumed, on its market returns alone, 110,000 bullocks, 776,000 sheep and lambs, 210,000 calves, 300,000 pigs, 700,000 quarters of wheat, 16,600,000 pounds of butter, and 21,000,000 pounds of cheese. It also ate the fruit and vegetables of 14,000 acres of intensively cultivated market-garden land fertilized by dung from the London streets. In the same period it consumed 1,113,500 barrels of ale and porter, each containing 36 gallons, as well as 11,146,782 gallons of spirits. The division of this great quantity of food was left to the laws of supply and demand, but only a small proportion of it can have been consumed by the well-to-do. Most of it must have found its way into working-class homes.[2] One recalls the young Dickens's account of the meals of the Thames-side coal-heavers in the little, rickety taverns of Scotland Yard: 'Joints of a magnitude and puddings of a solidity which coal-heavers could appreciate,' washed down with huge draughts of Barclay's best entire and rounded off with 'large, white compositions of flour and dripping ornamented with pink stains giving rich promise of the fruit within.' Cobbett, using the measuring-rod of what was customary in his youth, reckoned that a working-class family of five – father, mother, baby, and two growing children – needed daily five

1. 'How different was this sententious and becoming manner at table from the one which now prevails around fashionable boards, where, if a person cannot or will not both gabble and gobble at the same time, he is looked upon as vulgar. Bamford, I, 98–9. See *idem*, I, 60, 94, 176, 223; Argyll, I, 58; Bewick, 37–8; Clapham, I, 118; Eden, 101–6; Howitt, 130; Sydney, II, 59.

2. Feltham, 37–41. A quarter of a century later the comparable figures, allowing for the great increase in population, were less favourable; Eden's figures of a decade earlier, so far as they are comparable, had been rather better. Eden, 107; Partington, 7. In other words, England was growing poorer in food-wealth as she gained in other and machine-made forms of wealth – a process she tried to check in the middle of the century by cheap imports from abroad.

pounds of bread, two pounds of bacon and one pound of mutton, and a gallon and a half of beer.[1]

*

About nearly everything English there seemed an air of what, to a foreigner, was an almost insulting opulence. The verminous tatters of the Continental peasantry had no part in this tidy countryside. Such distress as existed was tucked away out of sight. One had, wrote Simond, who spent two years towards the end of the war studying the country's institutions, to go out and seek it. In sixty miles between Ormskirk and Kendal the only signs of it he could see were a few itinerant paupers – a crippled old man or a widow with a swarm of barefooted children – tramping back to their place of settlement. The clothes of English working folk looked as if they had come straight from the manufactory. The cottage wives in their grey stuff gowns, woollen petticoats, and checked aprons lacked the wretched, ragged appearance that so shocked Dorothy Wordsworth in the Low Countries. Their menfolk did not go about in bare feet; except in the north, where the clogs on the cobbles was traditional music,[2] even wooden shoes were regarded as symbols of poverty and popery. What particularly struck one foreigner were the scarlet cloaks and black silk bonnets of the country women in the market towns. 'When a class, so inferior, is so well dressed, who can doubt,' he asked, 'of the prosperity and comfort of the nation to which it belongs?'

Jolly country squires, beautifully mounted, with huge boots, snowy shirt-frills, and wide overcoats with capacious pockets; red-faced merchants and farmers in low-crowned, broad-brimmed hats and tail-coats of blue, buff, or brown; clergymen and lawyers in black silk gowns; sailors in reefer jackets with mother-of-pearl buttons, straw hats, and loose white canvas trousers; mechanics in striped shirts and leather aprons; gamekeepers in green coats and gold-laced hats; drovers in dark green slops with tin vessels jangling at their sides to catch the ewes' 'milk of the plains'; farmers' wives and milkmaids wearing combs and earrings, all spoke of the diversity, wealth, and cohesion of

1. *Rural Rides*, II, 366.
2. The turnkey of a Lincoln gaol begged a pair of clogs from an imprisoned Lancashire weaver to add to his museum of prison curiosities. Bamford, II, 329.

English society. The field labourer's wear was a straw hat and a round smock frock – blue, tawny or olive-green, but usually white – worn over leggings, breeches, and doublet. Beautifully hemmed and embroidered, such smocks were perfectly adapted for out-of-door work; Jane Austen's mother used to wear a green one for gardening. Most Englishmen at their callings dressed in clothes of the stoutest quality; yeomen in fustian coats, corduroy breeches, and ribbed worsted stockings, brewers in quilted coats of immense thickness; fishermen in striped jerseys, grey aprons, leather leggings, top-boots, and fur-lined caps; firemen in horse-hide lined with leather, quilted with wool and strengthened with metal. A Lancashire handloom weaver's working garb was a green woollen waistcoat with a silk neckerchief, his wife's a white linen mob cap, a cotton bed-gown and petticoat, a striped calico apron, and black hose and shoes. A young girl went to the Wakes in a 'gown made wi' tucks and fleaunces, new shoon wi' ston op heels, new stokins wi' clocks, a tippet wi' frills o reawnd, manny a streng of necklaces, an a bonnit made by th' new mantymaker, the prattyist at ever wur seen, wi' a skyoy blue underside and pink ribbins.' Even servant maids sometimes wore silk on Sundays, when the lanes were full of girls showing off their new pumps, caps, and ribbons. And the vagrant gypsies with their scarlet cloaks and bright tents and caravans were as colourful as the cottage gardens. Mr Petulengro sported a smartly cut coat with half-crowns for buttons, a scarlet and black waistcoat sewn with guineas, stuff velveteen breeches and fur boots, a silver-knobbed riding whip, and a high Spanish hat.[1]

*

English houses impressed foreigners like their food and clothes. Every traveller noted the contrast between the beggars and rural hovels of the Continent and the neat Kentish and Sussex villages – 'our own land of fair and handsome faces, well-fed inhabitants, richly cultivated and enclosed fields,' as Harry Smith, returning from the wars, called it.

1. Ashton, II, 220–1; Bamford, I, 30, 71, 94, 107, 132, 211–12, 214; II, 56–7, 259, 333; Clapham, I, 315–17; Cobbett, I, 17, 43, 53, 81; De Selincourt, *Middle Years*, II, 883; Eden, 108–9; Hill, *Austen*, 177; Howitt, 108, 117, 184; *Lavengro*, 36, 319–20; Meidinger; Newton, 166; Pyne, *Costume of Great Britain* (1808); *Romany Rye*, 44; Lady Shelley, I, 287; Simond, I, 3, 14, 181–2, 184, 226, 256; II, 224, 226, 256, 297.

Village greens with shouting children and fat geese, white-washed cottages exquisitely grouped round church and manor-house, roses, honeysuckle, and jessamine festooned over porch and casement, gardens full of flowers and embowered in trees, gave travellers the impression they were in a land where even the poor throve. So did the clean-scrubbed floors of the cottage interiors, the gleaming oak and copper, the inns with their neat, sanded parlours and plentiful fare. 'This,' reported a French American, 'is the land of conveniences.' After more than a year travelling the country he found, at Barnsley, its first bad inn, and even this, he thought, would have been deemed excellent in France.[1]

In the south the countryman's cottage was generally of stone or brick, half-cast and timber, with a thatched roof and from three to four rooms. It was built of local materials blending with the landscape. The casements, Simond noted, instead of being left open to the weather or stuck up with rags, as on the Continent and in America, were leaded and glazed. In the far north and west, where much lower standards prevailed, single-room turf-cabins of the Continental type were common. Yet even these were usually white-washed and had casements with gardens and flowers, indicating, a traveller thought, a remarkable degree of ease and comfort among the labouring classes. Over most of the country the standard of visible building was so good that it was hard for foreigners who did not penetrate under the surface to conceive where the poor lived.[2] The interiors of the wayside cottages were furnished with elm and oak settles, tables and chairs, iron-hooped harvest bottles, pewter and stoneware utensils, shelves for cheeses,

1. Ashton, II, 220–1; Bamford, I, 43, 94, 99, 209–11, 214, 219; II, 68–9, 260, 331, 333; Bury, I, 242, 245, 263; II, 15; Clapham, I, 220; Cobbett, I, 43, 61, 81; Colchester, II, 502; Lord Coleridge, 223–4; Cooper, 16, 19–20; De Selincourt, II, 283, 883; Dino, 165; Eland, 12, 19; Farington, VII, 125; VIII, 197; Lady Holland, I, 105, 320; Howitt, 131, 202–3, *et passim*; W. Irving, *Sketch Book*; Jekyll and Jones, 51, 80, 98; *Lavengro*, 2, 330; Leigh Hunt, *Autobiography*, II, 153–4; Letts, 65, 211–12; Meidinger, I, 315–17; Mercer, I, 37; Mitford, *Our Village*, 7–9, 14, 16–18, 32, 43, 65, 70–1, 74–5; *Old Oak*, 57–68; *Romany Rye*, 65, 162–3, 175–8; Lady Shelley, I, 287; Simond, I, 2, 3, 10, 12–15, 16, 17, 217, 221–2, 225–6, 256, 297, 338, 354; II, 56, 62, 78, 86, 115, 146, 182, 201, 224, 228, 234–5, 245–6, 251–2, 283, 297; Smith, I, 108, 334–5.

2. Simond, II, 224. 'There are a few cottages to be seen, but the pots of geraniums inside the windows and roses outside seem to place them outside the reach

herbs and bunches of yarn, and on the walls brass bosses, horses' face-pieces, and coloured plumes and streamers. The homes of the better-to-do weavers on either side of the southern Pennines – daub and timber cottages with low wooden latches overhanging crystal streams or stone houses in rows on the hillsides, with open doors 'inviting the stranger to glance at their neatness, cleanliness and felicity' – usually had a room in front, a loom-shop behind, and two or three sleeping chambers above, or else a large loft where the family worked. At Leek the silk workers occupied airy, well-furnished apartments approached by stairs, with carpets and oil-cloths; Cobbett passing through Durham and Yorkshire noted the excellence of the miners' and cutlers' homes. 'There were a dozen good rush-bottomed chairs, the backs and rails bright with wax and rubbing,' wrote a weaver's apprentice of his master's house, 'a handsome clock in a mahogany case, a good chest of drawers, a mahogany corner-cupboard all well polished, besides tables, weather-glass, cornice and ornaments, and pictures illustrative of Joseph and his brethren.' At the time of the peace, Howitt recalled, the Derbyshire and Staffordshire workers had so much furniture in their houses that they could scarcely turn round.[1]

If English peasants and artisans could take pride in their dwellings, those socially above them had every cause to do so. 'A nice farmhouse in a dell sheltered from every wind,' was Cobbett's definition of human felicity. In Miss Mitford's village the vine-covered cottage of her neighbour, the retired lieutenant, looked 'the image of comfort and content'; so did the white dwelling of the mason opposite and the old farm at the end of the hamlet with its pointed roofs and clustered chimneys. Her own cottage was full of 'little odds and ends of places, pantries and what not, all angles and of a charming in-and-outness; a little bricked court before one half and a little flower-yard before

of common labourers; those of America with double pay and provisions at half-price have no such habitations, at least as to neatness and good repair.' Simond, II, 283. See *idem*, I, 12, 184, 221, 256; II, 228; Bamford, II, 33; *Romany Rye*, 162; Woodward, 9.

1. Bamford, II, 260. See *idem*, I, 43, 68, 94, 169, 193–4; II, 68–9, 259; *Ann. Reg.* 1816. Chron., 111; Clapham, 28–9, 32–3, 36–7; Daniel, I, 28–9, 31; Darvall, 31–2; Eland, 12, 19, 21–2; Howitt, 107, 132–3, 202–3; Jekyll and Jones, 51, 98, 100; Leslie, *Constable*, 84; *Old Oak*, 48; Simond, I, 256; II, 10, 95, 213, 256; Walker, *Costume of Yorkshire* (1814); Woodward, 32–3.

the other; the walls, old and weather-stained, covered with holly-hocks, roses, honeysuckles, and a great apricot tree, the closets full of contrivances,' and the little garden full of flowers. It seemed built, she said, to show in what small compass comfort could be packed.

Where the labourers' homes were neat and those of farmers snug, the houses of the gentry were princely. Almost every parish possessed at least one fine seat on which successive generations of skilled builders, craftsmen, and gardeners had been employed by a connoisseurship which scarcely ever lacked taste and a sense of proportion. In most, the impress was classical; the lore of the ancient world and Renaissance Italy had been ransacked by the land-owning classes and applied with innumerable insular and local variations, Palladian, Baroque, Rococo and, more lately Pompeian and Grecian principles, being blended with the national genius for diversity and the pastoral background of hill, grove, and stream. Others, like the cottages and farms at their gates, were relics of a less sophisticated and purely native culture. Such was the many-gabled black and white mansion of Lady Shelley's childhood with the family arms carved in stone over the door, or the old hall at Middleton built of plaster and framework, with its massive beams and black oak carvings and walls hung with matchlocks, swords, and trophies of the chase. Many of these older houses had fallen into decay or become farms like moated Parham in Suffolk and Boston Hall in the Fens, their rafters exposed, the gilding peeling off the galleries, the vast doors and chests turned to humble rustic purposes, cooking utensils hanging on nails which had held the swords of crusaders, and pigs and chickens ranging the uneven floors. Owing to a new craze for romantic antiquities those that were still lived in by their owners were surprisingly becoming objects of new interest; the house-party in *Mansfield Park* made an expedition to view the beauties of Sotherton, though its improving owner intended to up-root the avenue and modernize the gardens *à la Repton*.

The most impressive thing about England's country houses was their number. They ranged from palaces like Blenheim, Petworth, and Castle Howard to unassuming residences of pilastered stone, brick, or white stucco little bigger than the houses of the professional classes in the county towns, but set amid the common denominators of park, lawn, and drive. They were, above everything else, the distinguishing ornament of the landscape.[1] A gentleman stranded on the road could be sure of shelter under the roof of one of his own kind, where he would find, though with infinite variations, the same classical or Gothic architecture, the same fine furniture of mahogany, walnut, and rose-wood, the same oriental carpets and china and their English counter-parts, the same ancestral worthies in gilded frames flanked by master-pieces or pseudo-masterpieces from Italy and Holland, the same libraries of leather-bound books containing the solid culture of three centuries. And outside would be the cedars, the close-mown lawns, the flower-beds, conservatories and ice-houses, the vistas cunningly blending the artificial with the natural, lawns, parks, water merging into the landscape which they commanded and to which they belonged.

Such houses were maintained in flawless order. The Earl of Bridge-water at Ashridge employed five hundred men in his gardens, con-servatories, and workshops. Nothing was allowed to be slovenly; everything was planned to give the highest possible return in elegance and comfort. The gardens of Jane Austen's Northanger Abbey had countless walls, villages of hot-houses and potting-sheds, and a whole parish at work on them. Nor was the author drawing on her imagina-tion; when she and her mother visited cousins at Stoneleigh Abbey the house was so large that they were unable to find their way about. It had forty-five windows in front, several drawing-rooms, dining-rooms, parlours, galleries and staircases, all hung with velvets, brocades, and family portraits, twenty-six bed-chambers in the new part of the building and more in the old. 'Every part of the house and offices,' wrote Mrs Austen, 'is kept so clean that were you to cut your finger I do not think you could find a cobweb to wrap it up in. In the kitchen garden the quantity of small fruit exceeds anything you can form an idea of. This large family, with the assistance of a great many black-birds and thrushes, cannot prevent it from rotting on the trees. The ponds supply excellent fish, the park excellent venison; there is a great

1. Simond, I, 201, 220–1; II, 86, 100, 254; Washington Irving, *Sketch Book*. Wansey, travelling in France in 1814, counted only twenty country houses in a day's journey; in the same distance in England, he reckoned, he would have seen three hundred.

quantity of rabbits, pigeons, and all sorts of poultry. There is a delightful dairy where is made butter, good Warwickshire cheese, and cream. One manservant is called the baker and does nothing but brew and bake. The number of casks in the strong-beer cellar is beyond imagination.'[1]

Within these stately houses went on a life designed for enjoyment and content. It seemed a paradox that their inmates, as mirrored in their letters and contemporary novels, should have suffered the usual human lot of anxiety, envy, longing, and even, sometimes, of despair. Amid furniture 'in all the profusion and elegance of modern taste' and the masterpieces of an unbroken civilization, on lawns shaded by cedars of Lebanon and rolled and scythed till they resembled green lakes,[2] surrounded by avenues, temples, and parks cropped by deer, with terraces for sun and groves and fountains for shade, with walled gardens and hot-houses that poured out a never-ending flow of peaches, nectarines, grapes, melons, and pineapples, with coverts full of game, cellars of choice vintages, side-tables of gleaming mahogany groaning with game, hams, and cheese, these elegant, favoured creatures, with the stimulus and wherewithal for the cultivation of every social, aesthetic, and learned taste, still contrived on occasion to be bored and out of humour.

Yet, on the whole, as Squire Lambton reckoned a man could do on £40,000 a year, they managed to 'jog along'. Sitting at the pianoforte in some great sunlit room filled with buhl and ormolu, pier glasses and statues, elegantly *dérangé* sofa-tables from Gillow's fashionable warehouse, Sèvres china, breloques, and singing clocks, little Tom Moore would sigh out his enchanting melodies, now gay, now melancholy, to companies of dandy men and exquisitely dressed women. The gentlemen hunted, raced, shot, fished, read, played at billiards, cards, and *écarté*, looked after their estates, sat on the Bench, and rode, danced, and joined in charades with the ladies; the latter gossiped, sketched,

1. Hill, *Austen*, 163–5.
2. 'The mowing, or rather shaving of this smooth surface, is done once a week and even twice in warm rainy weather. ... The grass must be wet with dew or rain and the scythe very sharp; the blade is wide and set so obliquely on the handle as to lie very flat on the sod. The rollers are generally of cast iron, 18 or 20 inches in diameter and 2½ or 3 feet long, hollow and weigh about 500 lbs.; ... those drawn by a horse are three or four times heavier.' Simond, 1, 154–5.

made scrapbooks, embroidered stools, looked at engravings, walked in the gardens and inspected the greenhouses, played with their children in the nursery wings, devoured the novels of Walter Scott or Lady Morgan, constantly dressed and redressed, and displayed their elegant accomplishments to the gentlemen. 'Lady Asgill established herself in an attitude with Sir Thomas Graham at her feet,' wrote Lady Shelley; 'in the next room Lady Jane and Miss Russell at a harp and a pianoforte (both out of tune) played the Creation.' At Knowsley, where from June to November there were never less than forty guests, the princely host restricted the gentlemen to five brace of partridges apiece to ensure their return to drive with the ladies in the afternoon, a concourse of carriages and horses parading after luncheon for the purpose. At Woburn breakfast was served from ten o'clock onwards, every guest being furnished, under the supervision of the groom of the chambers, with a separate teapot at any hour he chose, before parading for the great liveried battues. Here after dinner the 'lively, easy young Duchess would collect her romping force of girls and young men' and, advancing through an enfilade of half a dozen rooms hung with Canalettos, pelt the gentlemen at their whist with cushions and oranges. And though during the London season the enchanted groves and flowers in the shires wasted their sweetness on the uninhabited air, their owners always returned to them in the end with delight. 'Tixhall is in radiant beauty,' wrote Harriet Leveson Gower, 'all over roses, rain, sunshine, and a new fireplace in the hall. I really do love it beyond expression.' 'After having been at a ball until three o'clock,' Lady Shelley concluded her journal of a metropolitan July, 'Shelley, Mr Jenkinson, and I drove down to Sutton in the barouche and at nine o'clock we mounted our horses and galloped over that delightful turf. ... As I breathed this pure air my jaded spirits were restored. I was exalted by a sense of happiness which only those who love and understand the beauties of nature can fully enjoy. ... From Sutton we rode across country to Maresfield which "in all its blueth and greeneth" reproached us for our absence. Thank God! I can leave the vanities of London without a sigh and return to my dear home with every good feeling unimpaired!' An English squire wintering in Rome in the first year of peace told a friend that he had seen nothing among its southern profusion equal to Cowesfield House. 'Never mind the climate – stay where you are; all their tinsel and show can never be put in comparison with the solids and substantials of England.'[1]

1. *Paget Brothers*, 271–2. See Mrs Arbuthnot, *Journal* (23rd Jan., 1822, *et passim*); Austen, II, 369–70; Bamford, II, 215; Broughton, I, 174; Byron, *Corr.*, I, 298; Lord Coleridge, 241; *Creevey Papers*, I, 296; Farington, VIII, 17, 141, 143, 301; Gronow, II, 91; Gore, 57; Hill, *Austen*, 163–7; Harriet Granville, I, 35, 128–130, 151–2, 197–9, 202–3, 219–20; Howitt, 1–28; *Lieven Letters*, 18–19; Lockhart, V, 337–9; Mitford *Literary Life*, 26; Newton, 24, 159–60, 199, 204; *Sea-Bathing Places*, 46, 501–2; Simond, I, 9, 73–4, 154–5, 198–9, 223; II, 74, 78, 85, 99, 119, 219, 254; Lady Shelley, II, 12–13.

CHAPTER 6

THE PEACEMAKERS

> The victories of mind
> Are won for all mankind;
> But war wastes what it wins,
> Ends worse than it begins,
> And is a game of woes
> Which nations also lose;
> Though tyrant tyrant kill
> The slayer liveth still.
>
> EBENEZER ELLIOTT

> *It would have been to be wished ... that at the end of so long a struggle the several Powers might have enjoyed some repose, without forming calculations that always augment the risks of war; but the tone and conduct of Russia have disappointed this hope and forced upon us fresh considerations.*
>
> CASTLEREAGH *to the Duke of Wellington,*
> 25 October, 1814

THE summer of 1814, that saw a rich and secure Britain celebrating the peace, saw Europe licking her scars. For twenty years the nations of Christendom had been trying to destroy one another, invading and ravaging, and jettisoning the system of exchange which had rendered their separate assets common to all. By doing so they had forced one another back towards poverty and barbarism, driving husbandmen, craftsmen, and miners from creative callings into those of war, and forcing the capital which employed them into the same destructive channels. A battalion of Frenchmen, Germans, Italians, and Poles captured at Cadiz were found to have been nearly all master craftsmen before they had been conscripted; men – many of them with a wonderful facility for languages – who when off duty, avoiding drunkenness and idleness, occupied themselves in every kind of skilled work, carving bone, plaiting hair-chains, repairing watches, and making busts.[1] In their crusade for an abstract brotherhood of man the French Revolutionary leaders had damaged the mechanism on which real brotherhood and civilization depended.

1. Leslie, 232–3

The devastation of the Continent, however, had not been wholesale. In the absence of machine power, man's capacity to destroy had been limited. He could fire no farther than the range of his cannon and muskets, could ravage only within his immediate reach, could travel no faster than his own legs or those of his horse. But wherever the warring armies had been they had left behind them a slime of ruin, privation, and disease. It stretched from Moscow to Antwerp, from Lisbon to Toulouse, from Leipzig to the heights of Montmartre. Outside Britain and the remote corners of Europe which her sea-power had protected there was scarcely a town of any size that had not seen the French cavalry enter, 'wiping,' in Campbell's phrase, 'their bloody hands on their horses' manes.' When Lady Burghersh in the month after Leipzig travelled from Berlin to Frankfort to join her husband at Allied headquarters, she passed through every sort of horror, the ground emitting a sickening stench while flocks of crows fed on corpses along the ditches. Behind the sacrifices and romance of war lay a dreary landscape of decay and sadness: of dead horses and shattered homes, churches converted into stables and hospitals, deserted bivouacs covered with ordure, ashes, rags, and broken crockery. The sick and wounded lay on heaps of straw in village streets or dragged their mangled limbs along the highways; the filthy and reeking inns were filled with troops, the doors and window-frames were torn from the houses, the furniture burnt or smashed.[1]

The final stage of the war had been the worst. While the French army was on its outward march of conquest, it had ravaged and passed on. When it was forced to halt or retreat, as happened successively in Portugal, Spain, Russia, Germany, and finally France itself, the Revolutionary principle of making war support war entailed a fearful devastation. On such occasions its only resource was its leader's laconic order, 'Cause the commissary to be shot and you will want for nothing!' In the country round Dresden the houses were pulled down in search of buried food, the coffins dug up for firewood, and the rifled fields raked over again and again for roots. A few weeks after the French retreat Cam Hobhouse counted forty villages in ruins.

Behind the armies were the hospitals. The garrison towns of Europe in the spring of 1814 were crowded with sick and wounded; at Metz

1. See Stanley, 159-61; Brownlow, 66-75; Bury, II, 41.

alone there were more than seventy thousand. Multitudes died in the streets, the air was poisoned, pestilence spread through the countryside. The horror of the hospitals, without sanitation, dressings, chloroform or antiseptics, continued long after victory. An English traveller that autumn, passing through Champagne, was summoned to a church where, among hundreds of mutilated Prussians with gangrenous wounds, he found a dying British soldier captured at St-Jean-de-Luz, seated on a wooden cot with his legs shattered and his head suspended from a sling on the wall. There in the dark, amid the groans and ghastly countenances of the dying, he took down, by the light of tapers held by black-robed nuns, his countryman's last messages.[1]

The extremes of horror and suffering were reached in the fortresses of eastern and central Europe where Napoleon, refusing to relinquish what he had won, had ordered his garrisons to resist to the last man. Here, while the *Grande Armée* of which they were the farthest foam was swept backwards, the ramparts were manned by the dying and the streets piled with corpses; in starving Dresden living skeletons were thrown with the dead into the Elbe. At Torgau typhus raged with such fury that, when the survivors surrendered, the victors dared not enter. At Mainz the disease slew more than five hundred a day. During the next three years it spread westward into every country of Europe, stopping only at the Atlantic edge among the hovels of Connemara.

The misery entailed defied description. The most terrible trait in Napoleon and the reckless, uprooted race of Revolutionary warriors with whom he scourged Europe, was their complete indifference to human life and suffering. They considered them no more than the watching fishwives of Saint-Antoine had done in front of the guillotine. When after losing his entire army in Russia Bonaparte was reminded by Metternich that his new levies were conscripted from the school-room, he shouted back in rage that a man who had grown up on the field of battle cared nothing for the lives of a million men.

The war had led to an immense displacement of human creatures. By introducing the principle of national service the Revolution had made every able-bodied male liable to fight against his will in any part

<hr/>

1. Stanley, 166–8. See *idem*, 174; J. B. A. Hapde, *Tableau des Hôpitaux pendant la dernière Campagne de Napoléon*, Paris, 1815; St Cyr, IV, 178; Odeleben, *Témoin Oculaire*, II, 278; *cit.* Alison, XII, 184–5.

of the earth. In the closing stages of the war, as Napoleon's demands for man-power grew, the whole of his empire became a prison, with guards, inspectors, informers, closed roads, and armed searches. The fields were left to women and old men. No youth was safe: not even those whose fathers had compounded a dozen times to avoid the levies. Larpent's story of the Peyrehorade attorney's eldest son who had been seized as a conscript, wounded at Leipzig, and never heard of again, was a universal one. So was the spectacle of droves of deserters with shaven heads and pale faces, their thumbs tied together and their legs in chains, clanking their way towards some distant fortress.

Now, in the summer of 1814, the mournful procession was flowing the other way. Even in England the roads to the southern ports were thronged with released prisoners begging from door to door.[1] Many of those now returning to their homes bore ineradicable marks of suffering. They were of every European race and calling, and most took back to their native place a tale of inhumanities suffered at the hands of strangers. Those who had the farthest to go were those who, at the conqueror's command, had marched the farthest; typhus-stricken cripples – the remnants of the *Grande Armée* – begging and plundering their way home from Russian prisons. An English clergyman, travelling through eastern France, saw thousands of them, with death-pale faces, matted beards, ragged uniforms, and bleeding feet. Their bandit-like expressions often belied their natures: among those who begged a ride on the back of his barouche was a poor trembling fellow wrapped in a bivouac cloak who turned out to be a Trappist monk. This man, dragged with his fellow novices to the wars, had fought at Lützen, lost an eye at Leipzig, and been taken prisoner by the Swedes. He was now limping back to his monastery at Freiburg.

*

Before the end the universal tide of destruction had lapped the walls of Paris itself. For months after the morning when the Russians stormed the city, the valley between Belleville and Montmartre stank with half-buried corpses. During the last weeks of the war nearly three-

1. 'All had their hunger satisfied,' wrote kindly Elizabeth Ham of Bland-ford, 'at least if they stopped a minute before the door.' Ham, 188. See also Haydon, 1, 243, 258; Stanley, 98–9.

quarters of a million Russians, Prussians, Austrians, Germans, Swedes, Britons, Spaniards, and Portuguese had invaded France. Nothing could have been loftier than the declarations of the Allied Sovereigns. In their immediate entourage the strictest discipline was maintained and neither civilian nor property was injured. But those who marched under their banners had bitter wrongs to avenge. The most vindictive, apart from the savage Spaniards whom Wellington was forced to hurry back to their country, were the Prussian regulars and the Russian irregulars. At Château Thierry the Prussians pillaged every house, violated the women, and put the men to the sword. Everywhere they lived riotously on the country. Their worst crimes usually took place not in the towns, where under the eye of their commanders they preserved an appearance of discipline, but in the villages where they left little standing but chimney-stacks. They deliberately destroyed and defiled everything, tore down embankments and historical monuments, and scattered the streets with torn bedding and broken glass. An Englishman, visiting a château in Prussian occupation, found the doors and windows wrenched from their frames, the furniture thrown in a heap in the courtyard, the tapestries and pictures riddled with bullets, the walls defaced with filth and crude inscriptions of hate, the floors ankle deep in fragments of porcelain, and the noble trees of the avenue felled.[1] Nor was such barbarism confined to the rank and file – those fearful hinds from the wind-swept eastern backlands with animal faces and matted hair who made even Napoleon shudder. In Paris a young Prussian officer of good family, quartered on an old French couple who had loaded him with kindness, before leaving smashed all the furniture in his room and tore the bedding to shreds. When asked the reason, he replied that he wished his hosts to see in one room what their son had done in every part of his father's Berlin home.

The Russians varied. Their troops were of three kinds: the *corps*

---

1. Mercer, II, 75–8, 82–6. 'Shouts and laughter resounded through the building. The hussars were busy completing the work of destruction; and as we passed the magnificent stairs leading up from the hall, we narrowly escaped being crushed under a huge mirror which these gentlemen at that very moment launched over the bannisters with loud cheers.' See Mercer, II, 43–4, 56–7, 84; Gronow, I, 93–4, 130–1, 201–3, 206–7; II, 18–19; *Two Duchesses*, 391; Brownlow, 159; Lady Shelley, I, 108, 160; Colchester, II, 551; Croker, I 61; Creevey, *Life and Times*, 93; Festing, 197–8; Simpson, 98–9, 100–1, 111, 159.

d'élite – magnificent, wasp–waisted giants to whom instantaneous obedience, enforced by a ferocious discipline, was second nature; Cossack irregulars whose business was to scour the countryside ahead of the armies; and the stolid peasant masses who could only stand still in the place assigned them and be killed. Many of their officers were men of education who spoke good French and spent their time in Paris admiring statues and pictures. 'So far from looking brutal,' an English visitor wrote, 'they seemed the most refined of all the foreign officers in Paris, with fair complexions, soft hair, and expressive features.' But the Russians whom the ordinary villager encountered were the Cossacks. They were not in the least interested in art, and cared only for drink, fighting, and trinkets – which had for them a childlike fascination – and, when drunk, women, whom they raped with a barbaric disregard of age. These savage horsemen from the East, with their uncouth beards and long lances, their filthy, ragged ponies, their belts full of pistols and stolen bijouterie, were for a year the terror of Europe. Better the French as enemies, the German peasants on their line of march used to say, than the Russians as friends. The most expressive phrase a Frenchman could use after the invasion was to say that his house had been *cossaqué*. In one Seine valley town Cossack officers, after blowing up a woman on a pile of gunpowder, tried to roast the housekeeper of the château in which they were billeted for refusing to bring girls to amuse them.[1] Yet at times these fearful barbarians could show a touching simplicity and kindness. A Frenchwoman who had had an old Cossack billeted in her house, told a traveller that he was '*un bon vieillard, un bon papa.*' To their British allies they were nearly always friendly: tapping them on the shoulders, showing off their weapons and declaring with grins of approbation: 'You Inglis, moi Russe, we brothers!'

Strangely enough, the most unpopular invaders were the Austrians, whose discipline was almost as good as that of the British. Unlike the British, however, they did not pay for what they consumed. They

1. See a remarkable first-hand account written by a French girl living at Montmirail in 1814, of her own and her friends' experiences, and published in the *Cornhill Magazine*, July, 1906. See also Stanley, 105, 120, 154–5, 158, 161–5, 179, 209, 218; Wansey, 22; Lord Coleridge, 226; Larpent, III, 84–5; Haydon, I, 249–50, 256–7; Londonderry, 289.

damaged neither man nor house, but wherever they went they established a regimen of dull, legalized robbery. The French never laughed at the Austrians as, for all their fears, they did at the Cossacks. The cold, ineradicable detestation felt by the conquered for these tall, heavily-built, solemn-looking troops in their ill-fitting white uniforms transcended reason. Perhaps it was due to their forester's habit of decking their caps with green boughs which the French, who had so often beaten them, took for symbols of triumph.[1]

Of all the armies that ravaged France none was more cruel and rapacious than its own. In defeat this terrible host had degenerated into a band of *condottieri*. It burnt, ravished, and plundered indiscriminately. On the march from the Seine to the Marne it even sacked the château of the Emperor's mother. From the Imperial Marshal to the humblest *moustache*, pillage had become an ineradicable habit. Almost every English traveller's account of France in the summer of 1814 contains expressions of horror at the ferocious appearance of Napoleon's veterans: the swarthy, whiskered sentries in the streets and theatres, the gangs of braggart officers who clattered into the restaurants puffing enormous cigars and salving their wounded vanity by picking quarrels, the fierce swordsmen of the Imperial Guard who, if contradicted, stamped and pirouetted on their heels with the velocity of dervishes.[2]

*

Such was the crucible from which the statesmen of Europe had to distil the alembic of peace. Their first problem was with the country that had caused all this misery, unrest, and insecurity. For a quarter of a century the great amorphous mass of Revolutionary France, its components formerly quiet peasants and industrious artisans, had spread like a destroying lava across the patina of civilization. The business of the peacemakers was to restore quiet to the Continent, and enable habits of peace and productive industry to return to the most civilized and fruitful part of the earth's surface. To do so it was essential to clip France's wings.

Yet those who had defeated Napoleon were just and moderate men.

1. Stanley, 180; Simpson, III; Lord Coleridge, 226–7; Mercer, 231–2.
2. Stanley, 107, 147–8, 153–4, 157, 164, 196, 287; Mercer, II, 38, 215; Simpson, 86–7, 156; Lady Shelley, I, 94; Danilewsky, 242–3; Kausler, 408–9; Koch, I, 419 423; Fain, 164–5; *cit.* Alison, XII, 609.

Like their dead prophet, Burke, they did not wish to indict a whole people for the crimes of their leaders nor to impose punishments which would provoke worse iniquities. In the peace treaty, which less than a month after Napoleon's abdication they signed with the new government of France, they contented themselves with reducing her to the historic frontiers she had enjoyed before her armies had begun their career of conquest. Asked only to renounce her lawless claims to the Low Countries, Switzerland, Germany, Italy, and Malta, she was still left with territories greater than those of Louis XIV. Through an unparalleled act of magnanimity on the part of Great Britain she was given back all but one of the overseas colonies won from her in the past eleven years.[1] Despite Prussian protests she was not even asked for an indemnity or made to disgorge the stolen art treasures with which she had filled her galleries.

This forbearance by the rulers of monarchial Europe was not popular with their subjects. Even the easy-going British found it hard at times to stomach. Ever since most of them could remember, mankind had been tormented by this warlike race whom they had come to regard as a set of bloody-minded, thieving monkeys. The saintly Wilberforce himself thought the French should be made to pay an indemnity and suffer a little of what they had inflicted on others. But, like all the victors, Britain was governed by rulers bred from birth to great affairs and answerable only to those with their own advantages of education and independent property. They had been trained to take the long view and could afford to do so. Aware from experience of the follies of the past, they carefully refrained from rousing the French, as a generation earlier, by threats to dismember their territory. Their prescription for peace was a regimen not of punishment but of quietude.

For this they turned to the old monarchy which the French had repudiated. Nothing could be more pacific than the Bourbons who during the war had been sheltering in England. Wellington complained that the only field in which they seemed to wish to appear was in a good house in London. When the duc d'Angoulême arrived in Bordeaux his first request was for a British guard to protect him from

1. Of all her many conquests from France since 1793 Britain retained only Tobago, St Lucia, and Mauritius, the first two already ceded by the Peace of Amiens.

his countrymen. Such princes were scarcely likely, the rulers of Britain reflected, to lead France in a new crusade for military glory.

The difficulty was to make them acceptable to a people who, after so much upheaval and glory, had almost forgotten their existence. The head of the family was a stout, gouty, and prematurely aged man, Louis-Stanislas-Xavier, the brother of the guillotined Louis XVI. His ruling passion was gastronomy, of which he was almost as fine a connoisseur as Napoleon of war. It was his lament – though a needless one – that its practice had died with the Revolution, his pride that, amid the penury and shifts of exile, he had managed to keep it alive. His devotion to this civilized art had cost him the use of his legs: though still under sixty, he was so fat that he could not stand without swaying, while equitation, the traditional exercise of kings, had ceased to be possible for him except with the help of a crane. 'A perfect walking sore,' Wellington described him, 'not a part of his body sound; even his head let out a sort of humour.'[1] Under this enormous and feeble exterior, he concealed a kindly nature, a scholarly intelligence, much good humour, and a shrewd, cool judgement – virtues not unsuited to the rôle he was called upon to play. But as a symbol of loyalty for a warlike people, wedded to military glory, he lacked appeal. After *Napoléon le Grand*, a *Louis le Gros* was too much.

A few years earlier, the Comte de Lille, as he then styled himself, driven from his last refuge on the Continent, had seemed without a friend in the world. Then in 1811, after Wellington's expulsion of the French from Portugal, the Prince Regent, challenging the *parvenu* splendour of Erfurt with his own revivalist version of the *ancien régime*, had toasted him at a fête at Carlton House where more than two thousand hereditary princes and nobles sat down at tables ornamented with rivers bridged by jewelled pagodas. This symbolic breach with the policy of Pitt, who had always insisted that, in resisting Revolutionary aggression, Britain should support no government unacceptable to the French people, was partly inspired by the Regent's romantic wish to play the *grand seigneur* and pose as a patron of the legitimist conception. But it expressed also the growing conviction of Pitt's successors and of

1. Stanhope, 32. See Auckland, IV, 405; Nevill, 179–80; *Bonapartism*, 64; Havelock, 273; Greville, I, 179–80; Gronow, II, 38; Harriet Granville, I, 103; Wansey, 104; Lady Shelley, I, 54; Dudley, 255; Farington, VII, 243.

thinking Englishmen generally that there could be no peace while Napoleon remained on the French throne.

Yet, with their enemy controlling almost the entire Continent, anything more than a gesture would have been quixotic; whatever the Regent's chivalrous impulses, his Ministers were realists. The Comte de Lille and his suite of needy exiles withdrew for the next three years to a mansion in the Vale of Aylesbury where they lived a caricature of the vanished life of Versailles in a vast number of minute cubicles, erected to maintain the etiquette of court life. Here they shivered in the winter mists, hobnobbed with the local gentry, and consoled themselves with rumours.[1]

No one was more astonished than *Louis le Désiré*, as his more romantic supporters called him, when he learnt that Napoleon's Senate of wealthy profiteers and regicides had proclaimed him King. At the time of this apotheosis he was suffering from an attack of gout brought on by the consumption of a turkey stuffed with chestnuts. As soon as his legs permitted him to move he left

> *calm Hartwell's green abode,*
> *Apician table and Horatian ode*

on the first stage of his journey to his capital. After an uproarious yeoman welcome in Aylesbury market-place and a halt at the King's Arms, Berkhampstead, to pay his respects to his old wayside flirt, Polly Page, the landlord's daughter, he reached the Abercorn Arms at Stanmore just as Napoleon, bidding a histrionic farewell to the Eagles, began his ourney to Elba. Here the Prince Regent in full and florid wig, with postilions in white, was waiting to feast him with his chefs' choicest culinary. Then, with horse-trumpeters in gold lace and a troop of the Blues riding before and half the gentry of Middlesex behind, the stout royal pair drove together into the victorious British capital. Everyone in Hyde Park was wearing white cockades, the good-humoured Cockneys, as the disgusted Byron wrote, acclaiming Louis the Gouty as he wheeled into Piccadilly 'with all the pomp and rabblement of royalty.' At Grillon's Hotel in Albemarle Street he was lifted out of his coach, and, when he had recovered received his principal sympathizers, drag-

1. When Greville visited Hartwell in the summer of Salamanca he noted with a titter that after dinner every princess and duchess frugally tied up her napkin with a bit of ribbon and bore it away. See Auckland, IV, 418; Fowler, 107.

ging his vast body down the centre of a respectful avenue and sinking into a golden chair decorated with *fleurs de lys*. Fanny Burney, who was presented to him, was struck by the sweetness and dignity of his expression and the grateful way in which he signalled out the English before the French. He even made a little speech in which he declared that he owed his restoration to the throne of his ancestors solely to their victories.[1]

A fortnight later he entered his capital. The ceremony took so long that one spectator fell asleep in the middle of it. There was a great deal of embroidery and sheeting hung from the windows, the imperial eagles – now styled 'vile cuckoos' – were disguised in white silk cravats, and the streets were lined by the bourgeois National Guard. The cortège, which was led by the city fathers and a troop of young ladies in white ball-dresses strewing lilies, moved at a snail's pace and consisted mostly of returning *émigrés* in National Guard uniform. It was all a little marred by the unfeeling behaviour of a picket of Russian grenadiers who marched across the processional route changing guard, and by the sullen looks of Napoleon's veterans who presented arms with such ferocious emphasis that they almost caused a panic. After attending High Mass at Notre Dame, the King, bareheaded, drove past the spot on which his brother had been executed. In the courtyard of the Tuileries, where Napoleon had been wont to review his troops, he was laboriously lifted on to the saddle of a quiet horse from which he bowed – to the crowd – 'very gracefully for a personage of his size.' During the ceremony his niece, the Duchess of Angoulême, daughter of the murdered King, wept continuously.

For there was so much that this unexpected restoration could not restore. It could not restore the dead from the guillotine. It could not restore the estates of exiled nobles confiscated or sold for a song to land-hungry peasants. It could not efface the spectacle of traitors and regicides in high places. It had been negotiated under protection of foreign bayonets by the legal representatives of those who had murdered the King's predecessor. Its chief architect was Napoleon's Chancellor, the renegade bishop, Talleyrand-Périgord.

1. Ashton, I, 251–5; D'Arblay, III, 276–87; Fowler, 107–8; Havelock, 272–3; Moore, *Byron*, 248; Farington, VII, 240, 244; Nicolson, 106–7; *Creevey Papers*, I, 190; Berry, III, 11; Lady Shelley, I, 54; Gomm, 366.

It was a constitutional restoration on conditions – a return not to 1789 but to some elusive hour in 1791 when the responsible bourgeois leaders of reform and a humanitarian King were to have made a bloodless marriage between the old age and the new. This was not congenial to *émigrés*, who, having lost everything, had looked to the restoration of their properties and requital for their dead – satisfactions which such a compromise rendered impossible. 'This Senate of regicides is a bitter pass,' wrote one of them; 'if it was composed of honest people it might go down, but murderers and rogues are too much.' Still less was it palatable to those royalists, disciples of the great Chateaubriand, who in their imaginations had transmuted the sordid shifts and privations of exile into a glorious martyrdom and the dream of restoration into a second Redemption.

For the restoration was unreal. It was an attempt to restore a past no longer capable of restoration. After the *Marseillaise* there could be no going back to the *gavotte*. Elsewhere, now that the invader had been expelled, the embers of the eighteenth century could be fanned into new, if not enduring life. But in France the gulf between 1789 and 1814 was too wide. The pride and absurdity of the returning nobles could not be tolerated by a people who had proved the equality of birth in the bloodstained Paris streets and on a hundred battlefields. When Gaston de Montmorency declared that he would never marry in an age unworthy of Montmorencys, the French people merely laughed.[1] The great houses and salons of the Faubourg Saint-Germain were based on dying memories; the broad acres on which they had rested had been for a quarter of a century in the hands of a sturdy peasantry and could only be recovered by civil war. The glance of unutterable disdain cast by some old *Duchesse* of the Restoration upon the youthful belles of the Chaussée d'Antin or the widows of Napoleon's army of heroes, wrote Stendhal, was returned with amused contempt. It was an aristocracy, not of the living but of the grave. It could not even pay its way. Being needy, the returning *émigrés* were stingy. For a generation they had pinched in foreign lodgings; they went on doing so when they returned to the noble faubourg. A nation of materialists was not impressed.

1. The King's nephew, the duc de Berry, even spoke of Wellington as an upstart. *Dudley*, 290. Gronow, I, 111–12; II, 42–3, 286; Brownlow, 136; Festing, 196; Lord Coleridge, 253–4.

Nor had it much use for the restoration of religion. There were plenty of pious folk, especially among the elderly, to hang their houses with tapestry when the Host was carried through the sanded streets; in the remoter provinces there was even a revival of religious intolerance, and in the hot south a few Protestants were beaten up. But in most places the churches – some of them still bearing imperfectly effaced inscriptions of the Terror – were attended only by old women. The male population seemed to have grown indifferent to religion. The shops, after an attempt by the authorities to close them, continued open on Sundays; so far as the Sabbath was kept at all by the new generation of Frenchmen, it was merely as a holiday. When the King passed under the imperial frescoes of Austerlitz on his way to the Tuileries chapel, his tails upheld by Napoleon's time-serving Marshals and his broad stern and waist-band string exposed to the public gaze, the French people greeted the devout spectacle with a snicker. It was not the meek Galilean that they worshipped now.[1]

*

Many English folk, sallying across the Channel for the first time for eleven years, saw France in that summer of 1814. It was a strange sensation to land on a soil so long forbidden. Here were the voluble people the cartoonists had pictured; the little, bony, brigand-like soldiers in their ragged uniforms, patched breeches, and big cocked-hats; the screaming, chattering boatmen making more noise in five minutes than the crew of a British man-of-war in a year; the witch-like old fishwives, hook-nosed, snuffy, and wrinkled, with their short petticoats and wooden shoes – a species, Haydon thought, neither born of woman nor made for man, but adapted for no other purpose but to pull boats, drag wheelbarrows, and abuse Napoleon.

Much to English eyes seemed curiously old-fashioned, as though time had slipped back a generation. While in England social life had been forging ahead under the stimulus of an unparalleled individual energy, in so-called revolutionary France provincial society, dominated first by the Terror and then by a centralized military despotism, seemed to have stagnated. In contrast to the new Brighton with its

1. Mercer, II, 191, 232; Haydon, I, 269–72; Simpson, 160; *Marlay Letters*, 226–7; Wansey, 95–7; Alsop, 26; Stanley, 102, 139, 188; Lord Coleridge, 228; Farington, VIII, 206; De Selincourt, II, 902; Lady Shelley, I, 89.

elegant residences facing the ocean, its smart bathing-boxes, libraries, shops, assembly rooms, dashing tandems, and graceful terraces, Dieppe was an ancient, fishy, smelly, medieval town with its back to the sea and sewers flowing down its ditch-like streets. Visitors were assailed by packs of beggars with open sores and whining children who followed their carriages, throwing somersaults and screeching out what they regarded as acceptable anti-Bonapartist sentiments. The inns on the road were smelly hovels crawling with vermin, and even the grander establishments, though their furniture was gilded, had greasy floors, unswept hearths, and piles of horse-dung at the doors. There was little privacy and no sanitation, no basin-stands, no coffee, tea, or sugar. And though the main roads, straight as spears and lined with fruit-trees, had been improved out of recognition by Napoleon's military engineers, the means of private travel was antediluvian. Clumsy, ill-sprung *voitures* jolted over the *pavé* behind wretched cattle bestridden by dirty postilions cracking enormous whips, and the *diligences*, lumbering along like Noah's Arks at four miles an hour, took two days to reach the capital from Calais.

The countryside seemed to have been depopulated by the wars: one traveller calculated that there were twelve women working by the roadside to every man. In their high, white, conical, flapping bonnets, wooden shoes and scarlet petticoats these made a picturesque appearance, apt to be dispelled on a closer view by their wizened faces and moustaches. Their homes were mud hovels, and their methods of cultivating the interminable, hedgeless fields, with their horizons of straggling apple-trees, were by English notions primitive.[1]

As travellers approached Paris everything wore a deserted forlorn look. Compared with the elegant environs of London there was no bustle of trade, little to indicate the neighbourhood of a great city. Even the luxurious châteaux of the Napoleonic contractors were in ruins with shuttered windows and broken gates. The northern entrance was as sudden as it was dismal: a rough, wooden palisade to keep out

1. Haydon, I, 243–7, 250; Campbell, II, 246; Wansey, I, 5, 9, 21–4, 41–2, 108, 111, 114, 116; Bury, I, 242, 245–8, 263–4; Gronow, I, 90–1; II, 299; Broughton, I, 116–17; Harriet Granville, I, 60–1; Brownlow, 69; Dudley, 253; Jerningham, II, 54; Stanley, 100–4, 180; Larpent, II, 110; De Selincourt, II, 878; Lord Coleridge, 223–4; Mercer, II, 17–18, 22–3, 40, 204, 291–2, 302, 309, 328, 330, 334, 336; Simpson, 96–8, 138–9; Lady Shelley, I, 94, 118.

straggling Cossacks, a tall, ominous gateway guarded by soldiers, an idle knot of red-capped blackguards with enormous earrings glaring from a doorway, and then a labyrinth of high, crazy, crumbling, medieval houses, with pointed roofs and fantastic gables shutting out the sky. Down the centre of the narrow, villainously-paved roadways trickled streams of stinking water. Overhead ancient lanterns, slung from ropes, swayed in the wind.

In these dark streets, ankle-deep in mud, swarmed the fiery, excitable, braggart race which had conquered Europe. The babel of the crowds and the shaking of the carts was deafening. The men, with their tails dragging behind them, looked like monkeys: the women, ogling through their veils beneath gigantic casques of straw and flowers, were lappeted like Friesland hens. Nobody dressed for the filthy theatres: even the rich spat on the floor and used the points of their knives as toothpicks. A city of grimacing, posturing blackguards, it seemed to the English upper classes, in which no one had any sense of style except the little cocottes who, with neat ankles, twirling ruffles, and darting black eyes, minced among the filth and traffic as if they trod on needles.[1]

And from the foetid alleys and courtyards of the darker faubourgs – the terrible Quartier de Saint-Antoine, the PlaceRoyale, and the long blackguard suburbs of La Chapelle and Saint-Denis – fearful faces peered, recalling crimes which made respectable folk shudder. Here, recruited at a shilling a head, the guide would explain, the revolutionary mobs had poured forth from their abodes of darkness to fill the gutters with blood. It was clear from the glances cast at visitors that they were only awaiting a chance to repeat their exploits. The presence of foreign troops alone restrained them.[2]

Yet this 'bloody and ferocious capital', as Haydon called it, in which refinement and filth, murder and revolution, blasphemy and heroism had alternately reigned triumphant, was also one of idleness and pleasure. There seemed scarcely a counting-house in the place. Its chief

1. Haydon, I, 248, 251, 256–7, 270, 277; Wansey, 22, 24, 62, 93; Berry, III, 18; Stanley, 106, 109, 115; Simpson, 104–5, 127, 138–9. 173; Mercer, II, 17, 186, 227, 311; Campbell, II, 250–1, 257; Lord Coleridge, 229; Gronow, II, 140–3; Dudley, 255; Farington, VII, 283; Alison, XIII, 155; Lady Shelley, I, 104; Colchester, II, 54; Bland-Burgess, 340; Bury, II, 22.

2. Brownlow, 170; Gronow, II, 147–8; Mercer, II, 237; Campbell, II, 257.

industry, now that war and plunder had ceased, was amusement: a hectic, shameless gaiety, Britons thought it. The broad, tree-lined boulevards which encircled the old city were thronged with indolent people, sauntering about or sitting at open-air cafés watching fiddlers, mountebanks, and puppet-shows; the theatres, their boastful Napoleonic inscriptions painted over with *fleurs de lys*, played to packed houses; the piazzas of the Palais Royal rang with the odious propositions of brazen boys and meretricious ladies. It was not the Parisian home – a place were husbands and wives huddled together in nooks and corners to fly their separate ways at the first opportunity – wrote a horrified Scot, which was the heart of Parisian society,[1] but the restaurant. With his *piquante* sauces and *petits-plats*, his gilded mirrors, brilliant lights, and marble tables – so different from the smoky, wainscotted chop-houses of London – the *restaurateur* was the residuary legatee of the Revolution. There were gastronomic paradises like *Very's*, *Hardis*, and the *Quadron Bleu*; the *Café de Milles Colonnes*, where a magnificent, diamonded *Madame* in crimson velvet – reputed to have been a favourite of Bonaparte's – sat at a raised table among golden inkstands, flower-vases, and bells for summoning waiters; *Tortoni's* with its famous ices, where the great and fashionable supped and made love after the opera and where intending duellists could be seen breakfasting off cold *pâtés*, game, fish, broiled kidneys, iced champagne, and liqueurs; *Frascati's* and the *Jardin Turque*; the little *traiteurs* of the Palais Royal where at small spotlessly clothed tables one could dine for a few shillings on three or four dishes and a bottle of good Chablis or Chambertin; and that famous hostelry in the Rue Neuve des Petits Champs where the young Thackeray treated his love to *bouillabaisse*.

At the west end of Paris, close to the Seine, lay the great public buildings which Napoleon, extending the work of the Bourbon kings, had made the administrative centre of empire. These far surpassed anything to be seen in London. From this side the French capital presented an utterly different face: the noble bridge at Neuilly, the avenue to the Barrière de L'Étoile, the prospect from the summit across the Elysian

1. 'A French family has no notion of what we call a fireside,' Simpson, 112. See *idem*, 106–7, 111, 114, 135–6, 143–4, 156, 182; Stanley, 110, 141–2; Mercer, II, 136, 154, 216, 218–21, 222, 239, 256; Wansey, 21, 41–2, 46; Lamb, VI, 444; De Selincourt, *Middle Years*, 906; Farington, VIII, 197; Gronow, II, 283–4, 287–8; *Marlay Letters*, 265.

fields with the road descending through masses of foliage to the Tuileries in the hazy, dreamy distance. Emerging from the dark, cramped, turbulent streets of the city into this spacious over-world of vistas and buildings unstained by smoke, even the most stubborn John Bull could not help being impressed. Here was the venerable royal palace with its formal trees and gravel walks, the unstained banner of ancient France waving above it in the evening breeze, the Place de la Concorde and the Place du Carrousel, the pillar of victory in the Place Vendôme, the bronze Venetian horses riding above Napoleon's arch, 'the gilt chariot,' as Haydon with his poet's eye saw it, 'the Russian guard and the setting sun casting its glory over all.'

Here, everywhere, was the impress of Napoleon's personality: the huge marble bas-reliefs depicting his triumphs, the interminable bees, eagles, and laurelled cyphers, the orange trees drawn up in rows as on parade: the marks of all he had done to create an island of order and splendour in the midst of that dark, airless medieval jungle, and of all that he had meant to do when at last he wearied of war and had the time and labour to devote to the arts of peace. 'Ah, sir,' an old soldier exclaimed to an English tourist, 'the Emperor has done more fine things in ten years for the advantage of Paris than all our Sovereigns of a century past; had he reigned ten years longer he would have made Paris the finest city in the world.' The man whom a generation of Britons had come to regard as anti-Christ might have been a scourge and a tyrant, but at least he had been a tyrant of taste. It was a fine thing for a lover of elegance – and what English traveller in the year 1814 was not – to stand in Saint-Cloud, the Trianon, Fontainebleau, or the Élysée, those temples dedicated to genius and conquest, and see the imperial furniture of green and gold, the ostrich-feathered bed in which the great man had slept, the desk at which he wrote, all daubed with ink, the arm-chair in which he sat, though lacking the gashes which he was said to inflict on it in his fits of neurotic rage, the baths of white marble with cocks for hot and cold water and all their luxurious apparatus of washing.

But of all the evidences of Napoleon's glory, that which most impressed visitors was the palace of the Louvre where he had assembled paintings and sculptures such as had not been collected in one city since the days of Rome. It was something new, this gallery of stolen masterpieces that belong to a nation. Here, free as sunlight, the property of the public, were humanity's finest achievements. The idea made an irrestistible appeal to the English, even though its lawless origin embarrassed them. Instead of being hurried along, after soliciting for cards and bribing the butler, as in the private collections of England, one was allowed to dwell on any painting as long and as often as one pleased. It was there in the statuary hall that Mrs Siddons, on the arm of the poet Campbell, saw the Apollo Belvedere, his glowing marble unstained by time and the indignation in his countenance giving place to the assurance of victory. As she stood there gazing at it the whole gallery turned and stared at her: this noble Englishwoman in her sixtieth year, as perfect of feature, as poised, and as little touched by the years as the Grecian sculpture before her.[1]

But if the English admired the evidences of Napoleon's taste for art, they disliked intensely those of his love for war. The whole nation seemed to be vitiated by it; even the children wore cocked hats and strutted, drilled, and scowled. The Emperor's ambition to make the terms of man and soldier synonymous seemed to have succeeded. There was scarcely a driver of a *fiacre* or a waiter who had not served a campaign. There was scarcely a Frenchman, even among those who most reviled Napoleon, who did not regret his vanished military glory.

For the French were quite impenitent at the suffering they had caused. The only thing they regretted was that they had been defeated. Though they complained bitterly of the Allies' crimes, they dismissed their own with a shrug of the shoulders.[2] '*Après tout,*' they would remark of some blood-curdling horror, '*c'est le sort de la guerre!*' Their indifference to death was such that at Montmartre, where the Russians stormed their way into Paris over the bodies of the boys of the Military College, corpses were carefully preserved for sightseers, and houses,

1. Campbell, II, 261, 270–1; Haydon, I, 239, 243–4, 255, 262–6; *Marlay Letters*, 265; Wansey, 30, 33, 34, 50, 62; Stanley, 110, 113–14, 140, 148–9; Lord Coleridge, 221–2; Simpson, 118–24, 141, 146–52, 177–82; Mercer, II, 147.
2. 'No Tory ever believed more firmly in divine right,' wrote John William Ward, 'than the French believe in their right to plunder and insult all mankind without the smallest chance of retaliation.' *Dudley*, 289. See Brownlow, 80; Haydon, I, 258–9, 260, 296; Mercer, II, 175; Stanley, 106, 116–17, 140–1, 143, 157–8, 243; Simpson, 86, 134, 165; Wansey, 93; Campbell, II, 252–3; Granville, II, 512.

pitted with bullets, bore notices, '*Ici on voit la bataille pour deux sous!*'

Though they found much to admire, the English were disgusted at the cynicism of the French capital. All the Parisians seemed to care about was glory and pleasure. Now they had been deprived of the one, they thought of nothing but the other. On the night after the Allies' entry the theatres and public gardens were packed as though nothing had happened. The people regarded the *dénouement* of the bloody drama as a mere spectacle; instead of being chastened by it, they flocked into the streets to gape at their conquerors' uniforms. 'They appear,' wrote an onlooker, 'the same light, trifling, dancing people as ever; pleasure is still their idol, *vive la bagatelle* their motto.' Gambling was a universal relaxation; fagged out, slovenly in air and dress, both sexes crowded night after night into airless rooms where no sound was heard but the crack of the croupier's stick and the rattling of money. It shocked English visitors even more than the pornographic prints on the hotel walls.[1]

In some ways the country was wonderfully improved. The peasants, thrifty and industrious, were cultivating the holdings acquired from the sale of national lands; roads and bridges had been built; the law codified, and the foundations of an efficient, if over-centralized, administration laid. There was reason to hope, now that France had been freed from the drain of war-taxes and conscription, that material conditions would rapidly improve. But public morality had ceased, it seemed, to exist. It had been thrown into the basket with the heads of the priests and nobles. The Parisians were ready to betray or follow anyone or anything that suited their private interest. They would in one breath curse Napoleon for having led them to disaster, and in the next praise the crimes he had practised against their neighbours. Their only good seemed to be success.

For after two decades of centralized despotism and the suppression of independent opinion the people of the French capital, politically speaking, were without integrity. The faces of the men struck visitors as coarse and ferocious; those of their womenfolk in the restless boulevards as brazen. There seemed to be no gentlemen and, by English standards, no ladies; as Napoleon himself ungratefully observed, they

1. Harriet Granville, I, 67; Wansey, 101. See *idem*, 46, 100; Haydon, I, 251, 272; Simpson, 108, 125, 162–3; Mercer, II, 128, 144, 154, 216, 222.

were all rascals. 'Everyone appears intent,' wrote a visitor, 'on living what is called a life of pleasure ... splendour without taste and pride without dignity.' Self had become a religion; no one was prepared to play an uphill game or put himself in opposition to power except when it was falling. 'What have we to make us patriots?' a Frenchman asked; 'in England you have a Constitution to maintain under which you live securely and respectably, while we have nothing on which we can depend.' For a generation property in France had existed only by permission of the State, and conscience and conviction had been dangerous luxuries. The confiscation of noble and ecclesiastical lands, the abolition of primogeniture, the inflation under the Directory, the crushing taxation, had left only a tiny minority with any independence.[1]

So at least it seemed to Englishmen. The sense of despotism, Haydon wrote, preyed on the mind: in everything there was 'a look of gilded and bloody splendour, a tripping grace in the women and a ragged blackguardism in the men.' Life was regimented in a way undreamt of in England: the very cultivators' carts bore State-allocated numbers, while armed excisemen searched every wagon entering or leaving the capital. Napoleon's system of preventative tyranny had achieved its object: the restless, inquiring people who had made the Revolution were cowed. They did not even realize their own servility. 'Oh, no,' they would reply to those who commiserated with them on the ignorance in which the tyrant's Press had kept them, 'we had our Gazettes!'[2]

*

All this made British observers doubt the ability of the French to live quietly under a constitutional monarchy and parliamentary system. It was only a few months since a British Foreign Office official had reported that the Napoleonic government was so ruthlessly imposed and so efficiently centralized that it could never be destroyed. Now that it had suddenly collapsed, it was hard to see how the people could

1. Farington, VIII, 38. See Simpson, 85-7, 108, 115-16; Haydon, I, 256, 259-260; De Selincourt, II, 902; Stanley, 117, 243; Wansey, 93; Bury, II, 22; Harriet Granville, I, 64-5; Colchester, II, 554; Lady Shelley, I, 132; Neumann, 43.
2. Stanley, 105. 'The slavery of the Press had been so hideous a dream that they stared at our conversation as if awakening out of a dream.' Haydon. I, 259. See *idem*, 256-7, 276; Campbell, II, 246; Bury, I, 264; Mercer, II, 31, 263.

govern themselves without it. Their *Corps Législatif* was a joke; everyone wore uniform and members wishing to speak rushed to the rostrum like a charge of cavalry, shouting and pushing one another about while a gesticulating president vainly rang his bell for order. The nation had no more respect for it than it had for itself. 'Bah! Napoleon knew how to talk to such fellows,' a young officer told an inquirer. '"*Corps Législatif, je vous abolirai: sénateurs, garde à vous.*" That's the way!'[1]

For, having no independent local and national leaders, the French at the end of the Revolution and its wars were politically children. They obeyed only the rod. When Napoleon and his centralized despotism fell they were lost. They did not even attempt to defend their country against invasion. Those in authority transferred their allegiance *en bloc* to the new Government, though it was based on principles diametrically opposite to those to which they had so long adhered and sycophantically acclaimed. They were as sycophantic about the new. The higher placed they were, and the nearer the seat of power, the more so.

None were quicker to change than those who owed most to Napoleon. His marshals' titles and pensions had been guaranteed with the Restoration settlement. Now incongruously mingling with *émigré* dukes and marquises, they grouped themselves in their broad, red imperial ribbons around their new master, enjoying, as a lady from England wrote, their emoluments. They made him look, she thought, like Daniel in the lions' den. Except for the handsome Ney, with his fair curling hair, and Victor, who was admitted to have a gentlemanly appearance, they struck the English as an unprepossessing lot. The Duke of Dantzig squinted, Soult and Augereau were stout and vulgar, Davout had so cruel, cunning, and malevolent a face that he made an honest Hampshire squire feel sick. Though Masséna was conceded a kind of evil dignity and was said to be very gallant to the ladies, the plebeian faces of the rest were hard to distinguish from one another.[2]

It was symptomatic of the Bourbon genius for creating humiliating situations that of all Napoleon's lieutenants the King chose as Minister

1. Wansey, 30; Brownlow, 87; Stanley, 129-30; Simpson, 133-4.
2. 'In the character of almost all these French military leaders there are such blots and stains that one sickens at the thought of being of the same species.' Stanley, 196. See *idem*, 136-9; Wansey, 100; Brownlow, 97, 182; Lord Coleridge, 228; Granville, I, 516.

of War Dupont, the capitulator of Baylen. It was as though James II, recalled to the throne after England's defeat in a naval war, had sent Kirby and Wade to the Admiralty.

To the officers and men of the *Grande Armée*, trudging home in their thousands from captivity or relegated to half-pay to make way for white-feathered popinjays, the Bourbons and their hangers-on appeared a pack of traitors. Their looks showed what shift they would give them if their Emperor ever returned to lead them. '*Quinze, seize*,' the sullen veterans called out as their officers numbered the ranks, '*dix-sept, gros cochon, dix-neuf!*' Sent home to starve in their native villages, parade their wounds, and weave sagas of faded glories, they spread everywhere their contempt for the crowned *embusqué*. A British artillery officer, passing with his guns through a provincial town, tested the sincerity of the obsequious cries of '*Vive le Roi!*' by murmuring '*Vive l'Empéreur.*' Immediately men began to look at one another with sly, delighted expressions. '*Mais oui, monsieur*,' they cried, slapping their thighs, '*vive l'Empéreur, vive Napoléon!*'

Therefore, though royalist audiences called nightly in the Paris theatres for '*Vive Henri Quatre*,' '*La Belle Gabrielle*', and other Bourbon songs, few Englishmen who visited Paris in 1814 expected to see the Restoration last. King Louis might look an excellent man, as one of them wrote, very benevolent and soft, but he would never be able to control a people half monkey and half tiger. After a year or two of enforced quiet, they would be at their old tricks again.

*

Yet an unexpected influence was at work to tranquillize France. Few people liked Talleyrand, least of all those whom his treacherous feat of *legerdemain* had restored to the throne. Napoleon, whose Foreign Minister he had been, had once described him as filth in silk stockings. He was the most consistent crook of his age; a politician perfectly adapted to the prevailing moral climate of his country and a disordered Europe. He had been trained at St Sulpice – a priest of the *ancien régime*; in youth his epicurean self-indulgence while holding high church preferment had shocked even the amoral aristocracy in which he grew up. For a quarter of a century, through storm and terror, he had lived, survived, and triumphed by his wits. There were few crimes, including incest, of which he was not believed guilty. No one who saw his dirty, crafty, powdered face, with its half-closed eyes, villainous mouth, and slobbering, darting tongue, was left in any doubt as to the manner of man he was.

Yet he possessed an astonishing capacity for peaceful persuasion. Though with his club-foot and constant spitting and hawking he reminded some of an old, fuddled village schoolmaster, many of his countrywomen still found him irresistible. He had taken an exact measure of his fellow creatures. He had no wish to make them better or anything but what they were, nor did he attempt to impress them with his moral superiority. Instead, he addressed himself with unfailing tact and good humour to inducing them to do whatever should make him comfortable and secure. Being habitually idle, he relied on others for almost everything he did.

He had spent his youth in the most cultured society on earth, and his taste for pleasure and good living was exquisitely refined. He used to say that no one who had not lived before the Revolution had any idea how pleasant life could be. For all his coarse moral fibre, he was wholly civilized. Though he had contrived to live by democracy, he hated its drab social consequences. It followed that he wished, so far as was safe, to restore the life of privilege for his own enjoyment. As this was quite dissociated in his mind from any wish to ensure it for his class – for he was wholly without loyalty – he was able to do so while employing the revolutionary technique by which he had risen.

In this he served the future better than he knew or probably cared. After a quarter of a century in France that was *parvenu* and restless, he wished to spend his remaining years in one that, while still favouring the adroit and cunning, should enable them to enjoy their spoils in safety. He was the patron of the profiteer, the contractor, and the banker, of such aristocrats, old and new, as had made their peace with Power and wished to stabilize things at the highest possible level of good living: of all whose bread was well buttered and who, knowing that any further change must be for the worse, wished to keep things as they were. An artificial *ancien régime* of those who had been clever and sharp enough to survive the Terror and Napoleon was not likely to endure except on a broad bottom of popular prosperity. Talleyrand, therefore, made it his business to give it one.

His political aims were twofold. He sought to make France comfortable and prosperous and, by securing for its façade of legitimate monarchy an honoured and respectable place in Europe, to satisfy its wounded vanity. Though neither an orator nor an administrator – he was so indolent that he could scarcely pen a long letter or dispatch – he understood, like Wellington, what could be done with time. In his prescient patience he had outlasted Napoleon. He now set himself to outlast the legend of his conquests. By guaranteeing, by his presence near the throne, the Revolutionary gains of the new *bourgeoisie* and peasantry, he gave a reluctant France time to settle down and exploit those gains. The natural wealth of the country, its traditional civilization and the innate intelligence and capacity for enjoyment of its people, would in time, he saw, do the rest. They would turn to pleasure as flowers to the light.

For under the surface of the nerve-racked, turbulent France created by the Revolution was much that was gracious and instinct with new life. The frugal peasants toiling to improve their land, the industrious artificers in their neat clothes, the cheerful throngs of pleasure-seekers, oblivious of class or nationality, flocking to some *fête-champêtre* or gliding to music in painted barges along the tranquil rivers on summer holidays, were earnest of a happier future, if only the national mind could be deflected from thoughts of conquest. So were the puppet-theatres and the crowds, all bustle and loquacity, on the tree-lined boulevards, the delicate, elegant toys in the shop windows, the opera dancers with their skill and grace, the grisettes with their speaking eyes and tripping gaiety, the universal sweetness of address that marked the very gamins of the streets. 'Pardon, monsieur,' a beggar boy, rebuffed, cried with a bow to a Scottish visitor, 'une autre occasion!' For all their vices and blackguardism the French people were artists in living. Haydon, walking in the meadows near Magny, heard a violin and, on entering, found a party dancing in the cool of the summer evening with the grace inherent in their race. When a great mineralogist entered the lecture room at the Jardin des Plantes the entire audience rose to show its respect for learning.[1]

1. Haydon, I, 246–8, 249, 251, 260–1, 270, 277; Wansey, 12; De Selincourt, II, 902; Dudley, 255–6; Gronow, II, 299; Mercer, II, 30, 89, 128, 264; Simpson, 105, 107, 125, 143–4; Bury, I, 263–4; *Marlay Letters*, 265–6; Stanley, 99, 124–5. And see an interesting passage in Greville (Suppl.), I, 86–7.

By creating a moratorium on war and revolution Talleyrand gave such shoots the opportunity to grow. When a generation later another Napoleon seized the throne of France, the itch to conquer had gone out of her. The Grand Nation had become the land of the artist and academician, the peasant and the *bon-vivant*. By ceasing to be gigantic, in Talleyrand's words, she had grown great. It happened so gradually that no one realized it had happened at all; the French in 1870 still thought they were a conquering race. But when they left the theatre of Offenbach for the theatre of war, they found that it was not so. For all their valour they no longer enjoyed fighting.

In the international sphere Talleyrand's service to France was more spectacular. In diplomacy he had no equals. His country's conquerors were aristocrats by birth who had been belatedly made realists by experience: he himself had been both when most of them were in the schoolroom. He had dealt with them in the days of their collaboration; they had known him as their dreaded master's unjust steward who had done them favours on the sly and bid them say nothing. He could talk their language, whether of the *ancien régime* or the thieves' kitchen. His conversation, matching his furrowed, disillusioned face, was that of a cynic, but also a gentleman; he was without the professional wit's pedantry, yet every now and then could come out with some *mot* which was never forgotten. His genius lay in simplification and clarification: the Aladdin's lamp which brave men sometimes fashion for themselves in a revolutionary age.

It was Talleyrand who had prevailed upon the Czar to bring back the Bourbons and, in doing so, to grant France a liberal peace. Without his resource and address Castlereagh could not have persuaded the victorious war lords to agree to a restoration for which they had such scant sympathy and for which in France there seemed scarcely any support. But this limping renegade with his crooked face and body made the impressionable Alexander see that a Bourbon restoration was the way to tranquillize the country and that the only alternative was a Jacobin Republic. Anything in between, Talleyrand explained, would be an intrigue that could not last. Convinced by that beguiling tongue, the Czar abandoned his romantic projects of a Napoleonic Regency or of a new dynasty under his *protégé*, Bernadotte.

Having, as the restored King's Foreign Minister, negotiated a peace which left a vanquished France larger than in the days of the Grand Monarch, Talleyrand prepared to assert her right to a leading place in the councils of Europe. The objective he set himself was the destruction of the united front which Russia, Austria, Prussia, and Great Britain had formed at Chaumont. For unless he could dissolve this twenty-years league against France, her people, when they recovered from their defeat, were certain to challenge both it and the settlement it guaranteed. The old cycle of revolution and war would then begin again.

Since the enemy commanded the bigger battalions, Talleyrand formulated no detailed plan of campaign. Like Wellington under similar circumstances, he prepared to wait upon their mistakes and exploit them as they arose. His strength was that he knew exactly what he wanted and, representing a new Government, was not hampered by previous entanglements.

For those with whom he had to negotiate, though they had bound themselves to act together, had not freed themselves thereby from earlier commitments. These, since they conflicted, were bound to involve them in dispute. Russia, who had received Sweden's Finnish provinces as the price of earlier subservience to Napoleon, had in 1812 regained that country's goodwill by promising her Norway, the ancient fief of the pro-French King of Denmark. Britain, grateful for any ally, had underwritten this lamentable transaction. A year later Russia had secured Prussia's alliance by undertaking to restore to her territories as extensive as those she had enjoyed before Jena. Russia, Prussia, and Britain had acknowledged Austria's claim to the territories of the extinguished Venetian Republic and to suzerainty in Italy as compensation for her lost Belgian provinces. The Austrian Chancellor, Metternich, in return for an offer of military aid and in gratitude, it was rumoured, for the favours of his wife, Napoleon's sister, had secretly guaranteed to Joachim Murat – an innkeeper's son – his usurped Neapolitan throne. For, despite the claims of legitimacy, this promised better for a Habsburg hegemony beyond the Alps than a return of the lawful Bourbon house.

*

Of these conflicting commitments the most embarrassing was that by which Russia had bound herself to double Prussia's size and population.

Most of the promised increase was based on rights derived from flagrant aggressions during the early years of the Wars. By partitioning Poland two decades before, Russia, Austria, and Prussia had enlarged their territories at the cost of allowing France to dominate Europe. It had been their preoccupation in this which had enabled the Revolutionary armies to overrun Germany. The subsequent occupation of Vienna, Berlin, and Moscow had been a just retribution.

After Jena, Napoleon had seized most of Prussia's Polish spoils, including the former capital, and reconstituted them as the Duchy of Warsaw, making much play in his words, though not in his deeds, of Polish nationality and patriotism. To this he had added after his victory in 1809 part of Austrian Poland – Cracow and part of Galicia – placing the whole under the nominal sovereignty of his puppet, the King of Saxony. Early in 1813 all these territories – the whole of eighteenth-century Poland except the portion still remaining in Austria's hands – had been liberated and occupied by Russian armies.

Unless, therefore, Russia was prepared to hand back to Prussia the latter's Polish territory – and nothing had been said of this in the Russo-Prussian Treaty of Kalisch – she was committed to supporting an equivalent aggrandisement of that State in central and western Europe. It seemed unlikely, after her armies had been the chief instrument in liberating Europe, that she would now withdraw them without some compensation for the sacrifices she had made. Expansion to the west through Poland had been her goal for at least half a century.

Moreover, the Czar of Russia was inspired by progressive ideals. For many years he had had a Polish mistress and a Polish Minister. He profoundly regretted the rape of Poland by his grandmother, Catherine the Great, and her foreign allies. He wished to make amends by re-uniting and restoring that ancient kingdom. He wished to become its king. As its liberator, it seemed to him his duty to humanity.

It was never easy to turn Alexander from his duty to humanity. He loved, he said, to sit on his terrace and busy himself with the welfare of mankind.[1] He loved praise. He wished to satisfy his allies, the Prussians. He wished – within reason – to please the Poles; he wished to reward his subjects and free them from the bugbear of attack from the West. As the heir of Peter the Great, it was his mission to open the door

1. Havelock, 142.

of Europe to Russia. As God's vicegerent, it was his duty to extend his beneficent sway and liberate the oppressed.

It was difficult for statesmen of commoner clay to deal with a man so devout. He always seemed to have one foot in heaven and one on earth – and Russian earth at that. There were times when his attitude was scarcely of this world. When he entered Paris he assured the city fathers that he had come, not to conquer, but to learn the wish of France and to carry it out for the good of her people. It was not surprising that simple folk far removed from the realities of state regarded him as more than mortal.

Unfortunately the results of his actions were often different from those he intended. When by a magnanimous gesture he liberated – without the slightest provision for their journey – the French prisoners in Russia, they not only died in thousands on the roads but carried typhus into every city of Europe. When he chivalrously granted a safe-conduct to a beautiful Frenchwoman captured in the fighting near Paris, she was immediately raped by Cossacks. Holy Russia was like that. And, for all his liberalism and passion for western civilization, the Czar was a Russian and not a western ruler. He had acquired the Slav passion for arguing with flawless logic from premises arrived at by mysterious higher processes. And as he seldom stopped talking, was exceedingly vain and, when thwarted, invincibly suspicious, he presented a problem to his ministers and colleagues.

He suffered, too, like all autocrats, from the fact that no one in his entourage could safely contradict him. He was unused to opposition. When he encountered it from his equals, he reacted violently. This unsuited him for diplomacy. The events of the past eighteen months had greatly aggravated this unsuitability. Once he had taken the heroic decision to burn his capital and fight on, Alexander had marched from victory to victory. His natural irresolution and melancholy had been succeeded by a new decision and confidence; he who had been found sobbing after Austerlitz and had feared dethronement during the retreat to Moscow had become the arbiter of Europe's destinies, the prop, as he loved to be told, on which mankind leant. With God's miraculous aid he had ridden at the head of his armies into Moscow, Warsaw, Berlin, Leipzig, Frankfort, and Paris. His shining eyes were raised to Heaven, his high and noble forehead was crowned as with a halo. Tall, magnanimous, and dedicated to the service of God, he brought the jubilee. He could not be expected to give way over Poland.

*

Those responsible for British foreign policy failed at first to appreciate these factors. They knew the Czar as a man of high Christian faith and liberal sympathies who, after an unfortunate spell of collaboration, had helped them to liberate Europe and who now wished, with them, to pacify it. Like everyone in England they deplored the treacherous aggression that had led to the extinction of Poland twenty years before and would have liked to have seen its independence restored. But they knew that, strategically speaking, it was far beyond their power to challenge that twenty-year-old *fait accompli*. And after a generation of war a crusade by Britain against her allies was unthinkable. Her statesmen, as practical men, saw that the *status quo* of partition was the only way of avoiding disturbing and dangerous changes elsewhere.

When, therefore, during the preliminary discussions in London the Czar showed himself set on a solution of the Polish problem incompatible with inter-allied agreement and international law, they were much disappointed. They did not object to his proposal to revive a Polish state under his own sovereignty in the parts of Poland which had long been incorporated in Russia; on the contrary, they welcomed it as an instalment, however incomplete, of the restitution due to the Poles. Nor had they any objection to a reasonable expansion of Prussia in western Europe. Now that Austria had abandoned her old outpost in the Netherlands and withdrawn beyond the Rhine, it seemed wise to strengthen the only other German Power capable of resisting French aggression. For this reason the British were ready to overlook Prussia's seizure of Hanover during the earlier stages of the war. They remembered only that she was an old ally who had fought valiantly at the end and led the movement for German liberation.

But the Czar's unilateral claim to almost all Poland and his proposal to compensate Prussia with the entire domain of the King of Saxony struck at the whole system of European equilibrium and at that common action by the victor Powers on which Castlereagh and his colleagues believed that peace depended. To preserve the latter they tried hard to find a compromise that would satisfy the Czar. Being British, they hoped that good would somehow come out of evil. But the Czar, being an autocrat, disapproved of compromise. When the islanders attempted to reason with him, he replied that he had 120,000 troops in Poland and that no one could turn him out.

Such an argument awoke old suspicions which were difficult to still. Russian insistence on expansion in one direction implied Russian expansion in others. Britain, with her minute base and her roots in the ocean, had always been jealous of any Continental Power that sought ascendancy outside Europe. She had fought Spain, Holland, and France in turn on that score. Paramount herself in India and southern Asia, she saw in Russia a greater Asiatic Power stretching out tentacles towards every sea. What if, having occupied Finland, Bessarabia, and Poland, the northern colossus should now strike southwards across the central Asian deserts to the Indian Ocean? During their collaboration with Napoleon, its rulers had twice planned such a project. Now once again came reports from remote British consuls of Russian intrigue and infiltration; with the defeat of Napoleon the star of Muscovy was in the ascendant throughout the East.[1] It could be seen by the agents of the British East India Company as they rode in the vale of the Indus or were borne in their palanquins towards the Hindu Kush. They transmitted their fears to London.

Talleyrand also distrusted the Russians. A French eighteenth-century bishop was not to be fooled by a windy ideologue from the Neva. He knew when the Czar talked of the re-establishment of Poland, he was not thinking of giving up what he possessed of it but merely of acquiring those parts which he did not possess. And if Talleyrand did not wish to see Cossacks on the Oder, he had still less wish to see a predominant Prussia. He did not share the English view of Prussians. He had twice seen them in his country, with their stupid, swashbuckling officers, their grab and jackboot culture, their plundering, bullying ways. Their State – the Sparta of Europe – was built, like Napoleon's, round an army; their destiny, writ large across their brief, blood-stained history, to conquer or cringe. Talleyrand knew that if Prussia's

---

1. 'It seems to be the object of the Emperor of Russia to establish a predominant influence throughout Europe and particularly in those courts where Great Britain, by the assistance which she afforded to them during the war, has acquired a just influence.' Sir Henry Wellesley, Castlereagh, x, 180. See *idem*, 75.

population was increased from five millions to ten, it would merely increase her capacity for aggression. For it would double the size of her army.

There seemed a still greater danger in allowing Prussia to swallow a sovereign German State. In the ambition of the Prussians to unite northern Germany Talleyrand saw a threat to the future. If Germany was ever to be united and given nationhood, it must be under the aegis of a civilized, not of a barbaric, Power. For all her show of Lutheran piety, Prussia was a heathen State which recognized neither the Roman law nor the Roman morality. 'No scruples stop her,' Talleyrand wrote, 'convenience constitutes her only right.' If she were to impose her predatory, barrack-room conception of the State on the union or Germans which Napoleon had begun in the Rhineland and West-phalia, it might one day lay civilization open to a worse menace than Napoleon.

Elderly and hedonistic cynic though he was, Talleyrand therefore turned to the statesmen of England and Austria to safeguard the ideal common to them all – a stable and tranquil Europe. He took advantage of the British Foreign Minister's presence in Paris in August to propose that Britain and France should support one another at the approaching Peace Congress. But Castlereagh, though bitterly disappointed by his failure to reach an agreement with the Czar on the future of eastern Europe, refused to treat with France behind his allies' back. Only six months before he had pledged his country to act with Russia, Prussia, and Austria against French aggression, and he still regarded that alliance as the guarantee of European peace. He hoped that when the victors met that autumn at Vienna, wiser counsels would prevail, and that Russia would be prepared, like England, to make sacrifices for the common good. He pinned his hopes on the influence of Austria, the most civilized of the victor Powers, and in particular on the Austrian Chancellor, Metternich. He, therefore, continued his journey to Vienna without committing himself.

*

Between Castlereagh and Metternich there was a natural affinity. Polished, courtly, and handsome, the one forty-five and the other forty-four, both had consistently opposed the Revolution and the subversive violence which since their youth had threatened the world into which they had been born. Both, after prolonged perils and high courage, had seen their cause triumph. There the resemblance ceased. Castlereagh was a man of scrupulous integrity, incapable of deceit, simple, unaffected, home-loving, and by Metternich's standards, almost bourgeois in the propriety of his domestic life. His strength, like that of his country, lay not in intellect or adroitness, but in character. He dominated any society he entered not by graceful accomplishments but by his calm command of himself. Champion of a united Christendom though he had made himself, his boyish shyness, his awful French,[1] the long, stiff legs which he never knew where to put, his apparent constancy to his complacent-eyed, chattering wife, all proclaimed his insularity. Like every *rosbif* he was at bottom a provincial. Yet there was nothing vulgar in his provincialism. '*Ma foi*,' exclaimed Talleyrand after their first meeting, '*comme il a l'air distingué*.' With his tall, stately presence and frank gaze he personified the independence and assurance of the open-air ruling class of England.

Prince Metternich was as brilliant and accomplished as Castlereagh was reticent and patient. He was the doyen of a dancing capital. He prided himself as much on his *beaux yeux* and fascinating manners as on his cleverness. As great an *intriguant* in the boudoir as in the cabinet, he made his skill in the one serve his ends in the other. The wits called him '*le ministre papillon*'. He was the complete international character, equally at home in German, French, Italian, English, and Russian. Although a great upholder of the structure of Christian society, truth was alien to his nature; he sought the same ends as Castlereagh, but loved to achieve them by trickery. Napoleon, a connoisseur in such matters, remarked that he lied always and that this was too much. This, however, was because Metternich had proved the more successful liar of the two. Unlike the islander, Castlereagh, who had never had to fawn to the Revolution, he was an unconscious puppet of the lawless force he had set himself to destroy. Under a sincere show of principle, he was politically a trickster. He even out-tricked Napoleon.

Despite his love of pleasure, Metternich took himself very seriously.

1. 'How he gets on in French I cannot imagine. He called out to the *maître d'hôtel*, "*A présent, Monsieur, servez la diner*."' Harriet Granville, I, 62–4. He once remarked of his allies that they were all '*dans le même potage*.'

He saw Austria – a Christian and multi-racial State – as the microcosm of Europe. He sought to give the latter the stability enjoyed by the former. His political aim was to stop the hand of time. He did not believe it could be stopped for ever, only that by his own prescience and cleverness it could be stopped for his lifetime. *Au fond* he was a pessimist, for he believed that all change must be for the bad. He saw before the civilization he loved a long period of inevitable decline. Having witnessed in his lifetime so much violence, treachery, horror, and bloodshed, he appeared to have grounds for his belief. Meanwhile he meant to constitute Austria – and himself – a rock of order in a troubled world.

The State whose councils this conservative statesman guided had an even stronger interest in European stability than Great Britain. Austria was not a trading empire like Britain, but she was composed of many races. Before the war her hereditary ruler's domains had included Belgian and part of Western Germany, and his titles the great though nebulous office of Holy Roman or German Emperor. Since the conquest of Belgium by the Revolutionary armies and the dissolution of the Holy Roman Empire by Napoleon, she had turned southwards and eastwards and, abandoning the rôle of guardian of Germany against France – one which had proved beyond her military capacity[1] – had sought to fill the more profitable vacuum created by the receding tide of Turkish imperialism and the extinction of the Venetian Republic. The Habsburg Francis II ruled not only a Teuton Austria, a Magyar Hungary, and a Czech Bohemia, but over Italians in Lombardy and Venetia, Croats and Serbs in Illyria, and Poles and Ruthenes in Galicia. Such an empire was subject to every disturbing opinion and new idea. Being without natural frontiers, it was excessively vulnerable. Since 1796 its capital had been four times at the mercy of the French.

It was natural, therefore, for an Austrian Government to wish to avoid war and preserve the *status quo*. It was a police State presided over by a paternal dynasty and a rigid, well-meaning, and rather bovine

1. 'No reverses can correct, no experience instruct them.' Benjamin Bathurst, H. M. C. Bathurst, 175. 'Whatever their defects may have been, they bore their misfortunes with wonderful gaiety. Returning to Vienna after the battle of Austerlitz, Madame Pungstall heard the Emperor say: "Well! here we are; well beaten."' Broughton, 1, 61.

bureaucracy. It was not actively oppressive, but perpetually apprehensive and, therefore, meddling. Everything was censored, particularly newspapers and books. In Lombardy even excessive applause at the theatre was forbidden lest it should arouse national feeling. The imperial officials – mostly Teutons – drove the quicker-witted Latins, especially the Italians, almost frantic by their clumsy, rule-of-thumb pedantry. At Mantua, to get permission to leave the town, it was necessary to apply first to the officer of the Guard, thence to the Douane, thence to the Police, and, after half a dozen other officers, to the general commandant himself. When the latter's aides-de-camp had leisure to attend to the matter and had graciously issued a passport, the would-be traveller, retracing his steps, had to present it in turn to all these officers again. Such a system fostered neither commerce nor thought. It created – so long as men would tolerate it – a static society.

The supreme head of this far-flung State, the Emperor Francis, was a thin, dried-up, kindly little man, usually dressed in an old-fashioned and not over clean white uniform. Except when making toffee – his favourite relaxation – he was never so happy as when poring over police dossiers. He left questions of policy to his clever Chancellor and devoted himself to the ritual of the administrative priesthood of which he was the head. He was much loved by his Austrian subjects, a simple, pious folk who regarded him as their father and viewed his unceasing paternal concern for their affairs with grateful pride.[1] His capital and the brilliant aristocracy which thronged it made up for its lack of political responsibility by its intense love of music, dancing, and the arts.

In their attitude to Russian and Prussian pretensions the advisers of this good monarch were somewhat divided. The Chancellor, Metternich, felt a strong distrust of Russia and an even stronger dislike for the Czar – a rival in love as well as diplomacy. The Commander-in-Chief, Prince Schwarzenberg, and Count Stadion, the Finance Minister, were more frightened of Prussia. One group feared the Russian threat to absorb Galicia, the other the Czar's proposal to hand over Saxony and,

---

1. 'To redeem mankind, God gave his only son,' ran a Viennese illuminated nscription at the victory celebrations, 'to save Europe Francis gave his daughter. Glory to the Father and the Daughter!' Hon. Frederick Lamb to Lord Castlereagh, 18th June, 1814. Castlereagh, x, 56–7.

with it, the leadership of northern Germany to Berlin. The first would bring a neighbour of immense size and unpredictable ambition to the passes above the Hungarian plain; the second the hated martial State, which had seized Silesia from the Habsburgs, to the gates of Bohemia.

By the aristocratic and Catholic standards of Austria both Russia and Prussia were barbaric and upstart Powers. The Austrian nobility, who had been the guardians of Christendom from the Turk for two centuries, understood far better than the English how thin was the civilized veneer on which the values of the West depended. They knew how quickly it vanished as one moved eastwards into the plains and forests where Rome had never penetrated. It had been this fear of eastern barbarism that had caused the Emperor Francis to hesitate before dethroning his son-in-law, Napoleon. There seemed little advantage in exchanging the yoke of a Corsican brigand for that of a Calmuck chief.

Behind the Czar and his European Ministers lay Russia with her boundless territories and population. Her dramatic defeat of Napoleon had struck the imagination of Europe; her armies, triumphant on the Seine, stood revealed as the force of the future. It seemed a strange thing for eighteenth-century gentlemen to see 'a Bashkir Tartar with the Phrygian cap and bow' gazing about him from his ragged horse in a Paris street. The inscrutable, smiling barbarism of Russia both fascinated and repelled the West. Beneath the glitter of its elegant, Europeanized aristocracy, its people were still the savage, elemental creatures that ancient travellers had found beyond the Polish marches. When they spilled into Europe out of the remote plains and impenetrable forests from which Napoleon had roused them, they behaved like beings of a different species. They cut off the heads of their prisoners, drank the oil out of street lamps, and performed their natural functions in parlours. At one moment they would be standing like automata on parade, ready to be struck down by their officers if they moved a muscle, at another singing in unison in emotion-charged ranks before their incense-swinging priests; or capering about in dirty slovenly grey coats like herds of intoxicated animals. In all they did beauty and savagery were strangely mingled. To human life and the rights of the individual they seemed utterly indifferent; even a General whose men failed to keep their mechanical alignment at a review was punished with instantaneous imprisonment. Yet their fierce rhythm and sense of colour haunted the imagination of those who saw them. A British officer recorded his impressions of a Russian equipage in a Paris street: the bearded coachman with the brow and neck of a Jupiter, the beautiful boy outrider with flaming caftan and flowing elf-locks, the little, wild, long-maned horses that at a shake of the whip and a cry were off like the wind.[1]

A Power so impulsive and barbaric, with standards so different from those of the West, could not be allowed to dictate to Europe. Yet, having liberated the Continent from the Jacobin, it had become its strongest part. Both Castlereagh and Metternich saw that the preservation of peace depended on the maintenance of a common front by the victors. It was not by opposing Russia but by influencing her that European equilibrium must be established. And, as no one had been more insistent on the idea of an international order than the Czar, it was the task of western statesmanship to win him from his selfish insistence on purely Russian ends and recall him to the measures necessary to restore the balance and unity of Christendom.

Castlereagh's attempt to reason with Alexander, however, proved no more successful in Vienna than in London. When reminded that his proposal to publish a liberal Constitution for all Poles would not only put his allies, Austria and Prussia, in an invidious position but vex his own subjects who enjoyed no such Constitution, Alexander replied that the Constitution was the handiwork of a British liberal, Jeremy Bentham, and that by opposing it the British Foreign Secretary was flouting the conscience of his countrymen. This was awkward, for it was true. When Castlereagh went on to inform the Czar's Minister, Nesselrode, that it was not the resurrection of a free Poland that Britain opposed but of a puppet one under Russian control, he was curtly informed that Russia, already in occupation of Poland, possessed an army of 600,000 men.

On October 12th, therefore, Castlereagh addressed to the Czar a letter. After recalling that Britain could not condone a unilateral aggrandizement by an ally, he appealed to him to make the forth-

---

1. Mercer, II, 229–30. See Gronow, II, 19–20; Stanley, 178; Brownlow, 151–4; Granville, II, 476; *Paget Brothers*, 262; Dr Gray, *Autobiography*, II, 269; Haydon, I, 254, 257; Lady Shelley, I, 151.

coming Congress a blessing to mankind instead of 'a scene of discordant intrigue and a lawless scramble for power.' Simultaneously he sought common action with the other victor Powers to induce Russia to modify her claims. But his efforts broke down, not only on the King of Prussia's almost pathological subservience to the Czar but on the desire of Prussian statesmen for hegemony in northern Germany and their realization that this might be achieved with Russian but never with Austrian aid. Castlereagh, true to the traditional policy of the Pitts, could see little objection to an enlargement of Prussia, especially on the left bank of the Rhine where she could keep watch on France. He shared the view common to most Englishmen who had grown up in the eighteenth century that the Prussians were natural allies; they might be bellicose, but they hated the French.[1] But his proposal to give Prussia, in return for a stand against Russia, not only most of Saxony but the great southern German fortress of Mainz, was more than Vienna could stomach. She could not permit her rival to control the Main as well as the Elbe, Rhine, and Oder.

Meanwhile Metternich too had become embroiled with the Czar. When informed by the complacent Rhinelander that Austria would welcome a free Poland re-established by Europe but not a puppet state made by Russia, Alexander became hysterical with rage, accused him of insubordination, and threatened to force the Emperor Francis to dismiss him. He subsequently challenged him to a duel and, when this was prevented, declined to speak to him for three months. At the same time he made sure of the Prussians. On November 8th the Commander-in-Chief of the Russian Army of Occupation handed over Saxony to Berlin. A week later Alexander's brother, the Grand Duke Constantine, issued from Warsaw a proclamation calling on all Poles to unite and fight for their independence.

*

1. 'I know,' he wrote to Wellington, 'there may be objections to ... placing a Power, peculiarly military and consequently somewhat encroaching, so extensively in contact with Holland and the Low Countries; but, as this is only a secondary danger, we should not sacrifice to it our first object.' It was also widely believed – in England – that the Prussians loved the English. 'Every Prussian is thoroughly attached to England, and all the young Prussian Princes are *desperate* when they talk of Russia.' Duke of Cumberland to Prince Regent, 10th Jan., 1815. George IV, *Letters*, II, 4.

The eastern barbarians were thus aligned and the cloven hoof shown. If Castlereagh gave way Russia would not only secure a preponderance in eastern Europe so great as to overturn the balance of power, but would destroy the system of agreement between the Powers created at Chaumont. Yet not only was Austria by herself incapable of expelling the Russian and Prussian armies from Poland and Saxony, but the British people were utterly weary of war and unable for the moment to think of anything but the export market and the reduction of taxes. Such military force as they had chosen to retain was mostly on the other side of the Atlantic fighting the Americans, while the Opposition, heedless of geography and completely misled by the Czar's platitudes, was raising Cain over the Foreign Secretary's resistance to his bene-volent plans for Poland's constitutional progress. The Cabinet, con-scious of its weakness in Parliament, sent off dispatch after dispatch urging Castlereagh not to carry matters to extremities. Vansittart, the Chancellor of the Exchequer, struggling with the demand for lower taxes, was particularly insistent on the need for appeasement. 'We ought,' he wrote, 'to avoid irritating Russia by a pertinacious opposi-tion which is unlikely to be successful.'

But Castlereagh was unmoved. He had seen his country pouring out its blood and treasure for the ideal of international law for twenty years. He did not now intend to let that law be flouted with impunity by anyone, foe or ally. He would not allow a 'Calmuck Prince' to dictate to Europe. 'You must make up your mind to watch and resist him as another Bonaparte,' he wrote to the Prime Minister. 'You may rely upon it, my friend Van's philosophy is untrue as applied to him. Acquiescence will not keep him back nor will opposition accelerate his march.'

Having chosen his course, Castlereagh did not shrink from the measure to implement it. It was his habit, when threatened, to face danger boldly.[1] Having failed in his attempt to use the machinery of the quadruple alliance to restore European equilibrium, he called in an outside Power. For his ultimate objective was not the Grand Alli-

1. Walter Scott used to repeat, as an illustration of his courageous temper, a tale he had heard Castlereagh tell of how, approached by a giant spectre in a lonely Irish house, he had sprung from his bed and faced the spectre in an attitude of defiance, following it step by step across the room until it vanished. Lockhart, v, 213–14. See for his demeanour in the presence of a mob, Gronow, I, 221.

ance, but the purpose for which the Grand Alliance had been created.

Talleyrand's opportunity had come. He had gone to Vienna with two convictions: that an alliance of the great Powers from which a defeated France was excluded would produce not stability but instability, and that the westward expansion of Russia must be halted if civilization was to recover. As a Polish nation could only be re-created with safety to Europe if given the strength to preserve its independence, and as this was impossible, there was only one thing to be done: to return to the *status quo* and leave Poland divided between the original partitioning Powers. By throwing the weight of France into the scales to ensure this, Talleyrand could align her beside Britain and Austria and so end her isolation.

He had carefully prepared the way. The Peace of Paris, which referred questions affecting Europe as a whole to a conference of all the belligerent nations, had imposed on defeated France a secret article by which the four main victor Powers reserved to themselves the disposal of the non-French territories they had reconquered. This clause had never been communicated to the smaller Powers, who, being equally concerned in such general territorial dispositions, were bound to resent it. Relying on this, Talleyrand at an informal discussion on conference procedure inquired why the other signatories to the Treaty of Paris were not present as convening Powers, why, having pledged themselves to call an all-European Congress, the big Powers were setting up a council of four only, and why, five months after the restoration of the Bourbons, they were still using the invidious word, *Allies*. As by international law all sovereign States were equal, it was hard for those who were setting themselves up as the champions of public law to traverse this argument. The cunning Frenchman had thus been able to secure a reluctant admission that all eight signatories of the Treaty of Paris, including France, had a right to attend preliminary discussions on conference procedure. The only alternative answer was that might was right: the one argument which he knew Great Britain and Austria were determined to avoid.

Having gained France's admission on equal terms to the preliminary discussions, Talleyrand had put forward his own formula for the solution of the Congress's problems. It was that which the Allies had already, at his instance, applied to his own country. 'I ask for nothing,' he told them, 'but I bring something very important – the sacred principle of Legitimacy.' Based on the theory of government to which every hereditary Sovereign at the Congress owed his crown, it was almost impossible for them to reject. Yet it conflicted with vital dispositions the victors were trying to make. It involved both the restoration of the imprisoned King of Saxony, and the rejection of Austria's protégé, Joachim Murat of Naples.

Talleyrand had put the victors in a cleft stick. To break up the quadruple Alliance and align France with Britain and Austria he now sacrificed the interests of the French West Indian planters and agreed to the British demand that the Slave Trade should be forbidden at once everywhere north of Cape Formosa. He proposed, too, that a committee of the Congress should consider its universal abolition. Having won the goodwill of the British, he obliged Metternich by opposing the Spanish delegate's proposal for a European committee on Italy and so left Austria free to deal with that peninsula piecemeal. At the same time he ordered the partial mobilization of the French Army.

Thus armed, he offered his country's support to Great Britain and Austria at the very moment that Russia and Prussia were threatening to enforce their claims to Poland and Saxony by arms. Proclaiming that the dethronement of the Saxon King and the annexation of his dominions would undermine the whole principle of Legitimacy, he organized a collective protest by the lesser German States against the lawless liquidation of one of their members. To the Czar's rejoinder that the King of Saxony had forfeited his throne by treachery to the 'common cause', he replied that that was merely a question of dates.

This intervention by their country's hated enemy so enraged the Prussians that they threatened war unless their claim to Saxony was allowed. The effect on Castlereagh was immediate. If such a temper prevailed, he told the Prussian Chancellor, the Congress was no longer in a state of independence and had better be dissolved. At the same time he accepted Talleyrand's offer. Fortified by the news that a peace had been agreed by the British and American plenipotentiaries at Ghent, he signed on January 3rd, 1815, a secret treaty with Austria and France by which the three countries agreed to stand by one another in the event of an attack on any of them arising from the Peace Conference proposals. Austria and France were each to provide 150,000 troops and Great Britain an equivalent either in money or mercenaries. Bavaria, Hanover, Hesse-Darmstadt, and Piedmont were to be invited to join this western *bloc* against Russian and Prussian blackmail.

Meanwhile the wildest rumours circulated in Vienna and London. It was said that the Grand Alliance was dissolved, that the Russian army was on the march, and that Prussia was to occupy the English King's hereditary domain of Hanover instead of Saxony – this an entirely baseless report of the Russian Ambassador's wife who invented it to distract the amorous attentions of the Duke of Clarence in a coach. Even Napoleon joined in the clamour. 'If the Russians succeed in uniting the Poles,' he wrote from Elba, 'the whole of Europe ought to dread them. It will be impossible to foresee or limit the consequences. Hordes of Cossacks and barbarians, having seen the riches of more civilized countries, will be eager to return. They will overrun Europe and some great change will probably result from it, as has been the case in former times from incursions of barbarians.'

During these days Castlereagh remained calm. 'The climate of Russia,' he wrote, 'is often more serene after a good squall.' He knew that the Czar would bluff and bluster from gain to gain so long as he thought that the West was pacific and divided. Yet he knew that he wanted war no more than anyone else, that his troops were homesick and his people war-weary, and that Russia was embarrassed by internal financial and social difficulties.[1] He knew, too, that the Prussians, for all their threats, were anxious not to outrage Liberal German opinion which in the Catholic South and Rhineland was aligning itself with the forces of civilization and public law. Above all, he understood the moral prestige that his country enjoyed: her reputation throughout the world, even among those who least loved her, her renown for constancy and tenacity, her prodigious resources, and practical genius for achieving her ends. He therefore allowed the secret of his alliance with France and Austria to leak out discreetly. 'The alarm of war,' he wrote on January 5th, 'is over.'

The Russian and Prussian negotiators had learnt the strength of

1. H. M. C. Bathurst, 324; See Webster, 112–16; Webster, *Castlereagh*, I, 369, 370–1.

Castlereagh's character. They knew that he was a man of his word and that the conscience of Europe was behind him. Like everyone else they had been impressed by the news that the American war was over and that Britain's hands were free. With as little fuss as possible they began to climb down. On January 28th Metternich proposed that Austria and Prussia should agree to certain, though not sweeping, modifications of their pre-war frontiers in Russia's favour, and that part of Saxony should be given to Prussia in compensation, the remainder returning to its legitimate sovereign. Without a word the olive branch was accepted. The Concert of Europe was saved.

*

Early in February, 1815, a settlement was reached of the Polish-Saxon question. Austria retained her share of the 1792 partition except for the town of Cracow, which was relinquished by the Russians and made a free city. Prussia, of her former Polish lands, regained Posen but abandoned Warsaw to Russia, receiving as compensation the Duchy of Westphalia, Swedish Pomerania, part of the left bank of the Rhine, and about two-thirds of Saxony. The rest of the latter was reconstituted as an independent State under its legitimate King. Russia kept three-quarters of Napoleon's Grand Duchy of Warsaw – about 127,000 square miles with rather over three million inhabitants. Austria recovered the Tyrol and received Salzburg, the Illyrian littoral of the Adriatic and a free hand in Italy. A statistical committee was appointed to work out the exact frontiers.

'The territorial arrangements on this side of the Alps,' wrote Castlereagh to Lord Liverpool, 'are settled in all their essential features.' With Talleyrand's and Metternich's help the British Foreign Secretary had achieved his object: a readjustment of frontiers by general agreement which allowed time for a new European generation to grow up in habits of peace. Whether that new generation would accept the settlement or, by repudiating it, plunge Europe into new revolutions and wars, remained to be seen. For, in the nature of things, Castlereagh's prescription for peace was based on the ideals of the past. After a quarter of a century in which force and expediency had ruled the world, it seemed to statesmen enough to return to a framework of principle and law. Almost inevitably that framework was a reproduc-

tion of what they had known rather than an anticipation of the hopes
and beliefs of youth. The rough and ready work of governing mankind is not done by prophets or philosophers. The European settlement of 1814 was, indeed, a reaction from the disastrous consequences
of their speculations.

Its defect was that it enthroned a principle no longer universally
accepted. Its underlying belief – one going back to the Middle Ages –
was that an established succession of 'lawful' hereditary princes, bred
from infancy to their functions, acknowledging the Christian ethic,
and governing themselves by it in their relations with their subjects and
one another, was alone calculated to preserve peace and foster the
habits of social happiness. It afforded a foundation for stable government, justice – of a kind – and tranquillity. It was acclaimed by hereditary rulers of all kinds from emperors to village seigneurs, upheld by
the priests of the Christian Faith, and accepted, without question, by
the simple peasants of those lands to which an Allied victory had
restored familiar ways and traditions in place of a foreign despotism
imposed in the name of abstract equality. It was even acquiesced in,
though without enthusiasm, by the middle classes, whose hopes of a
more egalitarian and fluid society had been shaken by the massacres,
plunderings, conscriptions, and commercial restrictions of the Revolutionary Wars, and by the moral inadequacy, especially in Germany, of
some of the adventurers to whom in France's conquered provinces
power had too often been entrusted.[1]

Yet oppressive as Napoleon's bayonet rule had been, the ideas of the
germinating Revolution he embodied were not dead. They had
awakened men as well as scourged them. The static dream of centuries
had been broken. The old Order could never again be accepted without
question where men had seen the overthrow of the thrones and altars
they had believed eternal. The success of ragged armies led by men who
had had no place in the old order of things – poor sergeants, broken-
down attorneys, and inn-keepers' sons – had started thoughts, formerly
inconceivable, in the most submissive minds. For a whole generation,
Figaro had ruled Europe: a Figaro who in the last decade had assumed

1. For an amusing account of such a government see '*La Royaume de West-
phalie – Jérome Buonaparte – sa Cour – ses Favoris – et ses Ministres.*' *Par un Témoin
oculaire.* Paris, 1820, reviewed in *Quarterly,* XXII, 481.

an imperial grandeur and imposed a new order more impressive than anything known under the legitimate rulers of the past. However absurd it might seem to men of hereditary caste that clerks and trades-men should be tricked out in plumes and titles by Jacobin invaders, it did not seem so to those who belonged to these classes. The drums of Napoleon's armies had set men's minds marching along new roads. They continued to follow them even after the Emperor's fall. The transition from the music of Mozart to that of Beethoven, whose Seventh Symphony was conducted by the composer before the assem-bled diplomats at Vienna, is a measure of the troubled journey man had made, across the fields of Austerlitz and Borodino, from the peasant's cot of the *ancien régime*.

All this the peacemakers ignored. In their hour of triumph, like Napoleon himself, they treated what was unpalatable as though it did not exist. They tried to eliminate everything that had happened since 1789. Instead of making provision for the ideas of the young, they assumed that these had been discredited for ever by the crimes of Napoleon and the Jacobins. By refusing to compromise with the new, they made its ultimate rebellion certain. They thus undermined the world order they so carefully restored and left it exposed to great, though as yet remote, perils. In recasting the frontiers they had no re-gard to the racial feelings which the glorification of one nation by its citizens had aroused in others. The people of Germany, whose young patriots, with a new-found unity, had risen in the rear of the French armies, were herded back into the little ring fences in which they had lived before the Revolution, or consigned, without a chance to express their preferences, to some new ruler in order to achieve an equilibrium between Europe's lawful sovereigns. Being himself without racial pre-judice, Metternich – a Rhineland landowner in Habsburg service – thought only in terms of balancing the claims of princes so nicely that the hegemony of any one of them was impossible. So far as he sought to enlarge his master's dominions it was not in order that Austria should be strong, but that she should have the power to prevent anyone else from being so.

In this his aims were akin to those of the British Foreign Secretary. 'It is not the business of England,' Castlereagh wrote, 'to collect trophies but to restore Europe to peaceful habits.' For this he was prepared to sacrifice almost everything: revenge for wrongs done, the victors' spoils,[1] the logic of abstract justice, the isolation so dear to some of his countrymen, and the crusading liberalism so dear to others. His objective was a system in which international differences could be settled without bloodshed. 'He cared for nationality not at all,' wrote his disciple, Lord Salisbury, 'for the theoretic perfection of political institutions very little, for the realities of freedom a great deal, and for the peace and social order and freedom from the manifold curses of disturbance which can alone give to the humbler masses of mankind any chance of tasting their scanty share of human joys – for the sake of this he was ready to forgo all the rest.'

It was not that Castlereagh was indifferent to his country's interests. Like his master, Pitt, he was a patriot. But, like Pitt, he believed that England's first interest was the peace and stability of Europe. He fought strenuously to maintain her rights of search at sea, and insisted on placing outside the reach of future French aggression the naval base of Antwerp which would otherwise have entailed the charge of a perpetual war establishment. He sought this by the creation of a new Middle Power, a union of Holland and Belgium under the House of Orange. To give it stability he not only subsidized it from an overburdened British Treasury, but restored to it Java and the former Dutch East Indies – prizes ardently coveted by British traders.[2] And for the same end he restored to France and her former satellites the greater part of England's overseas conquests – the rewards of her many sacrifices.

Yet the conquests which Britain retained enabled her to play a wider part than ever before in guiding the world's destinies and preserving peace. Little thought of by Continental statesmen, who regarded a few square miles in Hanover as more important than a thousand in Canada or the Antipodes, they not only brought wealth and power to Britain but enabled her to insulate and localize every war for a hundred years.

1. 'It will be hard,' wrote his henchman, Edward Cooke, 'if France is to pay nothing for the destruction of Europe and we are to pay for saving it.' Castlereagh's mind rose above such considerations: his plea was for 'mildness and indulgence even to offending States.' See Webster, *Castlereagh*, I, 207–8, 273–4.

2. And by British humanitarians too. It was one of Raffles' dreams to emancipate the Malays from the unsympathetic and, as he deemed, degrading rule of the Dutch.

St Lucia, Tobago, Trinidad, Demerara, Essequibo, and Guiana on the western shores of the Atlantic, Mauritius and Ceylon in the Indian Ocean, the Cape of Good Hope at the junction of the two oceans, Malta and the Ionian Islands Protectorate in the Mediterranean, joined to her existing possessions, gave to her fleets an untrammelled command of the world's seaways. So long as she enjoyed this, it was impossible for any military power to conquer the world or even, while her statesmen and people maintained a sufficient deterrent strength, to embroil it. For pacific Britain's Navy made the waters that divided the land-masses of the earth corridors of peace.

It did more. In retaining a part of the gains won for her by Nelson and his contemporaries, Britain unconsciously signposted the human future. Alone in her consistent refusal to accept the Revolutionary thesis at the cannon's mouth, she yet secured and opened channels along which its ideas could flow. Her trans-oceanic possessions, unimportant as they seemed to European despots, were to witness, under her tolerant tutelage, the peaceful application of the very principles against whose armed enforcement she had fought. Even her claim to the 'Freedom of the Seas' – *anglice*, the right of search of neutral merchantmen in time of war – was to contribute to the expansion of the democratic belief. No one resented that claim more bitterly than the republicans of the United States who in 1812 had gone to war to challenge it. Yet it was the Royal Navy's grip on the Atlantic that enabled the infant Republic to consolidate a new libertarian order in the Western Hemisphere and to develop its immense resources without interference from the Old World. Nor was this service of England to her offspring entirely unintentional. At the very moment that victory in Europe freed her fleets and armies for major operations beyond the Atlantic, she showed her goodwill by seeking a settlement with the young democracy of the West. In the Treaty of Ghent she acknowledged its full territorial integrity in return only for a similar recognition of Canada's –[1] another potential democracy of poor men founded on the principles of liberty, equality, and fraternity.

1. The burning of the capital of Upper Canada in mid-winter by an undisciplined American army had led to the destruction of the uninhabited public buildings of Washington, though this retributory act – so stigmatized by a posterity which has forgotten its cause – was rightly deplored by many Englishmen, including the Prince Regent.

In like spirit England, lighted by the flame of Wilberforce's conscience, strove to secure the universal abolition of the Slave Trade, sacrificing territory and money to her allies and even her enemies to establish this fundamental canon of human equality. To those who did not understand the law of her being, the abolition of the Slave Trade – from which so many of her individual traders had profited in the past – appeared only as the hobby-horse of a little coterie of humanitarian cranks. Yet it was fought for as strenuously by British statesmen in Paris and Vienna as by the 'saints' of Clapham and Kensington Gore, and was supported by the entire public opinion of the country.[1] The repudiation by mankind of what Wilberforce described as the 'traffic in the person of our fellow-creatures' was the one trophy which all Englishmen insisted their representatives should bring back from the Congress. On February 8th, 1815, before leaving Vienna, Castlereagh obtained a joint declaration, signed by the eight convening Powers, condemning the Trade as repugnant to the principles of civilization and morality, and called for its universal abolition at the earliest possible moment.

For with its free system and tradition of toleration England could not close the door on the human future. 'It is impossible,' wrote the conservative Castlereagh, 'not to perceive a great moral change coming on in Europe, and that the principles of freedom are in full operation.' It was only his fear that the transition might be too sudden to ripen as yet 'into anything likely to make the world better or happier,' that caused him to mark time and align himself with the static Metternich. It was the essence of his country's politics that he could not commit her for long to such a policy. Already in Parliament and in the clubs and newspapers, English voices, though still only in a minority, were being raised in passionate protest against the settlement he had made. 'Here we are,' wrote Lord Byron, 'retrograding to the full, stupid old system – balance of Europe – posing straws upon Kings' noses, instead of wringing them off.' To him, as to other young Englishmen, the rulers of Austria, Russia, and Prussia were 'three stupid, legitimate old-dynasty boobies of regular-bred Sovereigns.'[2] Within

1. 'I believe,' wrote Castlereagh, 'there is hardly a village that has not met and petitioned upon it.' Castlereagh, x, 73. See Webster, *Castlereagh*, I, 413–24.
2. Just as when a male child was born, every woman in the house looked an inch higher, Lord Holland complained that, when a legitimate King was re-

a week of the Polish settlement the Leader of the Opposition was demanding that the Government should be arraigned for 'public brigandage,' while Sheridan, rousing himself from his vinous declension to the grave, spoke of crowned scoundrels cutting up Europe like carcass-butchers and England's conscience being silenced by the dirty bribe of a crown for Hanover. The transfer of Norway to Sweden, of the former Genoese Republic to Piedmont, of Saxons to Prussia and Poles to their former conquerors were all laid by British idealists at Castlereagh's door. So alarming did these parliamentary diatribes against him become that he had to hurry home in February to defend his policy in the Commons, leaving the Duke of Wellington to complete his work at Vienna.

*

With the general principles of a European settlement agreed between the Powers, the adjustment of frontiers was left to committees appointed by the convening States. The most important were the German Committee, and the Statistical Committee to ascertain the populations of the territories to be transferred. The former's duty was to draft a federal constitution to take the place of the defunct Holy Roman Empire and the French-controlled Confederations which had succeeded it. Consisting of representatives of Austria, Prussia, Bavaria, Württemberg, and Hanover – now elevated into a Kingdom – it was dominated from the start by the negative idealism of Metternich. Not wishing to unite Germany himself, he was determined that no one else should, neither a militarist Prussia nor a parliament of bourgeois doctrinaires – a class for which he had a high aristocratic disdain. He supported the separatist claims of the German sovereigns and ignored the rather heady patriotic fervour of their younger subjects. The Tugendbund had been well enough for recruiting a partisan army to overthrow Napoleon, but its windy aspirations could have no place in the Europe Metternich was seeking to restore. The Germany he loved was not the tribal Valhalla of nascent Teutonic legend, but the diversified and localized Christian polity of the Middle Ages, with princes and prelates in their castles and pious peasants toiling in the

stored, every sprig of royalty in Europe became more insolent and insufferable. *Creevey Papers*, 1, 206. See Moore, *Byron*, 201, 216; Broughton, 1, 206; Lord Coleridge, 243.

fields or chanting psalms as they rowed in Sabbath gala under the rocks of the Drachenfels. The wayside shrines and chapels which he loved to draw in the margin of his papers in committee were the symbols of that Germany.[1] Unfortunately they were not the kind of symbols that guaranteed the bourgeoisie against the conquering, plundering armies of the French. For this, Prussian guns and bayonets were more appropriate.

The Committee's solution of a titular German Federal Diet composed of the representatives of seventeen losely allied but completely independent sovereign States or groups, though it pleased the hereditary rulers, was a bitter disappointment to the young patriots who had taken arms to liberate their fatherland. It also disappointed the Prussian generals and bureaucrats, who had little use for intellectuals and visionaries but hoped to see Prussia the recruiting fulcrum of a centralized northern Germany. But it pleased England, whose ruler was a German sovereign and whose merchants required the pacification of their principal Continental market, and it was less displeasing to Talleyrand than a closer German union. Viewed as an essay in staying, if not putting back, the hand of time – the art in which Metternich excelled – it seemed an admirable expedient.

*

So, too, in Italy the old barriers, dynastic, military, and economic, which divided Italian from Italian, were carefully re-erected by statesmen in powdered wigs and silk-covered calves who were now once more living – in their imaginations at least – in the mannered, candle-lit world of the eighteenth century. The music of an almost unceasing succession of balls, concerts, *tableaux-vivants*, and masques attended by princely delegates of every description and their lovely ladies – or other people's – was the *symphonie fantastique* to which the *ancien régime* buried the still-born child of Italian nationalism. Sunk in dismal poverty, with flocks of famished sheep grazing off nettles in the Roman streets and verminous beggars swarming in every church and piazza, Italy with her beauty, sunshine, and artistic wealth was the Mecca of European nations. All, esteeming her the cradle of their culture, felt a

1. For a charming picture of this Germany as it still survived in 1814 see Stanley, 188; Brownlow, 139–40.

keen interest in making her conform to their purposes: Revolutionary
France seeing her as a forcing-ground for Cisalpine military republics,
Britain as a market and an academy of taste for her wealthy dilettantes
and sun-starved artists, Austria as a preserve for her solemn, well-
meaning bureaucracy. Spain, which a century earlier had been the
paramount Power in the peninsula, was no longer of importance; only
in Naples, where a branch of the Spanish Bourbons still lingered, and
in little Lucca did any link remain with the Iberian hegemony of the
past.

When the young Bonaparte had crossed into Italy like another
Caesar from Gaul, the ideal of Italian unity had seemed about to become
a reality. But it had soon become clear that he regarded Italians like
everyone else as persons to be exploited in the service of his destiny.
He had fined, plundered, and conscripted and, on occasion, shot them,
with such vigour that their enthusiasm for him quickly waned. None
the less, though the government of the French militarists was more
oppressive than any that had gone before, it had shaken Italians out of
their age-long apathy and subservience. For though Bonaparte might
manure the Spanish sierras and Russian plains with their bodies, his
very existence proved that the men of Italy could rule as well as cringe.
Even the poorest began to feel the shame of seeing his country parti-
tioned by alien princes; though Napoleon had carefully redivided the
country between his jealous satraps, a new feeling of unity had been
engendered, especially among the young. When the Germans rose
against the French, many Englishmen believed that the Italians would
follow suit; in the spring of 1814 the British Commander-in-Chief in
Sicily, Lord William Bentinck, went so far as to proclaim a national
rising. But, except for the hardy mountaineers of Piedmont, the
Italians were a gentle race. They refused as yet to fight for their
liberties.

It thus came about that with the fall of France, Italians, in Wordsworth's angry words, were 'transferred to Austria, to the King of
Sardinia, and the rest of those vile tyrants.'[1] The hated *tedeschi* reoccupied Lombardy, and transferred their patronage from the unreliable
Murat to the exiled Bourbons on the understanding that when they
returned to Naples they should look for guidance, not to London or

1. De Selincourt, *Middle Years*, 650.

Madrid, but to Vienna. The Austrian Emperor's daughter, Napoleon's grass-widow, received the Grand Duchy of Parma. Modena and Reggio went to an Austrian satellite; Tuscany returned to the mild rule of its former Dukes. Corsica remained French. The centre of the peninsula, including the capital, was restored to the Pope and the slothful, old-maidish despotism of the Roman priesthood. The extinguished republican oligarchies of Venice and Genoa, the only genuine Italian States of the recent past, were absorbed in Austria and Piedmont. Only in the mountainous north-west, where the House of Savoy ruled over martial Piedmont and Sardinia, was there a State which could be called wholly Italian.

There was one aspect of the Italian problem which everyone had forgotten. The diplomats overlooked, in their debates, the existence of the one great Italian of the age. While they had been talking and masquerading, the little Caesar at Elba kept a sharp eye on the Continent they were reshaping. His hope of a breach between them had been averted by Castlereagh; but Talleyrand's diplomatic victories in the drawing-room of Vienna had still to salve the vanity of defeated France. The wounds of her humiliation at the hands of her former victims were too deep: the spectacle of her inglorious Court could not be stomached by those who had so recently dictated to Europe. The possessors of national lands were scared by the foolish talk of the *émigrés*, the State's creditors irritated by the petty economies of an empty Treasury, the Army angered by popinjays in white feathers and laced uniforms who barred the democratic road to promotion and slighted the pride of the veterans of Austerlitz and Jena. A few months before, Napoleon had been reviled as the cause of all France's defeats and sufferings. Now the old *moustache*, home in his native village, quaffed the ashes of the eagles and muttered bloodcurdling oaths against the fat *coquin* in the Tuileries and the foreigners who had put him there. The Emperor, brave men whispered hoarsely, would return in the spring with the violets. And, as the hereditary boobies in Vienna undid his life's work and the London crowds queued outside the Panorama in Leicester Square to see the model representation of his island cage, the little man in the garden at Porto Ferrajo, with his telescope fixed on every passing sail, saw his opportunity. That February an English traveller was informed that Leghorn Jews were shipping eagled buttons to Elba.[1] The British Commissioner in the island sent a warning to London that something was afoot, the French Government pleaded nervously for the Emperor's removal to St Helena. But at Vienna, where the tinkling sleigh parties drove nightly home from the Wienerwald, the Congress was too busy to listen.

On the night of March 7th a great ball was to be held in the Austrian capital. That afternoon the Czar laid a wager with a lady as to who could dress most quickly. At a signal both left the room by different doors, the one returning reclad in a minute and a quarter, the other in a minute and fifty seconds. During the evening a courier arrived at Metternich's house with dispatches from Genoa. The Chancellor was tired from too much business by day and revelry by night. After resting for a while on his couch he opened the dispatch. Napoleon had escaped. In its well-bred inefficiency the *ancien régime* had let out the Corsican ogre.

*

Thereafter events moved at a terrible speed. On March 10th Napoleon, evading all attempts by the authorities to arrest him, appeared at Lyons, announcing that he had come to save the French from degradation and that his eagles, once more on the wing, would soon alight on the spires of Notre Dame. Unit after unit of the Bourbon army went out to stop him, and, on meeting that familiar, grey-coated figure at the head of his daring few, threw down their arms and welcomed him in a tempest of emotion. On the 14th he was joined by Marshal Ney, who had promised King Louis that he would bring him back to Paris in a cage. Six days later he reached Fontainebleau, where less than a year before he had abdicated and bade a last farewell to his veterans. That night he slept at the Tuileries, the King with a handful of courtiers tearfully scampering before him across the Flemish frontier. France had gone about again and the Revolution Militant was once more enthroned.[2] In Italy the impetuous Murat put his army in motion and the Pope and his Cardinals fled from Rome. So, except for a few fastidious Whig aristocrats, did most of the English tourists.

1. *Brougham*, II, 63–4. Holland, *Journal*, I, 232.
2. Cam Hobhouse was told during his visit to Paris that summer that the only change in the French capital after Napoleon's entry was that the newspapers and the pats of butter no longer had lilies printed on them.

The Sovereigns of Europe assembled at Vienna refused to accept the outrageous *fait accompli*. On March 18th they proclaimed the escaped prisoner an outlaw and 'disturber of the peace of the world.' Thereafter they ordered an immediate mobilization of the Continent's armies and appointed the Duke of Wellington to command the advance guard in the Low Countries – the doorway to the plains of France – until the immense forces of Prussia, Austria, and Russia could be mobilized. The flower of the British Peninsular Army – what remained of it after demobilization – was still in America or on the high seas returning from that country. But every man that could be raised was sent in haste to Flanders; even Ireland, despite the protests of Dublin Castle and young Robert Peel, was stripped of troops. Everywhere the trumpets were sounding again for war.

CHAPTER 7

WATERLOO

The British infantry are the best in the world. Fortunately there are not many of them.

MARSHAL BUGEAUD

What a happy consummation of his glory it would be to put the last hand to the destruction of Buonaparte's power in direct conflict with Buonaparte himself.

CANNING to Castlereagh,
28 April 1815

DURING the afternoon of Sunday, June 18th, 1815, the city of Brussels was in a state of panic. Since three o'clock a stream of fugitives had been pouring in from the plain beyond the forest of Soignes where, twelve miles south of the capital, Wellington, with 21,000 British and 42,000 Germans and Netherlanders, was barring the way of a victorious French army of 70,000 veterans commanded by Napoleon. Most of the English visitors who had invaded the city in the wake of their army had already fled to the north and were crowding the roads and waterways to Antwerp, where, on Wellington's orders, a state of siege had been proclaimed and crowds waited all day in the rain for news. But hundreds more, unable to obtain transport in the panic – for everything on wheels had been requisitioned – remained in the city without hope of escape. Every few minutes fugitives from the battlefield kept galloping into the town shouting that all was lost and that the French were at their heels. Once a whole regiment of Hanoverian cavalry poured in through the Namur gate with swords drawn and foam-flecked horses and rode through the town towards the north, upsetting everything in the streets on their way. There were other fugitives with bloody and bandaged heads, and cartloads of wounded, and occasionally, towards evening, an officer of high rank, British or Belgian, extended upon a bier borne by soldiers. As the dreadful afternoon advanced and the distant cannonade grew in intensity, the rumour spread – possibly circulated by French sympathizers, of whom there were said to be many – that Napoleon had promised his soldiery the sack of the city. Every woman knew what that meant. 'I never saw such consterna-

236

tion,' wrote Fanny Burney. 'We could only gaze and tremble, listen and shudder.'[1]

Yet three days earlier Brussels had seemed as securely held by British wealth and the martial power of united Europe as London. For weeks it had been a scene of gaiety and military pageantry, with the brilliant aristocracy of England flooding the city in the wake of her army and spending money with a profusion never matched by its successive Spanish, Austrian, French, and now Dutch rulers. The nearest French vedettes had been forty miles away beyond the Sambre, and between them and the Belgian capital two great armies had guarded every road on a hundred-mile front, growing daily in strength and commanded by the two most famous soldiers of the European alliance that had defeated and dethroned Napoleon. The Prussian host of around 113,000 men – almost as numerous as the largest striking force Napoleon could be expected to raise from an exhausted and divided France – had entered Belgium under Blücher to hold the frontier from the Ardennes to Charleroi, while a smaller joint British, Netherlands, Hanoverian, and Brunswick army had guarded it from Mons to the North Sea under the Duke of Wellington. Every week the young, under-strength battalions sent out in haste from England were being joined by the veteran regiments which had driven the French from Spain and which were now returning from America. Elsewhere more than half a million men, mobilized by the Sovereigns of Europe, were on the march, their vanguards already closing in on the French frontiers. The danger to Brussels and the Low Countries, so great three months before, seemed to have passed. Though no official state of war existed – Napoleon being merely treated as an outlaw under the new international system of collective security – it had been known that an invasion of France was to begin in July. It had even seemed likely that the French, republicans or royalists, would themselves throw out the usurper and so avoid the necessity of invasion. Napoleon's house, Wellington had told English visitors to the front, was tumbling about his ears.

On the night of Thursday, June 15th, there had been a ball in the

1. D'Arblay, III, 353. See *idem*, 354–60, 368. See *Near Observer*, 16–19; Costello, 195–6; *Creevey Papers*, I, 232–5; *Life and Times*, 78–80, 87–9; Jackson, 38–9, 81–3; Smith, I, 281–3; Picton, 104.

city. It had been given by an English milord of fabulous wealth, the Duke of Richmond, and the principal officers of the British and Allied army had attended it, including the Duke of Wellington and the leader of the Netherlands forces, the Prince of Orange, heir to the throne of the new kingdom. But during its course, and even before it had begun, it had become known that something was amiss. Several times Wellington had been interrupted by messages and was seen to write orders, and at an early hour many of his officers took their leave. During the small hours of the 16th the squares and streets of Brussels had filled with troops as trumpets sounded and drums beat to arms. Presently the troops – green-jacketed Riflemen, scarlet-clad infantry of the line and Highlanders, blue-coated Belgians, and Brunswickers in black – had moved off, laughing and joking in the early morning sunshine, and asking one another what all the fuss was about. The stolid Flemish country folk, rolling into the city in their carts, had watched them with curious eyes as they marched out down the Charleroi road. Everyone in command had seemed very composed and quiet; old Sir Thomas Picton, commander of the British 5th Division, with top hat and reconnoitring glass slung over his shoulder, cheerfully accosted his friends as he rode through the streets.

Elsewhere – at Enghien, Ath, Grammont, Nivelles, Oudenarde, and even as far away as Ghent – other troops, British, German, and Netherlandish, roused from their cantonments, had assembled to the sound of trumpets and bugles and, marching off along the hot, dusty highroads southwards and eastwards, had begun to converge on the assembly point. It had been a day of intense heat. As they emerged from the beech forests on to the great corn plain that fringed the Sambre to the north, the tramping infantrymen and jingling cavalry and gunners heard a dull, sullen sound like distant thunder and saw on the horizon columns of smoke arising.[1]

For on June 15th, after one of his incredibly swift and secret concentrations, Napoleon had sprung like a tiger across the Sambre and

1. 'There they go, shaking their blankets again,' said the old soldiers. Leake, I, 11; *Near Observer*, 2–4; Becke, 49 ff.; Bessborough, 240–1; Costello, 190; *Creevey Papers*, I, 223, 226–7, 229–30, 232; Lynedoch, 756; D'Arblay, III, 341–2, 347–8; Frazer, 520–4, 529–30, 536, 544, 572; Jackson, 6, 14–18; Kincaid, 153–6; Mercer, I, 47, 53–5, 103–4, 156–7, 198–202, 217–19, 230–9, 242–3, 284; Siborne, 3, 23; Simpson, 16–17; Smith, I, 226.

driven in the outposts of Blücher's army at the point where its right touched the left of Wellington's equally scattered force. When the first news of the crossing had reached the Prussian and British commanders, they had suspected it to be a feint. The hours Napoleon had thereby gained had given him the chance to drive a wedge between them. With 124,000 men he had placed himself between Blücher's 113,000 Prussians and Wellington's miscellaneous 83,000. His object had been to defeat one or the other before they had time to concentrate and then, forcing both back on their divergent communications, to enter Brussels as a conqueror. Thereafter, he had believed, the Belgian common people would rise against the Dutch, the war-weary French take heart and unite behind him, the Tory Government in London fall, and his Austrian father-in-law, deprived of British subsidies, sue for peace.

All afternoon on the 16th the people of Brussels had heard, through the hot, airless haze, the sound of cannonading from Quatre Bras, where twenty miles to the south Marshal Ney was trying to brush aside a weak Netherlands force from the crossroads which preserved front-line communication between the Prussian and Anglo-Dutch armies. By some miracle of tough, confused fighting, in which Picton's Highlanders had covered themselves with glory and the Duke of Brunswick had fallen, Wellington, reinforced by successive contingents, had held the crossroads and by nightfall assembled 30,000 troops in Ney's path. But owing to the delay in ordering his concentration – the result of faulty staff work – he had failed to join Blücher in battle that day against Napoleon. By nightfall, six miles away at Ligny, 63,000 Frenchmen under the great Emperor had beaten the 80,000 Prussians concentrated against them and inflicted 15,000 casualties. The seventy-two-year-old Field-Marshal had only narrowly escaped capture after being trampled on by French cavalry.

Yet Napoleon's victory had not been as complete as he had thought. Owing to the failure of one of his corps which, through contradictory orders, had marched and countermarched all day between the two battlefields without taking part in either, the Prussians had escaped annihilation and were able to withdraw in tolerable order into the night. Next morning, when the Emperor, detaching 33,000 troops under Marshal Grouchy to pursue the Prussians, had thrown the rest of his army against Wellington, the latter had withdrawn in good time up the Charleroi-Brussels highway. And though Napoleon had supposed that he had driven the Prussians back eastwards towards their communications, Blücher had in fact withdrawn northwards towards Wavre on a road parallel to the British only a dozen miles to the east. Unknown to Napoleon, the Allied armies had thus remained in touch and, though the Emperor had reduced their numerical superiority and shaken their morale, he had not, as he supposed, divided them. Nor, though the people of Brussels had expected all day to see the victorious French emerge from the Forest of Soignes, had the British withdrawal towards Brussels been on the whole precipitate. It had been brilliantly covered by Lord Uxbridge's cavalry and horse artillery, and by nightfall Wellington had concentrated his army on the ridge of Mont St Jean twelve miles south of the city. During the afternoon Napoleon's retreat had been increasingly delayed by torrential thunderstorms which had converted the Charleroi *chaussée* and the fields on either side into quagmires. It seemed, recalled one officer, as if the water was being tumbled out of heaven in tubs.[1]

The two armies had spent an uncomfortable night. The rain fell almost continually, with flashes of lightning and violent gusts of wind. The ground on which the men lay, drenched to the skin and shaking with cold, was sodden with wet crops. A few old campaigners made themselves tolerably comfortable by smearing their blankets with clay and making pillows of straw. Few of the newcomers to war, who in the Allied army outnumbered the old hands, got any sleep at all.

Dawn on the 18th was cold and cheerless. Everyone was covered in mud from head to foot. Presently the clouds began to lift, and the men managed to get their camp-fires lit and to cook breakfast. Afterwards, on the officers' orders, they dried their ammunition and cleaned their arms. Later, as the sun came out, Wellington rode round the lines, accompanied by his staff. They looked as gay and unconcerned as if they were riding to a meet in England.[2]

The ridge or rather rolling plateau on which the British army had halted was one which the Duke had long marked as a favourable

1. *Hamilton of Dalzell*, MS., 46–8, 77. See also Simmons, 364; Stanhope, 244; Tomkinson, 286–8.
2. Gronow, 1, 186–7; Smith, 1, 270.

position for the defence of the Belgian capital. It crossed the highroad from Brussels to Charleroi a mile and a half south of the village of Waterloo and the forest of Soignes. It was named after the little village of Mont Saint-Jean which nestled by the roadside in one of its northern folds. In the course of riding and hunting expeditions Wellington had carefully studied its gentle undulations and contours.[1] It was here that twenty-one years before, when he was a young lieutenant-colonel marching from Ostend to join a hard-pressed and almost identically circumstanced army, his chief, the Duke of York, had urged the Austrian generalissimo, Coburg, to give battle to Jourdan's levies after Fleurus. But Coburg had chosen to fall back eastward on his communications, leaving Brussels to its fate and the British to shift for themselves. It was because, after a generation of disaster and servitude, a Prussian Field-Marshal had learnt the necessity of unselfish co-operation between allies, that Wellington was able to take his stand here. For though his only reliable troops were outnumbered by two to one and though the French had nearly double his weight of artillery, he knew that he had only to hold his ground with one wing of an international army until the other under Blücher could reach the battlefield. Then, on the morrow, the whole mighty force could take the offensive and sweep Napoleon back to France.

Unlike Blücher at Ligny, who, in the normal Continental manner, had drawn up his army in view of Napoleon, Wellington – the greatest master of defensive tactics in Europe – had chosen a position where his infantry could inflict the utmost damage on the attackers while suffering the least themselves. Its reverse or northern slope, in whose undulations he concealed his forces, gave him precisely the cover and field of fire needed for an active defence. Behind it lay the forest which, stretching for miles on either side of the Brussels highway, constituted, with its close-growing beeches and freedom from undergrowth, an excellent temporary refuge into which to withdraw inexperienced troops if they proved unable to withstand Napoleon's attack. Once inside it, he remarked, he would have defied the Devil

1. 'If the Prussians are beat, which I think is very probable,' he told the Duke of Richmond on the night of the famous ball, 'that is the spot' – pointing at Waterloo on the map – 'where we must lick those fellows.' Lady Shelley, I, 171. For a first-hand confirmation of this story, see Granville, II, 538. See also Mercer, I, 194.

himself to drive him out.[1] But as, like his ally, he was thinking in ultimate terms, not of defence but of offensive action, he gave battle on the
open plain where the full strength of the Prussian and British armies
could later be brought to bear on Napoleon.

Until then, however, Wellington knew that his rôle must be strictly
defensive. At least half the foreign troops under his command could
not be trusted to manoeuvre. Kincaid drew the picture of a detachment
of them at Quatre Bras, behaving for all the world like Mathews the
comedian's ludicrous sketch of the American Militia; whenever, after
a careful explanation of their rôle, they were given the word to march,
they had started blazing away at the British skirmishers ahead – 'we
were at last,' Kincaid wrote, 'obliged to be satisfied with whatever
advantages their appearance would give, as even that was of some
consequence where troops were so scarce.' Later in the day, he admitted,
when they got used to the sensation of being fired at, they behaved
quite well. Many, however, having fought for Napoleon when Belgium, Holland, and Western Germany formed part of his empire, had
little stomach for fighting against him. Many more were boys and raw
landwehr, though, in the case of the Brunswickers, with good officers
and N.C.O.'s. Few were adequately equipped or trained.[2] Of the
42,000 foreign troops in Wellington's army only the 5500 men of the
veteran King's German Legion – an integral part of the British army –
could be described as first-line troops.

Wellington was, therefore, forced to do as he had done in early
Peninsular days; to stiffen his foreign formations with redcoats. In the
teeth of opposition, particularly from the King of the Netherlands, he
had tried to make his force as international in organization as possible;
to this end he habitually wore the national cockades of all the Allies in
his hat and forbade the playing of 'Rule Britannia' at regimental concerts. As at Talavera, the most immobile troops of all he stationed
among buildings and behind walls. Fortunately one of the features of
his position was the presence of villages and farms on either flank of
his two-and-a-half-mile front – Smohain, Papelotte, La Haye, and

1. ' It is not true that I could not have retreated. I could have got into the
wood and I would have defied the Devil to drive me out.' Mrs Arbuthnot,
Journal, 16th May, 1823. See also Cotton, 303.

2. Lynedoch. 764; Ellesmere, 216–18; Fortescue, 238, 243–7; Gomm, 363–4;
Basil Jackson, 10; Kincaid, 305, 329; Mercer, I, 93–4, 197–8, 281.

Frischermont to the east, and Merbe Braine and Braine l'Alleud to the west. In these he placed some rather uncertain Nassauers – who, however, defended them bravely – Chassé's Belgian division and the youthful Brunswickers who had suffered so severely at Quatre Bras. They thus served – an old device of Wellington's – both as flank guards and reserves.

The backbone of his polyglot, and what he afterwards described as 'infamous army'[1] was its 21,000 British regulars – of whom more than 2000 had arrived from Ostend only that morning – and their comrades of the King's German Legion. Yet of this vital 26,500 – a smaller force than any he had commanded since his first Portuguese campaign – only about half had been under fire. Several of its units were weak second-line battalions, scarcely out of the goose-step. Even most of the eighteen infantry battalions that had fought in Spain had been brought up to strength by recruiting from the plough before they left England. Probably not more than 12,000 had served in the incomparable army that had marched from the Douro to Toulouse.

Compared with his Peninsular army, Wellington's force was relatively stronger in cavalry than infantry. Its 7000 British and King's German Legion cavalry, though far outnumbered by Napoleon's cuirassiers and lancers, made an imposing spectacle, superbly uniformed and caparisoned – the Prince Regent saw to that – and mounted on the finest horses in the world. They could ride across country like a field of high-mettled foxhunters, for they came from a land where horsemanship was a passion. At a review they left Blücher speechless with admiration. 'It did one's heart good,' wrote a Rifleman, watching them on the retreat from Quatre Bras, 'to see how cordially the Lifeguards went at their work; they had no idea of anything but straightforward fighting and sent their opponents flying in all directions.' Their chief, the Earl of Uxbridge, was the Lord Paget who had commanded Moore's cavalry so brilliantly during the Corunna campaign, but whose service in the Peninsula had been cut short by an elopement with the wife of Wellington's brother. Apart from his amatory exploits,[2] he was an

1. Stanhope, 221.
2. When someone mentioned to Wellington that Lord Uxbridge had the reputation of running away with everybody he could, he replied, 'I'll take good care he don't run away with me.' In this anecdote, Fraser adds, he was compelled to soften 'the vigorous vernacular of the Duke.' Fraser, 186. See also Frazer, 520.

excellent officer, quiet, and incisive, though, like his command, rather too dashing.

What the British cavalry lacked, except for the King's German Legion and a few fine Peninsular regiments like the 23rd Light Dragoons, was experience of war and, in their high-spirited younger officers, discipline. Too many of the latter held their commissions, not because they wanted to be professional soldiers, but because a few years in a crack cavalry mess was a mark of social distinction. Their courage and dash was indisputable; their self-control and staying power less certain.[1] The troopers, magnificent fighting material, were what the officers – so much less experienced and realist than their humbler infantry colleagues – made or failed to make of them. The same witness of the Life Guards' charge during the retreat noticed with amusement that, whenever one of them got a roll in the mud, he went off to the rear as no longer fit to appear on parade.[2]

In artillery, though he only acknowledged it sparingly, Wellington was brilliantly served. Its mounted branch was magnificently horsed,[3] and, Horse and Field Artillery alike, officers and men were animated by the highest professional spirit. Only 96 of the 156 guns opposed to Napoleon's 266 pieces were British or King's German Legion, but they were probably better handled than any guns even on a battlefield where one of the commanders was the master gunner of all time. They were lighter metalled than the French guns, many of which were the dreaded twelve-pounders. Yet, thanks to the foresight of Sir Augustus Frazer, three of the seven mounted batteries had recently substituted

1. 'The real truth was that our cavalry never had much to do before this sanguinary battle; and the officers were, and always have been, very inferior to that of the infantry, being generally composed of country gentlemen's sons from the hunting counties of England. Such persons have no particular inclination for fighting but enter the Army as a genteel business, the oldest son being the squire, the second the parson, the next the dragoon.' *Hamilton of Dalzell* MS., p. 80. See Kincaid, 161; Stanley, 105; Tomkinson, 296, 318.

2. 'I thought at first that they had all been wounded, but on finding how the case stood, I could not help telling them that theirs was now the better situation to verify the old proverb, "The uglier, the better the soldier."' Kincaid, 334.

3. 'Mein Gott,' said Blücher, after inspecting Mercer's battery,' dere is not von 'orse in diss batterie wich is not goot for Veldt-Marshal.' Mercer. I, 217.

nine-pounders for the normal six-pounders. There were also some howitzers.

In the last resort, as Wellington well knew, everything depended on his British infantry. There were far too few of them; as he carefully sent them off after Quatre Bras before the rest of his troops, he remarked, 'Well, there is the last of the infantry gone, and I don't care now.' A few weeks before, Creevey, encountering him in a Brussels square, had asked whether he and Blücher could do the business. 'It all depends upon that article there,' the Duke had replied, pointing at a private of one of the line regiments who was gaping at the statues, 'give me enough of it, and I am sure.'[1]

He, therefore, placed his thirty-five under-strength British and King's German Legion infantry battalions where he thought the danger was greatest, but left no part of the battlefield without them. He had received in the small hours of the morning, before retiring to sleep, Blücher's assurance that he would join him in the course of the day with not less than two corps – a force as large as his own. His anxiety was, therefore, for his right rather than his left. Believing it to be to Napoleon's interest to shift the battle away from the Prussians' impending flank march, he expected him to incline to the west, possibly even striking as far as the Mons-Brussels road to seize the Belgian capital in his rear and break his communications with England. For this reason he had retained at Hal and Tubize, some ten or twelve miles to the west, 15,000 Dutch and Hanoverian and 3000 British troops to guard the Mons-Brussels road, protect the capital and keep open his lines to Ostend, where more veterans from America were expected. In the event of the battle shifting to the west this force might have an important effect, either against an offensive or in pursuit of a French retreat towards Maubeuge or Lille.[2]

There was a more immediate reason why Wellington felt anxious about his right. The unobtrusive but fine defensive position he had chosen had one flaw – a narrow, winding, shallow depression which, passing under the walls of a country house called Hougoumont in the

1. *Creevey Papers*, I, 208. See also Becke, 149.
2. As a similar Spanish force at Alba, had it only retained its position, would have converted his victory at Salamanca into a virtual annihilation of Marmont's army. See Ellesmere, 105, 183; Fortescue, X, 351, 355; Frazer, 267, 270; Greville (suppl.), I, 82–3; Tomkinson, 297.

plain below the ridge, afforded an approach by which a column could climb round the west shoulder of the plateau out of direct gunfire and debouch on to the reverse slope where his army was drawn up. For this reason he placed near the danger spot on the right of his front line the First or Guards Division and behind it, in reserve and *en potence*, Clinton's fine 2nd Division which, with its two brigades of veteran British and King's German Legion infantry, was the nearest he possessed to his old Peninsular Light Division – a force which could manoeuvre quickly. Beyond it he stationed at Merbe Braine and Braine l'Alleud his less mobile reserve of Brunswickers and Chassé's Belgians. In addition, since the winding hollow which his experienced eye had perceived could be commanded by musketry fire from Hougoumont, he adopted the unorthodox expedient of fortifying and garrisoning an outpost nearly a quarter of a mile in advance of his main position on the ridge. With its château, barns, orchards, gardens, park, and woods, the estate of Hougoumont formed a 500 yards square whose wooded southern border extended almost to the ridge occupied by the French. Without its possession Napoleon could neither move a column up the hollow nor, unless he divided his army in the presence of his enemy's best troops, envelop the Allied right. Wellington, therefore, placed seven hundred Hanoverians and Nassauers in the Hougoumont woods, and four light companies of the Guards, detached from the Guards' Division on the ridge behind, to hold the house, gardens, and orchard and command the sunken way. To the west, defending the avenue to the house from the Nivelles road, he stationed Mitchell's British brigade with some light cavalry in rear. Thus garrisoned, the Hougoumont estate outflanked from the west the plain between the rival armies; if it could be held till the Prussians arrived, Napoleon's position would become untenable. In the meantime it would gravely delay and impede his attack.

Having secured his right, Wellington strengthened the remaining two miles of his front in his usual way by placing his formations, except for the guns and skirmishers, on the reverse slope of the ridge. They were thus out of sight, though not out of range, of the enemy's cannon. They were deployed in broken and staggered lines and so disposed as to present single rather than double targets for the enemy's round-shot. The artillery, save for the reserve batteries, Wellington placed along the summit of the ridge, with orders to reserve its fire for the enemies' columns. The skirmishers and riflemen were stationed on the forward or southern slope, concealed, as were all his troops, in the corn which, almost shoulder-high, covered the entire battlefield. By this arrangement the French masses would have to advance through three successive zones of fire – the rifle fire of picked marksmen, the round-shot and grape of the guns, and, as they came over the crest, the musketry volleys of deployed and, till then, invisible infantry.

Apart from Hougoumont on the west, Smohain, Papelotte, and La Haye on the east, and the little farm of Mont Saint-Jean just behind the British lines, there were no buildings on the open ground Wellington had chosen for battle except the farm of La Haye Sainte. This lay a hundred yards or so down the slope on the southern side of the ridge, abutting on to the straight-paved *chaussée* from Charleroi to Brussels which, ascending the hill here through a cutting, intersected it and the British line at right angles. Here, in the centre of his line of skirmishers, Wellington placed a battalion of the King's German Legion under Major Baring. Behind it and at the top of the ridge the Charleroi-Brussels road was crossed at right angles by a sunken lane which, following the crest from west to east, joined, north of Hougoumont, another highway that fanned out of the Brussels road at Mont Saint-Jean and ran through a cutting south-westwards towards Nivelles. This road, like the orchards and woods of Hougoumont, had the effect of constricting the frontage on which the French could assail Wellington's right.

It was generally believed by the British – though not by Wellington, who knew his adversary's overweening confidence and impatience – that there would be no attack that day.[1] But in the course of the morning, it became clear that the enemy advance-guard, which had bivouacked during the night on a parallel ridge three-quarters of a mile to the south, was being joined by the entire French army. Presently the sun came out, and watchers could see the long lines of massed troops, with their glittering helmets, cuirasses, and arms, forming a magnificent spectacle, on the ridge of La Belle Alliance – named after the solitary,

---

1. H. M. C. Bathurst; Bessborough, 242; Frazer, 546; Kincaid, 338; Smith, I, 268; Gronow, I, 68–9; Leeke, 187; Gomm, 363–4; *Hamilton of Dalzell* MS., 49–50; Jackson, 7–8.

red-tiled public house of that name. At one time there was a burst of cheering, as a grey figure on a white horse, accompanied by a cavalcade, rode down the lines. For the French were not only intending to attack, but in their resolve to conquer, were partaking of a sacrament. Napoleon might not have France, or even all his anxious generals behind him, but there was no question of the devotion of his fighting men. Between him and his old *moustaches* was a bond to be found in no other army on earth. For all his grandiloquent pretensions, he and they were familiars. Cam Hobhouse, watching him review the Imperial Guard just before the campaign began, was amazed at the way he mingled with his troops, leaving the saluting base and marching in time beside each column; once he went up to a grenadier and affectionately pulled his nose. He might be prodigal of his men's lives, but, unlike Wellington, who was not, he valued his command of their hearts. It was the foundation of his fortunes. At that moment as he rode along the lines amid shouts of '*Vive l'Empereur!*,' Leipzig, the Retreat from Moscow, and the Abdication were as though they had never been.

Neither Napoleon nor his men doubted their ability to destroy Wellington's army and reach Brussels by nightfall. Their triumph over the Prussians two days before – achieved against superior numbers – had whetted their appetite for glory. They saw themselves, for all their difficulties, on the verge of a new Marengo. Nor was the urgent victory Napoleon needed the key only to political salvation. It would be a revenge for all the humiliations the English had heaped on him. Wellington was the one commander with a European reputation whom he had never beaten and the British the one army. 'Because you have been defeated by Wellington,' he told his Chief of Staff, Soult, who dwelt on the British capacity for recoil, 'you think him a great general! I tell you that Wellington is a bad general, that the English are bad troops and that this will be a picnic!' His only fear was that they would vanish before he could attack them, as they had done on the previous day at Quatre Bras and seven years earlier under Moore on the Carrion. As, however, they now appeared to be calmly waiting for him, their doom was certain. 'We will sleep to-night,' he told his officers, 'in Brussels.'

Owing to the usual dispersal in search of food and plunder the last of the French only reached their battle stations at midday, three hours after the time originally ordered. Napoleon, however, was not hurrying, since to make full use of his superior artillery and cavalry, he wanted the ground to dry. Despite warnings from those who had fought in Spain, he was quite sure that, once he struck in overpowering force, there would be little need to waste time in manoeuvring. Most of Wellington's foreign auxiliaries, he reckoned, would bolt at the start, and the stiff redcoats would then break under the triple shock of his massed bombardment, veteran columns, and discharge of grape at close range. 'I shall hammer them with my artillery,' he announced, 'charge them with my cavalry to make them show themselves, and, when I am quite sure where the actual English are, I shall go straight at them with my Old Guard.'[1]

As for the Prussians, he was so convinced that they had retreated eastwards, as he wished, that he never considered the possibility of their appearance on the battlefield at all. After the hiding he had given them at Ligny they were manifestly incapable of further fight for the present. Having detached Grouchy to shepherd them out of Flanders, he felt he could discount them. They could be trusted, as in the past, to act selfishly and leave their allies to their fate. It had never been his habit to keep faith with anyone unless it suited him. That a Prussian commander should endanger his army and strain his communications to keep faith with Wellington never occurred to him.

The Emperor, therefore, decided to open his main attack at one o'clock. In the meantime, while he massed eighty field-pieces on a spur of high ground in the middle of the valley opposite and about 600 yards short of the British centre, he ordered the troops on his two flanks to engage the extremities of the defenders' line at Papelotte and Hougoumont in order to distract attention from his impending blow, and probably – though of this there can be no certainty – to clear a way for the use, at the decisive moment, of the sunken hollow leading to the heart of Wellington's right. In that case, however, he was unfortunate in his adversary.

The first shots of the battle were fired at about half past eleven in front of Hougoumont. After a short preliminary bombardment, four battalions of Prince Jerome's division advanced against the wood to the south of the château. During the next hour they succeeded in driving

1. Foy, 278–9, 345.

out its not very numerous German defenders. But they then went on to attack the gardens and mansion and in doing so came up against a far more formidable adversary, the four light companies of the British Guards under Lord Saltoun. The attackers not only attracted the close attention of Wellington, but brought upon themselves exceedingly heavy casualties – 1500 in the first forty minutes, both from the steady aim of the British guardsmen, firing through embrasures in the walls, and from the accurate fire of Bull's howitzer battery stationed on the ridge behind the house. When the Guards counter-attacked and drove them back, Jerome threw another brigade into the assault and tried to gain a lodgement in the courtyard of the château. So furious was his attack that at one moment a detachment of his men broke open the great gate with an axe and swarmed in, only to be surrounded and destroyed inside, while four officers and a sergeant of the Coldstream closed the door behind them by main force. Once again the British counter-attacked with four companies of the Coldstream whom Wellington sent down from the ridge. 'There, my lads, in with you,' he said as they moved off, 'let me see no more of you.'

Jerome's answer and that of the commander of the French left, General Reille, was to undertake – a quarter of an hour before Napoleon's main attack on the centre was due to begin – a third attack on Hougoumont with still larger forces. For every regiment they committed, the frugal Wellington staked no more than a company or whatever smaller force was necessary to hold the position. All the while his guns continued to shell the wood with such effect that, as one unending column of fresh attackers poured into it, another –of wounded – as continuously poured out.[1]

So far Napoleon had been only partially successful. His diversion to the east had made little effect on the Netherlanders in Papelotte and La Haye, while the more important one to the west, though occupying Wellington's attention, had failed either to by-pass or capture Hougoumont. It was now one o'clock, the hour at which the bombardment of the Allied centre was due to begin. But before its smoke enveloped the battlefield, Napoleon, watching the preparations from a knoll beside

1. Stanhope, 47. See also Ellesmere, 105–6; Frazer, 556; Gronow, 1, 198–9; Greville (suppl.), 1, 83; Cotton, 51–7; Kennedy, 89–92; Houssaye, 187–9; Morris, 229–2.

the Brussels road, observed through his telescope a suspicious movement on the high ground towards Wavre, five or six miles to the east.
It might – at first it seemed to him that it must – be Grouchy, from
whom he had just heard that the Prussians were retiring, not on Liège
as both men had thought, but on Brussels. Yet this was scarcely likely,
as Grouchy in his dispatch, dated at six that morning, had announced
his intention of following them northwards on Wavre. And, as

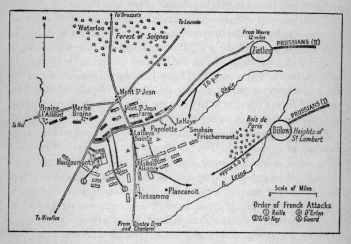

Grouchy, like Napoleon, had been wrong once about the Prussians'
movements, there was another and less pleasant possibility.

At that moment, this terrifying suspicion was confirmed. For a
Prussian hussar, captured by a French vedette to the west of the battlefield, was brought to Napoleon bearing a disptach from Blücher to
Wellington which showed that the troops visible on the heights of St
Lambert were Bülow's corps, advancing from Wavre, and that the
rest of the Prussian army had spent the night around that town, only
thirteen miles away.

Napoleon, in other words, had been 'making pictures' – the crime
against which he had always warned his subordinates. He had made
his dispositions to fight under conditions that did not exist. Instead of
having only the English and their feeble auxiliaries to contend with,

he would have, if he proceeded with his attack, to face before nightfall the intervention of another army. The attempt to separate Wellington's and Blücher's forces had failed, at least in any but the most temporary sense. The French must either withdraw – the prudent course – or defeat the British in the next three hours. For after that they would have to contend against two foes.

Being a gambler, and being, both politically and strategically, in desperate need of an immediate victory, Napoleon decided to proceed with the battle. It still seemed unthinkable to him that the breach he was about to blast in the British centre could fail to defeat Wellington, and, with him out of the way, Blücher could be dealt with in turn. Indeed, with Grouchy in his rear and his army committed to the muddy defiles between Wavre and Mont Saint-Jean, the old Prussian might end the day in an even worse disaster than Ligny. Napoleon, therefore, detached part of his reserve to delay the still distant Prussian advance, and ordered the attack on the British to proceed.

The eighty-gun bombardment, which opened at one o'clock, fully came up to expectations. Twenty-four of the guns were Napoleon's great twelve-pounders, with a 2000 yards range. It took away the breath of Wellington's young recruits and militia men, and surprised even Peninsular veterans by its intensity. Captain Mercer, commanding a reserve battery of horse artillery in a hollow several hundred yards and in rear of the British right flank, found, even in that sheltered position, the shot and shell continually plunging around him. One shot completely carried away the lower part of the head of one of his horses. Fortunately the ground was still wet and many shells burst where they fell, while the round-shot, instead of hopping and ricochetting for half a mile or more, frequently became embedded in the mud.[1]

But though very alarming, owing to Wellington's skilful dispositions, the bombardment did comparatively little harm except to a brigade of Belgians, whose commander, General Bylandt, misinterpreting his orders, had drawn it up, in the Continental manner, on the forward slope of the ridge. During its half-hour of bombardment in

1. Becke, 168; Cotton, 87–8; Fortescue, x, 360; Houssaye, 203; James, 223; Kennedy, 107; Kincaid, 341; Mercer, I, 294–6; Siborne, 327–8; Tomkinson, 297, 303.

this exposed position it lost one man in four, and, had it not been hastily withdrawn to a less conspicuous position, its loss might have been still greater. When, therefore, at halfpast one, D'Erlon in charge of the French right moved his corps forward to the attack, with all the panoply and terror of a Napoleonic offensive – drums beating at the head of dense column, bearded grenadiers marching four hundred abreast shouting at the top of their voices, and clouds of *tirailleurs* running and firing ahead – the customary conditions for success seemed to have been ensured. Four divisions of infantry – more than 16,000 men – each moving in close column of battalions at a quarter of a mile's distance, tramped down the slope and up the hill against the British centre and left through clouds of sulphurous smoke. Behind came companies of sappers, ready to turn the village of Mont Saint-Jean beyond the British centre into a fortress as soon as it was captured.

A hail of shot from the artillery on the crest greeted them. But it did not halt the men who had conquered at Wagram and Friedland. One column, supported by cuirassiers, swept round La Haye Sainte, encircling it and its German defenders and driving back the two companies of the Rifles – the most formidable marksmen in Europe – who were stationed in a sandpit on the opposite side of the *chaussée*. Another, to the west, forced the Dutch out of Papelotte and La Haye and temporarily occupied Smohain. In the centre about 8000 men approached the summit simultaneously. As they did so, Bylandt's Belgians – raw troops who had endured to the limit of their capacity – fired one hysterical volley at the advancing, shouting column and took to their heels, carrying away the gunners of the reserve batteries behind. They never stopped till they reached the Forest of Soignes, where they remained for the rest of the day.[1]

To Napoleon, watching from the knoll near La Belle Alliance, it seemed as though, as at Ligny, his adversary's centre was broken. But it was not a Netherlandish or even a Prussian army he had to dislodge, but a British. As the French bore down on the gap they had opened, Picton deployed Kempt's reserve brigade in their path. It was the

1. 'I peeped into the skirts of the forest, and truly felt astonished; entire companies seemed there, with regularly piled arms, fires blazing under cooking kettles, while the men lay about smoking as coolly as if no enemy were within a day's march. ... General Müffling, in his account of Waterloo, estimates the runaways hidden in the forest at 10,000.' Jackson, 47.

familiar story of every battle of the Peninsular War. 'The French came on in the old style,' said Wellington afterwards, 'and we drove them off in the old style.' The 28th, 32nd, 79th Highlanders, and the 95th Rifles – all veterans of Spain – held their fire till the head of the column was only twenty yards away. Then, from their thin extended line, they poured in a tremendous, disciplined volley, and, as the leading French files tried, too late, to deploy, charged with the bayonet. At the moment of his triumph Picton was struck in the head by a bullet and killed.[1]

Farther to the east, D'Erlon's two other divisions reached the summit. Here, after its heavy losses at Quatre Bras, Pack's brigade – Royals, 44th, 42nd, and 92nd Highlanders – could only muster 1400 bayonets. Slowly, against such odds, they began to give ground, while a brigade of French cavalry on their flank, having cut a Hanoverian battalion to pieces, swarmed on to the crest.

At that moment, Lord Uxbridge, waiting behind the British infantry with two brigades of heavy cavalry ready deployed, gave the order to charge. Leading the Household Brigade in person, he drove the astonished French cuirassiers into the ranks of the infantry behind, who, seeing the big, scarlet-coated Life Guardsmen slashing at them, turned and joined in the flight. It was the charge at Salamanca over again. Simultaneously the Union Brigade – consisting of Royal Dragoons, Scots Greys, and Inniskillings – swept down on another French column. Within a few minutes the flower of D'Erlon's corps was flying across the plain with 2000 British cavalry after it. 'Hundreds of the infantry threw themselves down and pretended to be dead,' wrote Kincaid, 'while the cavalry galloped over them and then got up and ran away; I never saw such a scene in all my life.' More than 4000 were cut down or taken prisoner. Many did not stop till they reached Genappe.

Unfortunately the pursuers did not stop either. The secret of cavalry is iron discipline. It was a secret that the British cavalry, though superlative in dash, physique, and horsemanship, had never wholly mastered.

1. Becke, 195–7; Belloc, 171–3; Fortescue, x, 360–4; Gomm, 351, 358–9; Gronow, 1, 188; Horsburgh, 249–51; Houssaye, 193–6; Jackson, 47, 88–92; James, 223, 228–9; Kennedy, 107–12; Kincaid, 344–6; *Random Shots*, 206, 273; Siborne, 19; Simmons, 365, 367; Smith, 1, 270–1, 277; Stanhope, 221; James, 228–35; Cotton, 59–62.

According to Hamilton of Dalzell of the Scots Greys, the troopers had been served with rum before the charge. They followed the French into the heart of Napoleon's position, sabring the gunners of his great battery and riding on to the ridge of La Belle Alliance itself as though they were after a fox. Having charged in the first line, Uxbridge was unable either to stop them or to bring up reserve cavalry in support. When the French cuirassiers and lancers counter-attacked in superior strength, the scattered, breathless men and horses were powerless and became themselves the pursued. The flower of Wellington's cavalry – the striking-force of his tactical reserve – having saved his centre, was itself needlessly destroyed. Sir William Ponsonby was struck down at the head of the Union Brigade, and nearly half the personnel of the six splendid regiments which had smashed D'Erlon's columns were killed or taken prisoner. Vandeleur's Brigade, which gallantly tried to cover their retreat, also suffered severely. Those who got back to the British lines were too few to intervene with real effect in the battle again. Some of the weaker brethren never returned to the field at all.[1]

*

But for this unexpected advantage, there would have seemed little object in Napoleon's continuing the battle. It was now three o'clock. Not only had one of his two corps of front-line infantry become heavily committed to an increasingly costly and still unsuccessful struggle in front of Hougoumont, but the British, contrary to expectation, had repulsed and shattered the other which, untouched at either Ligny or Quatre Bras, was to have breached and pinned down Wellington's centre until Lobau's reserve infantry, Ney's cavalry and, at the end of all, the Imperial Guard, had destroyed him. Instead, Napoleon now found himself committed to an impending battle on a second front, to avert or postpone which he was forced to detach, under Lobau, the very reserve of infantry which was to have followed up D'Erlon's expected success. With the Prussians approaching from the other side, he dared not commit this now to a left-hook against the

1. Lynedoch, 760, 762–3; Fortescue, x, 365–7; Gomm, 351; Gronow, 1, 78–80, 195–6, 204; 11, 3; *Hamilton of Dalzell* MS., 50–3, 70–1, 77–8; Haydon, 1, 311; Houssaye, 197 ff.; Kennedy, 110–11; Kincaid, 345; G. W. Picton, 78–80; Lady Shelley, 1, 173–4, 183; Siborne, 7–10, 16–17, 43–4, 72, 77, 81–2; Tomkinson, 300, 304.

British centre, the vital approach to which was still untaken. Apart from the small portion of Reille's corps still uncommitted to the unending fight round Hougoumont, he had no infantry left for a new attack on the ridge except the twenty-four battalions of the Imperial Guard. And these, in view of the growing threat to his flank and the, to him, unexpected revelation of British defensive striking-power, he was not yet prepared to commit. For the Guard was the last card that stood between him and ruin. He kept it, 13,000 strong, the apple of his eye, unused beside him.

For about half an hour there was a pause in the battle, except at Hougoumont, where Jerome and Foy threw ever more troops into the inferno round the blazing but still defiant buildings. Wellington took advantage of the lull to readjust his dispositions. Pack's brigade took the place vacated by Bylandt's Netherlanders, Lambert's brigade came up from the second line to strengthen Picton's battered division, and two more companies of the King's German Legion were thrown into La Haye Sainte. The Prussians were taking far longer to arrive than the British commander had expected. There had been a delay in their start, aggravated by a fire in the narrow streets of Wavre and the fact that Bülow's as yet unused corps in the van had the farthest distance to march. After the rains, the cross-country lanes were almost impassable for transport, and Gneisenau, the Prussian Chief of Staff, was reluctant to attack Napoleon, with Grouchy's troops in his rear, until he knew for certain that Wellington was standing fast. Only Blücher's insistence – for the old man, oblivious of his injuries, was with Bülow's advance guard by midday – carried the tired and hungry troops forward through the soggy defiles of the Lasne and the dense woods that lay between it and the battlefield. 'I have promised Wellington,' he told them as they dragged the guns axle-deep through mire, 'you would not have me break my word!'

Meanwhile, the French gunners had taken up their position again on the central ridge and, soon after three o'clock, reopened their fire. It was more intense than anything the oldest Peninsular veteran had experienced. The range was so accurate that almost every shot told, and after a quarter of an hour Wellington withdrew his infantry a hundred yards farther back from the crest. Under cover of the bombardment, La Haye Sainte in the centre was again surrounded. But

Baring's handful of German Legionaries continued to hold the walls, and with Kempt's and Lambert's men standing firm on the plateau above, D'Erlon's mangled infantry refrained from pressing home their assault. They seemed to fear a renewal of the storm of cavalry that had struck their comrades.

Suddenly the battle took a novel and spectacular form. For, mistaking the partial withdrawal of Wellington's infantry for the beginning of a general retirement, Marshal Ney decided to take a short cut to victory by sweeping the ridge with heavy cavalry. Of these – the finest in the world – his master had almost as many as Wellington's British infantry. He therefore ordered forward 5000 of them, including eight regiments of cuirassiers, drawing them up in the plain immediately to the west of the *chaussée* where the slope was easiest.

Wellington watched the splendid spectacle with amazement. It seemed unbelievable that the French would dare to assail a line of unbroken British infantry with cavalry alone. But such was plainly their intention, and, with his own heavy cavalry too weakened to counter-charge in strength, there was a danger that, if Napoleon was able to bring up infantry and guns behind them, the defenders, forced to remain in square, might be blasted out of existence by case-shot. The two divisions to the west of the Brussels road – the 3rd and 1st – were ordered to form battalion squares or oblongs[1] in chequer-wise pattern across the gently swelling, corn-covered plateau. They were aligned so that every face of every square had a field of fire free of the next. Until the attackers appeared over the crest Wellington ordered the men to lie down. Behind the twenty squares his cavalry, including the remnants of the two British heavy brigades, were drawn up in support.

Between and a little in advance of the squares Wellington placed his guns, bringing up his last two reserve batteries of Horse Artillery to inflict the utmost damage on the advancing cavalry. As Mercer's men, on the order, 'Left limber up, and as fast as you can!' galloped[2] into the inferno of smoke and heat on the plateau, they heard a humming like the sound of myriads of beetles on a summer's evening. So

1. The unusual but convenient formation chosen by young Captain Shaw Kennedy, a pupil of Moore and Craufurd, who was acting as chief of staff to Alten's third division. Kennedy, 98–102.

2. 'Ah!' said the Duke as he watched them, 'that's the way I like to see horse artillery move.' Mercer, I, 313.

thick was the hail of balls and bullets, wrote their commander, that it seemed dangerous to extend the arm lest it should be torn off. Their orders, in the event of the enemy charging home, were to run for shelter to the nearest square, taking the near wheel of each gun with them.

Mercer disregarded this order – one that could only have been given to gun detachments of the highest discipline and training – not because he doubted his battery's morale, but because he believed that the young Brunswickers in square on either side of him, who were falling fast, would take to their heels if they saw his men run. As soon as the French appeared out of the smoke a hundred yards away – a long line of cuirasses and helmets glittering like a gigantic wave on the crest of the rye – he ordered his six nine-pounders, doubly loaded with round-shot and case, to open fire. As the case poured into them, the leading ranks went down like grass before a skilled mower. Again and again, when the French charged, the same thing happened, and the Brunswickers who, before the battery's arrival, had stood like soulless logs in their agony and had only been kept at their posts by the gallantry of their officers, recovered heart.

Elsewhere, where the gunners obeyed Wellington's orders, the French cavalry, crowded in a dense mass into the half-mile gap between Hougoumont and La Haye Sainte, rode over the abandoned guns and swept round the squares beyond. They did not gallop like English foxhunters, but came, as was their wont, at a slow, majestic pace and in perfect formation, their horses shaking the earth. As they appeared the British infantry rose at the word of command, their muskets at the ready and their bayonets bristling like massed gigantic *chevaux de frise*. If the cavalry of the Empire were Atlantic breakers, the British squares were the rocks of an iron coast. The men, many of them rosy-faced youngsters from the plough, were much impressed by the splendid appearance of the hordes of legendary horsemen who suddenly encircled them and even more by their courage, but they were not intimidated by them, as Ney had intended. As their experienced officers and N.C.O.s seemed to regard the newcomers as harmless, in their stolid, unimaginative English way they did so too. The cuirassiers and lancers made a great deal of noise and glitter, brandishing their weapons like pantomime giants and shouting '*Vive l'Empereur*,' but they seemed infinitely preferable to the continuous hail of shot and shell which had poured from the French batteries till they arrived on the ridge.

Short of impaling their horses on the hedges of bayonets, Ney's cavalry tried every device to break the squares. Occasionally little groups of horsemen, led by frantic officers, would dash for the face of one, firing off carbines and pistols and hoping to draw sufficient fire to enable their comrades behind to break in on a line of unloaded muskets. But the British and Hanoverian squares preserved perfect discipline, withholding their fire until they received the word of command and then, with their volleys, bringing down everything before them. The loss of horses was prodigious; the poor creatures lay dead or dying in hundreds, their riders, many of them wounded, making their way in a continuous stream back down the hill, or sprawling in their heavy cuirasses in the mud, looking, as Wellington afterwards recalled, like overturned turtles.[1]

Whenever he judged that the intruders were sufficiently worn down and wearied, Wellington endeavoured to push them off the plateau with his cavalry, or, in default, by edging forward his squares in echelon towards the abandoned guns. He did not hurry, for he was playing for time, and he could not afford to let his light British and King's German Legion cavalry encounter the heavier armed cuirassiers until the latter were too exhausted and reduced to retaliate. The foreign Horse which he had brought up from the flanks and reserve to take the place of Ponsonby's and Somerset's lost squadrons proved, most of it, worse than useless, refusing repeated appeals from Uxbridge to charge. One regiment of Hanoverian hussars, led by its colonel,[2] fled as far as Brussels.

1. Someone once asked him whether the French cuirassiers had not come up very well at Waterloo. 'Yes,' he replied, 'and they went down very well too.' See Becke, 202–9; Croker, I, 330; Lynedoch, 759; Ellesmere, 98–9, 240; Fortescue, x, 370–6; Fraser, 558–9; Frazer, 559; Gomm, 373; Gronow, I, 69–73, 190–1; Houssaye, 204–14; Jackson, 48–51; Kennedy, 19, 20, 115–16; Mercer, I, 310–11; Picton, 81–2, 85–6; Siborne, 1–12; Tomkinson, 305.

2. 'The Aide-de-Camp ... seeing that the Hanoverian would not advance, said, "As you do not attend to the order given, I have another from the Duke of Wellington which is *that you fall back in the rear of the Army*." This the Hanoverian readily complied with, saying it was very considerate of the Duke when engaged in so much action to think of his Corps with so much care.

Even the British cavalry showed a reluctance at times to charge home in the face of such overwhelming weight and numbers, though several regiments, particularly the 13th Light Dragoons and the 15th Hussars, behaved with the greatest gallantry. The shock felt by men encountering for the first time the sights and sounds of battle – and such a battle – had in the nature of things a more paralysing effect on cavalry than on infantry whose men in square had the close support of officers and comrades. Once Uxbridge, whose energy and initiative throughout this critical time was beyond praise, was driven into exclaiming that he had tried every brigade and could not get one to follow him, and then, as he rode up to the 1st Foot Guards, 'Thank God, I am with men who make me not ashamed of being an Englishman.'[1] One of the officers recalled how, while Wellington was sheltering in his square, the men were so mortified at seeing the cuirassiers deliberately walking their horses round them that they shouted, 'Where are our cavalry? Why don't they come and pitch into these French fellows?' Such resentment failed to take into account the hopeless numerical inferiority of the Allied cavalry after its earlier losses, and was based on an incomplete view of the battlefield. All the hard-pressed infantrymen could see, amid clouds of thick, eddying smoke, was the outer face of the square on either side, and the hordes of encircling French Horse. They could not realize that the very presence of the decimated English squadrons in their rear helped to sustain the wavering morale of the Netherlanders and Brunswickers, and that the memory of their earlier and heroic onslaught accounted for Napoleon's failure to follow up his cavalry with infantry and subject their squares to case-shot at close range.

Five times in two hours the French horsemen were driven from the

Accordingly this Corps retreated, and it was from them that a report reached Brussels that the French had gained the victory.' Farington, VIII, 19–20. See also *Hamilton of Dalzell* MS., 73; Frazer, 560–1; Siborne, 14, 18–19; Stanhope, 221; Tomkinson, 296.

1. From a copy of a letter of Captain (later General) Horace Churchill of 24th June, 1815, kindly communicated by Brigadier C. E. Hudson, V.C., C.B., D.S.O., M.C. 'All that Churchill says in censure,' wrote Napier of this letter, 'was the common talk of the Army at the time.' See *Hamilton of Dalzell* MS., for a cavalryman's criticism, and Gronow, I, 73; Tomkinson, 318. Lord Uxbridge afterwards wrote in glowing terms of the conduct of the British cavalry as a whole. Siborne, 12, 16–17.

plateau; five times, after rallying in the plain, they returned. Whenever they disappeared the British gunners ran out of the squares and reopened fire, while Napoleon's guns resumed their cannonade. Some time after five o'clock Ney brought up the last cavalry from the second line – Kellermann's two divisions of cuirassiers and the heavy squadrons of the Imperial Guard. At one moment more than 9000 Horse assailed the ridge in a compact phalanx. This immense body was packed in the 800 yards front between the *chaussée* and the British bastion at Hougoumont, where the ground was a morass piled with dead horses. The front ranks, including most of the senior officers, were completely wiped out by the English batteries, and the weary mounts could only proceed at a walk. Yet they still continued to return.

Throughout this time and during the bombardments which preceded each assault the British infantry patiently endured their fate. They seemed in their steady squares to be rooted to the ground. Though it would have been hazardous in the extreme to have manoeuvred with some of the young second British and Hanoverian landwehr battalions, they showed themselves, under their fine officers and N.C.O.s, as capable of standing fire as the oldest veterans. Theirs, as Harry Smith said, was no battle of science; it was a stand-up fight between two pugilists, milling away till one or the other was beaten. Inside each suffocating square, reeking with the smell of burnt cartridge and powder, it was like a hospital, the dead and dying strewing the ground. The sufferings of many of the wounded were indescribable; one rifleman had both legs shot off and both arms amputated, but continued to breathe as he lay amid his comrades. Few cried out in their pain, and when they did so, their officers immediately quieted them;[1] it was a point of pride with Englishmen of all classes to take punishment without murmuring. Their stoicism was equalled by that of the French cavalry, who won the ungrudging admiration of the entire British army.[2]

1. 'The rear man made a considerable outcry on being wounded, but on one of the officers saying kindly to him, "O man, don't make a noise," he instantly recollected himself and was quiet. This was the only noise ... which I heard from any wounded man during the battle.' Leeke, I, 33.

2. 'Never was such devotion witnessed as the French cuirassiers. ... I could not help exclaiming when the mêlée was going on, "By God, those fellows deserve Bonaparte, they fight so nobly for him."' – MS. Letter of Horace Churchill, 24th June, 1815.

Nor was less courage shown by the defenders of Hougoumont. The flank companies in the burnt-out mansion among the charred remains of their comrades, the Coldstream lining the hedge and garden wall, the 3rd Guards in the orchard, all lived that day up to the highest tradition of the Brigade of Guards. They had made up their minds to die sooner than yield. Three times the wood was taken and retaken; every tree was riddled with bullets, and in the orchard alone more than two thousand bodies were crowded together. 'You may depend upon it,' said Wellington, 'no troops could have held Hougoumont but British, and only the best of them.'

*

During the last hour of Ney's cavalry attacks the sound of the Prussian guns had been audible on the British ridge in the lulls of firing, though few yet realized its import. By four o'clock, the two leading divisions of Bülow's corps had reached the western edge of Paris wood, just over two miles east of La Belle Alliance. Half an hour later, in view of the urgency of Wellington's messages, they went into action without waiting for their supports. Soon after five, when they had advanced to within a mile and a half of the Brussels road, Lobau counter-attacked and drove them back. But at six o'clock, two more Prussian divisions having emerged from the wood, Bülow again attacked, striking round Lobau's southern flank at Plancenoit, a village less than a mile from the French lifeline.

The situation was growing grave in the extreme for Napoleon. His troops had been marching and fighting almost continuously for four days; their losses during the afternoon had been heavier than in any engagement of comparable scale in his career. Again and again they had seemed on the point of carrying the ridge and sweeping Wellington's international flotsam and jetsam down the Brussels road. Yet whenever the smoke cleared, the stubborn redcoats were seen to be still standing. The Prussian shot, already playing on the *chaussée*, brought home to the Emperor that, unless he could break Wellington's line in the remaining hours of daylight, his doom was certain.

The Emperor descended from the mound on which he had so long watched the battle. Though, like his adversary, still in his middle forties, he had so far taken little active part in the direction of the assault. After a study of the battlefield in the early hours and the issue of orders for the attack, he had delegated tactical control to Ney. Exhausted by the exertions of the last three days, he had spent part of the afternoon in what seemed to onlookers a coma, and had not even intervened to stay the impetuous Marshal's abuse of his cavalry. But he now roused himself, to snatch, as so often in the past, victory from defeat.

He had to fight on two fronts. To the south-east 30,000 Prussians were striking at his communications; to the north 20,000 Britons and as many or more Germans and Netherlanders were still barring the Brussels road. Despite his casualties he still had between 50,000 and 60,000 veteran troops, though of Grouchy's 33,000 wandering somewhere in space to the east,[1] there was no sign. To clear his flank and gain time for a further assault on the British, he dispatched eight young Guard battalions of the Imperial Guard to reinforce Lobau and recover Plancenoit. Simultaneously he gave Ney peremptory orders to throw in infantry and capture La Haye Sainte.

Conscious that the crisis of the battle was at hand and that the interminable and futile attacks of the French cavalry must now be followed up by infantry, Wellington had already reorganized his line. Taking advantage of the lull after the last charge, he had brought up Clinton's division of Peninsular veterans from its place in reserve to a point at which, standing between the defenders of Hougoumont and Maitland's Guards, they could enfilade any attack on his right. Feeling that Hougoumont was now secure and that, as a result, no threat could develop from that quarter, he also summoned Chassé's Netherlanders from Braine L'Alleud and placed them in rear of his centre. Simultaneously, seeing that Ney's force was spent, he deployed his shrunken battalions from square, forming them four-deep instead of in the normal two-rank line so as to give extended fire-power against infantry while preserving sufficient solidity to repel what remained of the French cavalry.[2]

Soon after six Ney attacked in the centre with two columns of infantry and cavalry. They were driven back by a terrific fire from the British guns. But the French were fighting magnificently and with

---

1. Unknown to him they were at that moment fiercely attacking the Prussian rearguard at Wavre twelve miles away.

2. Becke, 211; Ellesmere, 207–9; Fortescue, x, 372, 378; Tomkinson, 308.

the recklessness of despair, and the young Prince of Orange, in charge of the defenders at this point, was without experience of command. Repeating a mistake made at Quatre Bras, he ordered one of Ompteda's battalions of the King's German Legion above La Haye Sainte to deploy in the presence of cavalry, with disastrous consequences. Their comrades inside the farmhouse were now down to their last round of ammunition[1] and at about six-thirty the key to the British centre was captured. Baring's remaining forty men fought their way back to the ridge with the bayonet. At about the same time the eight battalions of the Young Guard, sent to Lobau's aid, recovered Plancenoit.

This double success gave the French, at the eleventh hour, a chance of victory. Throwing sharpshooters and guns forward from the captured farm, they established themselves on the ridge and opened a destructive fire on the left of the 3rd Division and the right of the 5th. The Prince of Orange, who had by now completely lost his head, deployed another of Ompteda's battalions in the presence of cavalry with the same disastrous result. A few minutes later Ompteda was killed. His shattered brigade and that of Kielmansegge's young Hanoverians had reached the limit of their endurance and were on the point of breaking. Only the gallantry of the Rifles and a charge by the 3rd Hussars of the Legion prevented immediate disaster.

Had Napoleon been on the spot to exploit the opportunity, he might have turned the gap in the British centre into a chasm. But when, still watching from La Belle Alliance three-quarters of a mile away, he received Ney's urgent appeal for more infantry, he only asked petulantly whether the Marshal expected him to make them. At the crisis of his gamble his moral courage faltered; he was not ready to stake everything. And while the twelve remaining battalions of the Imperial Guard waited, unused, Wellington, summoned from his position with the Guards Division above Hougoumont, galloped to the spot, calling up every remaining available unit.

1. Through a failure on the Prince of Orange's part, and ultimately on Wellington's, to make adequate provision in time. 'The Duke lamented the loss of La Haye Sainte from the fault of the officer commanding there but immediately correcting himself, – "No, in fact it was my fault, for I ought to have looked into it myself."' Stanhope, 245. See also Ellesmere, 104, 208–9; Fortescue, 381–3; Kennedy, 122–3, 174–5; Siborne, 32–3; Tomkinson, 305.

The British commander-in-chief had received the news with his habitual calm and decision. As all the Allied leaders in the centre had by now been killed or wounded, he temporarily took over command there himself. Leading five young Brunswick battalions into the full storm of the French batteries, he rallied them when they broke under that hurricane of shot and brought them steadily back into line. Meanwhile, Vivian, seeing a new force of Prussians moving up from the east, arrived on his own initiative from the left of the ridge. Uxbridge galloped off to fetch Vandeleur's 11th, 12th, and 16th Light Dragoons, and Somerset, with the wreck of the Union Brigade extended in single rank to make the utmost show, instilled confidence and pressure from behind into Chassé's Netherlanders.

The bombardment had now reached a new degree of intensity as Napoleon brought up every available gun to reinforce his massed batteries. All along the Allied centre men were going down like ninepins; close by the crossroads 450 of the 700 men of the Twenty-seventh lay in square where they had fallen. In a neighbouring regiment – the Fortieth – both ensigns and fourteen sergeants had been killed or wounded round the tattered colours. The 5th Division, 5000 strong when the battle started, seemed to have dwindled to a line of skirmishers. Kincaid with the Rifles began to wonder at that moment whether there had ever been a battle in which everyone on both sides had been killed.[1] The stream of wounded and fugitives towards the rear was so great that a Prussian aide-de-camp, who rode up from Ziethen's oncoming corps to investigate, returned with a report that the British were defeated and in retreat. No one knew what was happening outside his own immediate vicinity, for in the windless, oven-like, smoke-filled air visibility was reduced to a few yards.

Yet Wellington's grip on the battle never relaxed. Unlike his imperial adversary he was used to commanding comparatively small armies and to attending to every detail himself. In his grey greatcoat with cape, white cravat, Hessian boots, telescope, and low cocked-hat, he rode continuously up and down the line, often alone and seemingly oblivious of the storm of shot. He neither avoided nor courted danger,

---

1. Kincaid, 352. See Ellesmere, 172–3; Fortescue, x, 396–7; Frazer, 139, 189, 219; Gomm, 359–60, 366; Gronow, I, 212; Basil Jackson, 75–6; *Autobiography of Sergeant Lawrence*, 239; Simmons, 375; Tomkinson, 308.

but, knowing that his presence was necessary to keep his young soldiers to the sticking point, showed himself, placid and unconcerned, wherever the fire was hottest. Everywhere he infected men, near the limit of endurance, with courage and confidence. Almost every member of his staff, including De Lancey, his Quartermaster-General, had by now fallen, but, though he looked thoughtful and a little pale, he betrayed no sign of anxiety.[1] Once, chatting with the commanding officer of a square in which he had taken shelter, he was heard to say, 'Oh, it will be all right; if the Prussians come up in time, we shall have a long peace.' But occasionally he looked at his watch.

'Hard pounding this, gentlemen,' he observed, 'but we will see who can pound the longest.' And when the smoke for a moment drifted away and the scanty lines of red were seen everywhere to be standing, a cheer went up from his tired countrymen that showed him to be justified. The hour for which he had waited had come. For streaming on to the west-end of the battlefield from Smohain, driving the French from the environs of Papelotte and La Haye and filling in the two-mile gap between Bülow's men before Plancenoit and the left of the British line came Ziethen's Prussian corps. Its intervention was far more decisive than Bülow's earlier but more distant attack on Plancenoit. As the Prussian batteries, adding their quota to the inferno on the ridge,[2] began to shell the ground near La Belle Alliance, Napoleon knew that the end was at hand. Already from his right rear news had come that the Young Guard had been driven out of Plancenoit. The field was closing in as it had done at Leipzig, and the night was little more than an hour away.

Soon after seven the Emperor took his final resolution. He sent two of the magnificent, untouched battalions of the Old Guard to recapture Plancenoit and prevent encirclement. Then, bidding his aides-de-camp announce that Grouchy had arrived from the west, he ordered a general

1. Afterwards he said that the finger of God had been upon him, adding simply that it was 'a near run thing' and that, if he had not been there, he doubted if it could have been done. Lady Shelley, I, 96, 103, 170; *Creevey Papers*, I, 237; see Broughton, I, 103; Castlereagh, X, 383; Ellesmere, 172-3; Farington, VIII, 32; Frazer, 263, 276; Gronow, I, 69-70; Guedalla, 275-6; *Hamilton of Dalzell* MS., 56-60; Kennedy, 126-9, 176; Picton, 88-9, 106; Jackson, 42-4; Smith, I, 271; Stanhope, 183.

2. Mercer's battery was almost cut to pieces by their fire. See Mercer, I, 325-30; Siborne, 21-2.

advance of all units. As its spearhead he brought forward the remaining battalions of the Imperial Guard, keeping only three as a last reserve. With these he descended the plain, marching at their head towards the British ridge. As he did so the French guns again increased their tempo.

The Guard, fresh from its triumph at Ligny two nights before, advanced with a deeply impressive *élan*. Its men were conscious that they bore the destinies of the world. The two veteran battalions who had been sent to recapture Plancenoit did so in twenty minutes without firing a shot. Those of the Middle and Old Guard advancing against the British were inspired by the personal presence of Napoleon. At the foot of the slope, in a sheltered hollow, he halted to let them pass, throwing open his greatcoat to display his medals and repeatedly crying out, '*A Bruxelles, mes enfants! à Bruxelles!*' They answered with shouts of '*Vive l'Empereur!*' and pressed forward with solemn tread and shouldered arms. In front of each regiment rode a general, Marshal Ney – '*le rougeout*' – with powder-blackened face and tattered uniform, directing. Cavalry moved on their flanks and in the intervals between the battalions came field-pieces loaded with case-shot. Ahead went a cloud of sharpshooters.

The Guard went up the hill in two columns, the one moving obliquely up a spur from the Brussels road towards the centre of the British right, the other using, so far as Wellington's dispositions admitted, the sheltered ground between La Belle Alliance and Hougoumont. True to the tactical conception that had dominated the earlier attacks, the frontal blow was to be clinched by a left hook. But with Hougoumont firmly held and Duplat's Hanoverians and Adam's brigade of Light Infantry deployed across the hollow way between it and the ridge, the front on which the attackers could operate was narrower than ever. And, with his unerring tactical sense, Wellington was waiting at the very spot at which his adversary's knock-out blow was aimed: on the right of the Guards Division where it touched the left battalion – the 95th – of Adam's brigade. Warned of the approach of the Old and Middle Guard by a deserting royalist colonel, he had ordered his men to lie down out of fire of the guns and *tirailleurs* until the French appeared; their long vigil of endurance, he told them, would soon be over.

In the general darkness and confusion, and because of the fire from the guns on the ridge, the leading battalions of the first column struck the British line at two points: where Halkett's battered brigade of the 3rd Division was drawn up in front of Chassé's Netherlanders, and immediately to the west where Wellington was waiting with Maitland's 1st Guards. As the huge bearskins suddenly loomed out of the darkness, the waiting British sprang to their feet in the corn and poured from their extended line a volley at point-blank range into the head of the advancing columns. The French tried to deploy but too late, and most of their officers were swept down. Then, while they were still in confusion, the British charged, Wellington himself giving the word to the Guards with a quiet, 'Now, Maitland, now's your time!'

But though the Imperial Guard recoiled, it did not break. Both parts of the column re-formed and opened fire on the oncoming British, their guns supporting them with case. To the east the remnants of the 33rd and 69th were driven back and at one moment almost broke, but were rallied by Halkett. A Dutch battery, behaving with great coolness and gallantry, raked the French column, and Chassé's Belgians, 3000 strong, came up in support. Gradually, the attackers isolated and, without support behind them, began to give ground. Meanwhile those opposed to the 1st Guards, though driven back for some distance, had also rallied. Maitland ordered his Guardsmen back, but his voice could not be heard above the firing, and some of them, mistaking his intention, tried to form square. In the confusion the two British battalions withdrew in disorder, only to re-form at the word of command with flawless and habitual steadiness on regaining their original position.

But before the battle between the rival Guards could be resumed, it was decided by the action of the most experienced regiment on the British side. Wellington always maintained that, if he had had at Waterloo the army with which he crossed the Pyrenees, he would have attacked Napoleon without waiting for the Prussians: 'I should have swept him off the face of the earth,' he said, 'in two hours.'[1] The first battalion of the 52nd, commanded by John Colborne, afterwards Lord Seaton, had served in John Moore's original Light Brigade; Colborne himself was Moore's finest living pupil. It had gone into action

1. Frazer, 38; Ellesmere, 106; Kincaid, 356.

at Waterloo with more than a thousand bayonets, being one of the very few British battalions which was up to strength – 'a regiment,' wrote Napier of its Peninsular exploits, 'never surpassed in arms since arms were first borne by men.' Owing to the skilful way in which Colborne had placed and handled it, its casualties during the French cavalry charges and the long hours of bombardment had been extraordinarily light.

As the second and westernmost column of the Imperial Guard after passing by Hougoumont pressed up the slope towards Maitland's unbroken line, the drummers beating the *rummadum, dummadum, dum,* of the *pas de charge,* Colborne, who was stationed in the centre of Adam's brigade to the right of the Guards, took a sudden decision. Without orders either from the Duke or any superior officer, he moved his battalion forward out of the line for a distance of three hundred yards, and then, as it drew level with the leading company of the advancing French column, wheeled it to the left with the order, 'Right shoulders forward.' He thus laid it on the flank of the French. By doing so he took the risk both of leaving a gap in the line behind and of having his men cut to pieces by cavalry – a fate he had experienced when, as one of Stewart's brigade commanders, he had moved up the hill at Albuera.

The reward of his daring was decisive. The Imperial Guard, taken by surprise, halted and poured a volley into the 52nd which brought down a hundred and forty of its men. But the British reply of this grave Roman battalion was decisive. It seemed as though every bullet found its mark. So heavy were the casualties in the dense, astonished column that the Imperial Guard did not wait for the 52nd to charge. It broke and fled. As it did so, the 52nd resumed its advance eastwards across, and at right angles to, the British front, with the two other battalions of Adam's brigade – the 95th and 71st – moving up on Wellington's instructions on either flank. A few hundred yards on they encountered another French column re-forming – the first that had attacked – and dealt it the same treatment and with the same results. Gradually, as the recoiling units of the French army streamed back across their path from the impregnable plateau, the British Light Infantry inclined to the right towards La Belle Alliance. Round them, out of swirling smoke, scattered units of British and French cavalry appeared in charge and counter-charge.

For from the ridge above them, starting from the right, the whole British line had begun to advance as Wellington, hat raised high in air, galloped westwards from one tattered, enduring regiment to another. The time for which he and they had waited had come. 'Who commands here?' he shouted to Harry Smith, Lambert's brigade major. 'Generals Kempt and Lambert, my Lord.' 'Desire them to form column of companies and move on immediately.' 'In what direction, my Lord?' 'Right ahead, to be sure.'[1]

It was now nearly dusk. But, as the French cannonade ceased and the smoke began to drift from the ridge, the setting sun cast a ray of light along the glinting British line, now motionless no more, and on the accoutrements of the defeated columns in the plain. The whole French army was suddenly dissolving with the landscape: entire regiments leaving their arms piled and taking to their heels. From the east the Prussians were pouring in a great flood across the battlefield, and to the south-west, where the Old and Young Guard were still fighting fiercely to keep Napoleon's life-line open, Bülow's men had swept through Plancenoit and were approaching the *chaussée*. 'I have seen nothing like that moment,' wrote Frazer of the Artillery, 'the sky literally darkened with smoke, the sun just going down and which till then had not for some hours broken through the gloom of a dull day, the indescribable shouts of thousands where it was impossible to distinguish between friends and foe.'

In that final advance, with little groups of French gunners and horsemen and the last unbroken squares of the Old Guard fighting gloriously to give their Emperor time to escape, a few score more fell, among them Lord Uxbridge, who, riding forward by the Duke's side, had his leg shattered by a shell. Most of the British regiments were so exhausted that they halted in the plain between the ridges. Only the cavalry and Adam's brigade, following the retreating squares of the Imperial Guard, proceeded through the heart of what had been the French position.

As Ziethen's Prussian cavalry from the east and Vivian's and Vande-

1. 'I never saw his Grace so animated,' Smith added. Smith, I, 272–3. See, Becke, 222–30; Cotton, 125–35, 305–6; Ellesmere, 183–4; Fortescue, x, 391–2; Gomm, 361–2, 367–73; Gronow, I, 73, 89–90; Houssaye, 221–32; Jackson, 69–70; Kennedy, 140–50; Leeke, I, *passim*; Moorsom, 256–65; Robinson, 611–14; Siborne, *passim*; Tomkinson, 311–15; Chesney, 210–13.

leur's British from the north met at La Belle Alliance, the union of the armies, fought for so fiercely during three days and nights, was consummated. Shortly after nine o'clock the two men whose good faith, constancy, and resolution had made it possible, met on the spot where Napoleon had launched his attack. They were both on horseback, but the old Prussian embraced and kissed his English friend, exclaiming, '*Mein lieber Kamerad*' and then, '*Quelle affaire!*' which, as Wellington observed, was about all the French he knew.

Then, in weariness and darkness, Wellington turned his tired horse towards Waterloo and the ridge he had defended. He rode in silence across a battlefield in which 15,000 men of his own army, including a third of the British troops engaged, and more than 30,000 Frenchmen lay dead, dying, or wounded. The sound of gunfire had ceased, but, to the south, trumpets could be faintly heard as the tireless Prussian cavalry took up the pursuit of their inexorable enemies. As their infantry, many of whom had marched fifty miles in the past two days, debouched from Plancenoit into the Charleroi highway, where the 52nd, with its tattered colours, was halted by the roadside, they broke into slow time and their bands played 'God save the King.'[1]

1. Leeke, 67; Moorsom, 267; Jackson, 57–9; Tomkinson, 315; Gronow, 1, 200; Simpson, 129; Stanhope, 245; Picton, 98; Gomm, 370–1, 375–6.

CHAPTER 8

PORTRAIT OF THE VICTORS

Great Britain ... in peace as in war, still watches for that liberty in which alone the genius of our isles lives, moves and has its being; and which, being lost, all our commercial and naval greatness would instantly languish like a flower, the root of which had been eaten by a worm; and without which, in any country, the public festivals and pompous merriments of a nation present no other spectacle to the eye of reason than a mob of maniacs dancing in their fetters.

THREE weeks after the battle, while Brussels stank with gangrene and the trampled Waterloo cornfields were heavy with death, a British army entered Paris for the first time since Agincourt. Groups of Guardsmen and Highlanders squatted under the trees or gaped at the boulevard puppet-shows, scarlet sentries paraded before sunlit façades, the Bois de Boulogne with its bivouacs looked like a fair. The Emperor had fled into the south-west to seek a boat, it was said, for America, and the exiled Bourbon – *Louis le Désiré* no more but *Louis l'Inévitable* – returned with his baggage-train to the Tuileries. So did his patrons, the rulers of Russia, Austria, and Prussia, and their paymasters, the robust aristocracy of Britain, from stout Sir Watkin Williams Wynn, who crashed catastrophically through the flimsy chairs of France, to little Lady Caroline Lamb in a purple riding habit primed for an attack on the victor of Waterloo. Even Dr Keate, the flogging Headmaster of Eton, was seen eating ices on the boulevards and dining with his former pupils, the young officers of the Guards.

During those rejoicing weeks while dukes, statesmen, bankers, fashionable littérateurs, and society hostesses rattled over the *pavé* in their carriages and packed the hot, grubby theatres and gambling saloons,[1] the victors showed their strength. At one review a hundred and sixty thousand Russians, superbly caparisoned, paraded before the Emperor of the North. A millennium of drill sergeants and Christian warriors under God's hereditary vice-gerents was now, it seemed, to

1. Croker, I, 63–4; Gronow, II, 15; Lady Shelley, I, 94–5, 107; Brownlow, 124–5, 129–33; D'Arblay, III, 381–2; Broughton, I, 305; Stanley, 197; Harriet Granville, I, 57, 66, 74; Williams, 258.

banish for ever the era of atheist mobs and revolutionary levies. The Russians kicked out their toes like rampant bears, the Prussians goose-stepped by like turkeys, the white-coated Austrians like supers at a German opera, the French royal guards pirouetted with the little steps of turnspits in the performance of their duty. All moved stiffly, with high, rigid collars and limbs that seemed mechanically jointed.[1] Only the British, taught in the school of John Moore, used the free and natural gait of man. As, with stained, shabby uniforms and bullet-ridden banners, they marched down the Champs Élysées past their chief – motionless on his horse like a Roman Emperor in all save pomp –they so impressed the Czar that he ordered the adoption of their system of drill by his Army.

Yet the British puzzled foreigners even more than they impressed them. While others meticulously rehearsed their reviews, they staged theirs without any preparation at all. The Czar having asked to see a representation of Salamanca, the Duke gave a few orders to the Deputy Quartermaster-General who, after a cursory look at the ground, passed them on without comment to the General Officers. The troops marched on to the field without even a plan of operations. The English seemed only interested in problems as they arose. They would not be troubled with theories, even those of their own victories.[2]

They had another peculiarity. They did not apparently think of themselves as conquerors. Wherever they moved, the Prussians, and to a lesser extent the Russians and Austrians, left a trail of shattered homes and trampled corn. They lived at free quarters on their enemies,[3] helping themselves to their best; at Épernay the Prussians watered their very horses on champagne. The Cossacks kept French crowds in order at a review by charging with drawn swords; a Prussian regiment, held up by traffic, knocked the coachmen off their boxes with their musket-butts. Blücher's officers entering a coffee-house would order out the natives with oaths of '*Faites place aux Vainqueurs, T—s;*' their

1. Blakeney, 304–7. See also Lady Shelley, 1, 116–17, 158–9; Croker, 1, 64, 72–3; Broughton, 1, 318; Brownlow, 126–8, 149–58; Gronow, 1, 97–8; Bess-borough, 252–4.
2. Lynedoch, 765; Brownlow, 161–2; Smith, 1, 294.
3. Blücher quartered himself in Napoleon's bedroom at St Cloud where he encouraged his dog to 'bivouac' in and soil a magnificent sofa. Simpson, 141.

commander levied a contribution of a hundred million francs on Paris and, when it was not paid, arrested the bankers and shut up the Bourse. The beautiful Bridge of Iéna was only saved from his engineers by a platoon of Coldstream Guards.[1]

Having suffered no depredations in their own country, the British behaved as they were used at home. When they came to a field of wheat, to the amazement of the natives, they broke rank and carefully followed the footpath in Indian file; when they had to requisition a house, they helped the inhabitants to remove their furniture. They quartered themselves in uncomfortable barracks or tents, paid on the nail, and often through the nose, for what they consumed, and, after the first few days, only entered Paris on passes. The least injury to civilian property was mercilessly punished.

For, though snobbish about many things, the islanders did not seem so about winning battles. Soldiers had a very modest place in their scale of values. Their rich milords and ladies behaved as though they had bought the earth, but their troops walked about the conquered capital as if they were in London, where soldiers were subordinated to the civil law. When French veterans muttered *sacré boeftake* under their breath, or trod on their toes, they looked the other way and even sometimes apologized. As to lampoons of themselves, these peaceable warriors seemed to enjoy them as much as the French. A ranting attack on foreign tyrants in the theatre only elicited from Wellington an expression of regret at his inability to understand French political allusions.[2]

'*Douces comme demoiselles!*' was the general verdict. It was hard to believe that these were the fellows who had chased the first troops in Europe from Spain and had now defeated the Emperor himself. There was quite a competition among French housewives to invite them to their homes. The Highlanders were particular favourites, though their

1. Thereafter, to his Allies' fury, Wellington kept a British sentry posted on it. See Stanhope, 119, H. M. C. Bland-Burgess, 345; Festing, 197–8; Creevey, *Life and Times*, 93–5; Croker, I, 62–4; Lady Shelley, I, 99, 104, 107, 110, 160; Colchester, II, 554; Brownlow, 172–5; Costello, 198–9; D'Arblay, III, 379 384; Gronow, I, 93–4, 98–9, 130–1, 206–7; II, 39–40; Broughton, I, 309–11, 316; Williams, 314–16.

2. Stanhope, 217–18; Kincaid, *Random Shots*, 240; Tomkinson, 323; Broughton, I, 302–3, 316; Creevey, *Life and Times*, 93; Colchester, II, 551; Gronow, I, 92–3; II, 15–16; Brownlow, 129; Smith, I, 294; Harriet Granville, I, 62–4.

kilts at first caused some consternation and even scandal among the ladies.[1] They helped with the household chores, played with the children, and rocked the cradles. A soldier returning to his billet would often be escorted by the entire household, jubilant at having regained its 'own Scotsman'.

*

Cohesion without coercion, wealth without slavery, empire without militarism, such was the spectacle Britain presented. 'I begin to be afraid, like the frog in the fable,' wrote an Englishwoman that summer, 'we shall all burst with national pride, for never, to be sure, did we stand half so high before.' Now that the revolutionary dream had flickered out in ruin, Britain's strength and prosperity was the wonder of mankind. She had annihilated the fleets of an enemy, who when the war began had nearly three times her population, defeated all attempts to keep her troops from the Continent, and, forcing Napoleon to expend half a million men in Spain, had roused and united Europe against him. In the closing months of the war she had subsidized the entire Grand Alliance.

Yet, while withstanding tyranny abroad, she had preserved liberty at home. It was this that made her the object of such universal interest. The dreams of a new birth of freedom founded on resounding phrases had proved in the past generation a bloody and destructive delusion. The French had shown themselves incapable of liberty. The authoritarianism of Prussia had broken, Austria had become a byword for defeat, the antique chivalry of Spain had dissolved under the hammer-blows of the Revolution. The smaller states of Germany and Italy had thrown in their lot with the conqueror. Even the Russians had proved barbarians in the grain. Only one kingdom had emerged victorious while assuring her people social order and freedom of choice. Britain might not be the Utopia of the philosophers, but she was nearer it than anything mankind had yet achieved.

*

Was the reality behind the splendid façade, the nation behind those proud white cliffs as strong and healthful as it seemed? There could be

---

1. '*C'est vrai! actuellement rien qu'un petit jupon – mais comment!*' remarked one excited Frenchwoman, lifting her hands and eyes, '*petit jupon – et comment!*' Stanley, 197. See Simpson, 11–12; Brownlow, 129; Gronow, 1, 80–1; Bury, II, 15; Gomm, 376; Broughton, 1, 312.

no doubt of her prosperity and social cohesion. The great mass of her people, Simond reported, appeared happier and more respectable than any other he knew. The good manners of her country folk, their open, friendly faces, the curtseys of the children on the roads and the raised hats of their elders, bespoke a society against which the waves of egalitarian revolution and the new creeds of envy and infidelity had beaten in vain.

The English plainly loved their country and found inspiration in serving it. They were free as individuals to rule themselves, which made them self-reliant, resourceful, and morally, as well as physically, courageous. They had a religion, deeply personal, which enabled them to set a course by conscience and secure the enduring strength of common standards of thought and behaviour. Together these things gave them an underlying unity which allowed for almost limitless diversity and was therefore far more stable than one enforced by a centralized and brittle authoritarianism.

Their belief in freedom was a passion, almost a religion. ''Tis liberty alone,' proclaimed their favourite poet:

> that gives us the flower
> Of fleeting life, its lustre and perfume,
> And we are weeds without it. All constraint
> Except what wisdom lays on evil men
> Is evil.

For the abstract liberty of the mass acclaimed by revolutionary France they had little use. The fabric of their law had been woven in the course of centuries to sustain that of the individual. The legal protection of his person and property against all comers, particularly against the King's officers, was, even more than Parliament, England's distinguishing institution. Parliament itself had been created to ensure it.

For this pragmatic race, hatred of power was an obsession. Even the occasional soldiers posted at street corners to restrain the crowds during the Allied Sovereigns' visit were denounced as intolerable. Keats at Naples felt unable to visit the opera because of the guards on the stage. 'The continual visible tyranny of this Government prevents me having any peace of mind,' he wrote, 'I could not lie quietly here; I will not even leave my bones in the midst of this despotism.' An English lady described how she and her husband, travelling through the dragooned French countryside after the war, chafed at the closed gates and the sentries who paraded the towns.[1]

Such hatred of constraint arose partly from a belief that power corrupted, and that it could not be safely entrusted, untrammelled, to anyone. For this reason the British Constitution was an intricate balance of rights and functions in which it was impossible to say precisely where power resided. The King having in the past tried to monopolize it, the King's powers had been drastically shorn. Though he still possessed great influence and could be a source of grave embarrassment to the Ministers whom he appointed, he could in major matters act officially only through them. His right even to a private secretary was questioned. Yet the Ministers who exercised his former powers were themselves dependent on the goodwill of Parliament. Without the support of a working majority of its members, they could not carry on the business of the country. And Parliament itself was a balance of conflicting powers: of rival parties and often rival Houses.

Nor did power reside in the people – that question-begging abstraction, so dear to the rationalizing philosophers of the eighteenth century, in whose name the French had drenched the world in blood. The House of Commons, like the House of Lords, so far as it represented anything definable, represented the interests and property of the country, though not as they were in 1815 but as they had been centuries before when the parliamentary system began. Little more than 400,000 out of the English and Welsh population of ten and a half millions enjoyed a parliamentary vote, and only 4000 out of two million Scots. And this restricted franchise was exercised on the most illogical variety of grounds. In the counties it was the prerogative of 40s freeholders, in many boroughs of a handful of occupants of particular tenements, in one or two constituencies of everyone who boiled a pot on his own hearth. More than a third of the House of Commons' seats were at the disposal of a couple of hundred landowners who virtually nominated the electors. Their right to do so was bought and sold, sometimes under

1. Lady Shelley, I, 215. It struck the Frenchman, Simond – even after his long residence in America – as remarkable that at the height of the War visitors to Portsmouth were allowed to pass through the walls and fortifications without being questioned. Simond, II, 247. See also Bury, I, 207; Keats, IV, 112.

the hammer, like any other species of property: a practice which, para-doxically, tended to correct the antiquated distribution of the franchise, since it enabled new forms of wealth unrepresented by geography to secure it by purchase – an example both of the conservatism of the English and of their genius for making the illogical work. Nor did the electorate even possess an absolute right to vote. It could be deprived of it by Parliament, which if the Crown consented might, as it had done in the past, prolong its own existence. For the English left every Parliament free to change the laws as it chose. They would not be bound even by a Constitution.

This baffling confusion was the aspect of their polity of which they were most proud. For it stressed the importance of the individual, for whom, in their view, all government existed. For there was another and indefinable force – one not counted but weighed – to which every legal power had at times to defer. It was the sum total of the political consciousness of the individuals who made up the nation. The most powerful Minister of the age, William Pitt, had been able to take office at the outset of his career with the King's support but without a parlia-mentary majority partly because public opinion, disgusted with those in office, was known to be behind him.

Even the views of uneducated individuals could at times influence political action in this extraordinary country. For, since there were no proper police and the only protection of Government in a capital of a million inhabitants were three regiments of Foot Guards and twelve hundred Horse, the London mob could subject Parliament and Govern-ment to a most unpleasant ordeal. In the seventeenth century it had more than once changed the course of history and, though the ruling aristocracy had learnt to humour and manage it, they could never wholly ignore it. Thirty years before, it had tried to burn down the capital in order to prevent a mitigation of the intolerant law against Catholics. During the rejoicings for Salamanca it had terrorized Lon-don for three nights, firing in the streets, setting coaches alight – in some cases with their occupants inside – and stoning the residences of the anti-war party. The iron railings outside London houses were not there for ornament. A howling mob round the door, a shower of brickbats at the windows, a lighted torch against the lintel were the statesman's reminder that, however irrational and ill-organized, the people had a will of its own.

Even in ordinary times the *mobile*, as it was called, played a part in politics. At every contested election the candidates had for weeks to run the gauntlet of a rough, drunken mob which paraded the streets, surrounded the hustings, and pelted speakers and voters. In the London suburb of Garratt near Wandsworth, a mock-election was held during every general election, in which all the most notorious characters of the metropolitan underworld appeared as candidates – a kind of political *Beggar's Opera*. For the sake of practical social convenience the right to vote was treated as a form of tenure, transmitted, like an estate or title, by inheritance or purchase. But the right to throw a dead cat at a candidate and to support one's Party with the full force of one's lungs and fists was regarded as fundamental, and inalienable.

> *Our man for ever, O –*
> *Yourn in the river, O!*

sang the Radical shoemakers of Towcester and the rival Tory poachers of Silverstone as they rolled up their sleeves before the hustings. 'The whole mob of Middlesex blackguards pass through Piccadilly twice a day,' wrote Walter Scott during a Westminster by-election, 'and almost drive me mad with their noise and vociferation.' Before it ended one of the candidates was wounded and another forced to hide for his life in a churchyard.

Only one thing could be said for certain of English politics. No power could be openly exercised without provoking a reaction. The greater the power, the greater the reaction. Even the mob was subject to this law of diminishing returns, since, whenever it went too far, it automatically created an alliance of law-abiding persons against it. England might canonize admirals – for their sway was too distant to threaten anyone's private liberty – but she never worshipped long at the shrine of any living statesman. Popularity with one faction was certain to arouse the enmity of another; vilification of William Pitt, the national saviour during the war, became the *credo* of Whigs and radicals for a generation after his death. It was symptomatic of this jealousy of power that the office of Prime Minister had no recognition in law, and that the Cabinet – the inner council of supreme office-holders, who were at once the Government and the managers of the parliamentary majority – was unknown to the Constitution. Its members modestly called themselves 'his Majesty's confidential servants.' They did not even possess an office or a secretary.

As for bureaucracy, what there was possessed no political power. The Civil Service was purely clerical and was nominated by the statesmen for whom it devilled. These viewed it chiefly as a means of rewarding supporters and providing for younger sons. Walter Scott praised Croker, the Secretary of the Admiralty, for never scrupling to stretch his powers to serve a friend.[1] Such patronage, though valuable for securing Party discipline, was no foundation for a strong executive· Ninety-nine Englishmen out of a hundred viewed with sturdy contempt a bureaucracy recruited by jobbery. The country gentleman who named a litter of puppies, Placeman, Pensioner, Pilfere, and Plunderer, expressed this.[2] Any attempt to increase the size and powers of the Civil Service was certain to be assailed. Even the Foreign Office had a staff of only twenty-eight, including the two Under-Secretaries and a Turkish interpreter. The Home Office consisted of twenty clerks. As every document had to be copied by hand, such administrators had no time for regulating other people's lives.[3]

It was a source of amazement to foreigners that a country so governed, without a regular police and with so small an Army, should be so orderly. At Brighton, a town in 1811 of 14,000 people, there were neither justices nor municipality, yet crime was almost unknown and the doors left unbarred at night. The capital, the world's largest city, was patrolled by a handful of police officers and a few hundred elderly night-watchmen. Little Mr Townsend, the Bow Street 'runner', with his flaxen wig and handful of top-hatted tip-staffs, constituted almost

1. 'If any office should be at your disposal,' wrote Wordsworth to Lord Lonsdale, 'the duties of which would not call so largely upon my exertions as to prevent me from giving a considerable proportion of my time to study, it might be in your Lordship's power to place me in a situation where, with better hopes of success, might advance towards the main object of my life; I mean the completion of my literary undertakings.' De Selincourt, II, 486; Lockhart, v, 306. See also *idem*, IV, 349; Mrs Arbuthnot, *Journal*, 8th March, 1822; Cobbett, I, 41; Granville, I, 22; Peel, II, 140; Lady Shelley, II, 90; Simond, II, 190–2.

2. J. E. Austen-Leigh, *The Vine Hunt*.

3. Woodward, 61, 189. See Emma Mount-Edgecumbe's account of how her uncle, Lord Castlereagh, sent for her to copy out a long dispatch to Wellington after Waterloo. Brownlow, 121.

the sole force for executing the Government's will. Everything else was left to the Justices and parish constables.

Yet the English were not a timid or submissive people. The brutality of an English crowd could be a formidable phenomenon. Even at royal levées there was so much shoving that the removal of fainting ladies from a 'squeeze' was a part of Court routine; when Carlton House was thrown open to well-to-do sightseers after a fête, shoes and fragments of clothing were gathered up afterwards in hogsheads.[1] In poorer districts fighting was almost incessant. Simond, staying in Orchard Street, was kept awake all night by Irish labourers having a free-for-all in a slum alley at the back. Above the noise of their rattles he could hear one old watchman calling out to another, 'If I go in, I shall have a shower of brickbats,' and the other replying, 'Well, never mind, let them murder each other if they please!'

To foreigners British liberty seemed always on the verge of degenerating into licence. In Edinburgh, hooligans roamed the streets at night with bludgeons, knocking down revellers with shouts of 'Mire him!'; English public schoolboys rose against their masters and had to be driven back to their class-rooms by the military. An attempt to raise the prices of the London theatres provoked the galleries to shout down every play for months and break up the houses.[2]

For the common people, though allowed a licence known to no other country, were, like the poor and uneducated everywhere, quite uninhibited. When their passions were roused, they acted passionately. Two Jews caught stealing in a Bristol stables had their hands tied behind their backs, their beards stuck together with pitch and their noses filled with snuff till they knocked each other senseless. A party of picnickers who fouled some fishermen's lines off Hammersmith, were pitched, with a stream of blasphemy, into the Thames. Nor, for all the

1. 'Many a delicate female was extracted from the mêlée nearly *in natura-bilis* and obliged to hide herself in a corner till a petticoat could be procured.' Simond II, 227. See *Ann. Reg.*; Mitford, *Life*, II, 187; The same thing had happened when Nelson lay in state at Greenwich a few years before. See *English Spy*, 219.

2. Simond, I, 89–91. See also Mrs Arbuthnot, *Journal*, 20th Feb., 1822; Ashton, I, 25; Bamford, I, 28, 127, 129, 131, 185, 245–9; II, 67; Bewick, 21–2; Scott, III, 61–2; Gronow, II, 225–6, 310; Keats, III, 282; Leigh Hunt, *Autobiography*, I, 190; Mitford, *Life*, II, 187; Simond, II, 227–60; Stanhope, 274; Woodward, 466.

deference of the race to rank, did the populace respect persons. The Chancellor of the Exchequer, when he attended divine service at the Millbank Penitentiary, was bombarded with stale bread by the aggrieved lady inmates. Appalling crimes of violence passed unpunished for lack of police. Lonely turnpike-keepers were robbed and beaten to death; gangs of smugglers and poachers fought pitched battles with keepers and revenue officers. Pickpockets surrounded the doors of the coaching inns for 'Johnny Raws from the country', and during fairs and public processions packs of thieves swept through the crowds emptying pockets, snatching purses, and even stripping men and women of their clothes.[1] Dusk round London was called footpad-hour. Yet the nimbleness and courage of its pickpockets was almost a matter of pride to Londoners. 'A man who saunters about the capital with pockets on the outside of his coat,' a guide-book warned its readers, 'deserves no pity.'

A little rough and tumble seemed a small price to the English for avoiding the ills of arbitrary power. 'They have an admirable police at Paris,' wrote Lord Dudley, 'but they pay for it dear enough. I had rather half a dozen people's throats were cut every few years in the Ratcliffe Highway than be subject to domiciliary visits, spies, and the rest of Fouché's contrivances.' The British attitude towards the agents of executive power was instinctively hostile; Stendhal on a visit to London was amazed to see soldiers jeered at in the streets. The Life Guards, who carried printed orders to avoid giving offence to civilians and repeatedly showed the most exemplary restraint under showers of stones, were known in the capital as the 'Piccadilly butchers'. Even the Prime Minister who reaped the glories of Vittoria and Waterloo viewed General Graham's proposal for a club for military officers as a threat to the Constitution.[2]

Foreigners could not understand the British attitude to popular violence; it seemed to them like the weakness that had precipitated the Terror. But the people who quietly obeyed their voluntary ring-

1. *Ann. Reg.*, 1819, Chron., 55; *Diary of Walter Trevelyan*, G. T. Warner, Harrow in Verse and Prose, 99. See *inter alia* Mrs Arbuthnot, *Journal*, 30th Oct., 1820; Bamford, II, 64; Colchester, III, 237; *Cranbourn Chase*, 35–7; Fowler, 122–3; Gronow, II, 309–10; Lieven, *Private Letters*, 78; Sydney, I, 122, 210; Leigh Hunt, *Autobiography*, I, 190.

2. Lynedoch, 748–51; Gronow, II, 220; Simond, I, 79, 91; II, 221, 280–1.

keepers at a rough boxing match chafed at the least restraint by arms. It was never really safe for a magistrate to use troops to maintain order. In the British Constitution there was no *droit administratif*; a shot fired in defence of public order by a servant of the Crown could involve both him and his superior in the penalties of murder.

It was in this that the English recipe for reconciling order with liberty resided. Social discipline was secured, in theory, by the rule of Law. A man might do as he pleased, but, if it infringed the liberties of others, he had to answer for it in the Courts. After the traditional chairing of the lord of misrule in north country villages, the constables spent the next day patiently inquiring who had kicked through a neighbour's door, smashed his window, or stolen his can. 'The strange medley of licentiousness and legal restraint,' wrote a foreigner, 'of freedom and confinement – of punishment for what is done and liberty to do the same thing again – is very curious.' At first it struck him as irrational, but in the end he decided that it approximated more nearly to natural law than the simpler and more arbitrary processes of other lands. The artificial composition of gardens in England, he noted, like that of her government, abridged only the liberty of doing harm.

For the judgement of their Courts the English showed an undeviating respect. The independence of the Judiciary was as much an article of their faith as the legislative monopoly of Parliament. No one, however powerful, could evade the Law; even the Heir Presumptive had his coach seized at a levée by sheriff's officers in distraint of debt.[1] The King's Ministers were as subject to this power as anyone else. A man arrested by the Executive could immediately obtain from the Courts a writ of *habeas corpus* compelling his jailors either to show lawful authority for his detention or release him.

Yet this, by itself, would only have increased the difficulty of governing such a country, but for the capacity of the ruling class for inspiring and evoking voluntary obedience. As there was no adequate standing army, police force, or bureaucracy to secure property and privilege, the gentry had to preserve these themselves. Their recipe for dealing with a rabble was to stand up and face it; it was the only attitude a rabble respected. Having no professional deputies as in more regimented lands to stand between them and those they ruled, they learnt

1. Holland, *Journal*, I, 125.

to command respect by force of character, courage, and good sense. Instinctive, unreflecting, and fearless leadership was a by-product of the country's libertarian laws. It was this, probably more than anything else, that enabled her to win the war.

Training for such leadership, like most things in England, was un-planned and unconscious. It began in boyhood, when future legislators and magistrates took part with the sturdy ragamuffins of the country-side in running, swimming, bird-nesting, riding the wild ponies of the commons, making midnight expeditions, climbing trees, rocks, and steeples.[1] They learnt to endure knocks and hardships, to face risks, conceal fear, be quick, bold, and adaptable. They acquired, before they inherited wealth and luxury, habits of hardihood such as early rising and cold bathing; John Mytton with his £20,000 a year, dressed in winter in a thin jacket and linen trousers without drawers, and once stalked wild-fowl all night on the ice stark naked. 'Can't I bear pain well,' he cried as he lay, skinned and scorched, after a debauch in which he had set his shirt alight to frighten away the hiccoughs.[2]

*

From their earliest years Britain's rulers indulged with passionate in-tensity in the field sports of the countryside. It gave them, as Walter Scott wrote of his countrymen, a strong and muscular character, saving them from all sorts of causeless fears and flutterings of the heart. Men who rode straight to hounds, shot duck in wintry marshes with breach-loaders, fished for salmon in moorland streams, learnt as boys to snare and kill wild-fowl, snakes, hares, rabbits, badgers, and all forms of game and vermin, and continued to do so, whenever they had a chance, so long as they could walk or stride a horse, were not likely to fail for lack of courage. Their versatility in sport was amazing. The great Master of the Quorn, George Osbaldeston – 'little Ossey' or, as he was called later, the 'Squire of England' – a shrivelled-up, bantam-cock of a man with short legs, a limp, a gorilla chest, and a face like a fox cub, excelled at every sport he touched, boxing, pigeon-shooting, steeple-chasing, billiards, was one of the six best amateur cricketers in the

1. Bamford, I, 85; Bewick, 16–17; Cooper, 20; Howitt, *Boy's Country Book*, 9–10; Lockhart, v, 80–1; Lucas, I, 33.
2. Mytton, 16–17, 127–9.

country, rowed for the Arrow club – the forerunner of Leander – beat the famous professional, Barre, at tennis, and kept harriers, gamecocks, and fighting mastiffs.[1]

The hunting field played a big part in such education. Under the famous East Midlands Masters a new form of foxhunting was superseding the slower and less specialized sport of the past. Its pioneers, establishing a new convention and discipline, were almost as much leaders in their kind as Nelson and Wellington. Their hounds ran from scent to view; 'neck or nothing,' 'a blazing hour,' 'the pace was too good to inquire,' were their watchwords. Their followers – for no man who wished to be respected spared either person or fortune in this pursuit – went like a scarlet streak across the green, enclosed shires. 'Throw your heart over and your horse will follow!'[2] the great Assheton Smith used to say. It was a rule gentlemen instinctively applied in time of danger, and to which the English people invariably responded.

All Britons admired what they called 'bottom.' 'God don't love those,' they were told, 'who won't strike out for themselves!' Little John Keats, affronted by boy or master, put himself 'in a posture of defence'; even the gentle Shelley fought a mill at Eton. Tickell the elder of that school, we are told, 'loved fighting and knew not what fear was; he went among his school-fellows by the name of Hannibal and Old Tough.' Byron used to thrash a pacifically-minded Harrow friend to make him thrash others 'when necessary as a point of honour and stature'; he himself fought his way out of the ridicule attached to a club foot by winning six out of seven successive battles. No one but a 'game chick' could thrive in this land.

Boxing was the national nursery of manliness. A gentleman was expected to be a 'proper man with his fists' and know how 'to clear a lane of men' with his 'morleys'. Thomas Assheton Smith, when Master of the Quorn, after a set-to in a Leicester street with a six-foot coal-heaver, clamped a raw steak on both eyes and sent his prostrated opponent a five-pound note for being the best man that ever stood up to him. Some foreigners landing at Dover were amazed to see a Lord

---

1. Osbaldeston, *passim*; *Creevey Papers*, II, 199–200; Dixon, 158–63, 166.
2. Dixon, 32. See *idem*, 17, 47, 154–63, 166–7; Allen, *passim*; Assheton Smith, *passim*; *Cranbourn Chase*, 42–3; *Creevey Papers*, II, 199–200; Lockhart, V, 81; Newton, 51; Nevill, 38–40; Osbaldeston, *passim*.

of the Treasury, dispossessed of his Ministerial box by officious customs men, put himself in a sparring attitude to regain it. Young noblemen took boxing lessons in Gentleman Jackson's rooms in Bond Street or walked proudly arm in arm with the bash-nosed champions of the 'Fancy'; an engraving of Tom Cribb was part of the normal furniture of an undergraduate's rooms.

A contest between two 'milling coves' was the most popular spectacle in the country. Its finer points were debated, not only by draymen and coal-heavers, but by men of culture; Keats, describing the match between Randall and Turner, illustrated its ups and downs by rapping with his fingers on the window. All England followed the fortunes of its 'men of science', those prize specimens of the race who met in the green ring by the river at Mousley Hurst or sparred before the 'Fancy' in the Fives Court. The heroes of the ring – Tom Hickman the Gas-Light man, Sutton 'the tremendous man of colour', the 'Flaming Tin-man', 'Big Ben Brain', the 'Game Chicken', Mendoza the Jew, Belcher 'the yeoman', and Tom Cribb, for ten years unchallenged Champion of England, were as great men in their way as the Duke of Wellington. And the lesser giants of the ring were only a little lower; Parish the waterman, the Giblet Pye, the game George Ballard, the tremendous little Puss, Shaw the Life Guardsman who fell at Waterloo, and the terrific Molineaux. What, asked Borrow, were the gladiators of Rome or the bull-fighters of Spain in its palmiest days compared to England's bruisers? With the ring formed, the seconds and bottle-holders in readiness, the combatants face to face, the English were in a kind of heaven. The gladiators, stripped to the waist, walking round each other with their fine, interlaced muscles and graceful strength, the naked fists, the short chopping blows delivered with the swiftness of lightning, the dislodged ivories, the noses beaten flat, the eyes torn from the sockets, the blood pouring on the grass, the pause between rounds when the 'pinky heroes', poised on their seconds' knees, were revived with brandy and water, the crashing blows delivered in the jugular with the full force of the arm shot horizontally from the shoulder, and the game, battered faces under punishment, impressed themselves on the memory of the islanders more than all their country's martial victories. 'Prize fighting,' wrote Pierce Egan, 'teaches men to admire true courage, to applaud generosity, to acquire notions of

honour, nobleness of disposition and greatness of mind; to bear hardships without murmurs, fortitude in reverse of fortune, and invincibility of soul.'[1]

Within the framework of law and property the English rule was that
a man should look after himself and have freedom to do so. If he failed
no one pitied him. It was his own fault; he had had his chance. The
islanders had not yet thought out the full implications of this rule; they
were to have opportunities for doing so later. But at the time it seemed
fair enough; it had the warrant of nature and the law of things. 'Fear
God,' said Isobel Berners to the Romany Rye, 'and take your own
part. There's Bible in that, young man; see how Moses feared God and
how he took his own part against everybody who meddled with him.
So fear God, young man, and never give in!' From the time they could
stand Englishmen were expected to fend for themselves. There was
nothing they valued like spunk. In men, indeed, they respected nothing
without it. 'Is not this being game to the backbone?' asked Walter
Scott, when he heard how a boy, punished by three months in a garret
on bread and water for shooting a cat, had spent his imprisonment
hunting rats on a new principle.

*

The religion of a people so libertarian was instinctively Protestant. An
Englishman's home was his castle; he wanted no priest, least of all a
foreign one, to share it. Popery to him was a symbol of tyranny,
absurdity, and inefficiency, for, since despotism corrupted, it followed,
in his eyes, that those who exercised it in religious matters must govern
badly. An English lady travelling in Switzerland declared she could
always tell when she was in a Protestant canton because the roads were
passable, the lands well farmed, and the cottages tidy. Jane Austen wrote
that she had 'a great respect for Sweden because it had been so zealous
for Protestantism.' For cardinals, priests, processions, fastings, penances,

1. *Boxiana, passim*; Assheton Smith, *passim*; Bamford, I, 28, 127, 131, 185;
Bewick, 20–2; Broughton, I, 96; Dixon, 22–7, 151–4; *English Spy*, I, 152, 338–9;
II, 199; Farington, VII, 25; Fowler, 192–5; Gronow, I, 120; II, 79–80, 214–15,
257; Leigh Hunt, *Autobiography*, II, 85; Keats, III, 282; IV, 304, 323–5; *Lavengro*,
48, 156–7, 166–9, 207; Leslie, 332; Letts, 212; *Life in London*, 37, 73, 173, 175;
Mytton, *passim*; *New Monthly Magazine*, Feb., 1822. W. Hazlitt, 'The Fight';
Old Oak, 161–8; Osbaldeston, *passim*; J. H. Reynolds, *The Fancy*, 1820; *Romany
Rye*, 98, 131–2, 141–2, 145, 194–5; Simond, I, 125–7; II, 194–8, 227.

'not forgetting anchorites and vermin,' the English had an inexpress-
ible contempt; the Reverend Edward Stanley at Aix-la-Chapelle was
nauseated by 'virgins and dolls in beads, and muslins and pomatum
and relics of saints' beards, and napkins from our Saviour's tomb and
mummeries quite disgraceful.' The average Englishman thought there
was nothing, however false and horrible, a priest-ridden nation might
not do.[1]

The font of English Protestantism was the authorized translation of
the Bible. This great book was the daily mentor of millions. Sir William Pepys told Hannah More that, with the exception of Revelation,
he read through the entire New Testament three times a year. Every
Sunday Mrs Cooper, the dyer's widow, took down her husband's
Baskerville edition of the Scriptures and, turning the pictured pages,
recalled for her little son what he had said of each. The Bible story lay
at the roots of the national consciousness. In country districts its words,
heard week by week in church or chapel, formed the mould of men's
minds. Its phrases strayed into their everyday speech; a gate-keeper's
application for a post on one of the first railways mentioned that he
and his sons could not only keep but carry the gates, 'yea, even the
gates of Gaza.' When Samuel Bamford returned from sea, his father,
the weaver, greeted him with the words, 'My son was dead and is
alive again, he was lost and is found.'

It was the last age in which a majority of educated men grew up without doubt. Walter Scott, in a dangerous illness, wrote that he could
look on death's approach without fear, relying on the merits and inter-

1. In militant Ulster, where English and Scottish Protestantism reached its
apogee, the fanatics of the Orange Lodges on the anniversary of the battle of
the Boyne gave expression to this sentiment in a toast:
'To the glorious, pious and Immortal Memory of King William III, who
saved us from Rogues and Roguery, Slaves and Slavery, Knaves and Knavery,
Popes and Popery, from brass money and wooden shoes; and who ever denies
this Toast may he be slammed, crammed and jammed into the muzzle of the
great gun of Athlone, and the gun fired into the Pope's Belly, and the Pope
into the Devil's Belly, and the Devil into Hell, and the door locked and the
key in an Orangeman's pocket; and may we never lack a Brisk Protestant Boy
to kick the arse of a papist; and here's a fart for the Bishop of Cork!' See also,
Romany Rye, 16–17, 400; Austen, 238; Bamford, I, 102; Castlereagh, X, 378;
De Selincourt, II, 578; Lady Shelley, I, 252–3, 287, 351–2; Stanley, 191; Wilberforce, II, 322.

cession of his Redeemer; Wordsworth trusted that God had received his child amongst the blessed. Often this conviction took a somewhat literal form; a Judge told a condemned prisoner that he would shortly appear before another and abler Judge. Fine speeches about religion were dragged into crude melodramas; a guide book on sea-bathing places broke off a disquisition on the scenery of Sussex rivers to compare them with the stream of time.[1] Such reflections were occasioned, not by a wish to increase the book's sales, which they could scarcely affect, but because they were natural to both reader and writer.

This sense of the validity of Divine law and of the judgements that accompanied its breach by man or nation, helped to give ordinary Britons a sense of proportion. It saved them from the pride which is the nemesis of success. They saw their transient present in a perspective of history. They did not, like their late enemies, believe in the perfectibility of man; they believed in his frailty and folly and the power of God to punish and redeem. Under their robust and often irritating self-assurance was a fund of deep personal humility; 'ours,' said Broke of the *Shannon*, 'is an unpretending ship.' A traveller from the United States at the climax of the war was astonished to find so little pride in the people who ruled the seas and held the East in fee. The most consistently successful of nations in battle, with conquered territories in every corner of the world, the British paradoxically were always in theory renouncing force. Believing they owed their being to something higher than themselves, they thought it wrong to use force except in defence of law and right. Castlereagh's Under-Secretary at the Foreign Office informed a colonial Governor that nothing was so repugnant to His Majesty's Government as a system of terror; Sergeant Broughton, the ex-champion of England, made a pupil promise never to fight unless compelled.[2]

1. 'And from this serious contemplation of the past the soul anxiously springs forward and anticipates that awful period when in an hour, in which it shall be least expected, while the labours of agriculture are going on as now before us, while the busy hum of men shall be ascending as now from the fields below, while all shall appear peace and security, a mightier destruction shall be ordained to nature, when the Heavens shall pass away with a great noise and the elements shall melt with fervent heat, and the earth also.' *Sea-Bathing Places*, 137. See also Bewick, 34; Gaussen, II, 344–5; *Lavengro*, 4.

2. Castlereagh, X, 217; *Romany Rye*, 198. See also Bamford, I, 185. The Peterloo leader tells us how he applied the principle himself. 'It was about this

It was this that made many foreigners think the English hypocrites and many Englishmen so critical of their country's policy. Almost any exercise by her rulers of her rights or interest was sure to be assailed on moral grounds by some other Briton. Cobbett thought it a duty to God and Man to put the Nabobs, those, that is, who were creating Britain's commercial empire in Asia, upon the coals without delay; they had long, he wrote, been 'cooking and devouring the wretched people both of England and India.' It was considered almost dishonourable for a member of the Opposition to stand up for his country. 'If it were not physically as well as morally impossible for Sheridan to blush,' wrote Mary Mitford when he supported the Government over the Peninsular War, 'his face should glow with shame for a month for his slavish speech on Friday: the vile, degenerate Whig!' The same instinct made poets like Campbell and Byron denounce the seizure of the Danish fleet as atrocious aggression and the dethronement of Napoleon as petty and reactionary spite.

Looking back over his experience of the politics of anarchical India and revolutionary Europe, Wellington declared that it was England's religion that had made her what she was: a nation of honest men. By this he meant one in which a majority of men could trust one another and which others could trust. For truth and straightforward dealing – except, perhaps, in the sale of horses – the English had an unusual respect. A liar or one afraid to avow his beliefs was despised; there was no place in their public life for a coward. Attempts to introduce a secret ballot into the electoral system were resisted as un-English on the ground that the franchise was a trust which an elector was bound to exercise publicly. 'Whatever he did,' Bewick wrote of a neighbour, 'was done in open day, for, as he feared no man, he scorned to sulk or to do anything by stealth.'

This insistence on frank dealing had a profound influence on Britain's overseas empire and trade. It caused peoples on whom the expansion of the English impinged, if not to like, to trust them. 'I would rather

time that I saw a young fellow beating a girl in the street.
' "Hallo, you fellow," I said. "What are you abusing that girl for?"
' "What's that to you?" said the blackguard.
' "I'll let you see what it is to me if you lay a finger on her again."
' "Oh, you will, will you," said he. "Come on then!"
So we set to, and in five minutes I beat him till he was dizzy and had enough.'

sacrifice Gwalior and every other portion of India ten times over,' Wellington wrote, 'to preserve our credit for scrupulous good faith.'[1] A Bordeaux merchant, on whom a penniless British officer was billeted, offered, unasked, to lend him any sum without security; he had complete faith, he said, in the word of an Englishman. 'Well, you are English,' said a Belgian peasant to a tourist who had offered her an unfamiliar coin, 'and the English never deceive.' Richard Hotham, the great hatter, made it a rule only to sell the best so that every new customer became an old; Samuel Archer, the inventor of imitation pearls, went to extraordinary lengths to prevent his products from being mistaken for the genuine article. Though cheats and knaves abounded as in every society, a bright skein of honesty ran through the nation; a poor Lancashire weaver almost starved on the road from Manchester to London sooner than risk not being in court when his bail was called. Among the Dorset quarrymen the saying 'on the word of a Portland man' was as good as a contract.[2]

*

At the beginning of the nineteenth century the national Church was suffering, like other English institutions, from a surfeit of material prosperity. With their genius for politics – for evolving, that is, institutions capable of withstanding the erosion of human nature – the English had rejected both the Catholic and Calvinist conceptions of religious society. In place of a priesthood uncontaminated by the ties of marriage but in danger of undermining the mutual trust of the home, they had licensed a sober married clergy with the same family responsibilities as other men. In place of a theocratic caste untrammelled by secular obligations and therefore a source of political intrigue, they had established a Church subordinate and allied to the State. But in their desire to give its ministers independence and social status, they had endowed them – and their wives and families – with opportunities for a larger share of this world's goods than was readily compatible with

1. 'Take care what you're about,' he observed of a scheme for national education, 'for, unless you base all this on religion, you are only making so many clever devils.' Stanhope, 261.

2. *Sea-Bathing Places*, 500. See also Bamford, II, 254; Bell, I, 184; Bewick, 33, 35-7, 46-7; Daniell, I, 51; Dixon, 66; Moorsom, 272-3; Simpson, 77; Woodward, 86.

spiritual humility and inspiration. Tithes and a monopoly of ecclesiastical preferments, enhanced in value by rising agricultural prices, had
blunted the edge of the spiritual sword. To men cast in a Puritan mould
– and many Englishmen were – the Anglican Church, with its decorous
but uninspired services, had become an affair of 'hassocks, footboards,
and lolling cushions.' Its bishops and higher clergy, though mostly
kindly and cultured men living decent lives, were far too well endowed,
dressed, and connected.[1] Those 'rosy-cheeked, homestalled divines',
whose faces Charles Lamb thought fragrant with the mince-pies of
half a century, with their sporting, literary, and farming tastes, had
lost the common touch. Zeal to them was the hall-mark of the under-
bred; when in 1814 the first Anglican Bishop was sent to England's new
empire in the East, the Archbishop of Canterbury warned him to
avoid enthusiasm.

Yet the tolerance of England, as always, afforded a corrective for
its conservatism. The vacuum was filled by the Nonconforming congregations. Of these there were many: almost as many, one visitor
concluded, as there were Englishmen. Their denominations were a
commentary on the national capacity for individual eccentricity. There
were Quakers – a most respected sect – whose founders, not content
with more normal forms, quaked in their devotions, Jumpers who
jumped up and down, Shakers who shook. Some believed in total im-
mersion in baptism; others that divine truth had been revealed ex-
clusively to some obscure, long-dead Englishman. During the past
half-century a new band of enthusiasts called Methodists, reacting
against the easy-going latitudinarianism of the Anglican Church, had
charted stricter roads to salvation which, offering no concessions to
worldly rank, made small appeal to the rich and powerful but a great
deal to the poor and humble. Preaching a crusade among the neglected,
Wesley's disciples had carried the gospel into the dark corners of what,
but for them, might have ceased to be a Christian land. In its remoter
parts there had sprung up a new religion of passion and poetry attuned
to the simplicities and superstitions of the poor. Borrow has left a
picture of a great multitude of rough men and women on a northern

1. Simond was amazed by 'the smart appearance of the English clergy.'
Simond, II, 134; Austen, II, 430. See Bamford, II, 211; Cooper, 15–16, 78;
Lamb, VI, 480.

heath – 'labourers and mechanics and their wives and children, dusty people, unwashed people, people of no account' – listening with strained, tense faces to a Methodist evangelist preaching from a wagon. On the wild Lancashire moors, whose valleys sheltered the chimneys of the new cotton factories, parties of pious weavers could be seen every Sunday making their way with sticks and lanthorns to tiny Bethels, where, amid groans and agonized confessions, they wrestled with the 'Powers of the Prince of the Air' and, crying for 'light' and 'grace', 'stormed the strongholds of Satan.'[1] Like the broadsides of the Nile and the raped breaches of Badajoz, they were a portent of the race's hidden fires.

Between these dissentient congregations and the old Church there existed a bitter enmity, theological, political, and social. Though the loaves and fishes, the power and the glory, belonged to the Establishment, the rival forces were closely balanced; of London's four hundred places of worship, nearly half belonged to the Nonconformists. Yet though scornful squires might forbid their tenantry to enter Methodist chapels, and Wesleyan missionaries – 'long-eared 'uns' to the profane – were sometimes thrown by village roughs into horse-ponds, nothing did more than Methodism to unite Britain in face of the Revolutionary peril. By convincing the more serious-minded workers of the validity of the Christian ethic, the great eighteenth-century rebel evangelists inoculated the English poor against the Jacobin fever that was sweeping the Continent. Only where there was hunger and intolerable injustice did the infidel virus triumph, and then only for so long as the more extreme hardships remained unalleviated.

The Terror temporarily opened the eyes of the British upper and middle classes. An age of comfortable rationalism was confronted with the depths of wickedness latent in human nature; there was a Devil after all.[2] The Evangelical revival within the established Church was its reply to the apathy of an over-indulged clergy and heathen indifference

1. Bamford, I, 115. See Clapham, I, 216–17; Cooper, 36–9, 79–86, 89–93; *Lavengro*, 161–3; Leigh, 319; Simond, II, 133.
2. 'The awakening of the labouring classes after the French Revolution,' wrote Lady Shelley, 'made the upper classes tremble. ... The parson no longer hunted or shot five days in the week, cleaning his fowling-piece on the sixth prior to the preparations of a drowsy sermon, delivered on the seventh day to a sleeping congregation.'

of the neglected poor. It was a spontaneous movement to arouse sluggish consciences and alleviate popular sufferings by personal charity. While England's rulers struck back at the Revolution militant with the sword of Nelson and Wellington, they resisted it at home, under the unofficial direction of Pitt's old friend, Wilberforce, with a flood of Sunday schools, tracts, free Bibles, benefit societies, soup and clothing clubs, and allotments. In 1811 the *National Society for Educating the Poor in the Principles of the Established Church* was founded; in 1814 the *British and Foreign School Society* for non-denominational Bible-reading. Admiral Cornwallis, the 'Billy-go-tight' of the blockade of Brest, refused, like a loyal churchman, to lease his land to a chapel, but gave it to the parish for a church school. While Elizabeth Fry, taking up the work John Howard had begun, strove with love and pity to reform the brutalized prisoners in Newgate – an example followed by the formation of prison committees in every English county town – and Hannah More, De Quincey's 'Holy Hannah', closed her life-work of charity with the building of cottages for deserving labourers with large families, young ladies like Jane Austen's sisters occupied themselves in visiting the poor, making them comforts, and teaching their children the Scriptures. Cobbett on the way to East Stratton – it was on a Sunday – met a little girl in a camlet gown, white apron, and plaid cloak with a prayer book in her hand, all given by the lady of the manor who had had her taught – to his disgust, for he did not like such patronage – to read and sing hymns.

There was nothing new in this; it was the repetition of a recurring pattern in the nation's history. Though its statutory institutions were no longer adequate to the size and energy of its population, its possessing classes and all those who, in its infinitely graded society, enjoyed property, status or privilege, felt, to a degree known nowhere else, the obligation to contribute personally to the alleviation of suffering and the elimination of vice, brutality, and disease among their poorer neighbours. This sprang partly from their Christian faith and the family life which, in England and Scotland alike, was its base, and partly from the necessity for individual responsibility inherent in a State which refused to tolerate either police or bureaucracy. The English had a talent for fighting fire because they regarded it as their duty and because they knew that in the last resort there was no one else to put it out but themselves. 'What stately edifices,' wrote the author of Ackermann's *Microcosm of London*, 'arise for the relief of every evil, corporate, moral, and intellectual, that afflicts the human species; diseases of every name, accidents of every kind, helpless infancy, friendless youth, decrepit age, moral infirmity, and mental derangement, find alleviation, restoration, reception, instruction, support, improvement, and renovation ... within these splendid receptacles.'

This was pitching it rather high; our ancestors' treatment of the beneficiaries of their charity was practical but spartan. The dining hall of the House of Asylum at Lambeth was floored with stones, lit by high skylights and fitted with long tables and benches, the fires at either end of the hall being carefully fenced round. Other furniture there was none, but everything was spotlessly clean and the inmates clad in neat white bonnets and tuckers and purple dresses. Here children, deserted or left bereft by their parents, were taught to mend their own clothes, make shifts and table linen, do needlework, and perform the business of house and kitchen. They also learnt to read the Bible, write a legible hand, and understand the first four rules of arithmetic. At the age of fifteen they were apprenticed for seven years to families approved by the governors.[1]

What was true of London was true also of the provinces. In Liverpool, a tenth of the capital's size, there was a *Blue Coat Hospital*, a *House of Industry*, a *House of Recovery*, a *Female School of Industry*, a *Seaman's Hospital*, a *Dispensary*, a *Welsh Charitable Society*, a *Ladies' Charity*, a *Lunatic Hospital*, a *Magdalene Society*, an *Institution for Restoring Drowned Persons*, a *Strangers' Friendly Society*, a *Society for Bettering the Condition and Increasing the Comforts of the Poor*, a *School for the Indigent Blind*, and a number of free schools, all supported by what was called public patronage. Every village had at least one ancient endowment; at East Burnham in Buckinghamshire there was a free school and a charitable trust with lands and £2600 in the Funds: at Gainsborough two educational foundations, one providing every scholar annually with a blue coat and a cap trimmed with yellow. Though there was little remedial

---

1. Ackermann, *Microcosm*, III, 119. See *idem*, II, 61–79, 137, 196; Ashton, I, 287; Berry, III, 308; Croker, I, 203; Leigh Hunt, *Autobiography*, I, 283–309; Partington, I, 9, 97–8; Festing, 193; Simond, I, 155–6.

action by the State outside the rather bleak Elizabethan Poor Law – itself, however, unique in a world which still viewed charity as a religious not a civic obligation – any national or international calamity was sure to provoke among the English a subscription for its mitigation. A fund started after Leipzig by Rudolph Ackermann, the print-seller, to relieve his ruined countrymen in Saxony, was over-subscribed in a few days. The 'Association for the Relief of the Manufacturing and Labouring Poor' during the Continental blockade had three royal Dukes and the Archbishop of Canterbury among its patrons. Even the careless Eton scholars competed in charitable contributions 'for a poor cad or the widow of a drowned bargee.' Most of this spontaneous charity was local; in the severe winter of 1814, for instance, the Quakers of Gainsborough organized a fund for distributing free soup, biscuits, potatoes, and herrings to the poor of the town.[1]

The effects of such humanitarian action, given a new impetus by the Evangelical revival, were felt in almost every sphere of national life outside the slums and factory towns. Its supreme achievement was the abolition of the Slave Trade, brought about in the teeth of vested interest after twenty years of agitation – a measure of incalculable benefit whose enforcement now became the task of the Royal Navy. Like so much that was best in the national life, it sprang from the protest of a minority of enlightened consciences at the suffering inflicted by the less enlightened. If there was freedom in Britain for men to commit social crimes, the same freedom fostered and helped men of active virtue to mobilize public opinion against them and bring about, after full exposure, their permanent suppression. The process even extended to the prevention of the callous cruelty perpetrated on animals by the unthinking multitude – the background against which man's inhumanity to man in early nineteenth-century slum and factory has to be set. This was no worse than in other lands, but it was very vile; a Loughborough bricklayer, for a bet, worried a hedgehog to death with his teeth, and a crowd cut off the horns of a baited bull and tortured it to death. Yet it was an English workman who, seeing in boyhood a hare's legs broken for sport, recalled that from that moment he became the friend of every

---

1. Cooper, 26. See *Fraser's Magazine*, XXXI, 457; Gaussen, II, 353; Halévy, I, 12–13; Ham, II, 168; *English Spy*, I, 35; Daniell, II, 87–93; Newton, 270–1.

living thing that suffered wrong and an enemy to every being who inflicted it. 'Humanity' Martin, who protested in Parliament against bull and bear baiting, was burnt by the mob in effigy, but as a result of his brave persistence the Royal Society for the Prevention of Cruelty to Animals was founded and the first Act against the ill-treatment of cattle and horses placed on the statute book.[1]

*

The English had a genius for voluntary co-operation. They based action, not on the State as in France, or on the Army, Church, or Dynasty as in Prussia, Spain, and Russia, but on the voluntarily created team. When after Waterloo the Allies entered Paris, 'the English gentlemen,' wrote Gronow, 'sought instinctively something like a club.' There was a Society for the Prevention of Vice and a Society for the Encouragement of Religion and Virtue; a Society of Antiquaries and a Mechanics' Institute; a Society for the Relief of Foreigners and one for the Conversion and Education of Negro Slaves: a Society for Protecting Trade against sharpers and swindlers, and a Society for giving Bibles to Soldiers and Sailors. It was hard to think of any object for which there was not some voluntary association of English men and women. And almost every corporate national activity, including the Army, was the result of a private contract voluntarily entered into by people of like mind.

Inside such self-chosen associations the English, normally so suspicious of authority, showed themselves astonishingly amenable. At the Beefsteak Club, where even royal dukes served their turn as 'boots', members were sworn in with the words, 'You shall attend duly, vote impartially, and conform to our laws and orders obediently: you shall support our dignity, promote our welfare, and at all times behave as a worthy member in this sublime Society; so Beef and Liberty be your reward!'[2] So long as they were not coerced from above but felt that they were co-operating of their own free choice, the English of all classes were prepared to contribute to their corporate activities a loyalty,

1. See Ashton, I, 83, 203–4; Bamford, I, 50; Bewick, 9–10; *Cranbourn Chase*, 64; *English Spy*, I, 72; Howitt, 415; Nevill, 213; Lady Shelley, II, 132; Woodward, 451; Smart, 206–7.
2. Nevill, *London Clubs*, 37–46.

enthusiasm, and readiness to serve capable of making any institution work. The Czar remarked after his visit to London that the high state to which the English had advanced was the result not merely of their laws and constitution, but of a temper of mind, a soberness of thought, a habit of reflection, collective and individual, possessed by no other people.

It was because they felt themselves to be freely associated in their country's service that the English viewed it with such loyalty and devotion. The poorest were entitled to discuss its affairs: the vote, like the seals of office, might be the privilege of the few, but the policy of the nation was as vehemently debated in market place and alehouse as in Parliament or Cabinet. Outside the new factory districts and the slum rookeries of the larger cities, this sense of national proprietorship was almost universal. Love of country was something that transcended class or rank. Looking at that landscape of splendid properties and at the country's mansions, banks, markets, warehouses, and factories, it was easy to account for the patriotism of the upper and middle classes. What was remarkable was the national pride of the poor, their instinctive belief in the superiority of their country and its ways of life, and their unfailing readiness to die for it. Theirs was a deep, sensitive love of its beauty, of its peaceful civilization, and free traditions. At farm feast or in village alehouse the artless chorus would rise, a warning to foreign tyrants who put their trust in lawless strength:

> *The race is not always got*
> *By them wot strive and for it run,*
> *Nor the battel to them peopel*
> *Wot's got the longest gun.*

For all its harshness and injustice, such simple folk thought there was no country like their own; they felt as Lord Dudley put it, that 'abroad was a poor place compared with England.' A Wiltshire peasant, sitting at his door on a summer's evening, recalled how, having heard the parson preach of Paradise, he had made up his mind that 'if there was but a good trout-stream running down Chicken Grove bottom, Fernditch Lodge would beat it out and out.' Even where the dark mists of industrialism were settling on the northern fells and moors, the love of England's beauty remained strong; the young lovers in Manchester in the early years of the century would seek out and walk together in Tinker's Garden, 'then a sweet bowery place.'[1]

*

In country districts rich and poor still joined in expressing their pride in the common achievements of the society to which they belonged. A Devonshire child born at the turn of the century recalled how all national celebrations began with a distribution of meat and bread to the poor; Walter Scott, the lion of fashionable Edinburgh, never failed to hurry home to join his rustic neighbours in a *gaudeamus* on the anniversary of Waterloo. 'As I came down here to-day,' wrote Lady Bessborough, 'I met a procession that I thought quite affecting – numbers of men without an arm or leg or variously wounded, with bunches of laurel in their hats, and women and children mingling with them. I inquired what it was and found it to be the anniversary of the battle of Talavera.' The sense of history had not yet been dulled by the impersonal segregation and ugliness of an industrial society; men still understood something of the march of their country through time, of its traditions and culture. When the Guards' band played the old martial airs of England outside the Palace, a foreign visitor noted that many in the crowd had tears in their eyes. It was not, Paley wrote, by what the Lord Mayor felt in his coach that the public was served, but by what the apprentice felt who gazed on it. To make men love their country, it was still thought necessary to make their country lovely.

For England still preserved a pageantry, beautiful and impressive though homely, that educated men in the meaning of society. The Mayor with his laced cloak, sword-bearer, maces, and aldermen, the gentlemen of the shire dining together in lieutenancy uniform, the humble beadles and criers in their cocked hats, flaxen wigs, and silver lace, the very postmen in red and gold were unconsciously teaching history. At Assizes the Judges drove into the country towns in scarlet and ermine, with outriders, javelin men, and halberdiers, while the bells pealed and the streets were thronged with gentlemen in dark-blue coats, glossy hats, and shining boots, and misses in white muslin and

1. Bamford, I, 102, 187, 195, 199, 209, 219; II, 187, 267; Bewick, 12–13, 31–2, 37–8; Brownlow, 21; Cowper, 22–3; *Cranbourn Chase*, 85–6; *Fraser's Magazine*, XXXI (1845), 192; Granville, I, 436; Haydon, I, 205, 282; Leslie, 228; Dudley, 309; Smith, I, 335.

their prettiest bonnets. In Edinburgh the Lord Justice Clerk and Judges passed through the city to their daily tasks in robes of red and white satin; in the grey streets of University and cathedral cities there was usually a flutter of gowns and a glimmer of wands and maces. From Windsor's keep, with its banners and martial music floating on the wind, to the local yeomanry jingling through market town and tented park with glossy horses and shining accoutrements; from the scarlet and buff of the Belvoir uniform flooding the grey, green Leicestershire fields to the ragged London sweeps marching through the streets on May Day with ribbons and trinkets, the English loved to preserve the symbols of their unity and corporate achievements.[1]

So, too, they commemorated their faith and the seasons of the pastoral year. Before Christmas the weavers of South Lancashire sang all night at their looms to keep themselves awake as they prepared for the holiday. In the West the yule-log was brought home and tales told over posset and frumenty, and the carollers and string-choirs went their frosty rounds:

> The holly bears a prickle
> As sharp as any thorn;
> And Mary bore sweet Jesus Christ
> On Christmas day in the morn.

With the farmhouses and cottages full of greenery and the kissing-bush hanging from the rafters, the traditional roast beef, plum pudding, mince-pie, and roasted crab of the great Feast were eaten, while the mummers in painted paper and floral headgear – King George, the Doctor, and the Turkey Snipe – recited traditional words and banged one another with their wooden swords. On New Year's Eve the was-sailers came round with garlanded bowls, cleaving the wintry skies with their song:

> Here's to our horse and to his right ear,
> God send our master a happy New Year;
> A happy New Year as e'er he did see,
> With my wassailing bowl I drink to thee!

1. Ashton, I, 215; Bamford, II, 80–1, 196; Dixon, 61–2; Howitt, 83–5, 417–8; Letts, 200; Lockhart, IV, 188, 204; Ackermann, *Microcosm*, I, 11; Newton, 206–207; Pyne, *Costume of Great Britain*; Simond, I, 3, 255, 269, 299, 361; II, 67, 72, 115.

and neighbours, made kindly by the season, sat in one another's houses, 'fadging' over cakes and wine. The same gatherings were repeated with differences on Twelfth Night, when fires were lit and the farm beasts and apple trees carolled. On Distaff's Day and Plough Monday the resumption of work was celebrated by labourers going round the parish in animal masks, blowing cows' horns, and cracking whips.[1]

Such feasts succeeded one another throughout the year, hallowed by memory yet sources of recurring excitement and activity. On Shrove Tuesday the miners of the north visited one another's houses to turn their pancakes and 'stang' whoever had not eaten theirs, carrying the laggards with laughter to the midden. Mothering Sunday was commemorated with a simnel cake, Good Friday by children going round with a fiddler 'peace-egging'. There were rituals that commemorated remote historical events, like the riding of the black man through the streets of Ashton-under-Lyne on Easter Monday, the torchlit procession of ropemakers at Chatham to celebrate the benefactions of Catherine of Aragon, the Pack Monday Fair at Sherborne on the anniversary of the completion of the Abbey nave. There were other days when the bonds of law were loosed, as at Michaelmas in Kidderminster when the gentry bombarded the Bailiff and Corporation with apples and for a 'lawless hour' everyone threw cabbage stalks in the streets, St Luke's Day in Cheshire when parsons were pelted with fruit, Tandering Day when school children barred out their teachers and men and women spent the evening drinking hot elderberry wine in one another's clothes, and the Mischief Meet on May Day when, so long as one was not caught, it was lawful to pay off old scores: to throw a neighbour's gate off its hinges, upset his cart or let out his cattle.

There were occasions, too, when the poor had a right to largesse from their neighbours, and when the hungry were filled with good things. There were rituals that marked the course of the farm year; the Whitsun Ale and the sheep-shearing festival, the Holy Night at Brough, when a burning ash was carried in front of the town band with everyone dancing and firing squibs behind, the hiring fairs when the markets

---

1. At Alkborough in Lincolnshire the masqueraders included a Fool, a Soldier, a Doctor, a Lady, an Indian King, a Hobby Horse, a Beelzebub and a character, met in many other parts of the country, called Besom Betty. *British Calendar Customs*, II, 97. See Howitt, 466–71.

were full of toys and ginger-bread stalls and young men and women stood in the streets wearing the emblems of their craft to sell their service for the next year. The greatest of all the farm feasts was Harvest Home when the Kern Dolly or Ivy girl, fashioned from the corn, was set upon a pole and borne home in the last cart, with music playing and the farmer and his men shouting in procession while the good-wife dished up the supper that was to crown the rustic year. There, at the long wooden tables, the reapers – 'with sunburnt hands and ale-en-livened face' – rejoiced over their beef, beer, and pipes, singing familiar songs and tossing down half-pint sconces with double forfeits for every drop spilt, until the time-honoured chorus was reached:

> Here's a health unto our master, the founder of this feast,
> I hope to God with all my heart his soul in Heaven may rest,
> And all his works may prosper that e'er he takes in hand,
> For we are all his servants and all at his command –
> So drink, boys, drink, and see you do not spill,
> For if you do, you shall drink too, for 'tis our master's will!

After which those able wound their way home, and those who could not slept where they lay, well content, in barn or stable.

Other dates in the calendar linked craft or calling to the Christian faith: the Spinners' Feast at Peterborough when workhouse children in white dresses and scarlet ribbons, the tallest girl in sceptre and crown, marched through the streets singing the spinning song; the processions of woolcombers on St Blase's Day in the cloth towns of Yorkshire and East Anglia, with their heralds, banners, and bands, wool-staplers on horseback, spinners in white stuff-waistcoats and silver sashes, wagoned pageants of Jason with Golden Fleece, Castor and Pollux, shepherds and shepherdesses, and good Bishop Blase in mitre and gown. Before the Lancashire Wakes, proclaimed by the bellmen in the churchyards on successive Sundays, every fold and hamlet vied in preparing the rush cart, decking its ornamental sheet with ribbons, streamers, and silver ornaments. With lanes resounding with fife, drum, and fiddle, the girls all flounces and frills in new kirtles and bonnets, the lads in jingling horse-collars and bright with ribbon and tinsel, the whole community followed the cart to the parish church, while the morris dancers leaped and spun before:

> *My new shoon they are so good,*
> *I cou'd doance morrice if I wou'd*
> *An' if hat an' sark be drest*
> *I will doance morrice w' the best.*

When Keats, in his *Ode to a Grecian Urn*, asked

> *What little town by river or sea-shore ...*
> *Is emptied of this folk this pious morn?*

he may have recalled the customary rites – doomed by the advance of an iron economy – of the Lancashire villages through which he had recently passed.[1]

Though all this pageantry was beginning to wear a little thin, and sophisticated folk to sneer and denigrate, it still served its purpose of enriching the imagination of successive generations. Men felt at one with their native place, loved its beauty, and took pride in its history. Old castles and monastic ruins, whose crumbling stones reflected the light of vanished sunsets, were sources not only of intellectual interest to the few but of wonder and poetry to the many. So were the rude signs in bright colours swinging over the tavern doors, of Admiral Keppel or Vernon braving the battle and the breeze, the Marquis of Granby in scarlet coat, or St George busy, with plumed helm and shield, slaying dragons. The rich might take the country's traditions for granted, but unlettered lads from Tyneside colliers stood 'beneath the wondrous dome of St Paul's with almost awful surprise,' and Bewick's neighbours, the Northumbrian peasants, spent their winter evenings listening to the tales and ballads of the Border. The earliest rhymes that Thomas Cooper, the Chartist leader, remembered were those of Chevy Chase. He used to repeat them until they made him feel as warlike as the sight of Matthew Goy riding into the town with news of a victory in the Peninsula or the scarlet-coated volunteers marching through Gainsborough on exercise days to the sound of fife and drum.

1. For an account of the Wakes see Bamford, I, 130–5, 146–7, 188, and Howitt, 493–5. See also for a detailed account of English social and ritual custom before it was destroyed by the Industrial Revolution, A. R. Wright's great compilation, *British Calendar Customs* (1936–40). See, too, Bamford, I, 120, 122–4, 127–8; Fowler, 250–1; T. Hardy, *Under the Greenwood Tree*; Howitt, *Boy's Country Book*, 93; *English Spy*, I, 97.

The English loved to voice their patriotism in a song. Bob Johnson, the jockey, after his victories on the turf, would climb on the table and strike up his favourite:

> *If ye ax wheer oi comes fra,*
> *I'll say the Fell side;*
> *Where fayther and mither*
> *And honest folk bide.*

The love of singing came out in the folk songs which, despite enclosure, lingered on in the villages like the string choirs and morris dancers.

> *Now when we did rise from that green, bushy grove,*

sang the old men recalling their days of love,

> *In the meadows we wandered away,*
> *And I placed my true love on a primrose bank,*
> *While I picked her a handful of may.*

In the alehouse or in the fields over the midday cheese and ale, country-men sang of their craft and skill, prizing them the more for the singing:

> *'Hold, gard'ner,' says the ploughman, 'my calling don't despise,*
> *Since each man for his living upon his trade relies,*
> *Were it not for the ploughman both rich and poor would rue,*
> *For we are all dependent upon the painful plough.'*

Often such songs, with their scope for character, would be acted, some elder piping up,

> *O true love, have you seen my gold?*
> *And can you set me free?*
> *Or are you come to see me hung*
> *All on the gallows tree?*

and the hearer, to whom the words were so familiar as to be automatic, joining in. They voiced the sentiment, honour, memory, poetry, and robust coarseness of the race. *So fleet runs the hare*, chanted the drovers at the Weyhill alehouse:

> *and so cunning runs the fox,*
> *Why shouldn't this young calf live to grow an old ox?*
> *O! for to get his living among the briars and thorns*
> *And drink like his daddy with a large pair of horns.*

The seamen, roughest and hardest-used of men, had their traditional songs and shanties, whose rhythm served their work and whose poetry sprang from the element they sailed:

> *Then a-weigh our anchor, my jolly, jolly tars,*
> *For the winter star I see.*

Having to make their own music, many Englishmen knew how to perform both vocally and instrumentally; at a homecoming, a wedding, a gathering of neighbours, a man would take down his fiddle or send for his neighbour's. Bamford's weaver father could read from the book and play both fiddle and flute, and even composed. The yeomen of Cranborne Chase gathered weekly at an inn on Salisbury Plain for instrumental music and part singing; the poor artisans of Lincoln formed a choral society to render Handel's Oratorios.

Deep down a vein of poetry, simple, sensuous, and strangely delicate, ran through this healthy, courageous, cohesive people.

> *Rosy apple, lemon and pear,*

sang the children of the Dorset villages at their traditional games:

> *A bunch of roses she shall wear,*
> *Gold and silver by her side,*
> *I know who'll take her as his bride;*
> *Take her by her lily-white hand*
> *And lead her to the altar;*
> *Give her kisses one, two, three,*
> *Mrs So-and-so's daughter.*

And in the sturdy north – the land of Bobby Shaftoe – the wives of Tyneside dandled their babies to the lilt:

> *Dance ti thy daddy*
> *Sing ti thy mammy*
> *Dance ti thy daddy*
> *Ti thy mammy sing!*
> *Thou shall hev a fishy*
> *On a little dishy,*
> *Thou shall hev a fishy*
> *When the boat comes in.*

There were songs that kept England's history bright; of ships with names like poems, of pastoral duties transformed by imagination into acts of significance and beauty, of courtship, tender, tragic, or bawdy, but always shot with the haunting loveliness of the green, peaceful land that gave them birth; of wild rovers and the misfortunes that befall poor men when passion sounds and the reckless heart tries to transcend the iron bars of destiny; of indignation against cruel laws and injustice and foul play; and, underlying all, the moral sense of a great people and their perception of the sweetness of love, courage, and loyalty to wife and home, and of the unchanging goodness of laughter and comradeship, striking, as the pewter pots beat time on the dark, dented, malt-stained alehouse table, chords that rose from the very depths of the English heart.[1]

*

Because of these things men respected learning and culture; they had not yet come to associate them with the superior privileges of an alien class. In the fly-leaf of old volumes treasured in farm and cottages, the familiar words could be seen:

> Unto this truth I set my hand:
> Learning is better than house or land;
> When house has gone and money's spent,
> Then learning is most excellent.

Poor children of parts committed Shakespeare and Milton to memory, not because they wanted to better themselves but because the literature of their native land was a heritage for their sharing. Young Thomas Cooper, inspired by the story of how Samuel Lee, the Hebrew scholar, had taught himself the classics when a carpenter's apprentice, learnt Ruddiman's *Latin Rudiments* by heart in his scanty leisure hours and, too poor to afford a fire, sat upon winter nights wrapped in his mother's

1. Proceedings of the *Dorset National History and Antiquaries Field Club*, XXXVIII, Rev. H. Pentin, *Dorset Children's Doggerel Rhymes*, 112–52. See also Francis Collinson and Francis Dillon, *Songs of the Countryside*; Ashton, 213–18; Bamford, I, 27, 87, 91, 97; II, 262, 274; Bewick, 52; Broughton, II, 153; Colchester, II, 503; Cooper, 107–10; *Cranbourn Chase*, 107–10; Dixon, 70, 201, 204; *Espriella*, I, 167; Fowler, 253, 264; H. Lea, *Thomas Hardy's Wessex*, 86; Leigh Hunt, *Autobiography*, II, 15, 207; Keats, IV, 91–2; Lamb, VI, 510–12; VII, 828; Lockhart, IV, 167; V, 16, 40; Dudley, 293–4; Mitford, *Our Village*, 67, 146; *Old Oak*, 187; *Real Life in London*, I, 158; Simond, II, 34, 83, 240.

scarlet cloak, spelling out Caesar's *Commentaries*. The rough, unlettered jailer at Horsemonger Lane treated Leigh Hunt with new respect when he found a Greek Pindar among his books; Keats's landlady at Carisbrooke had an engraved head of Shakespeare in the lodging-house passage, which, finding he was a poet, she let him hang in his room and afterwards gave him. In his native Scotland Walter Scott was treated by rich and poor alike as a prince; even in London a work-man stopped Charles Lamb in the street and, begging his pardon, asked him if he would like to see the great novelist crossing the road.

The wonderful accumulated wealth of seventeenth- and eighteenth-century England had been made by generations of hereditary craftsmen, who, though of humble status, were culturally the equals of those who employed them. It was still natural for English artisans to admire the best: to distinguish civilization from barbarism. It was no coincidence that both the artisan radical leaders, to whose autobiographies we owe much of our knowledge of working-class outlook in the period im-mediately preceding the Industrial Revolution, acquired early a love and knowledge of engravings. Natural good taste was widespread; Farington, the academician, staying in Norwich in 1812 was introduced to a house painter and a coachmaker who were connoisseurs of the arts; the former, he thought, was more genuinely devoted to pictures than anyone he had ever met. Constable's friend, the rector of Osming-ton, calling on a poor curate in a remote mud village on the Dorset coast found on the bare walls a coloured print of Stothard's 'Canter-bury Pilgrims' which its owner little less than worshipped. Even beg-gars were sometimes men of taste; Stephen Denning, the portrait painter who became curator of the Dulwich Art Gallery, began life in the gutter, picking up his craft from a colourer of prints to whom he had been apprenticed.

*

Compulsory state education at that time would have seemed to Englishmen an intolerable invasion of private liberty. But a miscel-laneous network of ancient Latin schools, charitable foundations, pri-vate academies, dames' and Sunday schools, however erratically staffed, and of monitorial schools which relied on the national passion for self-help and utilized pupils as teachers, afforded an avenue of advancement for genius and a means of maintaining a general level of culture. At Manchester Grammar School the boys of the English class sought eagerly for promotion to the Latin class, the key to a fuller life and better world; young Borrow learnt Lilly's Latin Grammar by heart in three years. For 6d. a week, or in many cases for nothing at all, a lad who was prepared to help himself could learn to read, write, and count, or, if he had the ability, get his feet on the educational ladder.[1] Based on the twin supports of the classical grammar school and craft apprenticeship, the country's educational system, like most British institutions at the beginning of the nineteenth century, was overgrown with antiquity, haphazard, and in urgent need of reform. Yet before it was overlaid by the growth of a new industrial society, it achieved results which have never been surpassed by any other civilization. In literature it produced, and almost simultaneously, Wordsworth, Blake, Keats, Coleridge, Burns, Scott, Jane Austen, Lamb, Hazlitt, Clare, Hogg, Crabbe, and De Quincey; in scholarship Porson, the son of a poor parish clerk and a village shoemaker's daughter who found his way to Eton and Cambridge; in medicine and science Humphry Davy, Faraday, a blacksmith's son, and John Dalton, a weaver's. In the arts it produced Constable and Turner – a barber's son – Girtin and Bonington, David Cox, the son of a Birmingham blacksmith who was apprenticed first to a locket-maker and then to a theatrical scene painter, Crome, Chantrey, a village carpenter's son, and Rowlandson; Raeburn, a jeweller's apprentice, Opie, also a carpenter's son, Hoppner, a Whitechapel chorister, and Lawrence, the son of a Wiltshire innkeeper. In the crafts it threw up that wonderful company of country lads who, building on the foundations laid by the great artificer inventors of the eighteenth century, transformed the face not only of Britain but of the entire civilized world. Though there was little social equality in that England, the career was open to the talents.

It was part of the irony of their achievement that so many of these rustic giants who charted the course of mankind's industrial future wanted in youth to become poets. The unspoilt countryside of Britain, its songs and folklore and religion created a natural instinct for poetry.

1. Bamford, I, 44, 80–9; Cooper, 5–7, 13–15, 32–5, 45–7, 55–61, 72–6; Farington, VIII, 81; Grote, 23–4; Leigh Hunt, *Autobiography*, I, 60–1; Lamb, *Essays of Elia*, Christ's Hospital; *Lavengro*, 38–9; Lucas, I, 31–2, 37; Ackermann, *Microcosm*, I, 69; Mitford, *Our Village*, 7, 67–8; Simond, II, 57–8, 96, 130–9; Woodward, 465–8.

Burns, apart from his genius, was no isolated phenomenon; he sprang from the conditions of his age. So did Hogg and Clare, both peasants, Keats the liveryman's son, Lamb the serving man's, Wordsworth, the petty yeoman's, Blake the poor artificer. Such a man as Bamford the weaver might lack their literary gifts, but he was cast in the same mould. His description of the midnight meeting in Grislehurst Wood of his friends, Plant the herb-gatherer, and Chim the bird-catcher, on the haunted eve of St John springs from the natural poetry of a high rural civilization. So does his account, reminiscent of Keats's delight in the wind in the cornfields, of the vision he saw in May, 1821, tramping home from prison with his wife across Hathersage moor:

"'I can see the wind,' I said. ...

"'See the wind! And what's it like?' said she looking up and laughing.

"'It's the most beautiful thing I ever saw. ... Look over the top of the brown heath with a steady eye and see if thou canst discern a re-markably bright substance, brighter than glass or pearly water, deeply clear and lucid, swimming, not like a stream, but like a quick spirit, up and down and forward, as if hurrying to be gone.'

"'Nonsense, there is not anything.'

"'Look again, steady for a moment.'

"'There is,' she said, 'there is; I see it! O! what a beautiful thing. ...'"

"'That is the wind of heaven,' I said, 'now sweeping over the earth and visible. It is the great element of vitality, water quickened by fire, the spirit of life.'"[1]

*

For all the new influences that were beginning to destroy it, there was still a strong hierarchical sense in the country. The people were not servile – in defence of their rights they could be excessively obstinate – but they took great pride in personal status and privilege and in the operational skills which these generally symbolized. In the country house – the headquarters of the nation's greatest industry and as yet its largest economic unit – an elaborately graded system existed in which every man and woman had his or her place. The housekeeper whom

1. Bamford, II, 334–5. See *idem*, I, 87, 102, 115–24, 236; II, 340; Cooper, 63–5, 91; Colvin, *Keats*, 135; Howitt, 206–8; Leigh Hunt, *Autobiography*, II, 2; Lamb, VIII, 580; Mitford, *Literary Life* 104–5; *Old Oak*, 75.

Simond encountered at Chiswick was 'a stately old dame, very cross, and surly'; she had her rights which she made it clear to the whole world she meant to keep. In the larger establishments of the higher aristocracy there were sometimes as many as a dozen servants' sitting-rooms, carefully graded to the status of their users. At Wentworth Woodhouse seventy sat down every day to dine in the servants' hall; at Blenheim there were eighty house servants and a hundred out of doors.[1] In its more elegant way all this somewhat resembled the Government departments of our own day, and grew on the same cumulative principle. To those impatient of delay and waste of human effort it could be very irritating; Wellington once remarked that he brushed his own clothes and regretted that he had not time to clean his boots, for the presence of a crowd of idle, officious fellows annoyed him more than he could say. To most, however, of the participants in this easy-going, rule-of-thumb English hierarchy the conventions seemed satisfactory enough. Simond found, not only that English domestics were more obliging and industrious than those elsewhere, but that they looked better pleased and happier. If their status was defined towards those above them, it was equally defined towards those below; they might sleep in attics but they lived on the fat of the land and shared the dignity of their masters. There was a decently modulated avenue of advancement that provided for both mediocrity and talent. Mary Mitford's friend, twelve-year-old Joe Kirby, promoted from the farm to the manor house where he cleaned the shoes, rubbed the knives and ran errands, 'a sort of prentice to the footman,' would, she predicted, one day overtop his chief and rise to be butler. His sisters went into service in the great house at fourteen and stayed till they married, learning there lessons of neatness, domestic skill, and respect for quality of all kinds. If deference were a product of English country house life, slatternliness was not. It graded men and women but civilized them. Like the monasteries whose social place it had taken, it made for comfort, culture, and order.

At the apex of this hierarchy was a type which, at its best, commanded admiration and often affection. The ruling principle of English

1. Simond, II, 84, 105, 119. See Bamford, II, 204; Creevey, *Life and Times*, 214–15; Farington, VIII, 98; Holland, *Journal*, I, 56; Howitt, 22–7; Newton, 93; Willis, III, 311.

society was the conception of a gentleman. Good breeding was not merely a mark of social distinction but a rule for the treatment of others. It made few concessions to the ideal of equality; men, it was held, were born to varying lots, and in 1815 one took these distinctions as one found them. But a gentleman was expected to treat his fellow creatures of all ranks openly and frankly, even when it meant sacrificing his interests to do so. A gentleman did not tell a lie, for that was cowardice; he did not cheat, go back on his word, or flinch from the consequences of his actions. When Lord Sefton succeeded to his estates he at once settled – and without question – a gambling debt for £40,000 alleged to have been incurred by his father at Crockford's.[1]

A man's reputation as a gentleman was looked on as his most valuable possession. Any action, or even association, incompatible with it was regarded as a stain which must be immediately expunged. This accounted for the extreme sensitivity with which public men reacted to any slight on their honour, vindicating it, if necessary, in some dawn encounter with pistols on suburban common or foreign beach. Pitt, Castlereagh, Canning, Wellington, and Peel all risked their lives in this way while holding high office. 'How constantly, even in the best works of fiction,' wrote a critic, giving his reasons for supposing the author of *Waverley* to be a gentleman, 'are we disgusted with offences against all generous principle, as the reading of letters by those for whom they were not intended, taking advantage of accidents to overhear private conversation, revealing what in honour should have remained secret, plotting against men as enemies and at the same time making use of their services, dishonest practices on the sensibilities of women by their admirers, falsehoods, not always indirect, and by an endless variety of low artifices which appear to be thought quite legitimate if carried on through subordinate agents.' It was one of the reasons for the immense affection in which Scott was held that he never deviated from honourable standards. A gentleman, at his best, was one who raised the dignity of human nature – noble, fearless, magnanimous. When the Governor-General of Canada, the Duke of Richmond, learnt that he was suffering from hydrophobia, he never breathed a word of his impending doom, but performed his social duties with the same calm and dignified bearing to the dreadful end. 'Throughout the whole of his career,' Gronow wrote of Wellington, 'he always placed first and foremost, far above his military and social honours, his position as an English gentleman.' The founders of Sandhurst laid it down that the professional education of British officers ought to aim at producing, not corporals, but gentlemen. So long as it did so, they knew it would produce the kind of leaders Englishmen would follow.

A gentleman was under an obligation to be generous; he held his possessions like his life on terms. The very flies at Petworth, wrote Haydon, seemed to know that there was room for their existence; dogs, horses, cows, deer and pigs, peasantry and servants, guests and family, all shared in Lord Egremont's bounty and opulence.[1] If there was anything the English despised more than a coward, it was a skint. 'It is not only a received thing,' wrote Simond, 'that an Englishman has always plenty of money and gives it away very freely, but no sacrifice of a higher kind is supposed to be above his magnanimity.' The Duke of Buccleuch in times of agricultural distress left his farm rents uncollected and refrained from visiting London that he might have the cash to pay his retainers; Lord Bridgewater never refused work to any local man, and during times of unemployment increased his Ashridge establishment from five to eight hundred.[2] Captain Sawyer of East Burnham – one of the older school of squires – always allowed his poor tenants as much driftwood and 'lop and top' from his plantations as they wanted. Though there were plenty of harsh landlords who rackrented their estates to finance their extravagances, and many more who, absorbed in their pleasures, refused to be troubled, there were thousands of others who, treating their poorer neighbours with kindness and consideration, preserved social distinctions by taking the resentment out of them. Tom Purdy, the Abbotsford gamekeeper, who weekly pledged the laird and his guests at their Sunday dinner in a quaigh of whisky, no more felt a sense of injustice against Walter Scott for being his master than did the latter's dog, Maida. Nor did the pageboy, whose exercise book the great writer regularly corrected.[3]

1. Haydon, *Life*, II, 140–1. Simond (II, 250) records that Lord Egremont allowed his farm workers to play bowls and cricket on his lawns and even write their names on his walls and windows.

2. Mrs Arbuthnot, *Journal*, 23rd Jan., 1822; Lockhart, IV, 218; Howitt, 56.

3. Long after, when this kindly tradition was no more and Sir Walter himself in his grave, old men recalled how the Galashiels weavers, then herded into

The ideal of equality which had so intoxicated the French, had as yet made little impression on the British mind. Whenever Squire Lambton, with his £70,000 a year, visited his northern home, the Durham colliers turned out in thousands to draw his carriage. It was injustice and tyranny that this pugnacious people resented, not privilege. 'Gentlemen are, or ought to be, the pride and glory of every civilized country,' wrote Bewick, himself a radical; 'without their countenance arts and sciences must languish, industry be paralysed and barbarism rear its stupid head.' Bamford, for all his life of rebellion, wrote with nostalgia of the freedom that had existed in his youth between the gentry and their tenants. 'There were no grinding bailiffs and land-stewards in those days to stand betwixt the gentleman and his labourer. There was no racking up of old tenants; no rooting out of old cottiers; no screwing down of servants' or labourers' wages; no cutting off of allowances, either of the beggar at the door or the visitor at the servants' hall; no grabbing at waste candle-ends or musty cheese parings.' For the English liked the rich to be splendid, ostentatious, and free with their money. It was what, in their view, the rich were for.[1]

*

They liked them, too, to share and excel in their pastimes. 'Nothing,' the Duke of Wellington declared, 'the people of this country like so much as to see their great men take part in their amusements; the aristocracy will commit a great error if ever they fail to mix freely with their neighbours.'[2] Sport in England was a wonderful solvent of class distinction. Even foxhunting, with all its expense and showy competitiveness, had still something of a rough democracy about it, at once exclusive and classless, of Master and huntsman, groom and whipper-in, dog-stopper and stable boy, meeting day after day on the level of a common love. The coloured prints that depicted its scarlet coats and glossy horses hung in village alehouses as well as manor houses; when the Manchester weavers, true to their country past and oblivious of their proletarian future, went on hunting on the Cheshire Hills, Sam Stott, factories and become embittered radicals, marched yearly with the banners of their craft to Abbotsford for their feast: 'the grand days of our town when Scott and Hogg were in their glory and we were a' teal Tories.'

1. Bamford, i, 38; Bewick, 31-2, 165, 182; Lamington, 6-7; Creevey, *Life and Times*, 158; Charles Dibdin, Songs No. 34, '*Nautical Philosophy*'; Simond, i, 306.   2. Stanhope, 87.

the huntsman, used to treat them to a warm ale and ginger.[1] On the cricket field too, the conventions of rank were forgotten; the best man was 'the hardiest *swipe*, the most active *field*, the stoutest *bowler*.' 'Who that has been at Eton,' asked the author of the *English Spy*, 'has not repeatedly heard Jem Powell in terms of exultation cry, "Only see me *liver this here* ball, my young master"?' The game was played by the Prince Regent – before he let down his belly – on his ground at Brighton, by the aristocracy who liked to gamble over it, and by the young farmers and labourers of almost every south country village. At East Burnham, until the sabbatarians stopped it, the common every Sunday afternoon 'presented a lively and pleasing aspect, dotted with parties of cheerful lookers-on, with many women, children, and old persons.' Mary Mitford from her Berkshire cottage window could see two sets of cricketers, one of young men surrounded by spectators, standing, sitting, or stretched on the grass, all taking a delighted interest in the game, and the other a merry group of little boys, shouting, leaping, and enjoying themselves to their hearts' content.[2]

For the English, as Hazlitt said, were a sort of grown children. They loved Punch and Judy and games like skittles and shove-halfpenny, leap frog, blind man's buff, hunt-the-slipper, hot cockles, and snap-dragon. When Nelson went round the *Victory*'s gun-decks before Trafalgar, the men were jumping over one another's heads to amuse themselves until they were near enough to fire. 'Cudgel-playing, quarterstaff, bull- and badger-baiting, cockfighting,' Hazlitt wrote 'are almost the peculiar diversions of this island. ... There is no place where trap-ball, fives, prison-base, football, quoits, bowls are better understood or more successfully practised, and the very names of a cricket bat and ball make English fingers tingle.' Nothing would deflect them from their sport; when 'Long Robinson', the cricketer, had two of his fingers struck off, he had a screw fastened to one hand to hold the bat and with the other still sent the ball thundering against the boards that bounded old Lord's Cricket-ground.[3]

1. Bamford, I, 189. See Hazlitt, 'Merry England,' *New Monthly Magazine*, Dec., 1825; Osbaldeston, 32.

2. Mitford, *Our Village*, 18; Assheton Smith, 21; *English Spy*, I, 28, 72; Grote 45; *Old Oak*, 132–43; *Sea-Bathing Places*, 120.

3. W. Hazlitt, 'Merry England,' *New English Monthly*, Dec., 1825; Bamford, I, 108; Eland, 19–23; *English Spy*, II, 332–3; *Life in London*, 27–8, 145, 180;

They liked, and honoured above all, what they called 'game, bone, and blood.' It was because their rulers possessed these qualities that, despite all their unimaginativeness and selfishness, they had so little difficulty in ruling them. It is this that makes so much of the economic interpretation of the time seem a little unreal; one is left at times with the impression that the people of Regency England had never seen a horse, snared a rabbit, or set a dog to a badger or sack of rats. Most Englishmen were far more interested in dog-fighting, coursing, hunting vermin, fishing and fowling, boxing and wrestling, than in the pursuit of equality or the class war. The man of the age was not the Benthamite philosopher, the radical martyr, or the wage-hungry cotton spinner – however important in retrospect – but the sporting type. *Jem Flowers*, the Eton boys sang of a local 'cad',

> *baits a badger well*
> *For a bullhank or a tyke, sir*
> *And as an out-and-out bred swell*
> *Was never seen his like, sir!*

The national norm was 'Joey' of the Westminster cockpit – 'a small man of about five feet high with a very sharp countenance and dressed in a brown jockey coat and top boots' – to whom Francis Ardry introduced the future author of *Lavengro*. After trying to sell the 'green one' a dog, this gentleman expatiated on the future of society.

'A time will come, and that speedily, when folks will give up everything else and follow dog-fighting.'

'Do you think so?'

'Think so? Let me ask what there is that a man wouldn't give up for it?'

'Why ... there's religion.'

'Religion! How you talk. Why, there's myself, bred and born an Independent, and intended to be a preacher, didn't I give up religion for dog-fighting. ... Religion! Why the parsons themselves come to my pit, and I have now a letter from one of them asking me to send him a dog.'

'Well then, politics.'

Haydon, *Table Talk*; Howitt, 495; Strutt, *Sports and Pastimes*, 522–44; *Real Life in London*, I, 81; II, 108 n.

'Politics! Why, the gemmen in the House would leave Pitt himself, if he were alive, to come to my pit. There were three of the best of them here to-night, all great horators. Get on with you, what comes next?'

'Why, there's learning and letters.'

'Pretty things, truly, to keep people from dog-fighting! Why, there's the young gentlemen from the Abbey School comes here in shoals, leaving books, letters, and masters too. To tell you the truth, I rather wish they would mind their letters, for a more precious set of young blackguards I never seed. ...'

'You show by your own conduct that there are other things worth following besides dog-fighting. You practise rat-catching and badger-baiting as well ...'

'Your friend here might call you a new one! When I talks of dog-fighting, I of course means rat-catching and badger-baiting, ay, and bull-baiting, too, just as when I speaks religiously, when I says one, I means not one but three.'[1]

*

One common denominator in particular linked Englishmen of all classes – the horse. The first goal of every boy or girl visiting the metropolis was Astley's circus. The friend who called Charles Lamb the only man in the country who had never worn boots or sat in a saddle, was only slightly exaggerating. Not that all Englishmen rode well; it was remarked of Wellington, though unfairly, that no conqueror ever combined more victories with more falls. Yet almost every Englishman born within sight of a highroad or a field thought it the height of felicity to be 'well mounted on a spunky horse who would be well in front.' The English loved horses. O'Kelly, owner of Eclipse, declared that all Bedford Level could not buy him. 'When you have got such a horse to be proud of,' the ostler told the Romany Rye, 'wherever you go, swear there a'n't another to match it in the country, and if anybody gives you the lie, take him by the nose and tweak it off, just as you would do if anybody were to speak ill of your lady!'[2]

1. *Lavengro*, 212–13.
2. *Romany Rye* 188. See Alken, *National Sports of Great Britain*; Bell, I, 170; Leigh Hunt, *Autobiography*, I, 134; Lamb, VI, 518; Newton, 220–1; Simond, II, 155.

'Something slap', a 'bit of blood', 'an elegant tit', were the phrases with which the English expressed this love. A smart or 'spanking' turn-out was, more than anything else, the symbol of national pride; there was no comparison, a visitor to Paris in 1815 reckoned, between French and English equipages; neatness, beauty, finish, lightness, quality, all were on the side of the islanders. 'The exercise which I do dearly love,' wrote Mary Mitford, 'is to be whirled along fast, fast, fast by a blood-horse in a gig.' During the first years of the nineteenth century the great coachbuilders of London and the provincial capitals turned out a wonderful succession of equipages, perfectly adapted for their purposes, from the fashionable landau and deep-hung, capacious barouche to the dashing curricle, tilbury, buggy and gig, and the phaeton 'highflyer' with its towering wheels and yellow wings. The most wonderful of all were the mail-coaches built for speed on the new metalled highways, with their blood-horses, bright brass harness, blazoned colours, horn-blowing guards, and coachmen with squared shoulders, vast capes, multiple coats, and nosegays.[1] Young aristocrats prided themselves on mastering the accomplishments of the professional knights of the road, even to filing and spitting through their teeth; to handle the 'ribbons' and be a first-rate 'fiddler' was passport to any company.

Supporting the noble institution of the horse was an immense community of grooms and ostlers, of sharp-eyed, wiry little men with bow legs and highlows and many a string dangling from the knees of their breeches, and lads in dirty pepper-and-salt coats and low-crowned hats with turn-up ears. They were members of an *alma mater* of which almost every English lad aspired to be a graduate.[2] Under its splendid clothes and yellow varnished equipages, Regency England stank of the stable and was proud of it. The fraternity of the curry-comb – that knowing underworld of inn tap-rooms and raffish-looking parties with hats on one side and straws in their mouths – stretched from Dover to Galway; without it, the economist's Great Britain of the early

1. *English Spy:* 1, 165, 275–6, 279–81; Gronow, 1, 129–30; *Life in London*, 37–8; *Real Life in London*, 1, 43–4; Simond, 1, 129–30; McCausland, *passim*.
2. Even factory lads, like Bamford in the Manchester warehouse, liked looking after their employers' mounts, and learned like him 'how to bed my master's neat tit down, to rub the bits and stirrups and sponge the bridle and girths.' Bamford, 1, 162–3.

nineteenth century seems as insubstantial as the two-dimensional world of the cinema. From it sprang the English poet whose mastery of sensuous imagery has only been surpassed by the offspring of the Stratford-on-Avon corn dealer. John Keats was the son of an ostler who married his master's daughter and succeeded him as keeper of a livery stable in Moorfields.

Horse jockeyship, the making of traffic in horseflesh, was 'the most ticklish and unsafe of all professions.' Coleridge heard a clerical Nimrod at Salisbury boast that he would cheat his own father over a horse. 'Then how would you, Mr Romany Rye', the ostler asked Borrow, 'pass off the veriest screw ... for a flying dromedary?'

'By putting a small live eel down his throat; as long as the eel remained in his stomach, the horse would appear brisk and lively to a surprising degree.'

'And how would you contrive to make a regular kicker and biter appear ... tame and gentle?'

'By pouring down his throat four pints of generous ale ... to make him happy and comfortable.'

The itch for horse-dealing and betting created, like everything English, its institutions. Weatherby's was to the Turf what the Bank of England was to the City, and Tattersall's, 'that hoarse and multifarious miscellany of men' below Hyde Park Corner, with its circular counter – a kind of temple to the goddess of chance – and its painting of Eclipse over the fireplace, was the Stock Exchange of the equine world.[1] A little Newmarket quizzing or hocussing was reckoned an essential part of a young gentleman's education for a rough, wicked world. It taught him, in the cant of the day, to keep his peepers open. It helped to give him and his race that strong practical sense – horse sense, they called it – that made them, wherever they went, the lords of the earth.

1. *English Spy*, I, 327–9; Dixon, 92–3; *Life in London*, 191; Lockhart, IV, 77, 290, 292; Ackermann, *Microcosm*; *Real Life in London*, 160–5; *Romany Rye*, 187–8, 335; Coleridge, *Miscellanies*, 236.

CHAPTER 9

THE OTHER FACE OF SUCCESS

An inventive Age
Has wrought, if not with speed of magic, yet
To most strange issues. I have lived to mark
A new and unforeseen creation rise
From out the labours of a peaceful land
Wielding her potent enginery to frame
And to produce. ... From the germ
Of some poor hamlet, rapidly produced
Here a huge town, continuous and compact,
Hiding the face of earth for leagues – and there
Where not a habitation stood before,
Abodes of men irregularly massed
Like trees in forests – spread through spacious tracts
O'er which the smoke of unremitting fires
Hangs permanent. ...

WORDSWORTH

WITH a society so constituted and with sons so self-reliant, resourceful, and loyal to creed and country, Britain had withstood the revolution in arms and defeated, contrary to all expectation, a martial State with a population, at the start of the war, nearly three times the size of her own. Even when all Europe was mobilized against her by an unparalleled military genius, she had triumphed, utterly destroying him and his power. And in the process, for all her immense sacrifices, she had grown rich – richer than ever before. The twenty-two years' struggle, though it had cost her seven hundred millions, had doubled her export trade and trebled her revenue. The carrying trade of the world was in her hands. Despite all her enemies' efforts, her merchant tonnage had risen from a million to two and a half million tons. Her commerce with the Spanish and Portuguese colonies in South America had increased fourteenfold. By her conquests in India, her occupation of the Cape, Ceylon, and Malta, her voyages of trade and discovery to Australia and the Far East, she had extended her tentacles into every part of the globe and raised the population of her empire from twenty to seventy millions. 'I doubt,' wrote Lord Dudley, 'whether any community ever attained to such a pitch of prosperity and glory.'

Everything testified to its wealth, power, and empire: the interminable masts in the Thames, Tyne, and Mersey, the Chinese, Persian,
Parsee, and Armenian traders in the Customs Houses, the Souchang
tea that Dorothy Wordsworth wrote for from Rydal to Twinings, the
rum with which the abstemious Wilberforce laced his bedtime milk.[1]
Even the humblest artisans seemed to share in that flood of prosperity
which their virtues and those of their leaders had unloosed. At the time
that Napoleon sailed, a prisoner in a British man-of-war, for St Helena,
wages in the manufacturing districts were higher than they had ever
been, save in the boom which had followed the short-lived Peace of
Amiens. Yorkshire woolcombers were earning five shillings a day,
coalminers almost as much. A few years earlier, Simond had found the
brass and iron founders of Birmingham, working by the piece, making
up to £3 and £4 a week – the equivalent of four or five times as much
to-day. Everyone with ambition was borrowing to launch out in new
ways; even humble Samuel Bamford, finding work for the handloom
so easily procurable, had given notice to his employer and, hiring
looms, set up on his own. A writer recalled how in the closing years of
the war, when Britain was manufacturing for all Europe, a vast working
population had been called into existence to supply every manner of
article to countries too busy in mutual slaughter to be able to make for
themselves. 'Everything,' he wrote, 'assumed a new and wonderful
value. ... The tables of mechanics were heaped with loads of viands of
the best quality and of the highest price: their houses were crowded
with furniture, till they themselves could scarcely turn round in them –
clocks, chests of drawers, and tables thronged into the smallest rooms,
looking-glasses, tea-trays, and prints stuck on every possible space on
the walls, and from the ceilings depending hams, bags, baskets, fly-
cages of many colours ... that gave their abodes more the aspect of
ware-rooms or museums than the dwellings of the working class. Dress
advanced in the same ratio; horses and gigs were in vast request; and
the publicans and keepers of tea gardens made fortunes.'[2] In the victory
summer of 1814 the weavers' wakes at Middleton were celebrated with

1. Farington, VIII, 22. See Alison, I, 78–9; Coleridge, *Unpublished Letters*, II,
72–3; De Selincourt, II, 558; Ackermann, *Microcosm*, I, 219; Pennant, *A Journey
to the Isle of Wight*, I, 11; Simond, II, 63; Woodward, 199.

2. Howitt, 202–3. See Alison, I, 80; Bamford, I, 122, 152–3, 188–9; Fremantle, I, 145; Letts, 134; Simond, I, 95–6; Smart, 414.

a hospitality and display never before known, six bands and eleven rush-carts perambulating the parish.

*

At the time of Britain's victory this material prosperity seemed the most assured thing in the world. Though chequered by spasmodic depressions, sometimes terrible in their intensity, the rise in production and trade had been continuous throughout the war. Now that peace was established over all the earth and her Navy's power to maintain it permanently was no longer even challenged, her statesmen, capitalists, and workers expected an even greater prosperity. They not only expected it; they felt they had deserved it. Their victory and the wealth that had come with it convinced them that the world they inhabited had been ordered by the God they worshipped to afford them ever-expanding prosperity. They did not wish to conquer that world like the vainglorious French; they merely wished to enjoy it and the fulness thereof. The richer they were, the more certain they became that this was their right. They were like the Jews of the Old Testament. They saw themselves as God's successful instruments for scourging those who broke his laws. Having emerged from tribulation into unbroken sunshine, they were totally unprepared for any reversal of fortune, for they could not conceive, having done so much for righteousness, how they could deserve misfortune. The shock, when it came, therefore, found them unprepared.

*

No one could gainsay the tireless energy with which the British worked to achieve success. The hours of the north country factories ranged from sixty-five to seventy-five a week.[1] The operatives who combed and sheared the cloth of the West Riding worked from four in the morning till eight at night; the children who pulled the trucks and emptied the baskets in the Northumberland mines did so with a fierce, daemonic rapidity. At Birmingham, a foreigner reported, no one spoke or thought of anything but labour. The London shops closed their shutters at midnight and opened again at dawn. When the first edition

1. Smart, 196–7.

of Scott's *Fortunes of Nigel* reached London from Edinburgh on a Sunday – the one day of rest observed by this nation of toilers – the bales were cleared from the wharves by one o'clock on Monday morning and 7000 copies distributed before ten. The wives of the farm labourers in the Vale of Aylesbury woke at four on summer mornings to plait straw for an hour before rising.

Punctuality and dispatch were almost universal attributes. 'With habits of early rising,' Cobbett asked, 'who ever wanted time for any business?' 'Sharp's the word and sharp's the action,' was the motto of the great carrier, William Deacon. In this the English resembled their hero, Nelson, who, as he was borne dying from the *Victory*'s deck, noticed something wrong with the tiller rope and ordered it, as was his habit, to be put right at once. The founder of W. H. Smith's built up his firm's fortunes by galloping the morning newspapers to catch the out-going mails. Even the postmen went from door to door ringing their bells 'with an indefatigable rapidity.'

There was something heroic about the energy of the English and Scots in their struggle for existence. Many resembled Wordsworth, whom Carlyle described as having 'great jaws like a crocodile cast in a mould designed for prodigious work.' George Stephenson's father looked 'like a peer o' deals nailed thegither an' a bit of flesh i' th' inside.'[1] A Northumberland pitman of Bewick's acquaintance was so strong that he thought it no hardship to spend his days at the bottom of a pit, breast high in icy water, filling buckets as they were lowered to him. Within this race of toilers burned a tireless and passionate intensity. Bewick himself set off at five every morning to walk ten miles to Newcastle, wading through streams and never troubling to change his clothes, even when they were frozen stiff. Even the gentle Charles Lamb, rusticating at Dalston, walked every morning into the Temple to get shaved, while Keats – a consumptive – tramped six hundred miles in a month through the Highlands, rising always before dawn to complete twenty miles by noon. A penniless widow in a little Lincolnshire town made and hawked pasteboard boxes for sixteen hours a day to feed and educate her son; her only respite was an occasional pipe with a neighbour who kept her children by sewing sacks for a factory, whereupon, her son wrote, 'the two brave women would go again to

1. Smiles, *Lives of the Engineers*, III, 17.

work after cheering each other to go stoutly through the battle of life.'[1]

They wasted little. The refuse of the capital was sold to the Essex and Hertfordshire farmers; the scourings of the streets were shipped to Russia to mix with clay for rebuilding Moscow. The great Walter Scott, who, to save cutting up a book worth a few shillings, would spend whole days transcribing passages in his own hand, taught his son-in-law his youthful expedient of sinking his wine into a well in the morning and hauling it up as his guests arrived for dinner. Frugality was the handmaid of industry; the possession of property, saved or inherited, was viewed as the one way a man could become master of his fate and the foundation of independence.

With energy and frugality went a high sense of enterprise and adventure. A nine-year-old Gainsborough boy, having raised fourpence by selling old bits of iron salvaged from the Trent, turned it into half a crown by begging a lift to Hull, fifty miles away, and returning with a bag of cockles for sale in his native town. From Peg Pimpleface, the costermonger's daughter, driving her donkey-cart round Poplar and Limehouse to sell vegetables from the Middlesex market gardens, to Captain Gordon of Calcutta chartering a vessel to penetrate the sea of Okhotsk and offer British goods to Siberian savages, the English were heroically on the venture. Wherever they went they fended, and expected to fend, for themselves. Simond, going over a West Indiaman, found her cabin hung with pikes, muskets, and pistols, and four great guns projecting from the cabin windows. In the same year – 1810 – he reported that 'the light troops of English commerce' were finding entrances to a forbidden continent, consigning their goods in packages which could be carried by hand and making them up to resemble the manufactures of the lands to which they were sent, even to the wrappers and trade labels; in a Leeds factory he saw the name of *Joumaux frères de Sedan* on broadcloth destined for export. A few years later, a clergyman, travelling behind the Allied lines, found all the uniforms of British make and even Prussian soldiers wearing brass lions in their

1. Cooper, 8–9, 26–7. See *idem*, 17; Bewick, 3, 35–7, 59–60, 95–7; Cobbett, *Rural Rides*, I, 28–9; Colvin, *Keats*, 293; Dixon, 66; Eland, 98; *Espriella*, I, 129; Farington, VII, 175; Hazlitt, 'The Letter Bell,' *Monthly Magazine*, March, 1831; Lamb, VI, 495, 581–5; Letts, 125, 133–4; Lockhart, V, 170; Lucas, I, 43–4; Simond, II, 77; Smart, 196–17; Sydney, 149; Woodward, 36.

caps. The Flemish burghers whom Dorothy Wordsworth saw after the war had their clothes made in Yorkshire. The very cottons of India were undersold by Lancashire on the banks of the Ganges.[1]

*

It was the blast furnaces that had made the armaments that had destroyed Napoleon. With the growing demand for iron – the main sinew of war – and the exhaustion of the south country forests that had fed the old charcoal furnaces and built the nation's wooden ships, steam-power, the invention of a succession of native geniuses, had been applied to the new coke furnaces of the North and Midlands. By the end of the war these were turning out between a quarter and half a million tons more than at its beginning. Coke, not charcoal, lit the funeral pyre of the armed Revolution. Simond in March, 1811 – the month in which Wellington's light infantrymen were shepherding Massena's starving army out of Portugal – was shown an ironworks in which three hundred men, operating enormous hammers driven by a 120-h.p. engine, produced 10,000 gun barrels a month. To feed the furnaces and the steam-power engines which inventors and capitalists were evolving in every industry to do with one man's labour what it had needed a dozen to do before, landowners and contractors prospected eagerly for coal and, finding it in abundance, made power-pumps and machinery to mine it and canals and iron-grooved or railed tracks to carry it to their customers.[2]

The British at the time were the most ingenious people on earth. A

1. Anderson, 117–20; Bamford, I, 201; II, 86; Bewick, 16–18; Cooper, 24–5; De Selincourt, II, 883; Lockhart, V, 100, 124; T. Moore, *Diary*, 3rd April, 1823; Pyne, *Picturesque Views*, Plates III, VII; Simond, I, 243; II, 77; Stanley, 185, 192; D. Walker, *General View of the Agriculture of the County of Hertford* (1795), *cit.* Ernle, 191; Woodward, 369, 444.

2. 'We crossed several iron railways leading from foundries and coalmines in the country to the sea. Four low cast-iron wheels run in an iron groove lying along the road. It is now, however, the general custom to place the groove on the circumference of the wheel, running upon the rail, which is a mere edge of iron, upon which no stone or other impediment can lodge. Five small waggons and sometimes six, fastened together, each carrying two tons of coal, are drawn by three horses, that is four tons to each horse, besides the weight of the waggon – about five or six times as much as they could draw on a common road.' This was in South Wales in 1810. Simond, I, 212. See Porter; Smart, 19.

society that venerated freedom of thought and action, peopled by an hereditary race of skilful mechanics, was a seed-plot for invention. Man in England was a tool-making animal. The first suspension bridge in Europe was built over the Tagus in 1812 by a major of the Royal Staff Corps to ensure swift communication between the two wings of Wellington's army. When, in a ship distressed at sea, a match could not be struck to fire the mortar, a young lieutenant was able to produce a bottle of sulphuric acid and a tube, primed with hyperexmuriate of potash and sugar-candy, to effect an instantaneous ignition. The school-boys at Harrow celebrated the retreat from Moscow at 'Duck Puddle' with cannon of their own making; Shelley at Eton hired a travelling tinker to help him build a steam-organ which, however, instead of filling the spheres with music, burst and nearly blew up himself and his tutor's house. Later, residing in Italy, he interested himself in building a steamer.

Lads of humbler parentage, heirs of generations of fine craftsmen, finding their ingenuity sought and rewarded, applied themselves to the evolution of new technical processes. Smiles' *Lives of the Engineers* is a saga of miraculous achievement wrought out of the native genius and character of a succession of Scottish and English country lads: Rennie, the millwright's apprentice who drained the Lincolnshire Fens and built docks and iron bridges; weavers and machinists like Crompton and Thomas Johnson who, backed by their employers, made lonely Lancashire the economic cornerstone of the world; the engineers, Bramah – a village carpenter's boy – Maudslay, Roberts, and Whitworth; Trevithick, the Cornish giant, and George Stephenson, the Northumberland collier's son who laid the foundations of the railway age. Steam-power to raise water and coal, and drive engines, ships, and vehicles, eliminating the horrors of wind-bound voyages and such winter exposure on coach tops as killed Keats; gas to light streets, shops, and houses;[1] safety lamps to prevent explosions in mines; water-closets

---

1. 'The effect of the new apparatus in the dining-room at Abbotsford was at first superb. In sitting down to table in autumn no-one observed that in each of the three chandeliers there lurked a tiny bead of red light. ... Suddenly at the turning of a screw the room was filled with a gush of splendour worthy of the palace of Aladdin. ... Jewellery sparkled, but cheeks and lips looked pale and wan in this fierce illumination; and the eye was wearied and the brow ached if the sitting was at all protracted.' Lockhart, v, 267–8. See *idem*, 263, 306,

instead of foul-smelling privies; wooden legs with elastic springs to reproduce the motions of nature, and pull-over bar-room taps, umbrellas and waterproof hats, patent folding carriage-steps, automatic cheese-toasters, chairs that sprang out of walking-sticks, and braces to keep up trousers, were all, in their different modes, manifestations of the tireless British will to tame nature for amenity and social betterment and grow rich in the process.

So were the ingenuities of the scientists –

> the varied wonders that tempt us as we pass,
> The cow-pox, tractors, galvanism, and gas[1] –

who, voyaging ahead of the practical possibilities of their age, were laboriously charting new courses for the future: young Faraday, the Newington Butts blacksmith's son, at his work on electricity; Dalton studying the combination of the elements and determining atomic weights while teaching mathematics at half a crown an hour; Sir Humphry Davy, who invented the safety lamp for miners in the year of Waterloo and thrilled fashionable audiences with his chemical discourses at the Royal Institution in Albemarle Street.[2] It was part of the same revolutionary urge that threw up in philosophy a Rousseau, in politics a Robespierre, and in war a Napoleon. Being a practical people, the English and Scots made their contribution to it in a utilitarian form. By doing so they did more to transform the material world than any of the other aspirants of the age.

Improved transport was the first condition of this revolution. The unlettered Derbyshire millwright, James Brindley, who with James Watt, the Greenock-born contriver of the expansive use of steam, was,

375; *Ann. Reg.*, 1816, Chron., 134; Clapham, I, 191–2; Colchester, II, 441–2; Farington, VIII, 211; Klingender, 88–9; Simond, I, 127; II, 94; Smart, 151–2, 405; Sydney, II, 5. The Speaker in 1814 opposed a similar installation in Westminster Hall. Colchester, II, 496.

1. Byron, *English Bards and Scottish Reviewers*.

2. 'The husband of a young lady who is very assiduous at the lectures said the other day he approved much of this taste in the sex in general; "It keeps them out of harm's way."' Simond, I, 34. In his popular lectures on light and heat in Edinburgh Professor Leslie electrified audiences by burning a cup of water into ice in seven minutes and then, like a good practical Scot, selling an apparatus devised for this useful domestic end at twenty guineas a piece. Simond, I, 378. See *Hamilton of Dalzell* MS., 168.

in his humdrum, practical way, the British counterpart of Rousseau, conceived the revolutionary idea of making canals independent of rivers on a nation-wide scale. He and his fellow engineers created radical, man-made waterways, straight and easily navigable, to take the place of God's, controlling water-levels, tunnelling mountains and bridging valleys with aqueducts. Before and during the war, more than three thousand miles of such waterways were built, enabling coal, iron, timber, pottery, and other heavy goods to be carried to any part of the country as easily and as cheaply as by sea.

At the same time the character of road travel was transformed. Before the war, even on the main trunk roads, postilions had to quarter ceaselessly from side to side to avoid huge pools of water and ruts deep enough to break a horse's leg; as late as the winter of 1797–8 the highway from Tyburn to Oxford was from a foot to eighteen inches deep in mud. The genius of two Lowland Scots, Telford, a Dumfriesshire shepherd's son, and Macadam, provided the country, during the first quarter of the nineteenth century, with smooth-metalled highways built on the principles of Roman science. Their engineered gradients, culverts, and bridges raised the speed of post-chaises and coaches from four or five to ten and even twelve miles an hour. The cost of such travel remained heavy; an inside ticket from London to Liverpool cost four guineas without tips and meals. But the gain to traders and men of money was immeasurable. Commerce and finance were given the speed and certainty required to control the fast-revolving machinery of Britain's new industrial production. The mail-coaches, with their chocolate-coloured panels, scarlet wheels, and melodious horns, became the national time-pieces. Such was their regularity that all along the roads men set their clocks by the 'Nimrod', 'Regulator', or 'Tally-ho'.[1]

*

Where Britain's own resources were insufficient for the needs of trade, men risked their lives and capital to seek them beyond the seas. Her

1. Dixon, 61, 72; Fowler, 216–17. See Ashton, II, 230; Austen, II, 423; Clapham, I, 59, 92–7; Creevey, *Life and Times*, 115; De Quincey, *Autobiographica Sketches*; Ernle, 203–5; Farington, VII, 97; VIII, 270; Hammond, *Rise of Modern Industry*, 75–9; Klingender, 13; Lockhart, V, 86; McCausland, 18–19, 23; Mitford, *Our Village*, 63; Nevill, 143–8, 153–4; Newton, 21; Simond, I, 17, 184, 201–2; Smart, 28–9; Sydney, I, 53–6, 58; Woodward, 4.

naval victories had given her a preponderating influence in all the outer continents and opportunities of illimitable commercial expansion. Even at the height of the blockade, when European ambassadors were almost unknown at St James's, there had been several bearded ones from Asia and Africa, and the streets of the capital had been brightened by Indian merchants with immense coloured umbrellas. Of the old European colonial empires Britain's alone survived the war. Though her statesmen seemed scarcely more interested in it than those of Vienna and Berlin, and political economists proclaimed that colonies were useless, trade still followed the flag. The Empire was the nation's chief overseas customer, even after the loss of the United States – the next largest. India and the West Indies, with their non-European populations, were still by far the most valuable part of it. Canada had only 300,000 French and 80,000 British settlers, mostly of the humblest kind. The Cape was a port of call, where a few officials and troops uneasily watched the growing bitterness between Dutch farmers and Kaffir tribesmen; Australia an empty and unconsidered continent fringed with a few pathetic convict settlements and sheep-farms – Newgate, jested Sydney Smith, become a quarter of the globe. Yet even here their traders penetrated, for wherever there was money to be picked up, Englishmen and, still more, Scotsmen were sure to come. And though the Empire made no appeal to the fashionable, and Harriette Wilson was bored to distraction by her first protector's drawings of West Indian cocoa trees, the imagination of the poor and the young were perennially fired by it. 'He used to tell us,' wrote a village boy, 'the most delectable tales about elephants and tigers ... of guavas, bananas, figs, jacks, and cashew apples, and your hat full for the value of a farthing! ... Miller and I often vowed we would go to that grand fruit country when we became men.'[1]

Britain's trade with India was a romance; so was the conquest of sixty million Indians by a chartered company of merchants who 'maintained armies and retailed tea.' A foreigner speculated as to the idea an Indian might form beforehand of the mighty Company and its august Courts, but thought he would be surprised as he approached the foot of his sovereign's throne in Leadenhall Street. Within its dingy walls

1. Cooper, 18. See Farington, VIII, 123–4; Halévy, II, 106; Leslie, 293–8; Harriette Wilson, 1–2; Woodward, 7, 350–2, 359–62, 368–9, 379–80.

the first prose writer of the age sat at his desk, totting up the price of tea, drugs, and indigo. Like the rest of the empire the Company's dominion and wealth depended on the Royal Navy, which, even after its reduction at the Peace, remained the controller of the world's waterways. Wellington, with his grasp of strategic reality, thought it indispensable that the capital of British India should remain at Calcutta or some place near the coast. Without sea-power the conquests of Clive, Wellesley, and Hastings and the trade they had won could not have been maintained for a month. With it there was no place within reach of flowing water where Britons might not venture and set up shop or factory. Some of them, out-distancing Marco Polo, traded broadcloth and shalloons for tea at the far ends of the earth with pigtailed Chinese.[1]

Year in, year out, the ships of maritime Britain carried her trade abroad, sailing from her estuaries under great wings of white sails, with manufactured cottons, woollens, hardware and cutlery, guns, wrought copper and brass, refined sugar, linens, lace and silks, saddlery and tanned leather, pottery, china clay, ironware, coal, and rock salt, and returning with raw cotton from the United States, timber from the Baltic, wine from France, Sicily, Portugal, and the Atlantic islands, sugar, rum, and mahogany from the Caribbean, tea and spices from the East Indies, cod from the Newfoundland fisheries. For England did not only enjoy her unrivalled sense of elegance and comfort; she exported it. From Wedgwood's famous factory at Etruria in Staffordshire went out the wares – 'neat, strong, and beautiful' – which were famed all over the world. In every good inn from Paris to St Petersburg, it was said, travellers were served on English ware.

*

For four miles from London Bridge to Deptford the forest of masts was almost continuous. Often there were two thousand sea-going ships lying in the river – more than four times the number a century before. Newcastle, Liverpool, and Sunderland, the next largest ports, had between them almost as many. Bernadotte, crossing to Sweden in 1810,

1. 'Dear father, Here I am comfortably settled in an arm-chair by the fireside in a Chinese temple which has been appropriated to the Embassy during their stay here and has been made to look like an English house by the kindness of the gentlemen of the British factory.' Hon. C. Abbott from Canton to Lord Colchester, 2nd Jan., 1817. Colchester, III, 13.

saw more than a thousand British merchantmen in the Belt convoyed by six men-of-war. The annual value of imports had risen during the war from nineteen to thirty-two millions, of exports from twenty-seven to fifty-eight millions. 'What are we to think of this trade,' wrote a foreigner, 'of which a whole immense city could not contain the stock and is merely its counting house. ... The mind forgets that the immediate object is sugar and coffee, tobacco and cotton, and sees only a social engine which rivals in utility, in vastness of operation as well as wisdom of detail, the phenomena of nature itself.'[1]

Even more remarkable than the volume of this trade was its continuous increase. Britain's exports in 1815 were small compared with what they were to become – the overwhelming bulk of consumption was still domestic – yet they were multiplying with every decade. The principal article exported was now manufactured cotton. This industry – trifling when the war began – had outdistanced even the cloth trade, for centuries the country's premier commercial interest, though this, too, under the impact of war and machinery, was expanding fast. Spinning had become almost entirely a machine and factory activity: the spinning-jenny and steam engine, it was said, together financed the overthrow of Napoleon. In Glasgow alone there were more than forty mills employing over two hundred workpeople apiece; Dale and Owen at the great New Lanark Mills – though this was exceptional – employed as many as sixteen hundred. Flax and worsted spinning were following the example of cotton, though weaving in all branches of the textile trade was still mainly done 'out'. But the steam power-loom, first set up in Manchester in 1806 as the rival of the handloom, was already proving a godsend to manufacturers trying to capture the markets which Britain's naval victories had opened. Three years after Waterloo two thousand power-looms were in operation; thereafter their numbers doubled every other year, rising during the twenties to prodigious figures.

*

The quality of the goods exported, and the integrity and dispatch with which British traders met their customers' demand, earned prodigious dividends. So did the ownership of land in the new industrial areas. The rent-roll of the Shakerleys, a typical Lancashire and Cheshire landed family, rose during George III's reign from £3000 to over £30,000 p.a. A traveller, passing through the Vale of Clwyd in the last year of the war, was shown the house of a formerly poor clergyman who enjoyed an income of £75,000 from a copper mine discovered on a barren piece of land of which he was part owner. Vast underground estates of coal and iron-ore, worthless a generation before, were transformed by the use of steam-power into properties bringing their proprietors rents and royalties transcending even those of high farming, and still greater fortunes to the thrusting, able men who developed them.[1] The Bridgewater Canal, which cost £200,000 to build, returned an annual profit of £100,000; the thirty-nine original proprietors of the Mersey and Irwell Navigation Company received their capital back in interest every other year for half a century. The first Sir Robert Peel, a dispossessed yeoman's son who invested in a few of the early spinning jennies, left nearly a million sterling. A Bristol merchant, worth at the beginning of the war under a thousand pounds, possessed half a million when Farington met him at its conclusion. A shopkeeper of the Exeter Exchange in the Strand amassed £100,000 merely by selling shilling packets of powder to sharpen razors.

*

The value of farm land had also soared with its use. A population which had grown during the war by thirty per cent had had to be supported by improved farming. In the decade between Trafalgar and Waterloo Lord Aberdeen's rents increased by fifty per cent. Arable in the Wye Valley, which in the seventeen-eighties had sold for ten pounds an acre, was letting by 1814 at forty shillings an acre per annum and selling at

1. Simond in March, 1811, wrote of a 5000-acre 'subterranean farm' for which a rent of £3000 p.a. was paid and a royalty or percentage on the quality of coals extracted which doubled it. 'When the estate in which this mine is situated was sold thirty years ago, the purchaser refusing to pay a trifling consideration for the right of mining, this right ... was reserved; not that either party were ignorant of the existence of coals, but the steam engine was not then generally applied to mining, and the other branches of the art had not then reached their present improved state. ... What is now worth £6000 p.a. was not deemed worth one year's purchase thirty years ago.' Simond, II, 61. See idem, I, 182, 206, 216, 230, 243, 331; II, 62, 72, 224, 242, 278, 292, 294; Farington, II, 145; VI, 142; VIII, 194–201; Newton, 184; Shakerley MSS.; Smart, 569; Woodward, 45.

thirty years' purchase. In the Lothians of Scotland, formerly the poorest of western European countries, rents rose more than fourfold in a generation. In the Vale of Festiniog, where embankment had been carried out by the gentry, rents had gone up from seven shillings to three guineas an acre, in parts of Essex from ten to fifty shillings, in Berkshire and Wiltshire from fourteen to seventy shillings. In Yorkshire the best land fetched as much as £8 an acre. At the summit of the boom in the last years of the war it could scarcely be bought at all.

One saw that illimitable wealth as one travelled the country: 'farmhouses in sight everywhere ... large fields fresh ploughed, black and smooth, others ploughing, always with horses, never with oxen; farmers riding among their workmen, great flocks of sheep confined by net-fences in turnip fields, meadows ... of the most brilliant green.' At the autumnal sheep fair at Weyhill more than a quarter of a million pounds changed hands annually to be borne home by plaided shepherds or their top-booted blue-coated masters who gathered over the 'ordinary' in the White Hart. At Falkirk Fair a tenant of Lord Egremont's bought twelve thousand head of cattle with £30,000 Bank of England bills carried in his pockets.[1] A man who could raise prize bullocks or grow outsize turnips did not need a pedigree; in their passion for agricultural improvement the English even forgot to be snobs. Members of Parliament and leaders of fashion spent half the year on their estates, planting, raising stock, experimenting in crops, and vying with one another in enriching their lands and country. After local ploughing competitions and cart-horse trials the worthies of a whole county, gentle and common, would dine together to discuss over roast beef and October ale the methods they had successfully pursued. The Duke of Bedford's or Coke of Norfolk's annual sheep-shearing were events as important as the Derby or the meeting of Parliament. Coke's rustic palace, Holkham, became a place of pilgrimage that rivalled Walsingham in the age of faith: the interminable drive, the triumphal arch, the lakes, the woods, the obelisk, the distant view of the sea, the overawed Norfolk church peering through its modest cluster of trees,

1. 'This is probably the only country in the world where people make fortunes by agriculture. A farmer who understands his business becomes rich in England with the same degree of certainty as in other professions, whilst in most countries a farmer is condemned by the nature of his trade to be a mere labourer all his life.' Simond, I, 174. See Cobbett, *Rural Rides*, I, 49.

the exquisite changes of autumnal leaf as the shooting parties, in green and buff and brown, moved like regiments across the landscape, the coverts with never-ending partridges rising out of wastes of sand bearded with stunted corn, and, all around, the wilderness flowering like a garden.[1]

No class had ever enjoyed such riches as the landed gentry of England. 'I have no occasion to think of the price of bread and meat where I am now,' wrote Jane Austen from Godmersham; 'let me shake off vulgar cares and conform to the happy indifference of East Kent wealth!' In Cheshire alone there were fifty landed estates of from £3000 to £10,000 a year, with a purchasing power equivalent to an untaxed income of at least five times as much in our present money. The greatest of all commanded revenues larger than those of reigning Continental princes; in July, 1813, the United States, then at war with Britain, was unable to borrow as much money as more than one English nobleman could raise on his private credit. The Duke of Northumberland's annual rental was over £150,000; the owner of Berkeley Castle's £180,000. Four-fifths of the House of Commons and almost the entire hereditary personnel of the House of Lords were landowners. Such was the respect for landed wealth that Englishmen felt reluctant to entrust political power to any man without it; Creevey, a radical Whig without birth or means, wrote with contempt of Canning and Lord Wellesley as 'fellows without an acre,' comparing them with his own Party's princely leaders, 'the Earl Grey ... the Russells and the Cavendishes and all the ancient nobility and all the great property of the realm.'[2]

*

One saw that wealth displayed in the west end of the capital, with its mile after mile of splendid mansions, wonderful clothes and horses, liveried servants and glittering barouches and landaus; in the new Edinburgh – a paradise, it seemed to contemporaries, of order, light, and

1. Lady Shelley, I, 38–9. See Aberdeen, I, 30; Mrs Arbuthnot, *Journal*, March 28th, 1820; Clapham, I, 223; Cobbett, *Rural Rides*, I, 97–8; Dixon, 240–1; 248–252; Ernle, 195–223; Fremantle, I, 140; *Hamilton of Dalzell* MS., 151–4; Howitt, 88–106; Newton, 107–8; *Paget Brothers*, 179–81; Simond, I, 331; Smart, 153–4; Toynbee, 92.

2. Creevey, *Life and Times*, 55; Austen, II, 243–4; Dudley, 211; Farington, VIII, 174; *Shakerley* MSS.; Simond, II, 56, 250, 295; Woodward, 87.

neatness – which had risen near Calton Hill, away from the crooked closes and stench of Auld Reekie; in the county towns with their crescents and railed squares aping London's West End, their exquisitely windowed shops and classical assembly rooms and fine ancestral residences, where the less metropolitan-minded county families spent the winter season for balls, local business, and race meetings; in the watering places, Bath and Tunbridge Wells of the mannered past and Cheltenham and Leamington of the dashing present, where the well-to-do flocked as much for pleasure as health. At Bath, wrote Pierce Egan, all was bustle and gaiety, 'numerous dashing equipages passing and re-passing ... the shops capacious and elegant ... libraries to improve the mind, musical repositories to enrich the taste ... and tailors, milliners of the highest eminence in the fashionable world to adorn the male and beautify the female.' In the Pump Room bands of music played almost continuously while the crowds promenaded. Elsewhere, along the sea coast, remote fishing villages were turning overnight into watering places of a new kind, with elegant villas, piers, assembly rooms, libraries, theatres, and bathing boxes where the genteel, and moneyed would-be genteel, could enjoy 'aquatic gratification.' The greatest of these was Brighton, which, with its royal palace, its half-hourly coaches to the capital, its immense promenade, its fashionable domes, bow windows and cupolas, was a kind of miniature West End by the sea.[1]

The dominant desire of all classes was to 'cut a dash'; to show 'style', to be 'elegant'. From Lady Londonderry going to a ball so covered with jewels that she could not stand and had to be followed round with a chair, to the poor Edinburgh widow who pinched to be buried in a coach and six surmounted with black plumes and followed by carriages and hired mourners, the British were increasingly becoming martyrs to display. 'The necessity of acquiring, not merely the real necessaries and comforts of life, but the means of living in style, a certain inveterate habit of luxury, inexorable vanity,' wrote Simond, 'answer in England the same purpose as the conscription in France; and the fondest mother thinks as little of resisting the one as the other.' To

---

1. Ashton, I, 143–4; Bury, I, 99; Clapham, I, 8–9; Creevey, *Life and Times*, 115; Daniel, I, 79; *English Spy*, I, 285, 305; Farington, VIII, 197, 201, 260; Leslie, *Constable*; *Sea-Bathing Places, passim*; Hill, *Austen*, 104–5; Simond, I, 266; Sydney, I, 39.

this universal principle of activity, though he doubted whether it secured private happiness, he attributed the country's strength, seeing it drive each generation as fast as it reached manhood into the Army, Navy, East and West Indies, and, he might have added, the Bar, the counting-house, and factory.

Almost everything the English rich did served the ends of style. It created both the external beauty whose survivals – houses, streets, gardens, parks, vistas, furniture, china, silver – still linger on into our own age, and the commercial, colonial, and industrial wealth that the Victorians both enhanced and exploited. It filled London and Brighton, Cheltenham, Leamington, and St Leonards, and the new suburbs of every ancient city with tree-lined avenues and Grecian and Pompeian crescents and terraces of white stucco with railed and green-painted jalousies, and fine assembly rooms, and Gothic lodges and cottages *ornées*. It spread itself across the countryside, adorning it with park-walls, crested gates, and castellated lodges, with Ionic arches and obelisks and Corinthian pillars, with metal turnpike roads traversed by beautiful equipages harnessed in all the pride of the loriner's art, with silver trappings and coloured housings and outriders in yellow and scarlet jackets. It filled the houses of the gentry with showy, lovely, and sometimes not so lovely, furniture, with buhl and bronzes and damask hangings, with great glasses and embroidered stools and rosewood tambour-frames; with Italian paintings and native portraiture, now reaching its high evening in Lawrence and Raeburn; with engravings and aquatints and the lovely art of the miniaturist; with Athenian marbles rescued by wealthy connoisseurs from the lime-burners in the pasha-ruled, robber-haunted Aegean.[1] At Powderham Castle, according to the guide book, the music-room was adorned with marbles and *bassi-rilievi*; the chimney-piece represented Apollo and the Muses and was copied from the sarcophagus of Homer.

1. Among them the Elgin marbles. 'There is not a classical nook,' wrote Simond, 'unexplored by these restless wanderers – they dispute with each other for the remains of Greece and Egypt, purchase antique marbles for their weight in gold, pack up and ship home a Grecian temple as other people would a set of china.' Simond, II, 148. See *idem*, II, 64–6; Mrs Arbuthnot, *Journal*, April 10th, 1822; *Sea-Bathing Places*, 217, 246–7, 286, 336–7, 447–8; Harriet Granville, I, 130; Gronow, I, 90–1; Hill, *Austen*, 40–2; Lockhart, IV, 337; McCausland, 22–4, 66; Lady Shelley, I, 48–9; Simond, I, 337; Wansey, 116.

Everyone who could afford it – and many who could not – was engaged in rebuilding and improving and emparking; 'my prodigious undertaking of a west wing at Bowhill,' wrote the Duke of Buccleuch, 'is begun.' Owners of ancient country houses, inspired by Repton's book on landscape gardening, were talking, like Henry Tilney in *Northanger Abbey*, of foregrounds, distances, second distances, side-screens and perspective, lights and shades. At Mamhead, Lord Lisburne's seat in Devonshire, the old error of torturing nature by raising gardens with terraces and making ponds and fountains on the sides of hills was corrected, we are told, and the ground restored – with infinite expense and labour – to its pristine natural beauty, with varied prospects of sea, river, and the country.[1] At Knowsley, Lord Derby's new dining-room, paid for by the rising wealth of Lancashire, measured fifty-three feet by thirty-seven, with an immense Gothic window at one end and two huge church-like doors at the other; 'Pray,' asked a guest, 'are those great doors to be opened for every pat of butter that comes into the room?' At Fonthill the interior was like a Gothic cathedral, only larger, fitted up with crimson and gold, with statues in every niche and immense gilded and jewelled boxes for relics. In the vast pseudo-medieval castle – a thousand feet in length with avenues radiating for miles in every direction – which the seventh Earl of Bridgewater employed Wyatt to build in place of the older Ashridge, the central stair-case, flanked with statues by Westmacott, rose to nearly a hundred feet, and the walls – a shrine to victorious aristocracy – were covered with immense pictures of the Allied triumphs at the close of the Revolutionary wars. The orangery was a hundred and thirty feet in length, and the conservatory, with its eleven Gothic windows, almost as long, and in the chapel, where daily services were held and two chaplains maintained, the elegance and snobbery of regency England reached an almost sacred apogee. 'The perforated oak screen which divides it from the ante-chapel; the mighty wrought Gothic ceiling, the windows filled with beautifully painted glass,' the house's contemporary historian wrote, 'demand our particular notice. ... The Pulpit and the

1. 'We cannot but admire the easy swell of the lawn, whose smooth verdure is relieved by groups of trees and shrubs, while at one extremity the eyes is attracted by General Vaughan's picturesque cottages. ... The river and the sea, in full prospect, gives a finishing touch to the whole and renders it a picture of enchanting sublimity.' *Sea-Bathing Places*, 463–4.

Reading-Desk are well placed, opposite to each other, and somewhat elevated' – a delicate compliment to the deity – 'above ... the richly carved canopies ... which form the seats of the Earl and Countess of Bridgewater. Beneath these stalls are the seats for servants. ... In this chapel was preached, in November 1817, the first sermon by the Chaplain of the Earl of Bridgewater, who had had the honour of compiling the pages of this history.'[1]

*

The assured, unquestioning snobbery of the rich which sprang from all this seemed as unalterable as the great palaces which housed them. The very approach to a nobleman's house was surrounded with an aura of respect; at Castle Howard visitors – for most of these places were open to gentlefolk on stated days – were expected to alight and respectfully walk the last half-mile through an avenue and deer-park.[2] An American staying at Gordon Castle wrote of the delightful consciousness that, whichever way the Duke's guests drove, the horizon scarcely limited their host's domains. 'The ornamental gates flying open at your approach, miles distant from the castle; the herds of red deer trooping away from the sound of wheels in the silent park; the stately pheasants feeding tamely in the immense preserves; the stalking gamekeepers lifting their hats in the dark recesses of the forest – there was something in this perpetually reminding you of privileges.' When Harriet Granville and her husband stayed by themselves at Trentham, six servants waited on them at dinner, while a gentleman-in-waiting and a housekeeper hovered round the door in case they should express any wish. Too often noblemen, building their lives on such deference, surrounded themselves with a horde of sycophants – led captains, toady dandies, and semi-professional wits – who obscured for them both their duties and interests; the fat, pasty-faced chaplain at Castle Howard scarcely dared give an opinion on the weather lest his patron, Lord Carlisle, should disagree.[3]

1. H. J. Todd, *The History of the College of Bonhommes at Ashridge*, 1823.
2. Simond, II, 73. See also *idem*, 65. It took a banker, however, Sir Richard Hoare of Stourhead, to invent the rule that visitors viewing the house should not be allowed to sit down. Simond, I, 200.
3. Harriet Granville, I, 48. See *idem*, I, 8–9; *Creevey Papers*, II, 49–50; Lockhart, 2–3; Willis, *cit*. Howitt, *Rural Life*, 27.

The rich had become almost too rich for reason. Lord Alvanley, whose dinners were said to be the best in London, had an apricot tart on his table every day of the year and, when his *maître d'hôtel* expostulated at the expense, sent him to Gunter's, the confectioner, to buy up his entire stock. At one fashionable breakfast-party the strawberries alone cost £150. The whole world, wrote a foreigner, was ransacked for the wealthy Englishman's dinner; Périgord pie and truffles from France, sauces and curry powder from India, hams from Westphalia and Portugal, caviare from Russia, reindeer tongues from Lapland, olives from Spain, cheese from Parma, sausages from Bologna. 'To live expensive and elegant' had become the end of existence; Lord Grey said he would not dress Lady Londonderry for £5000 a year. Her very handkerchiefs cost fifty guineas the dozen; a guest at Wynyard complained of being unable to sleep because the lace on the pillows and sheets so tickled his face. No one had any use for what was old-fashioned; everything in the *haut ton* had to be new, to use the Corinthian slang, 'prime and bang up to the mark.' A Colonel of the Guards used to give Storr and Mortimer, the Regent Street goldsmiths, £25 a quarter to furnish him with a new set of studs every week during the season.[1]

The acme of perfection, the *summum bonum* of style, was the dandy. The bright glories of the past were beginning to fade a little; even blue coats and brass and gold buttons were going out in London and being replaced by a sober black and white. But the quality of the cloth and the elegance and fit of the tailoring were superlative. A dandy was a formidable figure – the wide-brimmed glossy hat, always new, the spotless, white-starched cravat so tight and high that the wearer could scarcely look down or turn his head, and was for ever pulling it up and running his fingers along the bottom of his chin;[2] the exquisitely cut coat worn wide open to display the waistcoat of buff, yellow, or rose and the snowy embroidered cambric shirt; the skin-tight pantaloons or 'inexpressibles', gathered up into a wasp's waist and bulging like a succession of petticoats under the stays; the fobs, jewels, chains, and

1. Gronow, II, 83, 268–9; *Creevey Papers*, II, 132; *English Spy*, II, 19, 219; Gaussen, II, 355; Letts, 206; Lockhart, IV, 169; *Real Life in London*, I, 42; II, 67; Simond, I, 46–7.

2. Dandies sometimes cut their ears with their collars through moving their heads. Newton, 246–7. See also Harriet Granville, I, 158–9.

spotless gloves; the white-thorn cane – a hint of the broad acres that sustained the type – the wonderfully made boots whose shine rivalled the cuirasses of the Life Guards. Hoby, the famous bootmaker at the top of St James's Street – a Methodist preacher in private life – told the Duke of York that if Wellington had had any other bootmaker, he could scarcely have won his victories. The blacking of tops was a high art and mystery: two rival advertisers in a West End street, each holding up a varnished boot on a pole, claimed, the one, that his was the best polish in the world, and the other that it was so good that it could be eaten. Beau Brummell, asked for the secret of his, replied that it was made from the finest champagne.[1]

These bucks or swells – some of whom in youth had shared the friendship of the Prince Regent – ruled the world of fashion from their favourite vantage point in White's bow window. Their court was bordered on the north by Oxford Street, on the east by Bond Street, on the south by Pall Mall, and west by Park Lane, but their influence extended far beyond its borders. Byron rated Brummell's importance above Napoleon's. When, after bringing the Regent's soft muslin, bow and wadding neck-piece into contempt by appearing, to the amazement of the town, in a stiff collar, this remarkable man fled overseas from his creditors, he left his secret as a legacy to his country, writing on a sheet of paper on his dressing-table, 'Starch is the man.' The long morning hours spent by his disciples with their valets completing their toilets; their sublime lounge with every eye upon them down Bond Street, St James's, or Pall Mall; their exquisite French dinners; their invariable habit of being imperturbably late for every appointment; their condescending appearances at the great summer evening parades in Kensington Gardens or Hyde Park; their extravagant gambling and love of play; their generosity and occasional surprising kindnesses, and their unshakable self-confidence, were as much part of the England of the time as the fat cattle in the shires and the thoroughbreds on the turnpike roads.[2]

1. Gronow, I, 271–3; II, 52–3.
2. One of the greatest of all, 'King' Allen, had shown almost incredible energy and courage in the attack on Talavera. Gronow, II, 86. See Byron, *Letters and Journals*, II, 128; *Corr.*, I, 142; Broughton, II, 177; Lamington, 5–7; *English Spy*, I, 330–1; II, 218; Farington, VIII, 238; Harriet Granville, I, 158; Gronow, I, 52–3; II, 1–2, 58–9, 86, 238, 252–3; 268–9, 271–3, 294; T. Moore,

They shared their empire with the great ladies who controlled the *entrée* to Almack's assembly rooms and the balls and routs of high society. As evening fell the streets of London's West End became filled with an endless stream of wonderful carriages, each with its eyes of flame twinkling in the darkness. As with a sudden flurry of horses each drew up at its destination, the tall liveried footmen leapt down and set up a great rapping on the door. From six to eight, and again from ten till midnight, the noise of the wheels in cobbled Mayfair, Simond wrote, was like the fall of Niagara. The houses were lit from top to bottom; the windows from the streets framed a concourse of nodding feathers and stars under chandeliers, while gaping crowds stood at the doors and powdered, gold-laced footmen lined the steps. Every night in the season there were a dozen or more of such assemblies, in which there was seldom any room to sit, no conversation, cards, or music, nothing but glittering clothes and jewels and lights, shouting, elbowing, turning, and winding from room to room, vacant, famous, smiling, or evasive faces, and, at the end of an interval, a slow descent to the hall where the departing guests, waiting in their orders and diamonds for their carriages, spent more time among the footmen than they had spent above with their hosts. 'To the Duchess of Gloucester's rout,' Cam Hobhouse wrote in his diary, 'where was all London, and such a sight as was never seen. The Duke of Wellington and three Lord Mayors there; spent the night hustling to get the Misses Byng and Lady Tavistock to her carriage.' Lady Shelley, who was also present, mentioned that she was nearly squeezed to death and that many cried out in alarm: 'the Duke of Wellington, who was standing half-way up the stairs, called out to the ladies below that there was not the slightest danger, but the pressure was so great that many of them fainted. More than sixteen hundred persons had been invited to a house which is not capable of holding more than six hundred.'[1]

Fudge Letters; Nevill, 169; Newton, 246–7; *Real Life in London*, I, 42; Lady Shelley, I, 53, 64.

1. Broughton, II, 98; Lady Shelley, II, 12. See also Mrs Arbuthnot, *Journal*, May 31st 1822; July 3rd 1823; Broughton, II, 15; Lamington, 19; Harriet Granville, I, 28, 140–2, 152–4, 164, 205, 210; II, 80–1; Gaussen, I, 355; Gronow, II, 268–9; Holland, *Journal*, I, 65, 128, 152, 167–8, 173, 256, 332, 364–5; Leslie, *Constable*, 114; *Lieven Letters*, 18, 47–8, 112–14, 125–6; *Life in London*, 20–1, 234–46; Mitford, *Life*, I, 80; Moore, *Byron*, 291; *Paget Brothers*, 186–7, *Real Life in London*, II, 148; Simond, I, 26–8; II, 250.

There were breakfast parties in pastoral mansions among the Middlesex meadows and Surrey woods, water parties in carpeted boats with bands and delicately coloured awnings and Gunter's choicest suppers, *fêtes champêtres* in the gardens of aristocratic palaces, masked balls and music assemblies and dances where, after endless quadrilles and suppers in which every delicacy was served under Grecian lamps and festoons of exotics, white-gowned, high-bosomed graces relaxed, blushing in the arms of tight-pantalooned cavaliers, in the sensational new German dance, the waltz.[1] There were parades on summer evenings and Sundays in Rotten Row and Kensington Gardens where, through clouds of dust, hundreds of wonderful horses passed and repassed carrying with them the great world in taffeta, feathers and lace, uniforms, quizzing-glasses, and curving top hats. There were musical parties – it was the era of the young Rossini – when gifted young ladies vied over harp and harpsichord with singers 'in the public line', and nights at the opera in the Haymarket when Catalini's piercing voice drowned chorus and orchestra and, behind the red curtains of the boxes, all that was most brilliant and luxurious in the world congregated, with jewels, bare shoulders, and orders blazing under the light of thousands of candles, while, in the libertarian manner of England, frail ladies plied their trade in the galleries, and footmen, tradesmen, and sailors whistled, howled, and cracked nuts. There were other nights at the ballet when, as Vestris sang or Angiolini danced, even society forgot for a moment to admire itself:

> *While Gayton bounds before th' enraptured looks*
> *Of hoary marquises and stripling dukes:*
> *Let high-born lechers eye the lively Presle*
> *Twirl her light limbs that spurn the needless veil;*
> *Let Angiolini bare her breast of snow,*
> *Wave the white arm and point the pliant toe;*
> *Collini trill her love-inspiring song,*
> *Strain her fair neck and charm the listening throng.*

1. It was at first considered doubtful whether its shameless embrace was compatible, not only with female decorum, but with chastity: 'the breast', wrote Byron,

> 'thus publicly resigned to man
> In private may resist him if it can.'

There were *petits-soupers* and gay expeditions to Vauxhall:

> *when the long hours of public are past*
> *And we meet with champagne and a chicken at last,*

and *recherché* dinners when Luttrell or Rogers talked, and unforgettable evenings when Moore sang. 'It is not singing,' wrote Lady Charlotte Bury after a summer night in 1819, 'there is none of the skill of the mere mechanic in the art; it is poetry – the distinct enunication, the expression, the nationality of his genius – when heard, delighted in, and never to be forgotten.'[1]

Yet, though elegant and cultivated, society could often be stupid and vacant. At a dinner party at Lambton, in a dining-room hung with massive chandeliers and dark-coloured, heavily gold-fringed curtains resembling palls, thirty of the best-born people in England sitting at a long narrow table, the malicious Creevey recorded, ate in such a solemn silence that it might have been the Lambton family vault and the company the male and female Lambtons buried in their best clothes in a sitting position. Usually the conversation of the *haut ton* was of the emptiest kind, and concerned, except for politics, with dress, social precedence, and scandal. 'Shall I tell you,' wrote Creevey from Middleton, 'what Lady Jersey is like? She is like one of her numerous gold and silver musical dickey birds that are in all the showrooms of this house. She begins to sing at eleven o'clock and, with the interval of the hour she retires to her cage to rest, she sings till twelve at night without a moment's interruption. She changes her feathers for dinner, and her plumage both morning and evening is the happiest and most beautiful I ever saw. Of the *merits* of her songs I say nothing till we meet.' There was, as Jane Austen wrote, a monstrous deal of stupid quizzing and commonplace nonsense talked, but scarcely any wit. What there was of it lacked spontaneity; in the *salons* where the conversation of the rival wits 'raged', it was often tedious: famous talkers like Rogers, Luttrell, and Sydney Smith spent as much time preparing their *mots* as a fine lady her toilet. Scott, in London for a few weeks,

1. Bury, II, 201–3. See Austen, II, 140; Broughton, I, 94; Byron, *English Bards and Scotch Reviewers*; Lord Coleridge, 204; Croker, I, 66; *English Spy*, I, 164; Gronow, II, 120–3, 297–8; Lamington, 19; Leigh Hunt, *Autobiography*, I, 137–8, 142; Quennell, *passim*; *Real Life in London*, I, 16, 19; Lady Shelley, I, 64; II, 58; Simond, II, 198.

longed to be back at Abbotsford, away from fine company, champagne, turbot, and plovers' eggs; it was all very well for a while, he wrote, but it made one feel like a poodle dog compelled to stand for ever on its hind legs. Its conventions, though less tyrannical than those of a German Court, were rigid and oppressive; a young man of talent who aspired to a place in society had to spend half his time leaving cards and paying calls. To settle the precedence of going in to dinner required the tact of an ambassador and the pedantry of a herald.[1]

There was a universal sense of straining. 'I see her,' wrote Harriet Granville – herself a snob of finer, more gossamer texture – of Lady Shelley, 'with a sort of hoisted-up look in her figure, tight satin shoes, a fine, thick plait of hair, bloodshot eyes, parched lips, fine teeth, and an expression of conscious accomplishment in her face.' The little set who under the dictatorship of the vulgar, haughty, indefatigable beauty, Lady Jersey, managed the dances at Almack's had introduced, Cam Hobhouse thought, something new in English life: a rigid narrow pride as stupid as it was inhuman and uncharitable. 'It is not fashionable,' wrote the Countess Lieven, 'where I am not.' Stendhal, who visited London in 1821, found society divided like the rings of a bamboo, every class aping the manners and habits and striving to emulate the expenditure of the class above. The universal desire to get into a higher circle and keep out intruders vitiated it; people did not enter it with the desire of being agreeable but of being on the defensive against those less modish. Fashionable life at all levels was becoming a fearful hierarchy. Lords who kept open house for their county neighbours cut them in London; clubs and even provincial subscription newsrooms blackballed surgeons and estate-agents on the grounds that they did not admit professional men and servants. Gronow described a rich parvenu hostess who excluded from her parties in Portman Square everyone without a title. Strangers entering Stephen's Hotel, the haunt of fashionable officers and men about town, used to be stared out of countenance by the waiters. An English family whom Thomas

---

1. 'Mrs Allanson,' wrote the Reverend Benjamin Newton, 'seemed discomposed at my taking Mrs Guise out of the room before her, but, as baronets' sons have a degree in the scale of precedence, there can be no doubt but that Mrs G. ought to precede unless she chose to waive it.' Newton, 141–2. See also *idem*, 215; Broughton, II, 62, 188; *Creevey Papers*, I, 296; II, 280; Greville (Suppl.), I, 18–19; Lockhart, IV, 181; V, 370; Lady Shelley, I, 39–40; II, 16.

Campbell met on the Continent, reduced by some accident to the *diligence* and fearful of compromising their dignity, preserved throughout the two days' journey a sullen, timorous silence, never exchanging a word with either their English or French fellow-travellers. Good-humoured England was becoming what Borrow called 'gentility crazy'. 'The company are mostly of the superior ranks of society,' a guide-book assured its readers, 'the lower orders of the community not having as yet intruded themselves into Southend.' The feeling penetrated the very gaols; at Horsemonger Lane a warder told Leigh Hunt that his prison was not fit for a gentleman, since a person not used to 'low people' could not be expected to share their accommodation. Snobbery permeated even the ranks of radical reformers; 'Orator' Hunt, staying at a York hotel during the Peterloo trials, sent down a servant to tell a weaver's wife who wanted to shake his hand, that he was not at home. 'The same contemptible feeling of classism, the curse of England,' wrote Bamford, 'existed among the witnesses; there were the "broad cloth" and "the narrow cloth" ones, the rich and the poor, and the former seldom sought opportunities for inter-communication with the latter, but rather shunned them.'[1] Even the hunting-field was contaminated. 'These hounds please me,' wrote the Rev. Benjamin Newton, 'as they are attended by gentlemen, not farmers.'

Under the influence of this restless competitiveness class feeling was turning into a religion. To seem 'genteely connected', to boast a pedigree and titled relations was the supreme aim; 'it is to have the crest', wrote Jane Austen after the purchase of a Wedgwood dinner service. Even those whose self-esteem seemed in little need of such buttressing competed furiously for precedence; the owner of Stowe, with a dukedom and half Buckinghamshire, christened his son Richard Plantagenet Nugent Bridges Temple. The feudal fuss at times was almost intolerable. When the Duke of Atholl's heir was born at Alnwick –

1. Bamford, II, 204, 247–8. 'It filled the working classes with a fierce contempt and hatred for every one wearing a decent coat.' It later explained Karl Marx. See also Ashton, II, 63; Broughton, II, 186–7; Bury, II, 108, Campbell, II, 252–3; Chancellor, 51; Creevey, I, 14, 296; Dino, 110; Harriet Granville, I, 45, 112; Gronow, II, 221, 303; Howitt, 78–80; Leigh Hunt, *Autobiography*, II, 2; *Lieven Letters*, 25–61; *Life in London*, 148; *Johnny Newcome*, 160; Newton, 51, 226, 235; *Real Life in London*, I, 245; *Romany Rye*, 419; *Sea-Bathing Places*, 443–4; Lady Shelley, I, 37, 308, 359; II, 39; Stendhal, *Memoirs of an Egotist*, 71.

his mother's home – no bells were rung in the castle for a month, the servants were put into list shoes and the Duke of Northumberland forwent his daily exercise for fear of disturbing this precious offspring of two ducal houses.[1] Even clerics treated Debrett like the Bible; an Oxford tutor is alleged to have prefaced a rebuke to a pupil: 'The friendship I have for my Lord, your father, my respect for my Lord Bishop, your uncle, and the peculiar situation in which I stand with my Lord God!'

One of the disastrous effects of this epidemic of snobbery was to destroy the unity of the nation's educational system. The grammar schools, which had formerly recruited leaders for Church and State from all ranks, lost their upper-class pupils to those establishments which, abandoning their local connexions, took boarders at high fees and became called, with the English genius for illogicality, public schools. They mixed the older aristocracy with the new commercial and professional classes, but segregated both from the children of the poor. At the same time the country gentry ceased to send their sons to the university colleges which drew their revenue and scholars from their own shire and sent them instead to colleges where only the rich and titled were welcome. As a result, even though academic reform began to stir the surface of their eighteenth-century sloth, the universities ceased to be what their name implied. They became, instead, finishing schools for a class. 'You're a man of family,' a college tutor is reported to have said to an idle pupil, 'I'm a man of family; call it a literary transaction between two men of fashion!' Bamford thought it symptomatic that high walls were everwhere rising round rich men's gardens in place of the green sod ramparts and hawthorn hedges of friendlier days. Christian England was unconsciously falling a prey to the worst of all heresies: the worship of Lucifer and Mammon. Without birth or money a man was nothing; his only hope was to pretend he possessed them. Haydon, having run short of cash on a journey, flung his last sixpence to the porter at the coach stage so that it rang on the pavement; 'unused to such a present for looking after luggage,' he re-lated, 'he bowed and thanked me so much that all the passengers saw it, and so without sixpence in my pocket I got as much respect all the way

1. 'In short no child except the King of Rome ever excited such a ridiculous commotion as this boy.' Mary Mitford, April 2nd 1811. *Life*, I, 127.

home as if I had £100.' A bit of straw on a lady's petticoat, implying that the wearer had been forced to resort to a hackney coach, could set a room of fine people tittering. The effects of this disease were insidious. To be poor, since it was a mark of inferiority, was a matter for shame and to be hidden. It was this that caused Foscolo, the Italian patriot, when he visited England as an exile to write, 'The English are a humane people, but will have nothing to do with one who wants bread. ... Poverty is a disgrace which no merit can wipe off. ... Indigence would render Homer himself despicable in their eyes.'[1]

It was here that the nemesis of the contemporary passion for elegance lay: so admirable when as in the eighteenth century it had arisen spontaneously from a widespread love and craving for beauty, so dangerous when it became an obsession, driving men of all classes to a heartless, competitive extravagance. Like every social virtue it had become vitiated in the end by the faults of human nature and transformed from a blessing into a curse. It was at once the motive force and temptation of the nation: the stimulus and peril. It was increasingly attended by vanity, greed, and covetousness, and by the uncharitableness to which these gave rise. It reduced even good men from Christians to cads. It ceased to occur to gentlemen that there was anything ignoble in speaking of those socially beneath them with contempt. 'I never saw more ridiculous figures,' wrote Fox's great-nephew after a levée, 'tailors and haberdashers were among them.' 'King' Allen, the dandy, used to call his bankers his tradesmen, and the Benchers of Lincoln's inn resolved that writers in the Press were unfit to be called to the Bar. 'Mr Powlett,' a country clergyman noted in his journal, 'would not go to any place to dine where Mr Claridge was invited because he was a steward; how soon Mr Powlett seems to have forgotten that he is the son of a country attorney!' Lady Shelley's father was so disgusted at seeing a rich cotton spinner secure the best turbot at the local fishmonger's that he left his town house at Preston in a passion and never returned. She herself was unable to enjoy a fête at Geneva because some vulgar English were looking on, and felt a strong prejudice against Peel on account of his birth. Even so choice a spirit as Mary Mitford could not escape the in-

1. *Fraser's Magazine*, XXXI (1845), 401–2. See Ashton, II, 458; Bamford, I, 48; Broughton, 193–4; Newton, 72; *Real Life in London*, I, 19; Haydon, *Life*, II, 35 Woodward, 465–6, 469.

fection and wrote contemptuously of sitting next to the grocer's wife, jammed in between brewers and bakers and tailors and corn dealers. When the Prince Regent joined his servants at a Pavilion supper party, the Opposition Press made high jest at royalty condescending to 'cooks, scullions, dish-washers, lick-trenchers, shoe-blacks, cinder-sifters, candle-snuffers, etc.' A great poet like Wordsworth, a man whose life was dedicated to the contemplation of the eternal, could write of the disgrace – he was of yeoman stock – his brother had incurred by marrying his young housekeeper: 'a connexion with a servant, and that one his own.'[1]

*

Across the elegant surface of the national wealth ran a yellow streak. The cad – showy, heartless, deceptive, and bouncing – was a special product of the Regency; the Regent himself was one. So, for all his genius, was the most famous poet of the age, Lord Byron, who corresponded facetiously with the mother of the man he had cuckolded about her daughter-in-law's indiscretions. The dandies insulted their social equals and were offensively rude to their inferiors; a set of men, a contemporary recalled, who arrogated to themselves the right of criticizing the entire universe, who never condescended to laugh, always looked hazy after dinner, and sneered at everyone and everything. The air – the manner – the *je ne sais quoi* – of a Corinthian's quiz, 'the curled lip of contempt and the eye, measuring, from top to toe, his companions' became the glass of fashion at which young England dressed itself in the self-indulgent years after Waterloo. His imitators were 'the smokers, jokers, hoaxers, glass-cockers, black-legs, and fancy fellows of the town,' the Corinthian Toms, Jerry Hawthorns, and Hon. Tom Dashalls who figure with such gusto in the blackguard pages of the journalist, Pierce Egan, and who became a vogue towards the end of the first quarter of the century. Their motto was to be ripe for any spree, by which they generally meant any frolic that involved others in trouble. It was the result partly of too much food and drink, and, with the growing upper-class substitution of snobbery for religion, of too little sense of responsibility. Lord Barrymore, driving home from a midnight revel in his highflyer phaeton, cracked half the windows –

1. De Selincourt, *Middle Years*, II, 612. See Holland, *Journal*, I, 141; Mitford, I, 110–11; Newton, 89; Shelley, I, 3, 8, 236; II, 17; Woodward, 28, 541.

'fanning the daylights,' he called it – on either side of Colnbrook high street with his whip.

The older ideal of a gentleman was being obscured by one that, though based on elegance, high vitality, and courage, was both competitive and calculating: '*an out and outer*, one up to everything, down as a nail, a trump, a Trojan ... one that can patter flash, floor a charley, mill a coal-heaver, come coachey in prime style, up to every rig and row in town and down to every move upon the board from a nibble at the club to a dead hit at a hell; can swear, smoke, take snuff, lush, play at all games, and throw over both sexes in different ways – he is the finished man!'[1] Bamford, tramping through Oxford, was told in an alehouse that the undergraduates were courageous fighters, generous remunerators, and profuse spenders, all of which the company allowed to be gentlemanly qualities, but that, in intercourse with those beneath them, they were arrogant, wilful, and capricious and prone to lay on too hard when they got the upper hand. A heartless disregard for the feelings of others was the hallmark of the 'blood'. It was considered a joke to crowd timorous passers-by off the pavement, to throw a drunk in a dunghill, drop a live coal on a sleeper's head, rob a blind man of his dog, and swear in the presence of ladies and clergymen. 'What d'ye think of that for a lark, eh?' cried one of the type relating his evening at his parson brother's. '"Keep it up – keep it up, d — me," says I, so I sets down to the table, drank as much as I could – then I mix'd the heel-taps all in one bottle and broke all the empty ones and rolled home in *prime and plummy* order, d — me!'[2]

This notion of gentility had dangerous consequences when applied by the flashy sons of the rough, upstart employers and money-makers of the cotton and mercantile towns. Some Lancashire weavers' wives after Peterloo, who, wearied out on a tramp over the Pennines, boarded the York stage-coach, were greeted with coarse abuse by the young Manchester sparks aboard, and, when they sought protection from the coachman and guard, were ridiculed by these obsequious snobs. Below such 'gemmen' were the stable-boys, cadgers, pugilists, horse-croppers, and raffish hangers-on of the sporting world, with their cheap cigars, hats askew, and hands in pockets, swearing obscenely at street

---

1. *English Spy*, II, 217. See also *idem*, 219–21; *Life in London*, 35, 128.
2. *Real Life in London*, I, 90–1. See *English Spy*, II, 234.

corners or hanging about dog-pits or public houses making up their betting-books.[1]

Gambling – reckless and showy – was the crowning vice of the rich idler. Clubs like Crockford's and the Roxborough, with their exquisite furnishings and princely food and service, drained away more than one great estate and drove gentlemen to courses which damaged both their honour and their country. Lord Sefton – an upright and kindly man – after losing a small fortune at Brooks's, recouped himself, like others, by an enclosure-bill at the expense of his poorer neighbours. Sometimes the play at these establishments would continue for two or three days before the infatuated gamblers broke up. At Crockford's, during the parliamentary session, supper, cooked by the great *chef*, Ude, was served from midnight till five, every delicacy and drink that could gratify the most fastidious taste being provided without charge.[2] It was the green hazard table and the croupiers in their white neckcloths that maintained the club and made the fortune – more than a million pounds – of the old fishmonger who owned it. Humble men copied the vices of their betters; during the peace celebrations in Hyde Park the dicing tables in the gambling booths were continually surrounded by multitudes. In Dartmoor the poor perverts, shunned by their fellow prisoners and living apart under a monstrous king of their own choosing, gambled away their very clothes and food until they were left starving and naked.

1. Bamford, II, 210–11, 220–1; Byron, *Corr.*, I, 132–3; *English Spy*, I, 143–5, 247; II, 217–21, 234; Gronow, I, 227; Leigh Hunt, *Autobiography*, II, 173; *Life in London*, 35, 128; McCausland, 59–60; *Real Life in London*, I, 3, 26, 90–1 n.; Sydney, I, 131.

2. Those who chose, however, would throw a ten-pound note on the play-table at the end of the session and leave it there. Lamington, 11–12. See Lord Coleridge, 185–6; Ashton, 356–7; *Creevey Papers*, 36; D'Arblay, IV, 44–5; *English Spy*, I, 332–6; II, 13; Greville, I (Suppl.), 48–9; Gronow, II, 10, 81–6, 92–4, 282; Moorsom, 27; *Paget Brothers*, 177; *Real Life in London*, I, 196.

CHAPTER 10

THE UNDERWORLD

The carriage that glitters like a meteor along the streets of the metropolis often deprives the wretched inmate of the distant cottage of the chair he sits on, the table he eats on, the bed he lies on.

HAZLITT

If an empire were made of sand, it would be pounded to dust by the economists.

NAPOLEON

IN Spitalfields, once a village of pleasant gardened houses built by Huguenot silk-weavers, one saw the reverse of the London of elegance and splendour that the free institutions and the vigorous habits of the English had created. Here 50,000 workers, cut off from all direct access to the soil and the raw materials of their labour, and dependent solely on wages and the fluctuations of distant markets, were crowded in conditions of squalor which worsened as ever more newcomers poured into the place, its stately homes become overcrowded tenements, its mulberry trees cut down, and gardens obliterated by mean dwellings, its rustic lanes transformed into unpaved and sewerless streets.[1] In these nightmare extensions of London to the east and beyond the river, and in the rookeries and foetid courtyards that huddled behind the haunts of fashion and commerce, pallid, diminutive-looking men, women, and children dragged out their crowded existence amid heaps of garbage. The only cheerful places in such abodes of misery were the gin or 'blue ruin' shops. Here were the characters of low life that Corinthian Tom and Jerry Hawthorn, in their resolve to drain the last dregs of metropolitan pleasure, found revelling by night: Tinker Tom, dirty Suke, boggle-eyed Jem, and Billingsgate Moll, full of fire and fury defending herself with her fish basket, African Sall, flashy Nance and Bet, the ballad singer, 'rolling her peepers for a new fancy man'; the cadgers and flat-catchers of the Holy Land enjoying their 'peck and booze' after their eleemosynary labours; the lascars, jack-tars, coal-

1. F. Warner, *The Silk Industry, passim.*

heavers, dustmen, women of colour and remnants of once fine girls, who jigged together at All Max – that 'bit of life' at the east end of the Town – where the reckless could drown their miseries in 'Daffy', 'Ould Tom', and 'Stark Naked'.

Half the customers of such places lived outside the law. The thieves' kitchen was the natural flower of the London slum. The world of Fagin and the Artful Dodger did not spring from Dickens's imagination. Neither did the 'stout, broad-shouldered, sturdy-chested man' – with the broad-skirted green coat with large metal buttons and the pale, scared woman and emaciated children waiting for him outside the tap-room – who, as Bill Sikes, matriculated from burglary to murder. 'We never calls them thieves here but prigs and fakers,' the old apple-woman on London Bridge told the author of *Lavengro*. 'If you have any clies to sell at any time I'll buy them of you; all safe with me; I never peach and scorns a trap!' There were parts of the town like Tothill Fields and Seven Dials where by tacit agreement neither watch nor Bow Street runner ordinarily entered. In these 'flash cribs', or 'in-fernals', thousands of thieves and their female 'pals' lived in ancient tumble-down houses and narrow courts reeking with ordure. Across their horizons lay the shadow not of Paul's Cross but of the Newgate gallows and the gibbet. The most popular of London spectacles was a hanging; then the underworld, drunk on gin and horrors, shouted it-self senseless as Jack Ketch, the hangman, cut down the lifeless bodies.[1]

In the manufacturing districts vice and destitution lived, not in juxta-position with respectability and splendour, but far removed from them. Most of the steam-factory towns were situated on wild heaths and moors in scantily populated neighbourhoods little influenced by gentry or clergy. In these settlements, doubling in size every five or six years, with their filth, noise, and perpetual inflow of new inhabitants, the old framework of society, built round church, manor-court, and the village democracy of constable, way-warden, and overseer, broke down com-pletely. Here only the law of the jungle held. Just outside Birmingham, capital of the Midland hardware trade, was a squalid manufacturing

1. Ashton, *Old Times*, 246–7; Bamford, I, 67; II, 130–2; Cooper, 9–10; Dixon, 50; *English Spy*, I, 338; *Fraser's Magazine*, XXXI (1843), 335–6; *Lavengro*, 194–5, 289–91; Lucas, I, 45; Newton, 94; *Life in London*, 181, 207–31, 225–8, 271–3; *Real Life in London*, I, 295; II, 128–30; Sydney, II, 175.

village known as 'Mud City' whose inhabitants were the terror of the neighbourhood; a generation later Disraeli drew their savage offspring in his 'Wodgate'. The wife of one of Nelson's captains, passing through Nottingham a few years after Trafalgar, described with horror the drunken, riotous rabble that careered all night outside her inn.

For success in discovering new forms of livelihood was uprooting growing numbers from the country's traditional life. Though many thrived in that freer society, many more, the old props gone, went to the wall. Those swept into the slums of the capital or the squatters' towns around the steam factories could transmit to their children only a memory of the Christian traditions and influences among which they grew up. A generation after Waterloo a third of Manchester's children attended neither church, chapel, nor school. The stony places in which the dispossessed took root tended inevitably to make hard, cruel, reckless men and sluttish, depraved women.

*

Competition was the condition of English economic life. The end of competition was increased wealth and liberty for the individual. The virtues which made for success in it were largely those which had given England victory in battle and which were engendered by the free and Christian society in which the more fortunate of the English grew up. But the end of life was imperceptibly ceasing to be the pursuit of those virtues and was becoming instead the property and prestige which those virtues had created.

Nor were the qualities which made for such success – energy, faith, resource, happy co-ordination of body and mind – equally engendered in all. The distinction between the love of liberty and private selfishness was finer than Britons realized or cared to admit. English liberty, with its educative virtues, depended for its operation on the institution of property. Without it the boasted freedom of the individual had little real existence. A man without property, a man of straw, could preserve neither his own freedom nor that of others. The richer the subject, the more complete his liberty. A poor man could be incarcerated for debt, pressed, in time of national emergency, into the Navy, or, lacking the wherewithal to hire a substitute, called up for wartime service in the Militia. If the local Justices feared he might become a charge on the poor rates, he could be forcibly removed to the parish of his birth or 'settlement'. Even *habeas corpus* could not avail without the where-withal to fee a lawyer: 'an Englishman unless he can lay his hands on £25,' wrote Stendhal, 'is an outlaw.' In a country where tyranny was held in universal detestation and the right to liberty regarded as every man's birthright, the poor were almost inevitably at the mercy of the petty bully – the greedy employer, the embezzling tradesman or jerry-builder, the pawnbroker and usurer, the corrupt beadle or constable. There was no national organization to enforce order and justice; only twenty clerks at the Home Office. That and hanging! The substitute for a police force was the hundred to one chance that even the least offending malefactor might finish on the gallows. There were over two hundred capital offences; a man might hang for chipping the balu-strade of Westminster Bridge or impersonating a Chelsea pensioner. It was because the sanctity of property seemed so important to the Eng-lish – the sheet-anchor of all independence and virtue – that in 1810 the House of Lords, on principle, rejected Romilly's bill for exempting petty larceny from the death penalty. A man who stole five shillings' worth of goods from a shop counter, it was held, was undermining the whole structure of a free society and was not fit to live. As, however, the English were a humane and Christian people in their private re-lationships and instinctively reacted, when personally confronted with it, from the harsh reality to which their principles gave rise, the chief result of the bloodthirsty rigour of the laws with which they defended property was to ensure the acquittal of the majority of petty male-factors, judges and juries refusing to inflict death for such trifling offences.

It was the essence of all economic activity in England that it was un-controlled. Everything was left to individual enterprise. The very gardens in the new seaside resorts were laid out by speculating gardeners who recouped themselves by charging for admission and selling fruit and flowers. A service that was worth no one's while to provide – that did not offer profit to someone – was regarded as an activity not worth providing. Even the cleansing of the streets was left to the self-interest of men like Dickens's golden dustman who filled the suburbs with vast piles of stinking, fly-haunted rubble and manure which, regardless of their neighbours' amenities, they kept for sale to farmers and road contractors. Fire-fighting was left to insurance companies; London had to wait a generation after Waterloo before even its parishes were allowed to maintain a fire engine. All monopolies, it was felt, especially State monopolies, were bound to be inefficient and corrupt. 'An individual,' wrote Walter Scott, 'always manages his own concerns better than those of the country can be managed.'

Apart from the means of defence the State owned nothing; the very Ministers of the Crown regarded the official papers that passed through their hands as private property. Foreigners commented with surprise on the inadequacy of the public buildings; the benches and chairs in the London parks were invariably disfigured or destroyed. Even the royal arbours in Kensington Gardens were scribbled over with dirty rhymes. The cascade in Hyde Park below the Serpentine was blocked with duckweed and decaying branches; a large part of the metropolitan water supply – though the cost of a single week of the war could have supplied an aqueduct from the Surrey hills – was drawn from canals in which the poor washed or the Thames into which the sewers flowed.[1]

If London was badly off in public services, other places were far worse off. There were towns of ten thousand inhabitants which did not possess a post office or a postman. Their sanitary condition, a doctor reported, was like that of an encamped horde.[2] Birmingham – a city of 100,000 people and the fourth largest in the kingdom – was without even a charter and was administratively a mere agglomeration of squatters' dwellings, growing ever more congested and anarchical. Local government was a harlequinade; there were more than 250 municipal corporations in England and Wales and 15,000 parishes, and almost all corrupt. No one, except the very poor, showed the slightest respect for their authority or the antiquated regulations they feebly tried to enforce. Simond's first impression of England was the sight of the Falmouth beadles on a Sunday, in old-fashioned silver lace and cocked hats, trying to compel a Quaker to shut his shop, which reopened the moment they had gone.

1. Bury, I, 252; *English Spy*, I, 191; Lockhart, IV, 74; Partington, I, 27–8; Raumer, III, 142; *Sea-Bathing Places*, 429, 437; Woodward, 4, 41, 448.
2. Hutchins, *Public Health Agitation*, 64, *cit.* Hammond, *Town Labourer*, 44. See Clapham, I, 36–7; Fremantle, I, 46; *Sea-Bathing Places*, 349–51; Hammond, *Rise of Modern Industry*, 153; Letts, 123–5; Smart, 245–9; Woodward, 46, 432, 441.

In such a society scarcely anything was planned. Man was left free to act as and when it seemed fit to him to do so. In the hurly-burly of this untrammelled individual activity it was difficult even to unveil a statue or open a bridge without someone being crushed or killed. When Kean, the great actor, visited Liverpool a woman was trampled to death in the gallery; the King's brother, the Duke of Cambridge, taking his bride for a walk in Kensington Gardens, had to set her with her back to a tree to prevent her being smothered by the crowd. In the manufacturing districts, where the controlling forces of custom, Church, and ancient neighbourhood were lacking, English anarchy reached Homeric heights. When Messrs Hole, Wilkinson, and Garthside's new sheets were set out on the Manchester warehouse floor, the country drapers fought for the pieces with their fists.[1]

For here in the industrial North and Midlands was revolution – one more permanent and, to those who could comprehend its effect, more terrifying than any wrought by mob or guillotine. A whole society was being transformed by the impact of whirling wheels and grinding machines, while the nation's traditional leaders, far removed from the wild moors, mosses, and lonely valleys where the revolution was being enacted, stood aside and let it take its course. The new mechanical processes in weaving and spinning cotton, wool, flax, and silk, in smelting iron, mining coal, and making pottery, in harnessing steam power, the manufacture of tools, and the transport of goods, was creating a life of a kind hitherto unknown, where craftsmen and mechanics, instead of working as semi-independent manufacturers in their rural homes, crowded round large-scale factories as the wage-earners of employers with the capital to buy and maintain machines. The old domestic craftsman was a countryman, not only living within sight of the fields but frequently owning a stake in them. The competition of steam power either drove him, starving, from his home to seek employment in a factory town or turned his surroundings into one.

In the industrial districts the whole appearance of the countryside was changing. In south Lancashire and north-east Cheshire, in the West Riding, on Tyneside and Clyde, on the Warwickshire and Staffordshire heaths, the landscape was growing black, the villages were turning

1. Bamford, I, 227; See *Ann. Reg.* 1815, Chron., 71, 91; Lady Shelley, II, 15; Partington, I, 139.

into towns, and the towns were running into one another. Lady Shelley, after a journey in the West Midlands, wrote of 'that disagreeable, cold, and manufacturing county which for twenty miles smokes from a thousand steam engines, so that at night the whole country from Birmingham to Wolverhampton appears to be on fire': 'all the shining ewels of this wondrous cave,' another traveller wrote of Sheffield, 'shrouded in smoke and glaring red fire.' In Burslem the smoke was so dense that the potters had to grope their way to work.[1] A traveller from Rochdale to Manchester in the year after Waterloo found the houses as thick as in the environs of London, and 'smoke and trade and dirt' everywhere. The trout streams were being poisoned by dye-vats and the valleys studded with smokestacks; the willows and hazels of the Irk blackened and laid waste, the groves of birch, wild rose, and rowan and the green hills with the classical names and haunting rustic deities – Babylon Brow and Stony Knows – desecrated by money-grinders.

*

The character of economic relationships was changing with the appearance of the countryside. The weaver, spinner, stockinger, working in his own cottage with the help of his family and, perhaps, an apprentice, owning or hiring his own tools and selling the finished article to a capitalist wholesaler in the nearest town, from whom he also obtained the raw materials of his trade, was being superseded by the proletarian factory worker operating expensive power-machines owned by others and owning nothing himself but his labour. With every advance of the technological revolution the control of the capitalist over the conditions of work tightened. Before the end of the war the East Midland hosiers were letting out frames to stockingers in the Leicestershire and Nottinghamshire villages at thirty per cent per annum of their capital cost. Workmen who, rather than pay such rentals, tried to buy their own machines, found themselves shut out from both raw materials and markets. If they could not sell their wares promptly, their families starved. The decent hosier's standards were constantly forced down by

1. Wedgwood, *Staffordshire Pottery and its History*, 65, cit. Hammond, *Town Labourer*, 46. See Newton, 25–6; Bamford, I, 60, 71, 168, 223; II, 50–3, 80–2, 86, 115, 333; Clapham, I, 36; Darvall, 24; Newton, 25; Lady Shelley, II, 41; Simond, II, 76, 83.

the price and wage-cutting of his less scrupulous rivals. So were the good craftsman's.[1]

This process of transformation had still a long way to go. There were at least a quarter of a million handlooms in the country at the time of Waterloo. The three thousand domestic clothiers who rode every market day into Leeds, Bradford, and Huddersfield to sell their wares were still essential to the nation's economy; 'at Hathersage,' wrote Bamford, 'we heard the sound of a shuttle and my wife said we were getting near home.' The 'weaver's trade' was as much part of the English tradition as husbandry or seamanship; when the poet Blake wished to explain the mystery of life, he wrote that joy and woe were

woven fine
A clothing for the soul divine.

In 1811 four-fifths of the Midland stockingers' frames were scattered in more than two hundred and fifty villages with an average of twenty-two stockingers apiece, each operating three or four frames. Yet whenever markets dried up and competition intensified – during the Continental Blockade and American War, and in the more sustained deflation that followed the peace – the undercutting of the machines and of the capitalists who exploited them forced down the living standards of domestic workers and drove increasing numbers from their traditional life. In the trade depression of 1812 the average family earnings of Nottinghamshire silk workers dropped by a third, and the wages of Bolton cotton weavers fell to five shillings a week. Though a recovery always followed, each successive slump took its toll of independent 'manufacturers' – a word which was ceasing to denote a craftsman and becoming applied solely to employers.

It was a tragedy that at the moment when the introduction of labour-saving machinery effected this social revolution, the prevailing economic philosophy should have been so fanatically opposed to any protective regulation of conditions of employment. There were many regulations on the statute book dating from Stuart, Tudor, and even medieval times, but the political economists, who since the time of Adam Smith had monopolized the ear of Parliament, held them in

1. Darvall, 30–1, 35–7, 41, 47–8; Klingender, 42.

contempt. Even where they were not repealed, they were becoming a dead letter. The idea of regulating men's morals and social behaviour for their own good ran counter to the whole spirit of the age. Jeremy Bentham, father of utilitarian radicalism – the creed of every progressive for the next quarter of a century – maintained that all law was evil, since law was an infraction of liberty, and devoted his well-endowed life to exposing the unreason of past legislation. To him, as to Josiah Child before him, the laws of England were 'a heap of nonsense compiled by a few ignorant country gentlemen.' Every intelligent man subscribed to Burke's dictum that the chief inlet by which oppression entered the world was by one man pretending to determine the happiness of another. 'The right of the State to interfere to prevent a man from injuring himself,' wrote the economist, Nassau Senior, 'supposes that the legislator knows better how to manage the affairs of an individual than the man does himself.'

The effects of this theory could be best seen in places where the new industrial workers lived. 'The triumphs of the olive crown,' boasted a contemporary topographical guide, 'are not over kings or dynasties, but over material, inconsumable elements of nature, which, educated by a Newton, analyse the sunlight, or, directed by a Watt, force fire and water to the work of a thousand men's hands and unite the ends of the earth, bringing the scattered family of man into close and brotherly proximity.'[1] The closeness of that proximity had to be seen to be believed. In the first two decades of the century the population of Manchester increased from 94,000 to 160,000, of Bolton from 29,000 to 50,000, and of Lancashire from 672,000 to 1,052,000. The houses were put up by jerry-builders as cheaply as possible, with bricks so thin that neighbours could hear one another speaking, with roofs and floors supported by planks, without water pipes or drains.[2] In the sinister, sunless city beside the filthy Sheaf, whose forges, set against the bleak Derbyshire hills, made the world's finest cutlery, Bamford and his wife Mima were driven from their inn by the bugs which swarmed off the dirty walls and bedding. Fever caused more deaths in the industrial towns every year than Wellington's armies suffered in the

1. J. F. Murray, *Environs of London*, 205–6.
2. As late as 1842 four out of five houses in Birmingham were without water. Clapham, I, 164–5; Simond, II, 199; Woodward, 445.

Pensinsular War. Thousands, particularly where the Irish 'bog-trotters' congregated in search of subsistence, lived in foetid cellars and airless courts. Within a few months of their migration from a moorland village to Manchester, Bamford's entire family was stricken down by typhus.

In all the steam-engine towns – 'oppressive, smoky, noisy, riotous' – the creation of wealth and the perpetuation of poverty went hand-in-hand. In the vicinity of an inexhaustible supply of coals in South Wales the mouldering remains of Neath Abbey were populated by the families of the workmen employed in the neighbouring copper-smelting works. Obsession with external display was wholly lacking in the industrial districts. Despite the vast scale on which manufactures were conducted, the power and perfection of the machines, the capital invested in them, nothing was spent on appearance. The factory buildings were shabby and ugly, and added at different times without attempt at design or reference to convenience or beauty. Industrial capital was only employed in the creation of new capital. The sole end of all activity was profit. Success or failure turned on not spending sixpence more than was necessary.

Unfortunately the end was too narrow for the purposes of a continuing communal life. Cotton manufactory and coal mining – the trades on which England's new wealth was principally founded – were inherently unhealthy. The one confined men, women, and children for long hours in hot, vitiated, humid air which clogged the lungs with floating particles of cotton; the other banished them from the daylight. Accidents with primitive unfenced machinery were common; Pückler-Muskau saw workers with thumbs crushed into formless lumps of flesh. They were even more frequent in the mines, where explosions, floods, and landslides engulfed whole companies of colliers.[1] Half the workers in the Cornish copper mines, Ayton was told when he visited them in 1814, suffered from tuberculosis. Every year increased the numbers employed in the mills, mines, and foundries; every year their surroundings grew more squalid, insanitary, and hideous. And every year machines exerted a greater tyranny over men's lives,

1. For a terrible explosion in the year after Waterloo in the Heaton coal pit, resulting in the death by starvation of nearly eighty men and boys, see *Ann. Reg.*, 1816, Chron. 31.

forcing them to work yoked to automata which neither wearied nor rested.[1]

For the overall effect of machinery, though immeasurably multi-plying and cheapening consumer goods, was disastrous for man con-sidered as a producer. No longer was his work adapted in long-proved ways to his nature – to his physical needs, pride, skill, affections. Instead he was forced into the unnatural mould of forms of work dictated by the capacity of machines and the figures of machine-made accountancy. He was deprived alike of liberty, the control of his tools, and of his familiar home, of access to the fields and of the fresh fruits of the earth. Herded into factories like prisons and fever-haunted squatter towns like pig-styes, he saw his children grow up to a life utterly unlike that in which he and his forebears had lived. The old mould from which 'God's Englishman' had been made was broken. It was not surprising that the new mould did not always seem to cultured contemporaries a Christian or a kindly one.

Through the substitution of mechanical processes for human skill, it became possible to grow rich by employing unskilled women and children at low wages instead of craftsmen at high. Women and children had always been accustomed to work at wheel or loom in their own homes, where the 'drudgery of the bobbin wheel' was often enforced by the housewife's 'stout rod'. There seemed to contemporaries no harm in their doing so in factories. Work was regarded as the best of all activities for body and soul, and an extended means of employment was hailed as a national blessing. What was forgotten was that, while a woman working in her own home with her children around her could teach them the lessons of piety and good husbandry that she had learnt from her own mother, when she and they worked for twelve hours a day in a factory, the home and its culture were bound to be sacrificed. In his *Letters from England* Southey described how he watched children tending spinning jennies in the Manchester mills from five in the morning till six in the evening, till he was giddy with the noise and motion.

The early cotton-spinning mills, driven by water power, were

1. In one Manchester factory any spinner being sick and unable to find an adequate substitute had to pay six shillings a day for wasted steam. Hammond, *Town Labourer*, 20.

mainly operated by child-apprentices hired from poor-law overseers. Situated in the lonely upper reaches of Pennine rivers, there was no other way of staffing them. Steam power transferred the mills to large centres of population – generally in the neighbourhood of coal mines – where a plentiful supply of unskilled labour could be obtained, often from the families of skilled artisans who, being thrown out of work by machine competition, were forced to let their wives and children enter the factories. The process was exploited with ruthless realism. 'When a manufacturer,' wrote Walter Scott, 'wishes to do a particular job he gathers one or two hundred weavers from lanes, streets, and garrets without the slightest attention to character or circumstances or to any-thing but that they have ten fingers and can drive a shuttle. These men are employed perhaps for a fortnight and then turned off, the employer knowing no more or caring no more than if they were so many old pins or shuttles.'

Few of those who, by the power of employment, controlled this new society had been trained to lead or had been responsible for anyone save themselves and their families. They had been educated only for their craft, of which they were usually past-masters. Many were decent and kindly men, like the Manchester counterpane and bed-quilt manu-facturer for whom Bamford worked at the beginning of the century, or his successor, who read prayers to his family and apprentices every Sunday night, and whose wife nursed the latter through their illnesses. Peter Dixon, the 'Druid's' father, who had a cotton mill in Shad-dongate, Carlisle, visited his workpeople in their homes, looked after the sick and taught their children in Sunday school. Simond was much struck by the good nature and politeness of the large Birmingham industrialists round whose works he was escorted in 1811.

But most factory owners were small men, little removed in up-bringing or education from those they employed. They sprang from a rough, primitive, passionate folk who loved fighting, hard drinking, and simple, sensual pleasures. They had been uprooted from the pastoral communities of their forebears whose standards and beliefs they had either forgotten or repudiated as irrelevant in the wider world of clanging machinery and smoking chimney. With great virtues of energy, courage, native shrewdness, and industry, they were mostly thrusting, ambitious, ruthless types who succeeded because they were. As the machinery in which they had so boldly invested undercut their rivals and drove them into their factories, they found themselves in possession of great public and personal power. They used the former without a thought for the national good and the latter in pursuit of further wealth or the gratification of low, ignorant pleasures. 'They resembled,' wrote one who knew them, 'the man in the *Arabian Nights* tale whose eye had been touched with magic ointment and which presented to his mental vision an endless display of wealth.'

Under such circumstances the relations between employer and employed were bound to deteriorate. The old handloom weavers who worked for Messrs Broadbent of Manchester would rest, after their tramp from their moorland homes, on the seat thoughtfully provided for them before having a friendly check-up with the firm's 'putter-out', neither party trying to drive a hard bargain because of the other's necessities; perhaps afterwards buyer and seller would sit down together to a friendly glass of ale and a pipe at the 'Hope and Anchor'. Often in such old-fashioned firms, Bamford records, the master would take his men home to dine with his family on broth, dumpling, and baked pudding. But as machinery came in, the gap between capitalist and artisan widened. The snobbery that vitiated the society of the well-to-do, vitiated that of the industrial town. A man who worked with his hands, being increasingly prevented by the cost of machinery from becoming more than a wage-earner, was looked down on by those who enjoyed the increase wrought by the machines he tended. Hereditary skill counted for less and less as mechanical power took the place of craft. Phrases like the 'lower orders', the 'swinish multitude', 'the rabble', became habitual to men and women who felt themselves to be a different species from the poor toilers whose grandfathers and fathers had been the equals of their own. The filthier the workers' surroundings, the more deadening and brutalizing their conditions of labour, the more savage and pagan they grew and the more a race apart – a different and potentially hostile nation within the body politic. 'Their conduct on a Sunday,' a witness reported of juvenile cotton workers, 'is such that females as well as men insult their well-behaved superiors in the street, and that to a degree that well-behaved, discreet gentlemen, even if they meet the factory people, will, if possible, go on the other side of the street to avoid them.'[1]

*

This breach within the nation was allowed to develop and widen because the ruling class had been taught by the economists that the pursuit of self-interest was the key to national well-being. To buy at the cheapest and sell at the dearest was the commandment which in economic matters was taking the place of the original ten. Any restriction on what was called 'free' bargaining was repugnant to progressive, or as it was then called, 'enlightened', opinion. An Act of 1802, which confined – at least in theory – the hours of poor-law apprentices in water-driven cotton-mills to twelve hours a day, was not re-enacted to cover the steam-power factories which by the end of the war had almost completely taken their place. A Bill to make it do so, introduced in the year of Waterloo by a humane spinner, Sir Robert Peel – father of the statesman – was allowed to drop. Kindly employers, whose hearts were touched by the sufferings of children in their mills and in those of their harsher competitors, and who sought restrictive legislation to render humanity compatible with solvency, were able to do little against such a combination of solemn belief and self-interest. The nation which had repudiated the Slave Trade now accepted as inevitable a new and still more paying form of slavery.

The miracle of mechanical production had impressed sensitive contemporaries with such awe that they had temporarily lost their critical faculty. 'It is impossible,' wrote a visitor to Glasgow in 1810, 'to see without astonishment those endless flakes of cotton, as light as snow and as white, ever pouring from the carding machine, then seized by the teeth of innumerable wheels and cylinders and stretched into threads, flowing like a rapid stream and lost in a tourbillon of spindles. The eye of a child or of a woman watches over the blind mechanism, directing the motions of her whirling battalion.' The sight of gangs of maimed and exhausted children trailing daily into the factories and mines that supported England's new industrial wealth caused kindly and cultured men no astonishment, only a defeatist fatalism. In the great cotton manufactory at Lanark, employing 2500 hands, mostly

1. Evidence of George Gould, fustian merchant, *cit.* Hammond, *Town Labourer*, 162; Bamford, I, 110–11. See *idem*, 106–9, 251; Woodward, 6, 40.

children who had started work at the age of seven or eight, the hours were from 6 a.m. till 7 p.m., followed by evening school from 8 p.m. to 10 p.m. Some of the children's homes were close to the factory, but others, whose parents lived a mile away, had the additional advantage of a healthy night and early morning walk; they could be distinguished, visitors were told, by their brighter colour.[1] The long hours – in some places they were as many as fifteen a day for six days a week – were regarded as essential to enable manufacturers to compete against under-cutting and secure the markets without which their employees might be thrown out of work and starve. Viewed in this sense, the labour that crippled children's limbs, rotted their lungs, and stunted their minds, could be defended as a blessing, a means of preserving them from famine. Some supporters of the system went further, seeing in the children's ceaseless activity an inspiring spectacle. 'They seemed,' wrote one employer, 'to be always cheerful and alert, taking pleasure in the light play of their muscles – enjoying the mobility natural to their age. ... It was delightful to observe the nimbleness with which they pierced the broken ends as the mule-carriage began to recede from the fixed roller-beam, and to see them at leisure, after a few seconds' exercise of their tiny fingers, to amuse themselves in any attitude they chose till the stretching and winding-on were once more completed. The work of these lively elves seemed to resemble a sport in which habit gave them a pleasing dexterity.'[2] 'The mathematicians,' wrote a young officer of Wellington's army, 'from the dry bones of their diagrams, and the chemists from the soot of their furnaces bring with them dispositions which make them indifferent to the cause of humanity.'

This determinist philosophy – the precursor of Marxism – accorded perfectly with the requirements of landowners and manufacturers who,

1. On which Simond, who visited the factory in 1810, commented, 'Eleven hours of confinement and labour, with the schooling 13 hours, is undoubtedly too much for children. I think the laws should interfere between avarice and nature.' Simond, I, 278. See also Farington, I, 134, for a description of one of Arkwright's model factories where the children worked 13 hours a day, with 40 minutes off for dinner, to earn 3s. 6d. a week for boys and 2s. 3d. for girls, with chapel and Sunday school thrown in. 'The whole plan appears to be such as to do Mr Arkwright great credit.'

2. Andrew Ure, *The Philosophy of Manufactures*, 1895. See Gomm, 311–12. See Bamford, I, 111; Peel, I, 259–62; Woodward, 11.

needing ever larger sums for their competitive and showy society or for the enlargement of their businesses, accepted the under-nourishment and degrading surroundings of their fellow countrymen as an inevitable dispensation of Providence. It received its highest expression in the works of a clergyman named Malthus who contended that population automatically outran subsistence, nature's ruthless but beneficent law being to preserve the economy of the world by eliminating surplus mouths and hands by starvation. 'We are bound in justice and honour,' he wrote, 'formally to disclaim the *right* of the poor to support. To this end I should propose a regulation to be made declaring that no child born from any marriage taking place after the expiration of a year from the date of the law should ever be entitled to parish assistance. ... A man who is born into a world already possessed, if he cannot get subsistence from his parents on whom he has a just demand, and if the society does not want his labour, has no claim of right to the smallest portion of food and in fact has no business to be where he is. At nature's mighty feast there is no vacant cover for him.'

It was a proof of the extent to which educated and humane Englishmen were bewildered by the immense rise in the population – since 1750 it had almost doubled – and alarmed by the revolutionary events around them, that they accepted, and even with a kind of melancholy enthusiasm, this monstrous doctrine from a professor of the Christian Church – himself a most kindly and reasonable man.[1] If a natural law of increase made vice and misery inevitable for millions, there seemed no need for the ruling and possessing classes to reproach themselves for the increase of vice and misery which attended their own enrichment or to waste money trying to remedy it. It was like the fall of the leaves in autumn.

In this matter the poets were wiser than men of state and business. Writers of all schools of thought united in protest at Malthus's conclusions. Southey, the poet-laureate and an arch-Tory, denounced it as 'technical sophism and a physical assumption as false in philosophy as detestable in morals,' and Coleridge, in his rambling but prescient talk – delivered as from some lofty height from which he descried, invisible to all eyes but his, the course of human folly and frailty for a century ahead – remarked that if society disclaimed all responsibility

1. In a later work he considerably modified his own doctrine.

for the starving, the latter would reply that in that case they had no duties towards it and might take by force what was denied by humanity. Such arguments, however, made little impression on anxious rate payers forced to alleviate the growing pauperism caused by the wage-policy of manufacturers and farmers.

In the international sphere Britain's rulers had resisted the revolutionary claim that the strong possessed a natural right to ignore the mutual obligations of law. Yet in the economic sphere the same rulers, despite unavailing protests by the poor and in defiance of their country's historical tradition, accepted the revolutionary thesis that men had a right to enrich themselves without regard to social obligations and the continuing claims of the community. In England the legatee of the supremacy of natural right – the untrammelled liberty of superior energy and brain – was not the soldier of fortune, but the thrusting, broad-shouldered condottiere of commerce and finance. They, too, like Napoleon, regarded the world as their oyster and ravaged and exploited as they conquered. Like him, they made themselves rich and their country strong and glorious, but they uprooted and rendered millions wretched in the process. And to them was left, in accordance with the revolutionary doctrine that the pursuit of private gain must automatically enrich the community, the almost unfettered control of the ordinary Englishman's home, surroundings, food, health, and conditions of labour. Henceforward nothing was safe from the exploiters; a year or two after Waterloo, speculators started to seek for coal in the Thames valley below Oxford.

Such a theory of society made for a new kind of mind. Commerce was growing stricter, stingier. Charles Lamb, a clerk of the London trading company that had conquered India, wrote of 'this mercantile city and its gripple merchants,' and related how his employers, like the Bank of England, had cut down the old saints' days' holidays almost to nothing – 'the cold piety of the age lacks the fervour to recall them.' No longer, he told his correspondents, could he pass their letters through the Company's bag; the Directors, 'rascals who think nothing of sponging upon their employers for their venison and turtle and burgundy five days in a week to the tune of five thousand pounds in a year, now find out that the profits of trade will not allow the innocent communications of thought between their underlings and their friends in distant provinces to proceed untaxed.' So, too, in deference to the new outlook – cold, calculated, remorseless – his fellow clerk, Tommy Bye, coming into the office a little hazy one morning after an evening's debauch, found himself summarily dismissed after twenty-seven years' service. 'Clerk's blood, dam 'em! my brain, guts, skin, flesh, bone, carcase, soul, time is all theirs,' Lamb wrote, half in jest, but also in earnest, 'the Royal Exchange, Gresham's Folly, hath me body and spirit!' The apostles of Mammon were warming to their business, shutting up growing numbers of their fellows in factory and counting-house away from the fresh air and sunlight.

*

It was not only in the towns that man suffered on a cross of economic necessity. The British revolution, unlike that of France, did not arise from the corruption and inefficiency of an outworn society but from the country's very vigour and success. To overcome the opposition of the less well-educated peasantry and the wasteful overcropping of the soil under the old communal system of open farming,[1] and to apply the new methods of stock breeding and root-cultivation on a nation-wide scale, the land-owning class, having boldly invested enormous sums to increase agricultural production, had used its monopoly of political power to secure private acts of Parliament redistributing the arable fields and commons. With population rising by at least fifteen per cent in every decade, and grain imports stopped by the war, increased corn-growing had become both an urgent national priority and a means of vast private profits. Between 1796 and 1815 more than eighteen hundred enclosure Bills were passed, four hundred more than in the previous forty years. In no other way could the supply of home-grown food – and none other was available – have kept pace with the population.

The social, as opposed to the economic, consequences of this agrarian revolution were, however, disastrous. Growing numbers of husband-

1. 'The Goths and Vandals of open-field farmers must die out before any complete change takes place.' Arthur Young, cit. Ernle, 199–200. 'A great portion of the unstinted common lands remain nearly as nature left them, appearing in the present state of civilisation and science as filthy blotches on the face of the country, especially when seen under threatening clouds of famine.' William Marshall, *The Appropriation and Inclosure of Commonable and Intermixed Lands* (1801).

men who had enjoyed a small but vital stake in the land – a strip or two in the parish arable fields, pasture on the common for a few ragged cattle, pigs, and geese, the right to gather manure and fuel – found themselves deprived of them. Unable to face the initial costs of legislation, fencing, and drainage involved in enclosure, they were forced to sell their compensatory allotments to their richer neighbours. Those who possessed only squatters' rights on the manorial commons or waste received no compensation at all. Men with an hereditary talent for dealing with soil and beasts were requited with payment in a medium in whose use they had neither skill nor experience. As often as not, they spent it in the alehouse. Henceforward they and their children had no resource but that of the wages they earned. They ceased to be peasants and became proletarians, without security and therefore without liberty.

The rich welcomed the changed status of the rural poor because it made them easier to discipline. 'The land,' wrote a Scottish agriculturist, 'is divided into a limited number of great farms, and the tenants, men of capital and intelligence, are enabled to give the best effect to the virtues of the soil, and the great body of the people live quietly under them as farm servants and hired labourers, having no care but to do their own work and receive their wages.' The more profitable farming became and the more eager the rich to buy, the greater became the temptation of the poor to sell. Every year the amount of land in well-to-do hands increased. It was leased from them at high rents by a new race of tenant farmers who, operating under almost ideal conditions, with expanding markets, rising war prices, and cheap and abundant labour, could afford to operate on a far bigger scale than their fathers. Capital was found to drain, improve, and compost the soil, experiment in new root and grass crops, and raise the herds and flocks of fine cattle, pigs, and sheep that were the wonder of the world.

For the farm labourer on the other hand these improvements meant a fatal deprivation of amenities. He lost with the open field and common his milk, butter, poultry, eggs, and cooking fuel. Having no stake in what he raised, he gained nothing from its increased price.[1] On the

---

1. 'The labourer who sows and does not reap sees abundance all around him, creates it and does not partake of it.' Simond, I, 172-5, 'Shall we never cease to make him a miserable being, a creature famishing in the midst of abundance?'

contrary, having now to buy most of his own and his family's food, he was doubly the loser. Though his wages rose during the war, they did not rise as quickly as prices. The inflationary rise began for him at the wrong end, with the proceeds of labour instead of its reward. It was aggravated by the growing tendency of farmers, producing no longer for sustenance but for profit, to sell to middlemen whose profits had to be added to the price of his bread and ale. At the same time his family's supplementary earnings from domestic handicrafts were being reduced or eliminated by the growing competition of machines. The farmhouse where the young unmarried labourer had formerly boarded with the homely family of his yeoman employer became the residence of a finer kind of farmer, whose sons hunted and whose daughters played the piano and who could not be bothered with the board of farm domestics. Many of the smaller farmhouses disappeared altogether in the engrossment of farms which followed the enclosures. The landlords and their new tenants, Cobbett wrote in 1821, stripped the land of all shelter for the poor. Simond earlier noted the same phenomenon; the countryside swarmed with gentlemen's houses and opulent farms, but the dwellings of the real poor were hard to discover. Among the roofless ruins of Valle Crucis Abbey he saw peasants and their children squatting with pigs and poultry. 'The poor are swept out of the way,' he wrote, 'as the dust out of the walks of the rich.'[1]

Before enclosure the chief source of hired agricultural labour had been the smallholder or commoner, who devoted two or three days a week to looking after his own land and worked on that of a richer neighbour for the remainder. Though the latter was now becoming the peasant's sole support, the farmer who employed him, being in an advantageous bargaining position – for a man with a hungry family cannot stand on terms – was slow to raise his wages. By 1795 the rapidity with which prices rocketed under the triple stimulus of war, increased urban population, and a bad harvest temporarily threatened the landless labourer with immediate famine. In the face of this threat

Cobbett, *Rural Rides*, I, 592. 'The poor forger is hanged, but where is the prosecutor of the monopolising farmer?' See Ernle, 305–12; Hammond, *Village Labourer*, 97–145, 161–5; Woodward, 9, 158.

1. Simond, I, 222. See *idem*, II, 72; Fowler, 260–1; Grote, 26; Hammond, *Village Labourer*, 112–20.

the Berkshire magistrates at their meeting at Speenhamland that summer took a fateful decision. Instead of enforcing a minimum wage – a measure which, though empowered to take, they shirked out of deference to the new economic teaching – they fixed a basic rate of subsistence, based on the fluctuating price of corn and the size of the family, and authorized a grant in aid to all who were being paid less than this by their employers. By thus subsidizing wages out of rates, they pauperized the labourer.

Magistrates in many parts of the country had followed their well-intentioned example. Not only were farmers countenanced in their reluctance to pay an economic wage, but poor-rates had rocketed out of all proportion to the incomes of the smaller ratepayers, who had thus become saddled with part of the working costs of their richer neighbours. The decent employer was taxed to subsidize his unfair competitor and – since no man with savings could qualify for relief – the thrifty husbandman to maintain the unthrifty. By 1818 the annual national contribution to poor-rates, little more than £700,000 in 1750, had risen to nearly eight millions. More than a fifth of the rural population of England and Wales – Scotland had no poor-law – was in receipt of some form of parochial relief. Thousands of small husbandmen, faced by rate demands beyond their means, were also driven into the ranks of the landless workers and became themselves a charge on the rates. The poor-laws, wrote Malthus, had created the poor they assisted.[1]

The effect on the labourer was even more disastrous, for he was robbed of his self-respect. Having lost his proprietary rights, he found himself a member of a pariah class; a labour reserve from which landlords and farmers drew when it suited them without regard to human rights and feelings. In many places the overseers – generally farmers little above those they administered in birth and education – insisted that the grant of parish relief entitled them to a complete control over the lives of those whose wages they subsidized. They sent them round the local farms, including their own, in chains or gangs, as though they

---

1. Simond, I, 225. See *idem*, 229; II, 295. It was a system, said Southey, which converted the peasantry into the poor. See also Darvall, 46; De Selincourt, II; Dicey, 101; Ernle, 308–12, 327–8; Hammond, *Village Labourer*, 104; Porter, 88, 90; Smart, 137–8; Woodward, 431.

were serfs. A visitor from Jamaica who saw some of these gangs at work considered that his Negro slaves were better off.[1]

This accumulation of evil circumstances had fallen on the rural poor so rapidly, first in one locality and then in another, that few of those who were not directly affected were even aware of what was occurring. In most places its effect was not felt until the great agricultural depression set in after the war. But wherever it struck, it left the English peasantry, the traditional backbone of the country, suffering from a feeling of bewildered helplessness. Old England was tightening into neat-hedged and gated fields and high-walled parks; the sense of property was running mad and cruel, and there seemed no place in it save a serf's for the poor countryman whose ill-requited labour had wrought the transformation. Though many landlords and farmers maintained the old kindly, paternal relations with those who worked on their own farms and gardens or lived in their immediate vicinity, others, in their absorption in fashionable and sporting pleasures, increasingly left the management of their estates to professional intermediaries. The way in which bailiffs and land-stewards whittled away or ignored ancient rights was bitterly resented. In the manor of East Burnham, bought in the early years of the century by the great Whig family of Grenville, the latter's agent claimed an absolute rather than a manorial property in the soil, contemptuously refusing to fulfil the lord's duties of ringing pigs and maintaining fences, and selling the peat, wood, turf, and sand from the common to non-parishioners.[2] At Middleton Lord Suffield's steward broke up the village bowling green and turned it into a burial ground, because he could not keep its rustic frequenters in 'respectful bounds'. As he passed through Savernake Forest, Cobbett noted how many small farms had been swallowed up to add park after park to Lord Ailesbury's domain.

> Hence, yeoman, hence! – thy grandsire's land resign;
> Yield, peasant, to my lord and power divine!
> Thy grange is gone, your cluster'd hovels fall;
> Proud domes expand, the park extends its wall;
> Then kennels rise, the massive Tuscan grows,
> And dogs sublime, like couchant Kings, repose!

1. Farington, VIII, 39. See Cobbett, I, 94; Fowler, 246–7; Simond, I, 224–6.
2. Grote, 40–1, 44–6.

Lo! 'still-all-Greek-and-glorious' art is here!
Behold the pagod of a British peer![1]

The labourer's suffering was aggravated by the increasing rigour with which the game laws were enforced by landowners obsessed with the new mania for vast battues and game-bags. A Parliament of game-preservers, in the south of England at least, was banishing the peasant from the sports of his fathers. Men whose families were hungry and who saw pheasants, hares, and partridges swarming in every wood around them, could not resist the temptation of going out at night with gun and net to fill the pot or reap the rewards – far higher than their wages – offered by the agents of the London poulterers. When caught, they received short shrift from magistrates, who in this matter, so close to their hearts, could be utterly ruthless. By a savage act of 1816 a man caught at night in an enclosure with instruments for trapping game could be sentenced to transportation, by two magistrates, one of whom might be the injured property owner, while a blow, struck or even threatened in a poaching fray, could be punished by the gallows. The war between poachers and gamekeepers reached a terrible crescendo in the agricultural depression after the Napoleonic wars. Hundreds were killed or maimed in pitched battles in the woods or by the spring-guns and mantraps with which the more ignoble landlords protected their property and pleasures.[2]

Because of these things the peasant's unquestioning patriotism and respect for his feudal superiors were being replaced by a growing sense of injustice. At the time of Waterloo the social cataclysm which befell him was still far from universal. In the north, where the competition of the industrial towns for labour kept up wages, its effects had been comparatively little felt. And everywhere the sufferings of the poor, in this tremendous and little understood revolution, were modified by the decency and kindliness of thousands of worthy men and women, whose

1. Ebenezer Elliot, *The Splendid Village* (1833).
2. 'Nothing would induce me to put up boards threatening prosecution or cautioning one's fellow-creatures to beware of man-traps and spring-guns.' Walter Scott, Jan. 8th 1825. Lockhart, v, 399. See Cobbett, *Rural Rides*, I, 110–111; Coupland, *Wilberforce*, 428–9; *Cranbourn Chase*, 35–7, 39–41; Green, *Stendhal*. 183; Hammond, *Village Labourer*, 187–206; Woodward, 439.

sense of duty to their fellow-beings remained unaffected by opportunities of self-enrichment or by the new philosophy of *laissez faire*. Yet taking a broad view while the horizon had lifted for the rich and strong beckoning to an illimitable future of wealth and opportunity, for the poor it was fast darkening. The rulers of Christian England, and those who by their writings helped to form educated opinion, were blind to the changes which these new opportunities of enrichment had brought and were bringing, at an ever-increasing rate, to their poorer countrymen. They only saw their material manifestations – the new, neatly-hedged fields and smoking chimneys and the rising revenues of their estates and of the national Exchequer. They failed to see the hopelessness and hunger of the peasant deprived of his stake in the land and of the produce that had sustained his family. They failed to comprehend the agony of once independent countrymen imprisoned in the discipline of the factory and surrounded by the hideous squalor of the industrial town, or the mentality of children who grew up among these gloomy phenomena knowing no other. There was some excuse for their incapacity to realize the social consequences of the Industrial Revolution, since this, in the year 1815, was still in its lusty infancy and cradled in the most remote and unfrequented parts of the island. There was far less for their failure to understand the tragic social transformation wrought by the agricultural revolution at their park gates. They knew that by its means more food was obtained for their country and more rent for themselves. They turned a blind eye to its inability to produce the free and contented men and women who were the main source of England's wealth.

CHAPTER 11

THE YEARS OF DISILLUSION

The festal blazes of the war at an end, the sun of Peace is scarcely yet above the horizon; we must take care that during this cold and cheerless twilight the spoiler and assassin don't break in.

CANNING

Men of England: wherefore plough
For the lords who lay ye low,
Wherefore weave with toil and care
The rich robes your tyrants wear?

SHELLEY (1819)

YET it could be said in excuse of the rich that, while the war continued and prosperity with it, many poor men shared in that prosperity, and that when the war ended and the full force of depression fell on the landless poor, it was no longer in the power of the rich, struggling with lapsing leases and tumbling rentals, to help them. An observer of the English scene pointed out that a prodigal could not be generous. When rents and prices fell, the rich had to choose between reducing their extravagant but by now customary standards of living or allowing the poor to suffer. And, contrary to all expectations, prices fell even before the war ended. The cessation of Government buying to feed the armies and the opening of the European and American grain ports brought down agricultural profits with a run. The magnificent English harvests of 1813 and 1815, and that of 1814 in France, flooded the markets. Few farmers had saved money, for, unable to visualize anything but rising prices, they had re-invested everything in their land. The poorer soils that they had ploughed to satisfy wartime demand became economically unworkable with wheat prices dropping from 120s. a quarter – the 1813 level – to 76s. in 1815 and 53s. 6d. in the spring of 1816. The value of farming stock fell by fifty per cent.

Having undertaken leases on terms compatible only with wartime profits, farmers found themselves unable to pay their rents or to meet the interest on their loans and mortgages. The banks, fearful for the capital they had advanced, called in their money. Hundreds of tenants defaulted, and thousands sought rent remission. Rentals everywhere shrank, though to a level much higher than that of a generation before. The doors of the landed gentry were still guarded by armies of liveried retainers, their woods abounded with game, their wonderful horses shook the earth. But they were thrown into a flurry of anxiety and spoke of ruin, both national and personal.[1]

Their representatives in Parliament tried to bolster up prices by legislation. For twenty years the Corn Laws, which from time immemorial had prevented the export of corn in domestic shortages and protected the home-grower during foreign gluts, had been abrogated by war and blockade. Now they had suddenly become a necessity if the farmer was to pay his rent, taxes, tithes, and mortgage interest. On both sides of the House it was contended – though a few Whig enthusiasts for complete freedom of trade demurred – that the rising number of mouths to be fed necessitated more home-grown corn, even if it involved uneconomic tillage. To rely for part of the nation's food on foreign supplies was too risky; more than once during the war England had nearly starved. It seemed better that the people should pay more for their corn in fat years to be sure of it in lean. It was to their interest, too, it was argued, that prices should be stabilized – a traditional aim of the Corn Laws.

But the workers of England, dreaming, after all that they had endured, of the traditional first-fruits of peace – a cheap loaf – viewed these landowners' arguments with suspicion. So did the northern manufacturers, seeking to effect cheap sales abroad through reduced wages at home – a policy impossible to enforce while food prices remained at their wartime level. Why, asked a Whig member of Parliament, should importation of foreign corn be feared, since none could take place without a corresponding export of British manufactures? A stock-jobber named Ricardo, who brought out a pamphlet on the beneficial influence of low corn prices on industrial profits, went further and maintained that dependence on foreign corn could never

1. One Scottish earl, forced to reduce his rents by a third, told a friend that he had abandoned his carriage-horses, paid off his *chef* and was no longer called 'the great Lion of Galloway,' but added that he found himself as happy as before. Earl of Galloway to Sir Arthur Paget, Nov. 27th 1815. *Paget Brothers*, 285–6. See also Alison, I, 82–3; Ashton, I, 377; Broughton, I, 81; Byron, *Age of Bronze*; Colchester, II, 558–60, 584–5; Ernle, 174, 322, 318–21; Farington, VII, 215, 218; Halévy, II, 5; Howitt, 203–4; Smart, 406–9, 435–6, 445; Woodward, 58.

endanger Britain's safety, since no foreign Government would ever dare oppose the pressure of its farmers to grow for the British market. The House of Commons was flooded with petitions: one from Leeds bore 24,000 signatures, another from Bristol 40,000, others from Liverpool and Manchester 50,000 apiece. Despite, however, their reference to a select committee, a Bill excluding foreign corn until the price of native corn reached 80s. a quarter passed both Houses in March, 1815.

Legislators were left with no illusions about the measure's unpopularity. The degree to which the landed interest had been weakened by the destruction of the peasantry now became apparent. Outside Parliament landowners and farmers found themselves almost alone; even the peasantry, having nothing left to gain from high food prices, were apathetic or against them. There was a feeling that they had feathered their nests during the war at the expense of the nation, and that they now wished to do so indefinitely. It was a resentment which later found expression in Byron's *Age of Bronze*:

> *Safe in their barns, these Sabine tillers sent*
> *Their brethren out to battle – why? for rent!*
> *Year after year they voted, cent per cent,*
> *Blood, sweat, and tear-wrung millions – why? for rent!*
> *They roared, they dined, they drank, they swore they meant*
> *To die for England – why then live? for rent!*

At the time crowds surrounded Parliament, holding up halters and shouting, 'No starvation!' 'No Landlords!' The house of the Minister who had introduced the Bill was sacked. The Lord Chancellor, with the help of three sentries from the British Museum, drove out the undersized, undernourished hooligans who broke into his Bedford Square dwelling, and Castlereagh, calmly walking home through the mob that was stoning his windows, unconcernedly closed his drawing-room shutters with brickbats flying about his head. Even Wilberforce, who spoke in the House of the danger of dependence on foreign corn, had to garrison his country pleasance in Kensington with a squad of soldiers.[1]

1. They were asked to join in family prayers. Coupland, *Wilberforce*, 408. See also *Ann. Reg.*, 1815, 4–5; Brownlow, 190; Colchester, II, 527–8; Croker, I, 63; Festing, 195; George IV, *Letters*, II, 43–4; Gomm, 346; Gronow, I, 220–1, 346; Smart, 90–1, 365, 372–89, 406–17, 441, 446–60; Woodward, 58–9.

The feeling against the Corn Laws was aggravated because industry was also in trouble. There was no repetition of the boom after the Peace of Amiens. The Government, which had been spending fifty millions a year supplying the Fleet and Army and almost as much in subsidizing foreign States to buy British munitions and uniforms, went out of business. The bottom fell out of the armament market. The price of iron dropped from £20 to £8 a ton and of copper from £180 to £80. Other commodities fell in proportion. Exports, after a brief hectic rise, declined by seven millions, those of foreign and colonial produce from twenty millions to scarcely ten. After so long and destructive a war the European nations were too poor to buy.

*

This recession was turned into a disaster by the reckless way in which British exporters poured their wares into war-ravaged or under-developed countries that lacked the buying-power to absorb them. The fluctuating markets of the war had developed a gambler's spirit among the rough and adventurous men pioneering in mechanical pro-duction. The speculation that attended the opening of the South American market rivalled the folly of the South Sea Bubble of a century before. The Spanish colonies – now in revolt against the mother country – were deluged with improbable wares. The multiplying power of Britain's machines was not yet matched by the capacity of her merchants to forecast markets – a matter of great difficulty in days of slow communications – or of her customers to absorb goods. It was not even matched by the pockets of her people at home. From the moment the war ended a mounting shortage of purchasing-power developed in every department of national life. By 1816 two-thirds of the Shropshire blast furnaces had shut down. Steam-manufacturers, unable to meet their wage bills, either reduced wages or discharged hands. Needing not skilled men so much as machine-minders, of which the towns at their factory gates offered an inexhaustible supply, they felt under no obligation, economic or moral, to maintain their em-ployees. Simultaneously the labour market was flooded by thousands of ex-soldiers and sailors who, being without any income whatever, contributed no consumer-demand but, by their competition for employment, forced down wages further.

Finding itself short of money, the community turned on the Government and demanded reduction of taxation. If landowners, farmers, and manufacturers could no longer enjoy war prices, they could no longer stomach war charges. So long as the war lasted, Britons had borne their burdens with patience. In 1815 a population of fourteen millions was contributing £72,000,000 per annum or a fifth of the national income, as compared with the £19,000,000 paid in 1792 by one of ten millions.

The charge fell on almost every commodity. It was said that the Government owned one wheel of every coach on the road.[1] The price of glory, wrote Sydney Smith, was 'taxes on the ermine which decorates the judge and the rope which hangs the criminal – on the poor man's salt and the rich man's spices – on the brass nails of the coffin and the ribands of the bride. ... The schoolboy whips his taxed top, the beardless youth manages his taxed horse with a taxed bridle on a taxed road, and the dying Englishman, pouring his medicine which has paid seven per cent into a spoon that has paid fifteen per cent, flings himself back upon his chintz bed, which has paid twenty-two per cent, and expires into the arms of an apothecary who has paid a licence of a hundred pounds for the privilege of putting him to death.'

Every year in his budget the Chancellor of the Exchequer rang the changes on these omnipresent imposts. The result was always the same. The subject paid from every pore, and the poor man, having no reserve after satisfying his bare needs, paid relatively most of all. Beer – his chief drink – contributed a sixth of the revenue; Cobbett, travelling to St Albans on a hot day, reckoned that, in their exchange of beer for sweat, the haymakers in the Middlesex alehouses were contributing threepence-halfpenny on every fivepenny pot. The hardships suffered by the workers under this system – unguessed at by the rich – are described in Cooper's memoirs; of poor widows conspiring to outwit tax-collectors, who, knowing their straits, pursued them with indecent solicitations: of midnight removals of household goods to prevent distraint; 'the curse upon taxes and the tax-gatherer was in the mouths

1. Even travel in the Margate hoy was taxed, every passenger paying 2s. on his 9s., 11s. or 13s. ticket. Sea-Bathing Places, 375. See Alison, History, I, 78–9; Austen, II, 293; Clapham, I, 245–6, 319–20; Dowall, 239; Fowler, 219; Hammond, Town Labourer, 102; Simond, I, 51; II, 290; Smart, 433; Woodward, 61, 324.

of thousands.' At St Ives the populace celebrated the first Christmas of the peace by throwing a tax-collector out of the window.[1]

Among those with the power to show resentment the most hated impost was the ten per cent Income Tax which Pitt had instituted in the hour of national peril. He had undertaken that this inquisitorial measure, as it was deemed by those who paid it, should be repealed as soon as the war ended. But the Government, faced with the charge, first of the American War and then of Napoleon's escape from Elba, and anxious to contribute some force to preserve international peace, struggled for more than a year before abandoning it. The Opposition was furious; so were the Government's supporters. The young Whig, Lord John Russell, declared that the tax's continuance would erase the last vestiges of British freedom. Why, it was asked, should the country's military establishment be six times greater than in 1792, especially as France was disarmed and Britain now allied to all Europe. Brougham accused Ministers of plotting to alter the character of the Constitution and make it a military state. The Foreign Secretary, who was regarded as the villain of the piece, was charged with having imbibed so many Continental customs as to have forgotten England was an island.

On August 11th, less than two months after Waterloo, the Prime Minister wrote to Castlereagh warning him that the financial situation was too grave for the nation to be able to shoulder further foreign commitments. The Navy and Army were the first to be pared. Within eighteen months 300,000 soldiers and sailors were turned adrift.[2] A naval officer in charge of a Sussex coastguard station received sudden orders to discharge his men in the dead of winter, though they were on a hilltop miles from anywhere. The men who had fought their way from Torres Vedras to Toulouse were given neither pension nor

1. Broughton, I, 94. See Bamford, II, 110–11; Cobbett, *Rural Rides*, I, 78; Colchester, II, 527–8; Cooper, 26–7; Halévy, II, 60; Simond, II, 140–1; Smart, 3, 31–6, 43–4, 53, 67, 100–1, 112–15, 169–70, 277–81, 341–4, 360–2, 425.

2. 'We's all in mourning here for Mr Nap,' said the old tar to the 'Oxonian' when he visited Portsmouth, 'we've had no fun here since they cooped him up on board the *Bellerophon* and stowed him away at St Helena. Where's all the girls and the fiddlers and the Jews and bumboat-women that used to crowd all sail to pick up a spare hand ashore? Not a shark have I seen in the harbour, and all the old grog-shops with their foul-weather battens up and colours half-mast.' – *English Spy*, II, 184.

medal; the finest army England had ever had was dismissed without regret or gratitude.

*

Other wartime obligations were less easy to evade. Those who had fought England's battles could be relegated to a life of selling trinkets on the highways or sweeping the London streets,[1] but not those who had lent the State cash to pay them. It was the essence of the system of financing war by borrowing that faith must be kept with the public creditor; that is, with the rich investor. The war had raised the National Debt from £252,000,000 to £861,000,000: a 'poisoned dart,' Napoleon boasted, left in England's vitals. The annual interest was £32,645,618, half again as much as the total pre-war national expenditure, and five times more than the poor rates about which so much fuss was made.

This borrowing, added to every year and at rates lower at the end of the war than at its height, and the punctual discharge of interest, was regarded as a triumph of national strength and good faith. It profoundly impressed foreigners. So did the maintenance of 'a paper currency not convertible into gold and therefore not liable to be withdrawn, and yet issued in such moderate quantities as satisfied the wants of man without exceeding them.' Since Pitt's Government, by suspending cash payments, had given the privately-owned Bank of England – the principal proprietor of the National Debt – the right to issue paper currency unbacked by gold, there had been a huge increase in circulation. Yet it had been matched by the expansion in real wealth brought about by the machinery and improved farming which an enlarged currency had helped to buy into existence. Without it Britain, under her free system, might not have defeated Napoleon.

Yet though on the whole the Bank had exercised its privilege with

1. Officers of the Rifles, passing through Knightsbridge, were sometimes startled to see a tall, military-looking man picking up bones and to recognize through his rags one of the smartest and finest-looking men in the Regiment. See Anderson, 105-6, 128-9; Bell, I, 20, 35, 80, 114-15, 120, 149-50, 157-8, 193-4; Blakeney, 332, 364-7; Castlereagh, x, 477-9; Colchester, III, 247; Costello, 18, 65, 207-8; Farington, VIII, 35-6; Fortescue, x, 160; Gardner, 262-3; Grattan, 304; Gronow, I, 182-3; *Lavengro*, 86; Hammond, *Town Labourer*, 105; Harris, 102; Napier, VI, 175; George Napier, 195; Kincaid, *Random Shots*, 251, 290; Simmons, 379; Smith, I, 320-2; *Trade Winds*, 120; Woodward, 60.

patriotism and restraint, its directors, and the provincial bankers whose private note-issues had been rendered more valuable, would have been less than human had they not pursued their monopoly of creating money to a point where the increase in note-circulation exceeded the creation of real wealth. In 1810, when the House of Commons set up a Bullion Committee to investigate, £100 of paper currency was selling on 'Change for £86 10s. Yet even this modest depreciation, as the event proved, was due more to the drain of bullion to feed Wellington's army than to internal inflation. Though speculators did a roaring trade smuggling guineas abroad,[1] and at one time a premium of nearly thirty per cent was paid for gold, the latter started to flow back to England as soon as the war ended. Considering the Bank's opportunity, the degree of permanent inflation was extraordinarily small – a tribute both to the integrity of British bankers and the increase in national production.

*

In a great nation – the first industrial and trading Power in the world – a paper currency based on public credit had been successfully substituted for one based on precious metals. It had proved capable of financing not only the war but a novel multiplication of real wealth. The increased production of farm and factory Britain had needed for victory had not been retarded by any financial inability of the home consumer to buy it into existence. What was physically possible had been rendered financially possible. But, realizing neither the character of the transformation through which the country was passing nor the permanent need under it for an elastic system of creating purchasing-power, the British people repudiated their wartime financial expedient as soon as the war ended. Anxious at the drain of bullion abroad, bewildered by economic disasters caused by the transition from war to peace, and resentful of the immense fortunes made by bankers, they saw in their unorthodox, revolutionary currency the cause of their

---

1. 'In twelve days after we left Lisbon we found ourselves off Spithead. The number of Jews who crowded the vessel was astonishing. They all sought for gold. ... One solitary guinea was all I possessed. ... For this. ... I received 30s.' Grattan, 327 (April, 1813). See also Andreades, 206–39; Ashton, I, 67–8, 72–3, 110; Colchester, II, 562; Ernle, 213; Fortescue, IX, 94; Hammond, *Town Labourer*, 107; *Paget Brothers*, 154–5; Smart, 236–56, 270, 292–304; Walpole, I, 403.

troubles. The English had a sober respect, almost veneration, for gold; they despised paper. Since the latter was the creation of a Tory Government, the first demand for a resumption of cash payments came from the Whigs, one of whose leaders, Francis Horner, had presided over the Bullion Committee of 1810. It was resisted by the Government on grounds of expediency, but gradually yielded to by Ministers as the country's troubles deepened.

The clamour for a return to gold was naturally supported by the fund-holding class. The moderate inflation of the past few years had constituted a concealed tax on the fund-holder, which observers like Simond thought just, partly because the sums lent to the State during the war had been borrowed on terms highly favourable to the lender, and partly because the 'funds' were unburdened by charges like those on land and farm produce. But this modest depreciation of the investor's capital in favour of the owner and producer of real wealth had constituted an intolerable charge on the propertyless labourer, whose wages had failed to rise as quickly as prices. The new proletariat, both rural and industrial, shared neither in the enhanced profits of farmers and manufacturers nor in the fund-holder's discount and interest. Now, by artificially enhancing through a return to gold the value of the latter's claims on the taxpayer – the producer of real wealth on whom the burden of taxation ultimately fell – the Government increased the mortgage on the nation's productive capacity. For, though the payment of the annual debt charge – approximately half the revenue raised by taxation – was only a transfer of money from one pocket of the nation to another, the fund-holders or 'tax-eaters' were not necessarily the same people as the tax-payers. The new policy of deflation increasingly handicapped the latter in their struggle to produce.[1] 'There,' wrote Cobbett six years after Waterloo, 'is the Debt pulling the nation down like as a stone pulls a dog under the water.'

In deference to the Government's plea that so early a return to gold was impracticable, the change-over was fixed for the summer of 1818. The decision, however, caused an immediate restriction in circulation.

[1]. 'The tax-receivers have got a mortgage on the property, health, strength and skill of the rest of the community who pay the taxes, which bows their industry to the ground and deprives them of the necessary means of subsistence.' – Hazlitt, *Political Essays*, 260–1.

Commercial paper under discount at the Bank of England – more than £20 million a few years earlier – sank to £11½ million in 1816 and to less than £4 million in the following year. The circulation of country banknotes dropped in proportion. The restriction coincided with a phenomenal reduction in the world's supply of precious metals and a consequent fall in global prices. Civil war in South America had dried up the chief source of bullion at the moment that Britain, with her steam-power machines and improved agriculture, had evolved a new means of multiplying real wealth. In 1816 the quantity of gold and silver raised in the Spanish colonies was only a third of what it had formerly been. In a few years the population of the mining town of Potosi fell through revolution and pestilence from 150,000 to 8000.

*

Mass production – Britain's gift to the world – necessitated mass consumption. This could only be achieved through an expansive financial policy. The indispensable means in a free society to set the wheels of the new machines turning was buying power in the pockets of those who needed their products. If, through a restriction of currency, this was lacking, the increased wealth which mechanical science offered could not be brought into existence. Those who had been drawn by the demands of war into the service of the machines and had become dependent on them, were left workless and, having no alternative means of employment, deprived of the power of buying bread. This in turn halted an expanding agricultural economy and left farmers unable to sell their produce at a time when the industrial population was starving.

In their noble belief in the validity of human freedom and the inevitability of all things operating for the best, Adam Smith and the early economists had failed to foresee this. Nor had they reckoned on the disturbing passions, destruction, and dislocation of a generation of global war financed by State borrowing. They supposed that, through the operation of a just and divinely-inspired law of supply and demand, profits, prices, and wages must invariably find their true level; that it was only necessary to remove artificial restrictions on freedom of trade and contract to ensure a beneficial and progressive equilibrium. If under free conditions wages for any reason fell, prices must automatically fall too, and employers, enabled thereby to sell a correspondingly greater quantity of goods, would be able and anxious – seeing it was their interest to increase production – to pay out, not less, but more in wages. If a labour-saving machine threw men out of work, it would soon, by reducing the price of the goods they and others needed, recall them to the same or other work through the greater demand it created. But it was now found on trial that men who were thrown out of work by new machinery, or whose wages were reduced below a certain level, could buy nothing at all and starved or grew demoralized before the operation of the laws of supply and demand had time to restore things to their proper balance. So did their children.

These laws did not, therefore, appear to be so providential as Adam Smith had supposed. They were merely inevitable. Even though machinery offered man a swifter means of satisfying his needs, their operation involved impoverishment, hunger, and degradation. The less sanguine successors of Adam Smith explained this by Malthus's melancholy theory of population and by a new law which that kindly and ingenious clergyman expounded to the world for the first time in 1814 and 1815. By an inescapable dispensation of arithmetic, he explained, there existed at any given moment a fixed sum or fund out of which wages – and taxes – could alone be paid. It was useless for workmen to agitate for, or for employers to wish to pay, more, since the only result of their succeeding must be to diminish the amount available for wages elsewhere. This thesis, explaining and vindicating the terrible economic phenomena of post-war Britain, was expanded by Ricardo, who, in a work published in 1817 that became the capitalist's Bible, concluded, by a process of unanswerable deduction from false premises, that wages invariably depended on a ratio between population and capital. Any rise in wages, by automatically stimulating an increase in population, must not only defeat its own end but lead to a general decline of the wage-level.

What manufacturers who accepted this theory overlooked was that on this seemingly insufficient wage-fund depended, not only the livelihood of the starving weaver and sweated mill-hand, but the purchasing-power which could alone keep their own factories in full operation. It was its inadequacy to feed, house, and clothe workers who were also buyers that damped down their furnaces, stopped their revolving wheels, emptied their order-books, and threatened them with periodic bankruptcy and the nation with social misery and unrest. Out of this rigid wage-fund had to come, too, the capital needed to instal new machinery or the interest on it, which, while increasing future productive potential, diminished still further the existing purchasing-power that could alone, in the wage-earners' hands, afford an effective and continuous demand for maximum current production. It was because the workers did not receive a proper share of the wealth they helped to create that such wealth did not increase to the extent the means for creating it admitted. By using their ever-growing bargaining-power to keep the wages of their employees below the maximum level of production justified, manufacturers, without realizing what they were doing, put a brake on production.

The Government was responsible in that it took no steps to restrain such greed and enforce a reasonable standard of social justice. However understandably, it failed to perceive that, with the novel means afforded by machinery for increasing real wealth, the credit of the State might be used simultaneously to reduce taxation and enlarge consuming-power to a point that would equalize it with the power to produce. With agricultural and industrial production lagging behind both capacity and demand, an expansive financial policy might have changed the whole course of the nineteenth century. By using direct taxation to check inflation in boom periods and judiciously expanding the currency to facilitate reduction of taxation in a depression, a farseeing Government might have raised the workers' standards of living step by step with the rising wealth of the capitalists. Britain might then have emerged from the Industrial Revolution one nation instead of two.

*

But both the economic experience and administrative machinery for doing anything so revolutionary were wholly lacking. The nation's only resort in the *impasse* in which it so unexpectedly found itself was usury. Like a private subject in straitened circumstances, it resorted to the pawnbroker and the banker. The era of the Regency, under all its glittering brilliance, was the age *par excellence* of the moneylender; almost everyone was borrowing or lending. 'This declining age,' Mary Mitford called it, 'when too many worthy members of the community seem to have an alacrity in sinking.' Across rich, victorious England stalked a shadow: that of the seedy individual pinched for 'the needful', whom Charles Lamb called 'the deep insolvent'. It was no accident that to this deflationary era – that of the young Dickens's martyrdom in the blacking factory – belongs the genesis of Micawber. The shadows behind countless humble English homes were the dun, the tipstaff, and the debtors' prison. They menaced the great too; Rawdon Crawley's fate was not uncommon. Any man might be 'blown up at Point Non-Plus'; John Doe, Richard Roe, and the 'leary Bum-trap' were waiting at the end of many an avenue of promise. Even Lord Byron, who inherited an estate worth £140,000 and married an heiress, had an execution in his house. There were bailiffs discreetly disguised as footmen in ducal, spendthrift Blenheim; the Horsemonger Lane jailer remarked to Leigh Hunt of the royal brothers: 'They knows me very well, mister, and, mister, I knows them!'[1]

It was the age of the great bankers – the Barings, Hopes, Coutts, Hoares, and higher Smiths,[2] negotiating loan after loan and mortgaging and buying up everything around them, prototypes of that 'morose and rigid millionaire' who Charles Greville believed would never rest till he had stripped him of his property. It was the age, above all, of the Jews who, pouring into England from Italy, Spain, Holland, and Germany, found themselves with the wealth of a confused and warring world running – not without some of it remaining – through their skilful, sensitive fingers:

> *But let us not to own the truth refuse,*
> *Was ever Christian land so rich in Jews? ...*
> *All states, all things, all Sovereigns they control*
> *And waft a loan from Indus to the pole.*[3]

1. Leigh Hunt, *Autobiography*, II, 2. See *idem*, 26; Keats, IV, 21; Leslie, *Constable*, 97–8; Lamb, VI, 578; Lockhart, IV, 218, 236; Mitford, *Our Village*, 71; *Life in London*, 274–8; *Real Life in London*, I, 328, 373.

2. *Tom Smith lives here*
   Who is made a peer
   And takes the pen from behind his ear.

Lines pinned on Lord Carrington's door. Holland, *Journal*, I, 335. See *idem*, 44; Clapham, I, 266; Cobbett, *Rural Rides*, I, 83, 85, 235; Farington, II, 110–11; VIII. 113; Greville, I, 24; Simond, I, 85, 235; II, 173.

3. Byron, *The Age of Bronze*.

Money was their medium – the invisible river that flowed beneath the Emperor's palace and the weaver's hut. Wherever there was trade, luxury, and power and men stood in need of 'the ready', they were to be found with their whispered accommodations and the shekels under their gabardines or genteel modern equivalents. The persecution which had been their age-long lot but which in England they passed out of – the ghetto garb, the locked gates at night, the jeering Gentile children, the Bashaw's dungeon, the hunter's shouts of 'Hepp!' 'Hepp!', the brutal Slav or Teuton mob[1] – had made them quick, apprehensive, cunning, ruthless, and brothers to one another all the world over. It was remarkable how swiftly in this tolerant land of opportunity the Jewish trader, chaffering old clothes or tramping the roads selling trinkets – 'cringing, chattering, and showing his teeth,' like the poor pedlar in *Lavengro* – was transformed through his genius for adaptation and the handling of money into the man of property, the banker, and country gentleman.

The greatest phenomenon of the age after Napoleon were the Roths-child brothers. Meyer Amschel Rothschild, who started his career in 'the filthy Judengasse' of Frankfurt,[2] trading old coins and making himself useful to the rich Elector of Hesse in his money-lending trans-actions, set up his five sons, born in the seventeen-seventies, in the commercial capitals of war-divided Europe. Lacking the graces of the aristocratic societies they served, and contending against constant humiliations, these astonishing brothers possessed courage, energy,

1. 'When we got nearly through the town, we saw a surly-looking German driving a poor Jew forward with foul language and making frequent use of a stick he had in his hand. The countenance of the Jew expressed neither anger nor surprise nor agitation; he spoke with meekness and, unresisting, pursued his way … The soldiers who are stationed at the draw-bridge looked very surly at him, and the countenance of the bystanders expressed cold, unfeeling cruelty.' – Dorothy Wordsworth. De Selincourt, I, 93–4.

2. Meidinger, *cit.* Clapham, I, 37. See Brownlow, 5; Castlereagh, IX, 156; Clapham, I, 37; Corti, *passim*; *English Spy*, II, 123–5, 220; *Espriella*, II, 149, 181–3; Farington, II, 109; Gronow, I, 132, 136; II, 264–5; *Lavengro*, 8; Lockhart, IV, 342; *Romany Rye*, 422–3; Roth, 237–41; Smith, I, 209–10. Forty years later Charles Greville saw the old mother of the Rothschilds, then the richest men in Europe, emerging from the wretched tenement in the Judengasse, which nothing would induce her to leave, leaning on the arm of her granddaughter, the Baroness Charles Rothschild, whose smart *calèche*, attended by liveried footmen, was wait-ing at the end of the street. Greville (Suppl.), I, 205–6.

resource, and a profound knowledge of human nature. Never missing any opportunity of profit or of what they valued more than profit – a new connexion – they made themselves indispensable to those with wealth and power, discounting bills, collecting interest, making advances, acting as intermediaries between court and court, and spiriting bullion through the blockade and armies. Their greatest service, and their own chief source of profit, was the transmission from capital to capital, and from currency to currency, of the loans and subsidies with which Britain armed her allies. Ingratiating themselves with everyone, for they could afford neither friends nor foes, they used their family network, transcending frontiers, as an unofficial international clearing-house. With governments tumbling about their ears and armies crashing through their gossamer webs of usury, they never failed to fulfil, exactly and punctually, every obligation. In a time of universal impecuniosity the House of Rothschild, whose trading profits when the war began were only a few hundreds a year, raised themselves to a position of dominating credit in almost every capital of Europe.

The English representative of the family, Nathan, started business at Manchester in his early twenties with a few thousand pounds and without a word of English. In just over twelve years he built up a vast fortune by the skill with which he used the balances sent him for investment in England by his father's European clients, by conveying bullion through the heart of France to Wellington's armies, and by transmitting to the Continent the subsidies which armed the Grand Alliance.[1] Acting as agent for the paymaster of Europe, he was able to help his brothers establish themselves in similar positions at the Courts of Austria, Prussia, and Bourbon France. In keeping with the family tradition, he made it his business to offer private accommodation on easy terms to all in high place who needed it, including, it was believed, both the Regent and the principal permanent Secretary of the Treasury. It was Nathan's courier, outdistancing Wellington's dispatches, who brought the first news of Waterloo to London. Within a few years of the battle he was said to control the national rate of exchange.

What this great man achieved on an international stage, others did on a humbler. They did not succeed without arousing resentment and

---

1. More than £20,000,000 passed through his hands on this score alone. Herries, 108; Corti, 189.

envy. Cobbett in his blind rage at the debt system – IT, as he called it – which he believed was changing the values of the England he loved, wrote of 'dark, dirty-faced, half-whiskered vermin' to whose expenditure he attributed the alarming expansion of London, Brighton, Cheltenham, and other 'odious wens'. 'You may always know them,' he wrote, 'by their lank jaws, the stiffness round their necks ... their stays, their false shoulders, hips, and haunches, their half-whiskers, and by their skins, colour of veal kidney-suet, warmed a little, and then powdered with dirty dust.'[1] He did not confine his venom to Jews; Scotsmen in his view were as bad or worse. Instead, he complained, of a resident, native gentry attached to the soil, known to every farmer and labourer from childhood, practising hospitality without ceremony, a tribe of fund-lords, contractors, loan-jobbers, brokers, and bankers were buying up the entire countryside near the capital – 'a gentry only now-and-then residing, having no relish for country delights, foreign in their manners, distant and haughty in their behaviour, looking to the soil only for its rents, viewing it as a mere object of speculation, unacquainted with its cultivators, despising them and their pursuits, and relying for influence, not upon the good will of the vicinage but the dread of their power.'[2] It was from this class that the great economist, Ricardo, came – a most kindly, amiable man, inheriting a younger son's portion from his Dutch-Jewish father, starting life in a stock-jobber's office at fourteen and making a fortune before he was forty, when he purchased the estate of Gatcombe Park in Gloucestershire. Later, buying an Irish rotten borough, he entered Parliament where, despite his painful lack of oratory, he became immensely respected, his economic views being treated by all Parties almost as holy writ.

*

'According to the best information I can obtain,' wrote a correspondent in the October after Waterloo, 'the landlords will fall short of their Michaelmas receipts upon an average one half.' All over the country banks were calling in their money; some, like that in which Jane Austen's brother was a partner, had already closed their doors and stopped payment. The *Gazette* was crowded with bankruptcy notices and tradesmen's books with bad debts, and the table of the House of

1. Cobbett, *Rural Rides*, I, 68–9. See *idem*, I, 30, 38–9, 65.
2. Cobbett, *Rural Rides*, I, 33–4.

Commons piled with petitions from farmers and manufacturers. Cotton spinners in Lancashire and on the Clyde, hardware workers in Birmingham and iron-moulders at Merthyr Tydfil, Spitalfields silk-weavers, Leicestershire stockingers, and Nottinghamshire hosiers, all were hungry, angry, and clamorous.

As 1815 gave place to 1816 the situation grew worse. With bankers unwilling to advance or discount, no one, not even the rich, seemed to have any money to spare; by the spring ten thousand livery servants were said to be out of place. Among those who went down in the general ruin was Beau Brummell, the great dandy, who decamped for Calais with a few pounds. Another was Sheridan – 'the last of the giants'. Art prices fell to a level unknown in the history of the sale rooms; at Phillips's a Claude which had fetched a thousand guineas in 1813 went for £70. Even Sir William Beechey was forced to beg for a settlement of his account with the royal household, 'the unexpected alteration of the times making a shocking impression on the arts.' The only thing which seemed to sell in the universal ruin were Scott's novels.[1]

The summer of 1816 proved the worst in memory, though in a brief spell of fine weather at the end of May young Keats, after a day in the Hampstead meadows, wrote his sonnet, 'I stood tiptoe upon a little hill'. Six weeks later, in a torrential July, Jane Austen among the sodden Hampshire fields finished her last and greatest book. 'Oh! it rains again! it beats against the window,' she told a friend, 'we were obliged to turn back before we got there, but not soon enough to avoid a pelter all the way home. We met Mr Woolls. ... I talked of its being bad weather for the hay, and he returned me the comfort of its being much worse for the wheat.' Such a summer, her fellow writer, Mary Mitford, thought, was enough to make one wish for winter all the year round.[2]

1. Alison, I, 81; *Ann. Reg.*, 1816, 54; Colchester, II, 558, 560, 562, 584–5; Creevey, *Life and Times*, 102; George IV, *Letters*, II, 167–8; Hill, *Austen*, II, 244–5; Lockhart, III, 296, 333; IV, 2, 11; Lady Shelley, I, 186; Smart, 462, 512–13.

2. It is snowing and hailing eternally and will kill all the lambs to a certainty unless it changes in a few hours. At any rate, it will cure us of the embarrassments arising from plenty and low markets.' – Walter Scott, April 18th 1816. Lockhart, IV, 4–5. See *idem*, 9–10; Austen, II, 457–9; Colchester, II, 586; Colvin, *Keats*, 36; Hill, *Austen*, 249–57; Mitford, I, 333–4; Newton, 17, 27; *Paget Brothers*, 290; Smart, 490.

It was the same all over western Europe. The English visitors who flocked to the Continent that summer – the first without war in fourteen years – found sullen, pitiless clouds, and the crops destroyed by snow and hailstones. Such stupid mists, fogs, and perpetual density suggested to Byron that Castlereagh must have taken over the Foreign Affairs of the Kingdom of Heaven. Meanwhile, in every port British goods were piling up or selling below cost. During one week that year not a single entry for export or import was made at the London Custom-House – an event without parallel in its history.[1] The whole of the manufacturing districts seemed to be out of work. The unemployed colliers of Bilston Moor, with fifty men yoked to a wagon, set off with their coal for the capital to petition the Prince Regent; other teams of miners followed their example, and magistrates were kept busy intercepting them. A poor Lincolnshire widow, trudging from door to door trying to sell pasteboard boxes with her hungry boy trailing behind her, was followed by a blasphemous chimney-sweep who told her, with what seemed unanswerable logic, that if she did not sell the child for the two guineas which he flourished in his grimy hand she would soon be in the workhouse. In vain did Wilberforce and his friends revive the Association for the Relief of the Manufacturing and Labouring Poor, founded in the slump of 1812, and assemble the Archbishop of Canterbury and three royal dukes at a public meeting at the London Tavern. In such a deluge of ruin, private alms availed nothing; they could not distribute incomes.

*

In their tribulation the people turned to Throne and Parliament. They found small comfort in either. The old, blind king was irrevocably mad – immured with his medical attendants in a wing of Windsor Castle, 'with long, unkempt, milk-white beard,' talking incessantly, of the dead. The royal family was represented by his martinet queen and his seven stout, bald sons. The big man of all, Prinny, wrote Creevey, was ill in the bladder and afraid to show himself in the streets;[2] his brothers deep in debt and involved in ludicrous

1. *Morning Chronicle*, July 3rd 1816. See Creevey, *Life and Times*, 103–4; Farington, VIII, 83, 95, 100.

2. 'Not even the intoxication of that greatest of all victories, Waterloo, could extract from the Mob a single indication of applause for him on the day he

controversies and scandals; his wife – a pantomime source of ribaldry and indecorum – gallivanting round the Mediterranean with an amorous Italian courier and a court of rogues and buffoons. The Regent's girth was said by malicious gossip to have grown so vast that his doctors had advised him to give up stays and let his belly drop; the cartoonists portrayed him with dewlaps hanging like bags over his tight dandy's collar. To millions of decent folk his life seemed a perpetual scandal and his squandérous profusion, as a member of Parliament put it, more suggestive of the splendour of an oriental despot than 'the sober dignity of a British prince seated in the bosom of his subjects.' At the moment he was engaged on his most costly project – the rebuilding of the west end of his capital; a fashionable new park to bear his name and a sweeping avenue designed by his favourite Nash to give western London a north-south axis. That spring, while the sheep perished in the snows and an ailing Jane Austen, propped on two chairs, wrote and rewrote the closing chapters of *Persuasion*, he married his daughter, the heiress of England, to an obscure German prince; the bride could not help laughing at the words 'With all my worldly goods I thee endow,' for the bridegroom was so poor. A week earlier Lord Byron, publicly reviling his wife, attacked in a sensational novel by his mistress, and believed to be guilty of incest with his sister, left England in a blaze of notoriety.

*

If the Crown could not rally a distressed nation, Parliament provided an ineffective sounding-board for its grievances. Representing neither the small manufacturing middle class nor the hungry workers, its members had little understanding of the suffering caused by the crisis. Nor had the King's Ministers. 'Mouldy & Co.', as the young Whigs called them after the worthy, melancholy man who had stepped into the murdered Perceval's shoes, were still young in years – their leader was not yet forty-five – but the cares of war and revolution, continued throughout their adult lives, had robbed them of all spring. Lord

closed Parliament. They seem'd to think they did a great deal by maintaining a *dead silence* and no hissing, but they made loud and repeated applauses when the Duke of York's carriage appeared.' – Festing, 176–7. See Bury I, 262; II, 6–8, 20–4, 41, 50–3, 88–9, 92–3; *Creevey Papers*, I, 206–9; Creevey, *Life and Times*, 82; George IV, *Letters*, II, 97–8, 110–11, 120–1, 349; Gronow, II, 255–6; Dudley, 292; Stanhope, 174.

Liverpool, like most of his lieutenants, was of gentle rather than aristocratic origin – the son of Charles Jenkinson, Lord Bute's political
factotum. As Lord Hawkesbury he had been Foreign Secretary in the
well-meaning Addington Administration that had tried to appease
Napoleon, and he had never recovered his spirits after that early
blight. His high, stiff look, bold nose, strained mouth, the sorrowful,
blinking, rather defiant eyes, the long, awkward, slouching neck bespoke the character, not infrequent in the second generation of *arri-
vistes*, of a stubborn bewilderment. Like most appeasers who have been
humiliated by the object of their appeasement, he had become, in his
quiet, unemphatic way, an unshakable believer in the folly of compromise. He was thus the ideal leader of a party based on resistance to
change, and the worst for guiding a country through a revolution.

He was by nature a kindly and not illiberal man. But the horrors of
Revolution – he had personally witnessed the storming of the Bastille –
and of long battling with Napoleon had frozen his sympathies. He had
the virtue, desirable in the leader of an Administration, of being a
disinterested, honourable colleague, and of knowing how to keep his
mouth shut; Madame de Staël remarked that he had a talent for silence.
In his uninspiring way he held the reins of party firmly and fairly.
Though often testy and sometimes, when his royal master was
unendurable, querulous, he seldom lost his head and never snubbed
slower or stupider men into resentment, or aroused jealousy.

His colleagues were of a piece. They made no pretence to genius,
though one of them, Castlereagh – as trusted in the Commons as at the
Congress table – had great, if inarticulate, ability. The antithesis of the
daemonic, Napoleonic, or Byronic ideal which was the *ignis fatuus* of
the age, they appealed to quiet men of property and commerce; a
Ministry, as one supporter gratefully put it, without any of those
'confounded men of genius'. They represented 'the fear of democracy
and the general property of the country'; they were inexorably opposed to what they called 'the democratic spirit of the times' and
thought anyone infected with it either wicked or deluded. They stood
for Church and King, a 'Bible, Crown, and Constitution supremacy':
for Bishops, rectors, and Justices of the Peace, for Fellows of Oxford
Colleges and honest, old-fashioned shopkeepers and steady merchants,
for rents, tithes, and investments, for the *status quo* in thought and deed.

Their idea of the future was an unending extension of the present, though the old Lord Chancellor, Eldon – a rugged, self-made man of stoic character – dreamt of something more positive: a return to the tougher, more robust England of his youth before the French and American Revolutions.

Their enemies thought that they remained in office from love of power, their friends supposed it to be a habit of which they could not break themselves. They themselves attributed it to a sense of duty – 'shadows who work all day in the cabinet and wrangle all night in the House, baited like bears at the stake.' In this they were nearer the truth than the world supposed; for men of moderate ambitions, possessed of ample fortunes, there was nothing very attractive in guiding a high-spirited people through an interminable series of insoluble crises while enduring the vagaries of a spoilt unscrupulous Prince and the sallies of an irresponsible Opposition. It was their firm, unalterable conviction that they stood between the country and revolution; in this, by re-maining in office – pilots, in Byron's jeering phrase, who had weathered every storm – they conceived themselves to be carrying on her struggle against Napoleon and the armed Jacobin. From that war there was for them no discharge. They received the support of all who thought, like Walter Scott and Dorothy Wordsworth, that those who demanded change were 'rogue radicals' and 'incendiaries'.[1] They were also sup-ported by Wilberforce and his Evangelical 'saints', who believed that the nation should endure affliction with resignation, that the glory of the poor was to be patient in adversity and of the rich not to question the dispensations of Providence but to live piously and soberly in gratitude for saving mercies.

The Opposition represented the great Whig Dukes and land-owners – the Grenvilles, Cavendishes, Russells, and Fitzmaurices; the disciples of Fox, led by Lord Grey and Fox's nephew, Lord Holland; a sprinkling of young patricians of rather raffish, radical views; the respectable middle-class intellectuals of the *Edinburgh Review*; and

1. See Mrs Arbuthnot, *Journal*, May 1st 1820; Sept. 23rd 1820; Auckland, IV, 385; Brock, *passim*; Byron, *Age of Bronze*; De Selincourt, *Middle Years*, II, 569, 806–15; Farington, VII, 87; Leigh Hunt, *Autobiography*, I, 246; Keats, IV, 320; Lockhart, III, 112; IV, 125; V, 357; *Quarterly Review*, 1843, IV, 125 – Article by Rev. T. James; Simond, II, 161; Stanhope, 287; *Two Duchesses*, 362; Wood-ward, 50; Yonge, *passim*.

the Nonconformists. They enjoyed the rather disapproving support of the utilitarian radicals, the followers of the rich jurist, Jeremy Bentham, whose programme was the greatest good of the greatest number ascertainable by processes of strictly logical deduction never likely to be pursued by any political Party. Weak in numbers through their unpopular opposition to the war, the Whigs made up for it by their eloquence and capacity for faction. They were great hands at denouncing everything Government did, but fundamentally, except for the extreme radical left wing, believed in much the same things as their opponents. They supported the hereditary peerage, the rule of law, the sanctity of inherited property, *laissez faire*, the right of traders and capitalists to pursue their own unrestrained advantage, and the subordination of the lower orders to their social superiors.[1]

Like most politicians who have been too long in opposition and lack a leader, the Whigs found it hard to get on with one another.[2] Since Fox's death, ten years before, their only real allegiance had been to his ghost. Their most brilliant orator, Sheridan, had long drunk himself into a decline, while the rising hope of the Party, the lawyer Brougham, was too erratic, pushing, and plebeian to be trusted by his colleagues. Whitbread, the brewer, a shrewd honourable man, had committed suicide a few weeks after Waterloo. The titular leader of the Party in the Commons, George Ponsonby, was in failing health, and his lieutenant, Tierney, the son of an Irish wine merchant, was known to its irreverent younger members as Mother Cole.[3] The most distinguished Whig in the Lower House was Romilly, the advocate of penal reform and a foe of every form of cruelty and oppression.

1. Hazlitt remarked that the two parties were like rival stage-coaches; they splashed each other with mud but went to the same place.
2. 'They are a very powerful Party, indeed, if they would but abstain from fighting with each other ... which makes it so unpleasant to have anything to do with them.' – Dudley, 184. See *idem*, 198. See Broughton, I, 138, 179; Cecil, *Young Melbourne*, 210; *Creevey Papers*, I, 124, 164, 172, 192, 207, 324, 327; *Life and Times*, 55; Granville, II, 485–6, 493–4; Halévy, II, 53–4; Holland, *Journal*, I, 28; Moore, *Byron*, 182, 184, 345; Simond, II, 25, 35, 163; Stanley, 79–81; Woodward, 53–6, 76.
3. After his habit of referring to himself as a plain, honest man, like the lady in Foote's farce who presided over a female establishment in Covent Garden and loved to indulge in flattering references to her own character. *Creevey Papers*, I, 327.

For the Whigs the crisis was an opportunity. Only one of the Ministers – 'a good, quiet, easily-beaten set of blockheads' – was capable of a tolerable speech, and he, Canning – the fallen Tory arch-angel and the one man of genius among Pitt's followers – was so dis-trusted by most of his colleagues as to seem a negligible factor. 'Our ground,' wrote Brougham to Creevey, 'is clearly retrenchment in all its ways, with ramifications into the royal family, property tax, jobs of all sorts and distresses of the landed interest; in short it is the richest mine in the world!' The clamour for tax reduction became almost deafening. The Government, inundated with petitions from the com-mercial interest – assiduously collected by Brougham – and threatened by its own supporters, promised to reduce expenditure from a hundred to eighty millions and jettisoned the income and malt taxes. Castle-reagh, fearful for the peace of Europe, spoke sadly of an ignorant impatience of taxation; the Services were again drastically cut. The Regent, too, was forced to abandon his hope of crowning his metro-politan improvements with a new palace,[1] and the northward march of Regent Street was halted at Piccadilly Circus. Even the Elgin Marbles were nearly sent packing back to Greece. 'Economy is the order of the day,' wrote Walter Scott, 'and I assure you they are shaving properly close.'[2]

Yet, for all these measures, the distresses of the country increased. With the corn sprouting in October, wheat touched 103s. in Decem-ber. In Ireland, where the potato crop failed, the poor were reduced to stalks and nettles. Bamford saw an unemployed calico weaver's wife drop dead from hunger, with her babe at her breast, as she begged be-fore the Middleton overseers for relief. A Scotsman travelling across England at the year's end found half the houses along the road with placards announcing the sale of farming stock. Everywhere farmers were ruined, bankers failing, the bread like dough. The odious cotton and worsted mills, Dorothy Wordsworth wrote from Halifax, had become mere incumbrances on the ground. 'Few get more than half

1. 'Our fat friend will have to live within compass and fire off no more crackers in the Park.' – Walter Scott to J. B. S. Morritt, Lockhart, IV, 10–11.

2. Lockhart, IV, 7, 10–11. See Alison, 86–7, 94–7; Brougham, II, 303–5, 312; Colchester, II, 579; *Creevey Papers*, I, 247–8; *Life and Times*, 99–100; *Farington*, VIII, 77–8; George IV, *Letters*, II, 154–5, 158–9; Halévy, II, 6–8; Hansard, XXXIV–XXXV; Peel, I, 211, 216–17; Smart, 466–70, 497, 539.

work – great numbers none at all. ... For a time whole streets – men, women, and children – may be kept alive by public charity, but the consequences will be awful if nothing can be manufactured in these places where such numbers of people have been gathered together. It can never be expected, or even wished, I think, that the state of our manufactures should ever again be what it has been, but, if there be not a revival of trade in a smaller way, people and things cannot go on as they are.' The national debt, it was rumoured, was to be wiped out, and Parliament reformed.[1]

*

Humbler men, no more able to understand what ailed their country than their rulers, took their own remedy. Throughout 1816 a savage anger, unknown in England since the Civil War, spread through the labouring classes. It began in the early summer among the population of the enclosed villages. In Suffolk, Essex, Norfolk, and Cambridge-shire ricks and barns were burnt, some by night and others openly by day, while crowds surrounded mills and bakeries shouting for price reductions. The worst outbreak was at Littleport, where the cellars were broken into and the town subjected to a sack. Anxious Justices were sent galloping Londonwards for help, and cavalry was dispatched to the shires. At Cambridge, where the arrival of the fenmen was hourly expected, three hundred special constables were enrolled and the Vice-Chancellor prepared to arm the undergraduates.

Despite resort by a Special Commission to the gallows – Government's sovereign remedy for all ills – the rioting spread first to the south-west and then to the manufacturing districts. The pitmen of the Tyneside and Staffordshire, the Irish slum-dwellers of Glasgow, who, nestling in crowds about the Calton, Bridgeton, and Gorbals, were always ripe for mischief, the housewives of Sunderland, the Preston weavers, and Welsh iron moulders all attacked shops and factories. In October the employees of the Tredegar ironworks, faced by further wage reductions and rising prices, marched on Merthyr Tydfil to stop the blast furnaces. Later, 12,000 strong, they crossed the mountains to

1. *Ann. Reg.* 1816, Chron. 111–12, 167; Ashton, II, 97–8; Bamford, II, 56–8; Colchester, II, 584; De Selincourt, II, 765–8; *Hamilton of Dalzell* MS., p. 108; Hansard, XXXIX, 1430; Smart, 490, 492, 512, 540; Tooke, II, 12.

call out the colliers of Crundin, Newbridge, and Abercarne. Only the arrival of the military prevented worse.[1]

The most alarming outbreak of all came at the year's end. Throughout the autumn the radicals of the capital had been gathering strength. At a charitable meeting for the relief of the manufacturing poor organized by Wilberforce and presided over by the Duke of York, they shouted the royal chairman down and forced him to leave amid storms of booing. All over the country the revived Hampden Clubs, thrown open to the workers by penny-a-week subscriptions, met in alehouses and dissenting chapels to debate manhood suffrage and annual parliaments. Their proceedings were kept at fever heat by Cobbett, who, evading the stamp duty on cheap newspapers by issuing his *Political Register* as a twopenny pamphlet, sold nearly 50,000 copies of a single number. Thereafter he repeated his defiance weekly. Mass meetings occurred in all the principal industrial towns; at Manchester, Glasgow, and Paisley over a hundred thousand were reported to have attended. In the middle of November a still larger gathering took place in Spa Fields, London, when the orator, Henry Hunt, supported by the tricolour and a cap of Liberty on a pike, told an excited crowd that their all was being taxed to pension the bastards of the Tory aristocracy. He ended by promising to carry their petition – 'the last resort before physical force' – to the Prince Regent. A few days later Shelley, writing to Byron in Italy, predicted either radical reform when Parliament met in January or the triumph of anarchy and illiterate demagogues.

On December 2nd a further mass meeting was called in Spa Fields. It was preceded by a distribution of handbills proclaiming that death would be a relief to millions. Yet just as Hunt had stolen the earlier meeting from the parliamentary demagogue, Sir Francis Burdett, so Hunt's limelight was now stolen by a wagon load of fanatics supported by a gang of seamen with revolutionary tricolours. Two rabble-rousers named Watson, after inflammatory orations, asked who would follow them. Thereupon, before Hunt had even arrived, the sailors and a portion of the crowd set off for a gunsmith's shop and, after killing a merchant, marched on the City. They were opposed at the Royal

---

1. *Ann. Reg.* 1816. Chron., 60, 64–5, 67–71, 73–6, 79, 93, 100–1, 115–18, 127, 165–8, 173–4; Ashton, II, 89–94; Bamford, II, 11; Colchester, II, 595; Coupland, *Wilberforce*, 419–20; Halévy, II, 8–14; Newton, 34; Smart, 489, 492.

Exchange by the Lord Mayor with a small detachment of police officers, whereupon they made off with a great hullabulloo for the Minories, where they broke into two more gunsmiths' and acquired two small cannon. Later, after a futile summons to the Tower and a skirmish with the Life Guards in Aldgate High Street, they dispersed in small groups, whooping, breaking windows, and robbing passers-by.[1]

*

Across the sea, those who wished England well watched anxiously. In Dublin, Robert Peel was asked whether it was true that the Duke of York was at the head of the Guards leading the people against his brother. The Regent had his pictures at Carlton House valued and insured. All the world was awaiting the opening of Parliament in January when it was known that the reformers were to present petitions with half a million signatures. The National Convention of People's Delegates in London passed a resolution in favour of universal suffrage; the Lancashire delegates demanded annual Parliaments, manhood suffrage at eighteen, equal electoral districts, and the exclusion of placemen and pensioners.[2]

On the morning of January 28th, at the Golden Cross Hotel in Charing Cross, Hunt, in all the glory of blue lapelled coat, top-boots, and white hat and kerseys, handed the petitions to Lord Cochrane, who was to carry them to the Lords. The tribune of the people was in roaring spirits, rolling and unrolling the scrolls and exchanging greetings with the crowd. Later Lord Cochrane was borne shoulder-high to Westminster Hall, where it took him two hours to unload his petitions. Meanwhile the Regent, surrounded by Life Guards, drove to Parliament amid storms of abuse and ribaldry. As the royal cortège returned down the Mall, the glass of his coach was broken in two places, either by stones or by a bullet from an airgun.[3]

*

The attack startled the country. From the Government's point of view the effect was salutary. It made the Regent, in Scott's words, 'a good

1. Alington, 72–3; *Ann. Reg.* 1816, Chron., 190–1; Ashton, II, 122–30; Byron, *Corr.*, II, 20–2; Halévy, II, 18; Colchester, II, 581; Smart, 493; *State Trials.*

2. Bamford, II, 13–14, 24–6; Byron, *Corr.*, II, 31; Farington, VIII, 106; Halévy, II, 20–1; Moore, *Byron*, 330–1, 337; Peel, I, 235; Smart, 545–7; Trevelyan, *Grey*.

3. Ashton, II, 135–6; Bamford, II, 19, 21–2; Colchester, II, 599–601; Gronow, II, 308–9; Halévy, II, 21–2; Lockhart, IV, 43; Peel, I, 237.

manageable boy,' and sobered the House of Commons. For, as reports poured in from the provinces of designs for midnight risings, secret orders for pikes, and overtures to the armed forces, Whig and Tory alike stiffened against the reformers. If it was to come to a fight for hearth and home, Englishmen knew where they stood.

There was reason for alarm. The English poor were not weaklings; they were suffering almost beyond endurance. They were passionate, easily swayed by rumour, and uneducated. Behind the stubborn, rather bewildered, law-abiding artisan, marching with banners to demand bread or debating the Constitution in his penny Hampden Club, lurked a more menacing figure. The slums of London and the industrial towns swarmed with criminal types who, led by demagogues, were as capable of a massacre as their Paris prototypes. During that winter even the prisoners in Newgate rioted and attacked their jailers. The roughness of that outcast populace was a constant menace to a rich society. Such folk could not be ruled by milksops. Their blood was up; when Cashman, the man who committed the Spa Fields murder, was hanged, he shouted from the cart, 'Hurrah! my boys, I'll die like a man; give me three cheers when I trip!' and then to the hangman as the mob yelled encouragement, 'Come, Jack, you —, let go the jib-boom!'[1]

The rulers of England faced their peril with courage. Though unimaginative and narrow, they had strong nerves. They had not fought Napoleon and the Revolution to shrink from Orator Hunt and a pack of weavers. Even 'goody' Sidmouth – 'Britain's guardian gander' of invasion days – declared that no man was fit to be Minister to whom it was not a matter of indifference whether he died in bed or on the scaffold. Resolved to maintain public order, he and his colleagues made no concessions to popularity. Confronting committees of both Houses with widespread evidence of an intended insurrection, they suspended *habeas corpus*, stopped the unemployed 'blanketeers' who tried to march on London, and sent Bow Street runners to Lancashire to arrest the ringleaders. They enrolled special constables, strengthened the law against attempts to seduce soldiers from their duty, and took measures

1. Ashton, II, 98–9, 130. See Bury, I, 148; De Selincourt, II, 783–4, 813–15; Farington, VIII, 199; Gronow, I, 220–1; Dudley, 308; Lockhart, IV, 125, 128; Neumann, 36; Robinson, I, 389; Lady Shelley, I, 8; Woodward, 191.

to put down Cobbett, whose 'twopenny trash' threatened to turn every working man who could read into an agitator. Fearful of arrest for debt, the great journalist fled to America.

These measures – even the Cambridge Union Society had to suspend its meetings – were in quieter times condemned as alarmist. Owing to the inadequacy of administrative machinery, they were vitiated by the use of *agents provocateurs* and corrupt informers. But they succeeded in their object. Within a few months the epidemic of arson, strikes, and riots had ceased. Shelley wrote to Byron that Ministers had gained a victory undisturbed by a single murmur, 'save those of famine which they have troops of hireling soldiers to repress.' By the autumn most of the Government's measures were tacitly dropped as needless, though the suspension of *habeas corpus* continued till the beginning of the following year. Even in Ireland there was quiet.

Yet though England's rulers, in their fear of Jacobinism, closed down on the political aspirations of the workers, they showed little vindictiveness. Despite their lack of imagination and understanding they still behaved, even when scared, as members of a Christian society. Though Ministers, magistrates, and manufacturers were all convinced of the hopelessness of interfering with economic law, the Staffordshire gentleman who put himself and his family on short rations to feed the unemployed was characteristic of thousands.[1] It was still unnatural for Englishmen of different classes to hate one another. When the St Albans Justices stopped the Bilston colliers' march to Carlton House, pointing out that their action might result in a breach of the peace, the hungry, angry men listened with attention, admitted they had been ill-advised, and expressed their readiness to return home, and were helped to do so by a subscription. Bamford and his fellow radicals, though wrongly charged, were treated with courtesy and consideration by the Privy Council who examined them. The number brought to trial for treasonable conspiracy and libel was comparatively small, and most were acquitted, including Watson, the leader of the Spa Fields Riots, and the bloodthirsty Arthur Thistlewood, who had carried the tricolour in the attack on the Tower. Orator Hunt was not prosecuted at all.

---

1. *Ann. Reg.* 1817 Chron., 2, 239; Halévy, II, 28–9, 54–5; Harriet Granville, I, 129; Holland, *Journal*, I, 105; Lockhart, IV, 25–6, 98; Newton, 10, 78, 81, 85; Smart, 564–6; Young, 470–1.

And, after an intense but temporary spell of suffering, trade revived, as the economist Ricardo had always predicted. The prices of manufactures having fallen to rock-bottom, foreign customers began to buy again, and, employment improving as a result, internal purchasing-power became more plentiful. By the autumn the monthly average of bankruptcies was only a quarter what it had been at the beginning of the year. Agriculture revived, too, while the lovely summer of 1817 and moderate imports of foreign grain under the sliding scale kept the cost of bread within tolerable limits for the urban worker. Consols, which had been down to 63, recovered to 80. England was becoming herself again.[1]

*

She was still immensely strong and rich. A gentleman wrote that if he were to shut his eyes and open his ears he would believe the country ruined, but if he were to open his eyes and shut his ears, he would think it the most prosperous in the world. Even in the terrible summer of 1816, when her trade was at a standstill and her harvest ruined, Lord Exmouth with the Mediterranean Fleet stood in under the guns of the pirate stronghold of Algiers and, in pursuance of an international policy agreed at Vienna, destroyed, in an eight-hour bombardment, forts defended by 40,000 men, ending the cruel trade in Christian slaves which had terrorized the Mediterranean for centuries. On the second anniversary of Waterloo the Regent went down the river in his crimson and scarlet barge to open the new Strand bridge – London's fourth – while the throng of buntinged boats stretched from shore to shore and flags on enormous poles flew over the heads of watching multitudes. Another bridge of cast-iron was building a few hundred yards downstream, to be paid for like the other by tolls levied by the capitalists who erected it. During 1818 every building site on either side of Regent Street was taken, and the great avenue, halted at Piccadilly a year before, resumed its majestic sweep towards the Marylebone fields where Nash was laying out Doric-pillared crescents. In all the environs

1. *Ann. Reg.* 1817, Chron., 5, 16, 19–21; Alington, 73; Ashton, II, 141–2; Bamford, I, 10; II, 24–5, 31, *et seq.*; Colchester, II, 604–7; Cole, *Cobbett,* 217; Fortescue, *British Statesmen of the Great War,* 168; Halévy, II, 18–26; *Lieven Letters,* 1812–14, 30–1, 42; Mitford, *Life,* II, 1–3; Newton, 57; Peel, I, 237–8; Smart, 548–9; Woodward, 61–2.

of London neat, blue-slated terraces were rising on either side of the trunk roads, and pseudo-Grecian edifices of white stucco were replacing the red and grey bricks of the sober Hanoverian past. So were stately club houses with wonderful cellars and kitchens, vast docks with attendant slums, and grim prisons built on principles which made escape impossible. Soon, it was rumoured, Oxford Street was to be extended as far as Bayswater brook, making it the longest street in Europe. Gas was twinkling – still a little uncertainly – in shop windows, and steamers, blowing black smoke from high, thin funnels, were appearing in rivers and estuaries; Keats on a walking tour through the Highlands was astonished to see one on Loch Lomond. Others, with the help of sails, braved the waters of the Channel, or, despite an occasional tendency to explode,[1] carried parasoled ladies and top-hatted gentlemen on summer outings to Richmond and Hampton Court. And all the while the wheels of the north country factories turned ever faster and the smoking chimneys multiplied, and the ships of Britain carried goods to the farthest corners of the earth. Castlereagh, speaking in the Commons, described 1818 as 'the most splendid year ever known in the history of British commerce.' That autumn a vessel sailing from the Hooghly anchored in the river at Okhotsk and discharged her cargo, to the amazement of the inhabitants, into a Siberian warehouse.[2]

Yet underlying all this prosperity – the glittering streets and great houses where the 'fifteen hundred fillers of hot rooms called the fashionable world' supped nightly on ortolans and champagne, the ever-lengthening chain of mail coaches speeding across the land, the stupendous bridges planned to span the Menai Strait, Tyne estuary, and Avon gorge – the foundations remained troubled. In vain did the favoured architects of Society press forward with the new churches which Parliament had voted and towards which the pious were so liberally subscribing, so that, as Arthur Young put it, the poor might learn 'the doctrines of that truly excellent religion which exhorts to

1. 'As the steam-packet from Norwich to Yarmouth was pushing from its moorings the vessel blew up, eight persons were killed; seven had almost every limb broken; the whole were thrown in different directions, and to a considerable distance.' – *Ann. Reg.* 1817, Chron., 24. See *idem.* 54–5; Broughton, II, 133–4; Colchester, III, 91–2; Colvin, *Keats*, 287; Holland, *Journal*, I, 35; Woodward, 40.   2. *Ann. Reg.* 1818, Chron., 577–83. See Smart, 671.

content and to submission to the higher powers.' Discharged sailors and soldiers still begged, half-naked, in the gutters. Stendhal, visiting the capital, was shocked by the fear of starvation that haunted her outcasts; 'such,' he wrote, 'was the fruits of England's victory.' In the bitter winter of 1819–20 a poor woman who lived alone in Stewart's-rents, Drury Lane, in a room without bed or furniture, was asked by another still poorer creature – 'a heap of bones covered with rags and filth' – to let her boil a potato at her tiny fire where, being granted permission to lie down on the bare floor, she died from want of clothes and nourishment.[1] Many others, of whom there was no memorial, perished like her.

*

The boom of 1818 which followed the post-war slump was short-lived. In the summer of 1819 the same phenomena recurred – glutted foreign markets, slashed wages, shrinking purchasing-power and men and women unable to buy the goods whose sale would have given them the wherewithal to live. With their reappearance vanished the belief that the disaster and misery out of which Britain had so painfully climbed was something exceptional, attributable solely to the transition from war to peace. The storm had returned, and without explanation. Yet the Government's attitude to it remained one of invincible helplessness. 'Mr Bamford,' said Lord Sidmouth, when that honest weaver was discharged by the Privy Council, 'I would have you to impress seriously on your mind that the present system of distress of the country arises from unavoidable circumstances.' Convinced of this, Ministers and the ruling classes were bewildered by the growing bitterness of the poor; the kindly magistrate who visited Bamford in prison remarked that it was a pity that men should be so deluded. Yet, as the latter pointed out to Sidmouth, had the gentry investigated the conditions of their humbler countrymen, they would have seen that they were intolerable. It was England's tragedy that in the social revolution that followed the war those who had led their country so well in battle should have felt so little call to give them leadership in peace and have confined themselves to the negative task of repressing the

---

1. *Ann. Reg.* 1820, Chron., 7. See *idem*, 3, 5, 11. See also Ashton, II, 162–3; Colchester II, 561; III, 8; Coupland, *Wilberforce*; Woodward, 487.

disorder caused by the ensuing economic anarchy. Their only remedy – one instituted more as a safeguard for their property than as a cure for poverty – was to hasten the return to gold.

Proud and independent Englishmen who, through no fault of their own, had seen their livelihood destroyed, their savings expended, their homes sold up, did not take kindly to the cold, patronizing charity which was bestowed on them by the distant rich: to soup-kitchens, mendicity societies, workhouses, and the rates in aid of wages which condemned their children to exile and slavery and themselves to a detested surveillance. Even the good works of the untiring Evangelicals only embittered them the more. It was at this time that the man who had abolished the African slave trade became known to his poorer countrymen as Mr Cantwell. Major Cartwright, the kindly, middle-class counsellor of the radical artisans, recorded a conversation with Wilberforce in which the latter expressed the hope that they would meet in a better world; 'I answered,' commented Cartwright, 'that I hoped we should first mend the world we were in.'[1] Cobbett, writing from America, delighted his working-class readers with accounts of a land where there were not only no 'long-sworded and whiskered captains, no Judges escorted from town to town by dragoons, no packed juries of obsequious tenants, no hangings and rippings up,' but also 'no Wilberforces: think of that – no Wilberforces!'

For England's achievements and their own prosperity had a little upset the balance of her sheltered classes; in the face of their fellows' suffering their complacency had become outrageous. 'What mercies do we enjoy in the midst of a roaring ocean on all sides,' Wilberforce had written during the war; 'never surely was there so highly favoured a country as this, above all, our spiritual privileges.' Many earnest and worthy Evangelicals – though not Wilberforce himself – continued to think like this even when their starving countrymen were being mangled by steel traps or sentenced to life-long transportation for being found at night with poaching weapons. The treadmill struck Miss Berry as an excellent punishment; she watched the prisoners at Cambridge, twenty ascending the wheel at once, with a satisfaction bordering on enthusiasm. It was this heartless unconcern that provoked the young poet Shelley, after vainly seeking shelter one January night

1. Cartwright, I, 300.

for a poor woman found in a fit on Hampstead Heath, to address a deprecatory householder: 'It is such men as you who madden the spirits and patience of the poor; and, if ever a convulsion comes in this country, you will see your house, that you refuse to put the miserable woman into, burnt over your head!'[1]

To all this there was only one answer – growing and bitter resentment. When a Huddersfield manufacturer was shot at his door, a cheer went up from every rooftop in the neighbourhood. The class consciousness of the rich, Bamford wrote, had filled the poor with contempt for everyone with a decent coat. Even the unjealous Keats, Haydon related, developed a 'fierce hatred of rank'. The Leeds clothiers at a mass meeting on Hunslet Moor voted that the Savings Bank scheme, then being instituted by philanthropists to help the working classes, was an insult when nearly three-fourths of them were out of employ. Through the propertyless workers ran a growing consciousness of exclusion from the national heritage; the ex-convict in the *Romany Rye* said he could only hope to till the soil in Britain as a serf. More than anything else this explained the almost religious fervour of the new working-class radicalism. Bamford, visiting the Waterloo Museum, doffed his hat before that of Napoleon and reverently touched the sword of Ney. Only five years after the war such inveterate enemies of England had become for many Englishmen symbols of liberation. 'I went to the place,' wrote Leigh Hunt, 'where the guillotine stood – the place where thousands of spirits underwent the last pang of mortality; many guilty, many innocent, but all the victims of a reaction against tyranny such as will never let tyranny be what it was.' To such, Pitt was 'the great corrupter', Parliament 'the borough-monger crew', and the ruling classes a pack of placemen and pensioners battening on the taxes wrung from the people. During the post-war decade a legend grew which became an article of faith to millions: of a needless, horribly mismanaged war wantonly persisted in for twenty years against European liberty; of a crippling debt made by loans 'to support despotism under the guise of legitimacy': of a Court of hereditary flunkeys, a haughty, purse-proud aristocracy, an indolent, hypocritical Church – 'Christless, Godless, a book sealed' – and a

1. Leigh Hunt, *Autobiography*, II, 39–41. See Berry, III, 341; Smart, 725; Southey, *Espriella*, II, 145–6.

Government which, under an unjust Constitution, subjected the friends of freedom to spies, jails, and bastilles.[1]

Yet this movement, transformed by the English antipathy to violence, was later to become the mainspring of parliamentary liberalism. It derived from the middle-class reformers of the eighteenth century and the days when the young Pitt championed parliamentary reform. It had only spread to the populace because of the miseries inflicted by post-war deflation and industrial anarchy. Its leader was not Hunt or Thistlewood, but old Major Cartwright, with his long brown Hanoverian surtout and wig and philanthropic countenance – the Ancient Pistol of Byron's derisory phrase. 'Our venerable political father's maxim,' wrote Bamford, 'was "Hold fast by the laws".' The Hampden clubs, and the 'National Unions' which took their place, were the product of the denominational Sunday schools and night classes. Cobbett's wide circle of humble but law-abiding readers, ardently perusing sedition, derived from the same homely origins. Their goal was a reform of Parliament to ascertain the needs of, and represent, the People. It was the squalor and hunger of the illiterate slums which provoked the rioting and imperilled public order, not the simple-minded fraternal delegates with their biblically-worded and Utopian resolutions. The poor, as Bamford told the Privy Council, would have been perfectly content with the Constitution if they had been able to earn the necessities of life. Since it denied them this while preserving the fabulous wealth of the aristocracy, they assumed it must be corrupt.

*

By the middle of 1819 the plight of the textile operatives had again become desperate. The wages of the Glasgow handloom weavers, once twenty-five shillings a week, shrank that autumn to five shillings, or half what they had even been in 1816. In some places they were worse: at Maybole they fell to half a crown. The streets of the manufacturing towns and villages were silent and deserted, except where strikes brought thousands of sullen spectres clattering on to the cobblestones to stop the wheels and damp down the furnaces. To all thoughtful

1. Bewick, 149–52, 154–5, 169–71; Bamford, II, 126–7, 248, 299; De Quincey, III, 62; Halévy, II, 14, 55; *Hamilton of Dalzell MS.*, 185, 222–3; Keats, IV, 356; Leigh Hunt, II, 190; *Romany Rye*, 106; Rose, I, 144–5; Smart, 708.

men, and many thoughtless ones, too, an explosion seemed imminent.[1]

It was a summer of intense heat. The *Annual Register* reported that political agitators, taking advantage of the general misery, went about disseminating their doctrine through the great centres of manufacture. Hundreds of field-meetings were held to hear harangues on the iniquities of Government and the necessity of radical reform. At one, accompanied by all the outward symbols of Jacobin revolution – inflammatory banners, caps of liberty, and tricolours – 50,000 Birmingham artisans acclaimed a local radical landowner as their 'legislatorial attorney'. Leeds and Manchester attempted to follow suit.

All this could only end in one of two ways – revolution or repression. There was a naïvety about the reformers' leaders that played into their opponents' hands. They used the words and outward show of rebellion without either the intention to implement them by force or the realization that they must inevitably provoke force on the part of their rulers. Nor did they realize the roughness and indiscipline of many of their followers – not the sober, law-abiding majority, but the inevitable lawless minority, whose savage ferocity and predilection for plunder reminded even the liberal-minded Greville of the mobs of the Terror. 'Our worthy old Major,' wrote Bamford, 'seemed to have forgotten in the simplicity of a guileless heart, good old man as he was, that the people themselves wanted reforming, that they were ignorant and corrupt.' Scott related with glee how a young Edinburgh liberal was knocked down and robbed by rowdies at the very moment that he was declaiming against the impropriety of allowing constables to interfere with popular liberty. Even Byron could not refrain from poking fun when Cam Hobhouse – victor in the turbulent Westminster election of 1820 – had his watch pinched at the hustings.[2]

*

Most folk with property to lose were resolved to defend it. The Duke of Wellington, who had seen many popular ferments, remarked that

1. *Ann. Reg.* 1819, Chron., 31, 36–7, 54, 76–7; Halévy, II, 56; Hansard, XLI, 420, 1393; Smart, 690–2, 706, 720–1, 724–6.

2. *When to the mob you make a speech,*
    My boy Hobbie O,
    How do you keep outside their reach
    The watch within your fobby O?

the reformers' object was 'neither more nor less than the plunder of the rich towns and houses which fell in their way.' A peer declared that public meetings ought to be dispersed by grapeshot, the liberal John Ward thought that the first day of reform would be the first day of English revolution, and strikes were denounced as illegal combinations of foolish and 'refractory work-people' misled by Jacobin agitators – coercive attempts to dictate the wages paid by employers[1] and, therefore, gross interference with private freedom. 'I cannot,' wrote Walter Scott, 'read in history of any free State which has been brought to slavery until the rascal and uninstructed populace has had their short hour of anarchical government.'

As throughout the industrial North companies of workmen assembled to drill with bludgeons and pikes, sometimes under the tuition of Peninsular veterans – Harry Smith, on strike duty in Glasgow, reported that the weavers were organized in sixteen battalions based on streets – the Government urged magistrates to stand firm and marched its scanty Army into the manufacturing districts. And, as in the invasion years, it fell back on the spontaneous enthusiasm of those who felt their security at stake. A year or two earlier Wordsworth, in a letter to his patron, Lord Lonsdale, had urged the creation of an equestrian order of armed yeomanry; 'if the whole island was covered with a force of this kind, the Press properly curbed, the Poor Laws

> But never mind such pretty things,
>   My boy Hobbie O,
> God save the people: damn all kings,
>   So let us crown the Mobby O.

Toynbee, 140–1. See Bamford, II, 12–14, 20, 27, 33, 134, 280–1; Greville (Suppl.), I, 324; Holland, *Journal*, I, 33; Lockhart, V, 43; Lady Shelley, II, 28–30; Woodward, 60–1.

1. 'That kind of overbearing influence which is now most unjustly and illegally employed to deprive the master-spinners of the control of their own concerns.' – *Ann. Reg.* 1818, Chron., 104. 'After so long an absence from all profitable employment the workmen are convinced that they have neither the right nor the power to dictate, as a body, to their employers; and the latter, we believe, are sincerely disposed, now submission has been made, to pass over the attempt to take the management of their affairs out of their own hands, forgiving and forgetting the insults they received during the turn-out and the loss which so much capital, so long unemployed, had unavoidably occasioned.' *Idem*, 124. See *idem*, 90–1, 128–30; Halévy, II, 56–7; Dudley, 308; Lockhart, IV, 128; Newton 87.

gradually reformed, provision made for new churches to keep pace with the population, order may yet be preserved and the people remain free and happy.' Walter Scott, always to the fore when either volunteering or repression of Jacobinism was in question, busied himself in raising a company of sharpshooters from Ettrick and Teviotdale to march on the Tyne.

To those whose homes and factories were imperilled by a servile war such well-to-do volunteers, flooding into the shabby industrial towns with their bright yeomanry uniforms and handsome horses, were saviours, to be cheered and feasted for their patriotic self-sacrifice. To the workers they seemed heartless upstarts – young farmers or mill-owners' sons who, having risen in the world, treated their poorer neighbours like dirt and rode over them. Bewick wrote of 'the pride and folly which took possession of their empty or fume-charged heads when they got dressed in scarlet.'[1] To themselves, as they sharpened their swords in the village smithy and bade farewell to wife and sweetheart, they seemed heroes, ready to die for God, King, and country.

On August 16th the clash came. On that day, the culmination of weeks of drilling on the moors, from fifty to eighty thousand reformers – a force as large as Napoleon's at Waterloo – converged from all directions on St Peter's Field, Manchester, to listen to Orator Hunt and demand reform. They marched, unarmed, behind revolutionary banners, in columns of five and locked-step, to the sound of bugles and drums, followed by dense crowds of stragglers of both sexes. Their menacing looks and numbers terrified the sober and respectable. As they poured into the town they were received with wild enthusiasm by the poor, particularly the Irish weavers, who flocked after them to St Peter's Field.

As soon as Hunt began to speak the alarmed magistrates, watching from a neighbouring house, instructed their police officers to arrest him and ordered a detachment of yeomanry to force a way to the hustings. Jostled by the crowd, the yeomanry lost their heads and started slashing with their sabres. There was a panic, the hustings were

1. *Old Oak*, 104–5; see *Ann. Reg.* 1818, Chron., 129–30. Bamford, II, 146–54; Bewick, 154–5; Colchester, III, 101; De Selincourt, II, 585; Halévy, II, 63–4; Lockhart, IV, 310–20, 323–4, 328–32, 335; Smith, I, 325.

overturned and the people began to run, a few stalwarts fighting back. In the panic nine men and two women were killed, and several hundreds wounded. 'The field,' wrote the leader of the Rochdale column, 'was left an open and deserted space. The sun looked down through a sultry and motionless air. The curtains and blinds of the windows within view were all closed. ... Over the whole field were strewed caps, bonnets, shawls, and shoes, trampled, torn, and bloody. The yeomanry had dismounted – some were easing their horses' girths, others adjusting their accoutrements, and some were wiping their sabres. Several mounds of human beings still remained where they had fallen, crushed down and smothered. Some of these were still groaning ... all was silent save those low sounds, and the occasional snorting and pawing of steeds.'[1]

The country's immediate response was confused. It did not strictly follow class lines. Before the sabres flashed there appeared to be two Englands, both preparing to resort to force. The effect on the industrial workers was one of stunned shock, followed by intense indignation. The response of the other England was divided. The Tory party, the local magistracy which had precipitated the events, and the advocates of firm action everywhere, regarded the affray as the timely dispersal of a dangerous demonstration by a gallant handful. When Walter Scott heard the news he wrote that the yeomanry had behaved well, upsetting the most immense crowd that was ever seen and, despite the lies in the newspapers, without needless violence. There had been a blunder, it was true, in using yeomanry instead of regulars. But the meeting had itself been illegal, an organized conspiracy to intimidate for political purposes.[2]

Yet the Government had spilt blood, and the English did not like blood to be spilt. Military massacre was no part of their recipe for government. Because of this it became apparent that, instead of there being two Englands pursuing an unappeasable quarrel to its logical conclusion, there were three. The third consisted of an indeterminate majority which reacted against any Party that outraged its sense of

1. Bamford, II, 157–8. See *idem*, 149–57, 287; *Ann. Reg.* 1819, 106–7; Ashton, II, 203–5; Colchester, II, 82; Creevey, I, 332; Halévy, II, 64; Woodward, 62.
2. *Ann. Reg.* 1820, Chron., 85; Bamford, II, 161–2; F. A. Burton, *Three Accounts of Peterloo*; Colchester, III, 87–8; Lockhart, IV, 301; Lady Shelley, II, 71–2.

human decency. It comprised those in every class who, with the great Lord Halifax, regarded 'all violence as a kind of foul play' and instinctively trimmed the sails of state against those who resorted to it. They even included many employers, who, though they hated strikes and rioting, inherited their forebears' liberal instincts. This feeling was expressed by a large and by no means purely radical section of the Press, by the Common Council of London, who protested at the Regent's official message of congratulation to the Manchester magistrates, and by meetings up and down the country, one of which was attended by the great Whig magnate, Earl Fitzwilliam, Lord Lieutenant of the West Riding. Other Whig aristocrats, like the Duke of Hamilton and Earl Grosvenor, interested themselves in befriending the victims and the arrested organizers of the Manchester meeting.[1]

The reformers' leaders, who were nothing if not histrionic, did all they could do to exploit the anger of the people and the sympathy of the middle class. The printing presses poured out a stream of wildly exaggerated accounts of what became known as the Peterloo massacre. Hone's satire, *The Political House that Jack Built*, ran through twenty editions, and prints were hawked through the streets bearing inflammatory legends like, 'Down with 'em! Chop 'em down! my brave boys! give them no quarter; they want to take our Beef and Pudding from us!' When Orator Hunt returned to London in September, after his release on bail, an enormous crowd, running it was said to over a hundred thousand, met him at Islington. The procession included crippled heroes from Peterloo, red flags, emblems of mourning, a large dog with a collar labelled 'No dog tax', and an escort of horsemen. Among those who watched it with sympathy was the poet Keats.[2]

But, like the Government before them, the radicals overplayed their hand. Lacking all sense of responsibility and constructive statesmanship, they toyed with fire. The men they led were passionately angry, and everyone who lived near the manufacturing districts felt the hot breath of that anger and knew what it portended. For weeks after Peterloo the youth of industrial Lancashire was surreptitiously engaged in making pikes, grinding scythes, and converting hatchets, old swords,

1. Bamford, II, 214–15, 218; Berry, III, 189; Colchester, II, 94–5, 107; Halévy, II, 60–1, 64–5, 71–2; *Hamilton of Dalzell* MS., 122–4, 186; Keats, IV, 12–14; Lady Shelley, II, 87–8; Shelley, *Essays and Letters*, 289–90; Woodward, 62–3.

2. Ashton, II, 205–9; Halévy, II, 65; Keats, IV, 14; Lady Shelley, II, 90–2.

and mop-nails into weapons; 'anything,' wrote Bamford, 'which could be made to cut or stab was pronounced fit for service.' At Manchester a special constable was stoned to death. At Newcastle keelmen assaulted the magistrates with showers of brickbats and cries of 'Blood for blood!'[1] By inciting and advertising such activities the radicals, most of whom were men of boundless vanity, frightened the very middle-class allies who, by co-operating with them against the Government's rigid conservatism, might have made some measure of parliamentary reform possible.

*

The Government's remedy was to strengthen the laws. Before Christmas it introduced six Bills prohibiting private drilling, the bearing of arms, and certain kinds of out-of-door meeting, and virtually muzzling the cheap Press. Even the street ballad singers were temporarily suppressed by anxious magistrates. The feeling for strong measures was reinforced by the return to England of Wellington with the withdrawal of the occupying armies from France and his accession to the Cabinet at the end of the year as Master General of the Ordnance. Like a soldier, he saw the situation in terms of force, and knew that in such matters resolute decision was everything – a knowledge of which the Government's vain and noisy adversaries were devoid.

The sense of imminent doom was heightened that January by a change on the throne. Two years earlier, after a brief spell of radiant happiness as a bride, the Regent's only child, Princess Charlotte, had died in childbed. Her death left the English without hope of a crown they could respect.[2] A year later passed, with the Queen's death, the last royal symbol that enshrined the moral feeling of the nation; the weight had gone, wrote Scott, that slammed the Palace door on

1. *Ann. Reg.* 1819, Chron., 58, 70, 76–8; Bamford, II, 161–5, 197–200; Colchester, III, 83–4, 93, 95–6, 102–3; Dyott, I, 338; Farington, VIII, 233; Lockhart, IV, 323–6, 335; Lady Shelley, II, 89.

2. 'One met in the streets people of every class in tears, the churches were full at all hours, the shops shut for a fortnight (an eloquent testimony from a shop-keeping community), and everyone from the highest to the lowest in a state of despair.' – *Lieven Letters*, 34. Brougham wrote that it was difficult for persons not living at the time to believe how universal and genuine the national grief was. Brougham, II, 312–3. See Bamford, II, 138; Burghersh, 22; Bury, II, 144–5; Colchester, III, 26–7; D'Arblay, III, 418–22; Farington, VIII, 146–9, 151–2, 155–6; George IV, *Letters*, II, 209–12; Harriet Granville, I, 132; Newton, 108–9, 113.

whores. At the beginning of 1820 the old King drew himself up in his bedclothes, said, 'Tom's a cold!' and turned his face to the wall. His only son with surviving legitimate offspring, the Duke of Kent, preceded him to the grave by a few days. A week later his successor went down with pneumonia. At that moment the succession turned on five middle-aged brothers, every one of whom seemed to the nation either a bad life or a bad hat, and on the Duke of Kent's eight months' old child, Victoria. When King George IV was proclaimed and the officers of State and Judges dutifully waved their hats, the people, accustomed only to hiss and pelt him, stood silent and still.

As the bell of St Paul's tolled through the fog for George III's funeral, the news reached London that the ultimate heir to the French throne had been assassinated. With Spain, Italy, and Germany all stirring against the legitimist rulers imposed on them by the Vienna settlement, it seemed like the signal for the renewal of Jacobin revolution. At that very moment a fanatic gang led by Arthur Thistlewood, the ruined gamester who had tried to capture the Tower during the Spa Fields riots, was preparing the assassination of the British Cabinet. Their plan was to break in on them as they dined together in Grosvenor Square and, with a bomb and hand-grenades, to massacre the lot, including the Prime Minister, Castlereagh, Sidmouth, and Wellington. One of the assassins, a butcher named Ings, was equipped with a sack for the Ministerial heads which were to be exhibited to the mob and borne on pikes to the Mansion House, where Thistlewood was to be proclaimed President of a Provisional Government. But for the unreliability of two of the broken men to whom he entrusted his plan, the entire Administration might have perished over the walnuts and wine. As it was, the conspirators were surprised by police officers and a platoon of the Coldstream Guards just as they were about to sally forth from the hay-loft off the Edgware Road where they had secreted their bombs and cutlasses. Though the leader of the police was killed and Thistlewood himself and most of his gang escaped in the mêlée, they were quickly rounded up. Five of them suffered the fate they had prepared for the Cabinet, the executioner displaying their dripping heads to a groaning crowd.[1] They died maintaining that high treason had

---

[1] Thackeray heard as a child that, as one of the heads slipped and rolled across the scaffold, a cry went up of 'Yah! butterfingers!' – Oman, *Colonel Despard,*

been committed against the people of England and that, as patriots, they were justified in trying to exterminate the borough-mongering gang who were starving millions. Insurrection, Thistlewood declared, had become a public duty.

*

That spring the country prepared to crown its new King. The price of ermine soared, and Rundell, Bridge, and Rundell, the Ludgate jewellers, submitted estimate for embellishing the Crown jewels at a cost running into six figures. At the same time it became known that agents of the Crown had been making inquiries about the Queen's life in Italy. Rumours circulated of a green bag full of salacious details and of a large sum offered her to renounce the Crown. What was still more disturbing to those who knew, was that the King was again in love, this time with the buxom daughter of a rich London shopkeeper married to an Irish peer. His previous mistress, Lady Hertford, had been a constant irritant to the mob; a few months before, when his yellow chariot had broken down after a visit to her house in Manchester Square, they had besieged it for an hour, while he cowered behind its purple blinds, calling him and her all the naughty names in their robust vocabulary. Now, showering presents on Lady Conyngham and her daughter – for the lady, a lover of proprieties, insisted that her family should be honoured with her – the brandy-logged, dropsical monarch was not only insisting that his wife's name should be excluded from the Litany, but was urging his embarrassed Ministers to introduce a Bill of divorce. 'If he does,' wrote Harriet Granville, 'it will be the most tremendous piece of work that ever was made in a country!'

But Queen Caroline was no Josephine. Like her brother who had fallen at Waterloo, she was a fighting Brunswick, with a strong taste for melodrama. Five years before, when, on leaving England, she had first felt free to express her personality, she had toured Italy in a blue-lined gilt and mother-of-pearl phaeton, shaped like a sea-shell and driven by a child dressed as an operatic angel in spangles and flesh-coloured tights. Now, leaving behind the Italian courier whom she

22–48; Broughton, II, 126–7. See idem, 120; Mrs Arbuthnot, Journal, Feb. 23rd, March 7th, 8th 1829. Hobhouse, 15-16, 21–3; Lieven, Private Letters, 16; Neumann 17–19; Lady Shelley, II, 98–9; Two Duchesses, 343–4; Woodward, 63–4.

had promoted to be her chamberlain, she was on her way home, beside herself at her husband's decision to exclude her name from the Prayer Book, and appropriately clad in a low-cut bodice, short petticoats, and Hessian boots. She meant, she said, to secure her rights or blow the King off his throne.[1]

The efforts of the royal emissaries and of her own legal advisers to head her off were all in vain. On June 4th, 1820, she landed at Dover. All the way to London the church bells rang and cheering crowds lined the way. The people of the capital received her with intense enthusiasm. Their only regret was that she had not brought her lover Bergami: King Bergami they called him. They unhorsed her carriage and dragged it past Carlton House with indescribable din and tumult, smashed the windows of Cabinet Ministers' houses and let off thousands of squibs; several nervous persons were so frightened that they died. Everyone was forced to illuminate in her honour and doff their hats in the streets. The Duke of Wellington, stopped in Grosvenor Place by roadmenders with pickaxes, replied to their request, 'Well, gentlemen, since you will have it so, God save the Queen – and may all your wives be like her!'[2]

The Government had hitherto refused to proceed to extremities against Caroline, for, unlike their impatient, lovesick master, they realized what would happen if they did. They had only agreed to exclude her name from the Litany provided the divorce was dropped. But her return forced their hand and played into the King's. They did their best to negotiate an honourable compromise that would enable her to withdraw with profit and honour. But heartened by the mob, who stoned every Government emissary who visited her, she refused to yield a point and insisted on the inclusion of her name in the Prayer Book. As the only alternatives were an abdication or their own resignation – a step which they believed would be followed by immediate revolution – Ministers proceeded, though with the utmost misgiving, to introduce a Bill of Pains and Penalties to deprive her of her title

1. Bury, I. See *idem*, 80, 283, 342; Creevey, *Life and Times*, 102–4; Farington, VIII, 88; George IV, *Letters*, 350–2; Granville, II, 83, 535; Newton, 4–5.

2. Guedalla, 322. See *Ann. Reg.* 1820, Chron., 202–5, 206–8; 216–17; Berry, III, 238–239; Colchester, III, 87, 116–17, 131, 135, 137, 163; Croker, I, 160, 174; D'Arblay, III, 440; Farington, VIII, 247, 251–2; George IV, *Letters*, II, 339–43; Greville (Suppl.), I, 127; Halévy, II, 90–2; Hobhouse, 23–4.

round the House of Lords were barricaded under the Duke of Wellington's supervision, constables were enrolled and troops drafted into Westminster. The Duke treated the mob with contempt. More than once he wheeled his horse on the corner boys who followed him, putting them to flight with a flick of his switch. Outside London, except for a skirmish in July between strikers and yeomanry in western Scotland, the revolutionary fervour of the previous year seemed to have died away. Trade was reviving, the factories filling, and the price of labour rising. A radical attempt at Manchester to organize a Peterloo anniversary was a fiasco, for the potential marchers were back in the mills.

Even in London what had begun as a demonstration against the monarchy and ruling class was changing imperceptibly into a faction fight between the supporters of rival royalties and parliamentary Parties. The Queen's counsel being Whig, and the Opposition peers, including Lord Grey, making speeches on her behalf – not because they thought her innocent but because they thought the King guilty – the Whigs found themselves, not for the first time in history, the heroes of the populace. The good-natured Duke of Devonshire enjoyed an ovation twice a day as he rode in and out from Chiswick. 'Nothing can be more peaceable than the mob,' wrote Harriet Granville after seeing her Whig husband cheered through the barricades; 'darlings they are!' As anger went out of the proceedings, levity and boredom took their place, the long sultry days of August and September leaving both populace and judges a little limp. One blackguard, found asleep under a lamp-post, declared that he was tired, 'tired as a peer!' Even the Queen dozed during the long formal sessions, giving rise to Lord Holland's jest that, while formerly she slept with couriers, now she slept with the Lords. Outside in the hot dusty streets the costers sold Bergami apples and Caroline pears. Only the Italian witnesses continued to arouse excitement, making the peers laugh by the way in which they acted the evidence and provoking the mob, whenever they showed their swarthy faces, to paroxysms of anger; John Bull, someone wrote, looked on them as so many bugs and frogs. The poor men went in terror of their lives; when, after Denman's speech for the defence, the usher in charge, who was a dandy, entered their room running his fingers, according to dandy usage, along the top of his cravat, they assumed that their throats were to be cut and, plumping down on their knees, set up a yell of 'Misericordia!'[1]

The trial ended in a characteristic British anticlimax. On November 6th the bill affirming the Queen's guilt was given a second reading by a majority of twenty-eight. But the third reading on the 10th passed the Lords by only nine votes. The Prime Minister thereupon announced that it would be impossible with so small a majority to take the bill to the Commons. Later in the day Parliament was prorogued. The *mot* of the town was that the Queen and the Bill of Pains and Penalties were both *abandoned*. It amounted, as a Whig M.P. pointed out, to a decision that the lady was immoral and her husband a fit associate for her. The latter was so indignant that he lost all interest in the affair, asked for the Queen's allowance to be settled without further ado and even expressed his indifference to the insertion of her name in the Litany. In the angry recriminations between him and his Ministers, the latter almost resigned and the King almost sent for the Whigs. But in the end, much as they disliked one another, they stayed together. For neither could see any alternative.[2]

And though the mob in a three days' illumination celebrated what they chose to regard as the Queen's acquittal but was in reality their own triumph, and though even in the quiet Berkshire woodlands Mary Mitford and her family were forced by riotous villagers to light candles in the windows, the poor woman's cause was finished. She had ceased to be a pretext or even a joke, and had become a nuisance. *Most gracious Queen*, wrote a pamphleteer:

> *we thee implore*
> *To go away and sin no more;*
> *But if that effort be too great,*
> *To go away at any rate!*

The Queen fever was over. When Parliament met in January, 1821, a large majority voted against the inclusion of her name in the Prayer

1. Harriet Granville, I, 158–9. See *idem*, 155–6, 160–1, 164–6, 172, 179; Broughton, II, 134–5; Colchester, III, 164; Halévy, II, 99, 102.

2. Mrs Arbuthnot, *Journal*, Oct. 18th 1820, Feb. 24th, 28th 1821; Creevey, I, 319; Croker, I, 174–5, 179; George IV, *Letters*, II, 378, 386; Harriet Granville, I, 196; Halévy, II, 98; Hobhouse, 36–41.

Book. Her prestige slumped still more heavily when, having proclaimed that she would never touch a penny while the insult continued, she accepted an annuity of £50,000 per annum.

As the Queen sank, the King rose. That February, feeling perhaps that he had drained the last dregs of humiliation, he went, for the first time for years, to the theatre. He was very pale when he entered, but the whole house, including the pit, stood up and cheered him, singing the National Anthem again and again. There were only a few shouts of 'Queen!' and 'George, where's your wife!', and these were quickly drowned. He was so delighted that he repeated his success next night by going to Covent Garden where the same thing happened and where he laughed so uproariously at the jokes of Grimaldi, the clown, that he burst his stays.[1]

In its unaccountable way, the country had gone about. It had had a debauch and was now sober. Even Byron wrote from Italy repudiating the reformers and telling his friend, Hobhouse, not to be so violent.[2] The more dangerous radicals were safe under lock and key; the harmless ones like Bamford were released and allowed to return to their employment. Trade was doing well, food prices were low, the North was back at its looms and spindles. Everything was returning to normal; everything was apparently as it had been. A prime sporting dinner was held at the Castle Tavern, Holborn, where, after harmony, the stakes were laid for a match between Tom Cribb, the Champion of England, and a challenger; a new ballet dancer appeared at the opera – her price, the old lechers told one another, was £5000 – Constable exhibited four more pictures at the spring exhibition at Somerset House, including 'Hampstead Heath' and 'The Hay Wain'. Far away in a Roman lodging young Severn, the painter, bent over the bed of the dying Keats and heard the phlegm boiling in his throat.

*

1. 'I saw him trundle downstairs and I never saw anything look so happy.' – Harriet Granville, I, 206–7. See *idem*, 208; Mrs Arbuthnot, *Journal*, Feb. 7th, 8th, 1821; Farington, VIII, 274; Greville (Suppl.), I, 124; Neumann, 50–1.

2. 'It is not against the pure principles of reform that I protest,' he wrote, 'but against low, designing, dirty levellers who would pioneer their way to a democratic tyranny.' – Byron, *Corr.*, II, 147. See *idem*, 115–16, 134, 137–8, 142–3, 147–8.

That summer – the summer of Napoleon's death and Shelley's *Adonais* – they crowned the King. It cost a quarter of a million and was attended by every romantic excess of pageantry of which he and his age were capable. The Duke of Wellington, the Champion and the Earl Marshal backed wonderful horses down the feasting defile of Westminster Hall, girls in white dresses strewed flowers amid forests of plumes and gleaming trumpets, 'the nobles and sages of the land decked out in velvet and satin, gold and jewellery, passed in procession through countless thousands, the sun shining without a cloud, and all uniting to do homage to the Constitution.'[1] It was a lovely day and the populace was in the best of humours, cheering everyone, even Castlereagh, who, in his Garter robes and diamonds, was voted the handsomest man there. The King, looking a little pale after an operation, appeared like some gorgeous bird of the East. Much of the time he spent sighing and kissing his brooch to Lady Conyngham; 'anyone who could have seen his disgusting figure,' wrote a spectator, 'with a wig the curls of which hung down his back, and quite bending beneath the weight of his sixty years, would have been quite sick.' The poor Queen, attended only by a shadow of her former rabble, tried to get into the Abbey by a side door, but was driven away with shouts of 'Shame!' and 'Off, Off!'

A fortnight later she died, her supporters said of a broken heart, the doctors of an overdose of magnesia. The King, who was on his way to Ireland, with the tact of a perfect gentleman added a mourning band to his costume. Though the event produced one last glorious riot as the Home Office tried to stop the coffin from passing through the city, it was not allowed to interfere with the celebrations in Dublin. Here the King enjoyed the apotheosis of his career – coloured rags and streamers hanging from every window, whisky punch flowing in the filthy gutters, thousands of drunken Paddys shouting themselves delirious with joy. 'They clawed and pawed him all over,' wrote an onlooker, 'and called him *Ethereal* Majesty. ... They absolutely kissed his hands and feet. Alas! poor degraded country!' The only drawback – for the Vice-Queen, as Lady Conyngham was called, accompanied him – was

1. Mrs Arbuthnot, *Journal*, July 19th 1821. See *Ann. Reg.* 1821, Chron., 324–390; Colchester, III, 233; Creevey, *Life and Times*, 141; Farington, VIII, 291–2 *Hamilton of Dalzell* MS., 163–4; Haydon, II, 24–5.

what a correspondent of Creevey's described as an attack of
the wherry-go-nimbles in the royal stomach and the failure of the
stewards at the Curragh races to prepare a convenience with a large
enough seat. Byron from Italy commemorated the occasion in
verse:

> Lo! he comes! the Messiah of royalty comes!
>   Like a goodly Leviathan roll'd from the waves;
> Then receive him as best such an advent becomes
>   With a legion of cooks and an army of slaves!
>
> Spread – spread for Vitellius, the royal repast,
>   Till the gluttonous despot be stuff'd to the gorge!
> And the roar of his drunkards proclaim him at last
>   The fourth of the fools and oppressors called 'George!'

*

Events could not be expected to remain in so lofty a plane for long. If
the first year of the reign had been a nightmare and the second culminated in a fairy-tale triumph, the third posed a question mark. The
seventh anniversary of Waterloo saw English industry precariously
ascending the crest of another wave of short-lived, hectic demand and
English agriculture descending deeper into a trough of inexplicable
depression. The accursed system, wrote Cobbett, as he rode across the
green, anxious shires, was staggering about like a sheep with water in
its head, 'turning its pate upon one side, seeming to listen but has no
hearing, seeming to look but has no sight; one day it capers and dances,
the next it mopes and seems ready to die.'[1] Abroad, with the Holy
Alliance Sovereigns marching and counter-marching their armies like
fire-brigades across their neighbours' territories to extinguish one
national and liberal revolt after another, the Vienna settlement of
Europe achieved after so much blood seemed on the verge of collapsing.
The people of England, particularly its younger generation, were
growing increasingly hostile to such authoritarian interference by its
allies and increasingly critical of Castlereagh, who, as Foreign Secretary and Leader of the Commons, was at once the champion of
the collective system abroad and the pillar of repressive administration at home. This stately, honourable aristocrat, now Marquis of

1. *Rural Rides,* I, 7–8.

423

Londonderry, with his handsome face and impassive courtesy, had come to symbolize for them, not only the jack-booted Austrians and Cossacks who shot and jailed Italian and Polish liberals in the name of dynastic autocrats, but the slashing yeomanry of Peterloo and the spies and informers who dogged the footsteps of English reformers. The whole chilling array of luxury, display, indifference, and disdain which Britain's aristocracy presented to the victims of her industrial and agrarian revolutions seemed embodied by one man.

Yet that mask of cold indifference – a facet of the stoic courage with which the nation's rulers had faced Napoleon – concealed a deeply sensitive nature. Like his colleagues Castlereagh had borne without flinching the toil and peril of office in a revolutionary age too long, and, under that 'splendid summit of bright polished frost,' unguessed at even by his dearest intimates, the strain of overwork and public opprobrium had begun to tell. That summer he spoke of living amidst the ruin of empires and, riding one day in the Row, he told a friend that the business of carrying on the Government had become intolerable and that, once out of it, no power on earth would bring him back.[1]

In August after his Irish triumph the King set out on another progress. Before embarking for Edinburgh he gave an audience to the Foreign Secretary who was about to attend a Congress of European Sovereigns at Verona. The King was so struck by his Minister's distraught state that he spoke of it to Lord Liverpool. So did Wellington who had an equally disturbing interview with his colleague. Some mysterious fear seemed to be haunting that strong, calm mind; some obsession about a conspiracy to accuse him of a nameless crime.[2] During his conversation with Wellington he broke down and cried.

Two days later it was learnt that the Foreign Secretary, rising suddenly from a bed of fever, had cut his throat. To those who knew him intimately his passing seemed an inconceivable loss: that of the noblest and kindest of men and the wisest, most steadfast statesman of his time.

1. Broughton, II, 187; *Creevey Papers*, II, 38.
2. He had been much shocked by the disgrace of a wealthy Irish Bishop who had been caught with a guardsman in a London tavern, and believed that there was a plot to accuse him falsely of the same crime. Mrs Arbuthnot, *Journal*, August 5th, 6th, 7th, 9th, 10th 1820; Brownlow, 198; Croker, I, 224–5; Greville (Suppl.), I, 155–6; Hobhouse, Aug. 12th 1820; Lieven, *Private Letters*, 189–94; Stanhope, 272–3; Toynbee, 129–31.

Yet when the body of 'carotid-artery-cutting Castlereagh,' as the radicals called him, was borne to the Abbey door, a knot of rough-looking men in the roadway gave a fierce, exultant hurray.[1] '*Posterity*,' wrote Byron,

> *will ne'er survey*
> *A nobler grave than this:*
> *Here lie the bones of Castlereagh:*
> *Stop, traveller, and …!*

Tidings of another death reached London about the same time. 'Shelley, the great atheist,' wrote Charles Lamb, 'has gone down by water to eternal fire!' A few weeks earlier the poet had sailed from Spezia in a small yacht and was never seen alive again. His remains were burnt on the shore near Viareggio to conform with the Tuscan quarantine laws. 'Marble mountains touched the air with coolness and the flame of the fire bore away towards heaven quivering with a brightness of inconceivable beauty.' A Tory newspaper's comment was that the poet would now discover whether there was a hell or not.

*

Such eroding bitterness and division was symbolic. It sprang from the inability of those who ruled to cope with change. Being able to think only in patterns of thought which they had defended so long against foreign violence, they regarded with abhorrence all who found those patterns outworn, and were in turn anathema to them. Those who, suffering or perceiving injustice, demanded a reform of the country's laws and institutions, they denounced as Jacobins and potential assassins, and were themselves denounced by them as tyrants. By their defiant but pathetic conservatism, they made Crown, Church, and Constitution suspect to millions. They not only failed to find a common denominator for readjusting British society after the war; they failed even to realize one was needed. They could not reconcile, they could only denounce; they could not lead, they could only repress.

Because of this, Britain in the hour of victory, with as noble a material and spiritual heritage as any nation had ever had, faltered and

---

1. Cooper, 329–30. See *Creevey Papers*, II, 47; Croker, I, 226; Hobhouse, August 20th 1822; Peel, I, 321. For a tribute of deep affection to Castlereagh see Mrs Arbuthnot, *Journal*, August 25th 1822, *et seq.* and Brownlow, *passim*.

almost failed. With the means, physical and intellectual, of solving all her problems – which were not in reality very great – she staggered like a blind man from distress to distress. Yet she was not only immensely rich, but more advanced in real civilization than any other country. There was no land in Europe where so many were so free, and none anywhere where some had a freedom so complete and satisfying. There was none where men had such mastery over material phenomena and enjoyed such comfort, elegance, and happiness. There was none where man had done so much – in home-making, the shaping of landscape, and the manufacture of amenities – to adapt his environment to his nature.

But the dispossessed peasants starving in the midst of plenty, the pallid machine-minders at the closed factory gates, the poachers in the county lock-ups awaiting transportation, felt that they had no longer any part in that inheritance. *Suppose*, the flash coves sang in Salford jail after Peterloo,

> *the Duke be short of men?*
> *What would old England say?*
> *They'd wish they had those lads again*
> *They sent to Botany Bay!*[1]

For when the war, which had united men in sacrifice, was over, society was seen to assume a new face. The rich man in time of trouble withdrew to his castle and left the poor to fend for themselves against bewildering economic forces which made the rich still richer but engulfed the ancient communities of the humble like a flood. And the officers of the realm – princes, peers, legislators, judges, parsons, lawyers, lifeguards, bumbles – instead of endeavouring to rescue the poor from their unmerited plight, behaved as though the only purpose of the State was to preserve the wealth and property of the rich.

Yet the rich were not the oppressors the champions of the poor made out. They were seldom sadists or robbers or even tyrants. They were, for the most part, cultivated and kindly Englishmen, brought up in a Christian tradition and with a sense of personal responsibility and honour. Yet, intoxicated by their good fortune – the riches, luxury, elegance, and power heaped on them by the nation's triumphs – the

1. Bamford, II, 177.

gentlemen of England had unconsciously come to think of these as the end of their country's existence. They regretted that the poor must suffer, but when their economists told them that the wealth of the nation – that is, their own wealth – depended on the periodic unemployment, starvation, and degradation of their humbler countrymen, they accepted it as an inevitable dispensation of Providence and did their best, not unsuccessfully, to banish it from their minds.

Yet Wellington and his fellow officers had not applied the principles of *laissez faire* on the battlefields of the Peninsula. Nor had they shrunk from any duty demanded of them. In war they had been ready to suffer and sacrifice everything that their country might live. Throughout its struggle against Napoleon Britain had found its leaders equal to every need. All she now needed in peace was a reform of her financial system to harness and canalize the productive forces unloosed by her inventors, and of her laws and institutions to give renewed effect to the moral principles in which ninety-nine out of a hundred of her people believed. Those principles, founded on the Christian religion, were recognized by Englishmen of all classes. They were that a man should be free to live as he chose in his own home and follow his craft without the interference of arbitrary tyranny. They comprised a belief in the moral right of the individual to liberty, self-respect, and the ownership of property. A system of society in which so many were being deprived of their traditional livelihood, of their customary standards of living, and of any real freedom of choice by the action of remote economic forces over which they had no control, in which they were forced to work under conditions which robbed them of health and pride in their labour and to live in habitations which deprived them of self-respect, was a system which, by English standards, was in need of reform. It wanted the first essential of a society that could content Englishmen: it was unjust. For the broad framework of justice in which real liberty could operate was lacking.

EPILOGUE

THE ENGLISH VISION

It is not to be thought of that the Flood
Of British freedom, which, to the open sea
Of the world's praise, from dark antiquity
Hath flowed, 'with pomp of waters, unwithstood,'
Roused though it be full often to a mood
Which spurns the check of salutary bands,
That this most famous Stream in bogs and sands
Should perish; and to evil and to good
Be lost for ever. In our halls is hung
Armoury of the invincible Knights of old:
We must be free or die, who speak the tongue
That Shakespeare spake; the faith and morals hold
Which Milton held. – In everything we are sprung
Of Earth's first blood, have titles manifold.

WORDSWORTH

'Tis well an old age is out
And time to begin a new.

DRYDEN

TRUE aristocracy, after true religion, is the greatest blessing a nation can enjoy. Early nineteenth-century Britain possessed an unrivalled capacity for aristocracy. Her troubles arose because she was ruled by a counterfeit instead of the real aristocracy which her institutions evolved with such profusion. The subalterns and company commanders who had created a fighting force superior to Napoleon's were relegated to half-pay or placed under the command of young popinjays who had acquired their commissions by influence and purchase. Yet the rich country which wasted natural leadership with such arrogant careless-ness, continued to produce almost unlimited talent and genius. In every walk of life she threw up men who attained to the highest levels of achievement. In science and invention she towered above other nations, as she did in commerce, colonization, and discovery. Though the State applied to aspirants to public office the narrow measuring-rod of lineage and inheritance, men of enterprise in these years were creat-

428

ing new openings in a hundred spheres of spontaneous personal endeavour. While the Liverpools and Sidmouths were feebly governing England, their fellow countrymen, whom they regarded, except for purposes of war, as outside their pale, were policing Sicily, liberating Greece and Chile, pacifying the warlike tribes of Asia, and civilizing Malaya.

And if in Cabinet and Convocation inspiration was lacking, in the arts Britain was richer than she had ever been before. Not even in the time of Shakespeare and Milton had Britain produced such an astonishing harvest of literary genius. In the decade after Waterloo one might have met at one time or another in the London streets William and Mary Wordsworth, Coleridge, Blake, and Lamb, Keats, Shelley, and Byron, Jane Austen and Walter Scott, Hazlitt, Landor, Southey, Moore, Crabbe, Cobbett, De Quincey, Leigh Hunt, William Napier, Jeremy Bentham, Godwin, as well as a host of lesser literary figures like the elder D'Israeli, Haydon, and John Nyren. And Thackeray, Dickens, Carlyle, Fitzgerald, Tennyson, Borrow, Macaulay, George Eliot, Robert and Elizabeth Browning, the Brontës, Surtees, and the younger Disraeli were growing up – in the nursery or on the threshold of manhood.

> Great spirits now on earth are sojourning:
>   He of the cloud, the cataract, the lake,
>   Who on Helvellyn's summit, wide awake,
> Catches his freshness from Archangel's wing:

> *

> And other spirits there are standing apart
>   Upon the forehead of the age to come;
> These, these will give the world another heart,
>   And other pulses. ...

With the exception of Scott and Byron, none of these men and women were known at the time to more than a small circle of their countrymen. The blaze of genius was there, but it was a blaze in the garret. The great chandelier-lit rooms below were filled with magnificently dressed nonentities. It was her real aristocrats who, when the nation's official spokesmen were silent, gave her the answer she needed. The poets and philosophers recalled her to the enduring truths of her being. On the political issues of the time, in the narrow party sense, these great men were divided. Wordsworth, Coleridge, Scott, Southey, and De Quincey were Tories, Shelley, Hazlitt, Hunt, and Cobbett were radicals, Byron a Whig. Keats and Lamb, though conservative in instinct, were born too far below the social salt in that extravagantly snobbish age not to resent the pretensions of the ruling classes and translate that resentment into opposition. Yet all were at one in their advocacy of the moral truths which had made Britain great and whose oblivion by those in power threatened to make her little.

The most penetrating analysis of the shallowness of the rulers of Regency England came, not from a revolutionary or radical, but from the philosophic founder of nineteenth-century conservatism. Anticipating both the social-welfare Toryism of Disraeli and the Socialism of Ruskin, Coleridge poured scorn on the prevailing determinism of economists and statesmen. 'It is a mockery,' he wrote, 'of our fellow creatures' wrongs to call them equal in rights, when, by the bitter compulsion of their wants, we make them inferior to us in all that can soften the heart or dignify the understanding.' Distinguishing between conservatism as inertia and as a condition of organic life, he went to the root of the controversy between liberty and authority, finding the synthesis in his unvarying starting-point, the human soul. 'Man must be free, or to what purpose was he made a spirit of reason and not a machine of instinct? Man must obey, or wherefore has he a conscience? The powers which create this difficulty contain its solution, for their service is perfect freedom.'

The repression of Eldon and Liverpool had no part in this moralist's conservatism. 'No assailant of an error,' he wrote, 'can reasonably hope to be listened to by its advocates who has not proved to them that he has seen the disputed subject in the same point of view and is capable of contemplating it with the same feelings as themselves.' Sunk into easy and slothful living, pottering about Hampstead Heath between meal and meal, Coleridge seemed in his latter years to have become a rather futile person – 'the dear, fine, silly old angel,' as Lamb called him. Yet from 'that great piece of placid marble' flowed a never-ending stream of germinating ideas that were to stir and influence the hearts of men unborn: of a living and organic conservatism, a restored Church, and a society so morally knit that the gain of one class should automatically become that of every other.

At the opposite end of the pole to the quietist of Highgate stood, or rather rode, the radical pamphleteer, Cobbett. While the one had travelled from Jacobinism to Conservatism, the other had begun as a Tory and ended as a disciple of the republican Tom Paine. Yet the two men based their criticism of the ruling political philosophy on precisely the same grounds: that it was inhuman, un-Christian, and therefore un-English. Cobbett's lifelong object was to restore the yeoman England of his youth in which, or so he believed, the property of the poor had been held sacred. 'Then,' he wrote, 'should I hope once more to see my country great and glorious, and be cheered with the prospect of being able to say to my sons, "I leave England to you as I find it; do you the same by your children."' He saw dying all round him, of a poverty inexplicable in the light of the growing wealth of the rich, all the things he loved – good husbandry, craftsmanship, and social virtue – and threw his whole being into denouncing such poverty and those who tolerated it. For the repression of the helpless determinists in power he had nothing but a burning contempt. 'I was not born under the Six Acts; nor was I born under a state of things like this. I was not born under it and I do not wish to live under it; and with God's help I will change it if I can!'

Though secular in outlook and profession, in purpose all the great English writers of the day were religious. Where the Church failed to find an answer for the problems of an evolving society, the poets, like the prophets of the Old Testament, answered for her. When Shelley wrote 'atheist and philanthropist' after his name in the visitors' book at Chamonix and spoke of 'that detestable religion, the Christian', it was not because he was opposed to the ideals of Christianity, but because he was so passionately in favour of their practical application that he could not bear to be classed with the hypocrites who used the Church as a cloak for selfishness and intolerance. Even Byron, writing *Don Juan* in adulterous exile on gin and water and announcing that he was going to be immoral and show things, not as they ought to be, but as they really were, helped to restore the moral currency. *Go, dine*, he apostrophized the Duke of Wellington,

> *from off the plate*
> *Presented by the Prince of the Brazils,*
> *And send the sentinel before your gate*
> *A slice or two from your luxurious meals;*
> *He fought, but has not dined so well of late.*

In his great political satire, *The Age of Bronze*, and in *Don Juan*, he weighed the world he knew so well in the scales of justice, and with urbane, malicious laughter, refined the snobbery, vulgar pride, and inhuman callousness of fashionable society.

Unconsciously the poets and philosophers were setting standards of outlook which, though little regarded by the political and social leaders of their age, became, through the influence of their genius, the accepted canons of the next. The character of early Victorian England was not formed by its Prime Ministers, serving in 1822 their apprenticeship in junior Government office, or on the Opposition benches – Robert Peel, young Palmerston, Aberdeen, Lord John Russell, the future Lord Melbourne. It was profoundly influenced by the prophetic writers of the Great War and the Regency. The ideals of Thomas Arnold, creator of the Victorian public school, derived from Wordsworth, denouncing amid the luxury and display of the brief-lived peace of Amiens the luxury of English society.

> *Altar, sword and pen,*
> *Fireside, the heroic wealth of hall and bower*
> *Have forfeited their ancient English dower*
> *Of inward happiness. We are selfish men;*
> *Oh! raise us up, return to us again;*
> *And give us manners, virtues, freedom, power.*

Under the solemn dullness and pomposity of the gaunt, bony Westmorland prophet, the exclusive absorption in his own work, the huge crocodile jaw working in interminable monologue, the majesty of his poetry and doctrine worked like a leaven on the mind of the future:

> *inspiration for a song that winds*
> *Through ever-changing scenes of votive quest,*
> *Wrongs to redress, harmonious tribute paid*
> *To patient courage and unblemished Truth,*
> *To firm devotion, zeal unquenchable,*
> *And Christian meekness hallowing faithful loves.*

No nation whose ruling class based its faith on Wordsworth's philosophy was likely to fail its destiny through frivolity or lack of faith.

To this renewal of the nation's moral fibre in the spiritual exhaustion after the war all the great writers of the age contributed: Shelley preaching, through the flaming lyrics of his revolutionary advocacy, that men should love one another and that no society not built on love could endure; Blake, so obscure that only a few knew him, protesting against all that was rigid, unimaginative, and complacent in religion and morality and bequeathing from his rambling books of prophecy an anthem for the twentieth-century Welfare State; Keats, turning his back in a worldly age on every worldly hope in order to sustain – to the consumptive's death in the garret – his poet's creed that whatever the imagination seized on as Beauty must be truth. It was not that such men were apart from their country or possessed some superior virtue not shared by her people and rulers; on the contrary their vision sprang directly from her common faith and civilization. Jane Austen was as organic a part of the nation as a tree, Scott as his native Tweed. Genius merely enabled them to see her true course and to check the deviation of helmsmen with shorter vision. In a country that fostered freedom of expression, they operated as a magnetic compass. Walter Scott, wrote his political opponent, Hazlitt, by emancipating the mind from petty, narrow, and bigoted prejudices, and communicating to countless thousands his chivalrous and humane ideal of patriotism, was one of the greatest teachers of morality that ever lived.[1] Jane Austen, seeing life steadily across the quiet lawn of a country rectory, was as true a delineator of female honour as Scott of male. She once defined a lady as a mixture of love, pride, and delicacy, and in six great novels, never transcending the limits of human capacity, immortalized the type. Self-assertion was the cardinal sin in her calendar; the attributes she helped to perpetuate were self-discipline, moderation, a morality founded on tenderness and constancy, a readiness to shoulder the dullest and weariest burdens for those with claims of kindred and association, a quiet but unflinching opposition to everything lawless, coarse, brutal, and uncontrolled. But for these there could scarcely have been a Florence Nightingale or even a profession of modern nursing.

1. *The Spirit of the Age*, 165–6.

Even the essayists, Lamb, 'the frolic and the gentle', and the savage Hazlitt whom Wordsworth thought unfit for respectable society, helped to shape the outlook of the lesser professional and clerical classes on whose integrity the commercial empire of the Victorian was to rest. The one humanized and invested with poetry the common round of city life for an age in which cities continually multiplied; the other exposed, with compelling clarity, the wrongs and injustices of those without land, capital, or birth. Lamb, in his rusty stockings and unpolished shoes, preached the English creed of humorous and affectionate acceptance; Hazlitt, with his rapier thrusts, cleared a way for Thackeray and the young middle-class reformers of *Punch*.

*

Nor did the English vision stop at the English sea. For thousands of patriots in his own age and for millions in the next, England was typified not by Castlereagh, whose foreign policy, as the event proved, was writ in water, but by Byron. The latter's championship of liberty and nationalism, his aristocratic disdain for every form of tyranny, and his realization, so moving in a fastidious and sensitive man, that a nation has a right to its freedom, whatever its faults or vices, ran through the adolescent mind of European liberalism like fire. The little limping dandy who wrote the *Prisoner of Chillon* threw, like a lamp on the screen of the future, the form of Gladstone's speeches and Campbell-Bannerman's policy.

*

The splendours of Regency society, the power and wealth of early nineteenth-century Britain seemed brassy and eternal to the men and women of the time. So did the destitution and degradation that accompanied them. To poor and rich alike they appeared to be unchangeable – part of a divine, or, as many had begun to suspect, a diabolical ordinance. The poets taught otherwise. They could not change the laws or the harsh economic phenomena of the age, or arrest the cumulative evils to which those phenomena gave rise. But they could make men want to change them. 'If we are a Christian nation,' wrote Coleridge, 'we must learn to act nationally as well as individually as Christians. ... Our manufacturers must consent to regulations; our gentry must concern themselves in the education of their national clients and dependants – must regard their estates as offices of trust with duties to be performed in the sight of God and their country. Let us become a better people and the reform of all the public grievances will follow of itself.'

LIST OF ABBREVIATIONS USED IN FOOTNOTES

ABERDEEN – Lady Frances Balfour, *The Life of George, Fourth Earl of Aberdeen*, 1923.

ACKERMANN, *Microcosm* – R. Ackermann, *Microcosm of London*, 1808–1810.

ACKERMANN, *Repository* – R. Ackermann, *Repository of Arts*.

ALBEMARLE – George Thomas, Earl of Albemarle, *Fifty Years of my Life*, 1870.

ALINGTON – C. A. Alington, *Twenty Years*, 1921.

ALISON – Sir A. Alison, *History of Europe from the Fall of Napoleon to the Accession of Louis Napoleon*, 1852.

ALISON, *History, 1815–52* – Sir A. Alison, *History of Europe from the Commencement of the French Revolution to the Restoration*, 1850.

ALKEN – H. Alken, *The National Sports of Great Britain* (1903 ed.).

ALSOP – *Memorials of Christine Majolier* (ed. M. Braithwaite), 1881.

ANDERSON – Lt.-Col. J. A. Anderson, *Recollections of a Peninsular Veteran*, 1913.

ANDRÉADÈS – Prof. Andréadès, *History of the Bank of England*, 1935.

ANGELO – *Reminiscences of Henry Angelo*, 1830.

Ann. Reg. – *Annual Register*.

ANTON – J. Anton, *Retrospect of a Military Life*, 1841.

APPERLEY – C. J. Apperley, *My Life and Times* (ed. E. D. Cuming), 1927.

ARBUTHNOT – *The Correspondence of Charles Arbuthnot* (ed. A. Aspinall), 1941.

MRS ARBUTHNOT, *Journal* – *Journal of Mrs Arbuthnot* (ed. F. Bamford and Duke of Wellington).

ARGYLL – George Douglas, Eighth Duke of Argyll, *Autobiography and Memoirs*, 1906.

ARTECHE – General José Arteche y Moro, *Guerra de la Independencia*, Madrid, 1868–1902.

ARTZ – F. B. Artz, *Reaction and Revolution, 1814–32*, 1934.

ASHTON – John Ashton, *Social England under the Regency*, 1890.

ASHTON, *Industrial Revolution* – T. S. Ashton, *The Industrial Revolution*, 1948.

ASPINALL, *Brougham* – A. Aspinall, *Lord Brougham and the Whig Party*, 1927.

ASPINALL, *Princess Charlotte* – A. Aspinall, *Letters of Princess Charlotte*, 1949.

ASSHETON SMITH – Sir J. Eardley-Wilmot, *Reminiscences of the late Thomas Assheton Smith*, 1860.

AUCKLAND – *Journal and Correspondence of William Lord Auckland*, 1862.

AUSTEN – *Jane Austen's Letters to her sister Cassandra and others* (ed. R.W. Chapman), 1932.

AUSTEN, *Works* – *The Works of Jane Austen* (ed. J. Bailey), 1927.

BAIN, *Mill* – Alexander Bain, *James Mill*, 1882.

BAINES – E. Baines, *History of the Cotton Manufacture in Great Britain*, 1835.

BAMFORD – S. Bamford, *Passages in the Life of a Radical and Early Days* (ed. H. Dunkley), 1893.

BARANTE – P. Barante, *Souveniers*, Paris, 1882–9.

BARNARD LETTERS – *The Barnard Letters* (ed. A. Powell), 1928.

BARRINGTON – Sir Jonah Barrington, *Personal Sketches of his own Times*, 1827.

BATHURST – *Bathurst MSS.* (Historical MSS. Commission), 1923.

BEAMISH – N. L. Beamish, *History of the King's German Legion*, 1834–7.

BECKE – A. G. F. Becke, *Napoleon and Waterloo*, 1936.

BEER – M. Beer, *History of British Socialism*, 1929.

BELL – G. Bell, *Rough Notes by an Old Soldier*, 1867.

BELLOC – H. Belloc, *Waterloo*, 1915.

BENTHAM – *Works of Jeremy Bentham* (ed. J. Bowring), 1838–43.

BERRY – *Journals and Correspondence of Miss Berry* (ed. T. Lewis), 1865.

BESSBOROUGH – *Lady Bessborough and her Family Circle* (ed. Earl of Bessborough and A. Aspinall), 1940.

BEWICK – *Memoirs of Thomas Bewick written by himself*, 1924.

BIRKBECK – M. Birkbeck, *Notes on a Journey through France*, 1815.

BLACKWOOD'S – *Blackwood's Magazine*.

BLAKENEY – *Services, Adventures and Experiences of Captain Robert Blakeney*, 1899.

BLAND-BURGESS – *Letters and Correspondence of Sir James Bland-Burgess* (ed. J. Hutton), 1885.

Bonapartism – H. A. L. Fisher, *Bonapartism*.

BOOTHBY – C. Boothby, *Under England's Flag*, 1900.

BORROW, *Wild Wales* – G. Borrow, *Wild Wales*, 1901.

Boxiana – P. Egan, *Boxiana*, 1818–22.

BROCK – W. R. Brock, *Lord Liverpool and Liberal Toryism*, 1941.

BROUGHAM – *The Life and Times of Henry, Lord Brougham written by himself*, 1871.

BROUGHTON – Lord Broughton, *Recollections of a Long Life*, 1909.

BROWN – W. Brown, 45th Regiment; *Narrative of a Soldier*, Kilmarnock, 1828.

BROWNLOW – Countess of Brownlow, *Slight Reminiscences of a Septuagenarian*, 1867.

BUCKINGHAM – Duke of Buckingham, *Memoirs of the Regency*, 1856.

BURGHERSH – *The Correspondence of Lady Burghersh with the Duke of Wellington* (ed. R. Weigall), 1903.

BURGOYNE – *Life and Correspondence of Field-Marshal Sir John Burgoyne*, 1873.

BURY – Lady Charlotte Bury, *The Diary of a Lady-in-Waiting* (ed. A. Francis Stewart), 1908.

BUXTON – *Memoirs of Sir Thomas Fowell Buxton Bt.* (ed. Charles Buxton).

BYRON, *Works* – *The Works of Lord Byron* (ed. E. C. Coleridge), 1905.

BYRON, *Corr.* – *Lord Byron's Correspondence* (ed. John Murray), 1922.

BYRON, *Letters and Journals* – *Letters and Journals of Lord Byron* (ed. R. E. Prothero), 1904.

C.H.B.E. – *Cambridge History of the British Empire.*

C.H.F.P. – *Cambridge History of British Foreign Policy.*

C.M.H. – *Cambridge Modern History.*

CAMPBELL – W. Beattie, *Life and Letters of Thomas Campbell*, 1949.

CARTWRIGHT – *Life and Correspondence of John Cartwright* (ed. E. Cartwright), 1926.

CASTLEREAGH – *Memoirs and Correspondence of Viscount Castlereagh*, 1850–3.

CAWTHORNE & HEROD – G. J. Cawthorne and Richard S. Herod, *Royal Ascot: its History and Associations*, 1900.

CECIL, *Melbourne* – David Cecil, *The Young Melbourne*, 1939.

CECIL, *Metternich* – Algernon Cecil, *Metternich* (1943 ed.).

CHAMBERS, *Coleridge* – E. K. Chambers, *Samuel Taylor Coleridge*, 1938.

CHAMBRAY – Marquis de Chambray, *Histoire de l'Expédition de Russie*, Paris, 1839.

CHANCELLOR – E. Beresford Chancellor, *Life in Regency and Early Victorian Times*, 1926.

CHARLES NAPIER – Sir W. Napier, *The Life and Opinions of General Sir Charles James Napier*, 1857.

CHESNEY – Lt.-Col. C. Chesney, *Waterloo Lectures*, 1869.

CHURCH – E. M. Church, *Sir Richard Church in Italy and Greece*, 1895.

CLAPHAM – J. H. Clapham, *An Economic History of Modern Britain*, 1926.

COBBETT, *Cottage Economy* – W. Cobbett, *Cottage Economy* (ed. Chesterton), 1926.

COBBETT, *Rural Rides* – *Cobbett's Rural Rides*, II (ed. G. D. H. & M. Cole), 1930.

COCKBURN – Henry Cockburn, *Memorials of his Time*, 1856.

COLCHESTER – *Diary and Correspondence of Charles Abbot, Lord Colchester*, 1861.

COLE, *Cobbett* – G. D. H. Cole, *Cobbett*, 1947.

COLERIDGE, *Biographia Literaria* – S. T. Coleridge, *Biographia Literaria* (Bohn ed.), 1889.

COLERIDGE, *Essays* – S. T. Coleridge, *Essays on his Own Times*, 1850.

COLERIDGE, *Friend* – S. T. Coleridge, *The Friend* (Bohn ed.), 1890.

COLERIDGE, *Letters* – S. T. Coleridge, *Letters* (ed. E. H. Coleridge), 1895.

COLERIDGE, *Miscellanies* – S. T. Coleridge, *Miscellanies* (Bohn ed.), 1885.

COLERIDGE, *Table Talk* – S. T. Coleridge, *The Table Talk and Omniana* (Bohn ed.), 1884. (See also LORD COLERIDGE.)

COLMAN – George Colman, the Younger, *Random Records*, 1830.

COLQUHOUN – P. Colquhoun, *A Treatise on the Wealth, Power and Resources of the British Empire*, 1814.

COLVIN, *Keats* – S. Colvin, *John Keats* (New York ed.), 1917.

COMBE – W. Combe, *The Three Tours of Doctor Syntax*.

COOKE – Captain Henry Cooke, *A Narrative of Events in the South of France*, 1835.

COOPER – *The Life of Thomas Cooper* written by himself, 1879.

COOPER, *Rough Notes* – J. S. Cooper, *Rough Notes of Seven Campaigns*, 1869.

CORRY – J. Corry, *History of Macclesfield*, 1817.

CORTI – Count Corti, *The Rise of the House of Rothschild* (trans. B. and B. Lunn), 1928.

COSTELLO – *Memoirs of Edward Costello of the Rifle Brigade*, 1857.

COTTON – Sergeant-Major Edward Cotton, *A Voice from Waterloo*, Brussels, 1913.

COUPLAND – R. Coupland, *William Wilberforce*, 1923.

COURT – W. H. B. Court, *The Rise of the Midland Industries*, 1938.

CRABB ROBINSON – *Diary of Henry Crabb Robinson*, 1869.

Cranbourn Chase – W. Chaffins, *Anecdotes & History of Cranbourn Chase*, 1818.

Creevey Papers – *The Creevey Papers* (ed. Sir H. Maxwell), 1903–5.

CREEVEY, *Life and Times* – *Creevey's Life and Times* (ed. John Gore), 1934.

CRESTON – Dormer Creston, *The Regent and his Daughter*, 1932.

CROKER – *The Croker Papers* (ed. L. J. Jennings), 1884.

CROLY – George Croly, *Personal History of George IV*, 1846.

CUNNINGHAM – W. Cunningham, *The Growth of English Industry and Commerce*, 1912.

CURTLER – W. H. R. Curtler, *The Enclosure and Redistribution of Our Land*, 1920.

CZARTORYSKI – Prince Adam Czartoryski, *Mémoires et Correspondance avec Alexandre I*, Paris, 1887.

D.N.B. – *Dictionary of National Biography.*

DANIEL, *Rural Sports* – W. B. Daniel, *Rural Sports*, 1801.

DANIELL – W. Daniell, *A Voyage round Great Britain*, 1825.

DANILEWSKY – A. M. Danilewsky, *Campagne de 1814.*

D'ARBLAY – *The Diaries and Letters of Mme D'Arblay* (ed. A. Dobson), 1904.

DARVALL – F. O. Darvall, *Popular Disturbances and Public Order in Regency England*, 1934.

DE QUINCEY – *The Collected Writings of Thomas de Quincey* (ed. D. Masson), Edinburgh, 1889–90.

DE SELINCOURT – *The Letters of William and Dorothy Wordsworth, The Middle Years* (ed. E. de Selincourt), 1937.

DE VEGA – *Journal of a Tour made by Señor Juan de Vega, through Great Britain and Ireland*, 1830.

DICKINSON – H. W. Dickinson, *Matthew Boulton*, 1937.

Dickson Papers – *The Dickson Papers* (ed. Maj.-Gen. John Leslie), 1908–12.

DINO – *Memoirs of the Duchesse de Dino* (ed. Princesse Radziwill), 1909.

DIXON – J. B. Booth, *Bits of Character, A Life of Henry Hall Dixon*, 1936.

DONALDSON – J. Donaldson, *The Eventful Life of A Soldier*, Edinburgh, 1827.

DOWELL, *History of Taxation* – S. Dowell, *A History of Taxation and Taxes in England*, 1884.

DUDLEY – Lord Dudley, *Letters to 'Ivy'* (ed. S. H. Romily), 1905.

DUFF COOPER – A. Duff Cooper, *Talleyrand* 1932.

DYOTT – *Diary of William Dyott* (ed. R. W. Jefferey), 1907.

E.H.R. – *English Historical Review.*

EDEN – Sir F. M. Eden, *The State of the Poor* (ed. A. G. L. Rogers), 1928.

Edinburgh – *The Edinburgh Review.*

EGAN, *Life of an Actor* – P. Egan, *The Life of an Actor* (1904 ed.). (See also *Boxiana*, *Life in London*, and *Real Life in London*.)

ELAND – G. Eland, *In Bucks*, 1923.

ELLESMERE – Francis, first Earl of Ellesmere, *Personal Reminiscences of the Duke of Wellington*, 1903.

English Spy – B. Blackmantle, *The English Spy* (1907 ed.).

ERNLE – Lord Ernle, *English Farming Past and Present*, 1922.

Espriella – R. Southey, *Letters from England by Don Manuel Alvarez Espriella*, 1807.

FAIN – A. J. F. Fain, *Manuscrit de 1814*, Paris, 1823.

FARADAY – B. Jones, *Life and Letters of Faraday*, 1870.

FARINGTON – *The Farington Diary* (ed. J. Grieg), 1922–6.

FARMER – G. Farmer, *The Light Dragoon*, 1844.

FAY – C. R. Fay, *The Corn Laws and Social England*, 1932.

FEAVERYEAR – A. E. Feaveryear, *The Pound Sterling*, 1931.

FEILING – K. Feiling, *The Second Tory Party*, 1938.

FEILING, *Nineteenth Century Biography* – K. Feiling, *Sketches in Nineteenth Century Biography*, 1930.

FELKIN – W. M. Felkin, *History of the Machine-wrought Hosiery and Lace Trades*.

FELTHAM – J. Feltham, *The Picture of London in 1807*.

FESTING – J. Festing, *John Hookham Frere and his Friends*, 1899.

FORTESCUE – Sir J. W. Fortescue, *History of the British Army*, 1899–1930.

FORTESCUE, *British Statesmen* – Sir J. W. Fortescue, *British Statesmen of the Great War*, 1911.

FOSCOLO – E. R. Vincent, *Ugo Foscolo and John Allen*, 1949.

FOUCHÉ – J. Fouché, Duc d'Otranto, *Mémoires*, Paris, 1824.

FOWLER – J. K. Fowler, *Echoes of Old Country Life*, 1892.

FOY – *Vie Militaire de Général Foy* (ed. Girod de l'Ain), Paris, 1900.

FRANCIS – G. H. Francis, *Maxims and Opinions of the Duke of Wellington*, 1845.

FRASER – Sir W. Fraser, *Words on Wellington*, 1889.

FRAZER – *Letters of Col. Sir Augustus Simon Frazer, K.C.B.* (ed. Maj.-Gen. Edward Sabine), 1859.

FREMANTLE – E. A. Fremantle, *England in the Nineteenth Century*, 1929–30.

FRISCHAUER – P. Frischauer, *England's Years of Danger*, 1938.

FULFORD – Roger Fulford, *Royal Dukes*, 1933.

GALT – J. Galt, *The Lives of the Players*, 1886.

Gamonia – L. Rawstorne, *Gamonia* (1905 ed.).

GARDNER – *Recollections of James Anthony Gardner* (ed. Sir R. V. Hamilton and J. K. Laughton, Navy Records Society), 1906.

GAUSSEN – A. C. C. Gaussen, *A Later Pepys*, 1904.

GEORGE IV, *Letters* – *The Letters of King George IV* (ed. A. Aspinall), 1938.

GEORGE NAPIER – *Passages in the Early Military Life of General Sir George Napier* (ed. W. E. E. Napier), 1884.

GOMM – Sir W. Gomm, *Letters and Journal*, 1881.

GORE – John Gore, *Nelson's Hardy and his wife 1769–1877*, 1935.

GOURGAUD – General Gourgaud, *La Campagne de 1815*, Paris, 1818.

GRANVILLE – *Private Correspondence of Granville Leveson-Gower, Earl Granville*, 1916. (See also HARRIET GRANVILLE.)

GRATTAN – W. Grattan, *Adventures with the Connaught Rangers*, 1847.

Great Britain Illustrated. – *Great Britain Illustrated from Drawings by William Westall*, 1830.

GREEN, *Stendhal* – F. C. Green, *Stendhal*, 1939.

GREVILLE – *The Greville Memoirs*. A Journal of the Reign of King George IV and King William IV (ed. H. Reeve), 1874.

GREVILLE (SUPPL.) – *The Greville Diary* (ed. P. W. Wilson), 1927.

GRIMALDI – *Memoirs of Joseph Grimaldi* (ed. 'Boz'), 1846 ed.

GRONOW – *The Reminiscences and Recollections of Captain Gronow*, 1892.

GROTE – *Some Account of the Hamlet of East Burnham*, by a Late Resident (Mrs Grote), 1858.

GUEDALLA – P. Guedalla, *The Duke*, 1931.

GURWOOD – *The Dispatches and General Orders of Field-Marshal the Duke of Wellington* (ed. Lt.-Col. Gurwood), 1834–8.

H.M.C. – *Reports on the Royal Commission on Historical Manuscripts.*

HALÉVY – E. Halévy, *A History of the English People from 1815* (trans. E. I. Watkin), 1936.

HAM – *Elizabeth Ham* (ed. Eric Gillett), 1945.

Hamilton of Dalzell MS. – Manuscript Journal in the possession of Lord Hamilton of Dalzell.

HAMMOND, *Modern Industry* – J. L. and B. Hammond, *The Rise of Modern Industry*, 1925.

HAMMOND, *Skilled Labourer* – J. L. and B. Hammond, *The Skilled Labourer*, 1920.

HAMMOND, *Town Labourer* – J. L. and B. Hammond, *The Town Labourer*, 1920.

HAMMOND, *Village Labourer* – J. L. and B. Hammond, *The Village Labourer*, 1912.

HANSARD – *Parliamentary Debates*, 1814.

HAPDE – J. B. A. Hapde, *Tableau des Hôpitaux pendant la dernière Campagne de Napoléon*, Paris, 1815.

HARPER – G. M. Harper, *William Wordsworth*, 1916.

HARRIET GRANVILLE – *Letters of Harriet, Countess Granville* (ed. F. Leveson-Gower), 1894.

HARRIETTE WILSON – *Harriette Wilson's Memoirs* (ed. J. Laver), 1929.

HARRIS – *Recollections of Rifleman Harris*, 1848.

HASBACH – W. Hasbach, *The English Agricultural Labourer* (trans. Ruth Kenyon), 1908.

HAVELOCK – *Scenes of Russian Court Life* (ed. Grand Duke Nicholas, trans. Henry Havelock), 1917.

HAWTHORNE – Nathaniel Hawthorne, *Our Old Home*, 1863.

HAYDON – B. Haydon, *Autobiography* (ed. E. Blunden), 1927.

HAYDON, *Life* – *Life of Benjamin Robert Haydon from his journals* (ed. T. Taylor), 1853.

HAYDON, *Table Talk* – B. Haydon, *Correspondence and Table Talk*, 1876.

HAZLITT – *Collected Works of William Hazlitt* (ed. A. R. Waller and A. Glover), 1902–6.

HAZLITT, *Political Essays* – W. Hazlitt, *Political Essays*, 1819.

HAZLITT, *Spirit of the Age* – W. Hazlitt, *The Spirit of the Age*, 1825.

HENRY HUNT – *Memoirs of Henry Hunt*, 1820.

HERRIES – *Memoir of J. C. Herries* (ed. E. Herries), 1880.

HILL, *Austen* – Constance Hill, *Jane Austen; her Home and her Friends*, 1902.

HOBHOUSE – *The Diary of Henry Hobhouse* (ed. A. Aspinall), 1947.

HOLLAND, *Journal* – *The Journal of the Hon. Henry Edward Fox, afterwards 4th Lord Holland* (ed. Earl of Ilchester), 1923.

HOLLAND – 3rd Lord Holland, *Memoirs of the Whig Party in my Time*, 1852. (See also LADY HOLLAND.)

HOLLAND ROSE, *Napoleon* – J. Holland Rose, *Life of Napoleon I*, 1903.

HORNER – L. Horner, *Memoirs and Correspondence of Francis Horner*, 1843.

HORSBURGH – E. L. S. Horsburgh, *Waterloo*, 1895.

HOUSSAYE – H. Houssaye, *1815 Waterloo* (ed. A. Euan-Smith), 1900.

HOWE – P. P. Howe, *The Life of William Hazlitt*, 1947.

HOWITT – W. Howitt, *The Rural Life of England*, 1838.

HOWITT, *Boy's Country Book* – W. Howitt, *The Boy's Country Book*, 1939.

HUGHSON – David Hughson, *Walks through London*, 1817.

Huskisson Papers – *The Huskisson Papers* (ed. L. Melville).

IRVING – Washington Irving, *Works* (Bohn ed.), 1854.

JACKSON – Lt.-Col. Basil Jackson, *Notes and Reminiscences of a Staff Officer* (ed. R. C. Seaton), 1903.

JACKSON, *Diaries and Letters* – Sir George Jackson, *Diaries and Letters*, 1872.

JAMES, *Naval History* – W. James, *Naval History*, 1837.

JAMES – Lt.-Col. W. H. James, *The Campaign of 1815*, 1908.

JEKYLL and JONES – J. Jekyll and S. R. Jones, *Old English Household Life*, 1939.

JERNINGHAM – *The Jerningham Letters*, 1896.

Johnny Newcome – *The Military Adventures of Johnny Newcome* (1904 ed.).

JOURDAN – Marshal H. B. Jourdan, *Mémoires militaires sur la Guerre d'Espagne*, Paris, 1899.

Journal of A Soldier – *Journal of A Soldier of the Seventy-First Regiment*, 1822.

KEATS – *The Political Works and Other Writings of John Keats* (ed. Harry Buxton Forman), 1883.

KEATS, *Poems* – *The Poems and Verses of John Keats* (ed. J. Middleton Murry), 1949.

Keats Circle – *The Keats Circle* (ed. H. E. Rollins), Harvard, 1948.

KENNEDY – Gen. Sir James Shaw Kennedy, *Notes on the Battle of Waterloo*, 1865.

KINCAID – J. Kincaid, *Adventures in the Rifle Brigade*, 1830.

KINCAID, *Random Shots* – J. Kincaid, *Random Shots from a Rifleman*, 1835.

KLINGENDER – F. D. Klingender, *Art and the Industrial Revolution*, 1947.

KNOWLES – L. C. A. Knowles, *The Industrial and Commercial Revolution in Great Britain during Nineteenth Century*, 1941. (See ROBERT KNOWLES.)

LADY HOLLAND – *Elizabeth, Lady Holland to her Son* (ed. Earl of Ilchester), 1946.

LADY SHELLEY – *The Diary of Frances, Lady Shelley* (ed. Richard Edgcumbe), 1912–13.

LAMB – *The Works of Charles and Mary Lamb* (ed. E. V. Lucas), 1905.

LAMINGTON – Lord Lamington, *In the Days of the Dandies*, 1890.

LAPENE – E. Lapene, *Campagne de 1813–14 sur l'Ebre, les Pyrénées, et la Garonne*, Paris, 1834.

LARPENT – *The Private Journal of Judge-Advocate F. S. Larpent*, 1853.

LAS CASES – Comte de Las Cases, *Mémorial de Sainte-Hélène*, 1823.

Lavengro – G. Borrow, *Lavengro*, 1904 ed.

LEACH – J. Leach, *Rough Sketches of the Life of an Old Soldier*, 1831.

LEEKE – W. Leeke, *The History of Lord Seaton's Regiment at the Battle of Waterloo*, 1866.

LEIGH – *Leigh's New Picture of London* (ed. 1827).

LEIGH HUNT, *Autobiography* – *The Autobiography of Leigh Hunt* (ed. R. Ingpen), 1903.

LEIGH HUNT, *Correspondence* – *Correspondence of Leigh Hunt*, 1862.

LEITH HAY – A. Leith Hay, *Narrative of the Peninsular War*, 1879.

LENNOX – *Life and Letters of Lady Sarah Lennox* (ed. Countess of Ilchester and Lord Stavordale), 1901.

LESLIE – *Military Journal of Colonel Leslie of Balquhair*, Aberdeen, 1887.

LESLIE, *Constable* – C. R. Leslie, *Memoirs of the Life of John Constable*, 1845.

LETTS – M. Letts, *As the Foreigner saw Us*, 1935.

Lieven Letters – *Letters of Dorothea, Princesse Lieven, during her residence in London 1812–34* (ed. Lionel G. Robinson), 1902.

LIEVEN, *Private Letters* – *The Private Letters of Princess Lieven to Prince Metternich* (ed. P. Quennell), 1937.

LIEVEN, *Unpublished Diary* – *The Unpublished Diary of Princess Lieven* (ed. H. Temperley), 1925.

Life in London – P. Egan, *Life in London* (1821 ed.).

LOCKHART – J. G. Lockhart, *Memoirs of the Life of Sir Walter Scott*, 1837.

LOCKHART, *Peacemakers* – J. G. Lockhart, *The Peacemakers*, 1932.

LONDONDERRY – Marquis of Londonderry, *Narrative of the War in 1813 and 1814*, 1830.

LORD COLERIDGE – Lord Coleridge, *The Story of a Devonshire House*, 1905.

LUCAS – W. Lucas, *A Quaker's Journal*, 1934.

LYNEDOCH – A. M. Delavoye, *Life of Thomas Graham, Lord Lynedoch*, 1880.

MCCAUSLAND – Hugh McCausland, *The English Carriage*, 1948.

MCGRIGOR – Sir J. McGrigor, *Autobiography*, 1861.

MACREADY – *Macready's Reminiscences* (ed. Sir F. Pollock), 1875.

MALTON – T. Malton, *Picturesque Tour through the Cities of London and Westminster*, 1795.

MANTOUX – P. Mantoux, *The Industrial Revolution*, 1928.

Marlay Letters – *The Marlay Letters* (ed. R. W. Bond), 1937.

MARTIN – Sir T. Martin, *A Life of Lord Lyndhurst*, 1884.

MARTINEAU – H. Martineau, *History of England during the Thirty Years' Peace*, 1849.

MATHIESON – W. L. Mathieson, *England in Transition*, 1920.

MAXWELL – Sir H. Maxwell, *The Life of Wellington*, 1900.

MERCER – General C. Mercer, *Journal of the Waterloo Campaign*, 1870.

Metropolitan Improvements.—J. Elmes and T. Shepherd, *Metropolitan Improvements*, 1827.

MITFORD, *Life* – A. G. L'Estrange, *The Life of Mary Russell Mitford*, 1870.

MITFORD, *Literary Life* – Mary Russell Mitford, *Recollections of a Literary Life*, 1883.

MITFORD, *Our Village* – Mary Mitford, *Our Village*, 1891 ed.

MITTON – G. E. Mitton, *Jane Austen and her Times*, 1905.

MOORE – *The Memoirs, Journal and Correspondence of Thomas Moore* (ed. Lord John Russell), 1860.

MOORE, *Byron* – T. Moore, *Byron's Life, Letters and Journals*, 1838.

MOORSOM – Capt. W. S. Moorsom, *A Historical Record of the Fifty-Second Regiment*, 1860.

MORE – W. Roberts, *Memoirs of the Life of Mrs Hannah More*, 1836.

MORRIS – W. O'Connor Morris, *The Campaign of 1815*, 1900.

MÜFFLING – Freiherr von Müffling, *Aus meinen Leben*, Berlin, 1855.

MYTTON – *Memoirs of the Life of the late John Mytton, by Nimrod* (1915 ed.).

NAPIER – Sir W. Napier, *History of the War in the Peninsula*, 1834–40. (See also CHARLES NAPIER and GEORGE NAPIER.)

NAPOLEON, *Correspondance*—*Correspondance de Napoléon I* (ed. A. du Casse), Paris, 1878.

NEALE – J. P. Neale, *Views of the Seats of Noblemen and Gentlemen*, 1818.

Near Observer – *Battle of Waterloo by a Near Observer*, 1917.

Nelson's Hardy – John Gore, *Nelson's Hardy and his Wife*, 1935.

NEUMANN – *Diary of Philipp von Neumann* (trans. and ed. E. Beresford Chancellor), 1928.

NEVILL – Ralph Nevill, *The Merry Past*, 1909.

NEVILL, *London Clubs* – Ralph Nevill, *London Clubs*, 1911.

NEWTON – *The Diary of Benjamin Newton* (ed. C. P. Fendall and E. A. Crutchley), 1933.

NICOLSON – Harold Nicolson, *The Congress of Vienna*, 1946.

Old Oak – J. E. Linnell, *Old Oak*, 1932.

OLPHIN – H. K. Olphin, *George Tierney*, 1934.

OMAN – Sir C. Oman, *A History of the Peninsular War*, 1902–31.

OMAN, *Colonel Despard* – Sir C. Oman, *The Unfortunate Colonel Despard and Other Studies*, 1922.

OMAN, *Wellington's Army* – Sir C. Oman, *Wellington's Army*, 1913.

OSBALDESTON – *Squire Osbaldeston: His Autobiography* (ed. E. D. Cuming), 1926.

PAGET – *Letters and Memorials of Gen. the Hon. Sir Edward Paget* (ed. Eden Paget), 1898.

Paget Brothers – *The Paget Brothers* (ed. Lord Hylton), 1918.

Pakenham Letters – *Pakenham Letters* (ed. Lord Longford), 1914.

PARKINSON – C. Northcote Parkinson, *Edward Pellew, Viscount Exmouth*, 1934.

PARTINGTON – C. F. Partington, *National History and Views of London*, 1834.

PEEL – *Sir Robert Peel* (ed. C. S. Parker), 1891.

PELLEW – Hon. George Pellew, *Life and Correspondence of H. Addington, Viscount Sidmouth*, 1847.

PETRIE, *Canning* – Sir Charles Petrie, *The Life of George Canning*, 1930.

PICTON – G. W. Picton, *The Battle of Waterloo*.

PLUMER WARD – E. Phipps, *Memorials of the Political and Literary Life of Robert Plumer Ward*, 1850.

PORTER – G. L. Porter, *The Progress of the Nation*, 1851.

Proceedings of the Dorset Natural History and Archaeological Society.

PYNE, *Royal Residences* – W. H. Pyne, *Royal Residences*.

Quarterly – *The Quarterly Review*.

QUENNELL – P. Quennell, *Byron, The Years of Fame*, 1935.

RAUMER – F. von Raumer, *England in 1835* (trans. H. E. Lloyd), 1837.

Real Life in London – P. Egan, *Real Life in London* (1905 ed.).

RICARDO – D. Ricardo, *Principles of Political Economy and Taxation* (ed. E. C. K. Gonner), 1891.

ROBERT KNOWLES – *The War in the Peninsula: Some Letters of Lieutenant Robert Knowles*, 1913.

ROBINSON – Maj.-Gen. C. W. Robinson, *Wellington's Campaigns*, 1911.

ROBINSON, *British Tar* – C. N. Robinson, *The British Tar in Fact and Fiction*, 1909.

ROBINSON, *Picton* – H. B. Robinson, *Memoirs and Correspondence of General Sir T. Picton*, 1936.

Romany Rye – G. Borrow, *The Romany Rye*.

ROMILLY – *Memoirs of the Life of Sir Samuel Romilly*, 1840.

ROSE – *The Diaries and Correspondence of the Right Honourable George Rose*, 1860.

ROSEBERY – Lord Rosebery, *Napoleon, The Last Phase*, 1900.

ROTH – C. Roth, *History of the Jews in England*, 1941.

Rowlandson – *Rowlandson Drawings* (ed. A. Bury), 1949.

ST CYR – Gouvion St. Cyr, Marshal, *Mémoires*, Paris, 1830–1.

SCHAUMANN, – A. L. F. Schaumann, *On the Road with Wellington*, 1924.

SCHENK – H. G. Schenk, *The Aftermath of the Napoleonic Wars*, 1947.

SCOTT, *Visit to Paris* – J. Scott, *A Visit to Paris in 1814*, 1815.

SCOTT – *The Letters of Sir Walter Scott* (ed. Sir H. J. C. Grierson), 1932–7.

SCOTT, *Letter-Books* – *The Private Letter-Books of Sir Walter Scott* (ed. Wilfred Partington), 1930. (See also LOCKHART.)

Sea-Bathing Places – *A Guide to all the Watering and Sea-Bathing Places* (ed. 1815).

SEATON – *Life and Letters of Lord Seaton* (ed. G. C. Moore-Smith), 1903.

SEELEY – J. R. Seeley, *Life and Times of Stein*, 1878.

Shakerley MSS. – Shakerley MSS. at Smedmore House, Dorset.

SHELLEY – *The Complete Works of Shelley* (ed. R. Ingpen and W. E. Peck), 1926–30.

SHELLEY, *Essays and Letters* – *Shelley's Essays and Letters* (ed. Rhys), 1886. (See also LADY SHELLEY.)

SHEPHERD – W. Shepherd, *A Visit to France in 1814*, 1815.

SHIRLEY – Andrew Shirley, *The Rainbow*, 1949.

SHORE – H. N. Shore, *Smuggling Days and Smuggling Ways*, 1892.

SIBORNE – Maj.-Gen. H. T. Siborne, *Waterloo Letters*, 1891.

SIMMONS – *A British Rifleman* (ed. Col. Willoughby Verner), 1899.

SIMMONS, *Southey* – Jack Simmons, *Southey*, 1945.

SIMOND – L. Simond, *Journal of a Tour and Residence in Great Britain during the years 1810 and 1811*, 1815.

SIMPSON – J. Simpson, *Paris after Waterloo*, 1853.

SINCLAIR – *Memoirs of Sir John Sinclair*, 1837.

SMART – W. Smart, *Economic Annals of the Nineteenth Century*, 1910.

SMILES – S. Smiles, *Lives of the Engineers*, 1861–2.

SMITH – *The Autobiography of Sir Harry Smith* (ed. G. C. Moore-Smith), 1901. (See also SYDNEY SMITH.)

SOUTHEY – *The Life and Correspondence of Robert Southey* (ed. C. C. Southey), 1849–50. (See also *Espriella*.)

SRBIK – H. von Srbik, *Metternich*, Munich, 1925–6.

STANHOPE – Earl Stanhope, *Notes of Conversations with the Duke of Wellington*, 1888.

STANLEY – *Before and After Waterloo, Letters from Edward Stanley* (ed. Jane H. Adeane and Maud Grenfell), 1907.

State Trials – State Trials (ed. Howell), 1817–23.

STEWART – *The Life of Alexander Stewart* (ed. Sir Malcolm Stewart), 1947.

SUMMERSON – John Summerson, *Georgian London*, 1945.

SURTEES – W. Surtees, *Twenty-five Years in the Rifle Brigade*, 1833.

SYDNEY – W. C. Sydney, *The Early Days of the Nineteenth Century in England*, 1898.

SYDNEY SMITH – Sydney Smith, *Works*, 1848.

Times – The Times.

TOMKINSON – W. Tomkinson, *The Diary of a Cavalry Officer*, 1894.

TOOKE – T. Tooke and W. Newmarch, *A History of Prices*, 1928.

TOYNBEE – William Toynbee, *Glimpses of the Twenties*, 1909.

TOYNBEE, *Industrial Revolution* – Arnold Toynbee, *Lectures on the Industrial Revolution*, 1906.

Trade Winds – The Trade Winds (ed. C. Northcote Parkinson), 1948.

TREVELYAN, *Grey* – G. M. Trevelyan, *Lord Grey of the Reform Bill*, 1929.

TREVITHICK – H. W. Dickinson and Arthur Titley, *Richard Trevithick*, 1934.

TWISS – *Life of Lord Eldon*, 1844.

Two Duchesses – V. Foster, *The Two Duchesses*, 1898.

VARLEY – Adrian Bury, *John Varley of the Old Society*, 1946.

VAUDONCOURT – G. de. Vaudoncourt, *Histoire de la Guerre soutenue en 1813*, Paris, 1819.

VERE – Vere, *Marches of the 4th Division*.

VINCENT – E. R. Vincent, *Byron, Hobhouse and Foscolo*, 1949.

VIVIAN – C. Vivian, *Memoir of Richard, Lord Vivian*, 1897.

WALLAS – Graham Wallas, *Life of Francis Place*, 1898.

WALPOLE – Spencer Walpole, *History of England from the Conclusion of the Great War*, 1890.

WANSEY – H. Wansey, *A Visit to Paris*, 1814.

WEBB, *Local Government* – S. and B. Webb, *English Local Government*, 1658–1834.

WEBB, *Poor Law* – S. and B. Webb, *English Poor Law History*, 1927–9.

WEBB, *Trade Unionism* – S. and B. Webb, *History of Trade Unions*, 1894.

WEBSTER – C. K. Webster, *The Congress of Vienna*, 1934.

WEBSTER, *Castlereagh* – C. K. Webster, *Foreign Policy of Castlereagh*, 1931–4.

WEIL – M. H. Weil, *La Campagne de 1814*, Paris, 1891.

WELLINGTON, *Supplementary Dispatches* – *Supplementary Dispatches of the Duke of Wellington* (ed. 2nd Duke of Wellington, 1858–72). (See also GURWOOD.)

WEST – William West, *A History of the Forest or Chace known by the name of Cranbourn Chase*, 1816.

WHEELER – *The Letters of Private Wheeler*, Strand Magazine, March to May, 1949.

WILBERFORCE – *The Correspondence of William Wilberforce* (ed. R. A. and S. Wilberforce), 1840.

WILLEY – Basil Willey, *Nineteenth Century Studies*, 1949.

WILLIAMS – Helen Maria Williams, *A Narrative of the Events in France (from the landing of Bonaparte on 1st March, 1815, till the Restoration of Louis XVIII)*, 1815.

WOODWARD – E. L. Woodward, *The Age of Reform*, 1938.

WYNNE – *The Wynne Diaries* (ed. A. Fremantle), 1935–40.

YONGE, *Liverpool* – C. D. Yonge, *Life of Lord Liverpool*.

YOUNG – Arthur Young, *Autobiography* (ed. M. Betham-Edwards), 1898.

INDEX

Figures in italics refer to full descriptive passages

451

ACKNOWLEDGEMENTS

For kind permission to use certain copyright extracts the author and publishers are grateful to:

Messrs Edward Arnold for extracts from William Gratton's *Adventures with the Connaught Rangers* (edited by Sir Charles Oman), and from Sir Charles Oman's *Wellington's Army*; Messrs Faber & Faber for extracts from *Elizabeth Ham by herself* (edited by Eric Gillett); Messrs Jarrold for extracts from *Scenes of Russian Court Life* (edited by Grand Duke Nicholas); Messrs John Lane, The Bodley Head, for extracts from Constance Hill's *Jane Austen, Her Homes and Her Friends*; Messrs John Murray for extracts from *Services, Adventures and Experiences of Captain Robert Blakeney*, *The Private Correspondence of Granville Leveson-Gower, Earl Granville*, *The Diary of Frances, Lady Shelley* (edited by R. Edgcumbe), and *The Creevey Papers* (edited by Sir H. Maxwell); and Oxford University Press for extracts from *The Letters of William and Dorothy Wordsworth, The Middle Years* (edited by E. de Selincourt).

Other Penguin and Pelican
books are described on the
following pages

FRENCH ARCHITECTURE

PIERRE LAVEDAN

A329

This book, of which the French version has run into many
editions, is a history of French architecture from its origins
until the present day. In this Pelican edition it appears for the
first time in English. Unlike many writers on architecture,
Professor Lavedan does not subjugate the problems of technique and materials to aesthetic considerations. He sees that
almost every major architectural innovation has resulted
equally from technical and artistic demands. For this reason
the first chapter of the book provides a general account of the
materials and technique of building, which is not readily available in such a compact form elsewhere. The first part of the
book also discusses the important question of 'style'. The rest
is in the main divided into two sections dealing respectively
with the history of Religious and Civil architecture from
medieval times until the present. In addition there are chapters
on town-planning and the planning of gardens, biographies of
the chief architects discussed, and the book is illustrated with
line drawings in the text and sixty-four pages of plates.

ENGLISH FURNITURE STYLES

FROM 1500 TO 1800

RALPH FASTNEDGE

A309

This is a comprehensive, compact, and authoritative historical survey of the evolution of English furniture. In recent years interest in its makers has been growing. Legends have been dispelled, and new facts and material correlated so that our knowledge of the history of furniture design is now very much more exact. Chippendale, Hepplewhite, and Sheraton, for example, are seen no longer as fabulous, isolated figures, but in true perspective; and their famous pattern books (the *Director*, the *Guide*, and the *Drawing Book*), which have been known to collectors for many years, have been studied very closely. Quotations from old memoirs, diaries, and letters, which are often entertaining and very illuminating, help to re-create the social conditions under which the designers and makers were working. The book has several useful appendices, including glossaries of makers, woods, and specialized terms, and is illustrated by over 100 line drawings and sixty-four pages of plates.

SILVER

An Illustrated Introduction to
British plate from the Middle Ages
to the present day

GERALD TAYLOR

A306

Several recent exhibitions and the growing collections of plate in England and America have stimulated interest in the history of the British goldsmiths' and silversmiths' craft in many people who are not themselves collectors. As well as illustrated catalogues and descriptions of the plate in the major collections, and of church plate, several books of a more general scope have appeared. But to understand them the reader requires considerable specialized knowledge. Moreover many of them are expensive and difficult to obtain. This book is intended to fill the gap by providing an introductory explanation of the potentials of the two precious metals, silver and gold, and of their domestic use in England from the Middle Ages until the present day. It contains sixty-four pages of plates and many drawings, and abbreviated tables of hall marks of the London and main provincial assay offices provide a convenient means of dating plate from the sixteenth century onwards.

PETER QUENNELL

BYRON: THE YEARS OF FAME

This book describes the period of Byron's life that began in
1811 with his return from the tour of the Near East and ended
five years later when he left England for the last time. During
this period *Childe Harold* appeared, ran through seven editions
in five weeks, and Byron suddenly found himself famous and
became the darling of society. But lameness, financial difficulties, and debauchery led to a storm of public hostility that
drove him out of England. (982)

BYRON IN ITALY

The story of strange adventures is continued. Its background
is Switzerland and Italy during a period when Europe was war-
weary but still beset by fears of revolution. Byron himself
represented the spirit of change – wandering with his fantastic
household through Italy and dabbling in the activities of the
Italian Liberals. When he first left England he had been resigned to making a life of amusement, but a succession of
disreputable love-affairs was replaced by a calm domestic
relationship with the Countess Guiccioli. His decision to leave
Italy for Greece was made in no light-hearted mood. He
expected – perhaps he hoped – to meet his death there. (1057)

THE PELICAN HISTORY OF ART

EDITED BY NIKOLAUS PEVSNER

THE PELICAN HISTORY OF ENGLAND

While each volume is complete in itself, the whole series has been planned to provide an intelligent and consecutive guide to the development of English society in all its aspects. The eight volumes are:

THE PELICAN HISTORY OF THE WORLD

Each volume is written by a specialist, and the emphasis given to such matters as trade, religion, politics, foreign relations, intellectual and social life, varies and must vary between volume and volume, but the interplay of nationalism is as much part of national history as internal events, and it is hoped that *The Pelican History of the World* will be both a series of national histories and, in the true sense, a history of the modern world.

A HISTORY OF MODERN CHINA

Kenneth Scott Latourette

A302

A HISTORY OF THE UNITED STATES;

VOL. 1: COLONIES TO NATION;

VOL. 2: NATION TO WORLD POWER

J. E. Morpurgo and Russel B. Nye

(A313, A314)

A HISTORY OF MODERN FRANCE; VOL. 1

J. A. Cobban

(A403)

THE PENGUIN BOOKSHELF

In answer to many requests over the years a bookshelf specially designed to hold Penguin Books is now in production. Available in two models – for the floor or for the wall – in light oak or dark brown mahogany, this bookshelf is strong, elegant, and modern in appearance. It is made by Beaver & Tapley Ltd and designed by Frank Height, M.S.I.A. A feature of the Penguin Bookshelf is the nine internal divisions which keep small numbers of books separate, upright, and tidy.

The dimensions are:

FLOOR MODEL
2′ 4″ wide   2′ 10″ high   5″ deep
The legs are 6½″ deep

WALL MODEL
2′ 4″ wide   2′ 4″ high   5″ deep

The price is 92s. 6d. including Purchase Tax

The Penguin Bookshelf is on sale at most furniture shops and bookshops too. In case of difficulty please write to:

PENGUIN BOOKS LIMITED

HARMONDSWORTH · MIDDLESEX